Pierre Samuel Du Pont
de Nemours

Pierre Samuel Du Pont de Nemours

by

Ambrose Saricks

The University of Kansas Press

Lawrence 1965

Preface

The name "du Pont de Nemours" has come to have more significance in the history of the United States of America than in the history of France. When Eleuthère Irénée du Pont established his first powder mills on the Brandywine in 1802, he could not know that he was laying the foundations for one of the modern world's industrial marvels and for one of America's most famous families. Because his strenuous and diligent labor did lay such foundations, the story of the company and of the family has often been told. Through such accounts most readers first learn about the father of the company's founder, Pierre Samuel Du Pont (de Nemours), whose energetic career is part of the most influential period in modern French history—the Enlightenment, the Revolution, and the Napoleonic era. This book is about that man, the first Du Pont *de Nemours,* and about his relationship to some of the major events of the late eighteenth and early nineteenth centuries.

It is not the first full-scale study of his career. It is an attempt, within the limits of the author's abilities, to use for the first time all the available kinds of material—family manuscripts, archival documents, contemporary materials in print, and later scholarly treatises. In confronting this mass of information, I have had advantages—and disadvantages—beyond those of my four predecessors, who have not had all this material at hand. Its great bulk, especially that part comprising family manuscripts, could not be so completely absorbed as I had hoped during the time which I could devote to the task. Still I can claim, and do, that this book relies upon more sources than were consulted by Gustave Schelle, B. G. du Pont, Denise Aimé, and Pierre Jolly. The reader must judge whether I have drawn sound conclusions from them.

Because I have done my best to produce a scholarly work, and because none of the previous biographies is properly annotated, I have attached a heavy freight of notes to the text of my book. Scholars may complain, as I have complained about other books, that the notes are printed at the end of the text rather than on the pages to which they refer. Two factors dictated this arrangement—the exigencies and economies of bookmaking and the likelihood that a plethora of footnotes on the pages of the text may scare off all but the hardiest of readers. Those who have no interest in the notes are less likely to be disturbed by the small superscript numbers referring to them.

No one undertakes an enterprise of this nature without owing much to the help of others. In expressing gratitude for this assistance, I do not seek to absolve myself from responsibility for my work. I have made my own decisions on the use and interpretation of all the material available to me.

Without the skilled staff and convenient facilities of the Eleutherian Mills Historical Library (formerly Longwood Library), the book could hardly have been begun; certainly it could not have been completed. There are found the rich collections of du Pont family manuscripts, photographic copies of essential archival documents, and the largest number of printed works by and about Du Pont de Nemours anywhere available. Present and past members of the Library staff have become cherished friends while rendering invaluable assistance. I am especially indebted to Dr. Charles W. David, first Director of the Library, Dr. Richmond D. Williams, present Director, Mr. Frank Battan, formerly Assistant Director, Dr. John B. Riggs, Chief of the Manuscripts Division, Mr. Earle Coleman, formerly Chief Bibliographer, and Mr. Victor de Avenell, formerly Translator. Special obligations to the last two are further acknowledged in the notes. Dr. David arranged a grant for a trip to Europe; Dr. Williams, one for a summer of uninterrupted work in the Library. Mr. Battan was helpful in so many ways—for example, in providing living accommodations and transportation to and from the Library—that any expression of gratitude seems inadequate. The erudition and experience of Dr. Riggs, and the always willing aid of his competent staff, have been essential in resolving many of my problems.

I add my name to the long list of Americans who have benefited from the knowledge and labors of M. Abel Doysié. Through the cooperation of the Eleutherian Mills Historical Library M. Doysié ransacked Parisian archives in search of documents concerning Du Pont de Nemours. He also searched in other French depositories and carried forward essential inquiries with departmental and municipal officials. He arranged for the photographing of a large number of documents which he turned up and for the transmittal of the photographs to the Library. When I was in France, he supplied valuable suggestions for my own researches in the Archives Nationales, the

Bibliothèque Nationale, and elsewhere. He also put me in touch with M. Léon Petit, who was my guide and adviser during my visits to Nemours, Chevannes, and Bois-des-Fossés.

A grant from the Penrose Fund of the American Philosophical Society made possible a period of research in the Society's Archives. The General Research Fund and the Endowment Association of the University of Kansas also provided the financial assistance necessary to enable me to devote several summers to research and to arrange for the typing of the final manuscript. The Editor of the *Historian* has kindly consented to my using in chapters V and VI several paragraphs which first appeared in my article in volume XVIII (1956) of that journal. Dr. Clyde K. Hyder, Editor of the University of Kansas Press, has patiently labored with me on the often wearisome details of transforming a typescript into a printed book.

The debt to one's wife and family is usually acknowledged last, because there is no way properly to state its magnitude. My wife, Reese Pyott Saricks, has not only cheerfully welcomed Du Pont de Nemours into our home, but, over the years, has developed such a sincere affection for the man that I have found greater pleasure in my own association with him. Under sometimes trying circumstances, she typed an early version of my manuscript and never complained that so much of this version had ultimately to be discarded or altered beyond easy recognition. My son and daughter have well concealed any resentment which they might feel toward Du Pont de Nemours when he has taken me away from them.

For all this help, and more which is here unmentioned through inadvertence, I am deeply grateful.

AMBROSE SARICKS

Lawrence, Kansas
April, 1965

Contents

Illustrations

Chapter I

In Search of a Career (1739-1763)

THE "RUE DE RICHELIEU" recalls the name of the famous cardinal who was the real ruler of France for eighteen years before his death in 1642. One hundred years later, however, there was little to distinguish it among the streets of Paris. Very close at hand was the Palais Royal, which got its name when the cardinal willed it to his sovereign, Louis XIII. The King had little time to enjoy the bequest, for, within six months he, too, was dead. Young Louis XIV lived there for a very short time, but subsequently the palace had become the property of the Orléans family. Philip, Duke of Orléans and Prince-Regent during the minority of Louis XV, had ordered extensive rebuilding and given to the pile of masonry the general appearance which it still bears. It was not yet, however, the center of attention and excitement which it was to become after 1780 under the rearrangements of the improvident Duke Louis-Philippe, the "Philippe Égalité" of the French Revolution. Farther north was the fine building which Cardinal Mazarin, successor to Richelieu, had purchased in 1646 from a president of the Parlement of Paris. No one could foresee that, in the long course of time, this building with extensive additions would house the Bibliothèque Nationale, one of the great libraries of the world. Within easy walking distance, beyond the Rue Saint-Honoré, where the Rue de Richelieu began, were the old royal palaces, the Louvre and, in the opposite direction, the Tuileries, joined along the Seine by the galleries completed early in the seventeenth century. Ever since Louis XIV had moved the court to Versailles in 1682, these famous edifices had fallen upon evil days. The construction which the king had planned came to an end

1

by the beginning of the eighteenth century; even necessary repair work was neglected. Before 1750 there was some talk of tearing down the derelict buildings. In the year 1739, therefore, the neighborhood of the Rue de Richelieu was a relatively quiet place. Along the street could be found the residences and shops of small traders and artisans. It was in that year and in such a house, that of a *horloger*, or watchmaker, that Pierre Samuel Du Pont was born on December 14.

The name Du Pont[1] means literally "of the bridge" and, as Du Pont de Nemours wrote in his autobiography, "is very common in every country and in all languages. . . . The name is applied equally to families who are descended from warriors distinguished by their defense of a bridge or from a caretaker who guarded the bridge or even from a child who has been found on a bridge. Everywhere there is a large number of men in one or another of these categories and especially among the latter. It follows that there are many Du Ponts of all professions and ranks, but the greater part are in the least-known class."[2]

Most of Pierre Samuel Du Pont's ancestors were indeed in the "least-known class." The earliest surviving records of his family date from the sixteenth century when three brothers, Charles, Pierre, and Jehan du Pont, were living at Rouen.[3] Except for the fact that these du Ponts became Huguenots nothing important is known about them. They seem to have undergone with fortitude the disadvantages and hardships usually accompanying the practice of their religion in Catholic France.[4] Merchants and small traders, they spent their days attending carefully to business details. Although some of their descendants emigrated during the reign of Louis XIV, most of them remained in France, lived long lives, and had many children.

Pierre Samuel was the fifth generation descending from the sixteenth century Jehan du Pont.[5] His father, Samuel, was one of eleven children, and apparently the first of his family to try his fortune in Paris, where he became an excellent watchmaker.[6] Du Pont later described his father as being a very handsome man about five feet, ten and a half inches tall, with brown hair and blue eyes, dignified in his movements, a good dancer and fencer.[7] These pleasing attributes must have been even more vivid in Samuel when he was a young man of twenty-six. It was then that he attracted the attention of Anne

2

Du Pont's parents and Du Pont as a child
Courtesy of the Henry Francis du Pont Winterthur Museum

Bust of Madame Du Pont (1743-1784)
Courtesy of the Eleutherian Mills Historical Library

UXOREM ET VIRTUTEM
AMABIT SEMPER.

Miniature of Du Pont as a young man, from his small book
of verse, *Les Amusements de l'Amour*
Courtesy of the Henry Francis du Pont Winterthur Museum

Alexandrine de Montchanin, member of an old and impoverished family allied with the prominent nobles, the Jaucourt-Epenilles, one of whom became a collaborator of Diderot in the famous *Encyclopédie*.[8] Possessed of a keen intellect, Anne was forced by straitened circumstances to work with her brothers, Pierre and Alexandre, at the watchmaking trade in their house close to Samuel's on the Rue de Richelieu. This propinquity in trade and in residence brought the young couple together. Surviving documents contain no details of their courtship. One may speculate that Anne was eager to exchange her status as an unenthusiastic assistant to her brothers, upon whom she was dependent, and that Samuel found in her a vivacity which he lacked. In any event, they were married early in 1737.[9] Their union was not destined to leave behind so many children as those of other Du Ponts. Only Pierre Samuel, their second child, and a daughter, Anne Alexandrine, born in 1742, survived infancy.

The name Pierre was probably chosen for the boy from that of his maternal uncle, Pierre de Montchanin,[10] for whom he later developed a great admiration.[11] Pierre Samuel was christened in the Roman Catholic Church "when but a few hours old" in order to secure his "civil status," a ceremony regarded by the Huguenots as a purely civic function. Protestant baptism normally followed and Pierre was apparently baptized by a Huguenot chaplain attached to the Dutch embassy at Paris.[12] From the very beginning of his life, it seems, he was the cause of quarrels between his parents. The first arose over the question whether, as custom among city families then dictated, he was to be "boarded out" with a country nurse. As a matter of course such arrangements had been made by his parents for their first child, a boy, who had lived only a very short time. Anne was determined to nurse her second child herself but finally yielded to the insistence of her husband and her elder sister and sent the boy off to a wet nurse at Savigny-sur-Orge, fifteen miles southeast of Paris. Pierre's "foster mother" had no milk and fed him sparingly on boiled cow's milk and flour, almost starving him to death before he was rescued by his parents. Despite his mother's protests, he was at once placed with a second nurse, who gave him much better care. The woman's husband decided to help with his rearing by feeding him brandy. He proudly displayed young Pierre's taste for liqueur before his neighbors at various cafés. On one of his visits to his parents' he must not allow a simple private educator thus to present in public a child who had not attended classes in any college."[20] The remarkable intellectual acumen and the supreme confidence denied expression on this occasion were to abide with Du Pont throughout the rest of his life.

The sorry outcome of Viard's overambitious scheme brought more than disappointment. Samuel now insisted that obviously Pierre's education had gone far enough and that the time had come for him to take his place at the workbench of the watchmaker's apprentice. Mother and son wept and plotted to escape such an end to their years of planning and effort. Anne was equal to the occasion. She proved to her husband that a child had never been admitted to apprenticeship before he had made his first communion in the Church. Pierre's further education was disguised as preparation for this first communion. In order to enlist the active help of the clergy Anne let it be known that her son proposed to become a Huguenot minister, an undertaking which in Catholic France had to be attended with secrecy. Paul Bosc d'Antic, who had received training in theology at the seminary in Lausanne,[21] agreed to tutor him, and Pierre went happily on with his studies. He was, of course, set to work on philosophy and theology in preparation for a clerical career. These studies had a profound effect on his own convictions. According to his later account, they led him then to reject completely the basic teachings of Christianity, a religion which, he held, was "founded entirely on original sin, by reason of which one supposes that God has damned everyone for four thousand years; and this opinion that God could doom one man for the faults of another, billions of men for a fault of one alone, seemed to me . . . the most impious and the most atrocious calumny that could be imagined against the Divinity." He had even stronger words for his denial of the "absurd doctrine" of believing that, "in order to appease God, it was necessary for an inconceivable mixture of God-man to be put to death" and concluded "that a pious man and one of good sense could be neither Protestant nor Catholic, that it is necessary to respect the uniform and divine morals in all religions, to despise dogma in all [of them]; and, as to cult and ceremonies, to submit to the custom and the law of the country," wherever one may be.[22] There is no way to be certain that Du Pont's acceptance of Deism dates from this early period of his life. In these sentences he presents some of his mature convictions, which, while rejecting Christianity, upheld the reality of a divine being and the inviolability of private conscience despite the occasional necessity of yielding, publicly, to the custom and law of a country.

The first communion could not be postponed forever. Inevitably the day came, and now what was to happen to the schemes for education? Anne scored her last triumph when she finally convinced her husband that their son should be taught mathematics, since this discipline could be valuable in watchmaking. Although he knew no mathematics himself, Samuel remembered very well that his own master, Julien LeRoy, was a competent mathematician. The famous D'Alembert, then busy with the *Encyclopédie*, was consulted. While considerably impressed by Pierre's intellectual abilities, he had no time to do more than to recommend as a tutor a Monsieur Roussain, under whose guidance Pierre made excellent progress in the elements of geometry, algebra, and the science of mechanics.

At about this time a slight aberration from his rigid mental training occurred when his mother introduced him to one of her acquaintances, Madame d'Urfé, who dabbled in spiritualism.[23] This unusual activity appealed strongly to Pierre's young imagination, especially after Madame d'Urfé assured him that he had special powers. For a while he actually assisted Madame in her séances, at which she professed to be in communion with various invisible spirits. Before long, however, his reason conquered his imagination. One day he bluntly told Madame that he was convinced that all the images which he thought he saw in her magic glass were only reflections of objects in the room. In short order both Pierre and his mother were banished from the Hotel d'Urfé.

The banishment did not bother the young Du Pont, because he had just decided upon the career which would put his mathematics to best use. He would be a military engineer and become a great hero. He acquired and studied avidly the books of Vauban, Puységur, and others and set his imagination to building the courage expected of a famous military chieftain. A decision to prove this courage nearly brought him to his deathbed.

Living with the Du Ponts in Paris at the time was Pierre's cousin, Marianne Oulson, daughter of his paternal aunt, Marie Dupont.

This aunt had been married to an unlucky ship's captain who had died from exposure after a shipwreck off the Labrador coast. Left destitute, she eagerly seized upon the offer of her brother Samuel to take care of her daughter. Marianne was not an attractive girl either in appearance or in disposition, but, when she contracted a slight case of smallpox, Pierre insisted upon nursing her as became a man of courage. In the process he picked up the dread disease. He was at one time given up for dead by the doctor, but, under his mother's careful nursing, finally recovered. The severe attack had, however, a strange and permanent consequence, so affecting his vision that he remained ever afterward very nearsighted in his right eye. With his customary equanimity Du Pont later spoke of this defect as an advantage. "I call my left eye which sees far my eye for war and my right eye which is useful for fine work my eye for science and peace. I have therefore to thank nature and accident for having given me two eyes in the full scope of the term while other men have only one eye in two volumes."[24]

When he had sufficiently recovered, Pierre was put upon a daily schedule on which his father sternly insisted. Mornings were to be spent at the watchmaker's bench; afternoons would be devoted to geometry and evenings to fencing, Samuel's only hobby. His mother's kindness and encouragement were required to keep Pierre to this strict regimen in spite of his own inclinations and his father's harshness. Then came the worst calamity of his boyhood. After more than a decade had passed since she had borne a child, Anne had given birth within the period of a year to two daughters, both of whom lived only a short time. She had never regained her health, and died at the age of thirty-six, on July 21, 1756.

Her last appeal to husband and son, to make each other happy, was in vain. Bereft of the shield between himself and his determined and stubborn father, Pierre felt that existence now had lost its sweetness. His unhappiness was increased by the fact that his cousin Marianne, a formidable young woman of twenty-four, won sufficient ascendancy over his father to assume the management of the household. Pierre did not know where to turn. His sister, who had played little part in his life but from whom he might have found comfort, was then in a Protestant school in Geneva. Although his father's plans for him were certain, he could not himself decide upon a definite career. Everything except watchmaking seemed to interest him, and his diversified education did not help in narrowing the field of possibilities. He never forgave his father for not showing him the larger importance even of watchmaking. Only many years later did he come to recognize its significant relations to astronomy and navigation and "its use in all physical observations in general and in particular."[25]

Du Pont's wild hope for a career in the corps of military engineers was revived in 1757 when he met the philosopher D'Argenson, whose brother was minister of war. Patriotism, as well as personal ambition, probably had a part in these eager desires. France was again at war, in a desperate struggle of great powers which historians would later call the Seven Years' War. Without noble status, however much pride he might take in his mother's lineage, a young man of talent, Pierre knew, could hope for recognition only in such a service as the corps of engineers, where ability and training could overcome the disadvantages of being a son of middle-class parents. The meeting with D'Argenson came about through the hated watchmaking trade when Du Pont had been called to D'Argenson's house to adjust and repair the philosopher's clocks. But again his father stood in the way. When he learned of his son's fancy, Samuel asked D'Argenson not to do anything to further the scheme. A severe crisis in the relations of father and son could not be long postponed.

This crisis began with arguments over Pierre's infatuation for Mademoiselle Van Laan, whose father had been chaplain of the Dutch embassy before his death. Mademoiselle Van Laan continued to live in Paris with her widowed mother and apparently attracted so many admirers that she was the subject of uncomplimentary comments among the gossips. Samuel did not like to see his adolescent son acquiring what he considered bad habits by becoming part of her fawning retinue. He forbade any further visits and locked Pierre in his room at night. The young man could not, of course, tolerate this prohibition. He kept his appointments, leaving and returning through the window. His disobedience was discovered when his father got hold of a copy of a facetious sermon composed by Pierre to parody the strict and humorless Huguenot minister La Broue. This trifle, which drew profane conclusions from I John 4:7 about Christians' loving one another, much amused the gay little

9

band around Mlle Van Laan but made Samuel passionately angry. His son had disobeyed him not only by visiting a young woman of dubious standards but also by wasting his time in idle writing. These bad habits could no longer be borne, now that the boy could so light-heartedly make fun of holy subjects. Monsieur de la Broue was consulted. When that worthy saw how ridiculous Pierre had made him appear, he lost no time in impressing upon Samuel his sense of outrage. The distraught father lost control of his temper. He rushed home and denounced his son in violent terms, banishing him, as an outcast, from his room to the poorly lighted and ill-ventilated attic, to meditate upon his grievous sins.

This treatment was too much for Pierre. Life had become unbearable under such tyranny. Better to end it; and there by chance in the dark attic lay an old hunting knife, which he seized. Before he could turn it upon himself his cousin Marianne and the cook succeeded in getting it away from him and carried it at once to his father, with reports of the near suicide. Samuel was still in a temper and acted upon his first hasty instinct. In awesome wrath he ordered his son down from the attic and beat him severely. Pierre suffered the blows in silence. When they had ceased, he announced his intention to leave home. Three days later, on April 17, 1757, he penned a note of farewell and stole away in order to spare his father such scenes, "which ought to be almost as disagreeable to you as to myself."[26]

Flight did not solve his problems. He did find lodging of a sort near his home in the unused kitchen of Volpélière, one of his friends of the Van Laan circle. Volpélière soon undertook the task of attempting to reconcile father and son and began to make regular reports to Samuel. The father's heart softened to the extent of instructing Volpélière to pay his son's bills at the baker's if he were ever forced to seek credit. He took the occasion also to induce Volpélière to urge Mlle Van Laan to forbid any further visits of Pierre to her home. In all ways young Du Pont's condition grew worse. He was able to furnish his kitchen abode only by selling at a great sacrifice in cost and sentiment some of his prized possessions—his small silver sword, his natural history cabinet, some of his books. Then he was turned out of the Van Laan household. In delivering this blow, the young woman informed him of Volpélière's visits to his father. These seemed to him such a vile abuse of friendship that he challenged Volpélière to a duel, which the latter sensibly declined. Mlle Van Laan's cold dismissal convinced him that Volpélière had further deceived him by stealing away the girl's affections.

Looking back upon these events thirty-five years later, Du Pont ruefully wrote: "There I was alone, without a woman friend, without an acquaintance in the world, without money and almost without capacity to earn and nearly without property, given over to afflictions amounting to cruel misery and brought to this condition at about seventeen years of age by my pretensions, my self-esteem, my confidence in the happy appraisals which my mother and M. Viard had made of my talents and my disdain for the more substantial and less noble counsels of my father."[27]

He had cause to grieve. Until he could find work he had to continue as Volpélière's tenant. Through family acquaintances like Voisin, a Huguenot minister, du Busq, a distant cousin, and Doré and Madame Poly, friends of his father, he sought pupils to tutor in mathematics. He had no luck. The acquaintances to whom he applied thought him too young to be a satisfactory tutor and interpreted his requests to them merely as efforts to gain reconciliation with his father. He considered an appeal to D'Alembert but decided that his status was now too low to interest the great mathematician. Gradually he sold his other small possessions and more of his precious books in order to buy bread. Of his small library he had left only Rousseau's *Discourse on Inequality*, Montesquieu's *Spirit of the Laws*, and Caesar's *Commentaries*. In his wretchedness he even turned back to watchmaking. He spent three months painfully constructing a movement which a competent watchmaker would have completed within two weeks. A cousin of Mademoiselle Van Laan named des Rivières tried to help him by lending him an écu, most of which he immediately squandered on a losing lottery ticket.[28]

Since France was still at war, Pierre again nurtured his hopes for a military career. He would go to Canada, where, with less competition among the small number of French troops, his talents would more rapidly win him promotion to officer rank. Desiring to gain his father's approval of this venture, he consulted his favorite uncle, Pierre de Montchanin. Uncle Pierre was not sympathetic and saw the only solution to the boy's misery in a reconciliation with his father. After a conversation with Samuel, Pierre persuaded his nephew that, if he would yield to his father's wishes and beg his forgiveness, all would be well. Probably no one else could have brought the young Du Pont to accept this humiliation; unfortunately, Uncle Pierre had apparently misunderstood his brother-in-law. When, finally, young Pierre presented himself before his father for forgiveness, he was brusquely ordered to leave the house. This cruel rebuff led him to a firm decision. He would repay his father for his obduracy by becoming a skilled watchmaker and by producing a masterpiece which he would present to his father before abandoning forever the despised occupation. He would thus win his father's respect and "regain" his own liberty.[29] For five years he concentrated upon the achievement of his plan. And he carried it out with superb success despite various distractions.

Pierre first found a place in the *horlogerie* of a Monsieur Guizot, but this position lasted only two months before Guizot lost his wife and sent away his apprentices. Now regarding his son with more favor, Samuel found him another master, an Englishman named Prignan, who, although a better watchmaker than Guizot, did not like to work. From his new master young Pierre learned more about fencing than watchmaking. Fortunately Monsieur Fol, the most skilled of Prignan's workmen, undertook to instruct him. Pierre made such progress that his father was again willing to accept him, though he forced upon him a severe penance. He was ordered to give up his sword, to cut his hair short, and to dress soberly. To make his son even more conscious of his real status in life, Samuel would invite him to Sunday dinner and make fun of his appearance. With difficulty Pierre bore this humiliation stolidly, reflecting that it might be good for him, since he "had been too much flattered in childhood and youth."[30]

Prignan soon almost ruined himself by his neglect of business and retired with his wife to Passy. Pierre accompanied them and loyally shared their poverty. There he met Berneron de Pradt, who was to be one of his closest friends for many years. His frequent visits to the Pradt family helped him to live through these difficult months. With them he not only ate better than his own resources permitted but also spent pleasant hours that were a relief to his generally joyless existence. Eventually he found more permanent lodging in Paris, renting a room in the house of Monsieur Coupson,

12

another master watchmaker and a rival of Pierre's teacher, Fol. Both Coupson and Fol were pupils of Pierre Jodin, one of the famous horologists of his day, through whom young Du Pont met Denis Diderot, then still laboring on the monumental *Encyclopédie*. Nothing significant seems to have come from this association, which ended, as Du Pont later perhaps facetiously stated, because he did not sufficiently impress Diderot's wife and daughter. With the latter he feared he would fall passionately in love.[31]

His concentration on watchmaking now had its rewards. He learned to perform expertly enough certain specialized tasks which few Parisian jewelers had mastered and began to make a living at the hated trade. At this point, his interests turned toward another profession, which had not previously attracted him. He was then sharing his room with an unfortunate and unpopular young man named Paillard, whom his Uncle Pierre had induced him to take in. Paillard had picked up a venereal disease which under the ministrations of quacks soon developed into a serious ailment affecting his chest. When in addition he fell victim to smallpox, his condition became hopeless. An excellent physician, Jacques Barbeu-Dubourg, attended him, but Paillard died on Ash Wednesday, 1759. Distressed by his roommate's suffering, Du Pont became deeply interested in Barbeu-Dubourg's treatment. He asked many questions of the doctor, who, much impressed by the young man's intelligent concern, undertook to instruct him in the fundamentals of medicine and to encourage him to study further. With his characteristic energy Du Pont set out in pursuit of new knowledge. He read every book on medicine he could obtain and visited the Parisian hospitals. He even worked long hours in those hospitals after putting in the necessary time at the watchmaker's bench. His health broke down under this excessive activity. He was nursed by the kindly Pradt family through a short but severe illness, during which he must have given careful thought to the prospect of becoming a doctor. He finally decided against a medical career because, he said, he was not quick enough in grasping the right ideas and in finding the words to express them. Too poor to afford the regular training from the faculty of medicine in Paris, he could hope for nothing more than to be accepted by one of the provincial faculties. The only possible career, therefore, was to be a practicing physician, and he feared that he could not harden himself to endure the remorse which he would feel whenever one of his patients died because of his inability to provide proper treatment. When one calls to mind only in the Faubourg St. Germain what one should have prescribed in the Faubourg St. Antoine, he reflected, one is not born to be a practicing physician.[32] Still this exposure to medicine was to be of great use to him. His interest and knowledge put him on a closer footing with the man who was to be so important in his life, Dr. François Quesnay, and also made it possible for him years later, during the Revolution, to practice medicine in the country while staying clear of the police.

Not all of young Du Pont's time was devoted to these strenuous labors. He always needed some outlet for his natural energy and, despite his occasional feelings of humiliation because of his plain dress, his undersized frame, and his somewhat marred features, he participated actively in a society of young people in Paris. He took part in amateur theatricals, danced frequently, and posed for a drawing class of which his sister Anne Alexandrine was a member. Another member of this class was Jeanne Beçu (or Rançon, as Du Pont calls her, from the name of her stepfather), the young beauty who later became better known as Madame du Barry, last mistress of the King. With a possible note of regret, Du Pont remarked that he was "not among the numerous predecessors of King Louis XV."[33] During this time he tried creative writing, but with ill success. As he himself admitted, he "bungled" two tragedies, one concerning the sons of the prophet Elijah, the other *Clytemnestra*, in which he sought to rework the story of Orestes.[34] His romantic attitude toward women brought him to a serious quarrel with another young man whom he identified only as "St. Yriex," an assumed name. Incensed by St. Yriex's boasting of the favors which he regularly received from a young woman of Du Pont's circle, he challenged the braggart to a duel. St. Yriex was a good fencer and easily pierced his challenger's chest with the point of his sword. With less skill Du Pont broke his sword in a vigorous pass at St. Yriex's head. Part of the shattered blade became imbedded in St. Yriex's skull. Fortunately both recovered, but not before the young woman admitted that St. Yriex's boasting had been founded on fact.[35] Pierre had to be taken to his father's house to recover. There he remained for several months.

Upon his recovery he took charge of the shop for a month while his father went off to see his brother Pierre in England. Samuel was rather close-mouthed about the reason for this trip, but probably he was seeking counsel in finding a suitable husband for his niece Marianne. What advice he got is not known. He solved the problem of settling his niece by marrying her to Vaudry, one of his workmen, and by naming her his sole legatee. Pierre did not seem to have been much concerned by his father's action; he had become accustomed to such blows and, besides, he would never have maintained the horlogerie, as Vaudry might be expected to do. He left home again, not because he was unhappy over this arrangement, but because he had an opportunity to take a room with his good friend Berneron de Pradt. Samuel now looked upon his son as a grown man capable of taking care of himself and permitted him to go his own way.

Du Pont and Pradt had much in common—keen intellects, high spirits, romantic notions, Together they soon concocted a scheme which would make them great heroes. They would go to the island of Corsica, which for decades had been in revolt against its nominal overlord, the old republic of Genoa. Since 1755 Pasquale Paoli had been the most prominent leader of Corsican patriots resisting the inefficient Genoese efforts to resubjugate them. The French government became increasingly interested in the Corsican turmoil; eventually, at the request of the Genoese government, it intervened in the struggle and annexed the island in 1768, just in time for Napoleon Bonaparte to be born as a subject of the French king in 1769. The two dreamers in Paris had contemplated intervention much earlier—at least their own intervention. They would take over the scepter from Paoli and provide the Corsicans with an enlightened rule. Before their schemes became too elaborate, an unexpected development brought young Du Pont, with some reluctance, to abandon the project.

Like many Parisians of all ages he was eager, from time to time, to escape from the noise and bustle of the city into the peaceful countryside. When he could get away, he made extensive tours on foot, going as far as Nemours, some forty miles southeast of Paris, where Monsieur Doré, the family friend to whom he had earlier appealed for help, had now settled with his wife. Du Pont did not have a high opinion of Madame Doré, a "coquette," who, bored with country

15

life, had insisted upon purchasing the house in Nemours,[36] but he was attracted by her young cousin, Nicole-Charlotte-Marie-Louise Le Dée de Raucourt,[37] the daughter of a minor government official. Madame Doré was determined to make a good match for her young relative and did not look with favor upon a growing attachment between Marie and Pierre, who certainly had no great prospects. She decided to act rapidly. One day she announced her intention of arranging a marriage between her cousin and the local tax receiver, Desnaudiers, a widower of fifty-five who had, acording to the gossips, treated his first wife very shabbily. Pierre naturally entered a vigorous protest. He was now in a difficult position. Upon what grounds could he oppose this marriage? At first he did not wish to put himself forward as a suitable substitute for Desnaudiers, a man of some substance regardless of his poor reputation. He was fond of the young girl, but he acknowledged to himself that his love for her was not strong enough to object to her marrying another. He did not want to marry, because he hoped to carry out the great plans he had concocted with Berneron de Pradt. Corsica seemed then to offer greater attractions and opportunities. But further reflection told him that Desnaudiers was too old, too much a scoundrel; he could not permit his dear friend to be sacrificed to such an impossible husband. During a lonely and tormented walk in the large garden of the Doré property, he made his decision. He turned his back on Corsica and asked Madame Doré for the hand of her cousin. He admitted that he was then not sufficiently well-off and asked for two years to improve his prospects in the world. When she was informed of his decision, Marie was ecstatic with joy. Although not passionate by nature,[38] she easily fell in love with Pierre, assisted perhaps by her eagerness to escape the marriage earlier proposed by her aunt. She consented at once to the period of waiting and helped to win Madame Doré's approval. Pierre was probably more worried than happy by this turn of events. He could not yet know what a model wife he had thus won, almost by accident. He could only look without enthusiasm upon the collapse of his grandiose schemes and upon the necessity of formulating more realistic plans for his future.[39]

The first step was clear enough. He had to win complete freedom from his father in the manner he had earlier determined upon. He set to work in Paris to finish the beautiful watch which he proposed to present to his father as proof that he could qualify as a master watchmaker. Finally it was done and suitably engraved: "Du Pont Filius Composuit, Fecit, Dedicavit Patro Suo." On the first of January, 1763, Pierre had the great satisfaction of presenting this "talisman of . . . liberty" to his father and of taking his leave, a completely free man. Samuel was pleased. His son perhaps does him an injustice by attributing his delight to the "plausible motive" which he now possessed "to leave his shop to his nephew Vaudry."[40] Henceforth father and son would be friends but nothing more.

What now could Pierre do? Once more there pressed forward the schemes for military glory. Laboriously he drew up two *mémoires* containing detailed campaign plans for seizing Gibraltar from the British. One of the *mémoires* was worthless, as he himself admitted, and the other was rendered useless by the Treaty of Paris in February which ended the war with England. He did not abandon the idea of gaining the notice of someone in the government through recommendations which he made in long memoranda. His thoughts on general policies were turning in an important direction. Though there was little system in them his principal ideas came to be centered in the primary significance of land in any economic and social order. He never made clear how he arrived at this central idea, but it seems to have been firmly established in his mind before he had even heard of Dr. Quesnay or the Marquis de Mirabeau, who were then in the process of formulating an entire system of social thought on this fundamental tenet. It may well be that his walks in the countryside had turned his thoughts in this direction. From his early years he had constantly nurtured various grandiose plans which might make him famous. This ambition was undoubtedly one reason for his dislike of the tedious tasks of the watchmaker. Now he aimed at no less than the formulation of policies to regenerate the kingdom. At the close of the Seven Years' War many in France were engaged in this activity, and, indeed, the government of Louis XV was receptive to new ideas. Something, at least, had to be done to repair the almost hopeless condition of the Royal Treasury.

Although one can only guess at the origin of young Du Pont's views on these matters, one must recognize that he came upon them at a time most propitious for his future career. A great intellectual ferment of new and revolutionary ideas had long been in preparation.

In the last four decades of the eighteenth century it broiled in widening circles over the surface of France and of Europe. These were the years of the more radical Voltaire, of Rousseau, of the *Encyclopédie*, and of Quesnay and the Physiocrats. The term *physiocracy* was not yet coined, but the fundamental structure of this body of ideas had been put together. Du Pont's theories, which, according to his own account, he arrived at independently, almost inevitably brought him into Quesnay's circle. Equally important was his early conviction of the correctness of these ideas and of the duty "to make mankind happy" by putting them into practice.[41] At the age of twenty-three he stated the foundation of his creed in these words: "Land and water are the only sources of wealth, all combined in the harvests, and afterwards apportioned, distributed among all men by the various labors of society, [by] exchanges [of goods] and wages; whatever the constitutions [of societies] may be, [men] are never completely citizens, people whose interest is absolutely inseparable from that of the commonwealth and whose profits actually contribute to its maintenance, except those who gather the wealth and own the ground [*fonds*] which produces it, that is, the proprietors of the land; the interest of these proprietors requires the liberty, the happiness and the immunity of all the other inhabitants of the country and of all [kinds of] labor."[42]

The regeneration of France demanded, however, a wider and more practiced scheme than Du Pont could then draw from these abstractions. He set to work to prepare what he called a "fairly short" memorandum which he decided to present to the King's chief minister, the Duc de Choiseul, at one of the public audiences which the Duke held once a week at Versailles. If it ever existed, this *mémoire* has been lost; if it was short, it nevertheless covered a substantial number of items as Du Pont later described it. In several chapters it suggested methods of encouraging agriculture, of freeing commerce, of suppressing certain taxes (the *gabelles* and the *aides*) and of replacing their revenue, of recruiting the militia, and of constructing roads by the employment of troops rather than by the levying of the forced labor taxes, the *corvées*.[43] Exactly what methods he recommended in this *mémoire* cannot be known, but in support of each of these ideas he was to elaborate plans throughout the rest of his life. It must have been in the spring of 1763 that he went out to Versailles and found opportunity to present his manuscript to the minister. Choiseul was at first inclined to direct it unread to the controller-general of finances, since it seemed to treat mostly of matters directly concerning that official. Flattery had to be mixed with persuasion to win from the Minister a promise to read it himself. The promise was given, however, and the young author was elated when he was bidden to return in a week for another audience. Forthwith he composed an ode praising Choiseul for suspending the drafting of the militia, an action which he mistakenly understood that the Minister had taken.[44] While it shows some talent at versification, the ode is an undistinguished performance and rests, of course, upon a false opinion of Choiseul's virtues. This hopeful admiration of the Duke turned soon to bitterness and disappointment. Choiseul, with much else on his mind, was merely toying with him. There is no satisfactory explanation for Choiseul's conduct as Du Pont described it, though it is possible that he saw some promise in the young man. The Duke gave him the rather unusual permission of an entrée without appointment, saw him several times, and spoke vague words of encouragement. He had too much to do in maintaining his own position, which he owed largely to Madame de Pompadour, to give serious attention to an unknown youth of no influence. The keen disappointment which Du Pont experienced remained vivid as, years later, he wrote: "My hopes and, as I felt with great bitterness, those concerning my friend of which I was the depository, and my beautiful plans for Regeneration of the Kingdom were drowning quietly."[45]

More than his hopes and plans almost drowned. With a group of unnamed companions he welcomed the return of warm weather by swimming one day in the Seine. In preparation for his now abandoned Corsican plans he had been regularly practicing swimming, with emphasis upon distance rather than upon speed or grace. This day he overreached himself. After crossing the Seine several times, he suddenly tired in midstream and was swept along by the current. Had his friends not observed his plight, he would likely have been carried under.

Until he obtained the recognition which he hoped for from the government, he decided to make his way by his pen. He had been fascinated by writing for as long as he could remember, a fascination probably strengthened by his father's attitude to his literary efforts as time-wasting. A sympathetic friend of the family, Madame Poly, introduced him to the Abbé de Voisenon, who undertook to criticize and improve his poetry. He was also assisted by Poissonier, who sought to remove from his prose the "bathos and idle literary flourishes" in which it abounded. The Abbé de Voisenon was a well-known, if minor, figure in the literary and social world of Paris. He helped his young protégé to overcome some of his awkwardness by introducing him to his friends and by constantly encouraging him. He even tried to revive Choiseul's interest by suggesting a rather far-fetched comparison between Du Pont and Jean-Jacques Rousseau, once more very much in the limelight for his *Julie ou la Nouvelle Héloïse* and *Émile*, if not for *Le Contrat Social*, all published in 1761 and 1762. Both were the sons of watchmakers; both had warm hearts, extraordinary points of view, and romantic characters. The Duke is said to have replied about Du Pont: ". . . he should be happy with me, as I love him very much. He comes when he wishes. I accept all his nonsense, some of it good. He is a child; one way or another I shall do something for him."[46] But he never did.

The decisive incident which set Du Pont on his career came from another direction. The printing presses hummed busily, bringing out numerous brochures with suggestions for alleviating the serious financial burdens with which the French government and people were laden after the disastrous Seven Years' War. In May of 1763 there appeared one which created great stir in Parisian circles, *La Richesse de l'État*, written by Roussel de La Tour, a counselor at the Parlement of Paris. This pamphlet inspired others to publish replies and elaborations. The reason for the excitement was found in the daring tax proposals put forward by the author. He would abolish all the vexatious taxes in favor of one capitation levied on a progressive system according to the presumed wealth of the taxpayer. He divided taxpayers into twenty classes of 100,000 each, ranked according to wealth, and predicted from his suggested levies a tax yield of 698,366,666 livres. To this figure could be added the sum of 42,000,-000 livres from certain levies which the King would retain (customs duties, post, tobacco, church contributions, etc.), providing a total income for the government of about 740,000,000 livres.[47] When Du Pont read the treatise he was convinced at once that Roussel de La

Tour had committed a serious error in estimating the revenue which could be raised. Like many other readers he was attracted by the proposal to supplant the confusing and inequitable system of taxation with a simple one based upon a single tax. But the scheme was much too optimistic in its prediction of the number of individuals whose wealth could be taxed. Du Pont's view was conditioned by his now firmly held conviction that only the land could produce real wealth from which taxes could be paid. He decided that he must publish a reply to this brochure and thereby he set out on the path of his ultimate career.

As he planned his reply he realized that his first difficulty lay in the abstract nature of his ideas. He had little practical experience or knowledge with which to support his views. He admitted that the small amount of specific information in his possession was that which he had gathered through conversation with wagon-drivers along the way during his walks between Paris and Nemours. Lacking the time to carry on further extensive tours while preparing his treatise, he adopted an easier course of consulting the only person among his acquaintances who had sound ideas on rural matters—his father's cook! This good woman came originally from the province of Brie, southeast of Paris, and had been a servant in rural households and farmyards before she moved to the city. By questioning her closely Du Pont obtained "very pertinent information as to the number of persons and animals and the amount necessarily advanced for the exploitation of a farm."[48] He was pleased that this information confirmed his own estimates and he proceeded to set his observations down on paper. He sold his manuscript to a bookseller named Moreau for two louis, which he never collected, and with some trepidation saw his first published work appear anonymously in July, 1763, under the title *Réflexions sur l'écrit intitulé: Richesse de l'État.*[49] This pamphlet of thirty-two pages is obviously the work of a young author venturing rather hesitantly into the field of public controversy. It contains a humble dedication to L. A. D. V. (the Abbé de Voisenon) and ends with abundant praise for the zeal and good intentions of Roussel de La Tour. To introduce his subject, Du Pont used the device of an imaginary conversation with a farmer about the hardships caused by heavy taxes.[50] Here he was undoubtedly summarizing his prior discussions with rural carters and with his father's cook. He argued that the taxes of numerous workers and dependents were always, in the final analysis, borne by the farmers and the proprietors of land and that, therefore, the number of taxpayers assumed by Roussel de La Tour was incorrect.[51] He drew up a table to show that, from an assumed population of sixteen million there might seem to be as many as four million taxables but that seven-eighths of the traders and merchants (*commerçans*) and all the artisans and domestics not paid a salary but living at the expense of proprietors would have to be removed from the lists of actual taxpayers. How many could be counted in the ranks of proprietors (*possédans biens*), the only taxpayers? He leaves it to Roussel de La Tour to supply the answer.[52]

Du Pont's calculations were "crude" and in order to refine them he undertook another trip to Nemours, making a circle through Meaux, Château-Thierry, Coulommiers, and Provins. He stopped at several farms to seek information on income and expenditures and thus acquired a more detailed knowledge of the agriculture of Brie, especially of the cultivation of grain. By studying the situation at first hand, he ceased to be "an amateur of Paris."[53] In August his second anonymous essay was published as a *Réponse demandée par M. le Marquis de . . . à celle qu'il a faite aux Réfléxions sur l'écrit intitulé: Richesse de l'État.* Here he reasserted his general thesis and presented arguments in favor of freedom of trade in order to refute the anonymous marquis' false statement that Du Pont's own *Réfléxions* would be sufficient proof of the necessity of preserving import and export duties for the benefit of commerce and of revenue.[54]

At about the time these pamphlets were published Du Pont met a man who was to be of great importance in launching his career. Charles-Blaise Méliand, intendant of Soissons, was a relative of the Abbé de Voisenon and was introduced to the Abbé's protégé during a visit to Paris. Méliand was at once impressed by young Du Pont's earnestness and knowledge and offered to assist him in his endeavors. He set him to work to prepare routine reports on conditions in his intendancy and obtained his admission to membership in the Royal Society of Agriculture at Soissons.[55] Thus Du Pont had an opportunity to get practical experience in public administration and to keep in touch with members of societies concerned with the discovery of methods of increasing agricultural productivity. Societies like the one at Soissons often did not last very long and had only limited influence on public policy, but they did keep alive interest in agriculture and provided channels of communication for all those interested in farm problems.[56] The greatest service which Méliand performed for his young assistant at this time was undoubtedly to lend him books, among them Mirabeau's *L'Ami des hommes* and *Théorie de l'impôt*. In these two books Du Pont found opinions congenial to the disparate notions forming in his own mind. With the enthusiasm of the young student, he addressed a letter to Mirabeau at the latter's estate, Bignon, not far from Nemours. Mirabeau, who had read Du Pont's two pamphlets with approval, sent back an encouraging reply but, in writing of a "master greater than he," whose shoes he was not worthy to unlace,[57] he failed to identify the master as Quesnay. At Mirabeau's urging Du Pont went on to study carefully every tract on political economy which he could obtain, including the articles "Grains" and "Fermiers" which Quesnay had written anonymously for the *Encyclopédie*.

A more famous person than the Marquis de Mirabeau had earlier favored Du Pont with a letter. Acting on the suggestion of the Abbé de Voisenon, Du Pont had sent copies of his pamphlets to various prominent persons among the Abbé's acquaintances. One of those addressed was Voltaire, to whom Du Pont dispatched a few samples of his poetry, as well as his two treatises on taxation. The patriarch of Ferney replied on August 16, 1763, with a characteristically witty but inconsequential letter about this charming mixture of finances and poetry but showed no interest in the argument over taxation.[58] Almost all of Du Pont's biographers quote this letter in part,[59] but no great significance can be attached to the exchange of letters between Du Pont and Voltaire. Undoubtedly Du Pont was proud of this association and may have found encouragement in the substantial ground of agreement which he saw between his views and those of the famous *vieux malade* of Ferney. Voltaire was much more friendly to physiocratic thought than he appears to be in his *L'Homme aux quarante écus*, a humorous and caustic attack on the physiocratic doctrine of the single tax, published in 1767.[60] Thirteen of the sixteen letters which he later wrote to Du Pont were concerned with his enthusiasm for the reform program of Turgot in 1775 and

1776.[61] He was here using Du Pont only as an intermediary to get his questions and viewpoints to Turgot. Clearly Voltaire was not an important influence in Du Pont's life.

The first of the two men who exerted the greatest influence upon him was François Quesnay. Quesnay's duties as personal physician to Madame de Pompadour were never too onerous to prevent his perusal, however cursory, of new publications on financial and economic matters. These poured from the print-shops in increasing numbers under the enlightened censorship of Malesherbes, who was not alarmed even by the publication of Diderot's *Encyclopédie*. Du Pont's two pamphlets came to the attention of Quesnay, who was so struck by the similarity between his own views and those of the unknown author that he determined to seek him out. The search involved him in a comedy of errors which almost caused him to give up. Bertin, the Controller-General, told Quesnay that he remembered "a young man of Soissons" introduced to him by the intendant, Méliand, and presumed that he was the author of the pamphlets. Since the initials D. P. appeared on the pamphlets,[62] Quesnay wrote to the mayor of Soissons and requested a list of the best-known residents of the city whose names contained these initials. By chance there was a Soissons goldsmith named Du Ponchel. Quesnay wrote to him suggesting that, if his son would present himself at Versailles, he would find several people eager to meet him and to render him any possible service. Full of great expectations, Du Ponchel *fils* came to the palace and was warmly greeted by Quesnay and his friends. The first few questions soon revealed the ludicrous mistake. Du Ponchel of Soissons had never written anything and had not the vaguest idea of what was being talked about. Quesnay brought the embarrassing interview to a rapid end, recompensed the young man for his journey, and sent him back to Soissons with a strong encouragement to continue in his trade as a goldsmith. He decided to give up his quest in order to avoid another such trying scene.[63]

Several weeks afterwards, however, Mirabeau visited Quesnay at Versailles. In their conversations Du Pont's pamphlets must have figured, because at this time Mirabeau, who had already exchanged letters with Du Pont, supplied the Doctor with the correct name and address of the author. Quesnay immediately wrote a letter inviting Du Pont to Versailles and instructed a servant to deliver it in person.

Returning to his room one day toward the end of the year 1763, Du Pont was astounded to find awaiting him a messenger in the livery of Madame de Pompadour. He did not know what to make of this summons to Versailles and sought the advice of some of his Parisian friends, all of whom urged him to go.[64] On the appointed day, therefore, he presented himself at Quesnay's apartments and, by his replies to the Doctor's questions, soon reassured his host that another mistake had not been made. Quesnay was delighted and at once suggested that Du Pont busy himself with a study of the grain trade. Once the reason for the invitation to Versailles was clear, Du Pont had no hesitation in becoming another disciple of Madame de Pompadour's physician, having found in him a combination of his own deep interests, agriculture and medicine. Soon, therefore, Du Pont was associated with the formulators of a new school of thought, ever after to be celebrated as the *économistes*, or Physiocrats. "Let us take care of this young man," Quesnay said to the Marquis de Mirabeau, "for he will speak when we are dead."[65]

Chapter II

Du Pont and Physiocracy (1763-1774)

IT IS NO LONGER a simple matter to summarize the principal doctrines of the French *économistes*. In recent years numerous writers have not agreed with Eric Roll's judgment: "It is unlikely that an inquirer will today be able to discover any hitherto neglected aspect of their teaching, or to add anything of importance to what has already been said about individual points in their system."[1] This discussion must pass by many interesting ramifications of physiocratic thought[2] and limit itself briefly to an attempt to indicate certain features of the "system" and to describe Du Pont's part in its development.

By 1763, when Du Pont became active in the movement, the foundation and framework of the physiocratic structure had been erected. The chief architect was François Quesnay (1694-1774), who, as personal physician to Madame de Pompadour, was a well-known figure in the court at Versailles. The Marquis de Mirabeau (1715-1789) served as first assistant. Starting from somewhat different bases, these men found themselves working toward a similar goal. Both sought the establishment of a sound and prosperous agriculture as the essential basis of a healthy society.

This emphasis upon agriculture may have grown out of the obsession of the *philosophes* with a beneficent nature as the source of good. That occupation which was closest to, and most dependent upon, nature came in for considerable attention. The fruits of agriculture seemed in a very vivid sense to be the results of nature's work. From nature came the fundamental substance sustaining life and society. Nature was, therefore, the only source of real wealth.

Du Pont and Physiocracy (1763-1774)

The mercantilist predilection for commerce had come under attack not long after the death of Colbert. In his criticisms of the ancien régime, Boisguillebert (1646-1714) came to be celebrated by the *économistes* themselves as one of their precursors, though they reproached him for his shortcomings.[3] There were other writers, like Vauban,[4] from whom the founders of the school drew inspiration and ideas. Even John Law included in his treatises on finance maxims which the later Physiocrats could approve. Although Law was really a neo-mercantilist concerned mainly with the multiplication of money, his system did envisage a lightening of the burdens of agriculture and a rise in the price of land. Perhaps even more important, the fall of Law's system made apparent the enduring value of landed wealth at the same time as it cast into misery the landholders who had invested in his scheme.

Between 1720 and 1748, there was a dearth of such books as those of Boisguillebert and Vauban. A revival of interest after 1748 coincided with the increasing influence upon French thinkers of English practices and ideas. The new agriculture arising from the enclosure movement in England and the British legislation tending toward a freer trade in cereal grains were noted with some enthusiasm by students across the Channel. Of major significance was Richard Cantillon's *Essai sur la nature du commerce en général.* This Englishman had conducted a banking business in France for many years before his return to London, where, in 1734, he was murdered by a former servant.[5] Written in 1725, his essay was known in manuscript by a few, including the elder Mirabeau, upon whom its influence was decisive. It did not, however, appear in print until 1755. In his first sentence, Cantillon recognized the central position of land as the source of the wealth produced by human labor.[6] Such ideas stimulated Mirabeau to offer to the public in 1757[7] his treatise *L'Ami des hommes*, which had originally been planned as a commentary upon and a popularization of Cantillon's ideas. The overwhelming success of this work, subtitled *Traité de la population*, was undoubtedly due in part to its lively literary style. But its teachings also created discussion. Mirabeau believed that a large population is desirable as a stimulus to the increase of a country's wealth. Since land is the source of wealth,[8] the increase in production of the basic materials for the support of a large population would inevitably increase wealth. Population and agriculture are intimately bound together,[9] and agriculture must be freed of burdens and encouraged to expand.[10] The solicitude for agriculture aroused the interest of Quesnay, who induced Mirabeau to visit him at Versailles in July, 1757.

Quesnay's interest in agriculture dated from his childhood, for his family had a small farm in the village of Mére, where his father practiced law. His training had been primarily scientific and medical, and his first publications were medical treatises.[11] But he retained always "a lively taste, a decided inclination"[12] for matters connected with the cultivation of the land. In 1755 he purchased the large estate of Beauvoir in the Nivernais for his son Blaise,[13] for whom he had refused to intercede for a position of *fermier général* of taxes. More than ever, henceforth, his leisure time was given over to the study of rural economy. There are arguments that his economic thought was primarily shaped by Chinese influences which he concealed until 1767, when his *La Despotisme de la Chine* was published in the *Éphémérides*.[14] Like many other intellectuals of the eighteenth century, Quesnay was very much interested in China, but the extent of his indebtedness to Chinese thought will remain a point of disagreement not to be cleared by drawing parallels between his ideas and those of Mencius or other Chinese sages. Whatever the initial inspiration, Quesnay's absorption in agricultural matters was first reflected in the two articles, "Fermiers" (1756) and "Grains" (1757), written for the *Encyclopédie*.[15] Although they went practically unnoticed at the time,[16] these articles gave public voice to some ideas which became fundamental principles of Quesnay's system. Not yet dogmatically, or even clearly, put forward, four major conclusions were emerging from his studies: (1) that there is a "natural order" or natural law which should govern human societies as physical laws govern every organism; (2) that land is the only source of real wealth, since it alone, through nature's bounty, provides a "net product" (*produit net*), a surplus of wealth over and above the amount put into it; (3) that, consequently, the only productive classes are the proprietors and cultivators, all others being "sterile" and dependent upon the "producers"; (4) that all taxes should be levied directly upon the *produit net* of land, since any tax, whatever its nature, must fall, in the final analysis, upon the only surplus wealth available. The single tax (*impôt unique*) on the *produit net* would eliminate the expensive and vexatious nature of many taxes, as they find their way back to the only source which can sustain them.

In large measures, the completed physiocratic structure was an elaboration of these cardinal principles.[17] Around this core, essentially economic, Quesnay's disciples twisted the strands of their philosophy extending into political and social theory. If it were to succeed, any effort at reform must, they believed, first be directed to a solution of the problem of agriculture. Once freed of artificial restraints and allowed to develop in the "natural" way, agriculture would revivify human affairs in all directions.

To gain the adherence of Mirabeau, Quesnay had to demonstrate that the "ami des hommes" had placed the "cart before the horse" in advocating a large population before concentrating exclusively upon the increase of agricultural production which would make possible the end he sought.[18] Indeed, the goal was really a prosperous agriculture, because everything else followed from it. Mirabeau's conversion to this viewpoint was not very difficult, since he was much interested in agriculture. He owned numerous lands at Bignon, near Nemours, and elsewhere. Remembering, perhaps, that his father had lost 200,000 livres invested in Law's schemes, he had a horror of financiers and sought in large-scale agricultural enterprises a better investment of his fortune.[19] Considerably more effort was required to rid him of his feudal viewpoints regarding the privileges of the old nobility and of his doubts concerning the justice of the *impôt unique* on the income of landowners. Not until 1760 was sufficient headway achieved to turn Mirabeau into the first important popularizer of Quesnay's tenets.[20]

The "friend of mankind" undertook first to publish an expanded edition of the *Tableau Œconomique*, which Quesnay had drawn up in 1758.[21] A cumbersome attempt to put economic theory into tabular form, this *Tableau* was highly praised by the master's disciples.[22] By its use, one was supposed to be able to trace and to predict the flow of social wealth among the three classes into which, it is asserted, society is naturally divided: the proprietors, the farmers, and the sterile classes. The *Tableau* demonstrates the effort to place economic theorizing on the plane of scientific demonstration. Like many other "scientific" systems in the study of human society, it requires the deductive acceptance of its premises. Thereafter, it is coldly logical within its limits. If there is a natural order and if land is the basis of all wealth, it follows (1) that agriculture should be freed of all artificial restraints so that the natural order may prevail, (2) that those engaged in agriculture (as farmers and landowners) are the only real producers, (3) that taxes must fall upon the only surplus wealth created by society, the net income from land.

Mirabeau's next book created some disturbance and got him into trouble. His *Théorie de l'impôt* was a violent and inaccurate attack upon the existing system of taxation. It laid down some bold propositions calling, among other things, for the establishment of provincial estates which would assess and collect taxes, for the assessing of the *impôt unique* on the fruits of the land as the most just and natural tax, and for the abolition of the system of tax farming.[23] The taxation theories of the Physiocrats were obviously not popular with the ministers (who had to rely on the multiplicity of taxes for the revenue needed to run the Government), with the financiers (who were disturbed by attacks, frequently exaggerated and unjust, on the *ferme général*), or with the landholders (who had no desire to be burdened with the entire weight of taxation in the form of an *impôt unique*). For his strictures Mirabeau was imprisoned for eight days and then exiled to his estate at Bignon.[24]

No less unpopular with vast numbers of people were the physiocratic plans for complete freedom in the circulation of grain and other products. Frenchmen were accustomed to governmental control of prices and distribution, a practice deemed absolutely necessary in time of scarcity. But the ideas enjoyed some success. In 1761, Trudaine de Montigny, friendly to the school, became president of the Committee of Agriculture, recently established by the Controller-General. On his initiative, as well as that of Turgot, Bertin, the Controller-General of Finances, was induced to create, by the *arrêt* of February 24, 1761, the first Society of Agriculture properly so called. This action was very rapidly followed by the creation of many other societies.[25] On May 25, 1763, a solemn declaration proclaimed the freedom of the grain trade throughout the kingdom (except in Paris and its environs) and authorized limited exportation. Although this edict became largely a dead letter, the school now seemed really to be playing a role in public affairs. At this propitious time, November, 1763, there appeared the *Philosophie rurale; économie générale de l'agriculture réduite à l'ordre immuable des lois physiques et morales qui assurent la prospérité des nations agricoles,* a mature statement of the physiocratic viewpoint drawn up by Mirabeau under the careful supervision of Quesnay.[26] By the time their complete philosophy could thus be unfolded, Quesnay and Mirabeau had attracted several brilliant young disciples and collaborators. Among them was Du Pont, who spoke truly when he remarked, "I was only a child when [Quesnay] held out his arms to me; it is he who made me a man."[27]

The new disciple had at once to face some of the burdens of adulthood: the nagging annoyance of jealous and malicious criticism and the uncomfortable necessity of a major decision. Louis-Paul Abeille had enjoyed the favorite's role in Quesnay's circle and was then engaged in a study of the grain trade, which for over a decade had been a matter of widespread interest.[28] He naturally resented the attentions which the master lavished so quickly upon a novice and was probably taken aback by the news that Du Pont's first big assignment was to study the commerce of cereal grains, the very subject upon which he was at work. From that time forward Abeille, fifteen years older than the new favorite, never lost an opportunity to criticize and to ridicule Du Pont's writings, taking delight at the beginning in almost reducing him to tears before the master himself. Quesnay took the edge off these barbs and eventually Du Pont learned to bear up better under criticism, which he was to meet so frequently in his career. Abeille, who definitely broke with Quesnay in 1768, may have done him a service, however painful the experience was at first. The major decision concerned Choiseul, who had continued in his attitude of friendly encouragement unaccompanied by material assistance. Dutifully, Du Pont informed the Duke of his relationship with Quesnay and was rather alarmed by the reserve with which the news was received. What he did not know was that Choiseul had recently had a falling-out with the Pompadour and, as a result, now feared and hated Dr. Quesnay, who remained in the lady's good graces. One day, at the weekly reception, Du Pont boldly asked the Duke the reason for his chilliness. Retiring to an inner office away from the throng of courtiers, Choiseul stated blandly that he had not altered his attitude but that Du Pont's regard for him had obviously changed. Then came the fateful words: "M. Quesnay's friends are not mine: choose." While Du Pont declared that he would not choose, he made his decision by refusing to break with Quesnay. Any further hope of preferment from the minister had thenceforth to be abandoned. His future lay in the work which he could do for Quesnay and for Méliand.

The latter invited him to accompany him on a trip through his intendancy of Soissons. Quesnay urged him to go and gave him a long list of questions to investigate from the first-hand observations which he would be able to make during the journey. In his spare time, the Doctor said, he could work on his essay on the exportation and importation of grain. There was at first very little spare time. Du Pont participated so actively in the careful inspection carried out by Méliand in several of the districts (or *élections*) that he aroused the animosity of the intendant's first secretary and of various subordinate officials. Méliand appeared, however, to be well pleased with his efforts, especially with the reports which he wrote on different aspects of their investigations. For Du Pont the experience was valuable beyond words; he had an exceptional opportunity to observe the details of administration, to be present, for example, when the old and hateful tax known as the *taille* was assessed among the parishes of an *élection* and when judgment was rendered on the protests against specific assessments. After some weeks of this introduction to the practicalities of government, Du Pont began, however, to have pricks of conscience over his failure to produce the essay on the grain trade for which Quesnay was waiting. He induced Méliand to leave him behind in Soissons so that he could write in solitude while the intendant embarked upon another part of his tour.

Moving a small bed into the library attached to the intendant's office and arranging to have his meals brought in, Du Pont left his retreat only twice in three weeks. And during all that time he did very little of the writing which he had now assigned himself! Never before had he been surrounded by so many books with such exciting titles. For a fortnight he indulged in a veritable orgy of reading, hardly pausing to eat or to sleep. Exactly what books he went through he does not, unfortunately, state, but they drove from his head any thoughts of preparing his essay until just a few days before

Méliand was due to return. Then in four days he put together a rough draft of his essay on "the freedom of the grain trade," which, shortly afterward, he read before the Soissons Society of Agriculture. He was aware that the work was not yet ready for Quesnay's inspection; so, after another brief trip with Méliand, he begged for more leisure time in order to revise it. Knowing of Quesnay's interest in the work, Méliand granted his request.

Du Pont chose as his retreat this time the familiar house of the Dorés in Nemours. The chief reason for his choice was, of course, that he expected to find his fiancée, Mademoiselle Le Dée, there, but he explained it also as a matter of convenience. Since the court had temporarily moved to Fontainebleau, Quesnay would be rather close to Nemours. Du Pont was disappointed in his first expectation. Learning of his plans, Marie Le Dée's father came beforehand and took his daughter away. This action rather than removing a potent source of distraction almost wrecked the enterprise. Madame Doré was surly because Du Pont's visit thus led to the departure of her young cousin, and Du Pont was even more distraught. After several days, however, he made the best of the situation and used his leisure to turn out a much improved manuscript, which he carried to Quesnay.

The Doctor was well pleased with the work, which he believed could be printed after a few corrections. He decided, indeed, that the book would not be unworthy of bearing a dedication to his patroness, Madame de Pompadour. Such a dedication would have at least two advantages, that of blunting somewhat the strictures of those who would violently disagree with the viewpoints and that of finding for its young author a protector who could help him in his career. After having the whole matter explained to her, Madame, who counted agriculture high among her many interests, consented to the dedication and asked to have the author presented to her. Du Pont's elation was boundless; surely his career was now firmly established. Madame de Pompadour was gracious, calling him "our young agriculturist" and assuring him of her great interest in all efforts to alleviate the burdens of the people. There was talk of creating a special committee with Du Pont as secretary to study conditions and to make recommendations for action. When he returned to Nemours to make the necessary revisions in his manuscript and told Madame

Doré of this significant change in his prospects, he found her a much more pleasant hostess than she had been. While he worked on his manuscript, he took time also to read the *Philosophie rurale*. He was so well pleased with it that he paid a visit to the Marquis de Mirabeau at his estate of Bignon, only about twelve miles from Nemours.[29]

Here, for the first time, Du Pont met the tempestuous Mirabeau family, including the elder son Honoré Gabriel, who was later to be famous as one of the great leaders in the National Assembly during the early part of the Revolution. Almost ten years older than Honoré Gabriel, Du Pont was immediately attracted by the sharp intelligence of the young man. Mutual esteem formed the basis for a friendship sorely tested now and then by the irresponsible actions of the amoral Mirabeau, whose escapades became scandalous even in an age of greater tolerance of such conduct.

Another member of the Mirabeau household was Madame de Pailly, whose beauty thoroughly dazzled the visitor. During the following weeks she made a strong impression upon Du Pont. He was inspired to yield again to his penchant for versifying and to present to the lady several poems extolling her charms. These poetic outpourings were not without effect. Madame de Pailly, it appeared, expected them to be followed by more substantial demonstrations of Du Pont's affection. Rather belatedly the ardent poet came to appreciate that the relationship existing between Madame de Pailly and the Marquis de Mirabeau was such that the latter would not welcome any hint that another man was courting the lady. Out of respect and friendship for the Marquis, Du Pont now reminded himself severely that he was, after all, pledged to another and ceased his scribbling. An unhappy situation soon arose. Madame de Pailly did not appreciate this end to whatever expectations she may have had and, henceforth, exerted herself to turn the Marquis against this young man who had apparently been merely toying with her feelings. From that time on, to Du Pont's distress, there was a strain in his relations with the man who had been so important in encouraging him at the outset of his career. He was consoled only by the fact that at that very time the little notoriety which came to him through the publication of his *De l'exportation et de l'importation des grains* won for him the friendship of the man who was to mean more to him even than Dr. Quesnay. That man was Anne Robert Jacques Turgot, intendant of Limoges.

The book appeared, however, amidst very inauspicious circumstances. While the revised manuscript was going through the press, the great lady to whom it was to be dedicated and from whom so much was expected was laid low by a fatal illness, a congestion of the lungs, as it was said. Madame de Pompadour had long been in ill health but had insisted upon continuing without abatement all the numerous activities which filled her days at the court. As her health further declined, Choiseul, who detested Quesnay, won the King's consent that she be attended by another physician, a Dr. Richard. The latter sought to overcome the weakness of his patient by heavy doses of tonics and cordials. Du Pont was convinced that this overstimulation put too much strain on the heart and caused the death of the patient on April 15, 1764.[30] The loss of Madame de Pompadour was a disastrous blow to Quesnay and his young disciple. Choiseul was now in full command, and Quesnay no longer had any influence at court. There were chilling rumors that the first minister even proposed to imprison his rival, but they proved false. Quesnay and Du Pont were left at peace and alone, for all the courtiers who had previously filled the Doctor's small apartment to overflowing now scurried elsewhere. At least there was now opportunity for uninterrupted work.

Du Pont's powers of concentration were, however, undermined from another quarter. The sensation caused by the death of the favorite royal mistress set all sorts of wild tales afoot in the environs of Versailles. The probable disgrace of all those close to Madame de Pompadour was, of course, widely predicted. Such tales reached the ears of Madame Doré and of Marie Le Dée's father, who had to be concerned about his own position as collector with one of the royal tax farms. These two conspired to break off the understanding between Marie and Pierre, since all great expectations had now been borne to the tomb with the deceased protectress. This stern decision was a heavy shock to the engaged couple, who so recently had had good reason to believe that they would be able to marry before the two-year testing period had elapsed. Monsieur Le Dée had even had Pierre to dinner and had introduced him to other members of the family. Now he forbade his daughter ever to see him again. These parental prohibitions had the usual results: Marie and Pierre firmly resolved to maintain a secret communication.

Du Pont's book finally appeared late in April. It had been held up by the necessity of procuring authorization to circumvent the decree of March 28 which the new Controller-General, L'Averdy, protégé of Choiseul, had induced the Parlement of Paris to register. This decree forbade, on pain of extraordinary punishment, any writing on the past, present, or future administration of the finances. It was, fortunately, not very strictly enforced. *De l'exportation et de l'importation des grains* was a work of major proportions. With the appendix of two letters (one anonymous, the second by Forbonnais) reprinted from the *Gazette du Commerce* and Du Pont's reflections on these letters, the original edition extended to 173 pages. More important than the size was the carefully constructed text in which Du Pont used to good purpose some of the results of his investigations in the Soissons intendancy. It is difficult today to recapture the intense interest in the grain trade shared by so many intellectuals in the latter part of the eighteenth century. There are still stretches of the world where the abundance or scarcity, the storing and transport, of this basic sustenance may spell life or death for a vast number of human beings, but these matters are usually of small concern in areas where mechanization in its manifold applications has had significant impact. The so-called agricultural and industrial revolutions had not yet affected France, or most of Europe, when Du Pont wrote his book. In the field of agriculture, especially, England for peculiar reasons which could not apply elsewhere seemed to be ahead. Most students of political economy were then very much concerned with the English experience, and there was a growing communication between French and English writers. Already Du Pont had made some study of the English situation. The fourth chapter of his book[31] sought to estimate the effect upon prices resulting from the exportation permitted in England and to translate these estimates into calculations of the probable effect which exportation would have upon prices in France. The use of comparison or contrast between the two countries was, however, more clearly introduced in the pamphlet which his rival, L.-P. Abeille, published at about the same time, the *Réflexions sur la police des grains en France et en Angleterre*.[32] Both argued for free exportation—the view which was the more favored one between

1750 and 1770, after a long period during the first half of the century when views upholding regulation and restriction held the center of the stage.[33]

Against the advice of several of his friends, Du Pont insisted upon retaining the letter of dedication to Madame de Pompadour. Before the letter of praise he added a simple note which stated:

"It is believed that the sad event [which] occurred since the printing of this pamphlet ought not to bring the suppression of a homage which truth dictated.

"Woe to the man who would fear to fling a few flowers on the tomb of those to whom he offered his incense."[34]

The dedication did not detract from the book's popularity. Du Pont was able to call it "one of his writings which had most success." Within two months every copy had been disposed of at a good profit to the printer, P. G. Simon. The author received twenty-five louis and 150 copies of the book.[35]

The book's success was due at least in part to the climate of opinion favorable to arguments for removing restrictions on the commerce of grains. L'Averdy had not sought to revoke the declaration of May 25, 1763, calling for the freedom of the grain trade within France and for limited exportation. It is true that he did not try to attain the objectives proclaimed in the declaration, for he was not so sympathetic to this development as Bertin, his predecessor in the controller-general's office, had been. So long as the declaration remained official, however, the Government had not closed the door to the freeing of trade and seemed to invite further urging that it act. Du Pont's purpose was to supply reasons for governmental action in the direction of extending the area of freedom to include the exportation and importation of grain.

His book had merits of its own which contributed to its success. It is well organized into short chapters and written in a clear prose free of the literary flourishes which Du Pont sometimes attempted. It is not, and was not meant to be, an objective study of the problem. The author's conclusions were firmly in his mind before he began his study, but he does not seek to deceive his readers. The first sentence of his preface states openly that the matter at hand was "to prove the immense advantages which the nation would find in the general, entire, absolute and irrevocable freedom of the external

37

commerce of grains."[36] One feature lifts the book from the rank of being just another pamphlet founded upon abstract and dogmatic argument in a campaign to force government action. Du Pont cites actual figures acquired in his investigations in his consideration of the costs of production, in his estimates of average prices, and in his predictions of the probable effects of changes. He works out several tables to assist the reader in grasping these figures. While some of them were undoubtedly debatable, these statistical representations had decided impact upon many minds. A student today must often bemoan the unreliability of eighteenth century statistics. He must not forget, however, the growing interest during the latter part of that century in the study of whatever figures one could arrive at on governmental finance in particular and on economic activity in general. Only on the basis of information could realistic reforms be accomplished. It is easy to point out today that, because of the crude and uncertain methods of keeping records then employed, these figures could really be only estimates. Such considerations do not, of course, impede the eager reformer. Statistics can be overwhelming to those not initiated in what often seem their mysteries. Du Pont expended much care on his statistical tables and especially on the principal one found in his fifth chapter, which sought to predict the increase in agricultural productivity and revenue to be expected over a nine-year period from the free exportation of grain. He urged his readers to exercise their right to examine and to judge his figures but expressed the hope that those who did not, or could not, exercise this right would not dare to contradict him.[37] Here was an effective device for turning away possible criticism of parts of his argument. In a "Résumé" at the end he summarized the substance of each of his thirteen chapters. He had proved to his own satisfaction that freeing the external commerce of grains would triple the revenues, and add to the strength of the nation, the wealth of the rich, and the wages of the poor. All these advantages would be realized because freedom to trade would make easier the supplying of food for the people by increasing agriculture, population, and trade. Such liberty, he concluded, was indispensable to the true regeneration of the state and its finances.[38]

However impressive such arguments might be, there was one practical consideration which often prevented realization of a system of free trade in grain. When crops were abundant there was little significant objection to unrestricted trade. Let there be a bad harvest, however, and local officials and peasants called loudly for regulation so that they might assure sufficient supplies for their own minimum requirements. This ill luck was later to plague the efforts of the sincere reformer Turgot, who was to exercise the most powerful influence on Du Pont's life. It was the book on the grain trade that brought them together. In this fortunate event Du Pont found afterward the principal value and usefulness of his essay.[39] Immediately after reading the book Turgot made inquiries to discover the address of the author, identified on the title-page as an associate of the Soissons Society of Agriculture. Somehow he learned the address of the Du Pont shop on the Rue de Richelieu and made a personal call. Du Pont was deeply touched by the "esteem, confidence, and kind interest" shown in him by this well-informed man, who, however brilliant his theoretical insights, always drew upon his experience as intendant to temper abstract theory with the practicalities of administration. Du Pont came to feel himself more closely attached to Turgot than he had ever been to Quesnay. He later described his two masters in these terms:

The ideas of M. Turgot did not, perhaps, have as much depth as those of M. Quesnay, but in their range they were broader: he examined them less and connected them more. The doctor sought his principles in nature and in metaphysics; he said: "there is what ought to rule the world"; and he could be understood only by a small number of vigorous thinkers. The magistrate embraced in his [principles] the entire mass of human knowledge and the general history of the universe; . . . he could be followed provided that one was logical and had good sense. But what above all made M. Turgot more agreeable was that he was more affectionate. To please M. Quesnay it was necessary to have intellect and talent good for something. To be endeared to M. Turgot, it was sufficient to have a good, honest and sensible heart; however one did not immediately appreciate all the charm of his society. At first he appeared only wise, well-informed and gentle: it was necessary to have lived with him and in his home to know to what extent he was affectionate and tender.[40]

Turgot introduced Du Pont to Daniel Charles Trudaine, then one of the intendants of finance, and to his son, Jean-Charles-Philibert Trudaine de Montigny, who carried on some of the duties connected with his father's governmental position. His reason for this introduction was immediately evident. The Trudaines were then occupied with the drafting of an edict to consolidate the internal freedom of the grain trade and to extend this freedom to external trade. They were glad to have the assistance of Turgot and Du Pont in their labors. All four worked on the text of the edict and finally submitted it to L'Averdy. The Controller-General was not adamantly opposed to some further freeing of the commerce of grains, but he did insist upon numerous modifications that laid restrictions on the complete freedom for which Du Pont had argued. The edict was issued in July, 1764; it did permit exportation, but under certain conditions, such as that of requiring that grain for export had to be shipped from a few specified ports. Du Pont had been so dissatisfied with L'Averdy's modifications that, before the edict was promulgated, he had prepared under the title *L'Antirestricteur* a manuscript arguing against each of the restrictive changes upon which the Controller-General had insisted. The essay was never published in full and has been lost, but parts of it appeared in Du Pont's steadily increasing correspondence.[41] Having now seen some of his work in print and having won some little attention, he seemed to be gripped by a mania for writing. From this time to the end of his life his outpourings were prolific. At one point Quesnay sharply reprimanded him for wasting so much time on numerous and long letters to many correspondents. Thereafter he confined his personal letters to only a few persons outside of his family. The first of these was, of course, Turgot, to whom Du Pont, by his own estimate, wrote at least 1,800 letters and from whom he received about 1,000 replies.[42] Du Pont's various official activities from this time forward prompted a very large number of letters, usually long, which survive as originals or copies.

In his autobiography Du Pont mentions a letter to the committee set up by the Parlement of Aix (in Provence) to examine the edict on the grain trade. In sending them requested advice on this matter and on the best system of taxation he included in his letter most of the text of his memorandum against restrictions. This letter did not reach its destination, since it was intercepted by the government censors. In another letter to M. de Malteste, sub-dean of the Parlement of Dijon, he detailed his objections to the edict of March 28, 1764, which forbade any writing on the administration of finances.

He claims that almost the entire text of this letter appeared subsequently in the remonstrance of the Parlement of Dijon refusing registration of the edict. Eventually all the provincial parlements rejected it after it had been registered by the Parlement of Paris.[43] Undoubtedly Du Pont was flattered by the attention paid to him by men so much his senior in age and experience. The officers of the Royal Society of Agriculture of Soissons, of which he was a member, asked him to maintain regular correspondence with them. He did not get around to writing long letters to them until September, 1764, excusing the delay because of very severe illness, no record of which seems to exist elsewhere. His letters are detailed and technical, answering questions raised about specific points of his book on the grain trade, seeking additional information on agricultural practices in Soissons, and arranging to send a copy of his *mémoire* on restrictions.[44] Earlier he had written other letters on grain which were published in the *Gazette du commerce*.[45]

During the late spring or early summer of 1764 he prepared several reports for the Trudaines, who were now studying the problems involved in the suppression of interior customs lines and the establishment of a uniform tariff on the frontiers. Nothing came of these efforts at the time and his reports have not been preserved, but such studies added much to the store of information upon which he could draw in his later career. They served a more immediate function in that he received some payment for his services. He was able to scrape together enough money to take care of himself, but marriage was still out of the question. The substantial rewards which might have been hoped for from the Pompadour's patronage were now unattainable.

The mysterious illness mentioned in the letters to Soissons may not have existed except as a weak excuse for idleness. For about six months in 1764 Du Pont in his own judgment did nothing useful. Instead he threw himself into a round of dinners and parties. A welcome guest in the Trudaine households, he met many people, especially women, who flattered his ego. This ready acceptance into society must have gone to the young author's head. Too many of his afternoons and nights were spent in salons and dining halls and his mornings in bed recovering from the late hours of the night before. Of all his new acquaintances only one was of any value to him.

Through the Trudaines, he met Bouvard de Fourqueux, a friend of Turgot and a councillor of state attached to the royal councils of finances and commerce. He formed a close friendship with this experienced official, who concealed a profound knowledge behind an excessive modesty. Although Du Pont did not appreciate the modesty, which was foreign to his own nature, he must have profited considerably from Fourqueux's knowledge. Eventually he became dissatisfied with himself for staying so long away from his desk. One day he impulsively seized a pair of scissors and cut off the hair on the left side of his head. Thus rendered somewhat ridiculous in appearance, he had to withdraw from society. He went back to work.

Encouraged by Quesnay he produced a small essay on large- and small-scale cultivation of the land, published in the *Gazette du commerce* in January, 1765.[46] This insignificant piece blindly followed Quesnay's crude criterion for distinguishing between large and small tillage—i.e., whether horses or oxen were employed to draw the plows—but it did at least bring Du Pont back to his studies, leaving as his only distraction his courtship of Marie Le Dée.

The parental prohibitions had added spice to this courtship, which now became a conspiracy. In order to continue to exchange letters[47] and gifts and to meet occasionally, other persons had to be enlisted in the campaign to get around the barriers erected by Marie's father. Ready recruits were found in Marie's old governess, in Berget, the Le Dée gardener, in old Mother Saulnier, a midwife, and in Madame Benevault, Marie's great aunt. For a while everything worked splendidly. Deaf old Madame Benevault with her romantic notions furthered the course of young love by encouraging Du Pont with words and with money so that he could pay for the co-operation of his three other conspirators. Midwife Saulnier carried messages to Berget or to the governess, sometimes even to Marie. Berget (an "honest Drunkard," Du Pont calls him) was the chief intermediary in the exchange of letters. It soon became possible to have secret meetings at Madame Saulnier's, at the gardener's cottage and, for the touch of real excitement, even in the Le Dée household after Monsieur Le Dée had retired for the night. A light placed in a certain manner in a window summoned the waiting swain. A few dried peas thrown against a certain window announced his arrival. A door was opened and the lovers were united either in the dining room or the garden. Pierre's strange haircut was a welcome sign that he had forsworn all other women in favor of Marie and idle society in favor of work.[48]

Du Pont was happy and his sanguine temperament was again in command. He studied, he wrote, he consulted with Quesnay; with joyful expectation he awaited the opportunities which would bring him fame. His exuberance led him into a ridiculously naïve indiscretion. The actor and playwright Pierre-Laurent-Buyrette de Belloy achieved a great triumph during the winter of 1764-1765 when his *Siège de Calais* was produced in Paris. Du Pont was stirred by the play and saw it several times. After the text of the drama was printed at the end of the theatrical season in 1765, he read it carefully. He decided that it was really very badly written in "half barbarous" verse and undertook to help the author improve his piece so that it might enjoy even greater success when the theaters opened again. He made some 580 "corrections" in the text and sent them along with a friendly letter to Belloy. To his surprise he received no reply and subsequently learned that Belloy had been outrageously offended by his impertinence and would never pardon him! Worse was to come. Quesnay, who detested poetry as profoundly as Samuel Du Pont, heard that his favorite disciple was again wasting his time with such nonsense. He scolded Du Pont so thoroughly and so frequently that the latter decided to give up his pursuit of the muse. Not until four years later, under the kinder treatment of Turgot, who also liked to pen occasional verses, did he return to poetry and cherish it as the dearest companion of his leisure moments.

The most serious problem remained that of finding a position which would assure a regular income. Marriage was impossible so long as Du Pont had to subsist on the money which he could occasionally obtain by writing a book or by taking on special assignments. In 1765 he accepted an extensive assignment from Méliand, who hoped that a major achievement might forward his ambition to become a councillor of state. Méliand now proposed a detailed description of the economy of his Soissons intendancy, because the equitable and effective levying of taxes rested upon a complete knowledge of the necessary expenses and of the gross and net income of the many farms in the area. Du Pont was charged with carrying out this elaborate survey. He was given inadequate funds, only 1,800 francs, with which he was able to employ only five generally incompetent secretaries to assist him. Nevertheless he was overjoyed. Here was a huge task which, if successfully accomplished, would bring him renown. Furthermore Turgot requested him to make a similar survey of his intendancy of Limoges as soon as he had finished in Soissons. In his enthusiasm Du Pont saw opening before him the path which would bring him eventually to the office of controller-general or at least to that of intendant of finances.[49] He set off on the journeys throughout the intendancy which were necessary to collect all the information. But the job was never completed in the manner which he had first planned. Unexpectedly, still another opportunity arose.

In July, 1765, the proprietors of the *Gazette du commerce* began the publication of a monthly supplement bearing the name *Journal de l'agriculture, du commerce et des finances.* The columns of the biweekly *Gazette* had been increasingly filled with letters attacking and supporting the new ideas of Quesnay and his disciples. It was in order to give space to aroused public opinion while at the same time preserving their original intent to make the *Gazette* primarily an organ of information that the owners obtained official sanction for this supplement, whose principal function would be to open its pages on an impartial basis to the opponents and champions of the *économistes.* After the appearance of the first two issues, Du Pont was offered the editorship of the *Journal.* Although the exact circumstances of the offer are not known, it was probably made upon the recommendations of the Abbé Morellet and of Trudaine.[50] Its immediate importance for Du Pont was that it provided a position with some assurance of a regular salary which would permit him to marry. He accepted the offer at once and asked Marie to choose the day of their wedding.

But parental objections had to be overcome. Now that the problem of a regular position had been solved, Monsieur Le Dée objected on other grounds, those of religion. A pious Catholic, he could not, he now said, approve the marriage of his daughter to a Protestant. In a few weeks, however, his objections were overcome through the personal appeals of his daughter and through the letters of her fiancé, one of which, apparently, carried assurance that the young man was not a Protestant.[51] More time had to be given to winning the full assent of Du Pont's father, Samuel. At last all obstacles were overcome; the marriage contract was registered on January 26, 1766, with L'Averdy, the Controller-General, Trudaine de Montigny, Méliand, Mézieres, a Farmer General, and Du Pont's uncles, Alexandre and Pierre, serving as witnesses. The wedding took place two days later in the church of Saint Sulpice in Paris.[52]

This fruition of his rash promise of three years before brought Du Pont his greatest happiness during the difficult period when he was building the foundations of his career. Marie Le Dée was twenty-four when she was married, a gentle yet spirited and mature woman, well schooled in the arts of household management. Devoted to her husband, she encouraged his ambitions while relieving him of the details of household economy. She endured without complaint the material hardship of the first eight years of married life, which were full of disappointments. The first blow came before the year was out in the loss of the editorial position which had made marriage possible.

In view of the announced purpose of the *Journal de l'agriculture, du commerce et des finances,* the proprietors did not act wisely in naming Du Pont editor. He was conscientious and indefatigable but could, in no circumstances, assume an impartial attitude regarding the doctrines of the *économistes.* He was one of them and shared their delight in the prospect of access to a regular publication. He was soon doing everything possible to present the contributions of Quesnay and his associates—Mirabeau, Le Trosne, Saint-Péravy, Le Mercier de la Rivière, occasionally even Abeille—in a manner disadvantageous to opposing viewpoints. One method he used was to add notes disagreeing with the arguments contained in the unfriendly letters when he published them. After a few months the proprietors of the *Journal* ordered him to cease this practice. Thereafter he had, for the most part, to limit his own contributions to articles which he signed with the pseudonym "M-C."[53] All of them contained familiar physiocratic arguments dealing with such matters as freedom of commerce, especially of trade in grain, the central importance of agriculture in the maintenance of a large population, and opposition to monopolistic privileges in colonial trade.[54] Du Pont occasionally yielded to protests about the overemphasis upon physiocratic views

45

in the *Journal*; once he even had Quesnay prepare an article attacking his own doctrines. The real inclinations of the editor could not, however, be concealed. The owners of the *Journal* dismissed him in October, 1766, allegedly because of his refusal to censure the Parlement of Rennes for its support of its *procureur-général* La Chalotais in his determined opposition to the Duc d'Aiguillon, military commandant of Brittany.[55] Du Pont's dismissal effectively halted the project of turning the *Journal de l'agriculture* into a propaganda sheet for physiocratic viewpoints.

Quesnay and his group were not, however, to be without a regular outlet for publication. Since early November, 1765, the Abbé Nicolas Baudeau had been publishing the *Éphémérides du citoyen, ou Chronique de l'esprit national*, a journal of opinion, the separate numbers of which appeared twice a week.[56] Baudeau's economic ideas were at first a peculiar mixture of mercantilist principles modified by acceptance of the importance of a large population and of agriculture in assessing the wealth of a nation. Le Trosne and Du Pont seized upon these modifications and attempted to prove to the Abbé that these views must logically bring him to their side. From all accounts Du Pont played the most important role in "converting" Baudeau, who suspended his journal for two months in November and December, 1766, and began in January, 1767, to issue it as a monthly with altered emphasis and name as *Éphémérides du citoyen, ou Bibliothèque des sciences morales et politiques*.[57] Henceforth it was practically the official journal of the *économistes*. Only the Abbé Baudeau, the founder of the periodical, received any income from subscriptions. Du Pont had to rely once more upon the uncertain salary which might be earned by performing whatever tasks governmental officials would assign him.

Fortunately he could turn again to the uncompleted work which he had been doing for Méliand in Soissons. He had also the assurance of additional work for Turgot in Limoges. These labors for Méliand and Turgot supplied Du Pont with a wealth of practical information. In a later letter to Voltaire, he remarked that, in the course of his journeys, he had had the opportunity to see more than 3,000 farms and that he made a detailed description of around 400 of them.[58] While he carried forward the survey for Méliand, he undertook another project of importance in furthering physiocratic views. Fearing that many of Quesnay's writings, available in very limited editions like the *Tableau Œconomique,* or scattered in periodicals like the *Journal de l'agriculture,* might eventually pass into oblivion, Du Pont decided to publish a collection of the master's pieces. In addition to the famous *Tableau,* with various explanatory essays, he brought together a half dozen other papers. He wrote a long introduction to the entire work, prepared shorter prefaces to the individual essays of Quesnay, and added summary tables. Probably at Quesnay's suggestion he entitled the collection *Physiocratie ou Constitution naturelle du gouvernement le plus avantageux au genre humain.*[59] It appeared in two parts, or two volumes with consecutively numbered pages, in November, 1767.[60] The word *physiocratie* (formed from the Greek for "rule of nature") supplied the term by which the *économistes* were subsequently to be designated, although it did not become widely used during the eighteenth century.

Du Pont's "Discours de l'éditeur," covering 101 pages at the beginning of the first volume, sought to explain clearly and enthusiastically the substance of Quesnay's philosophy. There is some justice in Turgot's criticism that this introduction does not give a complete and accurate account of Quesnay's thought and that the development of the ideas is "too systematic."[61] Du Pont arranged Quesnay's writings in an "abstract and logical" order to display a consistency of thought not immediately apparent in a strictly chronological presentation.[62] He was attempting to put forward a coherent body of doctrine which, based upon an undiscriminating acceptance of the existence of a natural order and natural laws, would provide the framework for a science of society. His effort in *Physiocratie* was, however, considerably overshadowed by the work of Mercier de La Rivière, former intendant of the Windward Islands. Forced to leave his post in Martinique in 1764 because of objections to his liberal commercial policies, Mercier de La Rivière became an active supporter of Quesnay's teachings. In the summer of 1767 he published his *L'Ordre naturel et essential des sociétés politiques,* which Adam Smith later called "the most distinct and best connected account of [the] doctrine" of the school.[63] Du Pont was so stirred by the book, which he called "excellent" and "sublime,"[64] that he decided to prepare a concise summary of the "new science" discovered by Quesnay, a summary based upon Mercier de La Rivière's more detailed presentation of the tenets of physiocracy. One month after the publication of *Physiocratie*, this summary appeared anonymously under the title *De l'origine et des progrès d'une science nouvelle*.[65]

Early in this pamphlet Du Pont succinctly states the conception of the natural order which constituted the Physiocrats' frame of reference.

> There is a natural Society anterior to every convention among men, founded on their constitution, on their physical needs, on their obviously common interest.
>
> In this primitive state, men have *rights* and reciprocal *duties* of an *absolute* justice, because they are of a physical necessity and consequently *absolute* for their existence.
>
> *No rights without duties, and no duties without rights.*
>
> The *rights* of each man, anterior to conventions, are the *freedom* of providing for his subsistence and his well-being, the *property* of his person and that of things acquired by the labor of his person.
>
> His *duties* are the labor of supplying his needs and respect for the freedom, for the personal property, and for the acquired [*mobiliaire*] property of others.
>
> Conventions can be made among men only for recognizing and for mutually guaranteeing these rights and these duties established by God himself.
>
> There is therefore a natural and essential order to which social conventions are subject, and this order is that which assures to men united in society *the enjoyment of all their rights* by the observance of all their duties. The exact and general submission to this order is the single condition by which each one can expect and may with certainty hope for participation in all the advantages which society can procure for him.[66]

This statement reveals at once both the strength and weakness of the physiocratic approach. By the vigorous effort to seek a consistent order amidst the complexities of economic and social life the Physiocrats were able to mount an effective assault upon many contemporary institutions and practices which needed reform. The acceptance of this general framework by a group of able thinkers and writers inspired by Quesnay provides some justification for designating them as the first organized school of political economy. On the other hand, there is little that is original in their general orientation. The basic ingredients of Du Pont's statement can be found elsewhere—notably, for example, in Locke's second treatise *Of Civil Government*. What the Physiocrats supplied primarily was a doctrinaire emphasis upon these ideas, a confident assertion that these matters are necessarily part of nature. There is an easy confusion between the kind of *physical* law of nature which Newton put forward and a *moral* law of what *ought* to be but is not necessarily in operation. The conviction that there is a natural and essential order of rights and duties "established by God himself" was a source of courage to Du Pont and his associates in their bold attacks upon practices which interfered with this natural order. At the same time it could give to their arguments a rigid dogmatism which caused them to overlook the realities of their surroundings and to ignore the practical and gradual steps required on the road to reform. Du Pont's initial dogmatism was later considerably modified through his long experience in government. But he never lost the confidence of his conviction that he labored on the side of right and of truth.

After a brief survey of some of the principal publications which contributed to the establishment of the new science, Du Pont devoted the main sections of his pamphlet to a summary of the physiocratic doctrine of the primacy of agriculture and the wisdom of the single tax. Sections 19 and 20 present the physiocratic conception of the best form of government in a society established in conformity to a "natural and essential order." This view dismissed as undesirable both a democratic sovereignty and an elective monarchy because the agents of sovereignty in both cases are transitory and likely to be more swayed by private than by common interests. Only an hereditary monarch who is co-proprietor of all net product of the land can provide a permanent concern for the interests of the whole society and "perfect community of interests between a Monarch . . . and his people." "An hereditary Monarch associated with his nation by the proportional sharing of the *net product* of real property [*biens-fonds*] has a manifest interest [in seeing] that the *net product* be the greatest possible."[67] In order to assure this result, the monarch will, of course, take care that the "positive laws which he is obliged to promulgate" conform to "the divine laws of the natural order."[68] Although he later tempered his views on government, Du Pont was always solicitous about the prerogatives of the monarch, who might be this "legal despot," and suspicious of individuals' particular and private interests that would be contrary to the common welfare.

From the standpoint of conciseness and lucidity of statement, *De l'origine et des progrès d'une science nouvelle* must hold high place among Du Pont's works. It was reprinted in an expanded edition of *Physiocratie*, which appeared in 1768 and 1769[69] and was translated into German in 1770.[70] Du Pont was pleased by its success. Indeed, despite his financial uncertainties, these years were happy ones for him. He was busy at his writing table turning out page after page proclaiming the truths of the new science. He supplied Baudeau with several pieces for the *Éphémérides*, one of which—*De l'administration des chemins*—was separately published.[71] In this pamphlet he belabored the *corvée*, the tax paid in labor on the roads, as uneconomic and pernicious and argued for its replacement by a money tax levied on the owners of real property. The influence of Turgot, who had carried out this reform in his intendancy, is evident.[72] During these years also Du Pont was expanding his circle of acquaintances, which came to include two important foreigners, Adam Smith and Benjamin Franklin. Making the grand tour as tutor and companion of the Duke of Buccleuch, Smith lived in Paris for ten months between December, 1765, and October, 1766, and occasionally attended the regular meetings which Quesnay had with his group in Paris and Versailles. There Du Pont met him frequently but was not much impressed, since Smith had yet to achieve the fame which ten years later *The Wealth of Nations* brought to him.[73] Benjamin Franklin became an intimate of Quesnay's circle during his sojourn in Paris in 1767. Although Franklin expressed to Quesnay his interest in meeting Du Pont, the latter was so busy that he did not learn of this desire until the very day of Franklin's departure. Then it was too late. Months later he wrote to Franklin in London, sending along a copy of the *Physiocratie* and a shorter piece, probably *De l'origine*.[74] Franklin replied in gracious words which must have further stirred Du Pont's enthusiasm:

"I received your obliging Letter of the 10th of May, with the most acceptable Present of your *Physiocratie*, which I have read with great pleasure, and received from it a great deal of Instruction. There is such a Freedom from local and national Prejudices and Partialities, so much Benevolence to Mankind in general, so much

Goodness mixt with the Wisdom, in the Principles of your new Philosophy, that I am perfectly charmed with them, and wish I could have staid in France for some time to have studied in your School, that I might, by conversing with its Founders have made myself quite a Master of the Philosophy."[75] The exchange of compliments in these letters was the first of a series which passed between the two men during the next twenty years.

Personal contacts continued to be important in sustaining the morale of the group. Quesnay turned more and more from economic studies and ceased to meet regularly with his eager disciples, but the Marquis de Mirabeau filled the gap. Beginning in late 1766 or early 1767 he invited the group of *économistes* to his home in Paris every Tuesday for dinner and discussion. These weekly meetings, often attended by visitors, were important in clarifying and spreading the ideas of the school.[76] Du Pont could feel satisfaction in contemplating the continuing triumph of the new science. Everything seemed to be going along well. His family life also was happy. In October, 1767, his first son was born and Mirabeau consented to stand as godparent. The boy was, therefore, given the first name of his sponsor and baptized Victor-Marie.

In the spring of 1768 the Abbé Baudeau was tempted by the offer of a potentially remunerative position in Poland. He had first to relieve himself of the obligations incurred to the subscribers to the *Éphémérides* and now offered the editorship of the journal to Du Pont with a promise of full ownership within a year. Eager to forward the progress of physiocracy and to enjoy the prestige which this position would bring to him, Du Pont agreed to the terms, although Turgot, who wanted Du Pont to continue to work with him at Limoges, advised against it. With the assistance of others Du Pont believed that he could carry on the editorial tasks without seriously curtailing his other activities. After getting together material for the May and June numbers of the *Éphémérides*, for example, he accepted the invitation of the Duc de Saint Mégrin (later Duc de La Vauguyon) to accompany him on a journey to study conditions in several French provinces. Rather hurriedly he prepared material for two additional numbers for July and August and gained the consent of Baudeau and the Abbé de l'Ecuy[77] to produce the issues for September and October. The decision to leave Paris so soon after accepting these new responsibilities was not wise, because it gave Baudeau an opportunity to ignore the terms of his agreement. During Du Pont's absence, which extended from early August to late November, he failed to make the regular payments promised to the new editor and tried to bring in as an associate in the *Éphémérides* his friend the Abbé Roubaud. Through Roubaud's participation he hoped, in all probability, to keep hold of the journal instead of turning it over completely to Du Pont as he had at first proposed.[78]

Du Pont seems to have had two objectives in mind in making the trip with the young Duke. He was, of course, always eager to gather information in support of his views by direct observations of conditions in various parts of France. His work with Méliand, whose death Madame Du Pont had sorrowfully to announce to her husband in a letter of August 26, had shown him the value of such knowledge in giving substance to abstract theory. He was also favorable to Quesnay's idea of gaining the patronage of the Dauphin for the *Éphémérides*—and the Duc de Saint Mégrin was the son of the Dauphin's tutor. The determined opposition of the Marquis de Mirabeau eventually prevented the realization of this idea after all the necessary arrangements had been completed.[79] There were good arguments on both sides. Mirabeau feared a loss of freedom under official patronage; Quesnay and Du Pont believed that such patronage would surely lend greater prestige to the school. It is possible that the protection of the future Louis XVI would have given a longer life to the *Éphémérides*.

Du Pont and Saint Mégrin planned an itinerary including stopovers at Lyons, Marseilles, Nismes, Montpellier, Toulouse, Tonneins, Bordeaux, Cognac, and Limoges. They carried it out with two alterations. From Lyons they went on to Geneva and then to Ferney to visit Voltaire, who was much interested in the *Éphémérides*.[80] Near the end of the tour Saint Mégrin had to return to Paris, and Du Pont went on alone to Limoges, where he spent several weeks with Turgot. Meanwhile Madame Du Pont took care of young Victor, maintained the apartment which they had rented on the Rue de Faubourg St. Jacques, tended to the garden which had been planted before her husband left, visited relatives and friends, and wrote many letters in a neat and legible hand.[81] Du

Pont does not appear to have been much disturbed by long periods of separation from his wife and family. And Marie Du Pont, however much she regretted the long absences of her husband, reconciled herself to them as an inevitable part of his important work. Her contributions to his career were to encourage him constantly and to keep a neat household always ready for his return. It is doubtful that Du Pont fully appreciated her virtues until after her death.

The editorship of the *Éphémérides* kept him too busy to think of anything else. The burdens were so great, indeed, that he may perhaps be excused for his failure always to show good sense in managing them. After his return to Paris he soon discovered that Baudeau had not given exact information on the status of the journal. There were only 160 subscribers, not 400, and there was a mounting indebtedness, since the journal had been losing about 1,500 livres a year. As he went forward with the work, he had constantly to be concerned with the censorship, which required every article to be submitted for inspection before it could be published. The most irksome task was, however, to produce every month sufficient material for publication. Du Pont had himself to write a very substantial part of each issue. Over a four-year period, forty-eight volumes of the *Éphémérides* appeared under Du Pont's editorship;[82] for them he produced about 110 major articles[83] and some 40 smaller pieces and notes.[84] These herculean labors were insufficient to bring forth on time the amount of material needed for each month's issue. Du Pont had to call upon his friends and associates for help. Unfortunately, Quesnay had by now ceased active work in the new science in favor of absorption in bizarre mathematical speculations, a sign of senility to some of his friends.[85] But Turgot gave steady assistance in the form of encouragement, manuscripts, and even, occasionally, money. The Marquis de Mirabeau contributed long articles but did not submit gracefully to any editorial alterations. Baudeau, the founder of the journal, and others also came forward with material from time to time. Despite all these efforts, the *Éphémérides* fell as much as five months behind schedule. Du Pont was overworked and desperate. On at least two occasions he was guilty of ingratitude for the help which he received.

Answering Du Pont's urgent plea for more material in 1769, when the *Éphémérides* was two to three months behind schedule, Turgot submitted the manuscript of his *Réflexions sur la formation et la distribution des richesses*. He had first written out this important treatise three years before as a guide for two Chinese who had been brought to France and educated by the Jesuits. Since he regarded his effort only as a sketch which he would later develop more fully, he had refused to publish it. He yielded now somewhat reluctantly to Du Pont's need. The *Réflexions* appeared in three installments in the *Éphémérides* volumes for November and December, 1769, and January, 1770, although the actual publication of these late volumes occurred in January, February, and April, 1770. After reading the first two installments, Turgot was justifiably angered by certain changes which Du Pont had made in his treatise without informing him. What Du Pont had done was to alter certain points of Turgot's manuscript which did not entirely conform to physiocratic doctrine. Turgot had always disagreed with aspects of Quesnay's thought; he never numbered himself among the *économistes*. In a letter of February 2, 1770,[86] he protested explicitly against Du Pont's action and insisted that the final installment be printed without alteration. Furthermore, he insisted that, in the separate publication of the treatise which Du Pont planned, the text appear as originally written. Du Pont had, of course, to agree to these just demands.[87] His eagerness to further the cause of physiocracy hardly excuses his alteration of the manuscript. On another occasion he had to be admonished by Turgot because he had blithely proclaimed that Benjamin Franklin had "adopted the doctrines of our French economics."[88]

Du Pont was, of course, laboring under considerable strain in keeping the *Éphémérides* afloat. Personal sorrows were added to his editorial worries. He had to help nurse his son Victor through an attack of smallpox late in 1769, just before the birth of his second son, Paul François. Victor recovered but Paul lived only a few days. It was amidst this domestic care and tragedy that Turgot had agreed to send his manuscript. These hard blows visited upon the Du Ponts undoubtedly caused Turgot soon to overcome his initial anger over the manner in which Du Pont had treated his contribution. Throughout 1770 the *Éphémérides* continued to lag behind schedule. Towards the end of the year Baudeau agreed to prepare three volumes so that Du Pont might have time to accumulate sufficient material to catch up. Instead of devoting himself to this necessary labor, Du Pont now celebrated his temporary release from constant editorial duties by composing a play in verse about Joseph II, the enlightened Holy Roman Emperor, who was co-regent with his mother, Maria Theresa, over the Hapsburg realm. Again Turgot was upset when Du Pont sent him a copy of the play. His caustic criticisms of the drama were justified: there is not enough action to sustain the piece through three acts; the verse is undistinguished and is put to poor use in conversations about economic matters which contain only commonplace remarks.[89] There is little subtlety in the plot, which presents the exasperatingly good and high-minded Joseph II going about in disguise among his people and planning beneficial reforms. In the course of his reforming zeal he confounds the idle courtiers and rewards virtue by encouraging the love of Gelding, a young man eager to serve the Emperor, for Sophie Volsang, whose late father had been a brave officer in the Emperor's cuirassiers.[90] Wisely, if reluctantly, Du Pont took Turgot's advice, put the drama aside, and returned to work on the journal. Fifteen years later Du Pont acknowledged in a letter to the Marquis de Mirabeau that his comedy was worthless but that his intent had been to instill useful principles in the head of one who might some day accept them.[91]

Despite these occasional lapses, Du Pont's labors in behalf of the *Éphémérides* were remarkable. In addition to the large number of articles which he wrote he handled all the business details[92] and solicited and edited other manuscripts. Among his most valuable contributions to the study of physiocracy is the series of articles entitled "Notice abrégée des différents écrits modernes qui ont concouru en France à former la science de l'économie politique," which constitutes a critical bibliography of physiocratic literature published up to 1770.[93] He seized every opportunity to put forward physiocratic solutions to contemporary evils; "every article, every book review, every anecdote was in some way made an editorial...."[94] Thus, in a long review of Saint Lambert's popular poem *Les Saissons*, he included an extensive discussion of the evils and the unprofitable nature of slave labor.[95] He used the perhaps overworked device of criticizing French institutions indirectly by praising Chinese practices.[96] He championed the causes of freeing trade in grain,[97] of substituting for various indirect taxes a direct tax on land,[98] of abolishing the *corvée*,[99] of contructing canals with private capital,[100] and of ending monoply such as that enjoyed by the India Company.[101] The three articles which he wrote on commerce in general and the Compagnie des Indes in particular were brought together with additional material and published separately in 1769. This work may have assisted in the successful effort of the government in that year to strip away the remaining monopolistic privileges of the company.[102] Du Pont sought to point out the dangers "to which a State is exposed, which prefers the apparent gains of monopoly to the real advantages of competition."[103] He suggested the financial advantages to be gained by permitting freedom of trade and by ending the expenditures necessary to maintain colonies on an exclusive basis.[104]

In view of the close censorship to which the *Éphémérides* was subjected, it is remarkable that Du Pont was able to keep physiocratic views so definitely in the center of attention. During the period of his editorship, he had to contend with six different censors, most of whom had doubtful qualifications for the job.[105] On numerous occasions he had to yield to their demands for excision but succeeded more often than not, through flattery, deceit, and persuasion, in publishing articles in the form which he desired. Ultimately, of course, he failed, since Gardanne, the last censor, recommended the suppression of the *Éphémérides*. His past successes in getting around the censorship undoubtedly contributed to this ultimate failure, although an important factor was that the issues owed to subscribers were several months in arrears.

During these years of struggle the event which brought the greatest personal happiness to the Du Ponts was the birth of their third son in June, 1771. In February Turgot had agreed to be the child's godfather and, on May 24, sent a proxy for the baptism, suggesting in a letter that the child soon to be born be named Eleuthère Irénée "in honor of liberty and peace," names which could be used for either a boy or a girl.[106] The suggestion was accepted after some hesitation. Whatever apprehensions the parents may have had after the loss of their second son so soon after his birth were quickly forgotten. Eleuthère Irénée was a healthy and docile child.

In November, 1772, soon after the publication of the third volume for that year, the *Éphémérides* was suppressed by order of the Government. Maupeou, the Keeper of the Seals, and the Abbé Terray, Controller-General of Finances, who had co-operated to bring about the fall of Choiseul and his supporters in December, 1770, were now vigorously launched upon their program of strengthening the power of the Government. Since early in 1771, Maupeou had been waging a successful struggle to undermine the Parlements despite widespread protests, and Terray was engaged in various manipulations to improve government finances. Journals like the *Éphémérides*, which did not hesitate to question ministerial policies, were potential obstacles not to be tolerated in the difficult state of public opinion regarding the ministers' designs. Since it was seven months behind in meeting its obligations to its subscribers, the *Éphémérides* was especially vulnerable. Together with unpaid bills owed to Didot, the printer, these obligations amounted to about 15,000 francs, which were carried on the personal account of the editor. Two years later, when Baudeau succeeded in reviving the journal under the title *Nouvelles Éphémérides économiques ou Bibliothèque raisonnée de l'histoire de la morale et de l'économie politique*, he received 7,200 francs from the government treasury. Du Pont had no connection with this later journal and received no part of the sum paid to Baudeau. For years he had gradually to pay off the debts of the suppressed journal. His personal financial accounts early in 1775 show that he still owed Didot, the printer, 7,000 livres and various subscribers 1,500 livres for issues which he had not furnished.[107] Eventually he retired these debts, Didot agreeing to accept satisfaction without interest.

Some months before the disaster, Franklin had praised the *Éphémérides* in a letter to Du Pont, remarking: "You are doing a great deal of Good to Mankind, for which I am afraid you are not duly rewarded, except in the Satisfaction that results from it to your benevolent Mind."[108] This praise from London is indicative of the good reputation which the *Éphémérides* enjoyed among some readers outside of France.[109] Two enlightened rulers, Gustavus III, King of Sweden, and Carl Friedrich, Margrave of Baden, instructed their ambassadors in Paris to encourage Du Pont to continue his writing by sending them periodic reports on important developments in the "new science." They offered to pay him a small but regular salary for such reports. Desperately in need of money and eager to continue his efforts in behalf of physiocracy, Du Pont seized this opportunity by agreeing to write a fortnightly "Correspondence littéraire et politique," in which he proposed to review new books, to describe notable inventions, to discuss new works of art, and to analyze the acts of various governments from the viewpoint of their contributions to necessary reforms.[110] Friedrich Melchior Grimm's well-known *Correspondance littéraire,* which had been appearing since 1753, may have served as his model. Like the editorial positions, this "Correspondance" paid more in honor and reputation than it did in money.[111]

The Margrave of Baden, whom Du Pont had met during the latter's residence in Paris in the summer of 1771,[112] appointed him an "Aulic Councillor" on December 31, 1772,[113] and arranged for him to visit Karlsruhe periodically. Du Pont first traveled to Karlsruhe in October, 1773, and continued to write regularly to the Margarve,[114] often including in his friendly letters instruction and advice, some of which, like his counsel about finding a wife for the Margrave's son,[115] was probably not welcome. To this son, Carl Ludwig, Du Pont also wrote several long letters, seeking to guide his studies in preparation for the day when he would succeed his father as margrave.[116] In these letters he covered a great variety of subjects but naturally gave special attention to the tenets of physiocracy. He included three of the discourses which he had given during the Tuesday dinners at Mirabeau's house. One of these, entitled "De Courbes politiques," is significant as one of the earliest efforts in mathematical economics.[117] Here Du Pont attempted to draw a curve depicting the effect of excise taxes in reducing the remuneration of the first seller of a hypothetical product and, consequently, the means which he possessed of purchasing other products and services. By use of this curve he sought to prove at a glance that reduction or, best of all, suppression of excise taxes would greatly stimulate production of every kind. This attempt to apply geometry to economics is one of the best examples of the interest of the Physiocrats in using mathematics to support their claims that they had discovered an exact new science.[118]

In his letters to Karlsruhe Du Pont showed himself as an amateur art critic, as well as an amateur mathematician. For the Margrave's wife, Caroline Louise, he wrote accounts of three of the biennial salons held in the palace of the Louvre.[119] The three salons, of 1773, 1777, and 1779, described by Du Pont, are those for which Diderot did not prepare the regular critiques which, since 1759, he had been providing for Grimm's *Literary Correspondence*. While Du Pont's comments are inferior to the better-known *Salons* of Diderot, his descriptions of the exhibited paintings and sculptures are always clear and sometimes vivid. He was not equipped to judge problems of technique in composition and coloring, but he does not hesitate to express his opinion of many of the works and artists mentioned. His taste was eclectic; he displayed no definite preferences, though he believed that the sculptors were, in general, producing works far superior to those of the painters.[120] He did not, however, like at all the bust which Houdon had created of his friend Turgot.[121]

In the spring of 1774 came an unusual offer of employment which promised not only honor but also generous financial remuneration. Prince Adam Czartoryski, member of one of the most prominent families in the Kingdom of Poland, was then in Paris seeking tutors for his four-year-old son. Du Pont had, perhaps, been recommended to him by the Vice-Chancellor of Lithuania, Count Joachim Chreptowicz, who had been in close association with the Physiocrats during his sojourn in Paris in 1769.[122] After reading some of his works and conversing with him, [123] Prince Czartoryski asked Du Pont to accept the position as tutor and offered him, in addition, the title of Honorary Councillor of the King and the Republic of Poland. For these offices Du Pont was to receive an annual salary of 10,000 francs, living quarters, carriage, and traveling expenses, and after ten years a bonus of 100,000 francs.[124] This attractive offer undoubtedly owed something to the inspiration of the Abbé Baudeau, who, being now back in France, did not wish to return to Poland. When Du Pont hesitated, Baudeau arranged to have further inducements put forward. Du Pont was to be given also the position which had been offered to Baudeau in Poland, that of Secretary of the High Council of National Education and Director of the Academy, and was, furthermore, through Czartoryski's willingness to place a mortgage on property which he owned in Holland, to be enabled to acquire a landed estate in France.[125] This estate might serve as a present retreat for his father, who was in poor health,[126] and as a future patrimony for his sons. Du Pont could not refuse outright such exceptional advantages; yet he did not want to go to Poland. He set out instead for Karlsruhe, hoping that Carl Friedrich would decide that his services were too indispensable to permit him to travel so far away.[127] The Margrave made no such claim upon his services and he returned disappointed to Paris and reluctantly accepted Czartoryski's proposals. He continued to lament that Carl Friedrich had not insisted upon his remaining in Baden.[128]

Probably what most influenced him to accept the Polish positions was the opportunity of acquiring a landed estate. After years of theorizing and writing on the virtues and importance of agriculture, he would now have sufficient land to test theory by practice. For about 30,000 francs, paid to him in advance by Czartoryski, he purchased a farm in an area he knew well, not far from Mirabeau's estate of Bignon, and close to the village of Chevannes, near Nemours. The name of the estate, Bois-des-Fossés (literally, "Wood of the Trenches"), probably arose from the belief that ditches found in the woods on the property were the remains of Roman trenches. While not large, the property contained a well-constructed stone house and enough other buildings to carry on a modest agricultural enterprise.[129] He was able to spend only eight days on his new property before he set out for Poland, barely enough time to make the necessary arrangements with the tenant farmer but sufficient to make him feel "very content with [his] acquisition."[130]

With no enthusiasm for the Polish venture, Du Pont consumed more than a month in getting to Warsaw,[131] stopping off again at Karlsruhe on the way. He did not arrive at his destination, with his wife, two sons, and a secretary named Noyer, until the first week of September. The only one of his duties in which he was really interested was that of Secretary for Foreign Correspondence of the Commission of Education. With a firm appreciation of the importance of education in improving society and a mind full of plans, he went eagerly to work. He was convinced that the first important step which the Poles had to take in their efforts toward regeneration after the first tragic partition of their country in 1772 was the establishment of a sound system of national education. So busy does he appear to have been with the affairs of the Commission that he must have given little time to his duties as tutor to the young Czartoryski. Any neglect of the tutorial duties, which he abhorred,[132] probably made little difference, since Prince Czartoryski had apparently imported at least ten tutors for his two children.[133] For the Commission Du Pont prepared *mémoires* on many projects—on parochial schools, on universities and an academy of sciences, on the gradation of different schools from lowest branch to highest, on military training in the schools, even on the abolition of serfdom.[134] His original contributions cannot be clearly discerned and were probably limited, since, according to the principal authority on the Polish Commission of National Education, his *mémoires* were usually restricted to summarizing the views of the Commission.[135] All efforts were fruitless. As Du Pont remarked in a letter to Carl Friedrich, nothing beyond making proposals could be accomplished because of the niggardly fashion in which the inadequte funds available were employed.[136] A feeling of frustration overcame him, so that he was then probably too harsh in his judgments of the hopelessness of the situation in Poland. He was aware of the difficulties—lack of revenue, interference by foreign powers, jealousies among the Polish nobles —but was inclined to be impatient and indignant about them rather than to seek possible ways to overcome them. Fortunately for his sanguine temperament his stay in Poland was very brief.

In May of 1774, two months before the Du Ponts set out for Warsaw, Louis XV, no longer the "well-beloved," had finally expired. There was happy expectation that the new king, Louis XVI, would open a new period of accomplishment by effecting necessary reforms and improvements too often neglected by his grandfather. The new monarch showed an eagerness to do what was desired and sought for advisers and administrators who were honest and able. There was rejoicing among the Physiocrats when, in July, Louis brought Turgot into his Government as Minister of the Navy. When in the following month he elevated this brilliant and experienced administrator to the controller-generalship of finances, the most important post in the Government, Physiocrats and other reformers were convinced that a new day had indeed dawned.

Turgot expressed the desire to have his friend Du Pont assist him in the responsible position to which he had been called. In July he had announced his appointment to the naval ministry in a letter which Du Pont received soon after he reached Warsaw. He stated his eagerness to assign Du Pont to a governmental post, perhaps that of intendant of the Ile-de-France (or Mauritius), but agreed that his friend might prefer to remain in Warsaw.[137] With the co-operation of the well-intentioned young King, the necessary arrangements for Du Pont's recall were completed after Turgot became Controller-General. Turgot was able to promise that a financial settlement with Czartoryski would permit Du Pont to retain Bois-des-Fossés, his recently acquired estate. A formal command transmitted over Louis's signature[138] convinced the Polish government that Du Pont had no alternative but to return to France. Du Pont was eager to escape to this long-cherished opportunity—to participate actively in formulating and executing governmental policies in his native land. On September 21, Turgot had written: "You will have learned in your journey to appreciate our nation. It has now an advantage that few others possess—we have a king who is really an honest man and eager for the welfare of the country."[139]

Du Pont's appointment as Inspector General of Commerce, the position which Turgot now offered him, was dated September 20, 1774,[140] but almost three months elapsed before all the necessary arrangements for the return journey were made. Du Pont paused in Saxony on the way back in order to pour out his disappointments over the Polish venture in a long letter to his first master, Quesnay.[141] The letter was dated December 18, two days after Quesnay's death. Not until he reached Paris on the thirtieth did Du Pont have news of this sad event. The letter had dispatched the last remnants of his sense of frustration. He was again eager to go forward. The death of his master was the breaking of the visible link with his past as an apprentice. Now he entered upon a long period of governmental service which might determine how well he had learned his lessons.

Chapter III

Government Servant (1774-1787)

Du Pont's actual function in his minor post under Turgot was to serve as the Controller-General's private secretary.[1] During the twenty months which Turgot spent in the ministry, Du Pont was therefore in close contact with the details of government. His duties were heavier than might have been expected, for Turgot was ill of gout for seven of his twenty months in office.[2] To his superior Du Pont gave his complete loyalty in formulating plans for the regeneration of France. Turgot's theoretical solutions had been tested during his long service as intendant of Limoges. He was thoroughly familiar with the economic and financial problems of France and with the operations of the French bureaucracy. His approach to a problem was from the standpoint of the possible, not from that of the theoretically desirable. His eminent practicality undoubtedly exerted a healthful influence on some of his enthusiastic disciples. From the King he obtained approval for a limited program which was possible, if difficult, of attainment. It stressed economy based upon three essential points—no bankruptcy, no increase in taxes, no further borrowing.[3] While recognizing the necessity of removing abuses and inequities in the assessment and collection of the taxes, Turgot insisted that no reform was possible without economy in governmental expenditures.[4] Still, as Du Pont later pointed out, the new Controller-General had to accept as a "fundamental principle" of his administration the fact that significant improvement in the incredibly confused financial condition of the Government required efforts to increase production in France and to relieve the burdens of the common people.[5]

Du Pont and other Physiocrats looked forward, therefore, to larger reforms which they knew Turgot endorsed—complete freedom of trade in grain, removal of restraints on agriculture, industry, and commerce, the single tax on net income from land in place of the vexatious system of taxes in vogue, civil equality based on a hierarchy of representative assemblies for which only landowners would be eligible. They had, however, to admit the wisdom of Turgot's argument that not much could be done until the financial stability of the government was assured. The economy which this primary move demanded brought into opposition all those who profited through lax and lavish financial measures.

During his first year in office Turgot applied himself with some success to financial retrenchment. The annual deficit was reduced some 14,500,000 livres, anticipations (or the prior assignment of expected revenues to specific creditors) about 28,000,000 livres, and the long-term debt slightly over 20,000,000.[6] Because of his absorption in matters of governmental finance and taxation, Turgot could give his attention to only one major reform during this first year.[7]

That was the edict re-establishing freedom in the grain trade. Efforts to acomplish this reform had enjoyed but limited success in the past. In 1754 trade between provinces within France was relieved of many restrictions. In 1763 all restraints within France, except for Paris, were removed and limited exportation was permitted.[8] But these edicts were not uniformly or strictly enforced, and in 1770 new restrictions were decreed by the Controller-General, Terray. The *arrêt* of September 13, 1774, called for the re-establishment of the freedoms of 1763, except for the continuance of restrictions on export.[9] By remaining silent on the issues of liberty of exportation "until circumstances may become more favorable,"[10] Turgot hoped to weaken opposition to the reform.[11] There is no evidence that Du Pont had a direct hand in drawing up the preamble of this edict,[12] although it was, of course, very much in accord with his ideas.

As in the past, bad fortune followed this measure. Poor harvests led to a clamor for renewed governmental regulation and, in 1775, to a series of riots, sometimes referred to as the "flour war" (*la guerre des farines*).[13] Turgot remained adamant, however, used troops to quell the disorders, and continued to issue specific regulations aimed at increasing freedom in the grain trade.[14] Eight years later Du Pont asserted that it was upon his recommendation that Turgot employed force to put down these uprisings, which arose, he maintained, not from the misery of the people but from plots of grain speculators and others to embarrass the government by impeding the transport of grain to Paris.[15] During this period Turgot was faced also with the worst outbreak of murrain in eighteenth century France. He confronted this serious problem energetically by providing careful policing of cattle in regions invaded by the plague and by extending financial assistance and indemnities to those whose cattle died or had to be destroyed.[16] When corrupt subordinates threatened the success of the latter measures, Turgot called them to account. The poor harvests and the cattle plague forced him to disburse sums of money for public relief, which he attempted to systematize into work projects rather than into open charity. In small measure he sought to encourage, through grants of money, improvements in agricultural methods and inventions in industry. He brought substantial improvement in the system of posts and stages (*messageries*) by organizing a series of public carriages, which came soon to be known as Turgotines.[17]

On March 24, 1776, Turgot authorized the founding of the famous Bank of Discount (*Caisse d'escompte*) but was unable to bring about its firm establishment before his term of office came to an end. The Bank did, however, survive his fall and, although technically independent of the state, was later to be placed in such intimate relationship with the Government that it was frequently used to alleviate periodic financial crises. At first a simple bank of deposit and of discount, it was in 1777 granted the power to issue bank notes.[18]

In all these measures Du Pont did not take a leading part, though he was apparently busy behind the scenes preparing pertinent reports.[19] Early in June, 1775, his father died, but Du Pont did not even take leave of his duties at Versailles to attend the funeral in Paris on June 9.[20] He was apparently not much moved by his father's final illness and death, although his wife had kept him informed of the situation in her daily letters.[21] Samuel had not remembered him in his will, leaving the bulk of his estate to his niece, Madame Vaudry,[22] although some family property in Rouen eventually passed to Du Pont. If he did experience any grief at the time of his father's death, it was considerably alleviated by the news that he was to receive an honor of which he was ever afterward very proud. The Swedish Comte de Scheffer had written on May 23, 1775, to inform him that King Gustavus III desired to appoint him a Knight of the Royal Order of Vasa.[23] On June 25, 1775, Louis XVI signed a warrant granting his permission for Du Pont to accept the knighthood. The formal investiture by the Swedish Ambassador to France, the Comte de Creutz, took place on October 10 after Du Pont's return from a month's holiday with his family at Bois-des-Fossés.[24]

By order of Council on December 16, 1775, Du Pont was admitted to the Council of Commerce in an advisory capacity.[25] These special assignments do not appear to have been onerous, and he would have been free to devote much of his time to the direct assistance of his chief. Still, the extent of his contributions to the famous Six Edicts with which, early in 1776, Turgot sought to usher in a period of more fundamental change,[26] cannot be exactly determined. Only two of these edicts contemplated really major alterations in the old regime. Four were supplementary to the earlier effort to establish greater freedom in trade. One extended to Paris the provisions freeing commerce in grain; another suppressed a large group of minor officials of the Parisian ports and markets, whose activities produced more complications in trade than revenue in the Treasury; a third abolished the *Caisse de Poissy*, an institution originally designed to advance credit to facilitate transactions in the cattle and meat trade but, by 1776, controlled by financiers who perverted it to their profit;[27] the fourth reorganized the ancient tax on suet which had been a monopoly of the Guild of Chandlers. The last measure was necessary in the event that the first of the two major edicts should be successful, for this part of Turgot's plan sought the abolition of all guilds and the complete freedom of every man to enter whatever craft or occupation he might choose. Over several months Turgot built up a powerful case for this reform—a move directly in accord with the teaching of the Physiocrats. The other major revision sought the suppression of the unpopular *corvée*, which required the peasants to perform periodic work on the roads and highways of France. This reform had been one dear to his heart ever since his days as intendant of Limoges. With the apparent support of the King, Turgot had also in this matter long been preparing his argument. His final *mémoire* proposed to provide funds for necessary road work through a tax on the income of landowners, who could be expected to benefit most from good roads. Appealing to the sense of justice of the King over the selfish interests of the privileged orders, Turgot hoped to prevent evasion of the tax by the clergy and nobility.[28] Upon the insistence of Maurepas, nominally chief minister of the King, he agreed, however, to a compromise which would exempt the clergy.[29]

After long argument in Council, the King accepted all six edicts; but, bolstered by the Prince of Conti, the magistrates of the Parlement refused registration to all but the one abolishing the *Caisse de Poissy*. Despite the advice of the majority of his ministers, Louis decided to side with Turgot and forced registration of the edicts in a *lit de justice* at Versailles on March 12, 1776. This victory was Turgot's last. The court party, which had been intriguing against him from the time of his first move toward economy, now redoubled its efforts. While Turgot continued actively to perform his administrative duties, his enemies took up pen to wean Louis from his support. A number of libels appeared in print, castigating Turgot as a dangerous visionary and Louis as a feeble dupe. One of the most scurrilous, *Le Songe de Maurepas ou les mannequins du gouvernement français*, was generally thought to be the work of the King's brother.[30] A plot was hatched to place before the King forged letters purporting to be from Turgot to a friend in Vienna and containing uncomplimentary allusions to the King and Queen. Maurepas vouched for their authenticity, and Louis accepted his word. Every adverse criticism of Turgot heard in conversations or intercepted in the mails was carried forthwith to the King in order further to poison his mind against his minister. The derelictions of other officials were blamed upon Turgot. No opportunity was lost to present the Controller-General in a compromising or unfavorable position. It was the cumulative effect of all these petty efforts and the lack of any widespread popular support for Turgot which finally brought Louis to ask for his resignation on May 12, 1776. Great was the joy among the court party when this event occurred—an "indecent joy" as it was described by Du Pont,[31] who, of course, lost office along with his chief.

Turgot's dismissal occurred before he could lay before the King a plan for the creation of a hierarchy of representative assemblies, a plan which Du Pont drew up in accordance with Turgot's ideas and instructions. The purpose of the *Mémoire sur les municipalités* was to make the central administration more efficient.[32] In an often quoted passage, the *Mémoire* points out the basic weakness of the French monarchy.

The cause of evil, Sire, comes from [the fact] that your nation has no constitution. It is a society made up of different orders poorly united, of a people whose members have among themselves only too few social bonds —where consequently almost everyone is concerned only with his own exclusive private interest, where almost no one is troubled to fulfill his duties, nor to acknowledge his relationships with others. As a result, in this perpetual war of conceits and concerns which reason and reciprocal understanding have never regulated, your Majesty is obliged to decide everything himself or through his agents. . . . You are forced to enact laws on everything and most often by private desires, whereas you could rule like God by general laws if the component parts of your empire had a regular organization and well-known relationships.[33]

Outside of its context this passage seems to say more than it actually intended, and was so interpreted in later years when the demand for a written constitution found louder voice. The original argument, of which it is a part, was that, however beneficent and wise the King might be in attempting to apply the general laws of nature in the governing of his people, he could fail in his purpose through lack of the detailed and exact knowledge of actual conditions within his realm. This defect might be overcome by enlisting the aid of his subjects in gathering information and in supervising local administration. As the necessary foundation for such a plan, public education must be improved and extended. Then a hierarchy of assemblies should be established. At the base, in every village, a body could be set up to control assessments for taxation, poor relief, and public works. Every landowner with an annual income of 600 livres would automatically be a member of this body. If his income were in excess of 600 livres, he should have an extra vote for every additional 600 livres of income. Thus, a landowner worth 1,200 livres yearly would have two votes; one worth 1,800 livres, three votes, and so on. Those proprietors with less than 600 livres income a year could be gathered together in groups, each composed of individuals whose

Du Pont facing the bust of Turgot
Courtesy of the Henry Francis du Pont Winterthur Museum

Anne Robert Jacques Turgot (1727-1781); from
an oil portrait originally owned by Du Pont de Nemours
Courtesy of the Eleutherian Mills Historical Library

combined income amounted to 600 livres yearly, and each group could elect one member to sit in the local assembly. The principles thus established were that every 600 livres of income from landed property should be represented by one vote; that people outside the landowning class, being incomplete citizens, would not share in the government;[34] and, most important of all, that the traditional distinctions of privileged and unprivileged orders would not be recognized. Members of these bodies "were to take part in public affairs not as priests, as nobles or as commoners, but as delegates of the proprietors of the land; the *ordre réel* was henceforth to replace the *ordre personnel*."[35]

These local assemblies would elect intermediate or district assemblies; the latter, in turn, would elect provincial assemblies. Finally, bringing this method of indirect election to a logical culmination, provincial assemblies would elect delegates to the Grand or Royal Municipality, which, with the aid of the King's ministers, would co-operate with the Monarch in levying taxes, in arranging for public works, in discussing measures of reform. These assemblies were, however, neither to have exceptional powers nor to supplant any existing institutions. They were to be only advisory bodies, with no legislative or executive prerogatives. They could supply necessary information, they could counsel, but they could not act on their own initiative. According to a later statement of Du Pont, Turgot really believed that the assemblies could be given additional duties, such as supervision over different branches of the police.[36]

It is, indeed, impossible to determine how accurately many of the ideas in the *Mémoire* reflect Turgot's thoughts. Du Pont was at Bois-des-Fossés, his estate near Chevannes, when he was writing out the details of the project. His only contact with Turgot at the time was through correspondence. In one of his letters the Controller-General took him to task for spending too much time in developing his own ideas. "I have reflected too much on this matter for about fifteen years," he wrote, "not to have a multitude of ideas which you will not have been able to fathom."[37] Probably Turgot made substantial changes in the *Mémoire*. Whatever his attitude toward it would have been, the whole scheme was certainly impracticable. Even if the King could have been brought to approve it, the privileged orders would almost certainly have refused co-operation in any plan which ignored social distinctions. It would have had no more immediate success than the measures which Turgot actually put into operation. All were swept away when he fell from favor. The old order would have its revenge. But his general ideas did not die in the minds of some who thought of the future, or his detailed plans in the mind of Du Pont, who waited for another opportunity.

The reaction following Turgot's fall swept Du Pont into exile on his estate at Chevannes. Clugny, former intendant at Bordeaux, who now became Controller-General, set about removing all traces of Turgot's reforming ministry, including participation in the Government by Turgot's associates. His plan formally to remove Du Pont from his position as Inspector General of Commerce was blocked by the successful appeal made to Maurepas by the Duc de Nivernais and M. d'Angevilliers, who reminded the minister of the financial sacrifice which Du Pont had made in relinquishing his post in Poland.[38] It seemed to have been agreed that Du Pont would continue to draw his salary while remaining in retirement, subject to recall to duty as the Ministry might desire. The salary was not, however, paid regularly and, for the next two years, Du Pont continued to send letters and *mémoires* with supporting documents to Paris pressing his claims.[39]

Clugny confirmed his appointment and, after him, so did Necker, who entered the Government late in 1776, first as Director of the Treasury and, in 1777, as Director General of Finances, in which positions he actually did the work of the Controller-General, though this position was nominally held by Taboureau de Reaux as Clugny's successor. Very few, if any, payments came to the estate at Bois-des-Fossés. Except for the energetic and resourceful management of the estate by Madame Du Pont, the family's financial position would have approached destitution.

Du Pont tried to keep busy, but he was frustrated and depressed. Within three weeks of Turgot's dismissal, he had written a long letter to Vergennes, the Minister of Foreign Affairs, proposing that he be sent to America as a secret agent of the French Government, charged with furthering French interests in the colonies now in rebellion against the English Government. He put forward in detail what he considered his unusual qualifications for such an assignment: the fall of Turgot would lend credence to the idea that he was only seeking asylum in America and would remove any suspicion that he would be in contact with the French Court; he was not important enough to be noticed by the English but was sufficiently well-known to be able to make some impression upon the American Congress; he made much of his acquaintance with Franklin (which he portrayed as a very warm friendship—"Franklin . . . treats me like a son"); he was acquainted with other Americans; he was especially interested in encouraging a free and extensive commerce between France and America, an action which would greatly profit both countries. He was not, he wrote, thinking of himself but seeking to make himself most useful to his country. He could better serve in Philadelphia than in Paris, where his position as Inspector General of Commerce had only a limited utility. It would be easier for him to find an honorable retreat in Poland, Sweden, or Baden, but he was concerned only with contributing to the welfare of France.[40] Turgot was disturbed when Du Pont wrote to him of this American project but was comforted by his doubt that Vergennes would approve of it.[41] Turgot was correct. Nothing came of this first hope of Du Pont to go to America.

During this period of frustration even his health suffered.[42] After a fruitless trip to Paris in April, 1777, when he failed to see Trudaine de Montigny, who was ill at the time, Du Pont himself took to his bed.[43] The heaviest burden during this period was probably not financial difficulty but the feeling of frustration over the stifling of his ambitions to win renown and to serve his country in a position of consequence.

During these years he busied himself with the details of the management of his estate; engaged in some agricultural experiments; studied animals, insects, and birds; supervised the education of his sons, employing Philippe Nicholas Harmand as their tutor in 1778;[44] corresponded regularly with Gustavus of Sweden and with the Margrave and Margravine of Baden; maintained contact with Turgot and other associates in Paris; occasionally treated the sick in the neighborhood; and found spare time to begin a translation of Ariosto's *Orlando Furioso*, which was to provide mental relaxation for the remainder of his life. Paying regular visits to the elder Mirabeau at Bignon, he was drawn into the passions and animosities which divided the family of the Marquis. For years he was to try in vain to effect a permanent reconciliation between father and son. With the latter he was soon on very intimate terms and, if Mirabeau can be believed, was eager to give advice, even on details of how his young friend should conduct his notoriously extensive sexual activities.[45] Mirabeau was frequently confined in jail, often at his father's behest, during this period, and Du Pont sought to assist him in various ways, even serving as go-between in his wild affair with Sophie de Monnier. Mirabeau was later to repay these kindnesses with characteristic ingratitude.[46]

These activities did not satisfy. In the spring of 1778, Du Pont arranged for the publication in Paris of the *Table raisonnée des principes de l'économie politique,* which he had published in Baden in 1775 at the behest and with the help of the Margrave of Baden.[47] This *Table,* a broadside 38⅜ inches long by 30⅝ inches wide, attempted to include much more than was found in Quesnay's earlier *Table Œconomique.* It does work up (or down, as one reads the *Table*) to the basic physiocratic ideas on economics but presents them as part of a systematic framework of the evolution of mankind into stable and regular societies which arise naturally from man's sensations, faculties, and will. It is an excellent example of deductive reasoning from a few basic premises, the type of reasoning which is most significant in the science of physiocracy.

On December 13, 1778, Turgot wrote to Du Pont of an impending request from Necker for his return to active duty. Necker had found the records and statistics which were kept on foreign commerce, especially on the balance between imports and exports, in a wretched state. After long discussion in the Committee of Commerce, he decided to charge Du Pont with the responsibility of putting them in order. Turgot advised his friend to accept the assignment.[48] Although he continued to regret his exile from the center of really important happenings, Du Pont showed some reluctance to go to Paris. He shared Turgot's distrust of Necker, was not enthusiastic about the duties to be assigned him, and was suffering from a chronic cold which continued to cause him discomfort. Nevertheless, he recognized the wisdom of Turgot's argument that to refuse to serve would make his position more precarious and decided not to refuse.

He left Bois-des-Fossés in the capable hands of his wife and returned to Paris.

He was, however, not destined to spend much time there. He soon had other duties concerning the condition of trade in the region of Bayonne and the state of manufactures in various parts of the country and spent a very large part of his time in travel. He produced a *mémoire* on leathers which Turgot found good, except for minor revisions required mostly because of the mistakes of the copyist.[49] In the intervals between trips he rested at Bois-des-Fossés or visited Turgot in Paris. As Turgot's sufferings from gout grew worse and made him a chronic invalid, Du Pont took up residence in the house which Turgot had purchased on the Rue de Bourbon.[50] While in Paris he enjoyed the life of the salons and moved especially in the circles of Madame Blondel and the Duchesse d'Enville, two of Turgot's most intimate friends. Apparently at this time he became acquainted with the Abbé de Périgord, better known in history as Talleyrand.[51]

The translation of the first canto of Ariosto's *Orlando Furioso*, which had occupied so much of his leisure at Bois-des-Fossés, was published anonymously in 1781.[52] There had been many French translations of Ariosto's masterpiece during the previous 200 years, but few of them were in verse. Du Pont properly called his verse translation an *essai* and explained its publication as an effort to induce the Comte de Tressan to turn his prose translation, published in 1780, into verse. Tressan never did so. If he paid any attention to Du Pont's translation, he may indeed have concluded that prose was the medium to be preferred. Du Pont had labored diligently but must early have abandoned any hope of reproducing the polished ottava rima of Ariosto. He did not fulfill the statement in his preface that he had tried to give an "extremely literal" rendering, not only of Ariosto's thought but even of the very turn, movement, image, sentiment, tone, and words of the great Italian Renaissance poet. He could not match the division into exquisite eight-line stanzas; as a result he had also to abandon the rhyming scheme of the original. Du Pont's stanzas are not uniform in length; for the sake of his meter, which is not that of Ariosto, he had occasionally to add phrases not found in the original. Such departures are immediately evident to the careful reader, since Du Pont had the Italian text printed on the left-hand page facing his translation, on the right-hand page, throughout the slim volume. Despite his alterations his attempt to keep within the framework of the original impeded his freedom. His verse is often wooden and artificial. It has little of the flow and the vividness of Ariosto.[53] But who has succeeded in rendering the *Orlando Furioso* successfully into another tongue? Du Pont's effort is an interesting attempt. He continued to work at it for the rest of his life, publishing in 1812 a slightly revised edition of the first canto with his translation of the second and third cantos.[54] This edition, like the earlier one, contained notes of historical background or commentary on various parts of the poem. He loved *Orlando Furioso* and read it often, but found time, over a forty-year period, to translate only nine of the forty-six cantos.[55]

The year 1781 would not be remembered by Du Pont for the publication of his *Roland Furieux*, but as the year which brought him one of the most profound sorrows of his life. On March 18, after much suffering, his great friend Turgot died. Du Pont was often at his bedside, but lamented that he had not been present at the last moment. He had conducted Madame Blondel and the Duchesse d'Enville from the bedchamber in order to spare them the sight of the sufferings of their friend. His genuine grief was intensified by the thought that Turgot's final minutes of life may have been "affected by the sorrow of vainly desiring to be assisted or succoured by his faithful Du Pont, upon whose absolute devotion he had the right to rely. . . ."[56]

Du Pont was inconsolable[57] but probably found some relief in preparing material for a eulogy to be delivered by Du Puy, secretary of the Academy of Inscriptions and Belles-Lettres, of which Turgot had been president. As it turned out, Du Puy could use very little of the information in his brief discourse, and so Du Pont decided to publish his *Mémoires sur la vie et les ouvrages de M. Turgot*, which appeared in 1782. Some of the comments he makes on Turgot in this book might well be regarded as an expression of his own aspirations.

The fundamental principle of the administration of M. Turgot, by which he merited and justified the confidence of the Prince and that of the Nation, was always to seek the amelioration of the revenues of the State and the means of re-establishing the finances only in the augmentation of the riches of the Proprietors, in the comfort of the People, in the greatest facilities which one could give them for subsistence. He had the highest idea of the sanctity of the duties of the Government and the most religious respect for the rights of the Citizens entrusted to the care of the Authority which they have established, & which they sustain. He never gave advice to the Monarch with this formula: *That will be useful to you.* He always said: *That is just, Sire, & it will be a benefit to your nation.*[58]

Toward the end of his book he writes of Turgot's "three great needs": "that of seeking and recognizing truth, that of doing good to men, and that of being loved."[59] Undoubtedly he desired to think of himself in the light of these words, and sometime later selected as a motto under a portrait of himself the words *Aimer et connaître.*

The chief political event of 1781 was the resignation of Necker on May 19. As Director General of Finances, Necker had performed miracles, in the view of some of his contemporaries, by relieving the dangerous condition of the Royal Treasury, while carrying on a program of modest reform and even financing the heavy expenditures of French involvement in the War for American Independence without requesting additional taxes. His accomplishments were the result of economizing in court expenses, of adapting some of Turgot's programs to his own ideas, and of using his widespread connections in the financial world to obtain additional loans which, perhaps, no one else could have successfully floated. His popularity with the articulate public outside of court circles rapidly increased. In January, 1781, with the King's approval, he published his famous *Compte rendu,* which created a great sensation.[60] One hundred thousand copies were snatched up by the reading public; through it, for the first time, the reader could gain some idea of the state of the royal finances. It was not, however, an accurate idea, for Necker was principally interested in enhancing the favorable reputation which he enjoyed. He carefully concealed the extent of the continuing deficits by omitting, for example, from his accounts all war and "extraordinary" expenditures. Because, as a native of Geneva, he was regarded as a foreigner and a Protestant, Necker had not been appointed Controller-General, although he did the essential work of the office, and had been denied ministerial rank. Determining to seize upon the favorable state of public opinion, he now requested, upon threat of resignation, more power for his office and elevation to the Ministry. He soon learned that he had overestimated his value in the King's eyes and had underestimated the effect of court intrigues against him. Disliking his measures of economy, the court party, led by the octogenarian Maurepas, had been working to undermine his position, just as they had earlier conspired against Turgot. To his surprise, his resignation was accepted, but he left office triumphantly, with unsullied reputation in the opinion of many Frenchmen.

Necker was succeeded by Joly de Fleury, formerly intendant of Burgundy, and member of a family prominent in the Parlement of Paris. Joly de Fleury had been induced to accept appointment as Controller-General under the misunderstanding caused by Necker's *Compte rendu* that there was, finally, a surplus in the Royal Treasury. When he had unraveled the tangled accounts sufficiently to comprehend the actual situation, he found his position almost impossible. He struggled on until March 30, 1783, when he resigned, to be succeeded by Lefèvre d'Ormesson, a young Councillor of State, who held the office only seven months. Charles Alexandre de Calonne, an experienced official who had long coveted it, became Controller-General in November, 1783.

These changes in the controller-generalship had no important effect upon Du Pont's status. Since his return to active service he had regarded the Minister of Foreign Affairs, Charles Gravier, Comte de Vergennes, with greater admiration and affection than he could ever have for Necker. Vergennes became his intimate friend and supporter and, in 1781, made him a kind of unofficial adviser. For the next six years, until Vergennes' death in 1787, Du Pont addressed most of his official correspondence and reports to the Foreign Minister, who, in 1781, was also made chief of the Council of Finances. His official relationship to Vergennes' departments was not regularized until July 16, 1783, when an Order of Council assigned him duties among the ministries of Navy, Foreign Affairs, and Finance and also charged him with the task of collecting the laws of other nations concerning foreign commerce.[61]

Vergennes was twenty-one years older than Du Pont and had first come to know him during Turgot's ministry. After a brilliant career in the diplomatic service as French Ambassador to Constantinople and Sweden, Vergennes was appointed Minister of Foreign Affairs by Louis XVI in 1774. His dislike of England, which Du Pont came to share, led Vergennes to support the American colonies in their quarrel with the British Government. He yielded to the insistence of Beaumarchais that the French Government secretly supply the Americans with arms and volunteers and later concluded the treaty of alliance with the rebellious colonies. He was very much interested in strengthening commercial and other relations with America and assigned Du Pont various tasks relevant to the achievement of this goal.

One of these tasks was carried on in an unofficial capacity. Du Pont's published works, especially those in the *Éphémérides du citoyen*, had brought him into contact, it will be remembered, with many foreigners abroad who often wrote to him. From 1772 to 1778 he had carried on "a literary, philosophic, and political correspondence" with the London bookseller, James Hutton, who was a leader among the Moravian Brethren in England.[62] Hutton, who had become an intimate friend of Benjamin Franklin in 1757 during the latter's residence in London as the agent of Pennsylvania, was much distressed by the rupture with America because of its possible deleterious effect on the missions which the Moravians had established in Labrador.[63] In January, 1778, just before the signing of the treaty of alliance between France and the colonies, Hutton was in Paris to plead with Franklin for conciliation with the mother country. During this fruitless mission Hutton spent some time with Du Pont but did not, apparently, resume their correspondence after his return to London. Hutton had acquaintances in high places. As Franklin remarked in a postscript to his letter of February 12, 1778, to David Hartley, one of his closest English friends, enclosing his replies to a letter from Hutton, this "Chief of the Moravians . . . is often at the Queen's Palace and is sometimes spoken to by the King. . . ."[64] There is, however, no positive warrant for Du Pont's statement that Hutton had been sent over by the King to negotiate with Franklin.[65] If there was more than Hutton's personal concern for peace motivating his trip, it was his absorption in the missionary work in America. He had been one of the founders, and in 1778 was Deputy Chairman, of the Society for the Furtherance of the Gospel.[66]

When, unexpectedly, after a lapse of three years, Du Pont received a letter from Hutton in June of 1781, he immediately concluded that it was more than the merely personal letter it appeared to be. He looked upon it as a probing for some grounds for peace negotiations and as a document secretly inspired by Hutton's supposed friends in the British Cabinet. He therefore immediately sent it to Vergennes, together with the draft of his answer. He was convinced that any replies he made to Hutton's letters would get to the King and Ministry of England. Vergennes doubted that the letter from Hutton reflected any official interest in seeking peace and suggested that Du Pont couch his reply in generalities, avoiding any direct mention of peace and of his association with the Foreign Minister.[67] He came to share Du Pont's view that Hutton's letters were inspired by his friends in the Government but suspected that the object was not to lay a foundation for negotiation but to divide the French and Americans. For more than a year he devoted time to reading the letters from London and to suggesting slight modifications in the drafts of replies which Du Pont transmitted to him. The correspondence must, he counseled, be kept on a purely personal basis until, as did not happen, some definite proposals obviously dictated by the English Government should be forthcoming.[68]

Whatever ministerial connection with the Hutton letters may have existed was disrupted by the advent of the Rockingham ministry in March of 1782.[69] It is very doubtful that Hutton's letters were inspired by his Government and even more uncertain that the correspondence between Du Pont and Hutton had any influence whatever in the eventual preliminaries of peace concluded between England and the United States in November, 1782. No mention of it has been found in the available communications of the principal English negotiators of the preliminary peace or of the definitive treaty of September, 1783.[70] Since it never had official status, this omission might not, of course, be surprising. Still, there seems to be no firm basis for the assertions of previous biographers of Du Pont about the importance of this correspondence in laying the groundwork for peace between England and the United States.[71] There can be no doubt that Vergennes considered it potentially valuable and, in accordance with Du Pont's desires, exercised a general supervision over it. One of the specific interests sought in the correspondence was to lay some foundation for a freer trade among France, England, and America. A commercial treaty had accompanied the alliance treaty of February 6, 1778, between France and the new United States, and article 30 of that treaty had promised that the King would grant to the United States "one or more free ports" in Europe in addition to maintaining the freedom of the French ports in the West Indies.[72] So far as England was concerned, Du Pont early recognized the necessity of some French concessions if they were to get anything in exchange from the English.[73] The freeing of trade was one of Vergennes' hopes for the eventual peace settlement, and he kept Du Pont busy on various assignments connected with the problem.

One of the most complicated of these issues involved the situation of the port cities of Bayonne and Saint-Jean-de-Luz, and of the entire area southward, eastward, and westward to the Pyrenees known as the pays de Labourd. Traditionally this region held a peculiar and complicated status in matters of trade and provided a good example of the lack of uniformity in the administration of the ancien régime. Merchandise could enter the ports without payment of the general tariff duties but was subject to local levies, of which the most important was a *droit de coutume*, revenue from which was divided between the Crown and the noble house of Gramont. The Crown had leased collection of its part of the levy to the General Tax Farm; the house of Gramont held on to its part as an old feudal privilege. In the transport of most, but not all, goods from the region into other parts of the realm, Bayonne and its dependency, the pays de Labourd, were classed as *provinces étrangers effectifs*, thus subject to the general tariff duties. Such complications placed the area in a dual status in commercial arrangements; in some it was regarded as part of France, in others it was foreign territory. Its location afforded it obvious advantages in trade with Spain and the French colonies but, during the eighteenth century, trade had languished. In the eyes of the Bayonne merchants the chief reason for the decline was the continual interference of the General Farm with the privileges and freedoms enjoyed in the past. There were mutual complaints and legal processes between the Farmers General and Bayonne throughout the century.[74] The interest of the Government in attempting to end the conflicts was stimulated by the promise of article 30 of the treaty of commerce of 1778 to grant at least one free port to the United States. Because of its location and its prior privilege as a free port, subject, however, to local duties, Bayonne was a definite possibility for selection as the promised port. Just when Du Pont began work on the subject cannot be ascertained, though he seems to have been engaged in it before Necker's resignation. His frequent communications on it, all addressed to Vergennes, do not, however, commence until the spring of 1782.[75] During the previous fall and early winter he was able to do most of his work at Bois-des-Fossés,[76] where he was apparently reading and annotating everything which he could find on the problems of Bayonne.[77]

There would be no value in a detailed summary of all the work which Du Pont performed in seeking the resolution of these problems over a period of more than two years. After a careful reading of all of his reports and letters to Vergennes on the subject, one can arrive at certain conclusions. It is important, first of all, to insist upon the thoroughness and conscientiousness with which he carried on the task. These qualities are evident in all of his work in government office. This thoroughness had its disadvantages. In attempting to consider everything, Du Pont constantly involved himself in tedious details and complications which were as difficult for others to follow with interest then as they are now. The reform programs of the ministries before 1789, programs whose vigor and extent have too seldom been fully appreciated, were handicapped by the consideration which had to be given to the confusion of different privileges and interests in various parts of the kingdom. There was no orderly and uniform method by which reforms could be accomplished. Instead, government officials had to balance one local interest against another, to adjust their general objectives for the future to specific privileges inherited from the past. Substantial reform could be planned but could not overcome these obstacles. It had to await the sweeping away of these privileges and rights and the establishing of a more uniform system of administration. These ends were attained only after 1789. In his labors Du Pont showed himself willing to compromise with the existing situation. His effort was to seek conciliation of the conflicting interests, to accomplish the best that seemed possible. He was not blinded, as some of his contemporaries suggested, by his physiocratic viewpoints. He could be unhappy that the ideal was not attainable, but he could be content that something worthwhile short of the ideal might be achieved.[78] Undoubtedly, the doctrinaire approach evident in his early writings had been tempered in the school of Turgot, the practical administrator. If he was blinded it was not by dogmatism but by absorption in so much detail that he lost sight of the main outline of the problems at hand. He sometimes got out of touch with reality, not because his head was in a physiocratic fog, but because his eyes were not raised often enough from the rocks and ruts obstructing the road in front of him.

Du Pont did produce a plan for Bayonne, a plan which sought compromise among conflicting interests.[79] He would make Bayonne, St. Jean-de-Luz, and that part of the pays de Labourd on the left bank of the Nive River foreign territory in matters of trade, with two exceptions—the right of the area to get necessary grain even when the export of grain from France to foreign territory was prohibited and the right of free entry of codfish actually netted by local fishermen (though the fisheries remained under national regulation). To codfish Du Pont was willing to add the products of whaling. All products passing into and through the area designated would be free of toll, including the old *droit de coutume*, which the King would renounce for himself, while undertaking to indemnify in some way the house of Gramont for the loss of its part of the levy. The policing of the area by the General Farm would be substantially reduced and reorganized in a manner which Du Pont spelled out in detail. This reduction of police should bring economies in the administrative expenses of the Farm. The tax farmers were, however, to be compensated for the loss of revenue from levies formerly collected in territory now made foreign, even though the legal right of the Farm to most of these levies was in dispute. The tobacco monopoly would be extended over the town of Hasparren and fourteen parishes on the right bank of the Nive, in that part of the old pays de Labourd now made national territory, even though these localities had not been formerly subject to it. Finally, a financial indemnity would be paid to the Farm, its amount to be calculated after taking into consideration the new benefits now accorded to the Farm through economies in policing, extension of the tobacco monopoly, and certain arrangements regarding the transport of salt through the area.

This plan may seem unduly complicated, but, in comparison with what was to come of it as a result of further negotiation and compromise, it was a model of simplicity. All sorts of objections were raised. To a few determined reformers in the Government it was too solicitous of the Farmers General, a criticism which Du Pont was willing to endorse, but he believed such solicitude necessary if the opposition of the Tax Farm were to be overcome. The Farmers General, however, soon made clear their view that concessions to them were inadequate and they fought vigorously to gain more. Du Pont spent many hours in often fruitless negotiation with M. de la Perrière, chief agent of the Farm. Joly de Fleury, the Controller-General, was not enthusiastic because he was worried about further burdening the unstable Royal Treasury with indemnity payments to the Gramonts and the Farmers General. Only Vergennes steadily encouraged Du Pont to carry forward his efforts. Additional months of toil finally produced two drafts of very complicated decrees, one of forty-three articles, the other of thirty-six.[80] Not all the work was done by Du Pont, since he was closely assisted in this affair by Boyetet, an agent of the Bureau of Commerce. Du Pont preferred the shorter project of thirty-six articles as "infinitely better" and hoped that Vergennes could persuade Joly de Fleury to accept it.[81] He was still laboring over the specific affair of Bayonne and its dependent territory as late as December, 1783, when, opposing the claims of the Farm, he sought to suggest a definite figure as equitable indemnity.[82] Although it is impossible to determine from available documents the extent of the credit which Du Pont merits for the decision to declare Bayonne a free port early in 1784, evidently he did more work on this question than any other person.

For over eight months prior to the Bayonne decision he was engaged in other tasks relevant to the general issue of effecting greater freedom in trade. While he was very much concerned about expanding trade between France and the United States, he had no direct role in the arrangements concluded through the efforts of Lafayette, Franklin, and Vergennes to grant to American merchants complete freedom in the ports of Bayonne, Dunkirk, Lorient, and Marseille.[83] He was really more interested in attaining a general

82

freedom, as he made clear in a letter which he drafted in August, 1783, for Vergennes to send to Ormesson, successor of Joly de Fleury in the controller-generalship, regarding the freedom of the port of Lorient.[84] The object of granting free ports to Americans, he argued, was to attract their trade through the assortment of merchandise from all nations which could enter and leave without duty payment in a truly free port. To limit freedom to French subjects and American citizens would not really create a free port. Nevertheless, he worked diligently to facilitate American trade before and after the agreement on the four ports, gained principally through Lafayette's efforts, was announced early in January, 1784.[85]

The most serious problem facing the French Government at this time did not directly concern foreign commerce. It concerned the parlous condition of the Royal Treasury; here was the central problem with which all the controllers-general had to wrestle and before which eventually they had to bow in defeat. During his brief tenure of the office, Lefèvre d'Ormesson had to seize one expedient after the other to find the money necessary to keep afloat. He borrowed where he could at high interest rates and he drew upon the resources of the Discount Bank created by Turgot, converting it in effect into a national bank, with unhappy consequences to its own stability.[86] In his difficulties he also sought advice. Du Pont prepared for him several long memoranda on the finances and on the method of further borrowing. The one notable aspect of Du Pont's ideas in these detailed reports is his insistence upon the relationship of any plans for the amelioration of finances to the need for more general reform. The suppression of various indirect taxes, the rearrangement of others, the thorough reorganization of the Tax Farm, the establishment of a separately administered sinking fund for systematic repayment of loans—these changes, Du Pont argued, would not only increase available revenue but strengthen the credit standing of the Government so that more favorable loans might be obtained. The view that financial reform was impossible without general reform was one which Du Pont held to consistently and which was increasingly shared by others. Du Pont's schemes to tap sources for further borrowing within France and abroad were not particularly helpful and rested upon optimistic estimates of the amounts which might be raised.[87] Ormesson may have seized upon one of Du Pont's ideas, that of reorganizing the taxes and the Tax Farm, for in October he suddenly canceled the lease with the Farmers General. He got no further, however, because his action created such a disturbance that he was forced to resign a week later.[88] One can only speculate whether his later disdain for Du Pont was connected with this unhappy end of his ministry.

Two cherished honors recognizing his services came to Du Pont in 1783. The post of Baden chargé d'affaires in Paris became vacant late in 1782 when the Italian Santi, who had held the position for a year, resigned to accept a professorship at Pisa. Du Pont's friend, the Margrave Carl Friedrich, requested him to assume the office. This unusual arrangement by which an official of the French Government would represent a foreign prince was at first rejected by the King but, through Vergennes' intervention, was finally permitted if Du Pont served Baden without official title or formal recognition.[89] Du Pont continued his functions as unofficial chargé d'affaires for Baden until 1789 but had nothing very important to attend to on behalf of his client. His official letters to Baron Wilhelm von Edelsheim, the Minister of Foreign Affairs of Baden, are interesting principally for his comments on affairs in France.

Vergennes sought another way to honor him for his services by obtaining from the King, in December, 1783, a *lettre de noblesse* which raised Du Pont to noble rank.[90] Neither title nor material reward accompanied this recognition, but the privileges it granted were of some importance. It made Du Pont a social equal of most of his colleagues in the Government; it opened for his sons a wider choice of professions; it authorized him to add to his name the name of any *seigneurie* which he might receive; it permitted him to have a coat of arms. Du Pont never carried to fruition his claim to a *seigneurie*, that of Boudinville rather than of Chevannes, which his wife preferred, but he immediately adopted a coat of arms, displaying a crest of ostrich plumes with lion and eagle as supporters and the motto *Rectitudine Sto* ('Be upright"). With no apparent qualms he took the required oath that his religion was "Catholic, Apostolic, and Roman"—a description which perfectly fitted Madame Du Pont's religion and, at that time, his sons', but which can hardly be reconciled with his personal convictions. More important to Du Pont was the conception of honor and the obligations which the noble rank im-

Bois-des-Fossés, from a painting by C. Balké (1928)

Courtesy of the Eleutherian Mills Historical Library

Victor Marie du Pont (1767-1827);
from an oil portrait by Bass Otis
Courtesy of Mrs. Victor du Pont

Eleuthère Irénée du Pont (1771-1834);
from an oil portrait by Rembrandt Peale
Courtesy of Irénée du Pont, Jr.

posed upon the family. When his younger son, Eleuthère Irénée, reached his thirteenth birthday, Du Pont wrote out and enacted a formal ceremony in which the young man was given the sword to which his rank entitled him.[91] Throughout his life he always stressed the necessity of living true to the motto on the family coat of arms.

The little "domestic ceremony" involving his sons occurred just after they had suffered their greatest loss. For all of them life had by 1783 become more pleasant. Madame Du Pont's careful management of Bois-des Fossés brought material profit—she wrote happily in April of 1783 that they were out of debt.[92] They were well enough off for Du Pont to lease an apartment adequate in size for them all to be together for at least part of the year in Paris, where his numerous duties kept him chained to his desk. They were settled in the new place, in the Cul-de-Sac de la Corderie (now called the Rue Gomboust, not far from the Place Vendôme), when they received the happy news of Du Pont's elevation to noble status in December of 1783. There they remained until July, when Madame Du Pont and the boys returned to Bois-des-Fossés for the summer. They had carriages, better clothes, servants—many of the comforts and material possessions which might normally be associated with their rising position in society.[93] Then came tragedy. In late August at Bois-des-Fossés, Madame Du Pont complained of a slight indisposition but assured her husband in Paris that she would soon be well. In the last letter which she wrote to him on August 25, she did not even mention her illness. On September 3, 1784, she died, suddenly and unexpectedly, of causes never diagnosed, at the age of forty-one. It was bitter tragedy that she did not live long enough to enjoy to the full measure of her deserts the advantages which improved conditions might have brought after years of struggle. Her courageous spirit and capable mind had always been for her husband, as he now came forcefully to realize, bountiful sources of inspiration and of assistance. Du Pont was numb with grief. Even Mirabeau excused his friend for not writing—"he has lost his wife, one of the most sensible and most estimable mothers of a family whom I knew."[94] A few days after the funeral on September 4,[95] Du Pont wearily returned with the boys and their tutor to Paris and tried to ameliorate his sorrow by taking up again the many tasks assigned to him. Henceforth, he had also to supervise the rearing of his sons and to keep an eye on the operations of Bois-des-Fossés, left in the hands of a tenant farmer. It was a fortunate circumstance that he was kept exceedingly busy with these personal and governmental affairs, since he had less time for lonely and solemn meditation upon his loss. A year later, when the tomb which he had ordered for Marie's grave was ready, he attended a memorial service in the parish church at Chevannes. Church and tomb, both restored by his latter-day descendants, still stand prominently in the small village.[96] His expectation that he would be buried in the same tomb was not to be fulfilled.

Du Pont was eventually associated with the major reform program of Calonne, who had succeeded Ormesson as Controller-General in November, 1783. For the present, however, his chief contact in the ministry continued to be with Vergennes. The extent of his official duties was constantly increasing. In his letters to Vergennes he always adopted a freedom to comment on various subjects which did not specifically fall within the compass of his duties. He excused this freedom on the basis of his eagerness to serve his country and to learn all that he could from the Minister, whom he constantly praised. Vergennes tolerated this freedom, somewhat unusual on the part of a subordinate, and accepted the flattery because he had a very high regard for this eager assistant. He was more responsible than anyone else for the improvement in Du Pont's situation. This close association with one of the ablest ministers of the ancien régime probably caused Du Pont later on to exaggerate in his recollections the role which he played in the many projects for reform which filled these years. Writing to the Polish Count Chreptowicz on December 25, 1803, he gave this account of his activities during this period:

Monsieur de Vergennes gave me—with the title of Commissioner General of Commerce and under the combined direction of the Ministry of foreign affairs, the ministries of the navy and of finance—the general administration of foreign and domestic commerce and some authority in agricultural matters. My work had much success. We arranged for the suppression of internal customs; we established the franchise of Bayonne and of the Pays de Laboart [sic]; and we improved our commerce with Spain. We introduced whale fishing at Dunkirk. We formed the Compagnie du Nord and made the commercial treaty with Russia. We imported from Spain and England sheep and rams of fine breeds and supervised the flocks. We opened the Loire for commerce in wines and brandies. We suppressed the export duties on that trade. We encouraged the distillation of Cider, of Perry, of Hydromel and of grains. We created the manufacture of varnish. We developed the first mills for spinning cotton; the first French factories of muslins. We imported English machinery. We recalled the fugitive Protestants and encouraged their return by granting them special favors. We tripled the manufacture of printed cotton. We increased the pasture lands, both natural and artificial; extended the cultivation of potatoes; improved that of grains; doubled the quantity of fruit trees; restocked the forests with timber. . . .[97]

Although precise documentation is lacking for all of these claims, they deal with subjects with which Du Pont was obviously concerned in his many tasks. They are, furthermore, a good indication of the efforts which were made, often in vain, to achieve substantial reforms before 1789. Three obstacles blocked the road to change: the absence of a general program of reform, the opposition of vested interests in France, and the dangerous condition of the Royal Treasury. Calonne tried to remove the first obstacle but could not immediately overcome the other two.

Problems of agriculture consumed many of Du Pont's hours. He was a member of a special committee to make recommendations to the Controller-General on these problems. Between June 16, 1785, and September 18, 1787, this committee met at least sixty-nine times, and Du Pont missed only sixteen meetings. He delivered reports on the cultivation of flax, on the necessity for the establishment of a well-ordered department of agriculture, on the need for a thorough revision of the tithes, on a comparison between the condition of agriculture in England and in France, and on the regulation of the tax on veal.[98] Few of the recommendations were translated into immediate action, but a great amount of information probably useful to Calonne in the formulation of his reform program was accumulated. Among the five members of this committee was the celebrated chemist Antoine Lavoisier, whom Du Pont came to regard as one of his closest friends.

The work of the committee had to be fitted in with that of other committees which kept Du Pont busy. In October, 1785, he wrote to his son Victor: "I have scarcely any time. I am on a Committee with Monsieur Le Noire for several questions on commerce; another with Monsieur Boullogne; a third with Monsieur Fourqueux on commercial duties; and on that of agriculture with Monsieur de

Vergennes [nephew of the Minister]. With the office routine besides, I have little rest."[99] Here he was not exaggerating, for his tasks were many and varied. At the time he wrote to Victor he was working with Le Noir, Councillor of State at the Royal Council of Finances, on the draft of an *arrêt* to encourage the establishment of industries in France by foreign businessmen and manufacturers. An important part of the *arrêt* sought to remove some of the disabilities which attached to the profession of the Protestant religion in Catholic France so that foreign artisans might be attracted.[100] Most of his work, however, was concerned with foreign commerce.

Consistent with the views expressed in 1769 against the privileges of the old Compagnie des Indes, he argued against the plan to create a new East India Company with monopolistic rights. This time he was not successful, because there were too many in the ministry, including the Controller-General Calonne, who were convinced that French markets were not adequately supplied with eastern products by a trade left open to all without special privileges, as it had been since 1769. Although Du Pont produced tables to prove that there was no decline in trade between 1771 and 1782,[101] there does seem to have been a dearth of such products during the period of the war with England and the Government itself organized an expedition to replenish the markets in 1783. Finding that old arguments against monopoly were not very effective in this situation, Du Pont developed another plan which he had long had in mind. This impractical scheme he detailed in memoranda sent to Vergennes in late December, 1784, and early January, 1785.[102] He would create a Compagnie des Indes to operate ships which would actually be supplied by the King, although this arrangement would be disguised as a purchase by depositing the stock of the company in the Treasury. The company would be able to charge such low freight rates that it would soon attract the trade of other nations besides France. It would be granted the property of the old company and, depending on the King's wishes, might enjoy exclusive privileges, although they would not be needed, since the lower rates would attract all the business it could handle. The King would, of course, really retain the ships supplied to the company and could reclaim them as needed "when war or other circumstances interrupted trade." As profits mounted, more ships could be acquired and the King would eventually have an "India squadron" of respectable size that would cost him nothing, or at worst very little. These arrangements, which would have to be kept secret in order to conceal the hand of the King, would not only bring a great expansion of French commerce but might be expected to cut seriously into that of the English and Dutch.

Nothing came of his proposal then, or later. On April 15 Calonne had issued an *arrêt* establishing a new Compagnie des Indes as a purely commercial enterprise, with the exclusive privileges formerly enjoyed by the old company guaranteed to the new one for a period of seven years.[103] There followed other decrees defining its organization and operations. Du Pont continued to make suggestions[104] and even prepared early in 1786 a memorandum for Calonne reviving his project for a company of freight ships (*compagnie messagère*). He had the temerity to propose himself as one of the six directors of the proposed company. The Council of Finances wasted little time in rejecting his proposal as impracticable, and nothing more would have been heard of it had the Abbé Maury not somehow got hold of the manuscript of the memorandum in April, 1790, and made it public in order to embarrass Du Pont during the debate on revoking the privileges of the Compagnie des Indes. Then Du Pont had to extricate himself from Maury's trap by denouncing this publication of secret and personal papers as especially reprehensible in that it made useless the main objective of his plan—that of using the India squadron built up under his scheme for a sudden attack upon the English in Bengal should war break out again. This adroit maneuver won him the support of the Left in the Assembly at that time, though there is no hint of this objective in his original memorandum.[105]

Because his absorption in problems of foreign commerce necessarily brought him into contact with important government officers, foreign as well as French, Vergennes gave further recognition to his efforts in November, 1786, by persuading the King to raise him in official status by appointing him a Councillor of State.[106] At this time Du Pont was working very closely with Lafayette and Jefferson on increasing the trade between France and the United States. He was a member of what came to be called the "American Committee," set up early in 1786 at Lafayette's urging.[107] The committee's principal efforts were directed against the contract signed between Robert Morris and the Farmers General creating a monopoly in the supplying of American tobacco to the Farm, which, of course, controlled the sale of all tobacco in France. Franco-American trade had languished because of failure to carry out earlier agreements and because, by long habit, Americans were more accustomed to trade with England and drifted back into the old relations after the treaty of peace acknowledging their independence. Lafayette, Jefferson, Du Pont, and others associated with them hoped that, by breaking the exclusive Morris contract, they could create a "broad and favorable market for American tobacco."[108]

They had a difficult time against the opposition of the Farmers General and of Calonne, who had approved the contract. On May 13, 1786, Du Pont sent to Vergennes a résumé of the committee discussions on six memoranda aimed at cancellation or revision of the original deal.[109] Vergennes' assistance was important in bringing Calonne around to accepting a modification of the contract on May 24 during a meeting with the committee at his château. The concession gained destroyed the monopoly enjoyed by Morris by requiring the Farm to purchase each year an additional twelve to fifteen thousand hogsheads of American tobacco on the same terms as those accorded to Morris. Furthermore, there was agreement that no such contracts would be made in the future after the expiration of the deal with Morris.[110] It was a limited victory, further circumscribed by the failure of the Government to enforce and of the Farmers General to honor the agreement. The battle continued to be fought without attaining full victory throughout the following year.[111] The most prized benefit for Du Pont from his labors on the committee was the cordial relationship with Lafayette and Jefferson. The latter acknowledged that Du Pont had "rendered us essential services" in the efforts to facilitate American trade with France.[112]

Throughout these years Du Pont continued his intimate association with the Comte de Mirabeau, exiled from Paris by his father's wrath. His efforts to reconcile father and son were never successful, but he did what he could for his younger friend, even to the extent of trying to arrange loans for him. Soon after meeting Beaumarchais, for instance, he wrote to him about Mirabeau in support of a request for a loan which he had advised his friend to address to the celebrated dramatist.[113] For the most part, however, he had little time for affairs not connected with his work, in which he drove himself almost to the point of complete exhaustion. He had few diversions. Occasionally, he attended meetings of the Musée de Paris, a literary society founded in 1780 by Antoine Court de Gébelin,[114] but most of his days and many of his nights were spent at his desk.

The matter of greatest concern to Du Pont in 1786 was the completion of a commercial treaty with England. By Article 18 of the Treaty of Versailles of 1783, both nations had pledged themselves to reorganize their commercial relations within a period of two years. Vergennes had sent Gérard de Rayneval to London as early as 1782 to carry on negotiations, which dragged on beyond the stipulated two years. Rayneval was not particularly well versed in commercial matters and relied upon reports and memoranda prepared by other government officials laboring quietly behind the scene. There is no way to prove positively from contemporary documents the assertions of Du Pont, accepted without question by his biographers, that he did all the important work on the French side. The many reports prepared for the use of Rayneval are mainly in the neat script of copyists, although some have summaries in the left-hand margin and corrections in the text which are certainly in Du Pont's handwriting.[115] Vergennes was eager for a treaty and had obviously come to rely much upon Du Pont. Since some of the other subordinate officials, especially Du Pont's fellow Councillor of State Boyetet, were opposed to making concessions to the English, it seems likely that Du Pont would carry the burdens of detail. Indeed, there is one piece of contemporary evidence in addition to his own statements that clearly associates him with the principal *mémoires* in support of the treaty.

In 1789 Boyetet published a collection of his *mémoires* opposing the treaty. Several times in these documents he mentions Du Pont as the chief advocate against whom he is arguing. He points out that, before the arrival of the English negotiator William Eden, Calonne had requested him and Du Pont to prepare recommendations but had enjoined them to work separately. When the Controller-General was too busy to see them immediately on the day they were to communicate to him their first general observations, they exchanged their *mémoires*, which immediately made clear their opposed viewpoints. Although Du Pont expressed the opinion that their ideas were not so diametrically opposite that they could not work together, Boyetet rejected this view and consistently combated his colleague's arguments. He was disturbed when, he claims, Du Pont did not deliver to the Minister the first *mémoire* which he had prepared but rather a different one, largely devoted to refuting the arguments in the document which Boyetet had permitted him to read. He therefore printed Du Pont's *mémoire* so that he might in turn have the opportunity to refute his antagonist's views.[116] Boyetet may have published his collection because he was piqued that Du Pont's argument had prevailed over his. In fighting Du Pont he may inadvertently have placed his opponent in a more central position than the latter really occupied in the work on the treaty. Nowhere in the actual negotiations does Du Pont's name appear. He is never mentioned, for example, in the papers of William Eden, although Rayneval, Vergennes, and, less frequently, Calonne are.[117]

Commercial relations between France and England throughout the eighteenth century were in a state of confusion generally more advantageous to English merchants than to their French counterparts. The commercial treaty concluded in 1713 at the Peace of Utrecht had never been effective, because the English House of Commons had rejected the two essential articles which contained agreements for the two nations to treat each other as the most favored nation and to make reciprocal tariff concessions. When the Treaty of Paris was signed in 1763, the Duc de Choiseul was realistic, if technically inaccurate, in replying bluntly to a suggestion that he renew the Treaty of 1713: "The treaty never existed."[118] Regular and legal trade between the two countries continued to be beset by the old mercantilist practices of outright prohibitions and of excessively high tariffs. Merchants in both countries were accustomed to this regime of protection, which they regarded as the necessary safeguard of their interests. Despite these obstacles, trade was carried on, but much of it fell into the hands of smugglers, who were organized on a large scale. The French customs system was too complicated and too inefficient to stop the illegal importation of many English goods for which there was growing demand among French consumers. In the 1780's perhaps nearly half of the products of English origin reaching French markets evaded the prohibitions and customs duties.[119] France seemed, therefore, to be clearly at a disadvantage. Still, the necessity of French prohibitions and high tariffs was vigorously urged by certain manufacturing interests and governmental officials wedded to mercantilist views.

The best that could be hoped for under these circumstances was a series of reciprocal concessions which would expand the area of legal trade. As a good Physiocrat Du Pont was opposed to outright prohibitions, which he sought to replace with various levels of tariff duties on important goods. In intricate detail he balanced off one concession against another, arguing usually that France would benefit more than England. In a *mémoire* sent to Vergennes just after the treaty was signed, he did point out that ultimate advantages for France depended also upon internal reforms, such as the removal of disabilities burdening Protestant artisans, elimination of vexatious taxes, and the adoption of new industrial machinery and techniques.[120]

The documents on the French side of the negotiations display an eagerness to achieve agreement. They are the work of governmental officials, among whom Du Pont probably figured most prominently, and are not based upon any consultation with French manufacturers or merchants. Boyetet complained about this failure to consult with chambers of commerce in the provinces and exploited it to organize opposition to the treaty.[121] On their part the English appear to have taken every precaution to make the treaty as profitable to their interests as possible and to have carried out careful inquiries among businessmen beforehand. Their negotiator, William Eden, had mastered an immense amount of data and was able to take advantage of the French desire for conciliation.[122] He might, indeed, have pushed his advantage farther than he did, but he was himself eager for a treaty and was somewhat softened by the friendly attitude of the French Government.

There were reasons for this apparent weakness on the part of French officials, like Du Pont, who were laboring for the treaty. Vergennes hoped to make of it the first definite step toward a long period of peace and co-operation between his country and England. The impoverished condition of the Treasury and the desire to accomplish economic and political changes within France required such a period free of the fear of war with a traditional enemy.[123] The restoration of peaceful trade relations would not only destroy contraband trade, which had been disadvantageous to France, but would also serve, one might expect, as a spur to effect desirable reforms at home. Old methods could no longer continue undisturbed behind a high wall of protection.

The treaty, consisting of forty-seven articles, was signed by Rayneval and Eden on September 26 and was to go into effect for a period of twelve years after ratification. The need for additional agreements on specific points and for definite instructions to be sent to various officials postponed full execution of the clauses until as late as July 1, 1787. The treaty repeated the guarantees of the 1713 agreement regarding maintenance of normal commercial relations and protection of individuals and their property. It provided in article 6 for a lowering of duties on a variety of products, beginning with what seems at first to be a startling concession on the part of the English. Henceforth French wines imported into England would not pay "higher duties than those which at present Portuguese wines pay." This clause did result in a substantial reduction in the tariff paid by French wines but did not gain for them lasting equality with Portuguese wines.

The Portuguese soon claimed their rights under the Methuen Treaty of 1703 and obtained in March, 1787, a further reduction of one-third under the duties levied on French wines. There were also reductions on tariff rates on French vinegars and brandies and the establishment of maximum limits to rates chargeable on French olive oils and on a wide assortment of other products manufactured in either country—beer; hardware, cutlery, cabinetware, products of iron, steel, copper, and bronze; cotton goods and woolen goods, including hosiery; cambrics, lawns, goods of flax or hemp; saddlery; millinery; porcelain, earthenware, and pottery; mirrors and glassware. Article 7 provided that for products not listed duties would be those charged on such goods emanating from the European nation which, at the date of the treaty, had the most favored status in the tariff schedules of the signatory concerned. As Lafayette pointed out, the stipulation regarding the most favored *European* nation would not affect concessions granted by France to the United States.[124]

There were other important clauses, too numerous to summarize, erecting safeguards against rupture of the agreement. Except for French reservations in regard to Spain in conformity with the Family Pact of 1761 and for English reservations in regard to Portugal in accordance with the Methuen Treaty of 1703, each signatory pledged to extend at once, on a basis of reciprocity, any trade advantages accorded by it to another European nation. If either signatory in the future prohibited the importation of any products of the other signatory or raised the customs duties on such products beyond those provided by the treaty, the prohibitions and increased duties were to extend to those products coming from any European nation. If either signatory granted an export bounty to any of its products, the other signatory could proportionately increase customs duties on those products.[125]

In the brief period of its operation, the treaty did appear to work to the disadvantage of French interests. Many contemporary commentators and some later students tended to blame the treaty as the principal cause of the industrial crisis in France on the eve of the Revolution. There is no doubt that it provided a convenient scapegoat which could be held responsible for the difficulties which France experienced. A more balanced view is justified. There was sufficient reciprocity in the terms to provide positive gains for French industry had the treaty run its full course. Since its application was interrupted by the Revolution before it had been in effect for even half of the period foreseen by its authors, it cannot, indeed, be subjected to a definitive judgment. The fact is that France had entered an economic depression before the treaty became effective. After it did go into effect in 1787, French exports to England increased notably. The spectacular increase was, however, on the English side. One estimate is that French exports to England increased in value from 20 million livres in 1784 to 34 or 37 million livres in 1787, whereas English exports to France in these same years increased from 13,200,000 to 58 or 63 million livres. The statistics for 1784 do not show, of course, the considerable value of contraband goods which entered France.[126] The substantial increase of English imports was expected by the French authors of the treaty and justified, as has been suggested, on the bases of the favorable political effects of the expanded market and of the goad to reform which this competition would produce. The fate of the treaty was determined by the fact that neither of these expectations became actualities. Vergennes, chief architect of the peace policy, died on February 13, 1787, before the treaty was in effect, and shortly afterwards, diplomatic relations between the two countries were seriously strained by the conflict in Holland between the patriot party, supported by France, and the adherents of the Stadholder, supported by Prussia and England. Desired reform within France failed of full achievement because of the impasse which developed between Calonne and the Assembly of Notables.[127]

There was at first no widespread outcry against the treaty in France. Eventually opposition to it was voiced by chambers of commerce in Artois, Picardy, Bordeaux, and Normandy. In furthering his campaign against the treaty, Boyetet apparently was largely responsible for organizing this oposition.[128] The most substantial critique was that of the Normandy chamber of commerce, which sent out investigators to study the differences between French and English industries. Their findings, which emphasized the advantages enjoyed by the English, formed the basis of a report generally unfavorable to the treaty. The *Observations* of the Normandy chamber[129] had a wide circulation and Du Pont hastened to reply. His *Lettre à la chambre du commerce de Normandie* was published anonymously early in 1788.[130]

In a spirit of reasonable conciliation, Du Pont began his open letter by commending the Normandy chamber for publishing its *Mémoire* and by assuring it that many of the specific recommendations contained therein for improving French industry and agriculture had already been submitted to the Ministry before the signing of the treaty. Confusion arising from the meeting of the Assembly of Notables and changes in the Ministry had prevented positive action, but the future would bring results. The source of French disadvantages lay not in the treaty, but in the backward state of French industry compared with the English and in the inefficient administration of the French customs. General efforts must be made to improve both situations. The exclusive privileges of monopoly, ineffective prohibitions, and high tariffs could not effect the desired results. Freedom of any manufacturer to increase the quality and number of industrial machines, the end of smuggling and contraband by removing the stimulus of prohibitions and high tariffs—these were the paths of a revival of French interests. Real protection could come only through reasonable tariffs which could and would be enforced. In actuality, Du Pont argued, the English got from the treaty no advantage not previously theirs through the disregard of French prohibitions and customs duties. He concluded his letter by urging the fullest possible exchange of views on the subject and by praising the efforts of the King and his Ministry. To enrich information through an exchange of views is the duty of all good citizens, a duty which "will be fulfilled with more courage when it is seen that it is only a question of soliciting the promptest execution possible of the wise and beneficent views of the King and . . . of his principal minister."[131]

Du Pont's *Lettre* constitutes one of the best justifications of the Treaty of 1786 ever published. While admitting that certain interests have been temporarily damaged, it insists upon the ultimate benefits which will be certain after necessary changes have been carried out in France. Had these measures been effected, as the King and the Ministry desired according to the author, there would have been no ill results. The only complaints have come from a few areas where business does seem to have been hurt; public opinion in general was not unfavorable to the treaty.[132] Unfortunately, the major part of the printed pamphlet is devoted to explanatory notes, most of which seek to prove, by intricate calculations of the rate of exchange between the respective moneys and of the value of products imported and exported, that the balance of trade was favorable to France. The 117 pages (out of a total of 278) given over to statistical tables and long drawn-out explanations are tedious and hardly convincing, since the reader can follow them only with some difficulty. This burdensome freight at the rear casts a shadow over the bright impression created by the ninety-one page letter. One of Du Pont's failings is that of many writers: he too often passed far beyond the point at which he should have laid down his pen. His interests in such tables is, however, understandable, since one of his continuing duties was the preparation of statistical data on the balance of trade.

Months before his pamphlet appeared in print, Du Pont's ardent hopes for regenerative measures by the Assembly of Notables had been seriously injured, though he retained some of his usual optimism. To these hopes and to his part in the two Assemblies of Notables in 1787 and 1788, the following chapter must turn.

Chapter IV

Assembly of Notables (1787-1789)

CHARLES-ALEXANDRE DE CALONNE became Controller-General of Finances in November, 1783. Not until mid-August, 1786, did he outline before the King a general reform program seeking amelioration of the desperate financial condition of the Kingdom.[1] Months later, on February 14, 1787, just eight days before the opening of the Assembly of Notables, which had been summoned to consider the reform program, he called together several friends and associates to put into final form the recommendations for specific changes in finance and administration.[2] These apparent delays led his contemporaries, like Talleyrand, and most later commentators to indict him for irresponsibility and opportunism, to denounce him for seizing wildly upon hastily constructed and poorly co-ordinated plans in a last desperate effort to atone for his past errors and to retain his position. There is no doubt that Calonne was personally ambitious, but, in recent times, careful scholars have seriously challenged any completely adverse judgment of him and of his ministry. His program is now viewed as being well thought-out and long prepared, as reflecting a "novel . . . determination to apply fiscal, administrative and economic remedies simultaneously and [a] conviction that these reforms would not achieve their purpose unless the political structure of the ancien régime was itself remodeled."[3]

In view of this revised judgment of Calonne's program a present-day biographer of Du Pont would be delighted if he could rest content with Du Pont's assertions, repeated by his previous biographers, that he had prepared "almost all the plans proposed to the Assembly of Notables."[4] Unfortunately, such a sweeping claim cannot be sustained by reliance upon other testimony. That Du Pont was very busy during the years of Calonne's ministry has been demonstrated. That he was an important member of the group assisting the Controller-General in drawing up plans for reform is acknowledged by all students of the period.[5] There is some justice in the view that the shadow of Turgot hovered over many of the plans of ministers who succeeded him and that Du Pont was determined to vindicate the ideas of his late benefactor. "I have no projects," he wrote to the Comte d'Angivillier; "I worked on those of Turgot which were adopted by Calonne."[6] Still, it has long been clear that others labored in the ranks of the reformers, and it must now be conceded that Calonne provided more forceful leadership than has heretofore been appreciated.

Ministers and others less astute than the experienced Calonne realized that something must be done. Indeed, all of his predecessors in office had tried to do something. His contribution was to launch a wide-ranging scheme of reform in place of the previous half-measures and expedients of these predecessors. Undoubtedly Turgot would earlier have elaborated plans to push France in the direction of fundamental reform, had he held office long enough. That some basic changes were necessary had become clear to an ever increasing number of persons who were aware of the evolving situation. The old answers no longer sufficed for a France growing increasingly prosperous, powerful, and complex. Expanding energies did not rest easily within the limitations imposed by the old regime. While England forged ahead and while, even in more backward countries to the east, beneficent rulers boasted of their plans to improve their realms, no bold new program had found enduring official sanction in France. There much was written, much was spoken, indeed, on occasion, much was promised; but very little was done.

In France, on what proved to be the eve of revolution, all the factors for change were present: a political, social, and economic system which no longer met the needs of the people; numerous criticisms of the past and plans for the future from the minds of thinkers and writers; and a sufficiently advanced state of the people generally to bring an awareness of the possibility of further improvement. Resistance to gradual change on the part of those few profiting from the old order could, and did, bring the more violent and rapid changes associated with the word *revolution*. This resistance, a reflection of the so-called "seigneurial reaction" of the second half of the eighteenth century, culminated during the Assembly of Notables in what Mathiez and Lefebvre designated as the first of the series of revolts which, together, constituted the French Revolution.[7] Many of these features were not peculiar to France. Throughout much of the western world there was an upsurge of expectations, an increase in the demands for change.[8] It was in France, however, that they received their best-known expression.

Politically, the theoretically absolute monarchy of France had long passed the point of whatever usefulness it had in unifying and protecting the nation. It could no longer deal efficiently with the complex problems of government, even under a Louis XIV who worked conscientiously at his job. His successors may have had more sincere concern for the welfare of their subjects, but they had not his patience for the details of administration. Hence, the machinery of government moved ever more ponderously without intelligent direction. In the *Mémoire sur les municipalités*, Turgot and Du Pont had clearly pointed out the fact that, without more direct assistance from a greater part of his subjects, the King was almost helpless, however noble his intentions. Some fundamental reorganization of the administration was in order. Socially, the roots of discontent lay in the barriers separating the privileged from the unprivileged. These legal barriers, dividing the first two estates (the clergy and the nobility) from the third (the *Tiers*), grew higher toward the end of the ancien régime. At the same time, they grew more complicated because the social orders were divided within themselves. "In social manners and customs the nobility and the bourgeoisie were ranged in a multitude of layers and stages which never melted into one another, beginning with the prince of the blood, and going down to the humblest artisan. In respect of birth, public opinion held some recently ennobled persons far inferior to some members of the bourgeoisie with long pedigrees. . . . In society as constituted under the *Ancien Régime* there was what might be called a cascade of disdain, and it was this more than anything else which provoked the revolutionary movement."[9] However firmly they held to enlightened absolutism, the Physiocrats and Turgot were insistent upon the necessity of emancipating the individual. In their schemes for elective assemblies and for supplanting the *corvée* by a general tax on landowners, Turgot and Du Pont had sought to circumvent social distinctions. Earlier, in 1758, Forbonnais had declared: "France would be too rich if the taxes were equitably apportioned."[10]

The segments of the French economy did not show a uniform rate of advance. By present-day standards, agriculture was in a bad state. The peasants' primitive methods, lack of capital, and resistance to innovation kept productivity low. Yet Arthur Young admitted: ". . . France is in possession of a soil and even of a husbandry that is to be ranked very high amongst the best in Europe."[11] Recent investigation has shown that landholding was much more widely spread among the peasantry than was formerly assumed.[12] The problem was twofold: population was steadily increasing and individual peasant holdings were usually small and encumbered by seigneurial dues and obligations. Although there may have been no desperate "land hunger" in France among the peasants,[13] there was strong desire to increase landholdings, and to rid them of the burdens of the seigneurial régime, which became increasingly oppressive in the eighteenth century. "The love of landed property was one of the most powerful levers of the Revolution. It produced an immense displacement of wealth . . . [and] is the principal social question, bound to the struggle against the old landed régime, against the nobles and especially against the clergy. It concentrates in itself the most considerable interests and the most violent passions of the period."[14] Industry in France remained predominantly on a small scale, marked by an increase in rural industry in the eighteenth century. The greatest economic expansion lay in the field of commerce. Especially in foreign trade the advance was remarkable, being proportionately greater even than that of England. It was the commercial bourgeoisie, principally, who chafed under the vexations and restrictions of the established system.[15] Demands for the freeing of trade were heard throughout the eighteenth century. Physiocrats, interested essentially in freedom for agricultural products, had only to adapt familiar arguments for this part of their program.

The actual influence of such arguments, and of the varied critiques of the *philosophes*, was long a subject of debate. The weight of scholarly judgment appears to have decided in favor of the view that prevailing conditions were of primary importance in bringing demands for change and in shaping the thinking and writing of the *philosophes* and other critics. The latter, it may be argued, did assist in sharpening the understanding of undesirable conditions on the part of the reading public and in suggesting ideas upon which the minds of reformers could feed. The exact source of the viewpoints of any individual is usually difficult to trace. In pointing up abuses and in enriching the intellectual ferment of the time the critics did not labor in vain, although, undoubtedly, Du Pont was much too careless in his later declaration that, in commercial and financial questions, the Constituent Assembly, after violent invectives against the *économistes,* usually ended by adopting measures conforming to their principles.[16]

Whatever attitude various French ministries might take towards conditions and criticisms, there was always one issue which had to be faced—threatened or actual government bankruptcy. Bankruptcies, or repudiations of part of the national obligations, occurred in 1715, 1721, 1726, 1759, and 1770.[17] Temporary expedients, by which a Controller-General like Terray had been able to stave off total collapse, became increasingly less effective after the expenditures of the American War of Independence, expenditures against which Turgot had vainly protested. These outlays "cost the French nation from 1,000 to 1,200 millions. Cambon states the amount at 1,500 millions. No less than 220 millions were still due on this account in 1783 (Calonne) and 100 millions in 1784 (Necker)."[18] Under the heavy burden of the deficit, attempted economies were insignificant in ameliorating the condition of the Treasury. Besides, projected economies were so often combated by the Court party that they were never fully achieved. The only solution lay in substantial reforms which would extract revenue from the privileged orders.

Turgot's program was destroyed before it could produce important results. Necker next assumed the mantle of the reformer and undertook half-measures, which might have been aimed more at attaining personal popularity than at strengthening the Government. Without abolishing the guilds, he did increase the number of "free" trades. Without seriously disturbing the system, he did make more advantageous contracts for the farming of taxes. Without destroying social distinctions, he did establish provincial assemblies in Berry and Haute-Guyenne, with very limited powers of administration.

One-third of the members of these assemblies were appointed by the King, not elected by the landowners as Turgot and Du Pont had proposed. Half of the members were selected from the clergy and nobility, half from the *Tiers* of towns and rural areas. The third of the membership chosen by the King elected the other two-thirds. Class distinctions were retained. These assemblies met only once in two years, but were continued after Necker's retirement.[19] Necker effected some economies by abolishing useless offices and by checking the lavish grant of pensions. He also gained the King's consent to the abolition of serfdom on the royal estates. His most spectacular achievement, that of financing the war without an increase in taxes, was in reality a deceitful operation, since he concealed the deficit in his accounts. The falsity of his widely studied *Compte rendu* made more difficult the tasks of his successors.

When he learned the actual situation, Joly de Fleury did not hesitate to order an increase in various taxes and to establish a new one, the third *vingtième* authorized in July, 1782. The success of these measures was qualified by the opposition of the parlements, growing ever more sensitive to attacks on privilege and property. To carry on, Joly de Fleury had to have the usual recourse to loans, which he obtained with mounting difficulty. In co-operation with Vergennes, he set up a Council of Finances, whose duty was to discuss, in weekly meetings, ways and means of alleviating the deficit by economy in government expenses, by reforming the taxes, and by reorganizing the grant of pensions and gifts. Most of the Court party was not in sympathy with the last measure; as Calonne remarked, the Council would be "le tombeau des grâces."[20] Joly de Fleury resigned on March 30, 1783. The problems were too great for his successor, Lefèvre d'Ormesson, for whom Du Pont prepared detailed recommendations. Employing to the fullest his personal charm and his connections with some members of the Court party, the ambitious Calonne emerged successful from the intrigues surrounding the appointment of the next controller-general.

Calonne was an experienced and able administrator, but suffered the disadvantage of a bad reputation among many of his contemporaries, who regarded him as an unscrupulous intriguer and as a man of debased moral standards in his personal relationships. Although like faults could easily be charged to many of these same contemporaries, they served as convenient stones upon which to sharpen the barbs directed against Calonne by men like Necker and Lomenie de Brienne, Archbishop of Toulouse, eager to replace him in the Ministry. Calonne's analysis of the immediate situation was that, by policies of retrenchment, his predecessors had not only destroyed public confidence in the Government but had also undermined their own positions by arousing the opposition of the Court. The corrective was a display of governmental largesse, especially in favor of individuals like the King's brothers and the Queen. More money went for public improvements and for payment on the war debt. Calonne was at first convinced that his program was a success. Public confidence was so well restored that he could get much more favorable rates of interest on the large sums which he had to borrow to finance his projects. Soon, however, the unending succession of loans began to irk the parlements; the judges began to remonstrate. In 1785, Necker, the popular idol, presented his *Traité de l'adminis-tration des finances*, which convinced a large public that his good work had been ruined by incompetent successors. The same year brought the unhappy involvement of the Queen in the public scandal of the diamond necklace. After this unfortunate affair, Calonne may have held the support of the Court at less value. Meanwhile, the deficit continued to mount, and bankruptcy drew closer. But the situation was not hopeless, for, all during this time, Calonne, according to his own account, had been preparing a program of significant reform.

Why did he wait so long to present it to the King? For his enemies the answer was easy: he had been forced to it as a last resort in the face of mounting financial difficulties; it was his only hope to maintain his position. Calonne's explanation was different: he had first to make more secure his tenancy in office and to master the financial crisis; then he could proceed to elaborate plans for reform. He was brought to a realization that the financial crisis could not be overcome without wide-ranging reform, when he confronted the paradoxical situation of having to use borrowed money to create a sinking fund by which the debt could be gradually reduced. By early 1786 he could no longer postpone his schemes and turned to his associates, of whom Du Pont was one, for assistance in gathering information and in working out the details of his schemes.

The time was well chosen, for, by the end of that year, the third *vingtième* of Joly de Fleury was due to expire and the contract with the Farmers General for the collection of the indirect taxes was up for renewal. If resort to temporary expedients was to be avoided, a thorough consideration of the full ramifications of the financial predicament was essential. Du Pont seems to have had a hand in most of the studies which went forward in the spring and summer of 1786, but he was not the sole laborer. He worked with old friends like Fourqueux, Trudaine de Montigny, and Lenoir. Others contributed to the projects, so that it is impossible to determine precisely who should receive principal credit for specific projects. Calonne supervised their labors and modified their recommendations as he saw fit.

On August 20, 1786, he presented an outline of the proposals to the King. Louis is said at first to have protested that the program was "pure Necker." He might easily have called it "pure Turgot,"[21] for Calonne had no prejudice against incorporating into his views the ideas of others. With some misgivings Louis granted permission to carry forward the plans. In subsequent months Calonne was concerned not only with the elaboration of these plans and with the deteriorating financial situation but also with the problem of how best to make public his projects for reform. The opposition of the parlements was almost certain and, while the King might be induced to force registration of the necessary edicts in a *lit de justice*, this procedure had not saved Turgot, or his program. Calonne eventually determined upon a different approach, which might gain for his plans sufficient support to overcome the expected opposition of the parlements. He convinced the King that an Assembly of Notables should be convoked to consider the recommendations for reform. Such an assembly, consisting of members of the clergy, the nobility, and a few individuals from the *Tiers* representing municipal corporations, had not been called into session since 1626.[22] What Calonne hoped to accomplish by this revival of an old institution is not entirely clear. He probably thought that it would be more manageable than the parlements, since its members would be individually nominated and summoned by the King. Because it did include individuals from all three orders, even though clergy and nobility considerably outnumbered the *Tiers*, it might be looked upon as a quasi-representative body likely to have varied viewpoints differing from those of the robe nobility in the parlements. Should it nevertheless prove intractable, it could be dismissed by the King, and the final device of forced registration before the Parlement of Paris could be adopted. It was worth the risk in order possibly to circumvent this unpalatable alternative. Louis granted Calonne's request and authorized the transmission of letters on December 29, 1786, summoning the notables to assemble at Versailles on January 29, 1787.

Despite the months of labor which had preceded this summons, many of the specific proposals were not in order for presentation to the Assembly by the time of its scheduled meeting. The first session was successively postponed from January 29 to February 7, then to February 14, and finally to February 22. These postponements were explained as being due to the temporary indisposition of Miroménil, Keeper of the Seals, and of the Controller-General, although his opponents then and subsequently asserted that Calonne's illness was feigned, and by the fatal malady of Vergennes, who died on February 13. Talleyrand reports in his *Mémoires* that Calonne wrote to him on February 14 requesting him to come to Versailles in order to assist in drafting the recommendations which would be made to the Assembly. A similar request went to the Marquis de la Galaizière, a member of the Royal Council of Finances; to Nicholas de Saint-Genis, who was an expert in ecclesiastical law; to Pierre Gerbier, advocate at the Parlement of Paris; to M. de Cormerey; and to Du Pont. This group, according to Talleyrand, worked for a week in reducing to concrete plans the immense sheaves of papers and *mémoires* on various projects which Calonne transmitted to them. In his *Mémoires* Talleyrand castigates the Controller-General for the "presumption and carelessness" which had led him to neglect this necessary work for five months; actually, in 1787, just a month after the event which he describes in his *Mémoires*, he had indicated in a letter to Mirabeau his enthusiasm for Calonne and his program.[23] In the preparation of the final recommendations Talleyrand states that he worked with Saint-Genis on the *mémoire* on the payment of clerical debts and with Galaizière on the one regarding the *corvée*; Cormerey did all the work on the abolition of internal tariff lines, and Gerbier contributed "paragraphs" to all of them. As for Du

Pont, "he gave himself with all his imagination, all his soul and all his heart to questions which were more in line with his opinions."[24]

Du Pont was never modest in his own claims. He wrote to Edelsheim on July 7, 1787, that he had been responsible for eleven of the fourteen "operations," for which the *Gazette de France* had complimented Calonne.[25] A month earlier he had written to Ormesson that he had "concurred" in certain specific projects: the establishment of provincial assemblies, "according to the principles of M[r.] Turgot"; the regular collection of the *vingtièmes* in money; the modification of the *taille* and even its complete abolition as soon as possible; the freedom of the grain trade; the abolition of *corvées*; the suppression of interior customs duties; the complete suppression of the *gabelles* (salt taxes) and their conversion into "a tax on all orders of tax-payers." He had, he added, proposed to combine with these projects the suppression of the *aides* (beverage taxes), the *droit de marque* on leathers, and the lotteries. He further stated that, on almost all these points, the Assembly of Notables had found his ideas, which he had given to Calonne, preferable to the modifications which the Controller-General had believed necessary.[26] Calonne gave some recognition to his efforts by having him appointed second secretary of the Assembly. P. M. Hennin, another close associate of Vergennes, was chosen as first secretary. The two secretaries were accorded the honor of being personally presented to the King on February 4.[27]

The delay in opening the Assembly was unfortunate. It weakened Calonne's position and provided time for rumors to spread and opposition to organize. The rumor that the Assembly would be only a device to increase the taxes gained wider currency. The more sophisticated delighted in the witticisms which sought through ridicule to destroy the effectiveness of this Assembly of "Not ables" before it even met. There were reports of a placard which was tacked on Calonne's door announcing that ". . . M. the controller general has raised a new troup of comedians, who will begin to perform before the court at Versailles on Monday the 29th of this month. They will give the main piece *False Confidences* and for the small one *Forced Consent*. These will be followed by an allegorical pantomine ballet, of M. de Calonne's composition, entitled *The Cask of the Danaïdes*."[28] The figure of the leaking vessel of the Danaïdes was an apt representation of the condition of the Treasury, though undoubtedly the unknown author of the witticism meant to imply also that Calonne was responsible for the leaks.

Everyone outside the Government with any interest in the situation knew that something was wrong and found it easier to cast the blame on a person than to understand the complicated bases upon which the trouble rested. Many of the privileged were coming around to the view that they would have to accept some financial sacrifices, but they were determined to consent to them only at a price—a substantial strengthening of their political and social privileges.[29]

The assembled Notables early saw one approach which might give them some control: they would request from the Controller-General detailed financial statements, with the argument that only through a study of them could they really understand Calonne's problems. If they could force submission of the accounts, they were certain to gain an influence over what the Government could do. The issue was, therefore, posed before the first meeting. Calonne's program sought to make it possible for the absolute monarchy to operate with greater efficiency and freedom; the Notables sought to challenge the absolutism of Court and Ministry through increasing their influence in public affairs. Calonne's strategy was to present his projects as decisions already made by the King; the Notables might suggest changes in detail but could not question the substance. The Notables' reaction was to insist upon their right to know fully the situation which allegedly made the reforms necessary and to consider the wisdom and nature of each reform in substance as well as in detail.

The privileged orders were, of course, in control of the Assembly of Notables. Of 144 members less than thirty were drawn from the third estate.[30] They were by no means all of the same opinion about what should be done, though the view that the aristocracy must again have some formal power in government was strong. There were few, indeed, willing to follow the one eager and sincere reformer in their midst, the Marquis de Lafayette. They were pleased that in the opening meeting in the Salle des Menus-Plaisirs the old forms of ceremony were carefully followed and complicated rules of precedence meticulously observed. They were much less pleased by the long speech of the Controller-General, which began as an elaborate defense of his ministry. As Calonne read through the many improvements since 1783, some began to wonder why he had, in effect, admitted his difficulties by calling them together. Calonne had eventually to get around to the heavy deficit in the Treasury. He admitted vast outlays but justified them as necessary to restore public confidence and to construct necessary public improvements. The true cause of the deficit, he insisted, lay in the errors and abuses of the past. The present task was to eliminate the continuing source of evil—the abuses. As he launched into a vigorous denunciation of abuses, some of his auditors began to question in their minds whether he meant to draw a distinction between genuine abuses and justified privileges. What the King had to propose, Calonne conceded, was not new; the program was only a bringing together of projects long conceived by able statesmen. Up to that time efforts to put some of these plans into full operation had been thwarted "by the difficulty of conciliating a swarm of local customs, pretensions, privileges and interests opposed to one another."[31] He was undeniably correct in this analysis, but most of his audience were already determined to prevent the removal of all such obstacles to effective royal absolutism. Calonne provided a general outline of his projects in this opening speech, but everyone awaited the separate *mémoires* on each specific project which would be presented to subsequent sessions of the Assembly.

The *mémoires* were organized into four divisions, and the first of these divisions, containing six *mémoires*, was laid before the second meeting of the Assembly on February 23. The first *mémoire* dealt with the establishment of provincial assemblies; the second with a new tax on land; the third with the redemption of clerical debts; the fourth with the *taille*, the most disliked of the direct taxes; the fifth with the grain trade; and the sixth with the *corvée*. Of all these measures the first was the most controversial and was obviously an adaptation of the scheme which Du Pont and Turgot had worked on over a decade earlier. Calonne's attention was called to the *Mémoire sur les municipalités* by Mirabeau, who sold it to him as his own work in 1785 and then published it as Turgot's work in 1787.[32] It seems reasonable, nevertheless, to accept Du Pont's testimony that he prepared the plan for the Controller-General.

Du Pont was distressed by Mirabeau's unauthorized publication, but instead of denouncing his friend, he contented himself with attempting to rectify through letters to various journals the false impressions which he believed Mirabeau's edition would create. The plan presented by Calonne reproduced exactly the earlier project, except that it eliminated the grand or royal muncipality, the national assembly which would stand at the head of the hierarchy of local, district, and provincial assemblies. The radical aspect of the plan was, it may be recalled, that representation would be based not upon social distinctions but upon possession of an income of 600 livres. The traditional prerogatives of the nobility would be ignored. In an effort to weaken some of the criticism which this part of the plan would arouse, Calonne restricted this reorganization of local government to the *pays d'élections*, the provinces which did not already have provincial assemblies. Furthermore, as was true of the Turgot-Du Pont proposal, the assemblies were to have little real power. Essentially they were to assist the Central Government in matters of tax assessment, poor relief, and public works. The cavalier disregard of the hallowed division into "orders" or "estates"— clergy, nobility, commoners—was the point of contention for most of the Notables.

The proposal to establish a direct tax on landowners without exception was also one generally close to Du Pont's physiocratic predilections. He might very well have penned such sentences in the second *mémoire* as this one: "It is the land which produces; it is its productions which are protected and guaranteed by the Sovereign; it is therefore [up] to the land to pay tax[es]."[33] This new tax would take the place of two *vingtièmes*, or twentieths, still being assessed, the second of which, imposed in 1760, was due to expire anyway at the end of 1790. The land tax was to be proportional; that is, its yield would depend upon agricultural productivity. As the land produced more, the revenue from the tax would increase. It was also to be graduated so that the rich landowner paid more than the poor. With these features Du Pont could agree. He did not like the arrangement to permit the tax to be paid in kind, but Calonne defended it on the basis that it would not only lighten the load for peasant proprietors but also obviate the necessity of an expensive survey to determine the monetary value of products of the land in various parts of France. Not the tax itself but the nature of the assessment roused opposition among the Notables. A permanent tax proportioned to land productivity might afford the Government an ever mounting revenue which would free it from the limitations which parlements, provincial estates, and bodies like the Assembly of Notables might at times impose upon it because of its chronic financial difficulty. Unless the amount of tax to be collected were tied to the clearly perceived needs of the Government, a ready check upon absolutism would be surrendered. There was here an opportunity to request of the Controller-General that he justify his proposal by submitting financial accounts proving the needs of the Government. Furthermore, the plans for a graduated tax might undermine the right of provincial estates in the *pays d'états* to have voice in the assessment of direct taxes and would certainly destroy various local customs and privileges in this matter. For similar reasons collection in kind rather than in fixed amounts of money was also questioned.

The third *mémoire* re-emphasized the point that all land, including land held by the Church, would be subject to the new tax. To meet this assessment the clergy was instructed to redeem its accumulated indebtedness by permitting their serfs and tenants to relieve themselves of old obligations through regular payments in money. Capital accumulated thus, and by other means which the clergy was invited to suggest, could be used to retire the clerical debt by the end of 1790. Meanwhile, the King would pay the interest on the accumulated debt. This change in the financial position of the Church would have serious consequences for the corporate organization of the Gallican Church. No longer would it have a substantial debt to manage; no longer would it bargain with the Treasury over the amount of the so-called *don gratuit*, or free gift, which it contributed in lieu of taxes. Du Pont did not have a hand in this proposal, which Talleyrand claimed to have put in final form with the assistance of Saint-Genis. It was, however, one with which he could agree.

The fourth *mémoire*, on the *taille*, was very brief and did no more than provide for some reduction in its assessments as a tax on personal property. This kind of assessment Du Pont would have eliminated. If the *taille* could not be abolished, as he desired, it should be assessed only as a tax on land. The abolition of this oldest of French taxes did not seem to Calonne to be a very practicable measure and he did not propose it. The fifth *mémoire,* on the grain trade, concerned a subject upon which Du Pont had much experience. Once more he was disappointed in his hope to remove all restrictions on the exportation of grain. Calonne did agree to a freeing of the trade within France but permitted local restrictions on exportations when they should be requested. The Controller-General temporized also on the matter of the *corvée.* His sixth *mémoire* called for the conversion of this labor tax into a money tax assessable on all those subject to the *taille.* This restriction meant that the clergy and nobility would be exempt, since they were "non-tailleable." Du Pont preferred a tax levied on all landholders, since they would profit most from maintenance of the roads, the most common labor required by the *corvée.* Calonne could, of course, have argued that the privileged orders were not subject to the *corvée* and, hence, should not be subjected to the substantial money tax.

The Assembly of Notables was divided into seven committees or bureaus, each presided over by a prince of the blood, to consider Calonne's far-reaching projects. Du Pont was assigned as secretary of the second bureau, headed by the Comte d'Artois, the King's younger brother and a strong partisan of Calonne among the Court party. As in the full assembly, he had nothing to do here but to prepare a summary of the meetings of the bureau.[34] After each bureau had studied the proposal, the president and two delegates from each were to meet with Monsieur (the Comte de Provence), president of the first bureau, in order to review their judgments. After this meeting the Controller-General could be called upon for further elucidations. The period from February 23 to March 12 was given over to these meetings.

Vigorous dissent arose at once over the duration and method of assessment of the land tax. Calonne submitted to the bureaus a supplementary *mémoire*[35] declaring that the proportional and graduated assessment proposed was essential and not open for discussion and that the only point upon which the King was consulting the Assembly concerned the means of payment of the tax, whether it should be in kind or in money. This tactic did not succeed. Indeed, it stirred up sharper denunciation of Calonne in several of the informal gatherings, where opinions were more freely expressed

113

than in the regular meetings, inhibited as they were by some degree of ceremony and form. In an effort to prevent an early impasse, Calonne requested a conference at Monsieur's with delegates from each bureau on March 2. This conference was momentous to the fate of Calonne's entire program. The two secretaries of the Assembly, Hennin and Du Pont, prepared the detailed summary of this conference;[36] perhaps, the most useful copy of it is that edited by Du Pont and the Comte de Montchevrel, one of the regular secretaries of the Comte d'Artois, for inclusion in the collection of *mémoires* of the second bureau.[37]

This *procès-verbal*, as incomplete and prosaic as it inevitably is, contains clear evidence that the discussion was often heated. Calonne defended himself with calmness and skill against determined adversaries, prominent among whom was the ambitious Archbishop of Toulouse, Lomenie de Brienne. Without any genuine supporters, except for the Comte d'Artois, whose knowledge of the situation was limited, the Controller-General was forced into concessions. The very fact that he had requested the conference was to some a display of weakness and, at the very outset, he retreated from his earlier position that the bases of the tax and its assessment could not be points for discussion. On the one matter originally proposed for debate, the method of collecting the tax, he admitted the possibility that it might be collected in money rather than in kind. Compelled to prove the need for the tax, he announced a definite figure of the accumulated deficit—112 million livres. The problem of the deficit naturally brought up the *Compte rendu* of 1781, in which Necker had shown a surplus of ten million livres. There was a demand, especially from the clergy present, that Calonne explain the contradiction between his figures and Necker's. Calonne had no alternative to pointing out a disparity of fifty-six millions between Necker's published accounts and the actual accounts for 1781.[38] This demonstration was suspect to partisans of Necker among the conferees and, in any event, led to a demand for verification of the full accounts by a commission of the Assembly. The Comte d'Artois was shocked by this demand "to judge what the King has already judged," and no one put forward a firm proposal that the King be requested to submit the accounts.[39] But this hesitation was to be only temporary.

The conference made it abundantly clear that Calonne would win no ready acquiescence from the Notables. The hope for effective reform from the top had little foundation upon which to rest. The privileged orders might support some reform, might even consent to be taxed, but not without receiving something in return. The only parts of the first division of Calonne's program which the seven bureaus seemed inclined to accept without serious question were those involving the freeing of the grain trade and the suppression of the *corvée*.[40]

The third plenary session of the Assembly was held on March 12, when Calonne presented the second division of his projects. He provided more ammunition for his enemies when, in his introductory remarks, he made a foolhardy statement about how satisfied the King was to note that the objections raised to the first proposals were "principally relative to the forms [and] not contrary to the essential points of the goal" sought.[41] The Notables sat through Calonne's long presentation, during which he laid eight additional *mémoires* before them, but they would not proceed to a consideration of the new projects until they had won the King's consent to insert in the *procès-verbal* their complaints against Calonne's remark. Of the seven bureaus, only the second headed by Artois was willing to accept the remark without serious qualification. Each of the others insisted in their *reclamations* that their differences with the Controller-General extended well beyond the matter of the "forms" by which changes were to be brought about.[42] The fact that the King yielded to their pressure and permitted the inclusion of these *reclamations* in the official record of the Assembly indicated a weakening in his support of his Controller-General. Calonne's projects now had even less chance of success.

Most of the proposals in the second division were so close to Du Pont's interests and previous labors that his claim to have contributed to them must be believed. The first *mémoire* in this second division called for the abolition of interior customs duties and the establishment of a uniform tariff on the frontiers. The second sought the suppression of the tax (*droit de marque*) on the manufacture of and internal trade in iron products. The third provided for the abolition of various complicated taxes (*aides*) on wines, brandy, and other beverages, and the fourth demanded the suppression of duties on the

115

manufacture of oils and soaps. The fifth proposal concerned the suppression of anchorage taxes on ships and of other duties on maritime commerce and fisheries. The sixth discussed the levying in the future of uniform duties on colonial merchandise, and the seventh reviewed some necessary modifications in the privileges enjoyed by some provinces in the tax on tobacco. The eighth *mémoire* dealt with the vexatious salt tax, or *gabelle,* which many, including Du Pont, desired to abolish in favor of some other tax. Calonne summarized his opinion on the impracticability of replacing it with another tax and outlined complicated arrangements by which the *gabelle* could be modified to the advantage of taxpayers without disrupting the Treasury through loss of revenue.[43] The principal objective sought in all these projects was obviously the removal of various restraints on trade and manufacture. An economy free to expand without limit was essential to support the expanding demands of the Treasury. The permanent resolution of the financial crisis required an overhaul of the economic as well as the political system.

Calonne's moderation in his recommendations on the *gabelles* provided the Notables with an unexpected opportunity to pose as even more ardent reformers than the Minister. All seven bureaus protested that the *mémoire* on the *gabelles* did not go far enough, that the goal should be the total abolition of this detested tax and of the agencies of enforcement which accompanied it. The second bureau adopted Lafayette's humane proposition to petition the King that, with the abrogation of the *gabelle,* he release all individuals sentenced to jail or to the galleys for smuggling and other evasions of the salt monopoly.[44] The sincerity of most of the Notables can, of course, be questioned, but their expression of views like these explains why Du Pont could later state that the Assembly was more sympathetic to his ideas than to the modifications made in them by Calonne. He failed to admit that he had no exclusive claim on most of the ideas which he held; obviously, others had adopted them independently of his influence. The Notables were now conducting an astute delaying operation to force further concessions from Calonne without appearing to be merely blind obstructors of change and selfish defenders of their privileges.

Calonne was fully aware of their strategy and launched as a counteroffensive an appeal to public opinion to force the Assembly's approval of his projects. He reprinted the fourteen *mémoires* of his first two divisions, bound them together with an *avertissement* prepared by Gerbier, the lawyer who had earlier assisted him, and arranged for their distribution throughout the realm.[45] This publication appeared on March 30, the day after the third division of his *mémoires* had been laid before the fourth plenary session of the Notables. He had the *avertissement* separately printed and sent in bundles to all the curés, so that, if they did not read it from their pulpits, they could distribute copies to their parishioners.[46] Subsequently a larger publication followed, in which the *mémoires* of the third and fourth divisions were included with the others. This propaganda campaign failed because Calonne badly misjudged the state of public opinion. The disdain which had first greeted the Assembly of Notables had been considerably tempered by their professed attitude of favoring reforms even beyond those proposed, but of refusing to accept without question the dictates of the Minister. Calonne had no reservoir of personal popularity upon which he could draw. His reputation had just been further damaged by the publication of Mirabeau's *Dénonciation de l'Agiotage,* a violent attack by this clever opportunist on stock exchange manipulations, in which Calonne was rumored to have been involved. He was, therefore, doomed, but under different circumstances his strategy may have made sense. An alliance between an enlightened ministry supported by the King and an informed public opinion demanding reform might have overcome the resistance of the privileged orders, who were divided in their opinions. Calonne had not the strength of position nor, perhaps, of character to shape the issues so pointedly. The *avertissement,* indeed, repeated his tactic of March 12 when it alleged that the Notables agreed in principle with all the proposals and that "it would be wrong if reasonable doubts, observations dictated by zeal, expressions of a noble freedom would give rise to the idea of a malevolent opposition."[47] These remarks now had no other effect than to "bring about the greatest uproar in all the bureaus" and to elicit from all of them more or less violent protests.[48] It is ironic that popular distrust of the ministry nourished the widely held idea that the parlements and the Notables, the bastions of the privileged, were defenders of the "rights" of the people. They were then, of course, the only well-known institutions in which opposition to the absolute government could be organized and voiced.

The Notables' consideration of the two *mémoires* in the third division was interrupted by the Easter recess. The first of these *mémoires* proposed the "infeudation" of land on the royal domain through perpetual leaseholds and a reform of tenancy regulations. The objective was to stimulate more fruitful cultivation of the domain through more advantageous arrangements for tenants without legally "alienating" it from the crown. Short-term leases subject to sudden cancellation had never encouraged tenants to improve the land. The second *mémoire* provided for a reorganization of the administration of the royal forests to make possible profitable exploitation without waste.

These were to be the last proposals which Calonne presented as Controller-General. It was already abundantly clear before he read them to the Notables that he would not get from them the approval which he sought. Louis XVI was faced with a situation similar to that of 1776, when he had to decide whether to continue his support of Turgot or to request his resignation. Sincerely interested in the regeneration of his kingdom but pitifully indecisive, he was as ineffectual now as he had been then. His inclination was to stand by Calonne, just as he had wanted to support Turgot, but he could not remain steadfast against the pressures exerted upon him by others. Since Vergennes' death Calonne could find no real defender in the ministry. The support of Artois was feeble defense against the attacks of Lomenie de Brienne, Archbishop of Toulouse, seconded by other prelates. The rumors that Calonne was about to attempt a purge of the ministry and of the most recalcitrant of the Notables were given some substance when, on April 8, Miroménil was relieved as Keeper of the Seals in favor of Lamoignon.[49] When the Queen was brought into the camp of Calonne's enemies, Louis decided that he would have to find a new controller-general. Late in the evening of that Easter Sunday, he asked for Calonne's resignation. If Brienne's ambitions to enter the ministry were to be thwarted, an immediate successor had to be found. Old Bouvard de Fourqueux, one of the Notables and a friend of Du Pont, was chosen.

Fourqueux was ill and did not want the job. Du Pont hurried to the Fourqueux residence in Paris to convince his friend that he had to accept the appointment if the program of needed reform was to be saved. Without allowing the reluctant old man time to dress, Du Pont rushed him back to Versailles to receive the King's orders.[50] Talleyrand relates how, at 11 o'clock at night, Du Pont dashed into Calonne's chamber, where, surrounded by his personal friends, the disgraced minister was gathering up his papers, with the happy shout: "Victory! Victory! M. de Fourqueux accepts and he will follow all the plans of M. de Calonne."[51] The joy was premature, and Du Pont later regretted, as he had reason to, his precipitate action in overcoming Fourqueux's hesitation. Had he been able to foresee the consequences, he would not have acted as he did.[52]

Fourqueux's ingrained modesty was intensified by his age and ill-health. Calonne's hope that he might continue to direct the course of events through his successor was destroyed when he was forced into exile by his enemies, who continued to unearth unsavory details of his personal life. These circumstances, added to the constant machinations of Brienne and Necker, both eager to gain appointment to the ministry, combined to make Fourqueux's tenure of office brief. On April 23, with the King present, Lamoignon, the new Keeper of the Seals, presented to the fifth general session of the Notables the fourth and final division of Calonne's *mémoires*. These were proposals for an extension of the stamp tax on a large variety of documents and for the redemption of the unfunded debt through additional borrowing at fixed periods.[53] Repeating the argument that they could not intelligently discuss additional taxes and loans until they had a clear vision of the need for them, the Notables finally succeeded in getting the King to submit to them some of the current accounts.[54] They then busied themselves with suggesting many economies which could be made.[55] They harried old Fourqueux with minute questions which he could hardly answer without the assistance of Calonne.[56] It became obvious that a stronger hand was needed and Fourqueux's resignation was accepted on May 3. Brienne's desires were now fulfilled when, on that same day, he was appointed head of the Royal Council of Finances. Necker had to wait, because the King, displaying rare strength of will, refused to recall him. Instead, on May 6, Laurent de Villedeuil, intendant of Rouen and another of the Notables, was named

Controller-General.[57] No one doubted, however, that the actual direction of affairs was in Brienne's hands.

Du Pont soon had occasion to appreciate this fact. At first he had some hope, since, to the consternation of many of the Notables, Brienne seemed willing to go forward with much of Calonne's program. In the Archbishop's eyes, however, Du Pont had been against him in supporting Calonne and Fourqueux and deserved punishment. He announced his intention to remove him from all his offices, but eventually changed his mind, when he found that many, including Artois and the King, spoke in praise of Du Pont's zeal and loyalty.[58] He agreed to reserve final decision until Du Pont drew up a memorandum on all his past services and on the operations of his principal office, that of Inspector General of Commerce. The documents making up this memorandum repeat all of Du Pont's claims concerning the extent and importance of his work, claims which can be sustained on the first point but must be somewhat discounted on the second. They show also that, among the thirteen employees of his office, he had found places for the friend of his youth, Volpélière, who had suffered business reverses, and for his elder son Victor, who, as one of the three *sous-chefs* of the office, made extensive trips throughout France to collect useful information on affairs of commerce.[59] The *mémoire* achieved its immediate goal of inducing Brienne to retain Du Pont as an adviser, but, subsequently, Brienne's thorough reorganization of the agencies dealing with commerce separated Du Pont from significant participation in public affairs until the meeting of the Estates General.

Brienne's first problem was not to dispose of Du Pont, but to attend to the financial crisis. There was such relief over the fall of Calonne that he was soon able to float a new loan for sixty-seven million livres to get him over immediate difficulties pending the achievement of a general plan. Brienne had no practicable alternative to adapting to his purpose much of Calonne's program, which had been spelled out in detail. His apparent willingness to do so, despite his prior attack on Calonne, did not please many of the Notables. He had to make important concessions to their views, so that, eventually, nothing was left of the original program beyond what the Notables would accept.

Assembly of Notables (1787-1789)

The most significant of these concessions was made on May 9, when Brienne called a conference of representatives of all the bureaus, similar to the conference of March 2. Here he accepted the position of the Notables that the proposed land tax should not be a proportional levy tied to the productivity of the land but a levy of a stated amount payable in money and conforming to the needs of the Treasury. He asked for an augmentation in revenue of fifty million livres, promising that, if this amount proved to be more than was needed, subsequent levies would be decreased. He promised further that an annual account would be published so that the Treasury's need could be generally known.[60] The significance of this change was clearly stated by Du Pont two months later in a letter to Baron von Edelsheim. In his view, the entire constitution of France had been altered by adoption of the "English principle" that revenue ought to be proportional to expenses in place of the principle that expenses should be governed by revenue. With a fixed revenue in a period of rising prices, the King would continue to be burdened by a permanent deficit and would be hampered in what he could do for the regeneration of the Kingdom. He would constantly have to call upon his subjects for financial assistance. Du Pont put the situation in these terms:

> On the first of May 1787 France was still a monarchy, and the first of Europe. On 9 May 1787, in the conference held at Monsieur's in the presence of the two brothers and two ministers of the King, France became a republic, where there remained a Magistrate, decorated with the title and the honors of royalty, but perpetually obliged to assemble his people and to request them to provide for his needs, for which public revenues would be perpetually insufficient without this new national consent.
>
> The Notables and the ministry appeared to be interested in necessary precautions to prevent the deficit from ever arising again and much paper has been scribbled over on this subject. The Notables and the ministry were [actually] busy with means of managing that there would be a constant deficit, impossible to cover without new requests of the government and new grants of the nation.
>
> The King of France became a King of England. I regret it, much regret it; for I love the King, his family and the truly social constitution which I saw on the point of being established and beyond which we have passed.[61]

These remarks elucidate not only Du Pont's fundamental belief in the necessity of a powerful monarch but also the very essence of what later commentators named the aristocratic revolution. Here was a basic attack upon the presumed prerogatives of the absolute monarchy.

The bureaus of the Assembly of Notables devoted much attention to the tax proposals and the condition of the Treasury.[62] When they were finished with their examination, all but one of them rejected the land tax, despite Brienne's concessions. They declared that they had no power to authorize additional taxes, thus implying that only the Estates General had that power. In the second bureau Lafayette had gone even farther. He concluded a speech on the financial crisis with an appeal to the King to convoke a national assembly. Almost all of his colleagues, however, heard this appeal in silent consternation.[63] All that could be won from the Notables was approval for the commutation of the road *corvée* into a money payment, for the exportation of grain, with provision for local restriction if necessary, and for provincial assemblies, with retention of distinctions among the orders. This project for local assemblies was closer to that of Necker than to that of Calonne, Turgot, and Du Pont. Obviously Calonne's hope for tangible approval of a general reform program had been ill-founded. There was nothing further to do but to dismiss the Assembly and to get on with the inevitable struggle with the parlements.

By May 23 Du Pont had put in order the minutes of the fifty-one meetings of the second bureau. His summary of the work was submitted to a committee for revision of some details. Lafayette, a member of this committee, seized the opportunity thus presented to suggest additional resolutions not previously considered. He won approval for resolutions petitioning the King to restore civil rights to Protestants and to effect a thoroughgoing revision of the criminal law code.[64] Such liberal proposals, added to the diligence which the Notables had shown in their deliberations, led Du Pont and Lafayette to regard the efforts of the Assembly with greater favor and hope than the situation warranted. On May 25, the day of the sixth and last general session of the Notables, Du Pont wrote enthusiastically to Edelsheim that "France will have recovered from a moment of crisis, more powerful, better constituted and happier than it has yet been."[65] Lafayette was equally mistaken in his recommendation to the Duc d'Harcourt, the Dauphin's tutor, that, in choosing history books for his young charge, "he would do well to begin his history of France at the year 1787."[66] Both were to be disillusioned within a few months. What they were forgetting was that Brienne had still to deal with the parlements.

The tale of Brienne's failures, of the continued resistance of the parlements to his projects, of the repeated appeals of the privileged and commoners to the Estates General, of the mounting deficit, has been often told. At first Brienne had no difficulty with the Parlement of Paris, which accepted without protest the projects approved by the Notables: the freedom of the grain trade, the commutation of the *corvée*, and the establishment of provincial assemblies. These assemblies did not seem to promise much. One-half of their members were to be chosen by the King, the second half being elected by the first. After three years one-fourth of the original body were to retire in favor of new members chosen by a very restricted and very indirect elective process. Not until 1790, therefore, would there be any elections. Brienne somewhat weakened the aristocracy's support of the plan by imitating the system prevailing in Languedoc, where the *Tiers* had double representation and where voting was by head. Supplementary decrees were issued to set up elective assemblies at the parish and district (or *election*) levels. The right to vote and eligibility for election were dependent upon the amount of taxes paid, and distinction of orders was retained. Despite these weaknesses, these local assemblies as finally constituted served as useful "bridges" to the local governmental bodies set up by the Revolution.[67] If Brienne was encouraged by these successes, he was soon brought face to face with reality.

The Parlement of Paris would go no farther than the Notables had gone. It presented remonstrances against the stamp tax and refused registration of the land tax, arguing that only the Estates General were competent to levy new taxes. Brienne had to call upon the King to order registration in a *lit de justice* on August 6. The Parlement declared the action void, and Brienne had to proceed to the second step available to the Government to discipline the parlements. On August 14 he got Louis to sign an order exiling the magistrates of the Parlement to Troyes. The provincial parlements at once raised an outcry in support of their Parisian colleagues. There was popular unrest in Paris. On August 17 the King's brothers were enlisted in support of the monarchy. The Comte de Provence was dispatched to the Chambre des Comptes to order registration of the edicts on the stamp duties and land tax; the Comte d'Artois went before the Cour des Aides to perform the same duty. Monsieur, whom the mob mistakenly believed to be in favor of reform, was applauded, but Artois was so hissed at and jostled by the crowd that his guards had to draw their swords. The Chambre des Comptes and Cour des Aides imitated the action of the Parlement by declaring forced registration illegal and insisting that the power to authorize these taxes rested with the Estates General.

Overwhelmed by financial difficulties which had to be met, Brienne now had four possible courses of action. He could yield to the Parlement and seek some kind of compromise, he could attempt a reorganization of the judiciary depriving the parlements of their powers, he could accept their challenge and summon the Estates General, or he could resign. The last possibility he rejected out of hand, especially when the King, bowing to Marie Antoinette's insistence, named him First Minister on August 28. He saw too many uncertainties and delays in reviving the ancient Estates General. He was not yet strong enough or desperate enough to suppress the parlements as Maupeou had done in 1771. There remained only conciliation.

Events outside of France helped to force him into the latter course. A serious crisis arose in the Dutch Netherlands, where republicans and partisans of the House of Orange had been at odds for several years. French policy had supported the patriots, or republicans, in expectation of increasing French influence in the Netherlands. An alleged insult to Wilhelmina, a Prussian princess married to William V, head of the House of Orange, was used as the excuse for Prussian intervention on behalf of the Orange party. Brienne blocked the designs of Segur and Castries, Ministers of War and the Navy respectively, to oppose the Prussians with force. Such action would have multiplied the ills of the Treasury. Segur and Castries resigned their positions and were soon joined by Villedeuil, the Controller-General. Brienne took charge by appointing his brother Minister of War, and Lambert, who had been a member of the second bureau of the Assembly of Notables, Controller-General. For Minister of the Navy he chose the Comte de La Luzerne, who, since he was then serving in Santo Domingo, would be unable to assume active control of the office for several months. Brienne's peace policy was therefore triumphant, but the prestige of France suffered gravely. It had to submit to the erection of the hereditary stadtholdership in the Netherlands and to the loss of the Dutch alliance.

Unable to fight abroad, Brienne now called off the battle at home. The Parlement was called back and, on September 19, agreed to a compromise. It registered a decree continuing the two *vingtièmes* without exemption after Brienne agreed to give up the stamp duties and land tax. This arrangement could be only temporary. The additional revenue of the restored *vingtièmes* would come into the Treasury with too great a delay and in too small amounts to improve the general financial situation. Brienne was forced to seek authorization for additional borrowing. Some of the magistrates laid down the condition for approval—a definite promise to convoke the Estates General. Du Pont's prediction of July was being exactly fulfilled. The Government would be compelled to make periodic appeals to this kind of "national consent." Its activities would be vigorously circumscribed, if not rendered completely impotent. There would no longer be an absolute monarchy.

The magistrates were no more sincere than most of the Notables in their appeal to the Estates General. They were conducting an astute campaign of evasion. They were confident that they could count upon the reluctance of the King and his ministers to revive a representative body which had last met in 1615—over 172 years ago. Even if the unexpected occurred and the King did call the Estates General, the privileged orders could take comfort in the traditional organization of this body, an organization which kept the three Estates separate and required vote by order (or estate), not by head. Thus the clergy and the nobility in the first and second estates could always protect their interests against the third. There was good reason for the consternation aroused by Lafayette's call for a *national assembly*, which would not follow the ancient customs. Neither Brienne nor the parlements really desired to convoke the Estates General, which, as it had sometimes in the past, might get out of

hand. Still they played out the game. Brienne needed some assurance of money over a long period; he asked for 120 million livres
to be raised over the next five years, at the end of which period, in
1792, he promised to convene the Estates General. This commitment
was so momentous that he lacked the courage to permit its full effect
to be measured. Instead he seized upon other alternatives. He
persuaded Louis to hold a royal session of the Parlement on
November 18; here, as in a *lit de justice* which differed chiefly in
method of convocation, the King personally ordered registration of
an edict authorizing the loan. There was immediate protest, and
even the exiling of the obstreperous Duc d'Orléans and two coun-
sellors of the Parlement did not silence the outcry. The Parlement
used its popular appeal to discourage subscriptions to the loan.
Somehow Brienne struggled through for six more months, but some
of his actions did not strengthen his position. In January, 1788,
he reluctantly induced the Parlement to register an edict restoring
limited civil rights to the Protestants, an action for which Lafayette
had long been striving in association with others, especially the
Protestant minister Rabaut St. Étienne. It was a reform which Du
Pont had also been vainly advocating for years, but he could claim
no credit for its achievement. It inevitably aroused the hostility of
many of the Catholic clergy, who found it particularly bitter in that
it came during the ministry of an archbishop. There were rumblings
on all sides when this same archbishop shortly afterward evidenced
his persistent care of his personal ambitions by arranging for his
transfer to the archbishopric of Sens, much more remunerative than
the archbishopric of Toulouse. Amidst discord that seemed almost
universal, Brienne had finally to seek help in turning to more
extreme measures.

For some time Lamoignon, the Keeper of the Seals, had been
laboring on a plan to reform the judiciary. On May 8, 1788, with
Brienne's approval, Louis ordered registration of six edicts, prepared
by Lamoignon, effecting a reorganization of the entire judicial
establishment. The most important of the edicts bearing upon the
conflict was one which transferred the power of registering edicts to a
new "plenary court," to be composed of princes and officers of the
King. Four months of discord followed this drastic move.

The aristocracy made common cause against the reform and organized popular resistance. Grave disorders broke out in Paris, in Rennes, in Pau, and notably in Grenoble, where, during the "Day of Tiles" in June, the populace assaulted the garrison from the rooftops. The clergy drastically reduced the amount of its "free gift," upon which Brienne had been heavily relying. Too late the harassed minister saw the wisdom of attempting to break the unnatural alliance between the privileged orders and the Third Estate. On June 28 he issued an order of council suppressing the protests of the parlements and other bodies as seditious attacks on royal prerogative and as efforts to deceive the people regarding the King's intentions. Then he turned to the Estates General. On July 5, he announced that this ancient body would soon be summoned, and he requested the provincial estates and assemblies which might have information about its convocation and composition to transmit their knowledge to the King. This invitation provided the opportunity for the publication in subsequent months of a veritable flood of pamphlets which evaded the loose censorship by assuming the guise of responses to the Minister's request. Potentially there was wise strategy in this move. It implied that the traditional organization of orders as followed in the last Estates General of 1614-1615 might be set aside. It encouraged hope among reformers outside the privileged orders. It seemed almost to urge them to a co-operation with the King against all who opposed fundamental change. Such ideas were not, however, in Brienne's mind, and any wide misconception that they might be was made impossible by another order issued on the same day. This *arrêt du Conseil* confirmed the immunities of the clergy and was called forth by Brienne's hope that the clergy might yet be persuaded to make a substantial contribution to ease his financial burdens. His important announcement did not, therefore, enhance his popular prestige. In vain he went further and, on August 5, announced another decision that the Estates General would definitely meet on May 1, 1789, and that, meanwhile, the establishment of the plenary court would be postponed. As general criticisms against him continued and he remained paralyzed through lack of money, Brienne had left only the final choice, which he refused to take. He would not resign voluntarily and encouraged a scheme to bring Necker, the financial wizard, back into the Government. After his experience of seven years earlier, Necker could not be persuaded to return in a subordinate capacity. Brienne's last hope for some resolution of the Treasury crisis was therefore destroyed. On August 16, he finally had to admit the inability of the Treasury to meet its obligations unless it made part of its payments in special paper notes bearing interest. If outright bankruptcy were to be averted, Brienne would have to go. The King requested his resignation on August 25 and, with little enthusiasm, summoned the popular idol, Necker, to be Minister of Finances and Secretary of State. Under the circumstances there could be no quibbling about granting Necker ministerial status. Even in disgrace Brienne salvaged his personal ambitions. He gained promises that some members of his family would be provided for and that he would receive a cardinal's hat at an early opportunity. He was duly made a prince of the church in December.

Necker's appointment aroused great enthusiasm outside the Court. His first measures were carefully calculated to maintain his popularity. He revoked Brienne's order of August 16 and restored the Treasury's ability to make regular money payments by drawing again upon the Caisse d'escompte. Here he succeeded, where others would have failed, because of the general confidence in his talents. Lamoignon, author of the judicial reform edicts, fell from office on September 14. On September 23, Necker published the decision of the King that the Estates General would convene in January, 1789, and that the parlements would be re-established in the full exercise of their powers. Thus the order of May 8 was withdrawn and the conflict over the proposed plenary court ended. The Parlement of Paris was welcomed back amidst joyful demonstrations by the populace. It proceeded at once to destroy most of its popularity by including in its ordinance of September 25 registering the King's orders the decision that the Estates General should be "convoked and composed according to the form observed in 1614."[68] For the issue of most importance was, of course, the form of the convocation and composition of the promised Estates General. The problem of the representation of the *Tiers* was the one of special concern. Ardent reformers demanded that it be granted at least as many representatives as the other two orders combined and that votes be counted by head and not by order. Without these alterations there was no hope that any significant reforms could issue from it. And these issues were now more pressing, since the date for the meeting of the Estates General had been moved up.

To consider these questions and others regarding "the best manner of convoking the Estates General," the Notables were ordered on October 5 to reassemble in November.[69] Du Pont was assigned to the same position which he held in the earlier Assembly,[70] although Necker and Villedeuil had tried to give it to someone else.[71] His role remained a very minor one. Although he cherished it as a mark of honor, it brought no material rewards.[72]

Du Pont's personal fortunes had noticeably deteriorated ever since the death of Vergennes, who had been his strongest supporter. Brienne had treated him shabbily. In the reorganization of offices, he had abolished the position of Commissioner General of Commerce, which Du Pont had shared with Boyetet since 1785, and created five Inspectors General, assigning Boyetet to the first and Du Pont to the fifth (and least important) position. He decided that the secretaries of the Assembly of Notables should not be paid despite the demanding clerical work which they performed and despite the fact that they had to live at Versailles during the period of meeting. This secretarial position, therefore, cost Du Pont "very dearly," since he had to continue to pay for his apartment in Paris, in addition to his living expenses at Versailles. He could not make ends meet and asked Edelsheim to lend him some money.[73] Worse was to come, as Du Pont made clear in a long letter to his elder son.

When he was Minister[74] the last time, Monsieur Necker said "I wish neither to help nor to harm Monsieur du Pont—to give him nothing and to take nothing from him." He still feels the same and it is easier now because there is nothing that he can take from me. The Archbishop took everything. This is his arrangement of my affairs: I keep the place of Inspector General of Commerce with the salary, but the 4000 francs granted to me by Monsieur de Maurepas from the Caisse de Commerce has become a pension from the Royal Treasury and is therefore subject to a stoppage of three tenths; in other words reduced to 2800. So that I am 1200 francs a year poorer than I was twelve years ago when we lived at Bois-des-Fossés. I am obliged to live in Paris which is much more expensive and has not the same opportunities for a land owner. I have my two great children, both of them expensive in different ways; and I have not your good mother, who knew so well how to manage my money.[75]

His "two great children" he had been able to launch upon potentially valuable careers, though neither received any salary during what may be called their apprenticeships. Victor, to whom he wrote this letter, had been sent a year earlier to the United States in the suite of the Comte de Moustier, French envoy to the new republic. He had carried with him a letter of introduction and recommendation from Jefferson to Robert Livingston.[76] This fortunate opportunity had arisen soon after Victor's position in his father's government office had been eliminated, as were most of the others, by Brienne's reorganization of commercial affairs. Du Pont was disappointed that Victor did not take fuller advantage of it by using his diplomatic status to meet prominent Americans like Washington.[77] Obviously, he did not appreciate the humble status of an unpaid assistant in a diplomatic post. Eleuthère Irénée, then seventeen, was sent to study with Du Pont's friend Lavoisier, head of the French powder works at Essone.[78] The three years which the young man spent with the great chemist laid the foundation for the enterprise which eventually changed the fortune of the entire Du Pont family.

Du Pont himself undertook various economies. He moved to a smaller and less expensive apartment in another part of Paris, number 17 on the Rue du Petit Musc, not far removed from the Arsenal and the Bastille. He considered renting Bois-des-Fossés but could not bring himself to give up full control of his land. Instead he discharged some of his servants, keeping only two, one at Bois-des-Fossés and one in Paris. He gave up his carriage and got about mostly on foot "with heavy shoes and an umbrella."[79] He prepared an estimate of the value of his material possessions which might pass to his sons at his death. His personal property he valued at 30,450 livres, subject to debt of 18,548 livres, which would reduce the net to 11,902. He held real estate worth 71,000 livres (60,000 in Bois-des-Fossés, 11,000 in two houses in Rouen), with 16,300 in unpaid mortgages, leaving a net value of 54,700 livres.[80] Du Pont's accounting must always be treated with caution, but, if he is close to being accurate here, he was hardly destitute of capital. His net worth in terms of today's values would probably exceed $50,000. His problem in 1788 was the reduction in regular income and, perhaps even more, the reduction in potential influence which he might have on events.

He did not like what he saw as he moved about the city in October, 1788. "There is now no safety in Paris except that which is enforced by the courage, the coolness and the swords of the citizens. The Guard dares not come when it is called lest it be attacked by the mob. Every night they take away half of the Guards and send troops to reinforce the others; the Guards can scarcely protect themselves. The Parlement has instructed them in writing to behave with *moderation, consideration and humanity* towards the mutinous crowds, and thereby shown its sympathy for the demonstrations for which it was the pretext. Altogether, for the last six months we have had a helpless Government and no administration." His patriotism, he remarked, was "deeply hurt."[81]

Despite his concern for personal and public troubles, he always found time for a variety of interests. He was constantly writing. When he was not turning out voluminous reports and *procès-verbaux*, he was filling pages on many topics and occasionally publishing the results of his scribbling. In 1786 he had published a eulogy of Pierre Poivre, famous traveler and former intendant of the islands of Mauritius and Réunion. He had met Poivre, who had a deep interest in agriculture, at the outset of his own career twenty years earlier. He also knew Poivre's widow, Françoise Robin, but did not then foresee the important place she was to fill in his later career.[82] The same year brought from the press his *Idées sur les sécours à donner aux pauvres malades dans une grande ville,*[83] a systematic statement of ideas which he had first proposed to a committee of the Academy. The inspiration for this pamphlet also went back about twenty years when, in the *Journal de l'agriculture,* he had first speculated on the best method of caring for the ill with inadequate resources to care for themselves. He submitted his ideas to the Academy committee in 1786 to counter the proposal of a M. Poyet, who had argued before the Academy the necessity of establishing a large general hospital to which the indigent sick might be assigned. Du Pont believed firmly in the wisdom and economy of treating such unfortunates in their own homes or places of residence, drawing to the greatest extent possible upon the funds of private charity. As in the case of public education, he did hold that society had an obligation to make some provision. There were, apparently, some things which could not be left to the beneficent laws of nature.

It is curious that the ideas expressed in this little brochure were also to have an influence on the activities of his later years. In January, 1788, he became a member of the Association de Bienfaisance Judiciare, which sought to provide for the gratuitous defense of indigent prisoners and for the indemnification of the needy who were acquitted.[84]

During the period of almost a year when he was not assigned many governmental tasks, he gave considerable attention to the constitutional problems being discussed in the new republic to which he had sent his elder son. He decided to compose a treatise on the true principles which would assure the welfare of a federal republic like the United States. He probably never completed the manuscript of his "Observations sur les principes et le bien des républiques confedérées"; only a part of the eighth chapter is available today among his papers.[85] There is too little of it to judge the outline of the treatise which he had in mind, but he sent an extract from the uncompleted work to Franklin in December, 1787, with the request that it be translated and published in America. Franklin replied, on June 9, 1788, gently pointing out that seven states had already ratified the new federal Constitution and that "others being daily expected to do the same, after the fullest discussion in convention, and in all the public papers, till everybody is tired of the argument, it seemed too late to propose delay, and especially the delay that must be occasioned by a revision and correction of all the separate Constitutions." He did hope that Du Pont's treatise would be completed by the time the first Congress discussed various amendments to the Constitution, so that its principles might be useful in guiding the debate.[86] There the matter rested. Du Pont was searching eagerly for ways to be useful during this period of practical impotence at home. He welcomed a letter from Granville Sharp, who had been informed by Franklin of his interest in the work of the London Society for the Abolition of the Slave Trade. Sharp promised to send him the Society's publications.[87] Du Pont was always eager to maintain all such contacts. He kept in touch with Stanislas of Poland by sending him copies of his published works.[88] There remain several manuscripts showing Du Pont's absorption in diverse interests at the time. He prepared remarks on the observations which the Marquis de Mirabeau had made on the declaration of rights in the constitution of Virginia. Here he stated his long-held conviction of the essential importance of such a declaration, which established "the principles of natural legislation." He prepared a review of the French edition of Kirwan's *Essay on Phlogiston and the Constitution of Acids,* translated by Madame Lavoisier and accompanied by notes of Lavoisier, Laplace, and others refuting Kirwan's views. His constant interest in agriculture and commerce called forth an elaborate analysis of the value of French agricultural products; an opinion read in July, 1788, at the Royal Society of Agriculture opposing a motion to suppress a committee on the administration of agriculture; a defense of the proposition that all landowners should be assessed the money tax levied to supplant the *corvées*; and a tract supporting the wisdom of permitting the products of American whale-fishing to enter Dunkirk. The last piece must have been a protest to the order prohibiting the importation of foreign whale oil after the English had taken advantage of the more liberal trade policy by flooding the market.[89] So he might have gone on, probing here and there for worthwhile activity, had he not been called to his tedious tasks in the second Assembly of Notables.

What did the Government hope to accomplish by this second convocation of the privileged, among whom were even fewer genuine representatives of the Third Estate than there had been in the first Assembly?[90] One reason for the action is clear: many problems had to be answered in arranging the details for the convocation of an Estates General. The Notables, divided into six bureaus,[91] could be set to work on these problems. Indeed, a substantial portion of the answers which they provided were later incorporated in the electoral ordinance of January 24, 1789.[92] The efforts of the Notables were not, therefore, useless. But there was undoubtedly another reason in Necker's planning. While he was certainly not prepared to accept the full demands of the Third Estate for "double" representation and for vote by head, he was hopeful that the Notables, conscious of public opinion and made aware of the many changes which had occurred in the population of the local electoral units (*bailliages* and *sénéchaussées*) since 1614, would recommend some plan of conciliation. The order of council of October 5 which summoned the Assembly made explicit reference to the inequalities in size and population of the *bailliages* and *sénéchaussées* and to the lack of any uniform methods of choosing deputies from the three estates.[93] Necker's hope in this Assembly proved, however, to be as ill-founded as Calonne's hope in the earlier Assembly had been. The Notables resolved the difficulties but not in any spirit of conciliation.

Only one of the six committees, or bureaus, of the Assembly favored "doubling of the third." This was the first bureau of Monsieur, who sought conciliation, and there the decision was carried by the narrow vote of thirteen to twelve.[94] There is a delightful story that the vote could have gone the other way, had not one of the Notables, the old Comte de Montboissier, been asleep during the vote-taking. Awaking with a start he demanded of his neighbor, the Duc de La Rochefoucauld, "What are they saying?" La Rochefoucauld replied, "They say yes"; and Montboissier apparently agreed without knowing what was going on.[95] In the questionnaire which Necker prepared for the Notables he did not specifically raise the issue of the form of deliberation which the Estates General should follow. Inherent in this issue was the obvious problem of whether the three orders should meet together or separately with the corollary of vote by head or by order. This vital issue was included in the revised questionnaire prepared by the general committee of the Assembly which, following the arrangement of 1787, met at Monsieur's under his presidency. The answer was overwhelming. Only twenty-one members of the first bureau believed that the decision should be left up to the Estates General; all the others upheld the separation of the orders, though some were willing to have certain deliberations in common if each order *separately* agreed to such procedure.[96] Three of the bureaus did depart from the strict order of business laid before them to accept a statement in favor of the principle of equality in taxation.[97] But this was the only gesture of conciliation. What little effect for good it may have had was destroyed by a letter signed by five princes of the blood and sent to the King at the close of the Assembly. This letter called upon the Third Estate to cease its attacks upon the rights of the first two orders and to restrict its complaints to seeking decreases in the taxes with which it was burdened; if the Third Estate thus restrained itself, the first two estates, "recognizing in the third, citizens who are dear to them, will be able, by the generosity of their feelings, to renounce prerogatives which involve a pecuniary interest and to consent to support public burdens in the most perfect equality."[98]

Du Pont's heaviest task during the Assembly was not the exacting one of preparing with Hennin the *procès-verbal*, but that of keeping the minutes and papers of the second bureau of Artois, the same responsibility which he had in 1787. It was in the bureaus that the decisive deliberations of the Assembly occurred. He could take no part in the discussions beyond reading aloud for the members various documents submitted by the Government to guide their labors. The voluminous manuscript minutes of the twenty-six meetings of the second bureau provide a more illuminating view of those labors than the *procès-verbal* of the Assembly.[99] They do not, unfortunately, cover the debates in detail and do not indicate how the individual members voted, but they do make clear that the bureau was diligent and serious in its work. The majority of the second bureau must be ranked among the more conservative Notables. The only liberal gesture was inspired by the president, the Comte d'Artois, in his advocacy of the principle of equality in taxation. Lafayette was again a member of this bureau, and must have championed the liberal cause. His activity is, however, not disclosed in the minutes.[100]

After the Notables had concluded their sessions, their recommendations went to the King and his Council. Necker established a special committee to put in order a detailed regulation for the convocation of the Estates General. Meanwhile, he carried successfully before the Council the decision at which he had arrived after much thought, and was able to promulgate it on December 27. Because of the date of its publication it became popularly known as "Necker's New Year's gift to the nation." It announced that there would be at least 1,000 deputies in the Estates General, that, insofar as possible, the distribution of deputies would be in proportion to the population and taxes of each *bailliage*, and, most important of all, "that the number of deputies of the Third Estate will be equal to that of the other two orders combined and that this proportion will be established by the letters of convocation."[101] Undoubtedly, Necker was encouraged to take this daring step by manifestations

135

of support from influential places. Even the Parlement of Paris had, by a narrow vote on December 5, retreated from its adamant position of September, when it expressed its confidence in "the king's wisdom to decide upon the measures necessary to effect the changes that Reason, Liberty, Justice, and public opinion may demand."[102] He was, however, not prepared to go farther. He left undecided the crucial issue of the manner of voting, whether by head or by order.

There was strong support for his action from another quarter, though whether it actually influenced his action cannot be determined. By the time of the meeting of the second Assembly of Notables, a group of able and important men had organized themselves into what would now be called a lobby with the intention of bringing pressure upon the Notables to make liberal decisions. With the Notables the group failed; with Necker they may have been partially successful. This group, which met regularly at the Paris home of the forward-looking Adrien Duport, eventually had a membership of about thirty-five and was later spoken of as the "Society of the Thirty" (Société des Trente), though at the time it seems to have been referred to only as "the Society meeting at Du Port's." Du Pont was part of it from its beginning and found himself amidst a brilliant coterie reflecting the progressive spirit among some of the nobles, clergy, and upper bourgeoisie. Its distinguished membership included noblemen like Lafayette, La Rochefoucauld-Liancourt, Montmorency-Luxembourg, and Condorcet; clergymen like Talleyrand and Sieyès; prominent members of the Parlement like Duport and the Lameth brothers, Alexandre and Charles; able lawyers and officials like Target, Roederer, Le Chapelier, and Trudaine; bankers like Panchaud and Clavière.[103]

So many of these men are known to have belonged to lodges of the Free Masons that a belief arose explaining the name "Thirty" as referring to a presumed qualification for membership—that of having achieved the thirtieth Masonic rank of Chevalier Kaddock (or Kadosh).[104] The fact that at least a dozen could not be proved to be members of Masonic lodges was inconvenient but was passed over with the assumption that this minority were necessarily Masons.[105] Du Pont is among them. Only by such assumptions and by slight indirect evidence can one assert that he was a Free-Mason.[106] The question has less importance since the exaggerated claims of

Masonic influence on the French Revolution, stemming from the partisan work of the Abbé Barruel,[107] have been largely discounted by modern scholarship.[108]

The Society of the Thirty held vigorous debates on the measures which should be taken to regenerate the Kingdom. In such a group of talented individuals unanimous agreement was not to be expected, but they all profited from the sharing of views on current events, the latest publications, and future plans. They early accepted the scheme of doubling the representation of the Third Estate and were disappointed when the Notables rejected it. They continued their meetings into the new year, and, since most of them were chosen to be deputies to the Estates General, their discussions must have contributed to the formulation of the opinions which they later expressed. In considering the best means of handling the debt, for example, they put forward the plan for nationalizing the lands of the Church.[109] Du Pont must have been active in this vigorous exchange of views, but there is no record of the sessions.

The absence of records makes it impossible to assert with confidence that the inspiration for an important publication arose in the discussions of the Society of the Thirty. The interests of the group suggest that they may have encouraged a refutation of the famous panegyric of the British constitution published by the Genevese Delolme as long ago as 1771 but enjoying a renewed popularity as constitutional questions pushed to the front in France. Although Du Pont did not consider the British constitution evil, he believed it was worse than the constitutions of the thirteen American states, and he did not want it to serve as a model for the future constitution of France. He joined with Philip Mazzei and Condorcet in preparing for publication a French translation of John Stevens' *Observations on Government Including some Animadversions on Mr. Adams' Defense of the Constitution . . . and on Mr. Delolme's Constitution of England.*[110] In 1787 Jefferson had sent Du Pont a copy of John Adams' *Defense of the Constitutions of Government of the United States of America,* which, to Du Pont, "seemed to have a terrible erudition and to seek in the opinions and examples of men what Philosophers and Legislators should find in the nature of things and of the human heart, in right, in justice which does not depend on times or places." Good government consisted, he thought, in laying down right principles, which would become clearer as human enlightenment increased; forms and institutions were of less importance.[111]

The translation of Stevens' book was published in January, 1789, under the title *Examen du gouvernement d'Angleterre comparé aux constitutions des États-Unis*. Twenty-eight anonymous notes, prepared by the three collaborators, were appended and covered more than twice the number of pages required by the translation itself. By the time the book was ready for the printer, the news had arrived that, with the ratification of more than the required nine states, the new Constitution of the United States had been put into effect. The editors then hurriedly prepared as a supplement a French translation of the American Constitution. When they finished their labors, they had on hand a substantial volume of 291 pages.

The notes launch a vigorous attack upon the tyranny of the British legislature, which, though it was not truly representative of the British people, had gathered unto itself all the effective powers of government. There existed in England as a consequence no real liberty of thought, of commerce, or of persons. This sad condition resulted from a failure to recognize the principle that "all legislation is completely enclosed in a good declaration of rights." No legislature has authority to *make* law; it can only issue regulations to assure as much as possible the conservation of rights; only in this limited sense may there be said to exist a *legislative authority*. Every citizen must have the right to discuss freely the question of whether such regulations conform to the declaration of rights. A necessary safeguard is to require that a "considerable part" of the "legislature" should be elected each year, reserving to the electors freedom to re-elect those whom they desire, since there is a "rather grave inconvenience" in constantly entrusting public affairs to "new and inexperienced men."[112]

This insistence upon a clear declaration of rights and this fear of possible legislative tyranny were among Du Pont's cherished convictions. That his hand was active in preparing the notes is also indicated by a long quotation from an article which appeared in the *Éphémérides du citoyen* in 1769 and by the mention of "the profound thinker Quesnay."[113] The notes to the *Examen* seemed to stress the necessity of a legislative council chosen by the citizens and bound by a declaration of natural rights. While there is wisdom in some separation of the agencies of government, there is no need for an elaborate system of checks and balances. So long as the fundamental principles prevail, there is little to fear from king or aristocracy, though undoubtedly the selfish interests of the latter must be curbed if they are not, as in England, to be destructive of true freedom.

The book, though only one in the stream of publications issuing from the presses, attained sufficient notice to be praised by the Abbé Sieyès in the third edition of his famous pamphlet *Qu'est-ce que le Tiers État?* and to be referred to frequently in the later debates in the Constituent Assembly.[114]

On October 21, 1788, Du Pont had written to his son Victor, ". . . we will have the Estates General at the end of January and I will do all I can to be a member."[115] In accordance with the system of indirect elections decreed for the choice of deputies to the Estates General, inhabitants of the parish of Chevannes were to elect two men to represent them at the assembly of the *bailliage* of Nemours. Each electoral unit was to prepare a *cahier*, a document containing grievances, views, complaints, petitions, instructions to delegates, and other matters.[116] Du Pont returned to Bois-des-Fossés in February, 1789, and drew up the parish "instructions" for the representatives to take to Nemours. This document is in general a remarkable summary of some of his principal viewpoints. It begins with an "exposition of the rights of all citizens," including freedom to do anything which does not harm others, freedom to work at reasonable recompense, free and equal access to justice, right to private property which can be taken for public purposes only upon payment of reasonable compensation. It goes on to call for the limitation of all taxes to those necessary to assure the defense of the state, the costs of justice, the expense of public instruction, the building of roads, canals, bridges, ports, and fortresses, the care of the poor, and the maintenance of the King's dignity. The Estates General alone should have authority to levy taxes, which should be borne by all property owners in equitable proportion without any exemption. Specifically requested are the suppression of all privileges in payment of the *taille*, the suppression of the *corvée* in favor of road work for the poor at the expense of landowners, the abolition of the

139

militia and a return to voluntary recruiting, the reformation of the *aides* and other duties, the suppression of the *gabelles*, the removal of restrictions on the grain trade, the promulgation of a civil code, the revision of criminal law, the establishment of a school in each parish, the common deliberation of the three orders in the assembly at Nemours.[117]

In addition to this *cahier*, Du Pont composed *cahiers* for the four neighboring parishes of Egreville, Bignon, Bazoches, and Branles.[118] The election at Chevannes was a very calm affair, held in the parish church of Saint-Sulpice after vespers on March 1, 1789. After approving the "instructions," the "proprietors and inhabitants" unanimously elected Du Pont and Edme Page, a man of local reputation only, to represent them at Nemours.[119] Du Pont might have sat with the nobility at Nemours. Part of his property near Chevannes included the old fief of Beaumoulin. In accordance with the electoral regulations, he received a summons to attend the convocation of the nobles, but he preferred to sit with the Third Estate. He submitted a document naming the Vicomte de Caraman as his proxy in the meetings of the Second Estate.[120] His hope was to win approval of the recommendation of Article 16 of the Chevannes Instructions that the three orders deliberate together.

After the Mass which opened the Nemours Assembly and the verification of credentials on March 9, Du Pont was permitted to address the first general meeting.[121] In a long speech he called upon the three orders to meet together as evidence that they were "all animated by a common interest and . . . disposed by reason, affection, probity, religion, honor, to render complete justice to the legitimate claims of all."[122] Although the assembly then voted by acclamation to insert the speech in the *procès-verbal* and to have it separately printed, some of the deputies of the Third Estate were suspicious that this eloquent plea was part of a stratagem to limit freedom of discussion among the commoners. Their suspicion was probably increased when the Comte de la Tour-du-Pin, representing the Duc d'Orléans, supported the plea.[123] A few of the delegates of the Third Estate set out to discredit Du Pont as a noble in their midst who sought to undermine the just aspirations of the common people. When, in a separate meeting of the Third Estate, Du Pont moved for deliberation in common, some delegates rushed at him with the apparent intention of throwing him out of the window. Seizing hold of a fellow-delegate, who was exceptionally fat, Du Pont prevented his attackers from dislodging him. He explained to his stout anchor, "Every man for himself! They are going to throw me out of the window, and I intend to use you as a mattress."[124] This tactic gained him sufficient time to declare that, as representative of his constituents at Chevannes, he was only carrying out their wishes and that he would prefer death to being unfaithful to them. This statement turned the crowd in his favor, and the furor subsided amidst applause. But the Third Estate decided to deliberate separately.[125] Further attempts were made to raise suspicions about Du Pont's motives, but all were in vain.[126] Du Pont's part in the Nemours Assembly was an important one.

He was chosen first among sixteen placed on the committee to prepare the *cahier* of the Third Estate, which was to be a summary of the *cahiers* brought to Nemours from the primary electoral assemblies.[127] This committee held twelve meetings, but according to Eleuthère Irénée, who accompanied his father to Nemours, turned all of the work over to Du Pont.[128] Even his prodigious energy and knowledge were unequal to the task of finishing in the six days allowed by the Assembly the voluminous *cahier* which ultimately went to Versailles. Not until late afternoon on March 16 did he have the preliminary draft ready; then he consumed about three hours in reading it to the delegates of the *Tiers*. The clergy and nobility, who had earlier completed their work, were irritated by the delay and twice interrupted his presentation by sending delegations to request adjournment.[129] The *cahier* was approved the next day, with authority granted to make revisions and additions.

The Third Estate then proceeded to the election of their delegates. A final effort was made to eliminate Du Pont by a move to restrict the election to commoners. Du Pont succeeded in having it rejected by "unanimous vote" when he declared it would be contrary to right to tie the hands of the delegates, that they should be permitted to vote for those who they thought would best represent them and not be restricted to voting for those in whom they had less confidence. He was then elected on the first ballot, receiving 182 votes out of 208 cast.[130] Pierre Berthier, a Nemours lawyer, "a nice old fat gourmand,"[131] was elected second delegate with 155 votes.[132] On a third ballot Joseph-Étienne Bordier, mayor of Nemours, and Pierre-François Petit, of Château-Landon, were chosen as alternate delegates. The weary Assembly finally adjourned an hour before midnight on March 17.[133] A few days later Du Pont refused the fee granted to cover the expenses of each delegate in attendance.[134]

He was then back at Bois-des-Fossés hard at work on the final draft of the *cahier,* which he took almost a month to complete.[135] He was assisted by Pierre Denizet of Chevannes, who seems to have served as his secretary at Bois-des-Fossés.[136] In its final form this *cahier* fills 684 pages of manuscript[137] and 549 pages in the printed *procès-verbal.*[138] It follows the prescribed division into three parts: *Remonstrances, Moyens, Avis.* There is a general introduction to the whole, and a special introduction to each part. In addition to a detailed treatment of each item mentioned, philosophical reflections upon the true bases of society, government, and economics run throughout. The seventeen chapters of the first part are a mine of information on the inequitable taxes, tolls, and duties of the old regime. Also included are complaints regarding the militia, the lottery, and land leases. The second part *(Moyens)* begins by emphasizing the central importance of a declaration of rights and suggests thirty articles for such a declaration. Among these thirty articles, the following are notable: (1) every man has the right to do freely what does not injure other men; (2) every man has the right to the assistance of other men; (6) no authority can oblige a man to work without salary, or for a salary which seems to him insufficient; (7) every man ought to keep what he possesses, and what he has legitimately acquired by his labor, by gift, or by inheritance; (9) no man should be subjected to violence to his person or to his possessions; (12) every man ought to be protected by other men and by the whole body of society against all attacks on his liberty, his property, or his security; (13) liberty, property, security ought never to be violated with impunity; (25) proprietors who pay taxes should have representation in a general assembly to vote taxes.[139]

After a chapter devoted to the necessity of improving public instruction, the rest of the section on *Moyens* is concerned with the methods to be followed in making the Estates General an integral part of the government of France. Its concluding paragraph is actually a summary of some of Du Pont's cardinal principles.

The Third Estate of the *Bailliage* of Nemours thinks that if the Estates General would indeed give their attention to the propositions which it has made to them in this second part of its work; to equalize the representation among the different Provinces; to regulate the form of elections and the extent of the powers of the Deputies in their exercise and in their duration; to determine the manner of making motions, of debating them [and] of deliberating and of pronouncing upon them in the National Assembly; to state forever the imprescriptible right of the Nation to propose laws of any kind, and the eminent right of the King to give or to refuse his sanction to them; to base all these institutions on the most perfect and the most complete declaration of rights which the wisdom of the Estates General can draw up and approve; and to guarantee them by the best public and private instruction of which the freedom of the press is a part; they will have established the simplest and surest means of remedying all evils, of assuring the adoption and stability of all good.[140]

The *Avis* of the third part of the *cahier* provides detailed recommendations on the reform of civil and criminal law, administration of finances, and agriculture and commerce. The entire work is summarized in a general conclusion, which repeats the principal recommendations:

To declare what are the rights of men and of citizens.

To favor their being taught in all the kingdom.

To base [instruction] indispensably on morality and on justice, in order that positions to which public duties are entrusted may be open to all.

To make the Estates General periodic.

To charge them with the proposing of laws . . . .

To reserve to the King their approval . . . .

Neither to propose nor to maintain anything which can bring harm to liberty or to property.

To be concerned with the public treasury only after having determined by legislation for what public services it is necessary to spend money.

Not to allow any tax to continue which can lead to the violation of personal or of domiciliary liberty.

Not to admit any kind of privilege in the assessing nor in the allocation of those [taxes] which will be established.

Not to adopt any [tax], the revenue and cost of which cannot be perfectly clear.

To institute . . . an order which ceases to draw from the Provinces money which can be used there, [an order] which makes possible the rendering of an account of the financial situation whenever it may please the King or the nation to ask for it.

To reform the civil code, the criminal code, and the ordinances which may be needed to regulate the procedures, in a manner to guarantee in every particular the liberty, property, and security of anyone residing in the nation, or having just claims [upon the nation].

To make Agriculture and Commerce free.

To procure for them all the instructions and all the encouragements which can be useful to them.

To establish among all citizens a mutual correspondence of good offices and of reciprocal assistance.

Therein to assure gratuitous [care] to all those who are not able to reciprocate.[141]

In these words Du Pont's general program is fairly stated. His efforts in the Constituent Assembly were dedicated to establishing it in detail. It is a program closely allied to physiocratic objectives, but it also expresses, in greater detail than in most *cahiers,* the general dissatisfaction and hope of the majority of the advocates of reform.

Chapter V

The Constituent Assembly (1789-1791)

BY THE END OF APRIL Du Pont was in Versailles ready for the most important responsibility of his public career. In company with most of his fellow-delegates of the Third Estate, he looked forward to the meeting of the Estates General in eager expectation that it would be able to effect the changes necessary to revivify the nation. His labors on the *cahiers* had brought into order all his ideas on the reforms which he believed had to be accomplished. He arrived at Versailles early enough to find lodging at 55 Avenue de Saint-Cloud,[1] within walking distance of the Hôtel des Menus-Plaisirs, where, like the Assembly of Notables before them, the Estates General were to meet. Many of the deputies were late in arriving and the elections in Paris were taking longer than expected. The opening ceremony had to be postponed to Monday, May 4, but the King held separate receptions on the previous Saturday afternoon for the delegates on hand from each of the three orders.[2]

The costume which the delegates wore to the reception and to later sessions of the Estates General had been determined by a regulation proclaimed on April 27. This regulation was really the first victory won by the Third Estate. The contrasts in the costumes which it decreed would seem to nourish awareness of the distinctions among the orders. The cardinals in their red copes, the archbishops and bishops in their violet cassocks, the nobles in their gold-embroidered black cloaks and white-plumed hats certainly made a more brilliant appearance than the commoners in their black coats, vests, breeches, and stockings. The costume of the *Tiers* differed, nevertheless, from that first decided upon. There had been a vigorous protest from deputies of the Third Estate—who were, after all, mostly men of some substance, lawyers, officials, financiers—when word circulated that they were all to wear a cloak with pendent sleeves and a little black velvet cap (a *toque*) that had come to be associated in the theater with comic or foolish characters (like Le Sage's Crispin or Molière's Géronte). The Grand Master of Ceremonies, the Marquis de Brezé, sought compromise—some said at the urging of Necker, the hope of the people. The regulation of April 27 tried in words, therefore, to cover up the distinctions among the orders, to which the Third Estate had objected. In place of the cloak first mentioned and the *toque*, delegates of the Third Estate were to have "a short cloak of silk or voile, such as Persons [i.e., Nobles] of the robe customarily wear at Court, muslin cravat, a hat turned up on three sides, without braid or buttons, such as Ecclesiastics wear when they [are not in their vestments]."[3] It was a small victory, perhaps, but a significant one.

Young Irénée Du Pont left his studies at Essone to come to Versailles for the splendid ceremony inaugurating the Estates General. He described it in a letter to Victor on May 8.

> The Estates opened on the Fourth of May; the opening was delayed in order to wait for the deputies from Paris but at last they were given up. It was because Paris was given much less time than was necessary; the election of their deputies will not be completed for a week. The ceremony of the opening was very beautiful. The King, the Queen, the royal family and the whole Court, with the deputies of the three orders went in procession from Notre Dame de Versailles to the Church of Saint Louis. There they heard the Mass of the Saint Esprit and a sermon from the Bishop of Nancy that lasted for more than three hours; after that the Court left in superb carriages. Versailles was magnificent that day; nearly all Paris was there. The windows, filled with beautifully dressed women, rented for absurd prices.[4]

This inevitable pageantry completed, the serious reformers among the deputies eagerly awaited the first session on Tuesday, May 5. They were bitterly disappointed. "The King made a very good speech," Irénée wrote,[5] but he might have added that he said nothing which gave encouragement to proponents of change. He left up to Barentin, the Keeper of the Seals, and to Necker a detailed presentation of his desires. Barentin's remarks were inaudible ("No one heard him," wrote Irénée). It was just as well, because he did not offer much hope by his statement that, in allowing the doubling of the Third, the King had not meant to change the traditional form of deliberations; vote by head could be granted only upon the free consent of the Estates General and the approval of the King.[6] Everyone was waiting for Necker's speech, where, it was expected, vigorous recommendations for change would be set forth. But here came the greatest disappointment of all. Necker rambled on for more than an hour with a detailed statement of conditions; then his voice gave out long before he was finished. He had to turn over to an assistant the reading of the remainder of his speech, which consumed another two hours. At the end the dazed auditors could grasp nothing tangible which might stand as a direction-finder on the road to reform. This unhappy performance marked only the beginning of the ebb-tide in Necker's popular appeal.

The issue had to be faced at once. Barentin's last muffled words had instructed the Estates to assemble on the morrow to proceed with the verification of credentials. The majority of the Third Estate insisted upon verification in common, since they were determined not to concede the vital point of the separate meeting and voting of the three orders. From May 6, therefore, a seeming impasse arose which endured for more than a month. The Third Estate refused to begin verification of the credentials of its members until the other two estates met with them in order to pass on the credentials of all delegates to the Estates General. Twelve days after the first meeting Du Pont was named by the *Tiers* to a committee of sixteen for conferences with the first two estates in order "to seek the best means of verifying credentials in common."[7] He was appointed to draw up for the Third Estate the *procès-verbal* of the conferences. On June 5 he reported to the *Tiers* on the unsatisfactory progress toward a compromise and on the delay occasioned by the death of the little Dauphin the day before and the retirement of the grieving Royal Family to Marly.[8] The will of the Third Estate to hold firm had been strengthened on May 25 by the tardy arrival of the deputation from Paris, among which were prominent figures like the astronomer Jean-Sylvian Bailly and the renegade priest Emmanuel-Joseph Sieyès, whose *What Is the Third Estate?* had been the most widely read pamphlet among the many hundreds pouring from the presses over the last eight months. Everyone knew Sieyès' blunt answer to the question he had posed: the Third Estate was *everything*! The first two estates upheld their refusal to verify in common, though sentiment among the clergy, where the majority came from the lower ranks, was very closely divided. Necker now came forward with a compromise proposal that verification be done separately by each order but that the results be reported in common to all three orders so that any delegate might present objections to the credentials of any other delegate in any of the orders; if disagreement arising as a result of such objections could not be resolved by the delegates themselves, the King would make the decision. The nobility relieved the *Tiers* of the embarrassment of turning down this proposal by rejecting it themselves, except as it might apply to the few delegations which, as in Dauphiné, had been chosen in common by the three orders.

On June 10 the Third Estate seized upon another plan, put forward by Sieyès, to resolve the deadlock. The Commons, the designation now preferred by the Third Estate, would call the roll of all the delegations, noting in the record the absence of clerical and noble deputies. As his name was called, each deputy would submit his credentials. The roll call began on June 12 and ended on June 14, Du Pont submitting his credentials on the thirteenth.[9] A few priests joined in the roll call, but no nobles appeared. Committees were established to pass upon the credentials. Du Pont submitted the report of the fifth committee on June 15.[10] At that time he was first subjected to attacks from some of his colleagues. He objected strenuously to the mandate of the delegates from Brittany, which specified that no decisions of the Estates General would be binding in that province until approved by the provincial estates. His point was sound—namely, that general laws must be binding throughout the realm—but he spoke at too great length and severely reproved the Bretons. Some delegates thought that he was merely trying to confuse and to delay the business at hand in accordance with the wishes of the aristocrats in the Ministry.[11] The criticism directed against him was so loud that he sought to explain himself before the Breton delegates at their favorite meeting place outside the assembly, the Café Amaury on the Avenue de Saint-Cloud.[12] This was his first appearance before the group which, it is generally agreed, formed the nucleus of the later Jacobin club. He also sought to justify his stand in a long letter to his constituents.[13]

At the end of the roll call, the Commons debated at length the question of an appropriate name for an Assembly, no longer, in their judgment, composed of three separate orders. Of various suggestions presented, two received the most attention. The Abbé Sieyès first put forward the designation "Assembly of the Known and Verified Representatives of the French Nation," but Mirabeau thought it too complicated and suggested the briefer "Representatives of the French People." For some the latter title was too blunt and provocative, if not completely illegal. Mirabeau defended it with passion but was not yet able to exert the influence which his powerful oratory later brought him. Jean-Joseph Mounier, who proved to be more conservative than many expected him to be in view of the fact that he represented Dauphiné, where the three estates had met in common, now proposed another name: "Legitimate Assembly of the Representatives of the Major Part of the Nation, Acting in the Absence of the Minor Part." This title may have correctly described the situation, but it was even more complicated than Sieyès' original proposal. Nevertheless, Du Pont supported it and still preferred it to the name finally adopted.[14] In the evening session on June 16, Sieyès changed his mind and moved for the adoption of the name "National Assembly," which Du Pont says was first suggested by "M. le Grand, deputy of Berry" (i.e., Jérôme Le Grand from the *bailliage* of Bourges). On June 17, without further debate, the Commons adopted this name by a vote of 491 to 90.[15] They added emphasis to this momentous decision by again inviting the privileged orders to join this "National Assembly." Bailly, who had been elected "dean" of the Commons on June 3, became provisional president of the National Assembly.

To the consternation of the bishops a majority of the priests on June 19 declared in favor of uniting the three orders. The privileged orders now called upon the King for assistance. Even Necker agreed that something had to be done and supported a decision of the Council of State to hold a Royal Session (i. e., one in which the King would be present) on June 22. When the Commons assembled before their meeting place in the great hall on the morning of June 20, they found the doors locked and guarded by soldiers.

Placards announced that the hall was closed in order to prepare it for the Royal Session. To many of the deputies this action posed the threat of the use of force to dissolve the Assembly before any reform could be accomplished. Determined upon united opposition to such a plan, the Commons withdrew to the nearby indoor tennis court and there, almost to a man, subscribed to the famous Oath of the Tennis Court, by which they vowed not to separate until France had a constitution. Without hesitation, Du Pont affixed his signature to the Oath when it was written out.[16]

This action of the Commons increased the disagreement in the Council of State on what should be done. The Royal Session had to be postponed to the twenty-third. Necker, who had finally come up with a definite program, was outvoted in Council, but his compromise scheme for the verification of credentials was adopted. What else was to be proposed was finally worked out for inclusion in the King's speech and the declaration which Barentin would read. The Royal Session on June 23 had an atmosphere of tension which the presence of numerous soldiery around the Hôtel des Menus-Plaisirs did not help to dissipate. Under these circumstances the King's program, though he conceded much more than he had indicated himself willing to do on May 5, came too late. The Commons could not retreat from the decision of June 17.

When, as expected, the King concluded his remarks by instructing the Estates to separate and by implying that, if they did not obey, he would dissolve the assembly, the Commons remained stolidly in place as the Nobility and most of the Clergy left the hall after the King. Dreux-Brezé, the Grand Master of Ceremonies, repeated the King's orders. Some deputies wavered and may have drawn back from open defiance of the royal will. Here it was that Bailly, Sieyès, and Mirabeau arose to provide the leadership, or at least the words, needed to keep their fellow-deputies united. There are no completely reliable records of what they said,[17] but the exact words are not so important as the fact that the Commons stood firm. On June 24 the majority of the Clergy joined them and then, next day, forty-seven nobles, led by the Duc d'Orléans, followed. The Court party gave up the fight—for the time being. On June 27, the King ordered the remainder of the Clergy and Nobility to unite with the other representatives in one body. The Estates General was dead!

The National Assembly, the Constituent Assembly, which was to give France a written constitution, was established! Thus was accomplished what some have called the second stage of the Revolution—the bourgeois revolution.[18]

Meanwhile, despite the deadlock, other matters had to go forward. One of increasing concern was the food shortage especially in Paris. Du Pont was named to the Committee on Subsistence charged with discovering means to alleviate this situation. He prepared and delivered the report of the committee on July 4. The report was rather roughly handled by the Assembly. Adrien Duquesnoy of Bar-le-duc found it "detestable, of infinite length, presenting false, perhaps dangerous, views."[19] Du Pont expressed doubts about how far the committee could go in assuming powers to relieve the needy. He thanked the King for efforts to encourage charitable associations, parishes, and communities to furnish gratuitously all they could to the old and infirm. He urged all governmental bodies—the provincial estates, municipalities, and others—to do what they could, while the committee continued to study the problem, especially to find means of assuring the internal free trade and equitable distribution of grain. He finally suggested six possible courses of action, all of which would take time to carry out, including public subscriptions, local taxation, freeing of internal grain trade, government loans, temporary prohibitions of the export of grain, and a careful study of all problems related to the grain and cereal trade. Mirabeau and others expressed their dissatisfaction with the report, declaring it inadequate on several counts. The discussion brought no definite action.[20] Decision was not made easier by Du Pont's second report, where he reviewed nineteen projects for decrees which the committee had received. The best remedy, he held, was freedom of trade but admitted that it was difficult to bring about under the conditions then existing.[21] The only significance of these reports is that Du Pont was again subjected to a vigorous attack on his proposals. Now, as later, these proposals were too often enclosed in lengthy analyses and summaries of complicated details. Du Pont early became accustomed to such attacks and did not alter his methods.

Various factors undermined his effectiveness in the National Assembly. He was, first of all, a moderate reformer and, hence, open to the attack which extremes of left and right have usually launched upon defenders of the middle way. He did not yield to opposition, for he had definite views and the courage to uphold them. Despite an inevitable note of self-righteousness, there is more than a grain of truth in what he wrote later about his position in the National Assembly. ". . . I was entirely independent, honest and proud as liberty itself. I wanted only the Constitution, the assurance of the rights of man and of the citizen, the security of finances, justice, humanity, respect for the laws we have made, order, and peace. I detested, I defied, I fought on right and left all the factionists on both sides. I earned their hatred and the respect of honest men."[22] In the second place, Du Pont made himself an easier target for attack by speaking too frequently on too many subjects. There were times when he wearied even this Assembly of notable talkers.[23] His long speeches were carefully prepared, with occasionally neat turns of phrase, and bolstered by fact and statistics. Although they might at times be attentively followed because of the information which they contained, most of them could hardly be described as eloquent or exciting. Du Pont did not regard it as worthy of his effort to strive constantly for vivid phraseology or colorful witticism in order to gain popularity with the mob. That was the demagogue's method, which he detested.

Those who wished to attack Du Pont found other ready weapons. Physiocracy had come into ill repute with many reformers because of its predilection for land and landowners and its solicitude for the prerogatives of the monarch. Enlightened despotism did not appear to open the way for reform; and the unhappy experiences of Turgot, Necker, and Calonne "contributed much . . . to discredit the physiocratic conception of the good despot."[24] Du Pont was, of course, widely known as the disciple of Quesnay and hence was condemned as the captive of a "system" which limited his views. This criticism, though unjust, was often made.[25] Furthermore, Du Pont had served under various ministers and still retained his government post as Inspector General of Commerce. These connections were enough to bring accusations that he was the tool of the Ministry.[26] In defending himself on one occasion against the epithet "ministerial," he displayed a characteristic which turned many against him —his high-minded self-righteousness. He was always convinced that he labored unselfishly for the public good: "I have always remained free and independent of every other passion, of every other interest than that of the public welfare, among [the ministers] as among you [in the Assembly]."[27]

Despite the criticism to which he was subjected, Du Pont retained the respect of a large number of delegates. His obvious ability and his tremendous capacity for work led to his appointment to many important committees. On July 3 he was chosen as secretary of the twenty-seventh of the thirty committees into which the Assembly was divided.[28] He played a small part in the stirring events which confirmed the victory of the Commons. The Court party had no intention of yielding docilely to the decision of June 27. They induced the King to bring to Paris troops stationed at some distance from the city, since the garrisons on hand, closer to the restless people in the old capital, might not be completely reliable. Throughout the first part of July, the movement of troops, which could not be concealed, and the mounting food crisis increased unrest. Most members in the Assembly were not satisfied with the King's assurance that the troops had been brought in to guarantee public tranquillity by preventing disorders. Once the soldiery had been placed in and around the city, the Court party made its next move. On July 11, Necker and two other ministers thought to be his friends were dismissed and replaced by three others regarded, perhaps unjustly, as opponents of reform. Necker was instructed to leave the Kingdom but did not reach the frontier. The news of the ministerial change was abroad by July 12 and rumbles in Paris grew louder. Since that day was Sunday, the Assembly was not in session. The disturbing situation was the principal concern on the thirteenth. After long but inconclusive debate, the Assembly appointed a deputation to call upon the King for assurance that the troops would be withdrawn. Du Pont was named as one of the members.[29]

The rumblings in Paris grew into riots, as crowds of people set about to search for arms to defend themselves against the soldiers. The riots culminated in an attack upon the old fortress and prison known as the Bastille. Although it then had only a small garrison and confined only seven prisoners, none of them there for political reasons, the surrender of this grim fortress overlooking a workers' section of Paris on July 14 soon became symbolic of the overturn of the old order. It was not so much the fall of the Bastille, at first only an incident in the riots, that gave birth to this symbol; it was rather the King's reaction to the fearful reports reaching Versailles of the situation in Paris. The angry mood of the crowd inevitably led to cruelty and bloodshed—to the lynching of De Launay, who had surrendered the Bastille, and of Flesselles, provost of the merchants, chief official of the Parisian government. The rioters were only a small minority of the people of Paris, but it seemed as if the whole city had risen. Available troops were inadequate to restore order; indeed, their use could only add to the bloodshed. Rejecting the advice of his brother, the Comte d'Artois, and of others around him, the King abandoned the struggle. He decided to withdraw the troops from Paris and to agree to the establishment of a "bourgeois guard." This civilian guard, the embryo of the National Guard, had been set up on July 13 by citizens with enough property to be concerned about the looting of shops by the rioters. Du Pont on that day handed a note to one of the two deputies sent to Versailles by the electors of Paris to report to the National Assembly, requesting that he be enrolled, together with his son Irénée, in the citizen militia if it were established.[30]

He was very much disturbed by the reports reaching Versailles and at 11 P.M. on July 14 left the deputation calling upon the King in order to hurry to Paris himself. By a quarter past two on the morning of July 15, he was at the Paris City Hall and announced the favorable replies of the King to the deputation[31] several hours before the royal decision was made public. He spent the rest of the night among the aroused people, "speaking reason and calming its fury at the risk of turning it against" him. His desire to return immediately to Versailles in order to report upon what he had seen was thwarted by a regiment of Swiss guards stationed on a bridge across the Seine. He finally seized a boat and rowed across the river, pursued by some of the guards. He did not get back to Versailles until July 16.[32] That was the day when Louis XVI recalled Necker. The complete victory of "the popular revolution"[33] was confirmed the next day when Louis went to Paris, accepted the revolutionary cockade of three colors (the red and blue of Paris, the white of the Bourbon monarchy), and approved all that had been done. This approval included the reorganization of the Parisian government,

154

with Bailly as the Mayor, and the establishment of the National Guard, with Lafayette as the Commander.

The King's capitulation did not bring an end to popular disturbances. There were more lynchings in Paris. The scarcity of food increased the fear as well as the misery of the people. Frightening reports came to Versailles of continued rioting in the provinces. Throughout various parts of the realm, apparently spontaneous uprisings of the peasantry occurred in the latter part of July. Fed by wild rumors of brigands about to descend upon them, the peasants flew to whatever crude weapons of defense they could find. Their pent-up passion was sometimes directed against the château of the local lord, when the fancied brigands, allegedly inspired by a plot of the aristocrats, failed to appear. In the burning of châteaux in various localities there was apparently the naïve design of the peasantry to destroy the feudal rolls, the *terriers*, upon which were inscribed all the obligations owed to the lord. The destruction of the record of their duties would mean, so the peasants may have believed, the destruction of the duties themselves. In many cases the attack upon the property of the local nobility was merely the release of long-suppressed hatred. This "great fear," which, growing out of six isolated incidents, seemed to be sweeping the countryside,[34] could not be ignored. It had momentous consequences. Throughout France it quickened the pace of change. Other localities followed Paris in reorganizing the municipal governments and in forming contingents of the National Guard. In some areas these new safeguards of property succeeded in putting down the peasant riots by force. Many of the worried deputies in Versailles decided to adopt another course. They planned to stage a dramatic renunciation of privileges in the evening session of the Assembly on August 4 and, thus, so they hoped, to appease the peasants and to end the disturbances. Their limited plans got out of hand when, unexpectedly, the Vicomte de Noailles, a landless noble from Du Pont's district of Nemours, reached the rostrum first and went much farther in renouncing privileges, most of which he did not have, than had originally been planned. Caught up in a surge of deep emotion, deputy after deputy now rose to sacrifice his privileges, and those of others, to the national good and common welfare. During this impassioned session on the night of August 4, Du Pont was one of the few deputies to retain his composure.

In his view, the procedure underway was unsound and unworthy. He demanded instead that severe measures be taken to restore order in the provinces, thus incurring the displeasure of many of his contemporaries and of later commentators.[35] His conviction that nothing constructive could be accomplished amidst disorder and disregard of law caused him to speak out on this occasion in terms somewhat different from those used by other speakers. "A universal disorder," he said, "has taken possession of the nation by reason of the inaction of all agents of power. No political society can exist a single moment without laws and without courts to guarantee liberty, security of persons, and preservation of property. I insist on the necessity of maintaining and of not abandoning laws, which, however imperfect, have for [their] object the preservation of general order." Consequently, he offered a motion "to declare that every citizen is obliged to obey the laws in respecting the liberty, the security, and the property of other citizens; that the tribunals ought to act ceaselessly for the execution of these laws; and that . . . the citizen [*bourgeois*] militia and all military bodies lend assistance for the re-establishment of order and of peace, and for the protection of persons and of property, whenever they will be requested by the municipalities and civil magistrates."[36] On August 5, he once more called attention to this motion.[37] Obviously he had not been moved by the emotion-charged atmosphere of the night session just ended.

Although his proposal was not adopted at either session, the majority of the deputies came to believe that emotion had carried them too far beyond reason on that famous night. As they put together the decree which would make official the concessions which they had made, they began to draw back from the full implications of their action. The "decree of August 4," which was actually passed on August 11, drew a neat distinction among the privileges surrendered. Those which were personal obligations, binding man to man, were alone abolished without qualification. This meant that serfdom, where it still existed in France, was ended. But there were hardly more than a million serfs in all of France. Most peasants were concerned about real obligations, those which inhered in the land and which exacted dues and services from the holder of the land.

This type of obligation the Assembly did not abolish categorically. Instead, it provided that landholders subject to such obligations might redeem them through regular payments over a period of years. This arrangement, if they understood it, did not please the peasants. Most of them were unconcerned, for they ceased meeting the old obligations without a thought of redemption. The "peasant revolution" brought to France, therefore, a greater transformation than had been contemplated. A trend long in operation, that of transforming the peasant into a small, but independent, landholder, was greatly accelerated.

Du Pont's activities during the remainder of the session of the Constituent Assembly must be treated selectively. An attempt to cover them in full, or in chronological order, would be completely exhausting to both the author and his readers. It would, furthermore, require a chapter as long as the entire book. During these two years Du Pont served on eleven regular committees and did important work as adjunct member of the Committee on the Constitution. He was listed as a member of these standing committees: (1) Agriculture and Commerce, (2) National Treasury, (3) Examination of Accounts, (4) Public Assistance, (5) Public Taxes, (6) Examination of Caisse d'Escompte, (7) Imposts, (8) Ecclesiastical, (9) Finances, (10) Alienation of the National Domain, (11) Tithes.[38] Even with his boundless optimism, self-confidence, and amazing energy, Du Pont could not, of course, give equal attention to all these assignments. His labors on financial matters were so extensive that they must be considered in a separate chapter. Here, his general ideas on other subjects, especially touching upon the Constitution, will be treated.

In preparation for the important debates of August and September, which would lay down the foundations of the kind of governmental structure desired by the Assembly, Du Pont wrote out and published his views in a pamphlet entitled *De la périodicité des assemblées nationales*.[39] In launching his ideas, he used the convenient device of the social contract, which writers like Locke and Rousseau had made familiar. "Political societies," he wrote, "are formed of citizens who join together their means and their efforts to increase their common security, to extend and to guarantee reciprocally the use of their liberty, to preserve their properties, and to put themselves within reach of creating or of acquiring other [properties], with more peace and less hardship. The principle and the source of sovereignty are therefore manifestly in the citizens," who alone found a public power from the union of their private powers and a rule of conduct, or a law, from the union of their intellects and wills. In the government of this political society, Du Pont stated, legislative and executive powers must never be joined, else government will be arbitrary. One "ought equally to guard the people from ministerial despotism and from the turbulent aristocracy of its representatives." The best means of accomplishing this object would be to establish a national assembly, divided into two chambers, which would meet annually to make decisions by majority vote. Two chambers are necessary to give all measures the full discussion required to prevent force, intrigue, passion, or eloquence from being the decisive factors in legislation. The upper chamber should not be, like the English House of Lords, an hereditary body with the right of veto. A French Senate should rather be chosen without distinction of social orders and should have no absolute veto power. Its members should be really elders in the scope of their experience and learning, and might eventually be chosen by the electors themselves. A project for a law should originate in the lower chamber, or Chamber of Representatives, which could pass it after three readings and discussions on three separate days. Then it would go to the Senate, which by immediate approval could transform an "*Arrêté* of the Chamber of Representatives into a *Décret* of the National Assembly."

If, however, the Senate did not at once approve a measure, then a rather cumbersome procedure for ameliorating differences would be followed. Three times the Senate could refuse sanction to an *arrêt* persisted in by the Chamber of Representatives. If, unmoved by the arguments submitted by the Senate, the Chamber passed the measure a fourth time, it could, at the same time, invite the Senate to a joint meeting. The Senate would have no power to decline the invitation. Then, joined together as the National Assembly, the people's representatives could decide by majority vote whether or not to pass the measure. After all these obstacles, a decree of the legislature would still be subject to the absolute veto of the King! Theoretically, this power of the King must be unlimited, though it was hardly conceivable that his ministers would dare advise him to hold up for more than two years a measure obviously thought good by the majority of citizens. Frequent elections would make clear the will of the people, and prevent the sanctioning of the projects of clever and ambitious individuals, projects which might be contrary to public welfare.[40]

It may be doubted whether any proposal could become law by surviving these obstacles. A controversial measure might have to be passed by the lower chamber four times, then still be subject to final approval in a joint session of the two chambers and to final sanction by the King. On the surface, the arrangement appears to be carefully calculated to stop any important reforms. Yet such was not Du Pont's object. Some of his physiocratic predilections run throughout his scheme, which was obviously predicated upon an electorate limited to proprietors guided by enlightened self-interest and upon a king devoted to the welfare of his people. The selfish designs of ambitious individuals and the ignorant desires of the mass of the people must be guarded against. Arbitrariness—there is the enemy! "For the rights of men, their duties, justice [and] morality are not at all arbitrary. Their character created in Heaven can be recognized by every man who reflects and whom passions do not mislead."[41]

The position which he takes in this pamphlet foreshadowed the difficulties Du Pont was to encounter as a moderate reformer. With such fears of popular passions and of selfish ambitions, he could hardly expect to be a popular figure in the Constituent Assembly. However admirable in itself his determination to maintain order, to prevent "arbitrary" action, may be, it could be regarded by eager reformers as the refuge of timidity or of reaction. The fact that he was certainly neither timid nor reactionary tended, on the other hand, to bring him into disfavor with the opponents of substantial reform.

Toward disorder Du Pont's attitude remained consistent. He could never excuse it. He was convinced that behind every popular demonstration could be found dangerous agitators who stirred up the mob in order to further their selfish and evil designs. As sporadic rioting continued after the night of August 4, he renewed his efforts to enforce discipline among the people. On August 10, he proposed

159

that the Assembly warn the people not to take part in "seditious" movements on pain of being treated as rebels. He recommended that a proclamation be issued in terms similar to those of the Mutiny Act of England so that, if warning proved insufficient, troops could be used.[42] Since they believed that they were making adequate concessions in the decree which they were about to pass on personal and real obligations, the majority gave qualified approval to Du Pont's proposal. Later, on February 22, 1790, however, Robespierre led a vigorous and successful opposition to a similar project of Du Pont to invoke martial law against riots in the provinces.[43] It is notable that Du Pont never definitely laid responsibility for disorder upon the people. Always there were the ringleaders, the fomenters of riot, who should be sought out and punished. When, in July, 1790, there were mob demonstrations in his own district over payment of the tithe, Du Pont carefully explained to the Assembly that the people were misled by agitators. Harsh action should be turned, not against the people, but against the instigators.[44] Fortunately, the disturbances in the Gâtinais were easily suppressed by regular troops, whom Du Pont later congratulated for their exemplary conduct.[45]

This thesis that "agitators and anarchists" were the real culprits behind mass disturbances was developed at greater length by Du Pont in a speech on September 7, 1790. The immediate cause for his remarks was the rioting of the mob under the very windows of the Assembly meeting hall on the preceding Thursday (September 2). This demonstration had been, he asserted, the work of about forty fanatics and 400 or 500 men, who were paid twelve francs each to participate. The country and the Constitution had two kinds of enemies: those who sighed for the old order of things and those who sought to profit from anarchy and disorder. Both groups continued undercover seditious actions within France, because they could accomplish nothing openly. For one thing, said Du Pont, the courage and loyalty of the National Guard stood in their way. These enemies controlled bands of brigands from one end of France to the other, brigands most of whom were not French citizens but fugitives from justice. Alarmed by the threats of September 2, the Assembly agreed with Du Pont that repressive action against such individuals was immediately necessary.[46] With less success at two other meetings,

Du Pont urged measures against "incendiary" writings and against the posting of placards signed by a group or society, and not by individuals.[47]

The mob rioting, against which Du Pont protested, could now be a more prominent factor in the deliberations of the Assembly because, in October, 1789, it had moved from Versailles to Paris. In this move the Assembly had merely followed the King and his family, who had been triumphantly escorted back to the old capital by the Parisian market women and the rest of the mob which made its way to Versailles during these "October Days" (October 5 and 6). Behind this demonstration there were, in all probability, some of the varieties of agitators whom Du Pont liked to denounce. As is often the case, their presence is difficult to prove. The belief in the rumor of an aristocratic plot to starve the people into submission may have been sufficient to spur on the hungry housewives in their search for food. With the Royal Family—"the baker, the baker's wife, and the baker's boy"—in Paris, there was less likelihood that the alleged plot could succeed. There seems also to have been a political motive in the action—to bring pressure upon the King to sanction the decree of August 5-11 and the Declaration of the Rights of Man and of the Citizen which had been adopted on August 26. The royal sanction was obtained at Versailles on October 5, but it did not silence the demands that the King return to Paris with his people on October 6. Indeed, on the night before, Lafayette had arrived with the National Guard and two commissioners from the Paris Commune bearing the request that Louis move his residence to the city. Unless he yielded, Louis saw no way to get the mob out of Versailles. So back he came to Paris in a bizarre procession and was escorted with his family to the Tuileries. Henceforth he was practically a prisoner of the people of Paris.

These developments led to the first large-scale emigration of dissatisfied persons from France and caused the resignation of about two hundred deputies from the National Assembly, including Mounier, who went first back to Dauphiné and then into emigration. Although his high conception of the mission to which he had been called prevented Du Pont from even considering resignation, he could hardly have approved of the mob action witnessed on those October days. Unfortunately, there is no available record of his

161

thoughts at this time. All that is certain is that he moved back to Paris with the Assembly and reopened his old apartment on the Rue du Petit-Musc. The Assembly had a more difficult problem in finding space. When it became obvious that the King would be unable to return to Versailles, the Assembly appointed committees to seek out suitable meeting places in Paris. Not until October 19 did it officially transfer its seat. Then it took up uncomfortable quarters in the Archbishop's palace until it could move, on November 9, to the hastily refurbished riding school near the Tuileries.

More than a month before the removal to Paris, Du Pont had read to the Assembly his major speech on the Constitution. This was on September 4, nine days after the Declaration of the Rights of Man and of the Citizen had been adopted. Curiously enough, despite his keen interest in such a Declaration, he does not seem to have taken any part in the week-long discussion of it. The principal subject of debate early in September was the royal veto. While he dealt with it in his speech, Du Pont spent more time in developing his ideas on the organization of the legislature. He began with general reflections upon the necessity of a Constitution in order to prevent the rise of arbitrary power. Any people coming out of servitude demands such a guarantee, he asserted, so as not to fall into another kind of slavery. Then he combated the proposal to renew the Assembly every three years, declaring such a period far too long. "Men clothed with legislative powers for three years can allow themselves to give way to the inclination to dominate, so natural in the human heart." He called instead for yearly elections, with the right of re-election reserved to members of each Assembly. With somewhat more detail on a few points, he next outlined the suggestions for a legislature of two houses found in his pamphlet *De la périodicité des assemblées nationales*. He proposed that the electors choose from every three deputies the one whom they believed most mature. This deputy was to sit in the upper house, to be called the Senate "if you so desire," he added; the other two were to sit in the Chamber of Representatives. Under this system, in Du Pont's analysis, the Representatives proposed, the Senate discussed, the King sanctioned. When the King vetoed a decree of the National Assembly, he was to appeal to the electors for an expression of their view. If a plurality of the electors did not support the decree, it remained null and void. If, however, the larger number of votes were cast in favor of the law, the King could hardly refuse his sanction. Hence, the King's right of veto would be theoretically absolute, but in practice would surely be influenced by the desires of the electors and, thus, would be suspensive only. Without this safeguard, Du Pont implied, the people would have insufficient protection from the possible arbitrariness of the legislature.[48] Decisions on these points went definitely against Du Pont's views a few days later. Champions of the single-chamber legislature raised the question of why, after so much trouble in uniting, they should now vote to separate again. Bicameralism was firmly rejected on September 10. The next day the King was granted a suspensive veto power only, though by the terms of the decree the King might hold up legislation over a period of two legislatures, or four years, a longer period certainly than that contemplated by Du Pont, whose scheme rested, of course, upon the assumption that the theoretically absolute King would always yield to the desires of the majority of the electorate.

Du Pont stated his conception of the constitutional responsibilities of the Assembly in a letter written in February, 1790, to his son Victor, who had just returned to France upon the recall of Moustier's embassy. The letter was a reply to Victor's inquiry about the rejection of the motion of Cazalès, a noble deputy and a polished orator, that the Assembly set a definite date for adjournment. In Du Pont's opinion:

> The motion made by Monsieur de Cazalès was very dangerous and very unpatriotic. It might have left us with the Constitution half finished and the finances in desperate disorder. It involved the violation of our oath of June 20 that we would not separate till the Constitution should be finished, and the one we took later, to maintain it with all our strength.
>
> It is not sufficient to have overthrown an empire; it must be rescued and saved in its new form, since no other is possible. We must have a financial system, judicial authority, a King clothed with sufficient power to assure the execution of the laws; a Legislature in which resolutions cannot be acted on so hurriedly as they are in our Assembly or National Convention. We need periodic National Conventions which should receive instructions from their constituents concerning the changes and improvements necessary to our Constitution. Such conventions should be held not oftener than once in ten years and not less often than

once in twenty. The necessary work for arranging all that must keep us employed till October. . . .[49]

He was, as usual, too optimistic in his last statement. The "necessary work" consumed a year more than he expected.

Throughout this period Du Pont spoke on most of the important questions regarding the position of the monarchy. He argued successfully on September 17, 1789, against a constitutional article to exclude the Spanish Bourbons from succession to the French throne. It was best, he argued, not to debate this matter. Why try to decide something that may never have to be decided? Probably, it would in any event never be decided by a legislative decree. The French people should rather come more and more to demonstrate that those who can claim to rule over them must merit their esteem.[50] In most instances, Du Pont must be classed as a defender of the King's prerogatives. He held consistently to the necessity of a strong executive power as the best guarantee of the people's interests against arbitrary action by the legislature. During the discussion in the Assembly on July 9, 1790, concerning plans for the elaborate Fête of Federation on July 14 in celebration of the Bastille's fall, he displayed his solicitude for the royal prerogative even in a minor matter. He objected in vain to the first article of the proposal submitted by the committee on arrangements, which "invited" the King to take command of the National Guard and of the other troops sent to the celebration. Du Pont argued that the King, as supreme head of the nation under the constitutional articles already adopted, was automatically head of the National Guard, the *essential* army of France, Du Pont held, since the British principle of a standing army had been rejected. How could the King be "invited" to assume a command which he already had? Du Pont's question was brushed aside and the committee's article was accepted without modification.[51]

The lively debate on the Nootka Sound controversy which had just previously divided the Assembly gave Du Pont an opportunity to formulate his conceptions of the King's prerogatives in issues touching upon war and peace. This controversy arose when Spanish forces seized English ships and ejected English colonists from Nootka Sound on the Pacific Coast of North America within the limits of what is now British Columbia. Upon an English threat of war, Spain called upon France for help under the terms of the Bourbon Family Compact concluded in 1761. Seeing in the conflict nothing more than a possible intrigue on the part of enemies of reform to restore the King's power by drawing France into a foreign war, the deputies of the Left denounced the Compact and sought to reserve to the Assembly the sole right of declaring war and of concluding treaties. While he was preparing his major speech on this question, Du Pont tried to induce the Assembly to postpone for three weeks consideration of Alexandre de Lameth's vigorous proposal that the Assembly assert its exclusive right to declare war and to conclude peace.[52] Meanwhile, he urged the necessity of providing armament as nearly equal to that of England as possible in case of war. He had no love for England, which he regarded as a decadent oligarchy. Though they might talk peace, he remarked, the English could never be trusted.[53]

Du Pont stated his position fully on May 19 in a long speech, which was printed by order of the Assembly.[54] He argued that it is necessary to distinguish between offensive and defensive wars. "Offensive war is a crime; nations do not have the right to wage it. A power is not a right; it cannot be delegated to any one, not even to the King." War in defense of territory is a necessity recognized by everyone. In providing immediate measures for defense, however, a nation agitated by public deliberation would be in an evident position of inferiority. Only the executive power can act decisively and rapidly. The King must, therefore, be empowered to act, though he be restricted from declaring war. Treaties can be an effective way of providing for a nation's defense. Du Pont concluded by proposing a decree:

The French nation will not permit any offensive war; it will maintain in all arrangements, different treaties previously contracted; in the case where foreign powers threaten the empire, the King will take all necessary measures, even secretly, but cannot declare war; whenever hostilities begin he will arm the public force and will take action on the basis of reprisals; the King can conclude treaties of peace, if they do not contain any exchange or cession [of territories]; treaties of navigation and of commerce can be made by the King only with the consent and by the special authorization of the legislative body.

These carefully considered viewpoints provide a good example of Du Pont's endeavor to find what he judged to be a position midway

165

between the extremes of Right and Left. The defenders of excessive royal prerogative could not, it is clear, find much comfort in his proposals. With some justice, however, the Left could denounce his views as seeking to preserve too great an amount of initiative to the King. The immediate issue which forced upon the Assembly this acrimonious debate dissipated when the Spanish yielded to English demands after the Assembly refused assistance under the Compact. In a pamphlet remarkable for its comprehensive coverage despite the haste of its composition, Du Pont had defended the Family Compact as a treaty generally favorable to France. He believed that, with a few slight modifications in its original text, it should be maintained.[55] The debate on this issue led the Assembly to put in definitive form the constitutional articles regarding the King's power in war and peace. In general, the victory was won by those supporting the powers of the legislature. The Constitution of 1791 permitted the King to negotiate treaties, which required ratification by the representatives of the people. Furthermore, only the legislature could declare war.[56]

Du Pont's opinions on the type of ministry which the Constitution should provide were in accord with the majority decision. These opinions he pronounced in a speech delivered on October 20, 1790, before the Society of the Friends of the Constitution, now better known as the Jacobins. This society had grown from accretions to the group which in Versailles had formed around the Breton deputies. When the Assembly moved to Paris, it had joined with others to set up meetings in the old convent of the Dominicans on the Rue Saint-Honoré, not far from the Assembly's meeting place. The familiar name of the Dominicans in France (Jacobins) became the name by which the society was identified by contemporaries and by posterity. In its early years the Jacobin Society was a moderate group; only gradually did the trend of events turn it toward the more radical course with which the word *Jacobin* is more often associated. Du Pont seems to have maintained some sort of tenuous connection with the Jacobins, among whom were many of his acquaintances. He had little time to attend meetings of any kind outside the Assembly, however, and his presence at the meeting of October 20 was unusual, especially in view of the fact that for months he had been more interested in another group known as the Society of 1789, which had split away from the Jacobins. The issue under debate that day had aroused heated controversy, since it concerned an attempt of a large minority in the Assembly to pass a resolution expressing lack of confidence in the Ministry. Du Pont had been accused of evading the issue by leaving the Assembly meeting, and he was determined to make his view known.[57] He may, therefore, have chosen the Jacobin rostrum as a suitable one from which to put himself irretrievably on record. So that there could be no doubt left he went further by having his speech printed and distributed to the deputies of the Assembly.[58]

The Constitution did not, Du Pont noted in his speech, give France a *responsible* ministry in the English meaning of the term. Members of the Assembly—or any other French citizens for that matter—can state to the King that such and such a minister no longer merits confidence because he has done a *specific* wrong. The King has, however, the only real power over the Ministry. He selects and dismisses the ministers. The reason for this arrangement is that the French Assembly cannot, like the English Parliament, be dismissed by the King for an appeal to the people. Hence, it would be dangerous to give to such an Assembly control over the Ministry, because the Assembly might act contrary to the will of the people. That the Assembly is empowered to accuse and punish individual ministers guilty of proved wrongdoing is sufficient control. Furthermore, the decision of the Assembly to prohibit its members from accepting posts in the Ministry is a wise one, since it removes the possibility of ambitious intrigues. All these comments are, of course, consistent with Du Pont's constant effort to prevent legislative tyranny. He seldom found himself so completely in agreement with the constitutional decrees of the Constituent Assembly. In aligning himself on the side of those opposed to the selection of ministers from the ranks of the legislature, he widened the breach with his old friend Mirabeau, who believed sincerely that real co-operation between executive and legislative powers was possible only if the King chose ministers from the legislature, as was done in England. Mirabeau was here on ground more solid than that of Du Pont, but had been defeated on this issue a year earlier because too many feared that his proposal was a device to further his own ambitions to obtain a ministerial post.

Du Pont's views on the matter of eligibility for voting and for election to office were not the prevailing ones. In conformity with his long-held conviction, he tried on October 22, 1789, to persuade the Assembly that only proprietors should be electors, because they alone are concerned with the real problems of society. To qualify as an elector and to eligible for election to office were, in his opinion, two different matters. To be eligible for election "the only question is to know if one seems to have sufficient qualities in the eyes of the electors."[59] In practice, Du Pont could probably have reconciled himself to the restriction adopted by the Assembly. The amount of tax payments required to be chosen as elector might well assure that the electors would be proprietors, or would at least be sympathetic to the interests of property. He refused, however, to be content with the provisions which would demand the same requirements of eligibility for election to office as for the right to elect. On October 28, he restated his position on the question of eligibility for election. One must assume, he said, that electors are mature and responsible individuals. The only eligibility for election should be, therefore, to appear to the electors to be capable of handling their affairs. If a person did not pay taxes equal to the income of six days' work, would it necessarily follow that he could not have such qualities?[60] The Assembly was unmoved by his objection. Du Pont's independent judgment had, on this issue, brought him to a position which was somewhat more liberal than that of the Assembly. It is, however, a position consistent with his regard for the stability and the intelligence of the type of electorate which he envisaged.

The final debates on the Constitution in 1791 took place after an incident which undermined the stability of the new order and cast doubt upon the Constitution itself. On June 20, 1791, Louis XVI attempted to escape with his family to the frontier. This action had long been urged upon him by those who believed that the Revolution was the prelude to chaos. Only thus, they argued, could the King regain freedom of action, rally around him all Frenchmen who opposed violent change, and appeal effectively for help from outside of France. The Comte d'Artois, who had left France after the King's capitulation on July 17, and other noble émigrés had been attempting to stir up foreign intervention but had met with little success. Louis had persistently rejected the counsels to flee from his people and his kingdom. Now he listened to them and authorized the laying of plans for escape, because his continued participation in the Revolution seriously troubled his conscience. In April he was prevented by a crowd of Parisians from leaving for Saint Cloud to make his Easter confession to a priest who had not taken the oath prescribed by the Civil Constitution of the Clergy. Pope Pius VI had just publicly condemned this thoroughgoing reform of the Church in France. Another vital consideration had, therefore, been forced upon the King's mind—the salvation of his immortal soul. It was easier now for the Queen to gain his consent for her intimate friend, the Swedish Count Hans Axel de Fersen, to draw up plans for flight. The one man who might have dissuaded him from this disastrous course, the Comte de Mirabeau, who had been secretly on the King's payroll since the previous spring, was no more. This strong and dissolute life had come unexpectedly to an end early in April.

Fersen planned carefully but could not overcome all human miscalculation. The Royal Family was successfully spirited out of the Tuileries and set on the road late at night on June 20. The coach fell behind schedule, however, and the military detachments stationed along the way to escort the King became restless and withdrew, believing that the plans had been changed. The King was recognized and, at Varennes, so close to the frontier—and yet so far from it—was halted, and forced eventually to turn back to Paris. News of the flight caused consternation in the Assembly. For a brief moment many believed that the only solution now was to depose the King and proclaim the Republic. Indeed, Du Pont upheld this view in a gathering at the house of La Rochefoucauld on June 21.[61] He must have been shaken to the depths of his being by this desertion of the King. If he put his thoughts on paper at this time, he must not have preserved the document, since nothing can be found among his available papers. The thought of deposing the King was so foreign to his mind that, if he did entertain it briefly, he soon rejected it, as did most of his associates. The better solution lay in denying that the King had tried to escape and in attempting to strengthen the position of the Monarch in the new Constitution. Unless this effort were made, an important bastion against extreme radicalism would fall. The only hope of the moderates, it seemed, was to co-operate with the Right against the Left. The radicals could now be bolder. Demands for the Republic were heard for the first time in the meetings of the Jacobins. Du Pont was soon listed among those who sought to absolve the King in order to halt the turn to radical measures.[62] But the flight to Varennes could not be forgotten. It weakened the Constitution of 1791 before it was officially proclaimed in full, though many of its provisions had, of course, been earlier put into operation.

Du Pont was an active participant in the debates preceding the final passage of the articles of the Constitution. He criticized several specific parts, but did not succeed in effecting any changes. On August 9, 1791, he tried in vain to add an additional article to the Preamble, the Declaration of the Rights of Man and of the Citizen, guaranteeing to "all members of society, if they are needy or ill, [the] right to free assistance from their fellow-citizens" and to alter the wording of article 14 to give to citizens "the right to regulate, to determine taxation" rather than "the right of consenting" to it.[63] He next suggested a complete revision of the Preamble and here restated clearly an important tenet of his political philosophy. "It is necessary," he said, "that the *Declaration of Rights*, which is the real constitutional act, for all the rest is only the commentary of it—it is necessary that it have imperious brevity; it is necessary that it have philosophic clarity; it is necessary that it have profundity of ideas and exactness of expression. I ask you to reread it, and you will see that it lacks many of these things."[64] The Assembly could see no wisdom in revising a document already famous in its original form.

The day before, during a discussion of rural laws, Du Pont had expressed even more clearly his conviction that fundamental law could always be simply stated because its principles were universal. "It has always been said," he remarked, "that [general rural laws] were incompatible with the localities, habits, prejudices, [and] privilege of the different parts of the realm. It will be easy to show you that the principles of laws are extremely simple; that they are applicable everywhere. Rural laws like all other laws have no other bases than the common rights of men; one can reduce them to a very small number of laws which carry with them everywhere liberty and respect for property."[65]

Except for his objection to the cumbersome method of amendment provided for in Titre VII,[66] none of his other contributions to the debate is significant.[67] He was obviously not completely satisfied with the Constitution but gave no evidence then of the foresight which, years later, he claimed to have shared with other members of the Assembly. "You have woven the fabric of a republic," these far-sighted delegates are reported to have told their colleagues; "you wish to embroider a monarchy upon it; the needle will break, and you risk wearing out the stuff."[68]

More substantial than Du Pont's accomplishments in the general debates on the Constitution were those carried out in the Committee on the Constitution, of which he was an adjunct member. Few of his ideas on the type of government to be established under the Constitution were accepted, but his contributions to the reorganizing of the governmental subdivisions within France were notable. He was temporarily added to the Committee for the specific purpose of assisting in the division of the realm. He prepared, delivered, and defended a large number of the Committee reports on this matter. This responsibility required attention to intricate, seemingly infinite, details. Here again Du Pont displayed not only a considerable knowledge of the political and economic geography of France but an amazing capacity for work of a tedious nature. Perhaps his outstanding achievement was his defense of the plan to make Paris a separate department,[69] but he was very busy in delineating districts elsewhere.[70] To his son Irénée, he wrote on January 12, 1790, "What you saw of my fatigue was nothing compared to that which results from this division of the Provinces into Departments and Districts."[71] One estimate suggests that Du Pont was responsible for about one-third of the divisions of the Kingdom into departments and districts.[72] There is no firm basis for confirming or denying this estimate.

Du Pont's name appears later on many of the reports and decrees of the Committee on the Alienation of the National Domain.[73] Most of these reports reflect the tedious labor involved in compiling figures on land valuation, a kind of task for which Du Pont's demonstrated tenacity and patience would have fitted him. Here also there is, however, no way to determine how much of the committee work he did himself.

He was an obvious choice for membership on the Committee of Agriculture and Commerce, established by the Assembly on September 2, 1789. He was a landowner interested in practical agricultural problems, a Physiocrat long concerned with the theoretical position of agriculture in a nation's economy, and an Inspector General of Commerce with years of experience in government service. Because of this background, he could be "called to render double service to the committee."[74] He served as its *secrétaire adjoint* from September 7 to December 7, 1789.[75] His activity on this important committee was, however, to decrease noticeably in succeeding months. Most of his time outside the Assembly meetings and his government office came to be devoted to the heavy duties which he assumed in the reorganization of the taxes. Indeed, most of his reports before the Committee of Agriculture and Commerce were concerned directly or indirectly with his work on the taxes. Except for these financial tasks and the additional duties in the redistricting of France, he would undoubtedly have been an eager participant in all committee discussion. The *procès-verbal* of the committee shows, however, that he was present at only forty of the 258 meetings held between September 2, 1789, and September 23, 1791, and that he spoke at some length only about six times, usually in reporting on specific proposals regarding the replacement of indirect taxes.[76]

A bare mention of a few of the other matters, aside from finances, upon which Du Pont expressed opinions in the sessions of the Constituent Assembly will immediately display both the tremendous range of his interests and also one of his most serious errors. Undoubtedly, he talked too much on too many subjects, on many of which he could claim no special knowledge. He spread himself too thin, and frequently found the Assembly in no way influenced by his remarks. Concerning the annexation of Avignon and the Comtat Venaissin, Papal enclave within France, Du Pont advised caution, seeking to arrange for a fair plebiscite which could show the real desires of the inhabitants.[77] Although a plebiscite was agreed upon, the measures taken by the Assembly were, in general, sterner than those desired by Du Pont.[78] After his earlier labors on behalf of the freedom of the port of Bayonne, he naturally fought a proposal to end this freedom in order to destroy contraband trade. He argued on November 5, 1790, that the evil of ending free trade would outweigh the possible good of destroying the small contraband trade. Here he was successful in having indefinitely postponed consideration of the report of the Committee of Agriculture and Commerce which had raised the question.[79] A long speech and proposed decree on mines, presented on March 28, 1791, revealed Du Pont's defense of private property rights and his opposition to monopolistic concessions. He supported the right of a proprietor to mine his own land, but the Assembly finally approved Mirabeau's more stringent proposal which put coal, pyrites, and other minerals at the disposition of the nation, requiring special concessions to mine them, with the proprietor of surface land to be favored if he desired concessions.[80] On May 8, 1790, Du Pont spoke fruitlessly against André's amendment which would exclude from an administrative or judicial post in the government of Paris any member of the National Assembly until four years after the end of the Assembly. Such self-denying ordinances he regarded as unjust. "Surely," he remarked, "there is hardly a career where one can show oneself in a manner more advantageous to his fellow-citizens than that to which we have been called."[81]

These comments by no means exhaust the list of subjects to which Du Pont directed his attention. Except for financial matters later to be considered, only one other question merits specific treatment—Du Pont's part in the attempted settlement of the difficult problem regarding the position of Negroes in the French colonies. There was little sentiment among the deputies in favor of freeing the Negro slaves. Although he should have favored emancipation in accordance with views which he earlier expressed, Du Pont did not fight for it in the Assembly. His only pertinent comment was offered on May 21, 1791, as part of the instructions to the colonies, which he had been charged to draw up. Then he commended the "beneficent" project of the Spanish reformer, Count Floridablanca, by which Negro slaves might gradually purchase their freedom over a period of fifteen to twenty years.[82] More spirited debate arose over the rights of free colored people in the colonies. In its proposed decree, adopted by the Assembly on March 8, 1790, the Committee on Colonies, with Barnave as its chief spokesman, had attempted a compromise on the points at issue. The sense of this decree was to appease the Right by excluding any movement, even a gradual one, toward the suppression of slavery and to appeal to the Left by according full political rights to free colored people. Neither side was satisfied, but victory on the question of slavery encouraged the supporters of the white colonists to further efforts. Eventually they achieved complete success.

When one of the colonial assemblies in Santo Domingo declared its complete independence to legislate on the status of persons within its jurisdiction regardless of decrees of the National Assembly, the Left was able on October 12, 1790, to force passage of a resolution declaring this action illegal, disbanding the rebellious colonial assembly, authorizing the formation of a new one, and threatening the use of troops to restore order. But Barnave and the Colonial Committee had been won over to the side of the white colonists, and recommended that the Assembly pass laws on the status of persons in the colonies only upon the express request of the colonial assemblies. These circumstances set the stage for a great debate leading to another attempt at compromise.

Du Pont assumed a significant role in this debate. On May 13, 1791, he tried to force the Assembly to indicate clearly its stand regarding colored people. He reminded the Assembly of the great principles which guided it, principles which demanded the extension of political rights to free colored people. He faced directly the argument of the Right that the colonies might seek independence: "Do not fear the separation of our colonies. If it should take place, if you find yourselves in the pressing necessity of sacrificing either justice or humanity, I should say that your sole influence [must] tend toward justice; that, if you abandon this base, then you endanger the safety of much of the famous work which you have done for humanity; and that thus your interest, [the interest] of Europe, that of the world requires that you will not hesitate in the sacrifice of a colony rather than of a principle." He argued, however, that there was little to fear in any movement for colonial independence. The colonies would hardly go over to England, as some said, because England not only would be unable to furnish products needed by the colonists but also would regulate them much more strictly. Colonists probably would not be happy in a state of independence because it would cost them more to protect themselves than to enjoy the protection which France gave them. Even if they did remain independent, he concluded, they could hardly alter trade relations with France since their economic needs would be unchanged.[83]

The compromise decree of May 15, 1791, did, however, concede a point to the Right. The Assembly promised that the *Corps Législatif* would grant political rights only to colored people born of free fathers and mothers.[84] Nevertheless, the decree was so obnoxious to the colonial deputies that they ostentatiously withdrew from the Assembly. The next day Du Pont asserted that the Assembly had been more than just to the colonists, and supported the motion of Regnaud that specific instructions be sent with the decree to the colonies.[85] He was thereupon charged with the responsibility for drawing up such instructions.

Though he could hardly have agreed with the action of the Assembly, Du Pont prepared instructions of such a conservative nature that they were subsequently ordered revised by a special committee of four. They contained this statement: "[The Assembly] recognizes that the men charged with the labor of cultivation in the colonies are, by the defect of their intelligence and by their expatriation, in a state of prolonged minority which seems to require that the protection of the law be modified toward them, as toward children, by the immediate authority of the government of the family, and which seems to necessitate admission in the colonial constitution of some exceptions to general principles."

It is not easy to excuse Du Pont for an apparent departure from the general principles which he had so stirringly recalled in his speech just one week before. The instructions do assert that, under prevailing law, free colored people should be eligible to vote for colonial assemblies. They add, however, that the Assembly yields to the will of the colonists to have an intermediate class of persons enjoying civil but not full political rights. This status would be a sort of apprenticeship for full citizenship, and would comprise manumitted slaves and free colored men born of slave mothers.[86] Extensive revisions left in the final draft of the instructions only a few paragraphs of Du Pont's original work. Although most conciliatory towards the colonial white population, the final draft did reiterate article 4 of a decree of March 28, 1791, which stated that "without exception . . . every free person, proprietor or resident for two years, and *taxable,* will enjoy the right of suffrage which constitutes the quality of active citizen."[87] Although this decree of May 15, 1791, was not repealed, it had no effect, because the colonists refused to obey it and the Assembly found no alternative to passive acquiescence. Sagnac succinctly remarks: "The National Assembly was powerless to suppress inequalities of race in distant lands where it could not sustain its decrees by armed force. In the struggle between principles and realities, realities were the stronger."[88] The disappointed hopes of the colonial colored people, slave and free, led later to serious insurrections in the colonies.

While engaging in these heavy public duties, Du Pont found that the Revolution also brought important changes in his private life. It cost him almost the whole of his income from governmental positions. If personal sacrifice is a mark of the true patriot, Du Pont should eminently qualify for the title. During the period of the "patriotic gifts," he relinquished the salary of 8,000 francs, which he received as custodian of foreign laws relating to commerce and tariffs, while continuing to perform the duties.[89] A year later, he wrote to the Committee on Pensions, returning also the special allowance or "pension of four thousand francs that was given me in 1776 by Monsieur de Maurepas . . . because I accept the principle that no one should have both a position and a pension."[90]

Although he thus surrendered a large part of his own income, Du Pont was most assiduous in his efforts to obtain governmental pensions for deserving friends. At least twice he championed the cause of Madame Poivre, widow of his good friend, the former intendant of the Ile de France, and succeeded also in furthering the claims of the noted mathematician, Lagrange, also his friend.[91]

It was on a matter connected with pensions that Du Pont experienced his greatest difficulty in controlling the Assembly during his first day as president. This honor, accorded to no fewer than forty-eight deputies for brief terms of two weeks under the rules of the Assembly, fell to Du Pont on August 16, 1790.[92] On that day, a letter from Necker was read to the Assembly over the protests of several deputies. Necker questioned the wisdom of leaving the matter of pensions up to the legislative body and thus, in his view, weakening the Government. As president, Du Pont took a vote on whether to ignore the letter or to send it to the Committee on

Pensions. When he announced the majority vote in favor of the latter proposal, he was faced by loud and prolonged protest from many deputies to the effect that the question had been badly put to them, that they did not understand it, and that they had meant to vote to ignore the letter. Probably considering them only agents of disorder, which he detested, Du Pont dealt with them so brusquely that he did not succeed in restoring order.[93] The entire meeting was wasted. Although he was faced by no similar outburst, Du Pont cannot be considered a success as presiding officer. But he was not the only one to fail at this exacting task; keeping order in this Assembly overtaxed the powers of many presiding officers.

During Du Pont's term as president on August 24, 1790, the King celebrated the fête of his patron saint, St. Louis. In honor of the day, the Assembly authorized its president to head a delegation of forty-eight to wait upon the King. Du Pont's brief but carefully prepared speech to the King was very formal, but perhaps at least partly sincere, since loyalty to the Monarch was still the sentiment of the overwhelming majority of Frenchmen. In somewhat exaggerated terms, Du Pont compared Louis XVI favorably with St. Louis: the former had completed the task of destroying feudalism, a task which the latter had begun.[94] The King replied formally that he was sincerely touched by the sentiments expressed and that he flattered himself of being assured of the affection of the people by his constant concern for their happiness and by his confidence in their representatives.

Without breaking openly with the Jacobins, a group of moderate deputies around Lafayette, among whom Du Pont was numbered, organized on April 13, 1790, the Society of 1789.[95] While personal ambitions and factional fights within the Jacobin Society probably contributed to the formation of this new Society of 1789,[96] it did bring together a group of reformers who were troubled by the fear that change might go too far. Some were undoubtedly interested in holding reform at the point which would most likely benefit their own interests. Others, like Du Pont, were primarily concerned with maintaining orderly change. With no past tradition of gradual and peaceful reform upon which to rely, they were sincerely disturbed by the thought that too violent a rupture with the past might lead to chaos along uncharted ways. While desiring reform, they tended

177

to rally around the King as the surest tie with the past. Alarmed by certain radical tendencies of some of the Jacobins, men with these convictions withdrew to organize their own societies. Bailly, Mirabeau, Roederer, Le Chapelier, Talleyrand, La Rochefoucauld, Duquesnoy, André, Sieyès, and the Chéniers (André and Joseph) were other charter members of the Society of 1789. Pledged to King and Constitution, the Society grew in size as it attracted reformers of various degrees of moderation. It never aspired to become a really popular society, since it had a membership fee higher than that of the Jacobins and limited its membership to six hundred. It was frequently denounced by radical revolutionaries as a close-knit club of men of substance opposed to the will of the common people. It maintained rather sumptuous clubrooms in the Palais Royal and organized elaborate banquets for members and invited guests. The old Corsican patriot, Pasquale Paoli, was the honored guest at one such banquet.[97] Du Pont inscribed his sons, Victor and Irénée, as well as himself on the membership rolls of the Society.[98]

The Society published a periodical, the *Journal de la société de 1789*, edited by Gouvello and Condorcet, with the collaboration of De Pange and André Chénier. The *Journal*, made up principally of rather long and carefully composed articles, was more a review than a newspaper. In the fourth of the fifteen numbers published, a speech which Du Pont had delivered before the Society was printed by its order on June 26, 1790. Under the title *Considérations sur la position politique de la France, de l'Angleterre et de l'Espagne*, Du Pont's discourse was a denunciation of England's efforts to break the Family Compact during the Nootka Sound conflict. While recommending negotiation and mediation, he called for vigorous action on the part of France if England did not halt apparent preparations for war against Spain.[99] The *Journal* ceased publication after its fifteenth number (September 15, 1790), but the Society may have continued to exert some control over public opinion through other periodicals.[100] Whatever influence it may have had, however, declined markedly after the King's flight to Varennes. Moderate opinions linking King *and* Constitution were put more and more on the defensive. The more active defense provided by the *Feuillants* attracted many of its members, with the result that the Society of 1789 disappeared toward the end of 1791.

The Constituent Assembly (1789-1791)

This somewhat random description of Du Pont's miscellaneous activities during the period of the *Constituante* will, perhaps, offer support for some tentative generalizations on his personal viewpoints and conduct. Clearly he must be numbered among the most moderate of the reformers who wished to place a definite limit to the contemplated alterations in the French Government and society. Nothing beyond what is obviously necessary—this thought seemed to guide him. To go farther would merely substitute another species of arbitrariness for the one destroyed. Universal principles, not human desires and ambitions, should prevail. Such universal principles are capable of concise expression in a Declaration of Rights, which is really the fundamental constitutional document of any government. To safeguard rights a strong executive is indispensable. The tyranny of a legislature must be feared as much as the tyranny of a monarch, if not more. Dignity and order must prevail inside and outside the National Assembly, and popular demonstrations should be denounced and suppressed as the results of the evil intentions and actions of a few ambitious and dangerous demagogues. Government should be for, but not by, the "people."

Du Pont's multifarious activities display certain personal characteristics. Obviously, he had a tremendous capacity for work, which he never tried to avoid. He showed unqualified willingness to sacrifice himself to the important tasks demanded by the Nation. This sacrifice extended even to relinquishing a substantial portion of his income. He was intensely patriotic in furthering the interests of France as he saw them, even (as in the Nootka Sound affair) to the point of war. He had a high conception of the mission to which the deputies of the National Assembly had been called. He displayed courage in defending his ideas even in the face of attacks upon his wisdom and integrity. He had a strong conviction that he would ultimately be justified. His physiocratic conceptions may be discerned in many of his expressed viewpoints—the belief in universal laws, the support of a strong executive, the desire for a restricted electorate of proprietors, the solicitude for agriculture, the defense of free trade. It was, however, in the work more strictly concerned with public finance that his physiocratic training was most evident. There a final characteristic already evident in other connections is displayed—Du Pont's undoctrinaire willingness to compromise, to

179

accept the possible, if his vigorous fight for principles, for what he conceived to be desirable, had failed. His long experience in practical administration, and, perhaps, his reverence for Turgot, had undoubtedly tempered his judgment, and kept him from blind and stubborn insistence upon a set of theoretical postulates.

Chapter VI

Finances in the Constituent Assembly

THE OCCASION FOR CONVOKING the Estates General, the immediate issue which gave to the Third Estate the opportunity to wedge open the gateway to reform, was, of course, the hopeless state of public finances. The Constituent Assembly was, however, in no hurry to attempt a sound solution of this difficulty. Indeed, it never did achieve a sound solution. Many of its financial measures soon proved inadequate, and were largely swept aside by the current of events. Such a bald statement of fact needs some qualification. Most members of the Assembly could not, of course, foresee the chaotic times ahead and were content to design their program for a period of normal readjustment. Moreover, some of their work did endure, especially the destruction of much of the old fiscal system and the creation of a new type of direct taxation.

There were reasons for the general failure of the Constituent Assembly to solve the financial problem. Foremost among them, perhaps, was the inexperience of almost all its members in the field of public finances. "Do you think our finances would not have been administered better, more prudently, more economically, since the opening of the States General," asked one of the members in 1791, "if we had then possessed the experience which we have acquired?"[1] Du Pont was one of the few who might claim the right to speak with some authority on financial questions.[2] For some reformers the wretched condition of the Treasury seemed to be the strongest weapon at their disposal. They saw no wisdom in destroying this weapon by attempting at once to improve the financial situation; rather they would first use it to effect necessary reforms. Others

181

believed sincerely that finances were secondary to the great work of formulating a constitution. The resignation of Necker in September, 1790, removed an experienced hand from the Finance Ministry. It is true that he hardly deserved his earlier reputation and that he had come more and more to be regarded with suspicion by many deputies of the Assembly; nevertheless, his departure left the Ministry in the hands of less experienced, if not less able, men. Furthermore, continuity of policy was made more difficult by frequent changes. Necker was succeeded by Lambert, who served only three months. Delessart followed for five and a half months, and Tarbé held the office during the remaining four and a half months of the Assembly session. Changes in all the ministerial posts were frequent. Of all the former ministers only Montmorin in the Foreign Ministry retained his post throughout the period of the Constituent Assembly.[3]

It was less difficult to destroy the complicated, inefficient, and inequitable fiscal order of the ancien régime than it was to erect in its stead a new system adequate to the needs of the Government. By one of its earliest actions the Constituent Assembly had wrought even more disorder in the collection of public revenues. Its first "decree," proposed by Target and Le Chapelier on June 17, 1789, had proclaimed "all existing taxes illegal, as not sanctioned by the consent of the people, and therefore null and void in their creation, extension and propagation." Although the decree went on to declare that "the National Assembly provisionally and unanimously consents on behalf of the nation that [existing taxes] may continue to be levied as heretofore until the first separation of the Assembly, on and from which date the Assembly decrees that all taxes not expressly, formally, and freely accorded by it shall entirely cease in all Provinces of the kingdom, howsoever administered," many Frenchmen were happily convinced that former taxes had been abolished and immediately ceased further payments. To reassure and to gain the support of the powerful body of public creditors, this decree added that the Assembly, "as soon as it shall have fixed in concert with his Majesty, the principles of national regeneration, will occupy itself with the examination and consolidation of the public debt, and hereby places the creditors of the state under the protection of the honor and loyalty of the French nation."[4] The habit of not paying taxes

182

was easily extended in many cases to the new taxes decreed by the Constituent Assembly. The difficulty experienced in collecting taxes was, therefore, another of the serious financial handicaps faced by the new rulers of France.

The widespread dissatisfaction with, and even hatred toward, the old taxes provide sufficient explanations of why so many people joyously welcomed an excuse to stop paying them. However inadequate, they still brought in a revenue essential to the Government in its financial distress. To erase them from the statute books in one burst of revolutionary ardor before providing reasonable substitutes could never be judged the course of wise statesmanship..

There were three principal direct taxes (*impositions*) levied during the ancien régime: the *taille*, the *capitation*, and the *vingtième*.[5] The *taille*, an old feudal tax diverted to the Royal Treasury in the fifteenth century, was generally of two types. The *taille réele*, levied mostly in the *pays d'états* by the provincial estates rather than by the central Government, was assessed against the value of real property. Noble land was generally exempt. The *taille personelle*, a much more complicated tax usually levied in the *pays d'élections* (where there were no provincial estates) by the central Government, was assessed directly upon the individual, allowing some vague consideration of his ability to pay. Generally, the clergy and the nobility were exempt. Throughout the ancien régime, the number of *taillables*, those subject to the tax, continually decreased.[6] The method of collection led often to serious inequities. The Royal Council usually determined the gross amount of the *taille personelle* to be collected in each fiscal year; then it apportioned this amount among the *généralités*, *élections*, and parishes. This apportionment was hardly equitable, since frequently accident—or custom—ruled, and some localities were assessed much more than others of similar size and population. In each parish collectors were chosen, theoretically by popular vote but actually by the intendant in most cases; their task was to assess and to collect the tax in their parish. Although these collectors were commonly permitted to retain as recompense for their unpopular labors 2.5 to 5 per cent of the amount collected, many of them were ruined in the process. No sensible person sought election to the office of collector, because he would almost certainly be exposed to "endless bickerings and disputes, lawsuits and appeals."[7] Turgot had succeeded in suppressing the *contrainte solidaire,* by which delinquents were imprisoned and the wealthiest inhabitants made corporately liable for the whole *taille* of the parish, even though they had met their own payments. In the words of a pronouncement of the Constituent Assembly, this most hated of the taxes was responsible for "a negligence, a deprivation and an insalubrity in the majority of rural dwellings, most injurious to the comfort and even to the preservation of the tillers of the soil."[8] Well known is the touching story of Rousseau concerning the peasant who hid his little hoard and lived wretchedly through fear of the tax collector.[9] Although no completely satisfactory estimate can be made, the revenue from the *taille* has been figured at around ninety-one million livres on the eve of the Revolution.[10]

The *capitation,* a complicated combination of a poll tax and an income tax, dated from 1695, when it was first established during the War of the League of Augsburg. Suppressed after the Peace of Ryswick (1698), it was renewed in 1701 upon the outbreak of the War of the Spanish Succession, and, like many emergency war taxes, was destined to be maintained.[11] Under the system of assessment, also the cause of endless disputes, the inhabitants of the kingdom were divided into twenty-two classes according to their supposed ability to pay. The classes ranged from the Dauphin alone in the first class to common, unskilled laborers in the last class. As a rule of thumb, the apportionment was made usually according to the *taille personelle,* or, if no *taille* were paid, according to the public office or military rank held, or the business or profession practiced by the taxpayer. In theory, but often in theory only, the very poor were exempt. The clergy gained exemption from this tax until 1789 by granting a lump sum of twenty-four million livres in 1709. Most of the nobility and wealthier bourgeoisie escaped it by evasion. The revenue from the *capitation* has been estimated at more than fifty-six million livres by 1789.[12]

The *vingtième* ("twentieth"), theoretically a 5 per cent tax on incomes, also dated from periods of warfare. First imposed as a *dixième* ("tenth") by Louis XIV in 1710, it was abolished in 1717, renewed under Louis XV from 1733 to 1737 (War of the Polish Succession) and again from 1741 to 1749 (War of the Austrian

Succession). In 1749 it was made permanent at one *vingtième* and two sols the livre. A second *vingtième* was imposed in 1756, and a third from 1760 to 1763 (Seven Years' War) and from 1782 to 1786. Although the rate varied, it was, thus, more than a twentieth, or 5 per cent. The usual rate was probably closer to 11 per cent from 1756 on, increasing to around 16 per cent during the periods of the third *vingtième*. Because the tax was originally based upon property valuation and income declared by the taxpayer, the *vingtième* more closely approached a modern tax than any other assessment of the ancien régime. Decrees regulating the tax did not, however, succeed in preventing false declarations or in providing for upward readjustments based upon increased property valuation or income. Du Pont had castigated inequities in the assessment of the *vingtièmes* in the Nemours *cahier*.[13] Despite the facts that the clergy was generally exempt, that the types of income varied to the point of confusion, and that the nobility often escaped payment, this tax has been called one of the "most correct and least evil" of the impositions of the prerevolutionary period.[14] A rough estimate of its yield for the year 1785 is 2,500,000 livres derived from personal property and 74,000,000 livres from real property.[15]

Of the multiplicity of indirect taxes (*perceptions*) only the most important will be described. For the most part indirect taxes were not collected by the Government, but farmed out to private contractors. Such a system made even worse the prevailing inequities and worked great hardship on the mass of the taxable persons. The general rule was to effect a new contract with the Farmers General every six years. The controller-general of finances concluded an agreement with an individual who really represented a group of sixty rich financiers able to make a substantial advance to the Treasury in return for the privilege of collecting the taxes. It was expected that a good controller-general would seek to drive hard bargains. It might also be expected, as a result, that the Farmers would seek to recoup at the expense of the taxpayers. The complaints in the *cahiers* against the evil system are not to be wondered at.[16] Many criticisms directed against the Farmers General in the last half of the eighteenth century were, nevertheless, not justified. The profession of tax farmer was then an honorable one and enlisted men of unimpeachable probity like Du Pont's friend Lavoisier, the famous chemist.[17]

The most universally hated of the indirect taxes was, perhaps, the salt tax (*gabelle*), an excessively complicated levy. Its replacement was to force Du Pont to the most exacting labor which he performed in the Constituent Assembly. Outside of a special study of some length one cannot expect to do justice to any treatment of it.[18] There was actually a whole series of *gabelles* rather than a single uniform tax, because the realm was divided into six principal districts, each subjected to a type of assessment differing from that of the others. The price of salt, which was fixed, varied widely between districts, a circumstance that naturally encouraged smuggling.

Another type of indirect tax whose replacement or suppression Du Pont sought was the confusing series of excises—*aides* on alcoholic beverages (wine, brandy, cider, etc.) and various *droits* on gold and silverware, steel, iron, paper, playing cards, soaps, oils, starches, etc. Since most of these excise taxes originated in medieval times, there had grown up in the course of centuries the great diversity and inequity which characterized most of the taxes of the ancien régime. There were about twenty-five general *aides* as well as numerous local ones. In the *cahiers* the *aides* rivaled the *gabelle* for the reputation as the most burdensome assessment. One of the most forceful attacks is in the "Instructions" which Du Pont composed for the guidance of the Chevannes delegates to the electoral assembly at Nemours.[19] A similar complexity surrounded the *droits* on many products.[20] Regardless of the opinion one may hold about the quality of Du Pont's labors, one must respect the courage and determination of a man who would plunge into the intricate maze to find the path to uniform and equitable fiscal policy. It seemed an almost hopeless task, since the problem could not be solved simply by suppressing all such duties; it was necessary to figure the revenue yielded by them and to arrange some substitution which would not cripple the Treasury.

Somewhat similar to those *aides* which applied to the transport of goods were the *octrois*, generally duties on food collected at the entrance of many cities, and the *traites*, tolls levied for the benefit of municipal or ecclesiastical corporations, or of nobles, upon goods passing across the borders of their properties. The distinction between one type of duty and another was often merely a matter of legal definition or tradition. In the eyes of many, including Du Pont, they were only devices for restricting trade and for raising the cost of necessities. Still their yield was important for the general and local treasuries, and any attack on them ran afoul of the vested interests. Finally, the tobacco monopoly received some attention from Du Pont, although he tried to work out no general plan for revision. The entire tax system was subjected to such frequent attacks that, despite the financial exigencies, the Assembly was forced eventually to take action. Especially in the matter of indirect taxes, Du Pont did most of the work. In his own judgment he expended his most important efforts in that task.[21]

Du Pont served on the Committee of Public Taxation and on the Committee of Finances,[22] as well as on several smaller special committees concerned with financial questions. Among the latter were the Committee of Twelve to consult daily with the Minister of Finance[23] and the committee to study the operations of the Bank of Discount (Caisse d'escompte).[24] His labors were apparently highly regarded by the members of the Committee of Finances, for, on October 1, 1789, when the committee was divided into four sections, Du Pont was placed in the fourth section, which had the difficult and important responsibility of resolving disputed questions.[25] Yet the *procès-verbaux* of the meetings of the committee do not convey an impression of exceptional activity on Du Pont's part. In the 262 meetings covered, Du Pont is mentioned in the *procès-verbaux* of only twenty-nine, and he seems to have spoken only in sixteen.[26] The accounts of the meetings of the Constituent Assembly are a more accurate gauge of his exertions. There he is seen rendering numerous reports and making frequent remarks and speeches. Obviously a great deal of his detailed work was done in private study and in informal conferences. Except for his opposition to the assignats, his labors on financial matters seem generally to have been favorably regarded by the Assembly.

The device adopted by the Constituent Assembly for retiring the accumulated debt was, as is well known, the confiscation of the lands of the Church. The origin of this solution is not so well known, but it was not a sudden inspiration of a few members of the Assembly. There is a long history of the secularization of church property in

187

Europe,[27] and such secularization had occurred in Catholic France. The property of nine religious orders suppressed during the reign of Louis XV had been taken over by the Government. Calonne had looked with favor upon the idea of confiscation during his ministry, and a few of the *cahiers* had suggested it.[28] Although Talleyrand, who had been named Bishop of Autun late in 1788, is often credited with bringing the Constituent Assembly around to the idea of confiscation, he was certainly not the first to suggest it. During the debates after the famous night of August 4-5 leading to the formulation of the decree of August 11, Buzot, on August 6, and the Marquis de Lacoste, on August 8, both maintained that church property belonged to the nation. Alexander de Lameth supported Lacoste's argument that church property could be used as collateral in satisfying government creditors.[29] Although Du Pont was not the first speaker, therefore, to mention the idea in the Assembly, he was the first to include it in a carefully thought-out financial plan. This he did in a long speech on the financial situation on September 24, 1789, in reply to certain proposals which Necker had just personally presented to the Assembly.[30]

Du Pont specifically criticized as inadequate and impracticable Necker's project for a "voluntary" tax of a quarter of the gross revenue of all taxpayers. There were too few rich proprietors left to raise very much money for the Treasury. The disorders in the provinces had interfered with normal agricultural pursuits, and all proprietors have suffered. "Our rich are poor, our rich lack money, our rich are not paying their debts."[31] Another source of revenue had to be sought, he maintained, and it lay ready at hand: the great wealth of the Church derived from its landed estates. He rehearsed the familiar arguments that, since the Church had ceased to be a separate corporation as a result of the union of the three estates and the decisions of August 4 and August 9, the property which it held no longer had a master and thus reverted to the state. The Church had never had, he indicated, more than a right of usufruct[32] in the property it held and was pledged to use the income from it for the carrying on of "objects of public . . . or private utility" desired by the original endowers. The nation now could take over this property, but on the condition that it provide for all the religious and charitable work of the church previously supported by the income from the property. By various calculations, Du Pont concluded that, after taking over the church wealth and deducting all probable expenses, the nation would have a minimum of forty-eight million livres in revenue and an enormous capital sum in the form of non-usufruct property. Upon this security the Treasury would experience no further difficulty in obtaining favorable loans. As some of the church lands were gradually sold, the accumulated public debt could be retired. His was an essentially moderate proposal, seeking to meet a critical problem without disrupting the work of the Church or oppressing the clergy.[33] Still he believed that the improvement in the financial situation would be sufficiently marked to permit the revision or suppression of many iniquitous indirect taxes like the *gabelle* and the *aides*.

In a proposed decree added to the printed version of his speech[34] but, apparently, not presented orally he spelled out some of the arrangements that would have to be made. The nation would pledge definite amounts of money for the support of church activities, would reorganize the realm into 35,000 equal parishes—seventy dioceses, each with 500 parishes—would suppress collegiate chapters and religious orders, except for the Order of Malta, would reserve houses for those members of suppressed orders who wished to continue communal living, would provide clerical pensions and nontaxable salaries, would arrange for the redemption of the tithes, and then proceed with the sale of clerical estates—except for those of hospitals and colleges. These proposals were not voted as a decree at this time but contain suggestions later incorporated into the Civil Constitution of the Clergy and other clerical legislation. There is no way to measure the influence of these proposals on later decrees of the Assembly. While he clearly had no active part in the most important of them, the Civil Constitution of the Clergy, Du Pont deserves at least some mention in relation to this significant constitutional enactment.[35]

Against any plan for taking over the wealth of the Church the leading spokesmen of the clergy, such as the Abbé Maury and the Archbishop Boisgelin, argued vigorously. Their efforts, including the offer of an advance of 400,000,000 livres raised on the security of church property, were in vain. Bishop Talleyrand's support of the confiscation of the Church's estates in October may have swayed some wavering delegates, but the majority of the Assembly seems to have favored the idea as soon as one was bold enough to suggest it openly. Du Pont's speech of September 24 was still in press when Talleyrand made his move on October 10. Du Pont added a note to the printed version containing his own proposals, claiming that Talleyrand's project did not differ essentially from the one which he had prepared.[36] Whether Du Pont modified, or added to, his own proposals to put them in accord with developing opinion cannot be ascertained from available evidence. Neither Du Pont's nor Talleyrand's specific proposals were adopted in the crucial decree passed by a vote of 568 to 346 on November 2, 1789. Rather it was Mirabeau who formulated the law which placed the ecclesiastical estates at the disposal of the nation, with the guarantee that the nation would provide in a suitable manner for the expenses of worship, for the support of the clergy, and for the relief of the poor.[37]

The taking over of the church lands brought forward the problem of the tithes. As in the case of secular taxes, these church taxes had acquired over the years a complexity of types and were beset by many inequities. Although he had previously attacked their evils and abuses, notably in a *mémoire* read before the Committee of Agriculture in 1785[38] and in the *cahier* of the *Tiers* of Nemours,[39] Du Pont favored a plan to redeem the tithes because he saw no wisdom in depriving the state of a large amount of revenue. This viewpoint he expressed clearly on March 17, 1790, when he agreed with the Abbé de Montesquiou that the Assembly should hasten to work out a system for replacing the tithes. "If you suppress the tithes entirely," he said, "there will remain a frightful gap in the revenues. . . ."[40] On March 25, at the eighty-seventh meeting of the Committee of Finances, he won over the majority of the committee in support of a proposed decree calling for the abolition without redemption of all tithes whose collection required entrance into household gardens, but for the redemption on a progressively increasing scale of all other tithes.[41] The ancient tithes were, however, so universally unpopular that the Assembly decreed their abolition without redemption or replacement. Many delegates regarded Du Pont's stand as inconsistent with his earlier views. Despite some rioting in his own district over the tithe,[42] Du Pont remained firm in his moderate proposals.

No immediate solution to the financial difficulties would result from the confiscation of the ecclesiastical estates if the Treasury were forced to await the revenue available from the sale of the lands. The more practicable course was to use the lands as security for additional loans. Such was the plan favored by Du Pont, and, despite his fear of the consequences, was essentially the plan followed in the first issue of asisgnats. Originally, the assignats were in no true sense paper money, but merely interest-bearing Treasury notes. Many conservative financiers, among whom Du Pont may be numbered, saw in them, however, the first step toward an inflated paper currency. They would have preferred normal borrowing in the form of long-term Treasury bonds. Ever since the failure of John Law's ambitious program early in the reign of Louis XV, many Frenchmen had an intense dread of anything approaching the status of paper money. After 1789, however, political and financial exigencies overcame this dread in the minds of most of the members of the Constituent Assembly.[43]

Du Pont's opposition to the first issue of assignats was not so vigorous as his later stand. This first issue was, after all, to bear interest at 5 per cent, to be reasonably restricted in amount, and to be in large denominations inconvenient for use in normal exchange. The decree authorizing the issue of 400,000,000 livres in assignats was passed on December 19, 1789.[44] Actually, the resort to assignats was only part of the financial scheme established by this decree. The decree created a new institution, the Caisse de l'extraordinaire, in opposition to Necker's proposal to make the Caisse d'escompte a truly national bank. Into this new "extraordinary bank" were to be paid the proceeds of all exceptional taxation, like the patriotic contribution proposed by Necker and approved by the Assembly despite Du Pont's opposition. The principal source of its funds would, however, be the income from the sale of the lands of the Church. Lands to the value of 400,000,000 livres would be sold, and interest-bearing assignats to this amount would be issued against the Caisse de l'extraordinaire. These assignats should first be employed to reimburse the Caisse d'escompte for advances amounting to 170,000,000 livres made to the government. They were also to be given preference as payment in the sale of the confiscated lands and were to be canceled and burnt as they came in as payment for this land.

Unfortunately, this neat scheme was not successful. The Caisse d'escompte was not able to dispose of the assignats transmitted to it, and its own shares and notes continued to depreciate. The sale of land went slowly because prospective purchasers were fearful of the permanent validity of their purchases and because much of the land was still encumbered by debts and obligations, including the tithes upon the redemption of which Du Pont insisted. A practical reason for suppressing them absolutely was, therefore, to stimulate the sale of land. There was no appreciable improvement in the financial situation in the early part of 1790. Du Pont was much concerned. On February 6, he complained that the situation was worse than ever and warned the Assembly that this weakness could ruin the empire which they were trying to save, as it had ruined many others in the past. He urged his colleagues to clear the path to a solution by deciding upon the civil status to be accorded to the clergy, by seeking means to carry on necessary services and activities formerly maintained by the Church, and by finding a way to determine the resources available in the church estates which now belonged to the nation.[45] Three days later he proposed a decree that the Assembly occupy itself continually with financial problems, that it make some definite establishment of the Church, including provision of an honest pension for priests no longer needed, and that it set up a firm financial system. Until committees could report on these matters, the Assembly might proceed with its work on the division of the realm into new units of local government and on the creation of a new judicial system. He suggested that the Assembly meet every day, including Sundays and holidays, until these affairs were attended to.[46] The Assembly ignored the proposal as unnecessary and impracticable in view of previous arrangements adopted for their work.[47]

Eventually, in April, the Assembly approved two methods to alleviate the financial crisis. The first was to relieve the former church lands of most of the encumbrances which turned away private purchasers by authorizing the State to assume the debts of the clergy and all expenses of public worship. The second was to make assignats more attractive by giving them status as legal tender and by decreasing the interest. Reduction in the interest rate would tend, it was hoped, to make investors less eager to hold on to their assignats instead of exchanging them for land. Against the second measure Du Pont entered a vain protest.

Since the assignats were used to pay off the State debt, a reduction in the interest rate could only be regarded, Du Pont asserted, as a partial repudiation or bankruptcy. Besides it should be obvious that an assignat was only a promise to pay; it was not an actual payment. It was a dangerous delusion to think that the debt could thus be retired. "Payments cannot take place until the sale [of land upon which assignats are based] will be carried out." The proposal to make assignats paper money in place of the bills of the Caisse d'escompte would have disastrous consequences. During the period required for disposing of the lands, this paper money would inevitably decline in value in relation to metallic money. Sellers of goods were already charging higher prices because of the fear of a depreciated paper. Foreign merchants were being driven out of the market because of the prevailing uncertainty of prices. Really, the Assembly was just wasting time by indulging in unwarranted hopes and unsound measures. Du Pont proposed that it seek the solution in a definite financial plan. It should decree that it would authorize the use of assignats only for specific purposes, and that it would examine the possibility of establishing one or more banks where assignats might be exchanged at face value for specie. The Assembly should furthermore fix exactly the amount of annual expenditures and the list of properties standing as mortgages for the assignats.[48]

The majority of the Assembly brushed aside Du Pont's arguments and proposals. La Rochefoucauld and Roederer assailed his comments on paper money as irrelevant. The question was not, they declared, the creation of a paper money, but of making sound a paper money already established. They referred, of course, to the *billets* of the Caisse d'escompte, for which assignats were to be substituted. The decree passed on April 17, 1790, stipulated that the assignats "should be legal tender among all persons throughout the whole extent of the realm and should be accepted like metal currency for all payments both public and private."[49] From April 15 the interest borne by the assignats would be reduced from 5 per cent to 3 per cent. Assignats given as purchase-money for the national property were to be canceled and publicly burned. The first article of the decree formally acknowledged clerical debts as national obligations.

Du Pont accepted the decision without comment. He may have feared that further opposition would injure the plan now irrevocably adopted. Indeed, he turned his efforts toward facilitating its execution by proposing a method of keeping up the face value of the billets of the Caisse d'escompte in the provinces until the assignats which were to replace them were ready for distribution. The plan, which merely authorized the writing of the words "promise to furnish assignats" across the face of the bills of the Caisse d'escompte destined for the provinces, was added to the decree as article 16.[50]

Still, Du Pont's concern over finances increased. On July 27, he asked the Assembly to accept his resignation from five other committees so that he could conscientiously concentrate on the matters before the Finance Committee. His request was granted amidst much applause.[51] The bitterest fight over the assignats came in September, 1790, when the proposal substantially to increase the number in circulation and to remove the interest-bearing feature was in debate. Such an action would remove the last restrictions on the assignats and convert them into true fiat money. Du Pont's opposition was now vigorous and continuous. Early in September there appeared an anonymous pamphlet of four pages entitled *Effet des assignats sur le prix du pain*, which tried to put into simple terms for popular consumption the argument that great increases in the prices of necessities would be the inevitable outcome of the proposed policy.[52] This pamphlet was the object of an attack by Barnave in the Assembly session of September 11, 1790, at which time Du Pont publicly acknowledged that he was the anonymous author.[53] His major attack on the new proposal was, however, delivered before the Assembly in a long speech on September 25.[54] This discourse accurately predicted the future depreciation of the assignats, while combating the arguments advanced in their favor.

It was a delusion, Du Pont declared, to believe that the nation could pay its debts through the use of assignats, which were merely anticipations on the expected income from the sale of the national domains. "Since when," he asked, "can one consider synonymous the *deed* and the *promise*, the act of *paying* and that of *renewing* one's obligations?"[55] He went on to argue that, once begun, the

194

issue of assignats could not be stopped at any arbitrary limit. There will be constant demands for more to meet this or that payment. The effect of unlimited issues on the price of commodities was well known. Inevitably, prices would rapidly increase. Even these arguments are not accurate, Du Pont declared, for they assume that assignats would retain the same value at all times. Experience has shown that "it is above all human power to inspire for compulsory paper money, however excellent may be its security, the same confidence, to give it the same value, which metallic money enjoys."[56] The assignats already issued carried interest, he pointed out, yet they had lost 6 per cent of their value. "The most common arithmetic says that when there are eight or nine times more [assignats], they will lose as compared with silver at least eight or nine times 6 per cent or 48-54 per cent."[57] Du Pont maintained that it would be possible almost accurately to calculate month by month the inevitable decline in value of assignats and the corresponding rise in prices until the trend grew precipitate, got out of hand, and became incalculable. He cited the American experience with depreciated continental currency as a sufficient warning of what would happen.

The argument that the value of lands held would easily balance the value of assignats in circulation had little validity in Du Pont's view. Even if the values did balance—a very doubtful possibility— the lands had first to be sold and paid for, and that operation would take time. Meanwhile, the bulk of the assignats would remain in circulation with disastrous effect upon prices. This prospect, Du Pont asserted, had led some proponents of the assignats, like Mirabeau, to favor a limitation upon the total value of assignats which would be put into circulation. In any case, the majority of the bearers of assignats would not be able to purchase parts of the national lands. "No one can buy with the usual income which is needed for his daily consumption and to pay the co-workers in his employment; one purchases only with disposable capital which he has procured by the slow accumulation of savings."[58] Very few farmers and very few manufacturers had such capital. Clearly, therefore, the continued decline of the assignats would play into the hands of speculators who had a little capital to buy up depreciated assignats. The only way to prevent this development was to limit the issue of assignats to an amount sufficient to meet the balance due on current expenses and to cover the remainder of the public indebtedness by issuing interest-bearing national bonds, which could eventually be exchanged for land.

This careful discussion had no influence on those already in favor of the new issue. Two days after its delivery, Mirabeau launched a heavy counterattack. Old ties of friendship had long ceased to restrain this brilliant orator. Now he tried to cast scorn upon Du Pont for his denunciation of assignats after his previous defense of the paper of the Caisse d'escompte.[59] Mirabeau was here referring to an earlier exchange of views, when Du Pont had in November, 1789, vigorously championed the Discount Bank, the creature of Turgot, against the strictures of Necker, who wanted to convert it into a national bank, and of Mirabeau, who distrusted all banks.[60] The decree, finally passed on September 29 to provide for an issue of 800,000,000 livres of non-interest-bearing assignats for use in payment of the national debt, was generally in accord with Mirabeau's proposal.[61]

The determined attack of Mirabeau was more gentle than the assaults which beset Du Pont elsewhere. Desmoulins and Marat castigated him in their popular journals.[62] Indeed, the opposition did not content itself with words. When Du Pont left the meeting hall after his vigorous speech of September 25, he was surrounded and threatened by an angry mob. Against its taunts, he courageously maintained his stand against the assignats. Only the timely intervention of a detachment of the National Guard prevented his being thrown into the Seine as the mob pressed about him.[63]

In his first important speech on finances on September 24, 1789, Du Pont had urged that part of the increased revenue to be expected from the confiscation of church income and lands and from other sources be employed to replace or suppress various inequitable indirect taxes. The task of getting rid of these vexatious taxes did not prove easy. However iniquitous they might be, they did provide a sorely needed revenue. Hence much more was involved than their mere suppression. Du Pont came soon to appreciate the necessity of their replacement by other levies. The equitable assessment of the "replacement taxes" was to involve him in dreary complications that might well have driven lesser men to distraction.

Months of labor went into the first report on the replacement of the *gabelle* and other duties which Du Pont discussed with the Committee of Finances on March 3 and 8, 1790.[64] On March 11 with the committee's approval he presented to the Assembly his report and a series of proposed decrees.[65] The report was a masterly discourse, beginning with a general introduction on the importance of sound public finances, without which, Du Pont remarked, all is lost: "the greatest and boldest views, the most painful efforts, the most generous sacrifices, examples of which have been so multiplied in this hall." Then Du Pont took up at length the problem of replacing the salt tax. One might assume that, with true physiocratic insistence, he would argue for the suppression of all such taxes in favor of the *impôt unique* on the income of landowners. As a matter of fact, showing himself most solicitous of the interests of proprietors of land, he resisted such a proposal. Detailing some of the expenses to which landowners were subjected under the prevailing circumstances, he indicated that proprietors had little income left upon which taxes might be levied. He then discussed the iniquities of certain other indirect levies and argued for their replacement. He concluded with reflections on the amelioration of the postal service and read the texts of nine proposed decrees on all these matters. The report was frequently applauded, despite the fact that almost three hours were consumed in its presentation.[66] By order of the Assembly it was to be printed and distributed before any formal discussion.

The only important discussion, which began on March 13, was concerned with the proposal for the replacement of the *gabelle*. With minor amendments the other proposals were approved on March 22. The method adopted for the replacement of the numerous duties was essentially that found in the decree on the *gabelle*. The old duties were to be replaced by surtaxes on the tax rolls and on the entry taxes of towns. Districts which had not been subjected to the old duties were not required to pay the replacement costs in the form of surtaxes. The arrangement was to apply for one year.[67] The lively discussion on the *gabelle* decree need not be followed in detail, since the many changes in the wording of the proposed decree did not alter substantially the method of procedure which Du Pont had suggested.[68] Although the salt tax as such was suppressed, substitute levies were decreed to be added as surtaxes on the regular tax rolls, these levies to be paid "as an additional tax by all persons liable to taxation, either direct or indirect."[69]

These initial decrees by no means ended the work on the *gabelle*. In two directions much labor was still required. It was necessary to work out details to facilitate the execution of the "provisional" decree and to arrange for a permanent settlement of the replacement levies. These matters made up the subjects of numerous committee reports for which Du Pont was primarily responsible. The many technical points on administering the provisional decree are of no general interest,[70] but the establishment of a permanent plan for replacement taxes deserves some mention. Du Pont clearly bore the principal responsibility for the formulation of such a plan.[71] After weeks of tedious labor, he presented his program to the Assembly in a complicated report on August 14, 1790.[72] The method proposed in this report was to fix the direct levies replacing the *gabelle* and other duties in proportion to the population of the "departments and districts which formed part of the provinces formerly subject to the old duties. . . ." Places to be subject to these levies were indicated. Du Pont found no way to prevent a continuance of the disparity in taxation along the lines of the ancient privileges, and regions formerly exempt from the old taxes were not to be liable to the substitute levies. The Assembly took no action on this report, returning it to committee for further study.

The third, and final, formal report drawn up by Du Pont on the question of replacing the *gabelle* and other duties was presented to the Assembly on October 4, 1790.[73] The decree proposed in this report was essentially the one finally adopted by the Assembly.[74] Aside from the addition of more details, the decree followed the general lines previously evident. The amount of the surtax to be added to the direct tax rolls was in the case of the *gabelle* to be determined on the basis of salt consumed, estimated en masse in proportion to population. The Assembly was to have the advice and opinions of the local departmental and district directories, as well as of the municipalities, in establishing the exact amount to be collected. The regions to be subjected to the surtax were specifically listed in order to prevent confusion resulting from the reorganization of local governmental units. When the Assembly finally approved this decree, Du Pont was able to bring to a close his heavy labors on this subject.

Unfortunately, these labors were destined to be largely fruitless. The complicated method of replacement levies failed to achieve its purpose. After months of evading payment, the mass of French citizens were in no mood to revive the old charges under other names or by different methods of collection. Besides, the execution of the decree required a long period of tedious and exacting labor. Years later the National Convention assumed the responsibility of abolishing the surtaxes established by the decree of October, 1790, and of increasing the new direct taxes in order to obtain the revenue which had been lost.[75] At the time Du Pont could not pause to reflect upon these probable difficulties. He was too busy in tasks connected with the ending of other indirect taxes.

Undoubtedly Du Pont preferred the total suppression of the *aides* and *octrois*. Concerned, however, about the loss in revenue which would result from suppression, he put aside his theories to address himself to the onerous chore of seeking means to ameliorate these unpopular taxes which he had formerly so scathingly condemned. There is little point in tracing the tortuous progress of his labors, since again his endeavors were in vain.[76] The Assembly decided upon the total suppression of both *aides* and *octrois*. Years later, it is true, Du Pont stated that he had actually tried to effect this outcome.[77]

On the issue of ending the tobacco monopoly, which he had earlier fought, Du Pont once more showed himself more solicitous of the Public Treasury than of physiocratic theories. While opposing the monopolistic privileges in a speech on April 23, 1790, he concluded that a sales tax on tobacco must be retained in view of the needs of the Government. Since such a tax was on a luxury item, he accepted the viewpoint of many of the *cahiers* that it could be supported. He proposed a decree which, while seeking to end the monopoly, would preserve the public revenue from the sale of tobacco, would make collection and administration uniform, and would lower prices progressively to destroy privilege and contraband as this arrangement became possible with improvement in the public finances. He did hope that eventually the sales tax would become unnecessary.[78] His proposals were submitted for study to the Committees of Agriculture and Commerce and of Finances, but were never acted upon by the Assembly.

After this consideration of the principal financial measures in which he had an active part, what conclusions can one formulate about Du Pont's general attitude? The simple explanation that he approached every problem solely from the standpoint of physiocratic theories cannot be sustained. On many measures he was much more a realist than a theoretician. On others, notably his proposals on the *gabelle,* excessive thought and labor led him into impracticable complications. He remained ever aware of the desperate condition of the Public Treasury and accepted the necessity of compromise with existing circumstances and needs. The ideal arrangement could not be effected overnight, but had to be gradually prepared for. The first task was to find a way out of financial chaos and to build a sound foundation. Only then would real reform be possible. In finances, as in other matters, the moderate course was best.

There is an abundance of evidence to support Du Pont's own assertion that he sought the way of moderation and of justice.[79] He tried to save the taxpayers from excessive levies and demanded equitable assessment.[80] He opposed a too drastic reduction in payments made to the Farmers General and defended them against other attacks.[81] He drew up an elaborate plan for the employment and pensioning of the 30,000 persons discharged as the result of the suppression of various tax administrations.[82] He requested amelioration for certain proprietors of estates, the main income from which was in the form of seigneurial dues now abolished.[83] He opposed discontinuance of certain export duties and of *droits de circulation* on beverages until a definite plan for their suppression, modification, or replacement could be established.[84] In accordance with his belief in "the monarchical principles which the National Assembly has consecrated," he successfully attacked a proposal to have the Assembly select the director of the Treasury.[85] On the other hand, he failed to win approval for his proposal to reorganize the functions of the Treasury and to permit some degree of supervision by the Committees of Finances and of Public Taxation.[86] He held firmly to the belief that no measures to reform various state financial bodies could succeed without establishing more uniform methods of accounting and without recruiting more competent employees.[87] Such plans for the amelioration of the finances display a moderation which does not ignore the necessity of compromise.

Aside from occasionally urging the Assembly to decide upon a definite financial program, Du Pont appears to have had little direct influence in the preparation of the notable decrees establishing a new system of direct taxation. This situation is somewhat surprising because the important *contribution foncière*, decreed November 23, 1790, was a tax on revenues from the land and, hence, had a physiocratic flavor. It is true that, in presenting the report of the Finance Committee on September 11, La Rochefoucauld spoke against physiocratic theories, especially that one regarding the sovereign as co-proprietor of the land; nevertheless, he also said that the land, the source of all wealth, furnishes all the taxes.[88] The decree authorized a land tax from January 1, 1791, divided proportionately "on all land properties, on the basis of their net revenue, with no exception but those determined hereafter in the interests of agriculture." The tax was to be levied and collected in money by the local authorities. All land was to be taxed, even if it produced no income, although, in that case, the levy was to be moderate and regarded as payment for public protection.[89] This tax endured throughout the Revolution, although, from July 20, 1795, to November 23, 1798, payment in kind was authorized in part because of the depreciation of the assignats.[90]

Du Pont's failure to participate with his usual vigor in the formulation of this plan may have been due to a belief that attempts to follow physiocratic principles were premature until the ground had been adequately prepared. His only active intervention in the matter of the *contribution foncière* demonstrated his constant concern for assuring adequate revenue to the Government. On March 15, 1791, he successfully opposed a move to decrease by thirty million livres the amount to be raised through the levy of this tax.[91] His argument that the new taxes had actually afforded considerable relief to the taxpayers was later expanded into a long address which the Assembly ordered to be printed and distributed throughout France.[92]

There is no evidence to show that Du Pont played even such a small role in the establishment of the two other direct taxes decreed by the National Assembly. The *contribution mobilière*, adopted on January 13, 1791, was a complicated levy which, with minor modifications, was to last into the twentieth century. Essentially, this tax was an income tax assessed, not on the personal declaration of taxpayers as in present-day systems, but on external evidences of presumed income. Actually, the law established four types of tax: a *contribution personnelle*, a poll tax on every active citizen fixed at the income from three days' labor, exempting only those who received no wages and had no other income; a tax on *loyer d'habitation*, levied on the basis of 3 per cent of presumed income from rent; a tax on *chevaux et mulets*, generally restricted to pleasure-horses; and a tax on *domestiques*, varying in accordance with the number of domestic servants maintained.[93] The other direct tax, the *patente*, was established as part of the decree suppressing the *aides*.[94] With few exceptions, every person engaging in various trades, industries, and professions was required to purchase a *patente* or license at rates varying with the type of trade or profession. Suppressed by the National Convention on March 12, 1793, the *patente* was re-established in modified form during the period of the Directory on August 23, 1796.[95]

A tentative judgment on the influence of physiocratic ideas upon the reforms of the Constituent Assembly may now be possible. Two conclusions seem inevitable. There was, first of all, a widespread opposition among deputies of the Assembly to the doctrine of the Physiocrats. In the case of political ideas, this opposition was frequently and openly expressed in word and action, especially in connection with the physiocratic emphasis on a strong and independent monarch. There was, however, little opposition to some of the liberal tenets of physiocracy, tenets which sought, for example, the destruction of the old social inequities and the promulgation of a declaration of rights, based upon universal law. Here the majority of the deputies and the Physiocrats were thinking along the same lines. Yet that fact can hardly prove that physiocracy was the source of such ideas among the deputies. It would be easier to argue that individual deputies and Physiocrats reflected a significant trend of thought or opinion, since obviously the Physiocrats had no initial monopoly on these ideas. Perhaps all one can say is that their specific formulations of some of these ideas may have assisted in crystallizing the thinking of others. It is on this very point that the exact influence of the Physiocrats on the financial reforms of the Assembly is difficult to assess.

The second conclusion is that Du Pont, the only active Physiocrat in the Assembly, showed himself much more willing to hold his doctrines in abeyance in regard to financial matters than in regard to political affairs. His viewpoints on the latter seldom prevailed, but he fought for them strenuously. When he was considering fiscal affairs, however, he was often eager to postpone any clear application of physiocratic principles. His argument was that the public revenues had to be put in order, and their collection assured, before any fundamental reform would be possible.

It would appear, therefore, that doubt may be cast on the general assertions that physiocratic theories were very influential in the formulation of the reforms of the Constituent Assembly.[96] The argument that, if there was some conformity between the reforms and the principles, there must be definite influence is not entirely convincing. Du Pont himself was satisfied that there was such conformity between the decrees of the Assembly on matters of commerce and finance and the theories of physiocracy despite a general hostility toward physiocracy among the deputies.[97] Perhaps one cannot confidently go beyond this judgment of the chief Physiocrat in the Assembly.

Chapter VII

Private Citizen (1791-1795)

THE ADJOURNMENT of the Constituent Assembly forced Du Pont to confront serious personal problems. The self-denying ordinance of the Assembly, prohibiting its members from taking seats in the first legislature under the Constitution of 1791, made impossible further active participation in maintaining the reforms which had been effected. The decrease of income from his governmental positions made his personal financial situation almost as precarious as that of the Government. Eventually the positions themselves disappeared in the reorganization of the Government. Obviously Du Pont had to discover some definite means of support for himself and his family. Irénée, only twenty years old, added to his troubles by announcing his determination to marry Sophie Madeleine Dalmas, a charming but impecunious girl of sixteen. With characteristic energy he set about to solve these problems.

Even before the Assembly had closed its sessions, he determined upon his new career. He would become a printer and publisher. During his editorship of the *Éphémérides du citoyen* he had picked up from the Didots, the printers of the *Éphémérides* and one of the largest firms in Paris, a substantial knowledge of the technical details of the printing trade. He needed some outlet through which he could continue to comment upon public affairs. With his governmental career terminated, at least for the time being, it was not surprising that he should seek to make use of his earlier experience as editor and publicist. But he needed help from friends before he could proceed. Fortunately, some friends came forward. The printer Pierre Didot consented to give advice as requested and, more importantly, the chemist Lavoisier agreed to advance the necessary capital for the purchase of a print shop, accepting as security a mortgage on Bois-des-Fossés. Du Pont was then able to lease the printing establishment at the Hôtel Bretonvillers on the Rue de l'Ile St. Louis, formerly occupied by the now defunct General Tax Farm. For a rental fee of 4,800 livres, payable quarterly, he had use of a shop with twenty-five presses, conveniently just across the Seine from his residence on the Rue de Petit Musc.[1] On June 8, 1791, Du Pont drew up and distributed a long prospectus of his new venture. In it he summarized with satisfaction his important services of the past and asked support for his plans of the future. "I will take to my new work," he wrote, "the abilities that have always directed me. I will be attentive, industrious, honest; and, I admit, anxious to succeed. . . . I will work promptly for everyone. I shall be glad to end where Franklin began, and in no way humiliated that there is between him and me the distance of a whole lifetime."[2]

Regarding the marriage of Irénée, he labored earnestly, but in vain, to dissuade the young man from this precipitate step. In a long letter of August 26, 1791, he presented all the usual arguments against an early marriage: Irénée should not marry until he could surely support a family; his father's struggle with poverty in the first years of his own marriage should be a warning; Irénée could hope for no substantial help from his father because of present uncertainties and debts incurred in establishing the printing office.[3] He even wrote to Sophie's mother, emphasizing the unpropitious prospects— his indebtedness and his illness ("I have gout in the head, stomach, and intestines")—and requesting support in his efforts to postpone the marriage.[4] When these and other arguments[5] failed, he accepted the inevitable with good grace. Sophie and Irénée were married on November 26, 1791. Du Pont forgot his initial opposition, and became closely attached to the young couple. When Irénée lost his position at Essone after Lavoisier was transferred, he joined his father in the publishing business and, as events turned out, became the active partner and the chief support of the family. Sophie subsequently proved herself a capable manager of Bois-des-Fossés and became indispensable to Du Pont during his enforced period of seclusion there.

Although it never rivaled in size or importance such printing houses as those of Didot or of Moutard, publisher of the *Mercure de France,* or of Agasse, publisher of the *Moniteur,* Du Pont's print shop and bookstore enjoyed a satisfying growth during the first year of operation. By September, 1792, it employed forty-four printers and seventeen other workmen. Among the nine "officials" were Du Pont's brother-in-law, Philippe Jean Gudin de la Ferlière, husband of his sister Anne, and Philippe Nicolas Harmand, former tutor of his sons, and husband of a cousin of Du Pont's late wife.[6] Under Irénée's direction, the print shop continued to operate even after his father had been forced by the events of the Revolution to remove himself from active management. In October, 1792, the presses and other equipment were moved from the Hôtel Bretonvillers on the Ile St. Louis to the former monastery of the Capuchins on the Rue des Petits-Champs, facing the short street leading into the Place Vendôme.[7] A study of surviving imprints indicates that the Du Pont *imprimerie* published 100 pamphlets and books in 1791 and 1792, all but eighteen of them numbering fifty pages or less.[8] These pamphlets, a few written by the proprietor himself, covered a variety of subjects—finance and commerce, constitutional questions, education, literature, natural history, and others difficult to classify.

Du Pont and his associates sought orders for all kinds of job-printing and vigorously pursued government contracts. In March, 1792, Du Pont sent to the Committee of Public Instruction of the Legislative Assembly a copy of his *Table raisonnée des principes de l'économie politique* with the suggestion that it might be used as a textbook in the schools. The principal object of the letter which he wrote to the committee was, however, to obtain a commission to print "almost gratuitously" attractive and inexpensive editions of standard textbooks which the committee might order for the schools.[9] Since the accomplishment of educational reform then lagged considerably behind the valuable discussions and reports devoted to it, nothing came of this effort. Du Pont had much greater success in gaining contracts to print assignats, which he had so scathingly condemned before the Constituent Assembly. Four contracts signed in 1792 provided for the printing of 280,000,000 livres of assignats, for which the Du Pont press was to be paid 604,000 livres.[10] Principle had to be sacrificed in the face of this profitable business so necessary to keep the presses working and to make it possible to take on other commissions which could never provide comparable returns. Such a commission, for example, was the printing of the *Mémoires* of the Academy of Sciences. The volumes of the *Mémoires* for 1789 and 1790 issued from the Du Pont press, but their ultimate appearance was much delayed. The 1789 volume was begun at the end of 1791 but was not advertised for sale until March, 1796. The 1790 volume was finished in July, 1794, but bears the imprint date 1797, presumably when it was finally placed on sale. Indeed a notice in the front of this volume states that it had been withheld from public sale because of the depreciation of paper money (the assignats).[11]

From his publishing house Du Pont issued a weekly journal entitled *Correspondance patriotique entre les citoyens qui ont été membres de l'assemblée nationale constituante*, in which he sought to keep before the public the opinions of the architects of the new France. The journal, which had as its motto the bold words "Equality, Liberty, Property, Security," was composed of four parts —letters and *mémoires* of former members of the Constituent Assembly, of deputies to the Legislative Assembly, and of other citizens; extracts and notices of new publications; political news and reflections; and accounts of the meetings of the Legislative Assembly "with free observations, respectful but courageous. . . ." Du Pont's active editorship extended only over the first five volumes, which appeared between October 9, 1791, and June 1, 1792. Beginning with volume VI, the *Correspondance patriotique* was combined with *L'Ami de la Constitution*, a daily printed by Demonville.[12] Du Pont's participation in this volume, and in the two subsequent ones to August, 1792, was confined to that of printer.

This organ gave him a ready medium for the expression of his views. As long as he was active in editing it, he contributed more than thirty articles and comments. These varied in length from three to twenty-eight pages and covered a diversity of subjects— reflections on the Constitution of 1791, the general political situation, colonial problems, the organization of the army, the pernicious influence of the mob on the Legislative Assembly, the dangers of entering upon an unwarranted war against the Holy Roman

Emperor.[13] At least eight of his contributions were published separately as pamphlets. Undoubtedly Du Pont chose wisely in electing to become a publisher. He could never have been happy during this period of divorce from public affairs without the opportunity to believe that he might still have some influence in molding opinion. No burden was heavier for him than inactivity which made him feel removed from the course of events and, hence, completely impotent. He was always concerned about his place in history and could not bear the thought of being cast aside and ignored. He might occasionally seem to be reconciled to a quiet life, but showed his real sentiments by embracing eagerly any chance to return to active participation in public affairs.

From his editorial desk, Du Pont continued to defend the moderate course. This course had been placed more on the defensive after the vain attempt of the Royal Family to escape from its virtual imprisonment in Paris. Moderate projects were endangered by the hostile pronouncements and activities of some of the émigrés, who continued their efforts to stir foreign monarchs into armed intervention in France, and by the memory of the unfortunate incident of July 17, 1791, the "massacre of the Champ de Mars," when a detachment of the National Guard had fired on the mob to break up a threatening demonstration.

The Legislative Assembly, as the legislative body established under the Constitution of 1791 was called, faced many disadvantages from the time of its first meeting early in October, 1791. Since the Constituent Assembly had decreed that none of its members could sit in this first legislature under the Constitution, the Legislative Assembly was deprived of the services of many experienced men. It found itself seriously divided in its deliberations into bickering groups, with the very loosely knit group known as the Girondins coming more and more to favor an aristocratic republic and trying to supply leadership on the Left. Obviously, there were problems in attempting to carry on a government organized as a constitutional monarchy when there existed some doubt that the monarch would co-operate. The flight to Varennes was not forgotten. Louis XVI increased the doubt in November and December by vetoing punitive decrees against the émigrés and the recalcitrant clergy, who refused to subscribe to the oath required by the Civil Constitution of the

Clergy. Du Pont entered the lists in the arguments over the King's vetoes.

In the twelfth number of the *Correspondance patriotique* he upheld the King's right to veto the decrees and praised him for his courage in exercising this right. Whether he should have used it against the decrees in question, on the basis that they were unconstitutional, was a difficult question which could not clearly be determined until a later convention met to consider revision of the Constitution. Du Pont believed that the decrees on the émigrés and nonjuring clergy were unconstitutional, but admitted that, since the Constitution was so new, there was room for argument. For the present, one must support the right of the King to use his power of veto.[14]

In the early months of 1792, the Legislative Assembly found itself deeply involved in matters of diplomacy. The threat of foreign intervention was actually not so grave as it seemed, or as it was made to appear by those Frenchmen who sought in warfare the achievement of their own ambitions or plans. The movement to meet the threats emanating from the domains of the Holy Roman Empire to the east with a declaration of war was urged on by the Court party, by a group of moderate monarchists looking to Lafayette for leadership, and by the republican Girondins. Each group thought that war would open the avenue to its attainment of predominant power within France. Robespierre and his associates among the Jacobins, after some indecision, announced their opposition to a declaration of war, fearful that the advent of foreign war would undermine the pillars of the Revolution at home. Although not allied with them, Du Pont was equally opposed to war.

In the thirteenth number of the *Correspondance patriotique*, he argued that no legitimate cause for war existed. The only issue in controversy between France and the Empire was the protest of German princes, who had seen their rights in Alsace and Lorraine swept away by the decree of August 4-11 ending serfdom without compensation. It would be just, Du Pont held, to give ear to their complaints and to consider some reparation for their losses. Then, being persons of "honor and probity," they would cease to give any support to the émigré "rebels."[15] He continued to attack the warmongers, who, he asserted, were either émigrés or their friends in

209

France seeking to destroy equality or fomenters of anarchy desiring to ruin personal enemies and to attack liberty, property, security, and the Constitution.[16] The moderate course, in other words, must combat these extremes and seek the road of peace.

The move to war could not, however, be stopped. Eventually the "war parties" were successful. In April, 1792, the Legislative Assembly declared war against the Emperor. None could foresee the outcome of their momentous decision, which was to involve France in twenty-three years of warfare, with but two brief respites in that long period. Amidst the perils and alarms of invasion from without and of civil strife within, the moderate course was doomed. The hard fact of war, more than any other circumstance, pushed the Revolution to extremes. Du Pont tried to see the bright side, even after war was declared. He wrote on May 14 that peace would likely be soon restored. Radical clubs and factions within France would be suppressed, the French Government would offer an indemnity to the dispossessed German landlords and, perhaps, even to the Pope, and foreign nations, impressed by this display of responsibility and moderation, would eagerly agree to a general peace treaty.[17] He could hardly have been more incorrect in his analysis of the situation.

Without pause he continued to attack extremists who, he asserted, were attempting to influence events for their selfish profit. He was especially active in turning out polemics against Jérôme Pétion de Villeneuve, a prominent Jacobin who had succeeded Bailly as Mayor of Paris in November, 1791. His assault upon Pétion was called forth by the plans for a public celebration in honor of the Swiss regiment of Chateauvieux, which, eighteen months previously, had staged a mutiny in the Nancy garrison over the alleged pilfering of the regimental fund by its officers. Those mutineers who had escaped death had been sentenced to the galleys at Brest, but had been pardoned by the general amnesty granted at the close of the Constituent Assembly. They had come to be regarded by many as genuine martyrs, as courageous victims of hated tyranny. With his predilection for order, Du Pont was not, of course, among their admirers. He resented this glorification of disobedient soldiers. He was also undoubtedly antipathetic toward Pétion, who had been able to defeat Lafayette in the contest for Mayor five months earlier through an unfortunate split among the conservative electors. In an open letter to Pétion, dated April 13, 1792, he accused the Mayor of falsehood in several parts of the proclamation calling for the celebration.[18] He argued that Pétion had no constitutional power to initiate a public celebration. The statement in the proclamation that the fête was the desire of the majority of Parisian citizens and of the National Guard could not be true, Du Pont held, because the sections of Paris had not been convoked for consultation on the matter. If the celebration were, therefore, a private one, he asked Pétion to explain by what right he proposed to use public places and to decree how the citizenry should act during the fête. He looked upon the matter as a major constitutional crisis and employed strong language in posing it as a question whether the French people "would allow all powers to be usurped by men whom they had not chosen, by a small number of factious [individuals] who recruit themselves and who enslave, from one end of the kingdom to the other, the nation, its delegates and its representatives, by making use of calumny, pillage, fire, and assassination according to circumstances."[19]

For this "anti-revolutionary" letter Du Pont was denounced before the Jacobins on April 14.[20] Pétion was sufficiently aroused to make a public reply attacking Du Pont in various ways, especially recalling once again the fight against the assignats.[21] Du Pont had the final word. In a second letter on April 27 he warned Pétion that the celebration of force instead of law would bring havoc to all, including the Mayor and his associates.[22] After other writers entered into the debate, the affair ended, and the fête took place without serious incident. Du Pont's prediction of Pétion's fate was, however, ultimately correct. Within fourteen months Pétion was to be cast down with his associates among the Girondins and to escape execution of a death sentence against him only through suicide.

The war helped to bring more radical leaders to power and to put an end to the monarchy. Against the current Du Pont sprang actively to the support of the King. Some of his efforts in opposition to what he regarded as an organized attempt to overthrow the throne were directed to the composition and circulation of petitions of protest. These petitions were called forth by the demonstrations of June 20, 1792, when the Parisian mob invaded the Tuileries and threatened the Royal Family. The first, signed by 8,000 citizens, objected to the proposed formation in Paris of a camp of 20,000 *fédérés* from the provinces, who would come to the capital for the Fête of Federation scheduled for July 14, anniversary of the fall of the Bastille. This petition was followed by a larger one, allegedly bearing 20,000 signatures, protesting the events of June 20 and requesting the dismissal of the Commandant of the National Guard because of his failure to give clear orders to his troops.[23] This petition was personally presented to the Legislative Assembly on July 1 by "MM. Guillaume and Dupont, ex-deputies, Jaugé and two other citizens." Guillaume read the petition and made a speech demanding more stringent measures by the Assembly to prevent future disorder. The petitioners did not receive a friendly reception and departed "to the noise of murmurs of a part of the Assembly and of the galleries."[24]

These hostile demonstrations did not turn Du Pont from the course which he had chosen. He kept in print through three editions the vigorous letter which he had originally published in the *Correspondance patriotique* on May 14. Under the title *Avant-dernier chapitre de l'histoire des Jacobins*, this pamphlet accused the clubs of having overturned the Constitution by establishing themselves as a second legislative chamber, seeking to dictate to the single chamber established by the Constitution. These clubs, so falsely proclaiming themselves "friends of the constitution," must be disbanded. They were themselves unconstitutional, since the Constitution prohibited such associations, which tried to perpetuate themselves and to usurp power belonging only to the elected representatives of the people. Du Pont blamed them for the stupid and impossible orders which had gone out to the armies after the unfortunate declaration of war and defended his friend Lafayette, who had been denounced for his failure to set out at once with his troops on a campaign for which they were grossly unprepared. It is not surprising that Du Pont was again mentioned in a meeting of the Parisian Jacobin Club on July 6, when an unnamed spokesman protested against the rough treatment which he had allegedly received from employees at the print shop and declared that the proprietor had eagerly admitted the printing and distribution of numerous anti-Jacobin posters.[25]

Du Pont took up the sword as well as the pen. According to his own statement, he organized among "relatives and friends a little squad of fifteen men," with whom sixty others soon united themselves.[26] The little band called itself "The Grenadiers and Chasseurs of the Army of Paris." Du Pont wished to use it to close the Jacobin Club, but his plans miscarried when his grenadiers were scattered in a squirmish with 500 "men from Marseilles," who arrived in Paris for the celebration of July 14. The most important action of the little troop occurred in the defense of the King on the fateful day of August 10.

The opening campaigns of the war had been disastrous for the French, who met defeat on all fronts. Diplomacy had failed when the Prussians joined the Austrians in the war. Weakened by the large-scale emigration of noble officers, by lack of discipline among the rank and file, by inadequate training, by scarcity of arms and supplies, French armies had been routed. News from the front seeping back to Paris was all bad. The threat of imminent invasion by Prussian and Austrian troops, the rumor of treasonable communication between the Court and the enemy, the apparent collapse of French forces—all these elements in the situation kept the Parisian populace in a state of nervous fear and tension. The situation was made to order for enemies of the monarchical constitution. Popular leaders sought to organize demonstrations against the monarchy. The assault on the Tuileries on June 20, third anniversary of the Tennis Court Oath, had failed, in part because of insufficient planning and in part because of the unusual courage displayed by the King in facing the mob and in presenting himself as a friend of the Revolution. The demonstration of August 10 was better organized. The émigrés had helped to set the stage from without by inducing the Prussian Duke of Brunswick, commander of the forces marching against France, to issue over his signature a manifesto, which had actually been drawn up by one of the most recalcitrant of the émigrés. This document called upon Frenchmen to cease resistance to the invading forces and threatened to deliver Paris over "to military execution and total ruin," if the King or his family were in any way harmed or insulted. Although Louis immediately repudiated the manifesto, his voice was inaudible amidst the general clamor. The threats of the manifesto were, of course, a goad, not a

213

deterrent, to the popular leaders in the sections of Paris. Several petitions were presented to the Legislative Assembly demanding the immediate deposition of the King. When the Assembly hesitated to act, the populace seized the initiative. The events of August 10 were the result not of spontaneous rioting but of calculated planning to overturn the King, who was suspected of treason. Indecisive to the end, Louis failed to understand the seriousness of his situation and to provide sufficient protection. When the determined attacks of the armed mob assumed such dangerous proportions that they could have been blunted only by the expenditure of much blood, Louis drew back from ordering the troops around the Tuileries to fire upon the people. Instead he sought refuge for himself and his family in the meeting hall of the Legislative Assembly. His action embarrassed the Assembly but forced it to do something. It seemed clear to the majority that the existing government could not continue to function as a constitutional monarchy. The Assembly therefore voted to suspend the royal prerogative and to summon another assembly charged with deciding upon the type of government which France should have.

According to his own account, Du Pont and his little band of militia played a part in the poorly arranged defense set up to protect the King. Whatever chance for success this defense might have had was destroyed by the King's decision to leave the palace. By the time the defense had completely collapsed, Du Pont's grenadiers were no longer a disciplined group. They had been reduced to eight in number, including the captain and his son, Irénée. Did Louis, on his sad procession across the courtyard of the Tuileries, pause to exclaim, "Ah, M. Du Pont, one always finds you where one has need of you"? It is a proud family tradition, perhaps given birth by Du Pont, but there is no certain contemporary evidence for it.[27] Du Pont's small group escaped with their lives by calmly marching off under semblance of being a regular patrol. They got safely away from the scene of the rioting and bloodshed and disbanded for the last time. Du Pont had, however, laid himself open to retaliatory action by the republican victors. He yielded to the urging of his son and some of his friends that he go into hiding until any possibility of personal jeopardy had passed.

The faithful Harmand sought out the astronomer Lalande, chief of the Paris Observatory, and won his consent for Du Pont to conceal himself in the dome of the building which afterwards became the Institute. Here he remained uncomfortably for several weeks, without even a bed upon which to rest. He subsisted upon whatever food Harmand could smuggle in to him. Although he had been at his father's side throughout the struggle at the Tuileries, Irénée was, fortunately, not well enough known to have run any serious risk of future retaliation from the anti-monarchist factions. He was, therefore, able to keep the print shop in operation during the long period of his father's enforced absence. Before Du Pont had stolen away to the Observatory, he had executed a power of attorney authorizing Irénée to conduct the business.[28]

At the end of August Du Pont was placed in a more difficult position. Harmand was summoned to service with the army. Unwilling to expose Lalande to greater peril by accepting the venerable astronomer's offer to keep him supplied with food, Du Pont resolved upon escape from Paris. His opportunity came on September 2. On that terrible day there began the operation to clear the prisons of suspected royalists and conspirators before the troops left the capital for the front. People's courts were rapidly set up before each prison and the inmates were subjected to summary justice. If judged guilty, they were turned over to the vengeance of the mob. During the disorder attending these prison massacres, the gates of the city were left open and unguarded for a few hours. As soon as he heard of this circumstance, Du Pont left his place of concealment, and managed to get out of Paris without being recognized. He walked the ten miles to Cormeilles-en-Parisis, a small suburb northwest of Paris, where Harmand owned a little country house, which, of course, was made available to him.[29] Here, for two months, he played the part of an elderly physician who had no concern with politics. He partially covered his face with an eyeshade, and wrote out prescriptions for all who came to him. How useful now was his earlier dabbling in medicine! Within a month the general excitement fed by fears of imminent invasion had subsided. On September 20, the French Artillery had displayed sufficient firmness and fire power during the engagement in the fog near Valmy to discourage the Duke of Brunswick. The invading troops, weakened by illness, turned back. Paris was safe again. By early November, Du Pont decided that it was safe for him to go to Bois-des-Fossés and to trust to the goodwill of his neighbors to ward off any searching parties. Irénée's wife, Sophie, stayed with him as housekeeper, while Irénée carried on the business in Paris.

The new authorities seem not to have bothered about Du Pont for over a year. There were more important matters to engage their attention. On September 21, 1792, the new body which was to decide the future of France assembled. As its first important act, this National Convention proclaimed France a republic. Louis XVI became Louis Capet, private citizen, who was suspected of treason. The former monarch was arraigned and condemned by the Convention after a trial which was drawn out over a month. Many of the deputies were reluctant to pass sentence on the deposed King, but they were finally forced to a vote on January 15, 1793. Although there was unanimous agreement on Louis' guilt, the penalty of death was carried by a majority of only fifty-three votes. Twenty-six of the 387 who spoke up for the death sentence favored postponement of its execution, but it was not postponed. On January 21, Louis mounted the scaffold erected in the Place de la Révolution (now the Place de la Concorde). When the knife of the guillotine severed his head from his body, it drew a dividing line of blood across the Revolution. It forced would-be moderates either to accept the republic or to go into open opposition to the Revolution. Unfortunately, Du Pont's immediate reaction cannot be discovered. He was in hiding and carefully refraining from political comment. After the events of August 10, he may not have been too much surprised by the death of the King, whom he had vainly tried to protect. His decision obviously was to continue to remain out of sight of government agents. Public fear and fervor were again at high pitch. France was still at war and more seriously threatened after February, 1793, when the Convention declared war on England and Holland. An impressive coalition of powers was now arrayed against France. Amidst the mounting danger there were bitter struggles among the political factions in the Convention. These struggles were temporarily resolved in June, when the Jacobin faction of the Mountain, so called from the raised seats which its adherents occupied in the Convention meeting hall, was victorious.

With the help of Parisian mobs, it forced the arrest of its principal opponents and proceeded vigorously to carry on the Government under the Committee of Public Safety, a kind of group dictatorship, of which Robespierre became a member in July. Together with another group, the Committee of General Security, which exercised general supervision over police functions, the twelve members of the Committee of Public Safety set out to eliminate organized dissent at home.

Du Pont remained on the proscribed list. Danton accused him of counterrevolutionary activities in a speech before the parent Society of the Jacobins on June 12, 1793.[30] Although there was no basis for Danton's charges, the fact that they were made was proof of the danger which Du Pont faced. As they consolidated their power, the Jacobin rulers undertook an active search for individual enemies. There is a possibility that the new boundaries of the local jurisdictions in France caused sufficient confusion to save Du Pont from arrest for several months. Orders for his seizure would normally go to the Department of Seine-et-Marne, where Nemours was located. The village of Chevannes, however, had been detached from its former *bailliage* and incorporated in the Department of Loiret. In any event, Du Pont was free of serious harassment for another year. He later suggested that he escaped notice as long as he did because of a belief that he had perished in the prison massacres of September 2. An order for his arrest and lodgement at La Force, one of the Parisian prisons, had, he asserted, been signed on August 29.[31]

What did he do during the months he spent at Bois-des-Fossés? Soon after he arrived, he wrote to Irénée in Paris to assure him that "I shall do very well alone with both literary and outdoor work" and to request his son to send a copy of Plutarch, as well as shoes and shirts.[32] Although subsequent letters indicate that he was carrying out his announced program of "literary and outdoor work" by reading, writing, and tending to his farms, they are mostly given over to numerous instructions to Irénée about conducting the business in Paris.[33] The print shop, with all its equipment, had been moved from the Hôtel Bretonvillers to the old Capuchin monastery in October, while Du Pont was still in hiding at Cormeilles. On November 13 it began to issue a daily paper, *Le Républicain universal,* which it renamed *Le Républicain français* after its

217

fortieth number on December 24.[34] The very title of the paper shows a willingness to ride with the tide of public opinion. It is difficult to believe that Du Pont so suddenly shifted his allegiance, though he was later to assert that he was among the first republicans. As a general rule he kept silent about political affairs during these months. He seemed at first to be interested only in the profits which the *Républicain* might bring to the print shop and was distressed by the poor printing of the third issue, the first one which he had seen.[35]

In January, 1793, Harmand obtained a lease on the old convent of the Nouvelles Catholiques in the Rue Helvétius (now the Rue Grammont).[36] He immediately rented part of it to Irénée for use as an office and residence. Du Pont thought it would be safe for him to return quietly to Paris and lodge at this new address in order to be on hand to give personal direction to the print shop, and instructed Irénée to prepare a room for him in the Nouvelles Catholiques.[37] Because of the general perturbation and uncertainty after the beheading of the former King on January 21, he changed his mind and, probably at Irénée's urging, went instead to Harmand's house in Cormeilles, while Sophie joined her husband in Paris. The declaration of war against England and Holland in February did not improve the situation. Du Pont finally made his way back to Bois-des-Fossés in late February without setting foot in Paris.[38] Henceforth he would have to reconcile himself to directing the business by correspondence with Irénée, who tried faithfully to carry out all his instructions. Sophie returned to keep house for him.

From his farm he sent to Paris a constant flow of letters full of hopes and projects for the future of the enterprise. "We must try to secure some papers that have a ready sale. As soon as I am in Paris I will get to work at the *mémoires* and works of Mr. Turgot. That will employ two presses. And I will persuade Madame de Guibert to print her husband's works at her own expense; I will correct the edition. That will use two more presses. Mr. Lavoisier two, the Academy three, the *Républicain* two, odd jobs one; —that makes twelve, but I would like more."[39] For months he was burdened by worries more threatening than those regarding the success of his business. He was made uneasy by the complications over a certificate of residence demanded by the authorities at Rouen, old seat of the

Du Pont family. He sought the help of Irénée and of Harmand in assembling the necessary papers,[40] but feared that he was doomed.

The district of Rouen is correct, my child, when it says of the citizen of whom you write to me [i. e., Du Pont himself], "denounced for emigration," and he has been denounced only because of the action of that district and of the municipality of Rouen, where he never had a home; but nevertheless, on their own authority they put him on the list of émigrés and refused to take him off in spite of his offering them all the certificates required by law to which they invariably objected because of new laws not yet made public; so that because these gentlemen have not given an official certificate for the different papers that have been shown them, this citizen, who has never left France and has not been more than twenty-five leagues from Paris, may be guillotined at Rouen with his certificates of residence in his pocket.[41]

Such difficulties forced Du Pont to leave his estate for short periods during the autumn of 1793. These necessary journeys to Rouen, with a furtive stopover of a few days in Paris, were the only ones hazarded since his unsuccessful effort to return to Paris early in the year. Happily, the Rouen authorities finally accepted his proofs that he had not emigrated,[42] and he could return to Bois-des-Fossés to enjoy several more months of relative peace. As a result of this dangerous disagreement with the Rouen officials, he ceased to write letters himself. Except for an occasional note or postscript added to Sophie's letters, he did not directly communicate with Irénée, or anyone else, from October, 1793, to July, 1794. His son and daughter-in-law mentioned him in their letters to each other only in the third person as "our doctor" or "our friend."[43]

The reference to "our doctor" was accurate in view of Du Pont's efforts to relieve some of his pent-up energy by practicing medicine among his neighbors. On May 24, 1793, he asked Irénée to send him grains and scales for weighing, the lack of which "gives me much trouble with my medicines."[44] He confessed in another letter on September 5 that "my patients tire me out. No one has died yet, but there are always some in danger, and they are long distances apart."[45] Except for a severe attack of gout,[46] to which complaint he was long subject, his own health seems to have been good throughout these months of removal from the type of life to which he was accustomed. He was troubled by a feeling that the Lavoisiers,

219

his friends and benefactors, were becoming increasingly cold toward him.[47] Whatever disagreements there were seem to have been smoothed over by the spring of 1794, when the Lavoisiers were hoping to visit Bois-des-Fossés.[48] Then fell the terrible blow of Lavoisier's arrest, trial, and execution on May 5. There are no direct words of Du Pont available by which to measure his reaction to this shocking event. Since he had already decided to dedicate to the Lavoisiers the literary effort which he considered his major work, he must have been deeply moved. For Madame Lavoisier, who was twice bereft, since her father, Jacques Paulze, had been guillotined on the same day as her husband, Du Pont was ever afterward much concerned. She was the one, he wrote, "who most interests my intelligence, my chivalry and my heart,"[49] but he was frequently annoyed when she did not always accede to his wishes.

In the early summer of 1793 Victor returned from his second diplomatic mission to America and came to live with his father. A tall, handsome young man, with dignified bearing and polished manners acquired through his diplomatic experience, he should have been a source of strength and comfort to his father during this unhappy period. Instead, Du Pont found in him a cause for additional worry. The young men of Chevannes called to army service grumbled about this handsome, well-dressed stranger, who had not volunteered for service; they began to question the patriotism of his family. Victor solved this difficulty by enrolling in the local constabulary in order to escape a call to the army. Then he fell in love with Josephine Gabrielle La Fite de Pelleport, orphaned daughter of an impecunious noble and his second wife, who had been a commoner. Josephine retained her aristocratic and deeply religious sentiments and was horrified by the events of the Revolution. Her desire to enter a convent had been blighted by the reforms of the Constituent Assembly abolishing the Catholic orders and closing the monasteries and convents. She had sought escape by leasing with one of her half-sisters a quiet retreat in an abandoned convent in Ferrierès, near the spot where Victor's detachment of the gendarmerie was stationed. She was introduced to Victor at a fête in Montargis in late July, 1793. Some years later she wrote: ". . . I had never before seen, either at court or in town, a figure and face which so compelled attention and which sustained acquaintance so pleasantly."[50] She must have made an equally favorable impression upon Victor, for he soon began to court her with serious intentions.

Josephine's political and religious convictions stood in the way of her yielding to his desires for an early marriage. She was so much opposed to the Revolution that she could not marry a man wearing the gendarme's uniform; furthermore, she insisted upon being married by a priest, although there were very few left in the neighborhood and those who remained were fearful of performing an act which could compromise them with the secular authority. Victor was so determined, however, that these difficulties were overcome. He feigned illness, even staining his face with spinach juice, in order to be released from his constabulary duties. With some difficulty, he finally persuaded the curé at Branles to perform a secret marriage behind closed doors. Thus, unceremoniously, with Du Pont present and giving his consent, Victor and the hesitant Josephine were married by Catholic rite in March, 1794. Three weeks later on April 9, after all the required contracts and papers were prepared, the necessary civil ceremony was performed "in the former church of Chevannes, in the parish of Bois-des-Fossés" by a municipal official who, as Josephine pointed out rather disdainfully, was formerly a carpenter.[51]

Du Pont was eager to see his elder son settled into a promising career and hoped that marriage would bring to him a greater sense of responsibility than he seemed to have. He hoped that Victor might find employment with the government. But Victor took his time, awaiting an opportunity that was worthy of his attention. Meanwhile, with his new wife, he was most usually at Bois-des-Fossés.

Du Pont sought release from his worries by spending part of each day at his desk, turning out a variety of literary compositions. Unfortunately, he did not get around to completing the autobiography which he had begun at Cormeilles, because he had undertaken another work that he considered more important, a treatise attempting to state a philosophy of life. From the dates given at the beginning of the book, the *Philosophie de l'univers* was apparently written between December 20, 1792, and June 10, 1793. With the *Philosophie*, Du Pont included the *Oromasis*, a prose-poem which, according to his statement in the preface, was written while he was concealed in the Observatory after August 10. Although of inferior

221

quality, this little work displays the same sublime optimism which Condorcet was able to muster in somewhat similar circumstances while composing his famous essay on human progress. In Du Pont's "poem," Oromasis [Ormuzd] is creating the world and everything in it, while his immortal enemy Arimane [Ahriman] taunts him about all the evil which will grow in his creation. Oromasis is unperturbed. He creates the Good, while Arimane adds the Evil, but this addition merely completes the work. How can one enjoy good without the fact of evil; how have life without death? No matter how strenuously Arimane may exert himself, he cannot overcome the essential happiness of life.[52]

The *Principes sur la philosophie de l'univers*, written, as Du Pont remarked, in solitude, in the midst of a cold and rainy season, far from children, friends, persons whose society is habitually most necessary for happiness, in uncertain health, beset by troubles, annoyances, and privations, is also an optimistic statement. It suffers from wordiness, rhapsodical flights of fancy, and lack of precision, but remains a revealing portrait of the author. Like Montaigne, Du Pont, though lacking the literary charm of the great essayist, found that he could best answer the important questions of life by writing about himself. Without reserve, in numerous passages, he lays bare his innermost thoughts. True, Du Pont had never been especially reticent on this subject, but here he writes more familiarly, as if he were addressing only his friend Lavoisier, to whom his book is dedicated.

The basis of his "philosophy of the universe" is that nothing is done by chance. Providential laws direct the whole universe, as accords with good physiocratic doctrine:

There is no such thing as chance, even in a throw of dice; if we could learn how the dice ought to be placed in the box, how many shakes it is necessary to give them, in what direction and with what force for it to be double-six [*sonnés*] or double-ace [*bezet*], we would produce double-six or double-ace at will; for the dice are struck and thrown, fall and rebound, in accordance with very exact geometrical and physical laws. . . . Because we are ignorant of the manner of playing, we say that it is by chance and we even reckon the number of our blunders as hazards of the game, although these blunders are only the physical effects of physical causes set in motion by a not very enlightened intelligence.[53]

The rather materialistic view of the world to which such a starting point might lead is covered over by personal reflections upon morality often seemingly in direct contradiction to the basic conception. But Du Pont wrote as he felt at the moment. He was not writing a scientific treatise, and he allowed emotion to override reason and exactitude.

Instead of immortality, the Creator granted love to individuals, so that the immortality of the species might be assured. Love of life, love of other individuals—these instincts cause a creature to seek to sustain life and to guard against accidents which might bring death. This desire to sustain life requires work, and, from work, the necessity of knowing arises in order that one may be guided by the experience of the past.[54] *"To love and to know* are the principal aspirations of animated beings." There are, however, other powerful stimuli: sorrow, hope, self-love, liberty.[55] "There is *liberty* in every being who deliberates and does not decide without examination; there is *wisdom* in every being who prefers lasting and distant happiness to present and momentary pleasure; there is *morality* in every being capable of seeking and of finding his happiness in that of others." Morality arises from the conditions of existence imposed by the Creator. Although on an inferior scale, animals have an intelligence and a morality just as surely as humans. They likewise learn from experience, are guided by and make a choice of motives. When the primary needs for the preservation of species are met, animal morality is raised. Domesticated animals prove that, like man, animals desire to be loved and esteemed. There is only a difference of degree between animal and human instincts.[56]

Reflecting upon humans who had shown the highest development of these qualities, Du Pont was brought to inquire if "superior intelligences" did not remain after death to oversee the actions of those whom they loved and to guide them over difficult paths encountered in the course of life. He addressed an invocation to his "heroes."

August witnesses, if you have been pleased to impress in my heart an eternal and just recognition, if you have had indulgence for my faults, if you have had mercy on my weaknesses . . . I owe it, without doubt [to the fact] that you have found my spirit honest, pure and upright; that you have seen in my love an invariable constancy . . . a faithfulness full of zeal in friendship; the perpetual disposition to sacrifice my happiness to that of persons who have the right to count upon my affection; an inexhaustible ardor to serve my fellow-citizens, the human race, posterity; that these sentiments have made me industrious despite my laziness, and patient, although impetuous and angry; that they have prevented me from seeing in places [of] authority anything more than the duties which they impose and have made me keep my poverty carefully, knowing with all my senses the very real value of riches; that they have made me, without hesitation, prefer the public welfare, even to glory which I loved with folly.[57]

Towards the end of the *Philosophie* occurs a long passage arguing against suicide.[58] Here Du Pont reiterates his intense feeling on the necessity of sustaining life to the end. Suicide is never justified, however desperate or hopeless life may seem. No one can foresee the future. The worst may turn out to be best; even if it doesn't, and we as individuals are not spared, we must keep doing everything possible to better the future. Who can know the final result of even the smallest action? No one of perfect virtue will dream of cutting short his days. We must be an example for our children and fight on to the last.

The setting down of all these reflections was an important and necessary task during these years when Du Pont's world appeared to have collapsed around him. His high conception of the values of life and of his own position in the scheme of existence sustained him during periods of personal danger, of sorrow, of loneliness, and of frustration. It was not in his nature to turn a passive or indifferent face to life. The Good that is everywhere in life must be sought, followed, and fought for. This philosophy helped Du Pont to retain his equanimity and to carry forward work which he considered useful. His literary efforts at this time included several papers on natural history. Now that he was close to nature on his farm and in his woods, he could turn his attention more directly to this area of knowledge, which had long been among his diversified interests. He was usually not very scientific in his observations, even by the standards of his age, but, from this time forward, he composed various essays in this field, most of which were ultimately presented to the Institute.[59] In some of these a sympathetic sentimentality is more evident than any scientific exactitude, as in his comment midway in an essay on the sociability and morality of the wolf, the fox, and the wild dog: "Hard destiny, and more cruel than death, to acknowledge oneself impotent and vanquished, useless to those whom one loves, to those who ought to count upon the help of our genius, of our courage! But, disarmed and confined by men in our woods, let us not speak evil of our neighbors the wolves."[60]

Du Pont found time also to prepare a brief treatise on a system of national education, a work of which he was especially proud. He had Irénée print it as a pamphlet and sought to have it distributed among his friends and government officials.[61] The treatise begins as an effort to teach writing and reading to farm boys and town youths who have had to spend most of their time working; it soon expands into an elaborate, and ridiculous, scheme to organize instruction along military lines, with classes divided into platoons under sergeants and corporals, competing in "battles." These "battles" would take place once each decade (the ten-day week of the republican calendar) and would also provide the occasion for gymnastic and military exercises and for ceremonies designed to inculcate morality and sound republican virtue. The most interesting part of the treatise comes at the beginning, where Du Pont discusses the method which he had devised for teaching the letters of the alphabet by first learning to write them. Reading would not be taught separately but would evolve naturally through writing as the letters are formed into words with which each child is familiar. City boys would be taught the names of different trades; farm lads would be introduced to the words connected with farming and village chores, as well as the names of fruits, plants, and animals which they saw every day. Gradually, more abstract words ("work," "property," "justice," "economy," "wisdom," "happiness") would be brought into the lessons. Like Rousseau, Du Pont counseled that one should follow nature in education and should make lessons interesting, varied, and short.[62] He had used this method in instructing his own sons, but he could hardly justify the claim which he made that he had tried it successfully on two generations of youth.[63] His plan, he admitted, had only limited suitability for girls; it might be used to teach them reading and writing but, in its military aspects, could not apply to them, since their "honor and . . . happiness . . . are in the gentleness, the modesty, the charm with which they embellish a peaceful and retired life. . . ."[64] Some years later, at the request of

Thomas Jefferson, Du Pont more fully developed his ideas on a system of national education.

In July, 1794, Du Pont's career as a fugitive in his rural retreat was rudely ended. Since June 10, when the Convention had passed the Law of 22 Prairial, which gave almost unlimited power to the revolutionary tribunal, the number of arrests and of executions had rapidly increased. Robespierre and his Jacobin associates seemed determined to weed out the final remnants of opposition so that they could proceed with their program for the complete regeneration of France, now that the immediate danger of invasion had been ended by the victories of French armies. Dated 25 Messidor (July 13), an order of the Committee of General Security was transmitted from Paris for Du Pont's arrest and incarceration in La Force prison in the capital.[65] Nine days later a party of soldiers descended upon Bois-des-Fossés, put Du Pont under arrest, and immediately placed him under guard in a carriage bound for Paris. The soldiers rejected Sophie's plea to be allowed to accompany her father-in-law in the same carriage. Undaunted, Sophie placed her young daughter, Victorine, in the care of Victor and his wife, whose presence at Bois-des-Fossés now proved an advantage, harnessed a mule, and, assisted by a young lad of the neighborhood, set out that same night, which was a stormy one, to reach the public carriage in order to get to Paris.[66] She remained there throughout the period of his imprisonment. Fortune was on Du Pont's side—as he himself acknowledged in a letter from La Force addressed to Irénée on August 12: "Poor Alexandre Beauharnais was unfortunate enough to be the first arrival; as for me, by good luck, the Coach was *delayed*, and the order of the 25th [July 13] did not arrive at its destination till the 2nd of the following month [July 20]: Seven days—even four days earlier, and you would have loved, but you would have mourned your poor old father who would have gone to swell the number of murdered patriots."[67] Du Pont's life was spared by the fall of Robespierre and the ending of the Jacobin terror. Du Pont was arrested on July 22; Robespierre fell on July 27.

At the time of his arrest, Du Pont could not, of course, know that he was to be spared. He faced the ordeal courageously, refusing even to show passive resignation to a fate which he long reckoned might some day come to him. His indomitable conduct in this perilous situation is among the most attractive aspects of his career and may, perhaps, be considered the true measure of the man. Prison could not overcome his essentially sanguine nature nor keep him from the activity that principally sustained him. Count Jacques Claude Beugnot, who had come to know Du Pont during the period of the Constituent Assembly, recorded in his *Mémoires* much information on prison life in La Force. Du Pont's "arrival among us," he wrote, "was most helpful to us all. He outdid himself to scatter words of patience and hope, and he was sure to be found wherever any kindness could be done. We felt sure that he would not lose this chance of instruction in the science of economics. He opened his school; from evening till morning he talked or wrote and as everyone listened with interest or read with pleasure, no one was at a loss for scientific study in the retreat forced alike on master and disciples."[68]

Du Pont's prison career is best revealed in the numerous letters which he wrote from La Force to his son and daughter-in-law.[69] In these letters he assured them that he was well, was not being ill-treated, requested various items to add to his comfort and to make it possible for him to continue his work, instructed them on procedures necessary to effect his release, and gave advice on running the print shop. Actually, his life at La Force was very pleasant. He had considerable freedom, enjoyed witty companions, could exchange notes with his relatives outside, and was allowed to read and to write whatever he desired. The fall of Robespierre removed all anxiety for the future; thereafter, it was a question of being patient until the Thermidorian victors got around to releasing individual prisoners. In Du Pont's case, this matter was unduly delayed more than a month. His most trying experience was, therefore, in restraining his impatience as he witnessed the daily exodus of most of his fellow prisoners while he remained behind.

On the very day of his arrival at La Force (July 22), he wrote to Sophie requesting a bed, towels, and two housecloths.[70] He hastened to assure her the next day that he was "as well as one can be under the circumstances" and repeated his request for four towels and two housecloths, as well as "a little writing paper, a little box of white wood to hold my belongings, a straw arm chair, a little brush."[71] He was, in fact, determined to continue work as if nothing had happened

227

to disrupt the normal routine of his days. He asked Irénée on July 24 to send "four copies of my treatise on national education, and have one ready to send to each member of the Committee of [Public] Safety when I send you word."[72] On July 25, he sent to his son some work for the print shop ("a series of tables of the values of the old weights and measures in the weights and measures of the Republic" drawn up by General Guillaume), suggested the printing of Almanacs based on the Republican calendar, and concluded by requesting a paper chessboard and paper, pen, and some good ink to "continue and finish my work on national education."[73]

According to Beugnot, Du Pont displayed exemplary fortitude in prison. He refused to co-operate with a commission of the Revolutionary Tribunal by disdaining to fill out a long questionnaire which sought to establish the prisoners' political sentiments.[74] When news of the disorders attending the attack upon Robespierre reached La Force,

Du Pont addressed us about the danger with which we were threatened. As for him he intends to sell his life dearly. He exhorts us to do the same and tells us his plan of defense. There are twelve of us who can arm ourselves more or less well with the fire-irons, which fortunately had not been removed, the two daggers that we possessed among us, our knives and the legs of the chairs. We must adopt the ancient order of battle—that is to say, the strongest one shall be the front rank, two more the second, three in the third and four in the last. That disposes of ten men; the two remaining, chosen from the youngest, shall flank the army on the right and left to help wherever reinforcement is necessary. Then we must arrange for our retreat and we will make of our beds a strong barricade behind which we can collect our forces and where we can wait for help from outside. However alarming the situation, it was impossible not to laugh at the seriousness with which this good Du Pont arranged his line of battle.[75]

The decisive events of 9 Thermidor (July 27) brought even greater comforts of mind and body to Du Pont. He informed his son on July 29 that he now had "a little room with a fireplace . . . where I have but one room-mate. Here I can have more quiet in which to finish my work on national education." Then he added: "It is certain that if I had not been arrested eight days ago I would not be here now; and that is another reason for hoping to be given my liberty by those who have always known my profoundly

Republican patriotism."[76] There was little justification for this statement. Du Pont had, it seems evident, become convinced that the Republic must be accepted. In the absence of certain evidence to the contrary, one might conclude that his conversion was essentially a matter of expediency. After the beheading of the former monarch, there was little future within France for anyone desiring a public career who would not support the Republic. One may speculate that Du Pont's acceptance of the Republic must have rested upon a conviction that the Republic alone was capable of maintaining public order and of cleaving to a moderate course. Attempts to restore the monarchy or to revive the Jacobin "reign of terror" would lead only to chaos and civil war. In the future Du Pont would defend the moderate course within the framework of the Republic. He could hardly have believed, however, that his "profoundly Republican patriotism" would be widely known. Nothing in his past public record indicated adherence to republican principles. He could, it is true, recall his early support of the Republic after the abortive flight to Varennes, but he had clearly changed his mind very rapidly. He could, also, point out that he had been elected by his neighbors to be captain of the National Guard of Chevannes,[77] but this was a minor distinction. He may, of course, have been using the term "Republic" in the sense found in political writings of the eighteenth century—that of an orderly government regulated by definite laws, not by arbitrary authority. He set out, in any event, to emphasize his "Republican" zeal. In his letter of July 30, he enclosed a rough draft of a letter which he proposed to send to the Committee of General Security asking for a hearing or an opportunity to answer questions. "If I do not prove to you that the Republic has no citizen more zealous, more devoted, more faithful than I, dispose of me as you will," he wrote.[78]

Succeeding letters are filled with suggestions to his children on what might be done to get him out of prison. He assured them that he was comfortable, but confessed his irritation at the prolonging of his unjust confinement. He enclosed letters to be given to former associates—Grégoire, Sieyès, Treilhard,[79] Ramel Nogaret, Boissy d'Anglas, Merlin de Douai, du Pont de Bigorre[80]—urging that, with the letters, copies of his literary works (especially the treatise on national education) be included for wide distribution where they might do the most good. On August 8, he protested vigorously against certain phrases which Irénée had used in a note to him.

I have not been deceived; I have not *had my eyes opened*; I have done nothing *against the Republic*. I urged it before it existed, worked for it from its beginning. And what I did for the Constitution between those two epochs concerned the sacredness of the oath—unquestionable proof of my sincerity and my Patriotism, and of the confidence that the government chosen by the people should feel in both.

It is both base and stupid to excuse one's self when one has committed no fault; to seem to admit that what one has done which was praiseworthy was wrong; to ask pardon when one is in the right. It is much better to insist—especially when it is true and one can assert it with the firmness of a good conscience—that one has committed no fault, has never said nor done anything disloyal to liberty and equality. An unfounded admission of imaginary mistakes would give an opportunity to one's enemies, and would in history detract from the reputation of a man who has always been as honest and patriotic as he was fearless and who would not have trembled even under the tyrant's guillotine. Sophie can tell you how I accepted the arrest and that I showed no fear.[81]

This long letter is one of the most characteristic expressions of Du Pont's sentiments and general attitude. He was increasingly concerned with the reputation which he would have "in history." He was always eager to justify his conduct, to deny that he had made mistakes, so that posterity would find no blemishes in his actions and character.

On August 12 he wrote to Irénée about the prospects of gaining freedom through the action of organized bodies of his neighbors.[82] Three days later, however, he complained in a letter to Sophie that Irénée had shown too much zeal in attempting to get action from these groups. While appreciating his efforts, he asked if Irénée had not better remain in Paris to attend to business. Victor, who was at Bois-des-Fossés, could take care of matters at home. If a few days longer were required, what difference would that make? The prosperity of the printing business was more important than a few days' delay in getting out of prison.[83]

Toward the end of his prison sojourn, Du Pont displayed even greater patience. Freedom was certain to come in time.

Do not distress yourselves, my dear children [he wrote on August 22], if you find it takes longer than you thought to arrange my freedom. Do not let if affect your health nor interrupt your business. . . .

230

The only important thing is to be sure that justice will be given me and that I will be returned to you. The time, provided it is before the vintage, is unimportant.

I kept my fortitude when I felt my head under the Tyrant's axe and—what was harder to bear—when I thought your fortune in danger of cruel and unjust confiscation. I have quite enough good sense not to distress myself or wear you out, and not to destroy your business, which is at present your most important duty, especially as while I am waiting I am well lodged, well fed, in good company when I choose, free to have my room to myself when it suits me better; and working to help either those who are unhappy, or young men who will be more useful than I when they are old.[84]

The last of his letters from La Force is dated August 25 and is chiefly devoted to expressions of solicitude and of tender greetings to his "dear good children."[85] Shortly thereafter, the prison doors opened to readmit him into the world. Although exact details are hidden, it seems likely that his sons and friends had finally discovered the proper procedure to bring his release. From two of his letters one gathers that one of his friends had arranged for the necessary paper to be prepared in the office of the secretary of the Committee of General Security and to be signed by six members of the Committee.[86] In any event, he was able to return to Bois-des-Fossés in time for the vintage.

For the next few months Du Pont resumed the general routine which had occupied his time at Bois-des-Fossés in the two years before his arrest. He bowed to Irénée's insistence that it was not yet safe for him to return to Paris.[87] His letters during these months are very similar to those written between 1792 and 1794. They picture him continuing his studies and literary work, supervising the farm chores, carrying on his medical practice in the neighborhood, requesting various books and materials from Paris, and overseeing the operations of the print shop from a distance. He had further trouble with authorities at Cormeilles over a certificate of residence, and complained more often of poor health. He worried about Madame Lavoisier, who would not place herself under his guidance. Remarking on these worries in a letter to Irénée on September 25, he introduced a new idea. "[Madame Lavoisier] has embittered my life. I owe to her, we all owe her, all we can do for her. It seems impossible to give her my friendship again, and it was my delight

231

to give her unreserved affection. I wish I could forget her. But her husband, who was my friend, entrusted her to my care when he was about to die and long before his death. Sometimes I think I will end it all by writing to Citizeness Poivre, getting her to come here, and marrying her. But that is a very radical step to take. . . ."[88]

Unfortunately, there is no positive evidence in support of the conclusion which one may easily draw from Du Pont's correspondence available from this period of his life. It seems likely that Madame Lavoisier had not eagerly accepted Du Pont's tentative proposals for marriage. Undoubtedly he had sincere affection for the widow of his late friend and benefactor. He must also have calculated the advantages of marrying her, since she had inherited from her husband the mortgage on Bois-des-Fossés given as security for the loan which made possible the establishment of Du Pont's print shop. Madame Lavoisier had no love for Madame Poivre, widow of Pierre Poivre, another of Du Pont's friends. To marry her would be something of a "radical step," but Du Pont decided to pursue the possibility.

On October 1, 1794, he asked Irénée to send him Madame Poivre's address.[89] He remarked on October 6: "As for the Citizeness Poivre, it would comfort my old age to send for her—she would come; to consecrate my last years to her; and to live all together—three happy families. But I fear that under existing circumstances this action would seem to the woman [Madame Lavoisier] who always disliked the poor, unfortunate widow, a definite abandonment of her in the midst of her afflictions,—and indeed it would be so in some degree. I must then control my anger on one side and my affection on the other, and wait till God, time and events enlighten my mind and determine my conduct. I write letters—and burn them."[90] He turned and twisted amidst indecision, which is reflected in a letter of November 5, although he does not there mention the two widows: "I can arrange the happiness of the Republic and that of Europe and the world, because for them I have no doubt of what is just, useful and honest. I am not sure that I can arrange my own, because the situation is so complicated that it is difficult to know what is right. For whatever is the right step to take will be the happiest in the end."[91] Finally, on December 3, he admitted: "I have written frankly to the Citizeness Poivre, and if she still loves me as I have the hardihood to believe she does, we will have another member of the household in a few months."[92] On December 10 came the good news: "The good Poivre embraces you, my dear children. She still loves me; I scarcely hoped it. And it is necessary to me to be loved. That is why you are all so dear to me."[93] The decision had been made, but the marriage did not take place until nine months later. For "family reasons" Madame Poivre desired to keep their engagement secret for the time being.

The family considerations may have concerned the disposition of her property, in preparation for remarriage. Her daughter Julienne, the wife of Lafayette's friend Jean Xavier Bureaux de Pusy, was always very careful in protecting her rights. Madame Bureaux de Pusy, with a young daughter of her own to care for, had reason to be cautious. Her husband had accepted Lafayette's difficult decision to leave the army and France after the suspension of the royal power in August, 1792; he followed his friend into exile and, with him, fell into the hands of the Austrians. He was still a captive, as he was to remain, until 1797, when Lafayette was finally released. The possibility that Madame Bureaux de Pusy may have been responsible for her mother's hesitancy cannot be documented and must rest upon knowledge of Madame Bureaux de Pusy's later actions. Still, the marriage contract between Du Pont and Françoise Poivre, née Robin, as finally drawn up, explicitly excluded any community of property. Madame Poivre was to retain full disposition of her own possessions.[94] She consented to the publication of the bans of marriage in July, 1795,[95] and the marriage ceremony was performed on September 26.[96] Again Du Pont was fortunate, for his second marriage proved to be as happy and successful as his first had been. Although, years later, the actions of Madame Bureaux de Pusy were to cause some bitterness, the two families at first had no difficulty in joining amiably into one. Bureaux de Pusy was to figure importantly in some of Du Pont's subsequent plans.

Du Pont was much concerned about plans for his future in 1794 and 1795. Irénée remarked in a letter to his wife on October 16, 1794, that "there is a possibility that our dearest friend may be put at the head of the National Libraries."[97] Du Pont rose to the bait. "I would not object," he wrote three days later, "if your friend were given a literary position of which you wrote in your letter before the last. It is the one that would best suit his character, his customs, his position—though I do not think him sufficiently learned. But he learns easily and he would have every opportunity for study. I would, moreover, be in a position to help the printing house. Does the appointment seem probable?"[98] Unfortunately, the appointment was not offered. Du Pont hid his disappointment and kept busy at his desk, writing letters and *mémoires* which might open doors to suitable positions in the government for himself and Victor. Early in November he wrote to Treilhard about sending to the Committee of Public Safety "the beginning of a work on the political interests of the Republic" in the negotiation of a general peace and suggested that Victor be allowed to present his views in person before the Committee.[99] On December 23, he wrote to Boissy d'Anglas that he had been so incapacitated by gout that he had been unable to finish the writing out of his ideas on the general domestic and foreign policies which the Convention should follow. He wrote at length of his thoughts on commerce, upholding the ultimate advantage of suppressing tariffs but admitting that such action would be then premature. He stated his belief that the Convention should not entirely disband after it had finished its work. Only one-third should retire, since it was necessary that the Convention "still guide for two years the body which will replace it. Revolutions are too dear and cost too much blood. Let's not play this game any longer. . . ."[100] Du Pont here clearly favors, eight months before it was adopted, the provision that two-thirds of the members of the Convention would sit in the new legislature. He had never seen any wisdom in the self-denying ordinance of the Constituent Assembly, since it kept out of the Legislative Assembly the very men best qualified to supervise the execution of their own handiwork, the Constitution of 1791.

Du Pont was not immediately successful in finding a position for himself. Victor, however, obtained a place in the Bureau of Foreign Relations. Although he did not at first like this work, he found in it later an opportunity to return to America as first secretary of the French legation. He soon left this position to become French consul at Charleston, South Carolina.[101] Before these unexpected opportunities arose, Du Pont was disturbed by his son's apparent indifference. "I am vexed with Victor, my dear Irénée," he wrote on

November 5, 1794, "because he does not in the least realize the importance of the work with which he is entrusted nor the urgency of the needs of the Republic and of mankind. One would think he believes himself still in the old régime. The Republic has long been at a standstill, because she was pushed aside for a despotism; but now that it has fallen, all her steps will be giant strides, and the accomplishment of treaties, laws and great public works will be as rapid and as astonishing as her military victories."[102]

It was Du Pont's nature to be optimistic about the future, but his enthusiasm, like that of others, was heightened by the victorious course of the war. Everywhere French armies were advancing, as they had been since the late summer of 1793. Long past were the days of danger when many expected to see enemy troops in the streets of Paris. With the future showing brighter prospects, Du Pont could hardly have been serious when he wrote on December 14 that his best course was to retire from public affairs, leaving glory to the young, while holding himself ready to advise in the role of elder statesman.[103] Indeed, within five months he was back in Paris personally supervising the print shop and casting about for opportunities to enlarge his activities.[104] He reported to Felix Faulcon that he was "in requisition . . . to work on the regeneration of the finances," an undertaking which would be easy "if the convention didn't talk so much about it, or talked about it with more enlightenment."[105]

Now that he was back in the center of activity, he was busier than ever at his desk. He wrote and published anonymously several pamphlets giving his views on the political situation and on the kind of constitution which should be established. He defended the Thermidorian Convention from attacks on its actions in overthrowing Robespierre and ending the Reign of Terror. While still at Bois-des-Fossés he had put together extracts from Athanase Auger's translation of Lysias' eloquent oration against Eratosthenes and the Thirty Tyrants of Athens in 403 B. C. At appropriate places in the text he inserted in parentheses the names of former members of the Committee of Public Safety and of the Committee of General Security in order to show how Lysias' famous indictment might appear to a reader unversed in Greek history to be directed against the tyrants from whom France had so recently been delivered.[106]

235

He was, however, more concerned with the future than with the past. Responding to the general invitation issued by the committee appointed to work out a new constitution that all citizens present their views, Du Pont published a substantial pamphlet, in which, as in 1789, he outlined his own ideas about a suitable type of govern-ment.[107] In this anonymous pamphlet he argued that the only practicable government under existing conditions was a republic.[108] He suggested that the legislature be divided into two "sections" and detailed a procedure for reconciling differences, about as cumbersome as the one he had defended in his pamphlet of 1789. He was still afraid of arbitrariness. ". . . Nothing arbitrary in the future! . . . nothing arbitrary! may reason be our King!"[109] He returned to a favorite physiocratic argument that legislators could not *make* laws but only discover and make known those laws "which eternal wisdom has prescribed to common sense."[110] The executive power, he proposed, should be entrusted to a ministry of six men, each one responsible for a specific part of the administration. While conced-ing reasonably large powers to this small group, he sought to keep possibly ambitious ministers within limits by giving the legislature wide supervisory power, by restricting a minister's term to one year, and by making the president of the Senate, one "section" of the legislature, president of the Council of State, comprising the six ministers, with the nominal title of First Minister. This presidency, too, was limited to one year. He wanted a declaration of duties, as well as a declaration of rights, in accordance with one of his favorite maxims: "No rights without duties, and no duties without rights."[111] True sovereignty, he held, resided in the proprietors of the land, though renters of "a dwelling with fireplace" could be given full rights of citizenship, including the vote, upon favorable recom-mendation by the general council of their commune, and all inhabi-tants, even foreigners, should be eligible for any office to which they were elected "by vote of the people or the electors."[112] While he suggests no specific requirements for voter or elector, Du Pont clearly implies that the electorate should be composed of proprietors and others to whom proprietors might accord the vote. There should be no restrictions imposed upon the right of such an electorate to place in office whomever it chose. Du Pont did believe, however, that those elected as deputies to the national legislature should have proved themselves by fifteen or sixteen years of faithful and efficient service in successively higher grades of the departmental administration. Candidates for the legislature might be nominated by petition of six citizens during the first twenty days of the month of Germinal (21 March-20 April). Their names and qualifications would then be published in a brochure and in all the departmental journals. After a month, which would permit electors to study the candidates' qualifications, the electors would assemble on the last day of Floréal (May 19 or 20). Before the election, candidates or their friends might address the electors as a body, but could not converse with them individually. As in 1789, those chosen as electors in the primary assemblies of voters and those chosen by the electors as deputies should be given "instructions" by their constituents, but deputies should not be irrevocably bound by these instructions, if after presenting the desires of their local constituents, they become convinced that these particular requests must be sacrificed to "the most general interests, to reason, justice, demonstrated truth."[113] The term of office of legislators should be four years; each year one-fourth of the membership of the legislature should be changed by election.[114]

When the Committee of Eleven presented its proposed constitution to the Convention in August, 1795, Du Pont was not entirely satisfied. Anonymously he published another pamphlet of *Observations*.[115] While praising the committee for its "important service" in attempting to return "to the very point where we were on 15 July 1789," he found defects in its proposals.[116] He did not find that the new constitution explicitly enunciated principles which he considered essential for the future welfare of the country. "I claim," he wrote

For the proprietors of the soil, the sovereignty of the country, which they have conquered by buildings and cultivation;

For lease-holders who have patriotism and good morals, a right of representative citizenship;

For small communes, their conservation, the privilege of voting in their precincts, the right of naming electors and of giving to the latter instructions which they will transmit to the deputies charged with representing the people;

For the sovereign, freedom of choice.

For all men of merit and talent, eligibility [to office];

237

For the Council of Five Hundred and for the Senate, the obligation to explain publicly in writing the motives of their resolutions;

For the entire republic, means of discovering reason and justice and of making them the foundation of laws.[117]

Regardless of his opinion of the Constitution of the Year III (1795), Du Pont hoped, of course, to participate in the new government. From August to mid-October he was at Bois-des-Fossés, overseeing the harvest and making final arrangements for his marriage to Madame Poivre. As he moved about the neighborhood, he must also have weighed his standing with his former constituents. He made clear his desires in a letter to Irénée on August 24.

I have decided to go into the new legislature and the Council of Elders. I do not know that I can go to the preliminary assembly or the electoral assembly. But I hope that if my friends speak of Du Pont de Nemours who abolished the salt tax and the tax on wheat, and who so correctly foretold the end and the effect of the assignats, he will not be rejected.

I should like to be elected from the two departments—the Loire, and the Seine and Marne; the latter so that I may not lose my name de Nemours. The Electors from Nemours and from the communes of that district will certainly vote for me. I am sure too of some from Melun and from Coulommiers, in the same department. It is not impossible that I may have some votes in Paris.

I fully approve of the law that orders that five hundred members of the convention shall be reëlected and all wrong doers expelled. I would not like an election that would remove a majority of the convention; I would fear a royalist revolution which after thoroughly oppressing the country, would cause a Jacobin revolution.[118]

Du Pont's reason for supporting the unpopular "two-thirds decree," by which members of the Convention were to hold two-thirds of the 750 seats in the new legislature is thus explicitly stated in this letter. His words also reveal again his support of the Republic as the only possible middle course under the circumstances. He was determined to hold to the policy which he had earlier adopted, that of combating "on right and left all the factionists on both sides."[119]

Although his estimates of his chances for election by two departments were overoptimistic, he was chosen as deputy from Loiret.[120] He did not drop the "de Nemours" from his name, despite the fact that Nemours was in the department of Seine-et-Marne. Before his election he was married to Madame Poivre, who accompanied him to Paris when he went to take his place among the members of the legislature. The new government was organized in late October, and Du Pont was chosen to sit in the Council of Elders.[121] From this vantage point he would continue to champion the cause of moderation and of order.

Chapter VIII

Council of Elders (1795-1797)

ALTHOUGH THE CONSTITUTION of 1795 fell short of Du Pont's ideal, it contained many provisions which he could endorse. If it did not explicitly designate proprietors of land as the sovereign power, it was solicitous of property in its provisions regarding the franchise. Except for soldiers who had fought for the country, only adult males who paid a direct tax on landed or personal property had the right to vote. Urban and rural proletariat were thus excluded. A higher qualification was required of electors who had to own or lease property equal in value to wages paid at locally prevailing rates for from 100 to 200 days' labor. The maintenance of a system of indirect elections, in which the electoral assemblies would presumably be composed of men with substantial property interests, was certainly not contrary to Du Pont's desires. The electoral assemblies, not the voters, chose the men who would fill important local offices or be sent as deputies to the legislature.

The Legislative Body (*Corps Législatif*) was divided into two houses, another arrangement which Du Pont had consistently favored. The Council of Elders, to which he was elected, was to be composed of 250 men at least forty years of age and either married or widowed. The Council of Five Hundred was made up of men at least thirty years of age, who need not be married. The Council of Five Hundred was to originate all legislation, but its resolutions could be vetoed by the Council of Elders. The executive power was assigned to five Directors, who had to be at least forty years old and who would hold office for five years, except that each year one Director had to be replaced. The Directors were to be selected by

240

the Council of Elders from a list of nominees submitted by the Council of Five Hundred. With power thus distributed, a return to the Jacobin "dictatorship" was considered unlikely. This distribution of power was, however, the fatal weakness of the Constitution of 1795. It provided no definite method of resolving differences among the two Councils and the Directory. The result of this defect, which Du Pont did not foresee, was that serious differences were to be resolved by unconstitutional actions or coups d'état, the last of which brought the overthrow of the government by Napoleon Bonaparte.

The fact that the government of the Directory, for that is the name by which it has come to be called, was overturned in 1799 and was replaced by the brilliant reign of Bonaparte as First Consul, later Emperor, has given it a bad reputation in the estimate of most commentators. It did not preside over an inspiring period of French history, but it should not be held responsible for that situation. Inevitably, there would be a period of relaxation, of settling down, from the tensions of the Reign of Terror and Robespierre's Republic of Virtue. If the moral standards of some of the officeholders of the time were not very high, neither were those of many Frenchmen not in public office. If the Directory did not solve its major problems, neither had the governments which had preceded it. It inherited these—notably in the areas of finance, religion, and warfare; it did not create them. Some recent students of the period are inclined to see more merit in the efforts of the government of the Directory than many of its contemporaries and most nineteenth century historians found.[1]

The new government did not begin under very favorable auspices. Opposition to the two-thirds decree of the Convention had developed into a threatening demonstration, inspired for the most part, it seems, by royalist sympathizers, on October 5 (13 Vendémiaire on the revolutionary calendar). Barras, the former noble and terrorist, who had been charged by the Convention with the responsibility of defending it against the rumored attack, had wisely turned the command of the artillery over to a recent acquaintance, Napoleon Bonaparte, a young officer renowned for his feat at Toulon in December, 1793, when, by a masterful deployment of cannon, he had made possible the capture of the forts overlooking the harbor. Under menace of the guns from the forts, the British ships in the harbor were forced to evacuate, thus withdrawing their support of the insurrection in the city, which was soon reconquered by the revolutionary army. Bonaparte gave further proof of his ability; he saved the Convention by a "whiff of grapeshot," which scattered the mob descending on the Tuileries. Throughout October, however, there were minor disturbances and wild rumors in the capital.[2]

Du Pont's position in the legislature would provide ample opportunity for him to express his opinions on the actions of the new government. He also sought means to disseminate general information and personal viewpoints outside the legislative chambers. Such means could best be found in the regular issuance of a journal of news and opinion from his print shop. As early as September, plans for such a journal, to be called *L'Historien*, were well underway, and the first issues were being prepared.[3] Actual publication did not begin until November 22, but the first number contained a summary of the establishment of the new government and of the meetings of the legislative bodies from their first sessions through the previous day. *L'Historien* became a very useful journal, containing information and comment, letters and essays, on a wide variety of topics both foreign and domestic. It gave a rather full account of the debates in the Councils; beginning with number 181 (May 20, 1796), Du Pont's associate Jean Baptiste Bienaymé assumed sole responsibility for these accounts. Du Pont continued to be responsible for the literary and political sections. He enjoyed the collaboration of several distinguished men in his editorial labors—writers like Morellet, Forbonnais, and Peuchet; men of affairs like Jollivet and Lanjuinais. Although *L'Historien* claimed his chief attention, Du Pont also collaborated in the publication of other journals, especially the *Nouvelles politiques nationales et étrangères*, which had been appearing since November, 1792, and the *Journal d'économie publique, de morale et de politique*, which his friend Pierre-Louis Roederer founded in August, 1796.

Although he had given his approval to the two-thirds decree conceding to the deputies of the Convention a majority in the new government, Du Pont could never consent humbly to play a prescribed role. He would create his own role in the Government. He would confront issues on their own terms, not merely in accordance with the designs of the majority in control. At the

242

rostrum of the Council of Elders and in the pages of *L'Historien* he was determined to express his own opinions. These opinions came to be so frequently in opposition to the majority of the Directory and of the Council of Five Hundred that Du Pont is customarily ranked with the constitutional royalists who sought the overthrow of the regime.[4] As an ideal, Du Pont preferred a monarchical government, as his frequent defense of the royal prerogative in the Constituent Assembly made evident. But times had changed, and one must compromise with the existing situation. He had stated his fear that a royalist insurrection to restore the Bourbons would lead to chaos and anarchy, from which only the Jacobins might profit. A moderate course preserving right principles must be maintained. So long as this objective was pursued, the exact form of government was not so important. The Republic seemed now to offer the best hope for moderation; hence, as Du Pont said on January 10, 1796: "There are no royalists in the Council [of Elders]; everyone wants the constitution of 1795, which is republican."[5] Du Pont's opposition to the majority was an opposition to specific measures which he thought unwise or impractical. His objective was not to weaken and to destroy the Government, but to improve and to strengthen it. As a result of the efforts of Du Pont and others, the Council of Elders was sometimes induced to oppose the measures of the Directory. It is, therefore, not difficult to understand how in the eyes of some contemporaries and of later students, this opposition appears to be purely obstructionist in character, evidence of a desire to bring the Directory to a state of impotence in order more easily to overthrow it. Certainly, the majority of the Directory so regarded it, and felt justified in overturning the opposition by force. The fact was that the kind of moderation championed by Du Pont was no longer popular. Circumstances seemed to demand more forceful and positive action.

The work of committees was not so important in this legislature as it had been in the Constituent Assembly. Although Du Pont served on numerous special committees charged with reporting on resolutions submitted to the Elders by the Council of Five Hundred,[6] he was less burdened by such tasks than he had been from 1789 to 1791. This greater freedom gave him more time to devote to the preparation of his speeches in the Council. As a result, his oratorical style improved. Occasionally, he still spoke at too great length, but he more often succeeded in getting more verve and more color into his remarks. Sometimes they have a mordantly ironic tone which his earlier speeches lacked. His colleagues recognized his abilities by naming him one of the four secretaries on July 19, 1796,[7] and by electing him President of the Council of Elders on July 19, 1797.[8] In the latter office Du Pont served for one month, the prescribed term. According to some accounts, he had trouble at the beginning, showing the same tendencies to argue with speakers and to permit the session to get out of hand as he displayed during his brief period as President of the Constituent Assembly. After the first few days, however, he seems to have handled the meetings with more tact and efficiency.[9] He was proud of the honor shown him by his election to this office. On July 20, 1797, he wrote to his son Victor: "When you saw me go to have my head cut off, and when you grasped my hand as you said your last adieu, when you wept for me on the second Thermidor of the year two, neither you, nor our Josephine, nor poor Sophie who accompanied me, nor certainly I myself believed that in three years from then, day for day, I should take possession, not of the most powerful, but the most dignified position in the Country."[10] He could not know, as he wrote this letter, that, soon, he was again to be cast from the heights of glory and to be placed in grave danger.

The rather consistent opposition which Du Pont was to maintain against the majority of former members of the Convention was not long in showing itself. This majority in the Council of Five Hundred assured its control of the selection of the five Directors by drawing up a rigged list of candidates to be submitted to the Council of Elders. Of the fifty men nominated, only six were generally known. Except for La Reveillière-Lépaux, Reubell, Sieyès, Barras, Cambacérès, and Le Tourneur, they were men with only local reputations—engineers, mayors, judges, and other present or former officials in the local governmental units. Du Pont refused to ignore this subterfuge. He tried to delay the choice of the Directors, hoping, probably, that serious opposition would form if the matter were not rushed through the Council of Elders. He remarked on October 31, 1795, that the votes recorded after the names of many of the candidates clearly proved that the Council of Five Hundred had drawn up the list by plurality vote. When another member, Serres, and La Revellière-Lépaux, then serving as President of the Council of Elders, were able to demonstrate immediately that the Constitution called only for a plurality vote in this case, Du Pont had to withdraw his motion to postpone the final selection until the other Council had revised the list in accordance with the vote of the majority.[11] He next requested a few days' delay in order to get information on the unknown candidates.[12] "Far from us the thought," he remarked, "that in bringing together with a few celebrated legislators a large number of unknown men, it was desired to force the choice, to give to the country Directors who would not sustain the double test which the Constitution requires, and bring together the free sentiment of the two councils. Robespierre conquered France by force; this would be to conquer it by ruse! The action would not be less culpable."[13] The biting words were in vain. The five well-known men at the top of the list were elected by the Council of Elders: La Revellière-Lépaux, Le Tourneur, Reubell, Sieyès, and Barras. When Sieyès refused to serve, the same procedure was used to elect a replacement. A second list of ten candidates contained only two names which were known—Carnot and Cambacérès. Carnot was elected by 181 votes to 157 for Cambacérès.[14]

Failure never silenced Du Pont. A few days after the defeat of his effort to delay the choice of the Directors, he actively worked with Portalis, Tronchet, and Barbé-Marbois in the Council of Elders in opposing a scheme of the Directory to name judges in those localities where electoral assemblies had not yet filled such vacancies. Again his first attack was against the tendency to rush matters through the Councils. On November 14, he stated bluntly that it was probably "a question of violating the Constitution that urgency is asserted; . . . it is because of a desire to have these administrators and judges named in the manner of Robespierre. . . . But I—but all those like me who have taken an oath to the republican constitution—will not suffer it to be violated; we will not consent to confer on the executive Directory the royal prerogative which has been proposed to us."[15] Now that the monarchy was no more, Du Pont put a somewhat different emphasis on his arguments. He no longer stressed the necessity of a strong executive as a safeguard against legislative tyranny, but put forward more prominently the doctrine of the separation of governmental powers. This doctrine formed the core of his major speech on this issue on November 15.

> It is not without reason that in all countries where there has been [anxiety] for . . . liberty, the judicial power has always been separated from the executive power and from the legislative power. It is to the independence of the judiciary . . . that the security of persons and ownership of property most particularly tends. What founds tyranny, what characterizes and consolidates the despotism of the sultans and the king of Morocco, what particularly formed [the despotism] of Robespierre is the naming of judges from among men disposed to follow the wishes of [those who name them].

In any country free or half-free, he asserted, the executive power has not taken any part in the election of judges. He cited Montesquieu on the separation of powers and recounted his own experience: "I have served with zeal and courage a great republic, the loss of which I mourn today, the Republic of Poland, and I have seen all kinds of disorders born from the influence which the executive power took in decisions. . . ." This pernicious influence of the executive would be even more powerful in any situation in which the executive could choose the judges.[16] The majority of the *conventionnels*, however, gained the victory. With minor modifications, the resolution conferring this power of appointment upon the Directory was approved the next day.[17]

Du Pont was worried by what he regarded as a trend toward despotism on the part of the majority upholding the Directory. He supported the proposal of Barbé-Marbois to appoint a special commission to collect information on agriculture, industry, commerce, colonies, army and navy, revenues and expenses—indeed on any matter which might come before the Councils. He argued that the Councils needed this information in order to do their work properly; *agendi recte sapere, principium est et fons*, he declared, in an obvious misquotation of Horace, a fault of which he was frequently guilty.[18] He must surely have recognized the potential usefulness of such a commission in gathering data which could provide a means of checking upon the administration of the Directory. The same thought probably occurred to the majority, and it defeated the proposal.[19] Despite the fact that his views were usually voted down,

Du Pont seldom missed an opportunity to protest against the actions of the majority in the Directory and the Councils.[20]

At one time Du Pont sensed greater dangers in another direction. The day after the Directors appointed General Bonaparte to the command of the army of Italy, he wrote to Reubell: "Don't you know what Corsicans are? For a thousand years no one has ever been able to rely upon them. They are shifty [*mobiles*] by nature. They all have their fortune to make, and Pitt can give them more guineas than you can coin penny pieces for them."[21] Three months later *L'Historien* printed a letter, presumably written by Du Pont, defending the cannonade of 13 Vendémiaire and afterwards regularly published the proclamations and letters of Napoleon sent from Italy.[22] After the French occupation of Venice, *L'Historien* published the letter of commendation which the Directory sent to Napoleon, but, in the next number, Du Pont added a note that the printing of the letter should not be regarded as an indication that *L'Historien* approved of the action. Indeed, "the abuse of power by the general on this occasion was contrary to the French constitution and to the law of nations," and the Directory should not have despatched its letter of approbation.[23] There is no evidence that Napoleon saw these comments, but there is certainly the possibility that they were brought to his attention. His subequent treatment of Du Pont may have been influenced by the viewpoint expressed by *L'Historien* at the time when his victories were bringing him the first taste of glory.

Du Pont's interests as a member of the Council of Elders were as varied as they had been when he was a delegate to the Constituent Assembly. Financial matters again claimed his chief attention, but few others passed through the Council without stirring him to some comment. He continued to show his dislike for arbitrary action of any kind and his solicitude for the just treatment of individuals and groups. He protested frequently against the vague and general wording of resolutions before the Council, for he saw in such loose phraseology the cloak for arbitrariness and injustice. As in the Constituent Assembly, he seemed sometimes to carry his protests to ridiculous lengths. Even if an issue might appear petty, however, there is no reason for questioning his sincerity.

His attitude was early displayed in successful opposition to a resolution providing penalties for encouraging desertion from the army. He showed the necessity for distinguishing between individuals accused of actually hiring or recruiting deserters (*embaucheurs*) and those accused merely of encouraging desertions (*provocateurs*). The first crime was a serious and specific offense; the latter was very vague, could be extended to cover all sorts of circumstances, and would, therefore, open the door to arbitrary actions. In Du Pont's opinion, the Council of Elders had the special duty of assuring that laws would be just and exact, because it was "principally instituted to perfect not only the spirit but also the context and the letter of the laws." His forceful conclusion so completely stripped bare the weaknesses and inaccuracies of the proposed resolution that the Council was forced to reject it.[24] His stand on apparently trivial matters was shown in his strenuous objection to the designation of "patriots" assumed by the citizens of Montélimart in a congratulatory address to the Councils. Unable to prevent insertion of the address in the *procès-verbal* of the Council of Elders, he sought to modify the use of the designation *"les patriotes."* "You cannot approve that men call themselves exclusively patriots; this would be to re-establish a nobility, that of pretended patriotism, as under Robespierre; the constitution has proscribed all nobility. . . ." He refused to drop the matter until he succeeded, on the following day, in replacing *les* with *des* before the word patriots. All France is patriotic, he declared, and reminded the Council again that it had been Robespierre and his associates who had taken for themselves exclusively the title of friends of liberty and equality.[25]

Having himself endured what he considered unjust proscription, Du Pont was eager to obtain justice for others who were improperly subjected to hardships by the laws against émigrés, laws which had often been hurriedly promulgated. The time for calm reappraisal had come, he believed, and the clear duty of the Government was to judge cases upon individual merit and to rectify the errors committed by previous sweeping and arbitrary actions. On January 29, 1796, he tried in vain to win postponement of a resolution excluding four members of the Councils from their legislative functions until the Council of Five Hundred had revised the list of emigrés upon which their names had incorrectly appeared.[26] He waged a determined campaign against the law of 3 Brumaire, by one provision of which those listed among the émigrés were excluded from the general amnesty granted at the close of the National Convention.[27] The majority in the Councils favored revision of this law. Du Pont argued on November 18, 1796, that certain regulations, of which the misnamed "law" of 3 Brumaire was one, were provisional only, and once readmitted to deliberation, were no longer effective. Hence, in proposing six articles to maintain and to amend the "law" of 3 Brumaire, the Council of Five Hundred was out of order. The "law" was a dead letter, and entirely new proposals had to be submitted for consideration. He urged the members of the Council to accept this viewpoint by recalling at once Jean Jacques Ferrand-Vaillant of Blois (Loir-et-Cher), who had been expelled from the Elders in accordance with this law, and others who had suffered similar unjust discrimination. He was so eager for fair treatment of individuals that he conceded: "If you do not believe you are able in your own heart to act relative to the regulation of 3 Brumaire as in the light of a revoked law, I shall press you with all which God can give me of force and talent to approve the resolution [of the Five Hundred to amend the law]; for, in that case, the safety of the Republic and your glory will seem to me obviously united."[28]

Du Pont displayed a continuous interest in the problem of the émigrés. He was incensed by a resolution in January, 1796, to permit seizure by the State of that portion of a patrimonial estate which would have gone to a son who was an émigré. "From the moment that the resolution would be approved," he cried, "every corrupt youth, perfidious souls, scandalous women, would grab children arriving at manhood, and would say to them, you are master of a portion of your father's fortune." Such a situation would place fathers in an intolerable and unjust position. They would have to pay off extravagant sons who threatened to emigrate if they did not receive their portions of the estates; and they would lose those portions to the State if the sons carried out their threat upon refusal of the fathers thus to be blackmailed. "Citizens," he concluded, self-righteously, "do not prepare for yourselves regrets similar to those which will torment my colleagues of the Constituent Assembly. At that time [they] rejected the proposal which I made of using assignats only in payment for the national domains, and not making them current money. Today [they say]: Ah! if we had believed Du Pont de Nemours." In this matter the Council heeded his warning and rejected the resolution.[29] Months later, in August, 1796, Du Pont supported a resolution to stop the sale of estates owned jointly by émigrés and resident citizens. Although he admitted that the resolution was not well drawn, he urged its passage, since further delay would bring excessive hardship to co-proprietors. If the resolution, which provided, at least, a beginning of justice, were not passed, the Councils might not, in the press of work, get around to passing any similar decree, either better or worse.[30] Once again he had some success, for the resolution ultimately became a law permitting division of such jointly owned estates in order to protect the rights of a co-proprietor who had not emigrated.[31] He also won the support of the majority in seeking fair treatment for fugitives in the Rhineland. Many had been driven there by exigencies of war and necessity for seeking employment; they were not émigrés; they had been unable to get back to France within the short period allowed by the law of 22 Prairial (June 10, 1795); their merits should now be judged on an individual basis; they should not be arbitrarily discriminated against by a general disqualification.[32]

So numerous were Du Pont's remarks on a variety of subjects which came before the Council of Elders that many must go unnoticed. A consideration of his statements on some of these miscellaneous matters may be useful in judging the consistency of his views. He regarded himself as an opponent of all kinds of tyranny. He was, therefore, dissatisfied with the oath against royalty, which members of the Councils were expected to take on 1 Pluviôse (January 20-21). It was not sufficient, he thought, merely to state: "I swear hatred to royalty." He preferred to "swear hatred to royalty and intrepid resistance to every species of tyrants, whatever their number and their power."[33] Had he not feared disorder in the Council, he would have proposed an even more explicit formulation: "I swear hatred, or what is more effective and nobler than hatred, I swear intrepid resistance to royalty and to every species of tyranny, whatever may be the number and the power of tyrants. I swear zeal, fidelity, love, untiring service to the Republic, to liberty, to humanity, to equality, to property, to security, to justice, to the Constitution."[34] A year later, at the time of the oath-taking, he braved the displeasure of the

Council by insisting upon the alteration in the wording of the oath made by his colleague, Vincent-Claude Corbel. The prescribed oath in 1797 was in these terms: "I swear hatred to royalty and to anarchy; I swear attachment and fidelity to the Republic and to the Constitution of the year 3." Corbel had added, after the word "royalty," the phrase "in France and to all tyrannies," but withdrew this formulation after loud protests from other members of the Council. After he took the prescribed oath, Du Pont added: "I avow the exception made by our colleague Corbel, in order not to disaffect the kings who are our allies." This partly sarcastic remark further disrupted the session. Jean Dusaulx added to the disturbance, after he took the oath, by stating that he approved of the modification made by Corbel and Du Pont. After demands that they be called to order, Du Pont finally repeated the oath as prescribed, but would not withdraw his remark that he still agreed with Corbel.[35] His attitude was not based upon a desire to be merely sarcastic or obstructionist; he wanted to make clear his conviction that tyranny, tyranny of any kind, not royalty alone, was the enemy.[36] Such remarks did not win any friends for him among the old majority; instead, they strengthened suspicions that he remained a royalist in his deepest convictions.

These suspicions were not justified. Du Pont sincerely wished to support the Republic, but he could never relinquish his profound aversion to governmental measures which he regarded as arbitrary and dangerous to individual rights and justice. In July, 1796, he successfully opposed a measure to economize on pensions by decreasing the amount paid to widows of civil agents of the navy. Why should one group alone be discriminated against? He could easily agree that the pension lists needed revision in order to eliminate waste, but insisted that the revision should be a general one.[37] On the other hand, he won no support at all for his impressive attack in March, 1796, on the inexact phrasing of a law calling foreigners in Paris "more than suspect" and requiring citizens to inform the authorities of false declarations by these foreigners. Here, he believed, was a prime example of arbitrary action, "not worthy of any legislative body"; nevertheless, the Council of Elders approved it.[38] Again, in April, his sound arguments against part of a proposed law holding printers as well as authors liable for "abuses" of freedom of the press were disregarded. If that part of the law were adopted,

251

he pointed out, printers would have to assume a role similar to the old royal censors. They would have to read everything which they planned to publish; obviously this was an impossible task, even for the owner of a small print shop with only four presses. Furthermore, he reminded the Council, printers were often only artisans, subject to common human failings. How could they overcome the influence of ignorance and passion in judging the manuscripts submitted to them? The advancement of truth and knowledge could be seriously impeded, if this provision were retained in the law. His plea fell upon deaf ears.[39]

Although he disclaimed any personal interest, believing that "none of those who know me will suppose in me any motive which is not honest and strictly patriotic," he defended the attitude of proprietors of printing establishments toward the national print shop. No one, he asserted, wished to destroy the press of the Republic, but one could desire that it be better managed, more restricted in its operations, and subsidized by the Government to a much smaller extent. Private print shops could do most work better; yet the national print shop should be used for special jobs which were hardly likely to bring any profit. His argument was basically a defense of the rights of private enterprise.[40] In a similar vein, he had argued in January, 1797, for private ownership of canals. He did not believe that the State could afford to build and to maintain them; furthermore, he held that privately owned canals would be better managed. "What is it which men, even mediocre [men], administer well, with all their intelligence, with an indefatigable activity? Their affairs, their fortunes, their properties; those [things] which they hope to transmit to their children."[41]

Du Pont spoke strongly in favor of the promulgation of a civil code:

It is here that you have truly to fulfill the honorable title which you bear. Until the present, pressed by the results of the revolution and by the extraordinary circumstances in which the Republic found itself, you have made only administrative acts which are called *laws*, because our political dictionary is very imperfect. But in passing and in promulgating the civil code, you will really make a *law*, you will be truly *legislators*. A civil code ought to be, of all works, the most seriously labored over; it ought to be the masterpiece of philosophy, of morality and of justice;

it ought to impress respect, not only by the effect of the political power which obliges one to obey it, but, especially, by the incontestable sagacity of all its terms.

He wanted the Council to authorize all its members to have their observations on the project of a civil code printed on the national presses and distributed to the members of both Councils. When several members complained of the expense which this proposal would involve, the matter was turned over to a committee of four, including Du Pont.[42] Nothing came of it. The driving energy of Napoleon Bonaparte was to be required to make the Civil Code a reality, but the work done on a code during the period of the Directory was useful in the later efforts which led to the actual promulgation of the law codes.

Du Pont remained faithful to his convictions in taking a stand against imprisonment for debt as a practice subject to evil abuses,[43] against the lottery as an institution detrimental to sound morality,[44] and against highway tolls levied by the Government as obstacles ruinous to commerce rather than sources of adequate revenue.[45] He also displayed his usual concern for the efficient operation of the various departments of the Government. He opposed a resolution permitting free postage of letters from private citizens to members of the Government, holding further that the franking privilege of members of the Government should not be extended to include letters sent to private citizens or to constituents. The payment of postage on such communications would bring in a needed revenue, and remove any danger of returning to the evil practice of farming out postal concessions.[46] He spoke at some length on improving the organization and functioning of the national Treasury.[47] During the final week of his service in the Council of Elders, he criticized the Ministry of Foreign Affairs for excessive and wasteful expenditures, but argued that these expenditures had to be met, since they were made on the faith of the Nation.[48]

Throughout the period of the Constituent Assembly, Du Pont had maintained that financial stability must come first, that no enduring government could be successfully erected upon an unsound financial foundation, that nothing worthwhile could be accomplished until the public finances were in order. Holding to this view, he could never be happy under the government of the Directory, which had to operate on a very shaky financial foundation. In the disorders of the Revolution, the financial administration had become thoroughly disorganized; revenue from taxes had been disastrously declining; the value of paper money plunged downward to practically nothing; and there was a serious scarcity of metallic currency. The net income of the country had fallen, Du Pont was to assert, from 1,500 million livres in 1788 to 800 million livres in 1795, and there was little free capital available.[49] The Minister of Finances remarked despairingly that the manufacture of assignats could not keep pace with expenditures.[50] Except for the tribute laid upon conquered territory by victorious French generals, the Government would likely have faced total financial collapse. While it certainly did not ignore the problem, the Government of the Directory was unable to put forward a bold plan to solve it. In these circumstances, the part which Du Pont would play was clear. As he had done before, he would speak out against impracticable expedients and would plead for the vigorous prosecution of a general and consistent plan of public finances.

The first important scheme which the majority saw fit to propose was that of a forced loan levied on the "rich," the upper fifth of all taxpayers—that is, on those who paid the most taxes. The plan, proposed in November, 1795, sought to raise 600 million livres within a month by assessing definite amounts to be contributed by each individual in the twelve classes into which the eligible taxpayers were divided. The amounts assessed varied from 1,200 livres upon individuals in the first class to 100 livres upon those in the twelfth class. Payment was to be made in specie, in grains, or in assignats reckoned at current value.[51] The Council of Five Hundred approved the plan without serious discussion.

In the Council of Elders, Du Pont delivered a carefully prepared discourse against the proposal, which he refused to regard as a loan. A forced contribution without interest or positive assurance of repayment was actually a tax. He sought to demonstrate that the French people did not have the resources to pay such a tax. He reviewed at length the precipitous decline which the net income of the country had suffered as a result of the troublesome years of the Revolution. Entire branches of industry had disappeared, the colonies and Corsica were temporarily lost, the frontier departments and the Vendée were ravaged by war. While income declined, expenditures mounted. No one was "rich" any longer.

It seemed obvious that the income of the "least poor" citizens was not adequate to meet their assessments. The plan apparently assumed that most of the amount requested would come from capital. Where was the capital to come from?—Du Pont wanted to know. Landowners had no reserve funds; such funds had been absorbed during the Revolution by voluntary and compulsory contributions, by the imprisonment of property owners and their relatives, and especially by the depreciation of assignats. Manufacturers and merchants found themselves similarly hard pressed by the partial destruction of the principal centers of industry and of commerce in the flames of civil strife. The only free capital remaining was to be found among the contractors of the Republic established in Paris; and they were the very people upon whom the "loan" would fall with least rigor.

Du Pont held that, in all France, there was an insufficient supply of specie and of paper money to equal the total amount requested. According to his calculations, the value of metallic currency available could not be more than 300 millions, which was only half the amount of the loan. The remainder of the assessment would have to be paid in assignats at the rate of 100 to one. That would require thirty billions in assignats, and there were only twenty billions in circulation! The proposed law would, furthermore, demand payment of the assessment in three installments only fifteen days apart. Du Pont explained to the Council the serious difficulties which, despite apparent success, Pitt had experienced in England in launching a loan of 600 million pounds. The English statesman had had to employ all the devious arts of credit finance in the wealthiest and most industrious nation in the world in order to obtain in small daily installments the anticipated annual yield of his loan. How foolish, then, to believe that substantial sums, actually exceeding the amount of the two types of currency in circulation, could be realized in a few weeks by a similar loan among an impoverished and pillaged people! "To do the impossible," Du Pont declared, "is a noble expression which shows the individual sentiment of a generous heart; to order the impossible is not fitting to an assembly of legislators."[52] Disregarding his admonition, the

Council attempted the impossible by enacting the resolution into law. The forced loan proved to be a dismal failure. As in the matter of the assignats, Du Pont, although he had certainly painted a blacker picture than conditions warranted, was accurate in his prediction of the outcome.

In the main, Du Pont's solution to the financial derangement consisted of three points: no reduction in taxes, no new taxes, elimination of wasteful extravagances in the handling of public revenues. He seemed almost to be echoing Turgot's words of twenty years ago. On July 23, 1796, he presented to the Council of Elders the report of a special committee opposing a general reduction in the land tax, the *contribution foncière*. He argued that there had not been many complaints about the amount of the tax, that there had already been a reduction in rate, that the tax was too recent for one to be able equitably to determine its amount and incidence. The proposed reduction was, nevertheless, approved.[53] Commenting on a report by Laussat, deputy from Basses-Pyrénées, on June 2, 1797, Du Pont attacked the statement that personal and property taxes were too high. It was well to point out, he declared, that the taxes of the old regime brought in about ninety millions more than the present taxes did. Rather than reducing old taxes or fashioning new ones, the Government should seek to improve the situation by attending to a careful sale of the national estates, by increasing postal revenue through ending abuses of the franking privilege, by bringing a more efficient operation into the handling of public revenues. The coming of peace would also relieve many troubles. Only after these possibilities had been exploited to the full was it wise to think of tax reduction.[54]

His major attack on the financial waste of the Directory came on June 28, 1797. Speaking against a resolution which would permit the Directory to order *anticipations* (that is, to spend money before it was received, or even assured), Du Pont castigated it for wanton and profligate waste in the past. During this period when public services and public institutions were in a deplorable state, he sought to remind his auditors that the Directory had had available a larger revenue than at any time since the Republic was established. In addition to the ninety-seven millions from domestic sources, there were the vast sums which poured in from French levies on conquered territory abroad. ". . . the army of Italy, instead of costing [anything], brings in [revenue]; and [the expense of the army] of the North is almost entirely defrayed by the Batavian Republic; and [the armies] of Hoche and of Moreau live in part on the enemy countries." His sturdy onslaught induced the Council in this instance to disapprove the resolution on its second reading.[55] On the whole, however, his threefold program failed of sufficient support for it to become effective.

Du Pont's attitude toward paper money remained as it had been five years before. The depreciation of the assignats had exceeded his gloomy predictions. He was eager to liquidate the total issue as early as possible. In *L'Historien* he even tried to convince himself and his readers that there could be some good in the forced loan if it led to the destruction of the assignats. Since those subject to the loan could make payment in assignats at the prevailing value, they might use this method to get rid of the depreciated paper which could then be burned.[56] The Government was finally forced to extricate itself from the flood of depreciating currency. On February 19, 1796, the plates of the assignats were broken in a public ceremony. If the assignats were to be got rid of, some type of currency had to be substituted. After a lively debate in the Councils, a resolution continuing a system of paper money was approved as the law of 28 Ventôse Year 4 (March 18, 1796). The new law provided for the creation of 2,400,000,000 of *mandats territoriaux*, backed by the national estates and having the force of legal tender throughout the Republic. These mandats were to replace the assignats, which were stabilized at one-thirtieth of their face value, and were to receive special consideration in the purchase of land held by the State.[57] The mandats began to depreciate immediately. Through their use astute speculators picked up exceptional bargains in real estate. They did not, however, appear to Du Pont to be the solution to the financial troubles. He wanted to get rid of them as well as of the assignats. He sought vainly in August, 1796, to win support for a resolution providing that purchasers of land held by the Nation be *required* to pay in mandats, which they could get in exchange for coins. Such a measure, he argued, would bring to the Treasury a needed supply of metallic currency and would hasten the retirement of the paper currency.[58] In order to increase the stock of metal in circulation, he strove—again unsuccessfully—to end the charging of seigniorage in the coinage of metal and of mintage fees in the exchange of paper money for bullion. The collection of such fees, he held, discouraged individuals possessing metal from presenting it for use as currency.[59]

Amidst the financial disorder Du Pont thought that it was the special duty of the Government to guard against measures which might bring undue hardship to individuals. He protested in vain against a variety of proposals which would, he thought, betray this duty. He condemned a resolution which held the ten largest tax-payers in each district liable in case of delinquencies for the entire tax assessed in the district.[60] He attacked a proposal to pay State creditors in depreciated assignats at a rate of 100 to one.[61] He spoke against a plan for fixing the salaries of public officials paid in kind at a rate of two francs for each myriagram of wheat because of the difference in the price of wheat in different regions of France. This difference would lead to grave inequities. An official in one part of the Republic, Du Pont asserted, could live well on the same salary which brought starvation to an official in another region.[62] He argued against a plan to establish a definite scale of values for the depreciated assignats, holding that an accurate and equitable scale could never be worked out. It would be better, he believed, to leave this matter to the conscience and good sense of individuals faced with the problems in business transactions.[63] He delivered a long speech against a resolution extending for one year only a moratorium on the collection of private debts payable in specie. He held that the shortage of specie made necessary a longer time for equitable adjustments to be worked out. His stand cannot be regarded as contrary to his usual attitude on property rights, since, as he pointed out, very many individuals were both debtors and creditors. Besides, he believed that laws should not seek to favor either one group or the other, but to be just to all.[64] Du Pont failed in all of these issues to win the support of the majority.

His viewpoints on issues concerning customs duties, on the other hand, gained some success. As a Physiocrat he did not believe that there was such a thing as a good tariff. As a practical statesman, however, he recognized tariffs as necessary evils in the existing state of society. They were really "a species of reciprocal hostility between nations." Until the happy day foreseen by reason and philosophy when trade would be free, it was necessary to keep the "artillery of customs" in good order—that is, to make certain that tariffs accomplish only what they are expected to accomplish and do least harm to domestic industry, commerce, and agriculture. Every tariff schedule had, therefore, to be carefully prepared. Du Pont thought that the rates established by the Constituent Assembly in 1791 were the most efficient and the most equitable. Certainly they had been labored over for several years with the help of the best-informed merchants, farmers, financiers, and statesmen. These rates might be revised on the basis of experience, as they had been by the Legislative Assembly in 1792; but they should not be supplanted by some entirely new scheme developed by a special commission in a few weeks. Du Pont was determined to oppose the efforts of various interests to effect a general increase in rates. Unreasonably high rates, he held, destroy normal trade, since they are really prohibitive and tend to encourage smuggling. Such high rates could result only in a decrease of public revenue and a disruption of ordinary business with serious effects on the domestic economy.[65]

On December 17, 1795, Du Pont won the support of the majority in opposing a resolution to make customs duties payable in specie. "By its rarity," he declared, "metallic currency has no longer the same value as in 1791; in demanding metallic currency at the present rates, one is increasing the duties in a large proportion."[66] He failed, however, to prevent a substantial increase in certain export duties and in the list of items whose exportation was prohibited.[67] He was also defeated in his efforts to prevent an increase of import duties on leaf tobacco, an increase which he pointed out would distress "the Republic of the United States, our ally" and give encouragement to the "English party" in America.[68] It distressed Du Pont to see the hard work of a decade before on the issue of American tobacco thus undermined.

Of all Du Pont's discourses before the Council of Elders, the one which had the most physiocratic flavor was delivered on July 31, 1797, while he was President of the Council. During a discussion of a project for a land tax, Du Pont left the chair to present a lecture on the importance of the farmer-proprietor in any society. The healthiest society, he, of course, maintained, is one in which the farm is either owned outright or held on a long-term lease by the farmer who works it. The level of agriculture is thereby improved, and society draws from it more in sustenance and revenue.[69] As a general rule, Du Pont's speeches during his service in the Council of Elders were less concerned with abstract ideals. He concentrated more upon practical and specific issues facing the Government. While his basic orientation was still physiocratic, his willingness to compromise with some, but not all, of the existing conditions was more evident.

In addition to his work in the Council, Du Pont found other interests to keep him busy. He continued active supervision of his print shop, of course, and served as chief editor of *L'Historien*. His principal interests aside from his political and professional duties were centered in the National Institute and the new cult of Theophilanthropy. Du Pont was chosen as a member of the Institute soon after its establishment in accordance with article 298 of the Constitution of 1795. This assemblage of learned and talented men was divided into three classes, the first for physical and mathematical sciences, the second for moral and political sciences, and the third for literature and the fine arts. Du Pont was assigned to the second of these classes and attended most of its weekly meetings. He showed himself eager to submit papers on a variety of subjects, often resurrecting from his files *mémoires* which he had prepared years before. Of the five papers which he presented in 1796, for example, four had been written earlier; the fifth was a paltry note identifying the serpent in the third chapter of Genesis and in oriental mythology with love, which brought into life delights and pains to break "the cold uniformity which reason and geometry have generally prescribed."[70]

During his enforced sojourn at his country estate, Du Pont had given much attention to "natural history." He had not only done considerable reading on the structures and habits of plants and animals, but had also spent many hours in observing the various kinds of life in the countryside around Bois-des-Fossés. In his studies he gave free play to his imagination and sought always for parallels between human and animal life and habits. As he once remarked: "We are living creatures and the only creature whom we can examine in all its relationships. Our point of departure in understanding other creatures with whom we are surrounded, our single scale for comparing them, is ourselves."[71] He was convinced that animals possess intelligence, rather than mere instinct, and that each species communicates in a language which man, by careful study, could learn and translate in much the same manner as any unwritten human languge could be learned. He expended much labor on this fancy and wrote, in 1796, that he had "translated the caterwauling of two tom-cats and a female cat on a roof, and a conversation between two spiders in a prison,"[72] undoubtedly refer-ring to La Force, where he had been confined. The only example of his "translations" which he published was that of the nightingale's song during the hatching season,[73] although he explained the twenty-five words in the language of the crows, which he had learned by two winters of careful observation and listening despite "great cold in the feet and hands."[74] The method of imagining parallels with human society and institutions was further developed in Du Pont's long essay on the morality, intelligence, science, and social institutions of ants, which he presented to his class at the Institute on February 26, 1797,[75] and read before a public meeting of the entire Institute on April 4.[76] He concluded that the "civilization" of the ants was equivalent to that which "would be established in a society of our young boys of ten to twelve years old, when their understanding [*esprit*] and benevolence [*bonté*] had already undergone a rather large development, and when they are still neuter [*neutres*], before the period when their sex has become meaningful [*se fait entendre*]." He hastened to add that, if he had "the honor to sit in the principal Academy of a flourishing ant-hill," he would undoubtedly come to a different conclusion.[77] Du Pont was sufficiently well satisfied with this essay to include it as a note in the second edition of his *Philosophie de l'univers.*[78]

He spent so much time preparing this second edition of what he thought of as his major work that he drove Irénée, who had to arrange for its printing, to despair. "You have no idea," Irénée wrote to his wife, "of the troubles and annoyances with which I am overwhelmed and which increase every moment. It is a Penelope's task that I have undertaken, my beloved, in trying to finish dear Papa's *Philosophie.* I cannot get a sheet printed in less than three or four days. He changes, abridges, adds,—and then begins again.

I am in despair. There were to have been only two sheets of notes; there are four now and he has not finished the copy."[79]

Somehow Du Pont found time to participate actively in the effort to establish a new "natural religion," the deistic cult of Theophilanthropy. Although he did not like the name,[80] he eagerly embraced the principles of the new cult and served on the "committee of direction," which met every Wednesday evening to arrange the programs for the public ceremonies, celebrated once in each decade, the ten-day week of the Republican calendar.[81] The chief founder of the cult was J.-B. Chemin, a little-known writer, professor, and librarian, who published a manual on its beliefs and practices.[82] Theophilanthropy professed belief in God, in the immortality of the soul, in fraternity and in humanity. It was a nonmystical cult, embracing, so it was alleged, the truths of revealed religion accepted by all and confirmed by reason. Although, through their public ceremonies, the Theophilanthropists sought to enlist a wide following, they could attract only an elite of the educated. Du Pont was a strong supporter of deistic beliefs. He regarded religion as necessary to social stability[83] but had long been unable to accept the teachings of the traditional churches. Years later he continued to defend deism against charges that it was disguised atheism. "Deists and good Christians," he once wrote, "have an equal desire to conform to God's will, to obey his word. The only difference is that Christians, like Mohammedans, believe this word to be exclusively consigned in one book and Deists discover it in every page of the great book of nature. They say with Voltaire: 'Undoubtedly he has spoken, but to the universe'; and they add: *undoubtedly he still speaks* every day *to the heart, the reason, the conscience of the man of good will.*"[84]

At some point in the careers of many of the major and minor figures of the revolutionary period there enters a ubiquitous and influential personage—Anne Louise Germaine Necker, daughter of the former minister. Germaine had been married in 1786 to the Swedish ambassador to France, Baron de Staël-Holstein, seventeen years her senior. This marriage gave her an established position in society without interfering unduly with her freedom to pursue her own personal, literary, and political interests. From material at present available, it is, unfortunately, impossible to determine when

Du Pont first entered her circle.[85] He had, of course, known her father for a long time and probably found it easier to continue friendly relations after Necker left the Government, when his dissatisfaction with some of the former minister's policies would no longer stand between them. It is certain that Du Pont's friend Talleyrand was among the several men who shared Madame de Staël's interests, as well as her bed; possibly Talleyrand brought the two of them together in the spring of 1797, when Madame de Staël was allowed to return to Paris from exile in Switzerland. Madame had employed her influence before her own exile in late 1795 to gain permission for Talleyrand to return from exile in Philadelphia. The cautious Talleyrand took his time in getting back and did not arrive in France until the summer of 1796. By the spring of 1797, however, they had again joined forces. Their combined efforts gained for Talleyrand the portfolio of the minister of foreign affairs in July. From her drawing room in the Swedish Embassy Madame de Staël was by then using all her influence with various men to save the Republic from a rumored monarchist coup. Du Pont may have spent some time in that drawing room, though reliable evidence is lacking.[86] For the present the biographer must suffer frustration in his efforts to trace the inception and the development of the intimate friendship which later prevailed between this remarkable woman and Du Pont, who was only seven years younger than her father. Du Pont's first recorded remarks about her were certainly not favorable. In March, 1796, in a letter probably addressed to the younger Edelsheim in Baden, he wrote that Necker was "shut up in his château of Coppet, almost invisible and living in moroseness and solitude. His daughter, returning from Paris with two flunkeys, divides her time between her father's home and the balls of Lausanne. She is more lewd, more shameless, more foolish than ever. Her name is such a scandal and her extravagances are so dangerous that the constitutionals have totally abandoned her and let her frolic in her republicanism."[87]

Despite his failure to win effective support in the Council of Elders for most of his ideas and despite the possible dangers to which he was exposed by his rather consistent opposition to the Directorial majority, Du Pont was personally happy during most of this period. He feared the instability of the Government, but he found abundant outlets for his amazing energy. Unfortunately for him, this period of activity at the very fountainhead of events came rather abruptly to a close.

Dissatisfaction with the Government of the Directory had been growing in different parts of France. There had been no real improvement in the wretched lot of the majority of Frenchmen; the threatened bankruptcy of the Government disturbed the propertied classes; the opinion that only army contractors, speculators, and politicians were benefiting from the régime gained wider currency. The glory won by French armies appeared to many to be the only achievement of the Directory; and the generals, not the politicians, were responsible for that. To others the continued policy of conquest and expansion became distasteful; it promised to make war endless and to exhaust the resources and manhood of the country. The deep desire for order, peace, and stability worked its way to the surface of many minds. So long as the old majority in the Councils and the Directory prevailed, many Frenchmen saw no easy relief from the troubles and uncertainties of the times. This majority could not escape the necessity of submitting itself to the electors, in accordance with the provisions of the Constitution for the renewal of one-third of the membership of the Councils. In the elections of the Year Five the expanding discontent was registered.

The elections beginning April 9, 1797, in most localities were attended by widespread violence and disorder.[88] The pent-up dissatisfaction of the people broke into the open in a fashion which frightened the Directory. There was some discussion of proposing to the Councils that the elections be postponed.[89] No definite step in this direction was taken. The results of the elections were a decided blow to the old majority. Although it retained its hold in the Council of Five Hundred, only eleven of the 216 former members of the Convention who stood for re-election were returned to the Councils. The new members were a mixture of conservative republicans and of royalists generally hostile to the existing regime. Barthélemy, the new Director after Le Tourneur was retired by lot as the Constitution required, was not a partisan of the old majority. Together with Carnot, who, weary of violence, showed an inclination to oppose exceptional measures, he brought dissension into the executive body. After the members of the new third had taken their seats on May 20, the Council of Elders showed a threefold division among adherents of the Directory, supporters of the Constitution (among whom Du Pont should be numbered), and proponents of a restored monarchy.[90] This new grouping was reflected in the more independent course adopted by the Council. Not only were new measures urged by the Directory resisted, but also old laws were repealed. Undoubtedly, royalists found encouraging signs in the more tolerant attitude adopted toward relatives of émigrés and toward the nonjuring clergy. There seemed to be some ground for the belief that a Bourbon restoration was in the offing.

Led by Barras, the old majority sensed a favorable change in opinion. The presence in France of royalist conspirators, many of whom operated under the cover of "philanthropic institutes" in various parts of the realm, the brash activities of the royalist group forming the Club de Clichy in Paris,[91] the open boasting of notorious adherents of the deposed Bourbons—all these manifestations began to frighten and to displease influential segments of the population. Purchasers of the confiscated estates of the clergy and nobility foresaw the possibility of losing their property. Generals in the field, like Hoche and Bonaparte, indicated their anger toward a movement which would endanger their positions of glory. Barras, La Revellière-Lépaux, and Reubell among the Directors believed that the time was propitious for a coup which would deliver them from the constant harassment of their enemies. With the help of a general, they determined to purge the Councils and to arrest their intransigent colleagues, Barthélemy and Carnot. When Bonaparte in Italy agreed to dispatch to Paris General Augereau, a firm supporter of the Republic, the conspirators perfected their plans.

Asserting the imminence of a royalist coup d'état,[92] the three Directors ordered the Paris gates closed on September 4, 1797 (18 Fructidor an V). They issued a succession of orders which the soldiers under Augereau carried out. The brief notice which made up the whole of the issue of Du Pont's *L'Historien* for 19 Fructidor describes what happened at the meeting place of the Councils:

This morning the meeting halls of the Council of Elders and of the Council of Five Hundred were besieged.

At half past eight, officers of the general staff, bearers of the order of General Augereau, by force of arms, made the presidents and secretaries leave the platform and the two chambers and required all the members present to depart.

At noon, a large number of members of the Council of Elders, the president marching at their head, presented themselves at the door of their chamber and demanded that it be opened. They were repulsed a second time by armed force.

The same thing happened at the Council of Five Hundred.[93] By the time this notice appeared, hostile members of the Councils, editors and proprietors of opposition newspapers, and Barthélemy were under arrest. Forewarned of what was to happen, Carnot managed to escape.

Du Pont de Nemours was among those arrested in this coup d'état of 18 Fructidor. His frequent opposition in the Elders and his proprietorship of *L'Historien* made him doubly eligible for proscription. Early in the evening of September 5, while he was in bed suffering another of his periodic attacks of gout, he was arrested and carried off to La Force prison, together with his son Irénée.[94] They were freed within twenty-four hours,[95] but, during their absence, the print shop was thoroughly ransacked and many of the presses were damaged. Their release from prison spared them the fate of some of their fellow-prisoners—deportation to the prison colony of Guiana. There was no real case against Irénée, and Du Pont was defended by some of his acquaintances in the Council of Five Hundred and, probably, by Reubell, one of the victorious triumvirate on the Directory. In the debate in the Council of Five Hundred on the proscription of journals and the deportation of their editors, Tallien, a well-known Jacobin who, in 1792, had assisted Pétion in organizing the fête for the mutineers of Nancy, the plan vigorously opposed by Du Pont, denounced *L'Historien* and its editor, as he had done earlier in April, 1796.[96] A. J. C. J. Boulay from Meurthe and Jean-Marie Chénier, on the other hand, praised *L'Historien* as a journal whose obvious merits outweighed its faults and defended the patriotism of its editor, whose past services, they claimed, deserved consideration. Boulay spoke of Du Pont as "an old man of seventy years," and Chénier declared that the members of the Council owed some respect for "an old man of nearly eighty years." They succeeded in having the issue of proscribing *L'Historien* returned to committee for further study.[97] Madame de Staël later declared that she was responsible for inducing Chénier, who had, two years earlier at her request, "made the speech to which M. de Talleyrand was indebted for his recall," to take up Du Pont's cause. In her words, Chénier "ran to the tribune, where he succeeded in saving [Du Pont] by making him pass for a man of eighty years of age, though he was only sixty." She added, with perhaps a touch of malice, that "this artifice was not agreeable to the pleasing Dupont de Nemours, who, so far as the mind was concerned, had always strong claims to youth."[98]

That this "artifice" was significant in gaining Du Pont's release may well be doubted. Certainly he was too well known for anyone in the Government to be taken in by Chénier's remarks. He had not yet reached his fifty-eighth birthday; and while his baldness, his occasional sufferings from gout, and his round shoulders from so many years of bending over his writing desk had robbed him of any appearance of youthfulness, he could never pass for an octogenarian. He had wasted no time himself in striving for his release. The doors of La Force prison had hardly closed upon him before he penned a letter to La Revellière-Lépaux, then presiding officer of the Directory, protesting his arrest and demanding release, since he was innocent of any wrongdoing. He enclosed a copy of this letter in a note to Reubell.[99] Six years later he wrote that Reubell had "protected" him, so that he "got off" with no further indignities than spending one night in jail "with three robbers and an assassin" and having his house pillaged.[100] He gave no clear explanation at the time for the rapidity of his release. All he wrote about it in a letter to Victor on September 20 was that "my remoteness from every intrigue, my loyal attachment to the Constitution convinced the Directory and the Councils that I was entirely incapable of having taken part in any conspiracy." In this letter, he hints at his future plans by mentioning that he had been named by the National Institute one of the "traveling scholars" *(savans voyageurs)* charged with carrying on studies in foreign countries.[101]

It may be that Du Pont actually had no clear knowledge of why he had been so quickly freed. It is, however, also possible that his freedom resulted from a secret agreement which he could not disclose. One problem which occasionally troubled him and which gave the victors of Fructidor some hold over him was that his name had never formally been removed from the official lists of émigrés. He had been able to satisfy the Rouen authorities that he had never emigrated, but, for some reason, their clearance of him had not brought about his definitive removal from the central émigré list, to which he had been earlier reported. It is worthy of note that, on the very day that Du Pont officially resigned from his seat in the Council of Elders, his name was finally expunged from the émigré list. The likelihood is, however, that these events were related only through coincidence, since Du Pont seems to have been making plans for his future, plans which would not permit further service in the Council.

On September 13, 1797 (27 Fructidor An V), the Directory transmitted to the Council of Five Hundred a formal letter of resignation from Du Pont, who explained his action on the basis of his ill-health: "Citizens, colleagues, you have known my assiduity and my activity in all the time in which I believed [myself] able to concur usefully in your labors. You have seen the derangement of my health, [have seen] that all this month I left my bed only by an effort of courage to drag myself to the council. The sojourn, although temporary, which I have had in prison in this state of illness, has [resulted only in] the destruction of my strength. I beg you to agree to my resignation."[102] The letter was sent to the Council of Elders, which merely ordered that it be mentioned in the *procès-verbal* of the meeting of 28 Fructidor.[103] On 27 Fructidor (September 13) Du Pont's name was formally erased from the list of émigrés.[104]

Du Pont was undoubtedly suffering grave discomfort from gout, but he exaggerated the extent of his illness in this letter. Years later his friend, Boissy d'Anglas, described how Du Pont had, on the very day of his release, sought out his family and tried to comfort Madame Boissy d'Anglas and her children. "He offered to share with them all the money at his disposal and to undertake to have my two sons work under his eyes in America, where he had already a project underway to form an establishment."[105] The genesis of this project in Du Pont's mind cannot be determined, but the elaboration of it received his principal attention for the next two years.

Chapter IX

Du Pont and America

THE BUFFET TO HIS FORTUNES delivered in Fructidor was sufficiently severe to convince Du Pont that his hopes and his usefulness in France had come to an end. He refused, however, to despair. Soon after his release from prison, he retired to Bois-des-Fossés with a head full of new plans for the future. France might have nothing further to offer, but, across the ocean, there was the new world of America with its promise of refuge and hope to the unfortunates of the old world of Europe. In the third edition of his *Philosophie de l'univers*, which appeared in 1799, Du Pont was to write: "It is now America's turn. The temperate, moderate, judicious and republican government of the United States offers almost the only asylum where persecuted men can find safety, where fortunes can be rebuilt through work, where the prudence of heads of families may invest their last savings, the last portion of the subsistence of their children."[1]

The scheme around which Du Pont's mind revolved was most agreeable to his physiocratic predilections. Somewhere in the vast and fertile reaches of America might one not establish a model agricultural community operated on the best scientific principles and on a scale large enough to return substantial profits? Would it not be possible to interest European investors in the practicability of such an enterprise? Under wise and prudent management, which he was confident he could provide, such a project, he believed, could hardly fail. The more he pondered, the more enthusiastic he became, and he communicated his enthusiasm and optimism to his family.

If his dream of a happy and prosperous colony of *Pontiania*, stretching over a large tract of virgin land in an idyllic rustic environment, were to become a reality, practical questions had to be answered. How could he safely leave France without finding himself again proscribed among the list of émigrés? If the Institute would designate him as one of their *savants voyageurs*, authorized to carry on studies abroad, this difficulty might be avoided. He solicited support from his colleagues[2] and was successful in gaining this distinction. As he explained in a letter to Victor, who was still in America, "a savant who travels is not an émigré."[3] But what did he really know about America? The whole family must set about learning the English language and gathering information about the United States. As early as September 27, 1797, Irénée wrote to his wife from Paris about a long interview with Colonel Robert Fulton, who had just come back from the state of Kentucky and who recommended settling there. "Oh! how happy we would be," Irénée wrote, ". . . away from the volcano on which we live and established in the *promised land.*" On November 3, he reported in another letter that he was studying English. By that time Du Pont was back in Paris, sorting through his papers in preparation for the new venture. "He is still buried in his boxes," Irénée wrote; "he works at them from morning till night without stopping, and is nowhere near the end of his task, which was a very necessary one."[4] Du Pont was to consume fully two years in getting ready to depart. Years later Victor's wife, Josephine, remembered how *"bon papa* was talking very seriously of departure and not only not departing but not having yet made the least preparation for it, excepting to announce it to everybody. Involved in business and the writing of useless papers, in making visits and the approaching prospect of removal—it was very evident to his son and to all of us that it might be necessary to count our preparation by years before we could be ready to bid farewell to France forever."[5] Josephine was somewhat unfair in this description, for there was much to be done before departure. Still Du Pont did commit several errors in his long-drawn-out preparations.

Victor was the one member of the family who had personal knowledge of the language and of general conditions in the United States. Yet his advice was not sought beforehand. The entire scheme was projected, and modified—and Victor's name was prominently featured in public and private announcements—without consulting him. Du Pont did write to him in December, 1797, and again in March, 1798, but did not make clear exactly what he had in mind. In the first letter, he wrote of a commercial house in Alexandria, unless the new company should join with another firm, that of Odier and Bousquet, in which event headquarters would be in Philadelphia, and of a rural establishment in upper Virginia on "the south branch of the Potowmack." In the second he wrote that Victor would be his "first secretary" during his scientific mission for the Institute and that the projected company was necessary as a device to supplement available funds, since the Republic could not underwrite the expenses of the journey. The letters were chiefly concerned with problems of paying off debts and of settling affairs in France.[6] Not until a turn in his own fortunes brought him back to France did Victor learn what was going on. In 1798 he was appointed French Consul General to the United States and ordered to Philadelphia, then the seat of the Government. Relations between France and the United States had seriously deteriorated by this time to the point of an undeclared naval warfare between the two nations. President John Adams decided to issue no further exequaturs to French representatives. Victor was, therefore, unable to serve in his new post, and hurriedly arranged to return to France with his family in July, 1798. When finally he discovered what his father had underway, he wanted to oppose the enterprise. But plans were too far advanced to be recalled. Filial duty prompted him to go along, although he had hoped to find better employment for his talents in the diplomatic service.

Du Pont also counted upon the help of his old friend, Thomas Jefferson; yet he did not write to Jefferson until August 27, 1798, and, in his letter, did not disclose the real nature of his projected American venture. He merely stated that he was making the voyage as an official representative of the National Institute to further scientific knowledge, although he added that "it is my intention to prolong this voyage as long as my life."[7]

Du Pont did not seek advice from the two men most likely to be helpful because he had confidence in his own ability to launch a successful enterprise. In drawing up a lengthy prospectus, of which only an extended outline has been preserved,[8] he did not, however, hesitate to give them prominent mention:

> Our plan was conceived and will be directed by Citizen Du Pont de Nemours, who for twenty years was inspector general and general commissioner of commerce in France and who will go in the service of the National Institute and with the approval of the government on a cartel-ship and under the special protection of the belligerent nations; Citizen Bureaux de Pusy, an expert engineer, one of the three martyr-prisoners of Olmutz;[9] Citizen du Pont, junior, French consul at Philadelphia;[10] and his brother Irénée du Pont, a business man. The honesty and ability of these citizens are known and appreciated; they will be helped by the advice, support and cooperation of able business men of Switzerland and Batavia.
>
> Du Pont de Nemours and Bureaux de Pusy are investing the greater part of their fortunes in this enterprise, as are Latour-Maubourg and Lafayette, whose credit will be of great value in America. We expect the cooperation of Jefferson, Vice President of Congress, an intimate friend of Du Pont de Nemours whose negotiations for the American treaties cannot fail to insure his welcome by Wasingthon [*sic*] and by all the members of the American government.
>
> The purpose of the enterprise is *chiefly* to buy and sell land and incidentally to organize any commercial and industrial establishments that may contribute to the improvement of the estates and increase their value.
>
> The land will be purchased if possible in upper Virginia and the western counties.

There was much more. The alleged advantages of procuring land in Virginia and of establishing a commercial office in Alexandria were spelled out in detail. The Company was to last for twelve years with a capitalization of at least 200 but not more than 400 shares at 10,000 francs each.

As Du Pont spun out the ramifications of his project, he became more enthusiastic and optimistic. His exuberance, although it did infect most members of his family and inspire their efforts, was no adequate substitute for sound business sense. Du Pont displayed an unwillingness or an incapacity to weigh carefully all the practical difficulties. He regarded vague expressions of interest and promises to invest as cash already in hand. Thus he drew up lists of actual and promised shareholders to show that 214 of the 400 shares had been spoken for. The tenuous nature of the promises upon which he based his optimism is evident in one such list. Here Du Pont, Bureaux de Pusy, Lafayette, and Latour-Maubourg are marked for fifty shares among them; Bidermann, a Swiss banker resident in Paris, is noted as announcing his desire to invest in the company for at least thirty shares from funds available to him in Europe and America *after* the liquidation of the firm of Odier and Bousquet, of which he was principal shareholder; Johannot, Bidermann's partner, was stated to be interested " in the same way" for five shares; Adrien Duquesnoy had asked for two; Regnault St. Jean d'Angely had indicated an interest in taking two shares; men of business like Rousseau, Bisson Le Loup, and Bettefond had expressed a desire for a dozen shares but had not yet definitely decided; Beaumarchais, "if he enters for the portion of money owing him in the United States," a sum now in adjudication, *may* take seventy-five shares; Crillon, on what he can get from Lomassel of Philadelphia, who owes him more than 100,000 francs, might come in, but should not be counted upon for more than three shares.[11] So it goes down the list. It required a great deal of optimism, indeed, to launch a business on these possible investments.

Many of these promises were, of course, never fulfilled. A later list, while maintaining that, by subscriptions or promises both oral and by letter, more than 300 shares were bid for, states that Lafayette had withdrawn; that Latour-Maubourg, although he had not withdrawn, could not pay for his shares, because his wife, who had the money, did not care for the enterprise; that Beaumarchais, who had always promised to invest a third of the sums due him in America, was dead; that Albert Haller of Roche had written that someone had stolen his money; that Mosquenow of Cherbourg had withdrawn and requested return of his investment; that Homberg of Le Havre had not answered the letter asking him when it would be convenient to send the money for which he had given some hope; that, except for Jean Bernard Bicker, the Hollanders and Belgians had withdrawn. There were similar difficulties in the case of most of the other subscribers—Crillon and Hom, Necker-Germany (brother of the former Minister), Duquesnoy, Regnault de St. Jean d'Angely, Pourtales, etc.[12] Obviously there was no prospect of raising the desired minimum of 2,000,000 francs in capital. It is surprising that Du Pont was able to raise as much as he did—214,347 francs. Some of this amount came from the sale of the two houses in Rouen,[13] which Du Pont had inherited from his father, of the Beaumolin and Le Bosse farms[14] (which were dependent upon Bois-des-Fossés, but not part of the main estate), and, finally, of the print shop.[15] The exact sum available for investment from these sales cannot be determined, because some of the money realized went to pay debts and because Du Pont's financial records are confusing, if not inaccurate. He had some hope of retiring all his debts before he left France and contemplated the surrender of Bois-des-Fossés to Madame Lavoisier in satisfaction of the debt incurred for the establishment of the print shop.[16] Madame Lavoisier would not, however, accept this arrangement. Du Pont finally executed a power of attorney in favor of Harmand and J. B. Sirey, authorizing them to manage Bois-des-Fossés in his absence and, if possible, to sell it,[17] since he did not believe that he would ever return to France. The faithful Harmand took over the administration of the estate.

The capital raised was clearly inadequate to launch the venture as it had been originally planned, even after Bidermann had transferred to the company title to 56,000 acres of land in Kentucky.[18] Du Pont never saw this land, and his company never drew any advantage from it. There were conflicting claims to substantial portions of the acreage, little of which contained fertile and useful land. Except for 7,000 acres, later sold by Du Pont's descendants, the rest of the land covered by Du Pont's claims eventually went to Victor Du Pont's creditors.[19]

In view of the limited capital, Du Pont had to adjust his plans. The thought of giving them up completely never entered into his calculation. Indeed, he never lost his optimism. In a printed prospectus he announced that the operations of the firm of Du Pont (de Nemours) Père, Fils et Compagnie would be of two kinds: overseas commerce contracted for upon a commission basis and the purchase and resale of land. He claimed that various European merchants had already agreed to substantial and profitable commissions, most of which involved a triangular trade between Europe, the United States, and Santo Domingo. The company in America would receive cargoes of wines and brandies from Europe, exchange each such cargo for two cargoes of grain, carry the latter in two ships to Santo Domingo, where they would receive cargoes of sugar and coffee. One of the ships would then proceed back to Europe, while the other returned to America. Merchants owning these cargoes should, Du Pont estimated, at the least triple their capital, since his company would charge only freight and commission. The operations of the company would assure to every shareholder a substantial plot of land in America, size varying with the number of shares held. This land would bring to each investor additional profits, aside from the regular dividends and the ultimate distribution of profits upon dissolution of the company. For the first four years, the company would pay annual dividends of 4 per cent, for the second four years 6 per cent, and for the last four years 8 per cent. At the end of the twelfth year, when the company would be dissolved, each shareholder, Du Pont believed, would justly expect that his capital would have increased tenfold, at least. The smallest "shareholders will have acquired a sufficient comfort, and those who have invested in a large number of shares, will have made an imposing fortune."[20]

There was little warrant for such claims and expectations. Du Pont did not realize until too late that large investment in land in the United States was not even a reasonable gamble. The land speculation which was for decades to be rife in the United States was already well underway. Du Pont continued to believe, nevertheless, that land prices would adjust themselves to the point which would make possible the contemplated large-scale investment in land. Meanwhile, the commercial brokerage business, to which the Company would first be devoted, would, he was certain, bring substantial profits, thus providing regular dividends to the shareholders and increasing the capital which could ultimately be put into land. Perhaps it helped his physiocratic conscience to believe that the main objective was land development, though he does not seem to have denounced commerce as a sterile occupation. Indeed, he was determined to succeed in it for the benefit of the shareholders. So long as he was buoyed up by grandiose expectations, he was content and busy in his new role as businessman. He always believed that "by working with patience and determination one is sure to accomplish something worth while."[21]

For two years Du Pont was absorbed in the task of liquidating the past and preparing for the future. He later explained the length of this period as owing to the "break between the French and American

Republics,"[22] but he could hardly have been ready to leave any sooner had the best possible relations prevailed between the two governments. Weeks went by as he worked at arranging his voluminous papers for shipment abroad. Months passed as he attempted to balance and readjust his accounts and his plans when so many of the expected subscriptions of capital failed to come in. He convinced himself, and tried to convince others, that profits from the commission business would soon increase the meagre capital. The examples of his bookkeeping which survive are not very useful in determining the exact status of his enterprise. He constantly covered up the lack of capital by hiding the depressing figures of cash on hand behind a façade of optimistic expectations. Eventually he succeeded in confusing himself. As late as June, 1799, he remarked in a letter that he had to begin his accounting all over again, since he had omitted some items.[23] By that time he faced additional difficulties because the bank of Corsange, in which he had deposited some 36,000 francs of his accumulated capital, had failed. He had not got back this money by the time he sailed for America, although he had won judgment that this sum must be considered a deposit liability of Corsange and hence must have privileged position over the claims of the commercial creditors of the defunct banker.[24] This decision was later appealed,[25] and Du Pont never recovered the full amount of the loss.[26]

Amidst the hectic preparations for departure during these two years Du Pont found time to participate actively in the meetings of his class at the Institute. He submitted eleven *mémoires* on a variety of subjects,[27] including one arguing for the establishment of a primary school in each commune.[28] From September 23, 1798, to March 17, 1799, he served as president of his class.[29]

During these years he carefully refrained from participation in any political issue in order to prevent further complications which might interfere with his plans. The police of the Directory did not entirely ignore him. In November, 1797, the Ministry of Police received an anonymous report that "Du Pont de Nemours has retired to the department of the Loiret, where he receives visits from all the royalists of the neighborhood," and immediately ordered an investigation. The report of Saulnier, lieutenant of gendarmerie at Montargis, completely exonerated Du Pont. Saulnier wrote:

The minister of police was misinformed by whoever told him that this citizen is living at Chevannes. It is true that he was here in vendémiaire [September-October] last, but he stayed only ten or twelve days and more than a month ago he returned to Paris.

When he is in Chevannes, he practices medicine gratuitously; during his last visit he was busy with his vintage and did not receive visits. He is an intimate friend of the curé. This last is an old man of sixty-some years who has taken the oath, a careful observer of the laws of the Republic for his church and was unwilling, on Sunday, to say mass because a child had pulled the bell-rope.

Dupont is much loved at Chevannes. . . .[30]

He had no further trouble with government officials, except for a minor conflict over the payment of rent for his apartment at the Hôtel d'Angiviller in the Rue de l'Oratoire, near the Louvre. He had taken up residence there in March of 1796 but, after he had been designated a *savant voyageur* by the Institute, he argued that he should not be charged rent in advance. Threatened with legal action if he did not pay 2,000 francs within twenty-four hours, he penned the usual long protest, asserting that, in his official capacity, he should owe nothing. He had arranged with the noted explorer Bougainville for the latter to occupy his lodgings and to tend to his affairs while he was abroad; in return for these services he would later do the same for Bougainville. The threat of legal action involved, therefore, two members of the Institute.[31] He must have been successful in his plea, since he was not dispossessed or sued.

In the spring of 1799 Du Pont decided that the new venture could be launched by sending a small vanguard to lay the foundation in America. Du Pont's wife, her daughter, and son-in-law, Bureaux de Pusy, together with their small daughter Sara, were chosen as the pioneers. At the last moment, Madame Bureaux de Pusy, who was expecting another child, had to withdraw because of illness.[32] Du Pont accompanied the party to Rotterdam, whence, after being delayed by storms, it sailed on May 10.[33] Bureaux de Pusy carried with him a long, detailed letter of general advice and specific instruction prepared by Du Pont.[34] The instructions were not always very practical or realistic, but a tone of unqualified optimism was predominant throughout the letter. No obstacle was too great to be overcome. Subscriptions might bring in less capital than was needed, but profits from hard work in the commission business would make up the difference. No matter what the outcome, everyone would at least be active; and that is a virtue in itself. "And so," the letter reads,

each of us must be filled with a reserve supply of courage—and with quickness of judgment to meet unexpected or vaguely expected situations. We are waging war—we must be armed. *Nec pluribus impars.* The best of all arms are patience and confidence. No harm can befall us except such accidents as may come to any man, and we have already felt the most cruel of these possibilities. They are not fatal to us, we are unconquered. Worse things cannot happen; we have known it all. Let us keep our minds in peace, in gentleness, in firmness. We will not let ourselves be unhappy, for that weakens one's powers. So long as one is master of himself there is a remedy or a compensation for everything, and especially for men of wit and good humor. We must never lose our tempers; it is always useless—often harmful. Marcus Aurelius . . . says: "Do not be angry with men, for that will not improve them; and still less with things, for it will in no way affect them."[35]

Such a philosophy sustained Du Pont in the face of the inauspicious prospects of his company. Madame Du Pont and Bureaux de Pusy may also have had need of it, for bad luck accompanied them at the beginning of their journey. Although the ship on which they sailed set out to go north of the British Isles—a route which Du Pont thought was much better than by way of the English Channel[36]—it was intercepted by the English one day out of port and held for six weeks.[37] The voyagers eventually found passage on another ship and reached America just a few weeks before the rest of the Du Pont party set out from France.

Accompanied by Madame Bureaux de Pusy, Du Pont returned from Rotterdam by slow stages because of his stepdaughter's condition. Back in Paris by May 16, he plunged again into the task of closing up his affairs. The print shop was finally sold on May 21 at a price sufficient for him to be able to cover the five shares in the company which he had undertaken to purchase for his sons.[38] Victor set off for Rochefort, Saintes, and the island of Oléron to find suitable accommodations for the main party. He was attempting through his contacts in the Ministry of Foreign Affairs to free some American ships which had been interned by the French and to obtain inexpensive passage on one of them. While he was away, his third child, and second son, Samuel Francis, was born to Josephine, but lived only four days. The general grief was somewhat alleviated when Madame Bureaux de Pusy was safely delivered of a healthy boy. As both Josephine and Isle de France (Madame Bureaux de Pusy) rapidly recovered after their *accouchements*, they no longer provided reasons for delay. Irénée had to struggle through his own family problems amidst the hectic final preparations for departure. He was worried about the health of his three children, who were at Bois-des-Fossés with their mother, about the problems and dangers of having them inoculated against smallpox, and about the release of Sophie's brother, who had been drafted for military service. His father's demands upon his time were so heavy that he had little opportunity to concentrate upon these matters of important personal concern.[39] He had to drive himself hard to wind up affairs in France so that he could overcome his father's desire that he remain behind at least a month to take care of final details.[40]

Finally, in mid-September 1799, the family left Paris for the port of La Rochelle. A few days later the *Moniteur* briefly noted the departure,[41] and Félix Faulcon, a member of the Council of Five Hundred, contributed to *Le Publiciste* a letter full of praise of Du Pont. In taking his leave, Du Pont had remarked, according to Faulcon, "If France remains, or rather if it finally becomes free, I shall be honored always to carry the title of French citizen; if the kings overcome it, I shall immediately abdicate and declare myself a citizen of the United States of America."[42] These republican sentiments indicate that he had not given up all hope for the future of France. Earlier he had expressed satisfaction that Sieyès had been appointed to the Directory in what has come to be known as the coup d'état of 30 Prairial (June 18, 1799).[43] The momentous change, the coup d'état of Brumaire (November 9-10, 1799), by which Napoleon Bonaparte became First Consul, did not occur until after the Du Pont party was on the high seas. Inevitably, this change in government would have its effect on Du Pont's later calculations.

For the present, he was bound for America with his family and an immense accumulation of baggage, including pianos. The party consisted of eighteen persons. There were, first of all, the family members: Du Pont, his son Victor with his wife Josephine and two children, his second son Irénée with his wife Sophie and three children, Madame de Pusy with her new-born infant, and Charles

Dalmas, Sophie's brother, who had been saved from military service when his mother found a substitute for him.[44] In addition, there were three nurses, a young man identified only as "Jeandell, the son," and "a jockey thirteen or fourteen years old who . . . was given to Victor and recommended to him by friends from La Rochelle."[45] The final arrangements and preparations for sailing delayed the party in La Rochelle for a fortnight. Du Pont used one day to go over to the island of Oléron, where Boissy d'Anglas and other prisoners of the coup d'état of Fructidor were still awaiting transportation to the penal colony in Guiana. He urged the exiles to accompany him to America, where he offered to provide them opportunities for a new life. It was a grand gesture, which, fortunately for him, could not lead to any action, since Boissy d'Anglas and his companions could not accept the offer. The Du Pont enterprise could not have endured the added burden of so many more dependents. Yet it would be unjust to conclude that Du Pont was not sincerely concerned for his friends. He promised them to send a ship for their deliverance from Guiana, once they arrived there. This promise, too, was impracticable and never fulfilled. Nevertheless, the offers were made in good faith.[46] Only he who has never permitted feeling to disregard practicality is entitled to condemn Du Pont's action.

Toward the end of September the party boarded the *American Eagle*, an unseaworthy craft which, seized by the French, had been idle in port for two years.[47] Victor had succeeded in his efforts to get some of the interned American ships released. The captain of the *American Eagle* agreed as compensation for these efforts to carry the entire Du Pont party at reduced rates. He had no resources available properly to ready his ship for the voyage or to obtain a good cargo. Instead he accepted a larger number of passengers than he could adequately accommodate along with a cargo of salt. Finally, on October 2, he weighed anchor and committed his unworthy craft to the open sea.

As might have been expected, the voyage was a most trying experience for everyone. It extended over ninety-three days, a month longer than Columbus required to reach the New World. Winds were unfavorable; the ship leaked; the salt cargo melted; the captain was a poor navigator and lost his bearings; provisions ran low. These conditions turned the discontented crew into a mutinous band of thieves, who preyed upon the passengers. Three times the *American Eagle* was intercepted by English ships. The American *Marie* out of Boston came upon the distressed *Eagle,* when rations were so low that the passengers were eating horse beans, after cleansing them of worms. Captain Taylor of the *Marie* supplied water, biscuits, meat, and vegetables. The officers of the *Cleopatra,* the third British ship met with, decided first to convoy the distressed craft to Halifax, where it might lie over for the winter, but then released it to complete its wretched voyage.[48] Throughout all these trials, it is related, "Du Pont alone preserved his *sang-froid* and his gaiety; he consoled everyone and busied himself in making verses; but, with his sword under his arm, he watched at night so that the sailors would not restort to the last extremities against the passengers."[49] He even found time to do some work on his translation of the *Orlando Furioso.* The battered ship eventually docked at Newport, Rhode Island—which was not its original destination—soon after the start of the new year.[50]

Bureaux de Pusy and Madame Du Pont had reached New York five weeks earlier. They had bought a house and land at Bergen Point, New Jersey, opposite Staten Island. As Du Pont described the site, it was on the promontory separating New York Bay from Newark Bay, ten miles from New York, a distance which could be covered in one hour by sail.[51] Delayed in Newport by unfavorable winds, the new arrivals were unable to make their way to New York by packet boat until January 12. They set out at once for the Bergen Point estate, which Du Pont immediately named "Goodstay." Having realized that the house was too small to accommodate four families, Bureaux de Pusy already had ordered the construction of additional rooms. Victor and his family moved to New York, since it was necessary to establish an office in the city. They lived until May in a small house at 61 Pearl Street until a larger building, which could serve both as office and residence, was leased at 91 Liberty Street.

Victor, who knew most about America, had to assume the leading role in the family business. Soon after establishing the office in New York, he traveled south to investigate the prospects of opening what was expected to be the principal office of the company in or near the new "Federal City" of Washington. He decided, finally, that Alexandria offered the best advantages and purchased a warehouse there for $4,500. To gain legal sanction for the purchase he obtained from a state court an act of naturalization making him a citizen of Virginia, an irregular procedure, as he recognized, "for a citizen of the State of Virginia must be a citizen of the United States."[52]

With these acquisitions of property the company was ready to do business. After his arrival in America, Du Pont was easily convinced of the wisdom of his earlier reluctant decision to postpone indefinitely his scheme to buy and to develop land. A letter from Thomas Jefferson warned him of the "swarms of speculators who consider the stranger as lawful prey."[53] There was no immediate alternative to the concentration of effort in building up the business of the company as a commercial brokerage. Du Pont remained optimistic that the profits of this business would be substantial enough to pay regular dividends to the shareholders and to accumulate ample capital for investment in land once the mania of speculation had ended. But very little business could be found. Commercial relations between France and the United States had been badly disrupted by the disagreements between the two governments. The Du Pont company would not get very far if its business were to be limited to what it had on hand. This business consisted principally of attempting to collect on sometimes petty claims of individual French citizens against American businessmen. Large-scale operations involving governments were required for the kind of profits hoped for. Du Pont had no difficulty in drawing up grandiose schemes. He put seven down on paper toward the end of 1800, by which time there was better prospect of normal commercial relations between France and America. Napoleon, the First Consul, had signed a treaty with the United States on September 30. Du Pont at first believed that Napoleon's Government would bring great advantages, including prosperity, to France.[54] He was eager to do business with it.

Even before his arrival in America, he had planned to send one, or both, of his sons back to Europe to stimulate more business for the firm, once it was set up in the New World. By December he believed that his plans were well enough formulated for him to prepare a long letter to his friend and supporter, the Parisian

282

banker Jacques Bidermann, discussing the company's prospects with his usual optimism and outlining the separate schemes which his sons would seek to initiate during their business trip to Europe. The sons' voyage and this letter, which they would personally deliver to Bidermann, were, Du Pont thought, "of decisive importance for our enterprise."[55] Five of the seven projects which he had elaborated concerned various services which his company could perform for the French Government. These covered such matters as marketing sugar from Guadeloupe and French Guiana during the period of warfare between France and Britain, supplying the French navy, administration, and colonists in Santo Domingo during peacetime, operating packet boats under government patronage on a regular schedule between France and America, marketing merchandise which the French Government might send as a means of retiring its financial obligations in America, and handling a loan which, Du Pont suggested, the French might make to the United States. A sixth scheme sought to convince French mechants interested in sending cargoes to America of the wisdom of consigning them to Du Pont de Nemours Père Fils et Cᵢₑ, where they might be held and marketed, not at once, but as prices became most favorable for particular types of products. Obviously, Du Pont argued, American firms would not seek such favorable markets for French products. A seventh project involved two separate operations with the Spanish government. They were not spelled out in detail on paper, since their presumed success depended upon secrecy, as well as upon the continuance of the war. Only two ingredients were lacking for the spectacular success, estimated in millions of francs in Du Pont's expectations, of all these projects. One was the conclusion of the necessary agreements with the proper officials of the French and Spanish governments. The other was the raising of more capital to launch these allegedly lucrative enterprises. To Victor, the experienced diplomat, was assigned the responsibility of finding these missing ingredients. It was an impossible assignment which, nevertheless, Victor dutifully accepted.

An eighth plan was added to the original projects, a plan which Irénée had proposed and for which he was to assume responsibility. Through conversations with a guest of the Du Ponts, Colonel Louis de Tousard, one of the French veterans of the Revolutionary War who had remained in America, Irénée became interested in the techniques employed in the manufacture of gunpowder in the United States. He visited a plant in Pennsylvania which Colonel Tousard had mentioned—probably the Frankford mills of Lane and Decatur. He found that these mills, which had a contract to supply powder to the United States Government, produced powder much inferior to that which he had seen produced at Essone fifteen years earlier. The methods used had long been supplanted by better ones in France. He was certain that even a small establishment able to employ the improved techniques could compete successfully with the larger, well-established firms. Here was an unexpected opportunity for him to put to practical use the knowledge acquired during his years of study under Lavoisier. He had little difficulty in winning the approval of his father and of Bureaux de Pusy for his plan to raise in Europe sufficient capital to establish a separate company for the manufacture of gunpowder.

The two brothers sailed for France in January, 1801. Irénée's tasks were specific and definite. He knew exactly what he had to accomplish and prepared very clear and detailed reports outlining his plans.[56] Bidermann was favorably impressed by Irénée's presentation of the prospects for the success of the new enterprise. Du Pont's former colleague, Adrien Duquesnoy, also agreed to invest in the company. Their active support permitted Irénée to draw up in April formal articles of incorporation "for the establishment of a manufacture of military and sporting powder in the United States of America."[57] Under these articles the capital of the company was fixed at thirty-six thousand dollars in eighteen shares of two thousand dollars each. Bidermann and Catoire, Duquesnoy et Compagnie each subscribed one share apiece, while twelve shares were assigned to Du Pont de Nemours Père Fils et Cie of New York. Both Bidermann and Duquesnoy agreed to a separate arrangement, whereby "no one shall buy a share in the powder without at the same time taking two others of the same value in the Du Pont firm."[58] By this arrangement, Du Pont de Nemours Père Fils et Cie would be able to hold two-thirds of the stock in the powder company without drawing upon its already strained resources. Only four additional investors able to subscribe $6,000 each were needed. Unfortunately, they were not immediately found. Irénée thought that he had persuaded Louis Necker-Germany, brother of the former minister of finance, to take two shares in the powder company and four shares in the Du Pont Company. Victor, who remained in Europe longer than his brother, found that Necker-Germany was much more cautious than Irénée had supposed. Eventually he induced him to subscribe for one share only in each company. Victor also arranged a loan of almost $10,000 from Jacques Necker. This loan permitted the Du Pont Company to take up five additional shares in the powder works, bringing its holdings to eleven shares.[59]

While attending to these necessary financial arrangements, Irénée paid several visits to the government powder works at Essone in order to study improvements in machinery and techniques introduced since his apprenticeship there more than a decade earlier. He was delighted by the co-operation offered by the officials, some of whom he knew. The Government of the Consulate apparently saw in the establishment of a manufactory in America an opportunity to undercut the commerce of England, with which France was still at war. Irénée won the favor of the superintendent of the Essone works by agreeing to supply him with plantings of American trees, in which he was interested.[60]

Because of his keen interest in botany, which he had earlier studied for a time at the Jardin des Plantes in Paris, Irénée had brought to Europe a collection of the seeds of American plants and trees which he hoped could be cultivated in France. Most of these had come from the nursery set up in 1786 at Bergen Woods near the Du Pont estate of Goodstay, by the noted French botanist, André Michaux. As one of his duties for the Institute, Du Pont had inspected this nursery and discovered that, because of inadequate support from France, it had not properly been cared for. Paul Saulnier, the nurseryman, had nevertheless remained stolidly at his post, although he had to use some of the land to raise food crops for the support of his family, since he had not received the salary promised by the French Government. Du Pont and his son championed Saulnier's cause, especially when they learned of plans to close the nursery and dismiss the faithful attendant. They desired to preserve this potentially valuable nursery, together with another one which Michaux had established near Charleston, South Carolina. Undoubtedly, Irénée hoped to further the cause by bringing to France various seeds from the nursery.[61]

He did not permit this matter to divert him from his main task. He arranged with government draftsmen to draw plans for machinery and placed orders for the construction and shipping of the necessary equipment. Early in May, he set sail for the United States, leaving Victor and Harmand to oversee the execution of his orders. Although he was delayed for more than a week when the British intercepted his ship and forced it to drop anchor in Portsmouth, he landed at Philadelphia on July 14, eager to find a suitable location for the powder manufactory. He brought with him seven Spanish merino sheep which he hoped to breed in America. His father had already undertaken a journey to uncover a favorable site for the new enterprise near Washington. He did not find one but was able to visit with President Jefferson and to try to convince him of the usefulness to the American Government of the projected powder works.[62] Irénée took up the task. The list of stockholders was filled when Archibald McCall, a merchant of Philadelphia, and Peter Bauduy, a French émigré of Wilmington, each took two shares.[63] McCall soon withdrew his investment, but Bauduy was at first very helpful. He had a good knowledge of the language and of the business practices of the eastern United States. He wanted the Company to locate in Delaware, but Irénée insisted upon a personal survey of possible sites. When Lane and Decatur rejected his tentative offer to purchase their Frankford mills, Irénée spent months in traveling about New York and New Jersey and the area around Washington. He finally came back to Delaware, where the farm of Jacob Broom, spread out along the banks of the Brandywine, four miles west of Wilmington, seemed to offer the best prospects. Bauduy made the arrangements for purchase, enlisting the assistance of his friend William Hamon, a naturalized Frenchman. Since he was not yet a citizen, Irénée could not hold land in his own name. Hence Hamon came forward as the presumed buyer when, on April 27, 1802, ninety-five acres were purchased from Broom for $6,740.[64] Irénée at once plunged into the difficult tasks of hiring workmen, constructing buildings, and installing machinery. Bauduy tended to correspondence and sought out customers for the Company's product. On August 25, 1802, a separate agreement was entered into with Bauduy, an unfortunate action which was to be the source of much difficulty.[65]

By this time important decisions had been made about the future of the parent company. Victor's conscientious efforts in France and Spain had not been fruitful.[66] The vague and impractical nature of most of his father's plans and the changed conditions in Europe brought about by the signing in October, 1801, of preliminary arrangements for peace between France and England doomed his original proposals. He thereupon prepared a plan to modify and to combine some of these proposals in accordance with overtures which had been made to the Du Pont Company by Louis André Pichon, then French Consul General in the United States. Pichon had encountered increasing problems in contracting for supplies for Santo Domingo. He had to operate under drafts drawn on the French Navy Department and, because of growing indebtedness to American suppliers, he faced heavy discounts on such drafts. He hoped to work out better arrangements by using the Du Pont Company as his agent. Victor tried unsuccessfully to get a firm commitment tying the French Treasury into the financing of these drafts and guaranteeing regular payments to the Company should it honor Navy Department drafts at face value, at a cost to the French Government of a commission of only 5 per cent on the value of each draft. Despite the failure to get the guarantees he sought, he foresaw the possibility of sure profits in pursuing the business proposed by Pichon. His father carried forward negotiations with Pichon in America.[67] This alignment with Pichon was to prove a fatal mistake. Victor returned to America in December, 1801, to find the state of the Company's business even worse than he had expected.

As Josephine later wrote: "While [Victor and Irénée] were away . . . Mr. de Pusy and Papa did not do much business for the stagnation of all commerce was very serious, while the rental of their office, the salaries of the clerks, the expenses of the joint families were rapidly emptying the common purse."[68] Indeed, before Victor returned, Bureaux de Pusy decided to go back to France with his

287

wife, presumably to stir up more business for the Company but actually to seek a position for himself in the new government of the Consulate.[69] He was successful in gaining appointment as prefect at Moulins in the Department of Allier; shortly, thereafter, he became prefect at Lyon in the Department of Rhône-et-Loire. Du Pont was obviously surprised by Bureaux de Pusy's action, but he did not disapprove of his accepting the appointment: "One should never refuse to serve one's country under a fine leader." He expected his associate to use his new position to further the Company's enterprises.[70] Bureaux de Pusy's intention was, however, to break his active connection with the Company, regarding it as incompatible with his official position.[71] Subsequently, he not only ceased to work for the Company but, hard-pressed financially, he tried in vain to borrow money on the security of his shares and even to sell the shares. His wife became increasingly bitter over the failure to realize any gain from the Du Pont Company.[72] In later years she was to be the source of much grief and worry to Irénée.

Du Pont always seemed to retain his optimistic outlook and kept himself too busy to have time for worry. Except for an attack of gout in the winter of 1801-1802, his health throughout his sojourn in America was excellent. Only in letters to Harmand did he reveal any indication of discontent. These letters, some of them very long, are probably an accurate gauge of his feelings, since he seldom tried to hide anything from the man who had always shown him unhesitating loyalty and devotion. In writing to Harmand, he had occasionally to revive his flagging spirits by recalling his past accomplishments. Except for his constant concern over his responsibility to his shareholders, he found it difficult to retain an enthusiastic interest in his Company. He still looked beyond the petty commercial enterprises, to which the Company had had to repair, toward the vision of the land development and ideal colony which first he had proposed. Bureaux de Pusy's desertion must have been a blow, because he had hoped for the success of his European negotiations, although, as Du Pont did not admit, these negotiations never had a chance to succeed. Had they turned out as expected, Du Pont looked forward to closing his business career in two years and then turning either to the dream of a colony in the United

States or to philosophical retirement in France. He was distressed by Madame Lavoisier's changing moods and her complaints over the protection of her investment in Bois-des-Fossés. He confessed to a passionate attachment to this remarkable woman in the past, but admitted that it was now broken off on both sides.[73] He was tempted to go to Europe himself, where he thought he could accomplish more than his sons, but he resisted the temptation because he feared that his associates might interpret his leaving his post as a neglect of their interests.[74]

The doubts and uncertainties which he thus expressed to Harmand did not often come to the surface of his consciousness, buried as they were under layers of varied activity. Du Pont did not forget that his voyage was under the auspices of the National Institute and dispatched from America eight *mémoires*, which were duly read before his class at the Institute.[75] They contained his observations and reflections upon a variety of scientific phenomena —a kind of sea snail and marine plant picked up in mid-Atlantic on the voyage to America, the force of an eddy of the current from the Gulf of Mexico which had presumably driven the ship off course, the formation of water in living bodies, the islands at the mouths of the Hudson, Passaic, and Raritan rivers, the nature of the eastern seacoasts of North America, a theory on winds, and so on. They are not significant, except as a further indication of his wide-ranging curiosity. One of the papers discussed the New Jersey nursery and its usefulness as a source of certain American trees which might beneficially be cultivated in France. The paper has a practical interest in itself but must also be regarded as one of his efforts to induce the French Government to maintain the nursery.

Some of these papers were also submitted to the American Philosophical Society for the Promotion of Useful Knowledge in Philadelphia. Jefferson had sent to the Society Du Pont's paper on the analogy between vegetables and polypi and insects and nominated him for membership. He was elected to membership on April 18, 1800, and his paper approved for publication on May 2. He was very proud of this honor and continued to submit papers for consideration, some of which were published in the *Transactions* of the Society.[76]

Du Pont spent many hours on another project which developed from a specific request of Jefferson. As the latter described the matter years later in a letter to Madison: "At a time when I had a hope that Virginia would establish a University I asked Mr. Dupont and Dr. Priestley to give me their ideas on the best division of the useful sciences into Professorships. The latter did it concisely, but Dupont wrote an elaborate treatise on education which I still possess."[77] What Du Pont did was to work out in some detail his ideas for a complete educational system in the United States, from primary grades through the university.[78] He suggested the ideas which should be instilled in the young and perfected through the various stages of their education—ideas on liberty, property, justice, the value of mutual helpfulness, the sacredness of agreements, benevolence, sympathy, forbearance. He followed Rousseau in recommending that children be helped "to follow the natural road, to use their own intelligence, without demanding that they accept ours," though he thought that Rousseau had carried the "excellent maxim, *do not interfere*" too far. "Of all the children educated by [Rousseau's] method," he remarked, "not one was willing to work, not one of them had been taught how."[79] Du Pont's objective was to produce good republican citizens with sound principles.

He had a high regard for his treatise and hoped to have it translated into English. He was himself never able to master the English language. He was too busy to spend much time in concentrated study and was not unduly handicapped in most of his corespondence and personal contacts by his lack of facility in the language. Victor, Bureaux de Pusy, and eventually, Irénée had a firm enough command of English to take care of all business details which could not be conducted in French. Du Pont never got much beyond the stage of development shown at the beginning of a letter which he wrote from Philadelphia to his wife on March 28, 1800: "I am unworthy, my dear Soul, to receive an english letter from you. My progress in this tongue are least. I have lost my grammar of Peyson [?] at Bristol, and yesterday only j could another retrieve. Nevertheless, j begin to accustom me with the pronounciation, and j hope, if we help ourselves and one another to repeat our lesson, that we will be ables to become less ignorants. It shall be needfull that we would learn by heart, like the children, and recite to his companion. The one who will make one fault, shall pay one penny. This game shall be more profitable for us than the chess."[80]

After Irénée's return from France with good prospects of establishing gunpowder mills, Du Pont permitted his thoughts more and more to revolve around the idea of his going back to his native land, where he not only knew the language but also had many friends to whom he might appeal for assistance. When Bureaux de Pusy so quickly obtained a government post after his return, Du Pont easily convinced himself that he could do likewise. Thus, while trying to improve the fortunes of his Company in France, he might be assured of a steady income from the Government. Madame Du Pont grew more homesick after her daughter left and more frequently expressed her desire to leave America. Despite his avowals that he must think only of the welfare of his business associates, that he was determined to make a reputation as a businessman to add to his reputation as a government administrator and a philosopher, and that he wished "to die in the Republic of Commerce,"[81] he could not resist the attractions which, more and more clearly, he saw in France. He still had high hopes of the general good which could come from the Consulate under the forceful administration of Napoleon Bonaparte. Bureaux de Pusy wrote in January, 1802, that he had found the First Consul rather cold, but by no means malevolent, in his bantering remarks about Du Pont. Napoleon had asked his new intendant how Du Pont was managing the net product and had laughed when Pusy replied that "it is ineradicably in his principles and he says that it is not his fault if they are inapplicable almost everywhere." Pusy thought that whatever coldness there might be was due to Du Pont's absence from France. Madame Bonaparte, he wrote, was always obliging and had expressed her regret that Du Pont had believed it necessary to leave.[82]

Madame de Staël, who had not yet become completely disillusioned about Napoleon, also urged him to return. As early as May, 1800, she wrote to Du Pont that, once peace was established, he would find in France the best means of increasing the value of his investments.[83] A year later she wrote that Benjamin Constant (with whom she had formed an intimate liaison in 1795 or 1796) "this winter . . . several times had brought forth the idea of nominating you for senator, but one knew that Buonaparte didn't want these positions given to those who were absent; he is in too much of a hurry to await support even if it comes from afar, but if you arrive I am sure that the opinion Buonaparte listens to would instantly carry you to this position."[84] Such letters stirred Du Pont's latent appetite for public office and honors. When Victor returned from his largely unsuccessful journey, Du Pont became more convinced that he should himself go to France. Since he would leave his two sons in America to oversee the interests of his associates there, he would not really be deserting them; besides, he could certainly do more for them in France. His decision to leave America, at least for a brief period, became firm early in 1802. All that remained was to complete the necessary arrangements.

The E. I. du Pont de Nemours Company had already been established near Wilmington. Victor now set up another concern, V. du Pont de Nemours & Cie, with headquarters in New York. The parent company, which was to retain a controlling interest in the two other firms, transferred its headquarters to Paris. A formal notice of these changes was issued in English on May 1, 1802; somewhat later a circular letter in French was issued in Paris announcing the new arrangements.[85] By separate documents in French[86] Du Pont agreed to turn over to Victor $78,000 in the form of a loan from the parent company, $48,000 of this sum constituting the estimated valuation of the Kentucky lands, which were conveyed to Victor by a deed of indenture.[87] Most of the promised loan was not, however, paid over. Goodstay, the Bergen Point estate, was also turned over to Victor. With these details out of the way, Du Pont, his wife, and little Sara, the Bureaux de Pusy's daughter, who had been left with them, sailed for Europe on June 1, 1802.

The journey eastward on the *Virginia* was far more pleasant than the venture on the *American Eagle* had been. Accommodations aboard ship were comfortable, and Du Pont was able to work every day at his writing desk. He had planned to get his accounts in order, especially those covering the provisioning of French ships going to Santo Domingo, so that he could present a clear statement to his shareholders and to government officials when he pressed them for payment of drafts. He soon realized that, unfortunately, he had left behind most of the necessary papers; thus he turned, undoubtedly with a sigh of relief, to preparing several long notes for inclusion in the next edition of his *Philosophie de l'univers.* The *Virginia* dropped anchor in Le Havre after a crossing of thirty-two days' duration. Du Pont paused for several days in Le Havre, and for a few more in Rouen, in order to write letters to his sons in America and to many of his acquaintances in France, announcing his safe arrival and seeking ways to facilitate the business of his companies.

By the end of July he was back in Paris, rejoicing in the friendly reception accorded to him by everyone and, particularly, by persons of influence—Consuls Le Brun and Cambacérès, Madame Bonaparte, Ministers Talleyrand, Marbois, and Chaptal, Councillors of State Portalis, Roederer, Jollivet, Fermon, Fleurieux. He even had a long and pleasant interview with the First Consul, an interview which, "everyone" told him, was a "very distinguished" welcome. Napoleon spoke to him about the drafts for the Santo Domingo supplies, displaying a remarkably exact knowledge of the sums involved.[88] Madame Bonaparte presented to him a card of admission which entitled him to enter the Tuileries "whenever he may present himself."[89] Du Pont's optimism soared at these apparent marks of favor. He was confident that his business and personal ambitions would soon be fulfilled. His company, he believed, would have no difficulty in having its drafts honored by the Government and could expect more and profitable business. He would likely soon be made a Senator. Subsequent developments were to show that, once again, his optimism had no solid foundation upon which to rest.

On another matter, however, that of the crucial negotiations between the governments of France and the United States over the problem of Louisiana, Du Pont's optimistic outlook proved to be useful and important. When he learned that his old friend was returning to France, President Jefferson turned over to Du Pont some papers bearing on the negotiations.

The problem of Louisiana arose when news reached the United States that, by secret treaty in 1800, Napoleon Bonaparte had forced Spain to retrocede to France the vast territory of Louisiana, which the French had turned over to Spain in 1762. Many Americans were concerned about the possible loss of the only practicable outlet for the products of the western states and territories. If the Mississippi River were to be closed to American shipping, or if the right to "deposit" in warehouses in New Orleans products awaiting transfer to ocean vessels were withdrawn, the future development of the western United States into a region of prosperity would be fatally impeded. Jefferson recognized the danger and was determined to prevent a strong and ambitious power like France from controlling Louisiana. He wrote to Du Pont on April 25, 1802, before he had received from Du Pont a letter dated April 24, in which Du Pont had offered to assist in the rumored negotiations: "I wish you to be possessed of the subject, because you may be able to impress on the government of France the inevitable consequences of their taking possession of Louisiana."[90] He was convinced that this action by France would lead to war.

Napoleon's plans to re-establish a French empire in America were to suffer a serious blow when yellow fever decimated the ranks of the expedition sent to quell the insurrection in Santo Domingo, an expedition for which the Du Pont Company had provided some supplies. By the spring of 1803, another factor had to be brought into the calculations of the First Consul—the likelihood that the Peace of Amiens would soon come to an end and that France would again be at war with England. For an agonizingly long period, however, Napoleon refused to commit himself on his future projects regarding Louisiana. Robert Livingston, the American minister to France, endured months of frustration through his inability to obtain satisfaction in his interviews with Talleyrand and other officials of the Consulate.[91] Among some Frenchmen, often dubbed the Ideologues, there was an intense desire to keep France out of Louisiana. As adherents of republican and democratic ideas, they feared that the retrocession of the territory to France would lead to the inevitable weakening and, perhaps, even the complete collapse of the great republic across the Atlantic.[92]

Du Pont never shared the fears of these ideologues; he was convinced that negotiation could bring a mutually advantageous resolution to all the problems between the two countries. In his letter to Jefferson on April 24, he remarked that he had heard of a suggestion that the United States purchase Louisiana. If there was any truth in this rumor, he thought, the idea was "salutary and acceptable." Naturally, Du Pont believed that he could be of service in discussions between the governments and promised to see Livingston when he got to Paris. As he pointed out, he knew personally the French officials, understood "the customs of the [French] nation," and had resolved to entrust to America his children, his fortune, and his hopes for repose in his old age.[93] Indeed, he was peculiarly fitted to play a part in relations between his native land and his adopted country, and Jefferson recognized this fact, even before he received Du Pont's letter offering his assistance. How Du Pont picked up the rumor about the possible purchase of territory by the United States is not known. That the initial inspiration for attempting to resolve the issue in this manner did not come from him seems clear. It was being considered in Washington, and James Madison, Secretary of State, "had proposed to Livingston on May 1, 1802, before Du Pont's suggestion could have been known in Washington, that he negotiate for New Orleans and the Floridas."[94]

Along with his letter of April 25, Jefferson sent a packet of letters which he asked Du Pont to deliver. One was addressed to Livingston and left unsealed so that Du Pont might read part of it.[95] The President informed Livingston of this arrangement in a letter dated May 5, in which he explained his "unlimited confidence" in Du Pont. "His dispositions in favor of this country, as well as France, are unquestionable, and his talents so well known that I presume his opinions will have just weight with the French government." He did fear, however, that Du Pont had received "false impressions" from his letter and that he might be going beyond the purpose which the President had originally in mind.[96]

What Jefferson was protesting here was, apparently, Du Pont's recommendations contained in his letter of April 30. Although still in the United States, Du Pont had thrown himself completely into the Louisiana tangle and now proposed compromise and urged further the idea of offering the French government a good price for part of the territory on the left bank of the Mississippi, while conceding to France all territory on the right bank. He questioned "this uneasiness about the French who are quite disposed to leave you the ports of the Mississipi [*sic*] open with small customs and duties which could be determined by a commercial treaty, while the English, more jealous and disdainful, do not seem to bother or displease you in Canada, although they refuse you an outlet through the St. Lawrence, which would be almost as natural as one through the Mississipi. . . ."[97]

Jefferson's reply to this letter has been lost, but, from Du Pont's remarks in his letter of May 12, it seems obvious that the President had argued against the suggested purchase of territory because the condition of governmental finances would not permit it. Jefferson must have known of Madison's instructions to Livingston and, hence, was merely trying to cool Du Pont's ardor. Du Pont brushed aside such an argument and put forward a specific proposal for buying New Orleans and the Floridas, which were generally, though erroneously, believed to be part of the territory retroceded by Spain. "Agreement as to the price is the main thing. To arrange the matter of payment . . . is a minor matter which would straighten itself out." In this letter, Du Pont also pleaded for the United States to show gratitude to Lafayette for his past services by helping the General out in his present financial difficulties.[98] For a considerable period of time Du Pont seldom lost an opportunity to seek some assistance for his old friend.

After his arrival in Paris, Du Pont wrote to Jefferson on August 16. He was still optimistic about the satisfactory resolution of the problem, though he admitted the presence in France of attitudes hostile to the United States, a heritage, he believed, of the unhappy relations during the Presidency of John Adams. Livingston, he remarked, believed that he might be useful. Then he turned to other concerns—including another plea on Lafayette's behalf, a reminder of the potential value to America of the powder works, and a suggestion that his Paris Company could serve as the fiscal agent in handling American accounts.[99]

The most important letter which Du Pont wrote to Jefferson on the Louisiana negotiations was undoubtedly the letter of October 4, 1802. At that time the issue was becoming critical. Livingston was deeply distressed by the lack of progress and communicated his pessimism to his superiors in Washington. Du Pont, on the other hand, continued to be confident about the outcome. While admitting that the degree of success was less than he would have wished, he insisted that the situation was not nearly as bad as it seemed to Livingston, who was upset by the absence of firm written commitments, even though oral statements made in the discussions were favorable. Still confident that the French Government could be relied upon, Du Pont believed that, although it would probably insist upon taking formal possession of Louisiana, the Consulate would then not refuse to negotiate. Although Jefferson, who wanted to keep the French out, could hardly have been reassured by this statement, Du Pont went on to include the draft of a suggested treaty by which the issue might eventually be settled.

The four articles of this treaty provided that France would cede New Orleans and the Floridas to the United States for six million dollars, on condition that Frenchmen would receive in these regions the same commercial rights as Americans. Such rights were not to be extended to the citizens or subjects of any other nation. Furthermore, by the suggested treaty, France would reserve for herself all other territory adjacent to Louisiana proper on the right bank of the Mississippi. "If you are willing to go that far," Du Pont wrote, "I do not despair of success." In concluding he did not lose the oportunity to urge again some help for Lafayette, proposing that at least the United States Government should pay off Lafayette's debts to United States citizens.[100]

Subsequent developments indicate that these tentative proposals of resolving the issue by purchase of territory were inspired by sources within the French Government and that, therefore, Du Pont was building upon more than his own original ideas. Whatever the source, the possibility of peaceful accommodation which Du Pont's letter asserted had particular significance. When his letter was received in Washington on December 31, a very severe crisis had developed because, on October 16, Spanish officials announced the revocation of the American right of deposit at New Orleans. The uncertainty and profound concern aroused by this event might have led to a breaking off of further attempts at negotiation with the French and could have led to war, for, as Jefferson remarked to Du Pont in his letter of February 1, 1803, "The occlusion of the Mississippi is a state of things in which we cannot exist." Yet, in this letter, the President was notably calm despite the apparently increasing dangers. The conclusion that his calmness was in large part due to Du Pont's letter of October 4, 1802, is inescapable. Indeed, Jefferson now wrote in regard to that letter: ". . . I received [it] with peculiar satisfaction; because, while it holds up terms which cannot be entirely yielded, it proposes such as a mutual spirit of accommodation and sacrifice of opinion may bring to some point of

297

union." He announced that he was sending James Monroe to Paris to assist Livingston and urged Du Pont to continue to make himself useful. "It will often, perhaps, be possible for you having a freedom of communication *omnibus horis* which diplomatic gentlemen will be excluded from by forms, to smooth difficulties by representations and reasonings which would be received with more suspicion from them." Fearing that in such requests he might seem to be ignoring Livingston, the official negotiator, Jefferson implored Du Pont to burn this letter, together with those he had written on April 25 and May 5, 1802. He concluded by promising to consult with Albert Gallatin, Secretary of the Treasury, regarding Du Pont's suggestion that his Paris Company might become fiscal agent for the United States Government.[101]

The influence of Du Pont's letter is very clear in the instructions which Monroe carried with him on his mission. These instructions authorized the American negotiators to offer ten million dollars for the city of New Orleans, the island on which it was located, and the Floridas. They continued: "It is to be added that the overtures committed to you coincide in great measure with the ideas of the person through whom the letter of the President of April 30, 1802, was conveyed to Mr. Livingston, and who is presumed to have gained some insight into the present sentiments of the French cabinet."[102] Although the date of the letter here mentioned does not correspond to the date of Jefferson's letter delivered by Du Pont to Livingston (this letter was written on April 18 and transmitted to Du Pont on April 25), the President could hardly be referring to anyone except Du Pont.

If he was, as is almost certain, his presumption that Du Pont had gained an insight into official French sentiments was a safe one, for Du Pont was very active in cultivating all possible contacts. He wrote to Jefferson on March 3, 1803, that he had seen Talleyrand, the Foreign Minister, several times and Le Brun, one of the three Consuls, just recently. He assured the President that the French Government had no intention of depriving United States citizens of navigation of the Mississippi. It was seeking only to gain for Frenchmen similar privileges, such as the free entry of goods coming into the United States by way of the Mississippi and Ohio rivers. Once this arrangement was agreed to, Du Pont was certain that New

Orleans would be established as a free port, even though a small fee might be demanded for the right of deposit. He believed that no reasonable proposal regarding the acquisition of territory would be rejected.[103]

Meanwhile, the First Consul was coming to important decisions. He finally determined to offer for sale to the United States not just part of the Louisiana territory, but all of it! The dreams of empire had to be put temporarily aside. On April 8, 1803, the very day upon which Monroe landed at Le Havre, Napoleon had an interview with Barbé Marbois, in which he suggested the sale of all of Louisiana. Three days later Talleyrand startled Livingston by inquiring casually what the United State might offer for the entire territory.[104] From this point on, negotiations were set toward this large objective and were in the hands of the official representatives. Really only matters of detail had to be worked out. As the principal consideration was that of bargaining on the price to be paid, Barbé Marbois, as Minister of the Treasury, became the chief negotiator for France. Livingston and Monroe carried on the business for the United States, and Du Pont had no further useful part to play.

He had expressed to Jefferson on April 6 his continued hope for a happy resolution of difficulties. Then he thought that Bernadotte, one of Napoleon's marshals, was to be sent to America to conclude negotiations. He considered this prospect a happy one, because he looked upon Bernadotte as a true friend of liberty, an admirer of America, and a good friend of Lafayette. "I think," he wrote, "that Mr. Livingston will have told you that I have very actively employed my zeal for the United States. And he has not been able to tell you everything, for there are details which I have not told even to him and which I could confide only to you."[105] Yet Livingston was the official American representative and, supposedly, chief spokesman! He certainly did have just cause to complain, as he did, of the treatment he received from his own government.[106]

Bernadotte was, of course, never sent to the United States. Instead he went off to war in May, when the Peace of Amiens finally collapsed. Before then, the negotiators in Paris had reached agreement. The documents conveying to the United States title to all of Louisiana for the sum of eighty million francs were dated April 30, even though the actual negotiations consumed an additional week.[107] Twenty millions of this sum were to apply to the settlement of the claims of American citizens against the French Government. There was nothing further for Du Pont to do except to congratulate the United States and President Jefferson upon acquiring without bloodshed a territory ten times greater in extent and in fertility that what had at first been desired. He was especially happy that there was now joined to the United States a vast region whose language and customs he knew well, since it had formerly been French. He could not refrain from warning Jefferson against political adventurers who might covet a continued expansion of territory through the conquest of Mexico.[108]

In his letter of November 1, 1803, Jefferson formally thanked Du Pont for the assistance which he had given in relation to the Louisiana Purchase and assured him that, if possible, the United States would avail itself of the fiscal services which Du Pont had several times offered to have his Paris Company perform. Unfortunately, Jefferson added, at present no business remained to be done in that connection.[109] Business in general continued, indeed, to be bad for the firm of **Du Pont de Nemours Père, Fils et Cie**. Du Pont was either not fully aware of this situation or refused to acknowledge it. He kept busy and, though most of his early hopes went up in smoke, he did not soon return to America, as he had first stated he intended to do. The decade and more which he spent in France was a period of frustration for his larger ambitions. One may properly inquire why he did not yield to the repeated urging of his sons that he rejoin them in the New World.

Chapter X

In the Shadow of Napoleon

ALTHOUGH HE FOUND SATISFACTION in some of the numerous activities which kept him busy, Du Pont looked upon the years spent in Napoleonic France as a period of disappointment and frustration. He had sanguine hopes of receiving a government position that would afford a regular salary but not require exceptional labor and of settling his claims against the French treasury, thereby relieving his Company of financial burdens. Perhaps then he might quit the field of commerce, which he really did not enjoy, for the more attractive paths of government and philosophy. First, however, he wanted to establish his reputation as a businessman. In none of these major objectives did he succeed.

The first blow was the failure to obtain appointment to the Senate. Undoubtedly encouraged by some of Madame de Staël's comments in letters written to him while he was still in America,[1] Du Pont was confident that Napoleon would name him a Senator. Upon his return to Paris, he had attempted to ingratiate himself with the First Consul and had carefully renewed his acquaintance with prominent men in the Government. Months went by without the expected summons. Du Pont had finally to accept the distasteful fact that he would not be chosen. He sought for reasons to explain his failure to himself and to others. He wrote to Victor that his chances had been destroyed by "complaints sent to France of Pichon's financial operations," for, to Victor's distress, he had been defending Pichon despite the difficulties which Victor had with this unscrupulous agent of the French Government.[2] To the Polish Count Chreptowicz he explained in a letter of December 25, 1803, that, despite the "personal considerations" which he enjoyed, the Government no longer regarded him as a statesman, because of his two years' absence in America while he was attending to the interests of the shareholders of his Company. He confessed to Chreptowicz that he disliked the "multitude of business affairs," which devoured his life and his time in "a hopeless manner." He found in them no nourishment for his mind or his heart.[3] Later he informed his sons that involvement in the wretched Santo Domingo affair had excluded him from both the Senate and the Legion of Honor.[4]

His fruitless effort to be admitted to the Legion of Honor he later covered up in a not very creditable manner. In spite of considerable opposition on the score that he would be establishing another kind of nobility, Napoleon had created the Legion of Honor in May, 1802, as an institution to honor those who had performed distinguished military or civil services for the State. In December, 1803, Du Pont addressed a letter to Lacépède, Grand Chancellor of the Legion of Honor, suggesting that his name be included in the group soon to be nominated for membership on the basis of meritorious civil service. Lacépède replied on January 3, 1804, that Du Pont's request would be sent to the Grand Council of the Legion.[5] That was the last heard of it. Months later Du Pont sent to Irénée a copy of the letter of refusal which, he declared, he would send to Napoleon, if, as he feared, he might be included among the nominees to "his so-called legion of honor."[6] One would like to believe that his change of heart was due to the transformation of Napoleon from First Consul of the Republic to Emperor of the French, when the Empire was proclaimed in May, 1804. One might also believe that the increasing difficulties which Du Pont encountered in trying to get the French Government to pay his company what he thought was legitimately owed had brought a deepening disillusionment with Napoleon and made him no longer willing to accept an honor from the hands of the autocratic ruler. The eagerness with which Du Pont accepted knighthood in the Legion of Honor under the restored Bourbon king in 1814 presents some difficulty in accepting these possible explanations without reservation. He certainly coveted this honor in 1803 and early 1804 and must have been disappointed in being passed over. His letter to his son, written in one of the four different numerical codes which he devised for their correspondence, can, perhaps, be more easily interpreted as a not unusual reaction of the rejected suitor.

This entire period of his life was marred by his lack of success in settling his accounts with the French Treasury. The engagements entered into with Pichon, mostly by Victor, constituted a series of poor judgments and misunderstandings which might be regarded as a comedy of errors, were it not for the tragic consequences to Du Pont's hopes of proving himself a successful businessman. His failure, furthermore, destroyed the principal justification which he preferred to put forward for his return to France and temporarily embittered his relationship with his sons in the United States. The core of the difficulties in his business relations with his sons was that each man was primarily and necessarily concerned with the status of his own Company. Du Pont tended to look upon the enterprises of Victor and Irénée as subordinate branches of the Company which he had established. Victor and Irénée regarded the three companies as co-ordinate but separate entities. Because of the technical problems involved in establishing the powder works, Irénée could operate with a greater degree of freedom, although he was always solicitous of his father's wishes. Until 1811 he was not seriously handicapped by his father's activities in France. The only burden placed on his shoulders by his father's actions was one for which Du Pont cannot be gravely censured. In 1803, Du Pont entered into a contract with Charles François Parent, an experienced French powderman, who was well recommended by his superior in the government powder factories, to pay for the transportation to America of Parent and his family and to employ him as foreman of the powder works being constructed along the Brandywine. As it turned out, Parent arrived in Delaware too soon to be put to work, since the buildings were still under construction, and was immediately dissatisfied with the wilderness around him, so different from the conditions he knew in France. He began to believe that he had been tricked and set about to extricate himself from the undesirable situation. From the start, therefore, he became a troublesome problem for Irénée. He refused to work, even after Irénée put him in jail for three months for breaking his contract. Finally, in October, 1804, Irénée was forced to get rid of him by shipping him off to New Orleans with sufficient machinery to start a manufactory of his own, far enough removed not to compete with the Brandywine works. Irénée estimated that the unhappy Parent affair had cost him about $2,400, with nothing to show for it.[7]

At about this time there began the long quarrel between Irénée and Peter Bauduy, the result of their different interpretations of the nature of their partnership. This conflict, extending over a decade, was the most serious problem which Irénée had to face, aside from inevitable technical difficulties in the operation of the powder works. Victor strove for years to mediate the differences but could never do much more than patch up a temporary settlement. Irénée insisted that their agreement only made Bauduy a silent partner, an ordinary arrangement under French law, and that, on all important questions, he was to have the ultimate decision as organizer and manager of the company. Bauduy refused, of course, to accept this interpretation and regarded himself as an active and equal partner. The split certainly endangered the company. Irénée may not have had all the right on his side, but he had sufficient competence and determination eventually to win out.[8]

Du Pont was first informed of the quarrel by Victor in a letter of July, 1805. Since Victor was at the time in serious difficulties himself, Du Pont was much alarmed by this threat to the success of the powder company, which, more and more, he was coming to regard as his only hope. He had no clear idea of what was going on. His sons could not send him all the intricate details and, when they tried to inform him as fully as possible, he was too far removed to grasp the complete picture. Furthermore, the exchange of letters was even more delayed than usual because of the increased interference with neutral shipping brought about by the actions and counteractions of the French and British during the period of Napoleon's Continental System, that vain effort through a self-imposed blockade to keep British goods out of the Continent. Under these circumstances Du Pont worried more than was necessary and, of course, devised schemes, which, in turn, caused concern to his sons, since they did not know exactly what he was doing. Understandably, they pressed him even more urgently to return to

America and he began again to think of doing so. He decided, however, that he could not leave France until he had settled his accounts with his shareholders and completed his task of preparing a multi-volume edition of Turgot's works. These were not only responsibilities which he owed to posterity but also actions which would refurbish his reputation. He was much concerned, as he wrote later to Victor, "to leave us a name that is historic, philosophic and revered."[9]

After months of worry, Du Pont produced a plan which he revealed to Irénée in a letter dated May 17, 1806, and written partly in numerical code.[10] He would sell Bois-des-Fossés and repurchase the shares of Necker-Germany so that he might have another share in the powder company; he would sell the uncontested 16,000 acres of Kentucky land so that he could buy Bauduy's shares in the powder company; and he would obtain a substantial loan from his friend Talleyrand so that he might provide working capital for Irénée's enterprise. He hoped that a sufficient sum could be realized from these operations also to settle accounts with his shareholders. Only the third of these schemes—the loan from Talleyrand—eventually proved to be practicable. Madame Lavoisier, who held the mortgage, raised difficulties over selling Bois-des Fossés. The Kentucky lands, which had been deeded to Victor, were tied up in the liquidation of his company. It required considerable effort to negotiate the loan from Talleyrand, who at first refused to do more than to underwrite payments if Du Pont could find another lender. All hope seemed lost when Talleyrand resigned from his position as Foreign Minister on August 9, 1807. Unexpectedly, however, Talleyrand did agree in September to lend 100,000 francs. Why he suddenly agreed was never explained. Since he had made a fortune from his government posts, he certainly had ample funds to invest and he probably believed that, in the continuing war situation, a loan secured by a mortgage on the shares in a powder company held by his friend Du Pont was a promising investment.

There were so many difficulties in arranging for the mortgage, for the transfer of funds, and for methods of repayment that Du Pont was beset by additional worries about his present position and ultimate reputation. Actually, by the time the loan was negotiated, Irénée could have got along without it. In May, 1807, indeed, he had sought to discourage his father from continuing his efforts to obtain the loan.[11] Although he was hard-pressed, as he always was, he was not desperate and did not want his father to make arrangements which might prolong his stay in France. Du Pont had persisted, nevertheless, and, with the help of his friend and business associate Jacques Bidermann, completed the transaction in December. As it turned out, only about 60,000 of the 100,000 francs reached Iréné, who deposited it in a bank, gradually drawing upon it for the purchase of scarce saltpeter.[12] Of the remaining amount, 20,000 francs was used to purchase the one share in the powder company and the three shares in Du Pont de Nemours Père Fils et Cie held by MM. Catoire et Compagnie; 2,000 was paid to Beauquer de Grandval, who had earlier lent 3,000 francs to Victor on Du Pont's endorsement; about 1,300 went to Madame de Staël toward payment of the overdue interest owed on the loan made by her father Jacques Necker, who had died in 1804; 3,278 was withheld as the first interest payment on the principal. Du Pont retained 5,250 francs in his possession. Over 8,000 francs cannot be accounted for. They disappeared either in the normal manipulations of the transfer and exchange of the substantial sum or in the possibly deceitful manipulations of Jean Victor Augustus Menestrier, who acted as the straw man for Talleyrand in the final negotiations. Du Pont used 4,000 francs to cover the expenses of Henry Manigault, a young American from Charleston, South Carolina, whose education in France he had agreed to oversee. Manigault was the son of Madame Gabriel Manigault, a friend of Madame Victor Du Pont. He expected to recover most of this amount and presumably did, although accounts are not available. In short order over 1,100 francs went to meet his own personal debts or current expenses. He had left 110 francs surplus, a paltry sum indeed, in view of the grandiose expectations he had originally had of extricating himself from all difficulties.[13] The loan was, of course, never repaid during Du Pont's lifetime. Irénée eventually retired it after many additional difficulties and complications.[14] The only advantage which the loan ever provided—and that was far from sufficient to counterbalance the difficulties it caused—was that Irénée was enabled to buy expensive saltpeter in 1808 at more favorable prices than otherwise he would have had to pay.

With Victor, Du Pont naturally had closer and more constant business relations than with Irénée. Victor Du Pont de Nemours et Compagnie in New York expanded considerably the commercial brokerage business first undertaken by Du Pont de Nemours Père Fils et Cie now located in Paris. Most of the business activity of the latter firm, indeed, consisted of serving as European agent for Victor's company. In his handling of many transactions, however, Du Pont did not clearly distinguish the operations of the two firms. He put to the account of the parent company sums which Victor regarded as belonging to his company. Victor was constantly complaining to Irénée about their father's failure to grasp the nature and extent of their transactions, but he "determined not to scold poor Papa any more. . . ." Nevertheless, he decided to "send all large amounts directly to Mr. Bidermann, for I have never been able to get Papa to send me a single statement or a definite account—everything is approximated; but I say nothing about it and all my letters to him are encouraging and comforting."[15] Victor's objective, like that of Irénée's, was to persuade their father to return. "Much as I wanted Papa to go to France," Victor wrote to Irénée on May 16, 1804, "now that I find he has no credit there I wish even more earnestly that he were here with us at Bergen. It is absolutely necessary for me to have business relations with a good firm in Paris for a thousand different affairs, and while he is there I dare not establish them with anyone else."[16]

Victor was, indeed, engaged in a "thousand different affairs"—and more. A tall, handsome, vigorous man, with an attractive and outgoing personality, he continued, as he did all his life, to charm almost every person whom he met. He had mastered all the niceties of refined society and was a popular host in his own home and a welcome guest in the homes of others. He lived well, probably beyond his means, and believed that his standard of life helped his business. He would have been an outstanding salesman at any time, but he lacked the caution and sound business sense required by his actual position—the very qualities which Irénée had in abundance. He operated on a large scale and mostly on borrowed money. For years he was able to meet his notes as they came due, though he was increasingly beset by difficulties and had to resort to more and more complicated arrangements to stay afloat. Still he might ultimately have succeeded; others then and since eventually made their way to a firm footing through such operations. He encountered bad luck and finally decided to give up the struggle before he became hopelessly involved and involved others who had trusted him. His failure was not ignominious.

One of Victor's worst mistakes was his connection with Louis André Pichon. He entered into further and more complicated engagements with this French agent beyond those originally undertaken in co-operation with his father and with the firm of Louis Marie Noailles. Finding that the French Government had no credit with established American firms, Pichon had turned to French concerns more recently opened in the United States, like those of Du Pont and Noailles, to finance supplies, especially of flour, for Santo Domingo. Pichon appealed to the love of the Du Ponts for their native land in seeking their assistance toward the success of the French expedition to Santo Domingo. Patriotism did have a part, as Du Pont always maintained it did, in bringing them to the decision to advance substantial credits, accepting drafts on the French Navy and Treasury as security. Had all drafts ultimately been paid in full, the Du Ponts, it is true, would have realized good profits on the ventures. But much depended upon Pichon's integrity and intelligence, and Pichon was unreliable, perhaps even a "vile Scoundrel" as Victor finally described him.[17] By the time of this outburst, however, arrangements between Victor and Pichon had become so complicated, so susceptible to misunderstanding on both sides, that the judgment may be too severe. Pichon was, of course, interested in protecting his reputation in Napoleon's eyes, as well as in improving his personal fortunes. In these endeavors, which proved ultimately in vain, he did not always tell the truth.

One of Du Pont's primary objectives in returning to France in 1802 had been to get the drafts held by his company honored by the French Government. Additional drafts were held by Victor's company as the result of his continued engagements with Pichon. Some of the original drafts in the hands of Du Pont and Noailles were duly paid,[18] but growing suspicions of Pichon's operations in America led to delays in paying most of them until after thorough investigation. Some of the questions raised in 1802 concerned the justification for the prices and interest rates which Pichon agreed to pay for flour to be supplied by the Du Pont and Noailles firms. Even if the original rates were justified because Pichon could not make more favorable arrangements elsewhere, subsequent rates, after Pichon's credit was established, seemed out of line to government officials in Paris and led to the suspicion that Pichon and commercial houses like those of Du Pont, Noailles, and Francis Breuil of Philadelphia—who had become involved by refitting a French ship under guarantee of payment given by Du Pont—were conniving to defraud the French Treasury.[19] Napoleon's often expressed distrust of businessmen who obtained contracts to supply the army and navy at some profit to themselves made even more unlikely the ultimate payment of the drafts.

The refusal of the French Government to honor the drafts on sight increased Victor's difficulties. He had sought other methods to obtain payment on the credits extended by entering into arrangements with Pichon for the outfitting of frigates to carry cargoes for sale abroad. Both Victor and Pichon hoped to make profits on such cargoes, although Pichon's commission from the French Government certainly did not authorize such commercial undertakings. Pichon was willing to gamble on the ventures in the expectation of enhancing his stature with the Government by thus retiring the drafts which he had authorized and also, undoubtedly, of making a personal profit. Victor was unwise in suggesting these arrangements, but he was in such a vulnerable position that he, too, had to gamble. None of the ventures produced the expected profits. The chief result was a series of further disagreements between the two men, each of whom accused the other of not fulfilling his commitments. Pichon was especially devious in his interpretations of the agreements, since he had to try to hide some of his operations from his superiors in Paris.

Another grave miscalculation was Pichon's decision to assist Jerome Bonaparte during his residence in America. This irresponsible younger brother of Napoleon had entered the French Navy and been sent to the West Indies, whence he made his way to the United States. His relationship to the First Consul and later Emperor made him a popular figure in some segments of American society. He indulged to the full his taste for a life of luxury and, in 1803, at the age of nineteen, married Elizabeth Patterson, a celebrated young beauty of Baltimore. He easily forgot his naval duties and seized upon the round of pleasures available to him. His activities outraged Napoleon and, when he eventually returned to Europe in 1805, he was brought to strict account by his brother, the Emperor, and even forced to give up his wife. Napoleon refused to recognize the marriage, since Jerome was a minor at the time, and forbade Miss Patterson, the "woman he is living with," as Napoleon insisted upon describing the alliance, to set foot in France.[20] Pichon did not, of course, anticipate this violent reaction; he must have expected, indeed, that the favors which he extended to Jerome would be repaid by favors he would receive from Napoleon. Unfortunately, Victor shared this expectation. Jerome's support might at least aid in inducing Napoleon to authorize payment of the drafts. Although the young man did not in himself represent a very sound investment, Victor undertook to pay his expenses under a presumed guarantee from Pichon that he would be reimbursed. He wrote to Irénée on July 10, 1804: "[Mr. Jerome] has acted very badly for his own interests in not going to sea. In spite of the increased forces, he has given up the voyage and gone to a watering place. If Pichon pays I have no objection to keeping them there until the peace. They spend about 8000 dollars a month and have already spent 15,000 dollars in repairs."[21] This involvement with Jerome could only serve to weaken further the Du Pont cause in Napoleon's estimation.

Victor's personal engagements with Pichon became so unsatisfactory that, late in 1804, he began a lawsuit against the French agent, alleging the latter's failure to fulfill his promised payments on some of the frigates. Aware that his operations were creating growing suspicions in France, Pichon could not afford to expose them as fully as his defense against Victor's suit would require. He therefore tried to divert Victor by offering further drafts on the French Navy. When Victor naturally refused to accept additional drafts, Pichon gave his personal drafts on the French banking house of Perragaux, La Fitte et Compagnie, the drafts to be payable in London, an arrangement which would have been of great advantage to Victor's company. Victor therefore did not press the lawsuit, preserving, however, the threat to renew it, should the drafts not be paid.

Du Pont entered into the negotiations at this point and, if Bidermann was correct in his analysis of the situation, was able to induce Perragaux to accept some of the drafts, payable, however, in Paris, not in London.[22] Since two of the drafts remained unpaid, Victor's financial condition was not substantially improved. He complained that he never got full benefit from sums due him in Paris because his father drew on them to pay dividends to the shareholders of Du Pont de Nemours Père Fils et Cie. His complaints were, however, usually addressed to Irénée, not to his father.[23] Du Pont was firm in his conviction that his sons and he were equally obligated to the investors in the original company and insisted upon paying dividends whenever he could, even though his company had earned no profits on its initial capital.

By July of 1805 Victor was in such a desperate situation that he contemplated going himself to Paris in order to try to straighten out his accounts with Bidermann and his father. He decided, however, to send his confidential clerk, Raphael Duplanty, who carried with him a balance sheet showing, in Victor's words to Irénée, "that I have still more than 20,000 dollars without the Kentucky land; that I have lived rather expensively for three years; that I have had enormous losses—and that I began with 45 dollars less than nothing, except the real estate."[24] His one hope was that, on the basis of his accounts, he would gain financial support from Bidermann. The banker was not, however, able to offer this support. After learning in detail from Duplanty how precarious Victor's situation was, Du Pont was greatly disturbed. He appealed to Talleyrand for help. Perhaps believing that at least something could be realized from the drafts on the French Treasury Talleyrand seems to have agreed to authorize Victor to draw upon him for sums necessary to get him over his current difficulties.[25] This arrangement, if it could have been worked out, came too late to save Victor. On August 24, he came to the grim decision that he had to suspend payment on his notes. "My credit is quite gone," he wrote to Irénée, "and I have no way of saving it; I could do nothing now except by adopting a method of business absolutely contrary to the one with which I started. I began with nothing, I paid with audacity; I tried to bluff. Nothing can help me now except a firm foundation, months of cash purchases, &c."[26]

The suspension of payments destroyed for Victor's creditors the last remnant of confidence in his ability to attain financial solvency. His worst fears were realized and he had to give up the slight hope that, after temporary suspension, he might attain a "firm foundation." He salvaged very little from his disaster, only sufficient credit to purchase on time payments land along the Genesee River, near Angelica, in western New York, where he believed that he had an excellent opportunity to profit in the development of the "back country." He seized upon this very dubious prospect because he was determined not to become an additional burden upon Irénée, who was insistently urging him to join the powder works. Irénée, who was proving himself to be the only one of the family possessed of a sound business sense, was much opposed to this project in the Wilderness. Victor persisted, however, agreeing only to allow his wife, who was expecting another child, and his three children[27] to stay with Irénée, while he set up a farm and opened a general store near Angelica. His family later joined him there. For three years, they tried to make the venture a profitable one, but Irénée had, of course, been correct in his analysis of their prospects. They had to give up and, with Irénée's assistance, established a woolen mill on the Brandywine, on the bank oposite the powder mills. They were dependent not only upon Irènée's financial help, but also upon the flock of Merino sheep which he had reared there.

Du Pont was naturally distressed and confused over Victor's failure. He defended his son in statements to his business associates, placing the blame, where certainly in part it could be assigned, on the refusal of the French Government to honor the Santo Domingo drafts. In private communications, however, he was not kind to Victor. He believed that he could have held on until help had come from abroad or until substantial profits were realized on the sale of cargoes sent from Guadeloupe. He did not take into account that Victor had tried desperately and vainly for many months to obtain assistance from Europe and that Victor could not have known in time about the Guadeloupe transaction. As Victor remarked in a letter to Irénée on November 1, 1805: "Alas! how well I should be living now if, instead of always drawing back, Mr. Bidermann would have supported me loyally. Within two months that excellent Reseville has sent me from Guadeloupe forty thousand dollars worth of cargoes—but how could I have foreseen that? and could I have waited?"[28] Another reason for Victor's collapse, which Du Pont did not recognize, was his unfortunate relations with his father's company in Paris. Victor strove successfully to prove the independence of his company from the original partnership and from the powder mills, so that these concerns would not suffer disastrously from his bankruptcy. His comments in a letter to Irénée on September 10, 1805, are not only enlightening on his association with the company founded by his father, but also on the loose business procedures adopted by him and his father. "Between the French firm and me there are no relations whatever, except that it admits owing me a rather considerable sum of money which it agreed to lend me and never paid; so we are even there. Unfortunately, the money appears on my books and the acknowledgement of the loan is among the loose papers. As a matter of fact the Paris firm owes me several thousand dollars; it has in its possession now all my Santo Domingo drafts &c."[29] Du Pont sometimes blamed Victor's misfortune for his own lack of success in business. He once wrote to Irénée that all would have gone well if Victor had had as much enthusiasm for the land scheme of the original company as he had for commercial enterprises which went awry.[30]

Du Pont continued to hope that, eventually, the Government would make some payment on the Santo Domingo drafts which he held. This hope was shattered in late September, 1807, when the Council of State issued its decision. The arrangements between Pichon and the Du Ponts, Noailles, and Breuil were reviewed at length in the Imperial Decree of September 30 to the detriment of all parties. Pichon was formally dismissed from all his governmental functions and almost all the sums due to others in his accounts were rejected. Pichon's right to attempt recovery of excess charges and interest, for which he might remain personally liable, was reserved.[31] Du Pont refused to drop the issue. He prepared a *mémoire* even longer than the decree giving his own review of the various agreements with Pichon.[32] He submitted it to Napoleon, together with a petition requesting further study of the transactions by a special commission. He reported to his shareholders in April, 1808, that "the Emperor received my petition graciously and sent it to the Minister of the Navy [but] the Commission has not been named."[33]

Du Pont was here attempting to put the best possible front on the matter. One doubts that Napoleon was very gracious in his reception of the petition, upon which he intended to take no action. Not until after the fall of the Empire was Du Pont able to get anything done. On November 11, 1814, a decision of the Ministry of the restored Bourbon king Louis XVIII annulled the decree of 1807 and ordered a new examination of the Pichon accounts.[34] But nothing ever came of it.

After Victor's fiasco, Irénée provided the last hope which Du Pont could retain for ultimately extricating himself from his own financial complications. He had to paint for himself and others an optimistic picture of how well the powder works were doing. He did not know, and did not try to find out, the very serious problems which Irénée had constantly to face. Irénée did not, on his part, trouble his father with all the details of his own difficulties. He did urge him frequently to return to America, alleging that his assistance was badly needed. Du Pont was, however, so busy at a variety of tasks that he kept postponing his departure. Madame Du Pont's obvious reluctance to leave helped him to find excuses for postponement.

Most of what Du Pont did during these years in Paris is not important. His one enterprise of significance for the future was his editing of Turgot's works. The completion of this task was an obligation which he had quietly laid upon himself after the death of his great friend. He had never been able to find time for it. Hoping to do the work in the United States, he had carried across the Atlantic the large collection of Turgot's letters, manuscripts, and official papers. When he returned to France, he had, of course, to bring the papers with him. Now he was unwilling to submit them a third time to the hazards of an ocean voyage and decided, therefore, that he had to finish the work in France before he could return to America. The accomplishment of the task consumed much more time than Du Pont had at first estimated. There was an immense bulk of material, which eventually spread over nine volumes, and there were inevitable delays in the printing, the expenses for which were met by borrowing from Bidermann. Because of his involvement in other activities, Du Pont could not give his full time to the task. Volumes II through VIII were not off the presses until 1809, although volumes II through VI have "1808" on their title-pages as the date of publication. Volume IX appeared in 1810 and volume I in 1811. Volume I, the last published, was a revision of Du Pont's *Mémoires sur la vie et les ouvrages de M. Turgot* of 1782. It was meant as an introduction and guide to the entire edition, since footnotes refer to specific pages in succeeding volumes.

Du Pont's edition[35] has serious defects. Except for volume IX, which presents chiefly Turgot's literary essays and his translations from Virgil's *Georgics*, from Horace, and from Pope, the various writings are given in chronological order. This arrangement produces a confusing assortment of pieces on many different and unrelated subjects, a patchwork of the important and the insignificant. Even volume IX includes, along with the literary criticism and translations, Turgot's interesting paper on uniform weights and measures and some of his letters to different correspondents on diverse subjects. Volumes VII and VIII do have some unity because they cover the period of Turgot's service in Louis XVI's Ministry from 1774 to 1776. Unless he takes the time to go through the text and footnotes of volume I, the reader attempting a systematic study of Turgot cannot escape some perplexity and exasperation in going through Du Pont's edition. Du Pont was not always meticulous in reproducing some of Turgot's manuscripts. His most serious fault, previously mentioned,[36] was to print in volume V the text of the important *Réflexions sur la formation et la distribution des richesses* with his own alterations, against which Turgot had earlier so vigorously protested. In an unusual display of modesty, Du Pont did not include Turgot's letters to him. He did not want to draw the reader's attention away from the subject to the editor. Yet some of these letters are important in grasping Turgot's viewpoints.

Despite these defects the edition had genuine value. It was for more than a generation the only collection of Turgot's works and it contained useful notes contributed by the editor. When Daire and Dussard brought out their more systematic edition of Turgot's works in 1844, they included many of Du Pont's notes.[37] These earlier editions have now generally been superseded by the most recent collection prepared by Gustave Schelle,[38] but Du Pont's volumes will always retain historical interest to the student of physiocracy or of Turgot. In a mood of depression, Du Pont had written to Madame Lavoisier on June 30, 1808: "I would like to be present everywhere and do good everywhere—poor, vain, ambitious creature without the least assurance of being useful to anybody anywhere, if it is not by the publication of the works of the excellent Turgot."[39] His implied hope for at least this "assurance of being useful" was not entirely in vain.

The next most important of Du Pont's activities during these years was his work in the Paris Chamber of Commerce. The old chambers of commerce had been abolished by a decree of the Constituent Assembly on September 27, 1791. Napoleon re-established them in twenty-two cities by an order of December 24, 1802. Frochot, Prefect of the Department of the Seine, seems at first to have opposed the creation of a chamber in Paris, but this principal commercial center of France could not be ignored. By a separate order of the First Consul on February 25, 1803, Frochot was required to choose sixty merchants of Paris as an electoral body to select a chamber of fifteen members. Du Pont was chosen as one of the sixty electors on March 16. The electors cast their ballots on March 21 and, on the third ballot, Du Pont received twenty-five of the forty-six votes cast and was, therefore, selected as the thirteenth of the fifteen members of the Chamber of Commerce. His friend and business associate Bidermann had been elected to membership on the first ballot. At the first meeting of the Chamber on April 7, Du Pont was chosen by his colleagues to be secretary. He was elated by these successes.[40] They seemed to prove that his past services had brought him a lasting reputation and that his efforts since his return to renew his associations with many prominent persons had been effective. He naturally hoped that his improved standing in the world of commerce would bring material benefits to his company. He worked hard at the job, although whatever hopes he had for personal profit were not realized. During his years of membership, he missed only thirteen of 176 meetings.[41] He was re-elected when his term expired in March, 1806, but, owing to a decision of the Minister of the Interior that members were not eligible for re-election until at least one year after the expiration of their term of office, he had to retire. He was re-elected to membership in April, 1807, and served for three more years. On June 10, 1807, he was elected vice-president of the Chamber, the highest elective office, since the Prefect served ex-officio as president. He held this post until his retirement in April, 1810.[42]

Since Du Pont was an officer of the Chamber for almost the entire period of his membership, his name appears frequently on the official papers of the organization. The actual extent of his responsibility for most of the reports, resolutions, petitions, and other papers, which he signed as secretary and vice-president, cannot be determined with any degree of certainty. Some manuscript drafts in the archives of the Chamber have corrections and alterations in his hand, but these may often have been only editorial changes.[43] An interesting but perhaps insignificant change is evident in the manuscript draft of the letter of gratitude and praise sent in printed form to Napoleon on May 26, 1804, after the Chamber had learned of the Emperor's intention to create a special section of the Council of State devoted to questions of commerce. Du Pont, who alone signed the adulatory address as secretary of the Chamber, may have been the sole author, but the manuscript is not in his hand, except for the one word "étonnante," which he substituted for the word "grande" in that part of a sentence describing the Emperor as "un homme d'une aussi étonnante force que vous. . . ."[44] If the change and the entire address itself have any significance, they may be indicative of the fact that, for years, Du Pont retained some hope that Napoleon would be a force for good. The constant warfare eventually brought disillusionment.

At the time Du Pont began his service with the Parisian Chamber of Commerce, the brief respite of the Peace of Amiens was coming to an end. The disagreements between the French and British governments had not yet resulted in declarations of war, but hostile acts on both sides were increasing. The British were intercepting French ships and, in retaliation, Napoleon required inspection of all ships entering French ports to make certain that they were not carrying cargoes of British origin. In the deteriorating situation the Paris Chamber of Commerce had opened a successful subscription among businessmen for a sum of money sufficient to provide a warship to be named the *Commerce de Paris*. As secretary of the Chamber, Du Pont signed the published extract from the minutes and was probably responsible for its final form.[45] He became more actively concerned in the commercial quarrel when the Chamber heeded the protests of certain Parisian merchants who had assignments on cargoes aboard neutral ships sequestered at Dieppe. The Chamber decided to send a delegation to Napoleon, who was then supervising preparations on the Channel coast for a possible invasion of England, in order to petition for release of the cargoes. Du Pont and Jean-Joseph Rousseau, a Parisian banker, were chosen as the delegates. They traveled to Brussels in late July, 1803, hoping for an interview with the First Consul. Napoleon refused three times to see them, however, and they succeeded only in presenting their petition to Chaptal, the Minister of the Interior. The mission was generally a failure, since the Government undertook only to release each ship individually after its cargo was cleared.[46]

During 1803 and 1804 the Chamber carefully discussed the project for a code of commercial law and published its observations, which contained many suggestions for changes.[47] Du Pont probably put the *Observations* in final form before they went to the printer, but there is no way to determine his individual contributions. The consideration of the many suggestions received from interested groups like the Paris Chamber of Commerce was a heavy task laid on the Council of State. From the mass of detail it never did succeed in formulating a concise and clear code. The commercial code, finally promulgated in 1807, while containing much of value in consolidating practices and ideas of the Ancien Régime as well as of the Revolution, was the most incomplete and ill-organized of the Napoleonic law codes.

On two occasions Du Pont's labors with the Chamber incurred the displeasure of Napoleon. By 1805 France was again at war against a potent coalition. The disordered commercial situation and the expenses of equipping a large army had put a serious strain on finances. The Bank of France, which had been chartered in 1800, had to suspend payments in specie because the Government had made such heavy demands upon it to recompense army contractors. The Paris Chamber was naturally concerned about the sharp financial crisis which resulted. Du Pont prepared a report for the committee which the Chamber appointed to study the situation. This report on the bank was printed, but without the endorsement of the Chamber, which decided upon a cautious policy in the dilemma of war and financial troubles.[48] The argument of the report echoed the views expressed in Du Pont's defense of the Caisse d'escompte in 1789.[49] Banks get into difficulties when they are not permitted to operate as private enterprises but instead are tied into governmental operations. When their policies are conditioned by the needs of the public authority, they cannot conduct their business on sound principles. They must be kept independent of the state if they are to prosper. These views were judged subversive by the Napoleonic censorship and the printed brochure was seized by the police. No punitive action was undertaken against the committee or the principal author of its report.

In 1809 the Paris Chamber learned that Napoleon had modified the restrictions of his Continental System to permit American ships to enter Dutch ports. The change, made at the request of Napoleon's brother Louis, the King of Holland, would likely have little effect, since the Embargo Act was still in force in the United States and since the British would attempt to intercept any ships ignoring the embargo. Nevertheless, French merchants desiring a renewal of direct trade with America prodded the Chamber to protest this apparent favoritism. Their strategy was to seek the opening of French ports to American trade. Du Pont, then vice-president of the Chamber, was eager to use the issue as an opportunity to argue the advantages of free trade. The Chamber approved his proposal to write a letter to Fouché, then serving as Minister of the Interior as well as Minister of Police, expecting that it would be brought to the attention of the Emperor, who was then in Austria waging his fourth successful campaign against the Hapsburgs. Du Pont composed a rather dogmatic letter on the virtues of "freedom and stability" in commerce, stressing the importance of providing an export market for grain.[50] The letter did reach Napoleon, who replied vigorously to Fouché on July 28: "I have received a [piece of] trash which you sent me on the grain trade and which is entirely ridiculous. . . . It is a prattling of the economist." In the midst of assertions that no one in France opposed the grain trade, that he would be happy to receive American ships, that the American embargo and the British blockade were responsible for closing French ports, Napoleon had some sharp words on Du Pont. "I have no need of the drivel nor of the lessons of M. Du Pont de Nemours and a few merchants. . . . We do not need the lectures of the

Chamber of Commerce, and if we do need them, it is not M. de Nemours who should give them to us. Conversations with a few knowledgeable merchants can be useful but the deliberations of the Chamber are always useless and have serious disadvantages."[51] The references to Du Pont in this letter indicate that Napoleon had a very low opinion of him. From a broader point of view, however, they reflect the attitude which energetic men of affairs have generally displayed toward those whom they regard as dogmatic theorists unable or unwilling to grasp the realities of specific circumstances. Naturally, nothing came of Du Pont's protest. Napoleon continued to ignore him.

Many other matters claimed Du Pont's attention during his years with the Parisian Chamber of Commerce, but they are not of sufficient importance to deserve mention. These activities occupied only part of his time. His amazing energy remained undiminished despite his advancing years. In a letter to Victor on April 3, 1803, when relations with Napoleon seemed more propitious, he had described the busy course of his days:

Here is the arrangement of my time: One morning for the affairs of the Banque Territoriale and the afternoon for drives and visits or at the Chamber of Commerce or the Philanthropic Society or that of Statistics. The next morning for the business of my own Company, correspondence, accounts, investments, &c, in my office which is warm and comfortable, fresh air and good light, the afternoon like the one before. Twice a week, on Monday and Friday at the Institut from three o'clock till five; twice a week, Monday and Saturday the evenings at the receptions of the second and third consuls. Wednesday to Talleyrand and Madame Bonaparte, when her health permits her to receive. Every fortnight from noon till two o'clock on Sunday at the audience of the First Consul. I dine at home only on Thursdays. This arrangement, you see, is very regular, but energetic for a man who is never free from gout which shifts from place to place five and six times a day.[52]

He maintained such a full schedule over the years, although specific activities changed from time to time and he was less persistent in cultivating high society after the advent of the Empire.

Du Pont became connected with the Banque Territoriale, which he mentioned in this letter to Victor, in December, 1802, when he was made one of the directors along with his friend Bidermann.[53] Probably he owed his selection to an old acquaintance, André-Daniel

Laffon-Ladebat, director-general of the bank. This enterprise had been organized in May, 1798, to make loans to landowners secured by mortgages on their property.[54] The loans were in the form of bank drafts issued to the amount of one-half of the estimated sale value of the mortgaged property and were payable in ninety days. These drafts soon enjoyed a good standing among businessmen because they apparently had good backing—the mortgaged land having twice the value of the drafts outstanding—and because they were promptly redeemed upon maturity by the bank. At the end of the ninety days the mortgagor had the choice of either redeeming his property by paying off the loan with interest or of renewing his obligation, which might extend up to ten years, provided the mortgagor regularly renewed and paid interest. If he failed to do so, his mortgaged property was forfeit and could be sold. From proceeds of the sale the bank recovered the principal and interest due and returned any surplus to the defaulting mortgagor.

The scheme worked well at the beginning but was risky, since it rested upon a close and accurate assessment of the valuation of landed property. Lenud, one of the commissioners charged with verifying the value of the mortgaged property, and a Madame Baraudin, who had acquired the shares of Noiret, an original partner in the bank, were later charged with defrauding the bank for their own profit. Their alleged connivance resulted in an overvaluation of property offered for mortgage and in the acceptance of properties already mortgaged—operations which led to the temporary enrichment of their families and friends. The two culprits were eventually prosecuted, but the bank suffered a substantial loss. Then, in June, 1802, burglars made off with 400,000 francs in cash from the bank's vaults. They were subsequently caught, but more than 200,000 francs was never recovered.[55]

Du Pont had no suspicion of the parlous condition of the bank when he became one of the directors. The Lenud-Baraudin conspiracy was still uncovered,[56] and the notes of the bank were still being accepted. Indeed, the bank had issued a quantity of sight drafts payable immediately upon presentation. This part of its operations ran afoul of the law of April 14, 1803, suppressing the paper of private banks payable on sight. Obliged to retire such notes in a short period, the bank found itself with insufficient funds to redeem them, along with its regular ninety-day notes presented within the prescribed period. It suspended payments on May 24.

Du Pont's most active participation in the affairs of the bank began at this point. Once again his energies were to be exerted in a hopeless cause. He was chosen as one of the six members of an "intermediary commission," responsible for making equitable arrangements between the stockholders of the bank and its creditors, those who held its notes upon which payment had been suspended. He was made president of the commission and devoted considerable time to it for the next six months. He was never so happy as when he was busy, and activity in a position of some prestige and responsibility was especially delightful. Victor summed up the situation in a letter to Irénée: ". . . all his other affairs are going very badly; he has no credit; he has put himself at the head of a bank that is bankrupt and will never again be solvent. He is killing himself with work in the effort to accomplish everything; but perhaps this active life is good for him, for everyone who has seen him says that he is much better than he was here, where he had much less to do."[57]

For five months the six members of the intermediary commission had no apparent differences of opinion. By November, they had, however, split into two factions. Three of them, led by Du Pont, supported the plan of turning over to Chavagnac et Compagnie, a firm established by some of the bank's creditors, all of the assets of the bank, which would be liquidated, although Chavagnac et Compagnie would carry on the same type of operation as that of the former Banque Territoriale. The other three commissioners, led by Michel-Mathieu Lecointe-Puyraveau, vigorously opposed this plan. A war of pamphlets followed. Du Pont was determined to override the opposition, because he was convinced that the plan which he supported would best protect the creditors in the long run, and because he believed that continuance of a system providing loans to landowners was important to the progress and prosperity of agriculture. These were the arguments which he stressed in his pamphlets.[58] His arguments may have been made less convincing for some of his readers by the fact that his name appeared as one of the three "administrators-directors" of the new company which was to take over the Banque Territoriale. Lecointe-Puyraveau and Pierre-François Page, two of the commissioners opposing Du Pont, published vehement replies.[59] In general, they wrote in behalf of the creditors who did not want to be associated with their fellows in Chavagnac et Compagnie and argued that the plan being pushed through by Du Pont would result in substantial losses to all creditors.[60] The open split in the intermediary commission had one inevitable consequence. The creditors became alarmed and met in Paris early in December to review the controversy. The six commissioners proving adamant in their stand, three on each side, the assembly of creditors decided to replace the commission with another one, composed of three members only in order to prevent such an even split in the future. Under the circumstances it did not seem wise to place any of the members of the divided commission on the second. Du Pont's connection with the bank ended, therefore, on December 12, 1803.[61] The plan which he had already begun to put into effect was modified. Most of his efforts had, therefore, been in vain. Except as a vivid example of the frustration which was usually Du Pont's lot during these years, the entire incident of the Banque Territoriale hardly merits consideration.

The same judgment must be made on the *New Jersey* affair, which occupied much of Du Pont's time in 1805. The *New Jersey* was an American merchantman which carried a cargo from Philadelphia to China in 1797. On her return in 1798, during the undeclared naval warfare between France and the United States, she was captured by a French privateer and taken to Porto Rico. There she was judged lawful prize, but was released by General Hedouville, agent of the Directory in Santo Domingo, upon payment of a deposit of $203,000 by the insurers of the vessel and cargo.[62] A claim against the French Government was entered in the names of the owners of the *New Jersey*, Philip Nicklin and Robert E. Griffith, under the terms of the Convention of 1803 which set aside twenty million francs of the sum paid by the United States for the Louisiana Territory as a fund to be used in settling such American claims. The real claimants were not Nicklin and Griffith, but the underwriters of the ship and cargo who had actually paid the sum as a deposit, reserving at the time the right of appeal. The case appeared to be routine, and the Council of Prizes in France approved the full claim in September, 1804. At this point, for reasons not entirely clear, the American Minister to France, John Armstrong, entered the affair and recommended that the claim be disallowed. Various reasons for his action were later put forward,[63] but, initially, Armstrong appears to have acted on the rumor that Nicklin and Griffith were actually British subjects, and hence not eligible for restitution. This rumor proved to be false, but Armstrong persisted in his opposition to the granting of full restitution to the claimants. His view was that, since there were numerous American claimants for indemnities of various kinds, each claim approved could expect to receive only a proportion of the limited sum available. In this impasse Du Pont's Paris company was authorized to act as agent in the Paris courts for the American owners and insurers.[64] Du Pont worked ceaselessly, arguing the case before French officials and writing five *mémoires* over his name and that of a lawyer, De La Grange, also retained as agent for the insurance companies.[65]

Du Pont did more than argue the case in France. He presented his views at length in letters to Jefferson, especially in his very extensive epistle of August 28, 1805.[66] He was particularly incensed by Armstrong's conduct in the affair and castigated him unmercifully. On a higher plane, he argued that this base treatment of a just claim would inevitably lead to a weakening of American interests in general in similar negotiations. President Jefferson had entered into the case indirectly, although he apparently was under a misapprehension of the principal question involved. He instructed Secretary of State Madison to write to Armstrong and later to transmit to the Congress, together with other documents, his view that the rights of the shipowners under the treaty with France clearly passed to the insurers who had "paid the loss of the original owners, citizens of the United States."[67] Despite this concern for the affair on the highest governmental levels, the disposition eventually approved by Napoleon prevailed. In the existing state of disagreement, Armstrong and Barbé-Marbois, Minister of the French Treasury, were authorized to settle the matter. They approved the payment of 300,000 francs, less than one-third of the original claim.[68]

Du Pont's vigorous criticism of a high American official in his letter of August 28, 1805, was typical of the freedom he employed in sending along to Jefferson, and later to Madison, his viewpoints on the proper course for American policy to follow. He offered frequent and lengthy advice in his letters from France. He was proud to have given the United States, through his son, "the perfected art of gunpowder," and proposed, upon his return, to bring to similar perfection the techniques of tanning.[69] Among his numerous recommendations to the American Presidents were that Canada be annexed at all costs,[70] that defense establishments be increased,[71] that part of the militia be armed with pikes, if a sufficient number of guns was lacking,[72] that a good national system of education be established,[73] that the Floridas must be acquired, by force if necessary,[74] that manufactures not be developed beyond a point "absolutely necessary" for defense,[75] that plans for regular militia drills and for civic festivals be set up,[76] that the way be prepared for instituting the single tax,[77] that uniform books on the classics be prepared for the education of youth.[78] There were many additional pieces of advice in his usually long letters to America.

This correspondence with Jefferson provided an irresistible opportunity for Du Pont to present at length many of his firmly held ideas. The most notable opportunity came in 1812 when Du Pont read a book entitled *Commentary and Reviews of Montesquieu's Spirit of Laws* and at once decided that it was Jefferson's work. Actually the author was the Frenchman Destutt de Tracy; Jefferson had merely arranged to have the original French manuscript translated and published in 1811. Du Pont commented upon it at length in three letters to the supposed author. He labored to demonstrate to Jefferson where his thought was faulty, although he thoroughly approved the general philosophy expressed in the *Commentary*. In his letter of January 25, 1812, he entered objections to the argument of the book as he understood it concerning the equal importance of all types of labor in the production of wealth. This "false" theory of Adam Smith and J.-B. Say logically leads, Du Pont held, to pernicious systems of taxation, especially to the iniquitous income tax and excise taxes. He refused to believe that Jefferson could really hold such views. He took pains to explain again that the only production of new wealth belongs to God, not to man. Only through the bounty of nature can man's work really be productive. If the only positive productivity lay, therefore, in the proper cultivation of land, the only defensible tax was the single tax on the net product of the land. In practice, he asserted, there is nothing more important to organized society than establishing a reasonable system of taxation.[79]

On April 14, 1812, he repeated old arguments in favor of restricting the exercise of the governing power to proprietors. Those without property should be permitted to remain free of all political, military, and tax obligations in order to devote all their time, ability, energy, and capital to the improvement of their economic condition. To open to them the exercise of political power would be to admit into government dangerous popular prejudices, to put in "a shade of the *pure democracy* which you have acknowledged to be only the rough outline [*ébauche*] of a civilized society, and [which] cannot and ought not exist in a nation raised to a higher degree of moral science through a profound study of rights, duties, and the common interest."[80] In a postscript Du Pont repeated his belief that officials clothed with executive power should have some part in the legislative power, a view which the author of the *Commentary* did not seem to share. He had never been an advocate of the complete separation of powers, a theoretical situation which could never exist, though he had placed some emphasis upon it during his term in the Council of Elders. In this letter he argued for the necessity of giving to the executive power a right of remonstrance, consequently of suspensive veto, to decrees passed by the legislature. The executive should not be expected to administer a law which it considered evil. A suspensive veto at least would provide time for discussion of such ordinances and for the formulation of public opinion upon them. If the legislature persisted in approving such decrees, the executive did not have the *right* to continue its opposition beyond the period during which reasonable discussion of the issue was possible. Indeed, Du Pont stated, if the executive still believed that it had to oppose the decree, then it had the *duty* to resign. He was confident that during the public discussion made possible by the suspensive veto, reason would eventually triumph.[81]

The last letter devoted to the *Commentary on Montesquieu*, May 17, 1812, protested that the author had given Adam Smith credit for being the first to remark that human faculties are the only original property. Du Pont quoted and summarized extensively from his *Table raisonnée des principes de l'économie politique*, which he claims was printed in Karlsruhe in 1772 and in France in 1775.

Although he was apparently incorrect in his recollection of the dates of publication,[82] his assertion that he had expressed this view **before the publication of Smith's *Wealth of Nations* in 1776 is valid.** He had great respect for Smith, whom he regarded as a disciple of Quesnay, but he believed that Smith's only real contribution was the demonstration of the advantages of the division of labor. He was fearful, however, that the impetus to industry provided by this division of labor inevitably produced an unhappy, and potentially dangerous, class of workers.[83]

The abundance of advice and counsel which fills his letters to Jefferson during these years may partly be explained as an effort to convince himself that he could still be useful. Aside from his labors on the Turgot volumes, he found few significant opportunities to employ his restless and ambitious energy on projects which he could regard as beneficial to mankind and as helpful to his own reputation. One position which might have fulfilled his aspirations never became more than a plan or a hope. In 1805, when he expected that Du Pont would soon return to America, President Jefferson wrote to William Claiborne, Governor of the new Louisiana Territory, a strong letter of recommendation that his friend be made president of the academy which the legislature of Orleans then planned to establish. He informed Du Pont of this action on February 12, 1806,[84] but the proposed academy was not set up. With his intense interest in education, Du Pont considered this position most appropriate to his desires, especially in a region where a knowledge of the French language would have been an advantage. Here Du Pont believed that he could be most useful because his inability to master the English tongue would not be an obstacle.[85]

In his search for worthwhile activity, Du Pont engaged in a variety of enterprises. He maintained his interest in the Institute despite his dislike of the reorganization ordered by Napoleon on January 23, 1803. By this order the Institute was divided into four classes: (1) physical and mathematical sciences, (2) French language and literature, (3) ancient history and literature, and (4) fine arts. Du Pont was assigned to the third class.[86] He found this assignment less desirable than his former assignment to the class of moral and political sciences, which had been abolished by Napoleon's rearrangement.[87] Since the new regulations permitted each class to choose a limited number of members from the other classes, Du Pont nominated himself in April, 1803, for the first vacancy occurring in the class of physical and mathematical sciences. This vacancy had arisen in the section of anatomy and zoology when the renowned Cuvier had been chosen as permanent secretary of the class. Du Pont's candidacy was noted in the minutes but, "since he [was] already a member of another class," he was not formally nominated by the section of anatomy and zoology.[88] He had, therefore, to be content with his original assignment. There were, after all, friends like Talleyrand and La Revellière-Lépeaux in his class of ancient history and literature; he could still submit papers to the class of physical and mathematical sciences, even though he was enrolled in another class; and he received the annual compensation of 1,500 francs granted to members of the Institute regardless of their class. He was faithful in his attendance at the weekly meetings of his class and submitted papers on diverse subjects to his colleagues in the first and third classes.

None of his contributions is important, although, had he completed it, his history of British finances might have been worthy of note. He read the preface and two chapters of this treatise during three meetings of his class in April and June, 1805.[89] Apparently, he was unable to carry the project any further. Although he seldom missed a meeting, he had a really effective role on only one occasion. That was in 1810, when he opposed the recommendation of the prize jury that the work of Rulhière on Poland be awarded the Institute prize for that year. Rulhière's book had stressed the sad condition of anarchy in Poland, which had led to the dismemberment of that nation. Du Pont thought that Rulhière's strictures were too severe, and he presented before his class three observations against the book on August 24 and 31 and September 7, 1810. His three discourses were later published.[90] His opposition was undoubtedly important in causing his class, by majority vote on September 14, to reject the recommendation of the jury, although it did vote to award honorable mention to Rulhière's book, along with those of several other authors.[91]

Du Pont was also occupied in the labors of various other societies. He tried to assist the American Philosophical Society by ordering for it the printed accounts of Institute meetings and other books and journals.[92] He served as one of the two vice-presidents of the *Société d'encouragement pour l'industrie nationale* and was especially active in 1806 in urging efforts to improve the manufacture of iron and steel.[93] He was the *rapporteur* for the committee established by the *Société philantropique* to study the operations of various provident and beneficial societies organized by workingmen. Several of his reports commending such societies were published.[94] Some of them he presented to the Institute, along with reports which he had prepared on the general work of the *Société philantropique*.[95]

Late in 1807 Du Pont was appointed sublibrarian at the Arsenal. Apparently, he owed his appointment to one of his colleagues in the Chamber of Commerce, Benjamin Delessert, member of the Parisian banking family with which the Du Ponts had many dealings. On September 27, 1807, Delessert, who was in a position to know about Du Pont's financial difficulties, proposed to Crétet, then Minister of the Interior, that Du Pont be named librarian at the Arsenal. He remarked that "the very straitened position in which he presently lives imposes on his friends the duty of seeking to be useful to him."[96] The position of sublibrarian, to which he was named in October, was a poor substitute for the important governmental post he had hoped earlier to achieve. Nevertheless, he accepted it and regularly drew the monthly salary of 200 livres from November, 1807, to July, 1814.[97] The position was a sinecure, perhaps a humiliating one,[98] and Du Pont performed no duties in connection with it. He turned down an opportunity in 1811 to become administrator of the library, an office which would have increased his annual salary to 5,000 livres, proposing instead that the appointment go to another man, De Sales, who very much wanted it.[99]

His personal financial situation had not been much improved by 1811, but he had relieved himself of the heaviest burden which had oppressed him ever since his return to France. His constant concern was to meet his obligations to his associates in Du Pont de Nemours Père Fils et Cie. The collapse of Victor's company and the refusal of the French Government to honor the Santo Domingo drafts would have been fatal blows except for the fact that Irénée's company continued to operate. Upon it Du Pont placed all his hope to escape the disgrace of bankruptcy. On April 18, 1808, he prepared a long report to his shareholders, in which he reviewed at length the misfortunes which beset the enterprise. He defended his actions and those of his sons, but had to admit that "the Powder factory is today our only resource and my one hope of *perhaps* saving the capital of my associates. . . ."[100] How he proposed to protect his associates is made clear in his report. The number of shares in his company had been reduced from forty-six to forty by an early repurchase of three shares held by Abbema and by the recent purchase of three shares held by MM. Catoire et Compagnie. The latter purchase was made possible by the loan from Talleyrand, whom Du Pont, of course, does not name in this report. He writes only of borrowing 100,000 francs "from a generous protector." Also purchased from MM. Catoire was the one share which they held in the powder company. This acquisition brought to twelve the number of Du Pont's original company's shares in the powder mills. Du Pont does not state that these shares were never fully paid for, because he had for a long time become accustomed to ignoring this fact in his calculations.

He wrote thus of his "present hopes":

I think—I like to believe that when the Powder factory has had some improvement—especially a second stamping mill that will cost four thousand dollars—and when it has repaid the hundred thousand francs that I borrowed for it, each share will pay six hundred dollars a year and will therefore have a real value of six thousand dollars . . . that would be three times the original cost of each share of my Company.

And it follows that the twelve shares that my Company owns in the Powder Company would equal the thirty-six shares in the Company that bears my name—of which I am the head.

If I live till the time of our settlement, which should be in July 1812, I will be glad to sacrifice four of my six shares, so that my associates may receive their entire capital.[101]

He assured his shareholders that he had already made personal sacrifices for them. "As for me and my wife, not only have we refrained from drawing any interest on our investment, but for the last four years I have not even permitted myself to take the salary allowed me by the Company as its Director. I have lived by my own work, from some wood I have had cut, from some land that I have sold and several other trifling resources. . . . I want to make . . . every reparation in my power. And I will guarantee their repayment to the utmost of my shares and of what remains of my fortune. To be ruined at my age is not cheerful. But to be blamed, to suffer reproaches that have some apparent foundation, would be a thousand times more unbearable."[102]

Subsequent to this report, he was able to purchase the share in his Company held by the heirs of Necker-Germany, thus reducing to thirty-nine the number of outstanding shares. On May 18, 1810, a year before he actually carried out his plan, he described to Madame de Staël exactly what he would do. He admitted again that the only resource left was the powder works. He proposed to surrender three of the six shares which he held in his Company and, thus, be able to turn over to his associates the twelve shares in the powder works held by the Company on the basis of one-third share in the powder company for each of the remaining thirty-six shares in his Company.[103] The concern on both sides over repayment of the note owed to Necker, which Madame de Staël had, of course, inherited after her father's death, could not be kept out of the friendly letters which Du Pont and Madame de Staël exchanged during these years. Much of Du Pont's extensive correspondence had to be devoted to explanations of his unfortunate business situation. He was oppressed by thoughts of failure, or rather of the detrimental effects which failure would have on his reputation. It is not surprising that he sought relief in a variety of activities, hoping somehow to be useful and to enhance his standing. After a decade of worry, he sought finally to free himself of all business entanglements.

On June 1, 1811, he announced his plan in a statement to his shareholders. To each of the thirteen associates holding the thirty-six shares in his Company would go the twelve shares held in the powder company, distributed as shares or parts of shares in proportion to each individual investment. Thus, for his three remaining shares, Du Pont would receive one share in the powder company; Bidermann, who had thirteen shares, would get four and one-third shares in the powder mills; Madame de Pusy, who held five shares, would acquire one and two-third shares in Irénée's company. Similar distribution was made to each of the remaining ten shareholders.[104] In this manner Du Pont liquidated his own Company and put upon Irénée the burden of guaranteeing the investments of his associates.

Irénée had not been entirely unaware of his father's intentions and sought to dissuade him from making this distribution of shares. He feared that those who received them might sell them and that he therefore would run the danger of losing control of the powder works. In view of his disagreements with Bauduy, he was especially afraid that the latter might be able to acquire sufficient shares to remove him completely from the enterprise which he had labored so diligently to build up. He sent money to his father, suggested other methods for him to settle his business obligations, and urged him to return to America.[105] His efforts were, of course, in vain, since his father had already put his plan into operation. Because of the delays in sending letters across the ocean and the loss of some letters, he did not learn exactly what had been done until some eighteen months later. Gradually he discovered the actual state of affairs through his negotiations with his stepsister Madame Bureaux de Pusy, who had come to America late in 1811 to settle her claims in person.

The next three years were to be the most agonizing in Irénée's life, and he could not help blaming his father for many of his difficulties. Bureaux de Pusy had died suddenly in 1806 at the age of fifty-six, and his widow was naturally concerned for the future of her children. She had inherited the five shares in Du Pont's Company, which her husband had helped to establish; for them she eventually was assigned ownership of two of the powder company shares when Du Pont de Nemours Père Fils et Cie was liquidated. These two shares she regarded as her best hope for the future. Misled by Du Pont's misunderstanding of the status of Irénée's company and by his faulty bookkeeping, she exaggerated the immediate value of these shares. When she got to America, therefore, she was upset by Irénée's doubt about the actual value of her holdings. His own bookkeeping was not up to date because he had been too busy to attend to it carefully himself. He set Victor's former clerk Raphael Duplanty to work to try to straighten out his accounts. He wanted to be fair to his stepsister and to his other shareholders and could not put an immediate estimate on the current value of each share. Until his records could be untangled, he undertook, whenever he could, to meet Madame de Pusy's immediate monetary needs. These needs increased when she purchased a house in Philadelphia to await his accounting in reasonable comfort. A long series of misunderstandings now ensued. There were such glaring discrepancies between his records and those of his father that, even with Duplanty's assistance, he could not produce a clear accounting as soon as he had expected. Madame de Pusy waited impatiently and began to think that Irénée was deceiving her. She fell an easy victim to the malicious tales which Bauduy circulated.

Her suspicions were undoubtedly expressed in her letters to her mother and stepfather. Du Pont became convinced that Irénée was trying to keep Madame de Pusy and his other associates from what he considered their just share in the powder works. On October 14, 1813, he wrote a cruel letter to his sons in a special numerical cipher, accusing them of wrongdoing and threatening to sue them.

I will go to America [he wrote] that we may understand each other, since you pay no attention to my letters. And if I cannot get you out of this horrible situation I will attack you both in the courts—in my own name, for I still have three shares in my Company which is equivalent to one in the Powder, and in the names of my associates who will give me authority. We will sue you. Yes, my sons, we will sue you. I will bring suit against you both.

I will wash my hands of the stain that you have tried to make me share.

I will empty yours. I will see that every member of the association of Du Pont de Nemours père fils et compagnie is assured of his rights, which one of you saved and which I believed safe in his care.

If you resist, you will be ruined.

I know how to think, act, write, speak; I do not know how to yield to injustice or to leave it unconquered . . . .

Could I have believed that you would treat me so? Have I not been good to you, and gentle, and an honorable father? The dream of my life has been to make your name an honored one.[106]

Du Pont probably regretted this vehemence, which shows him at his worst. It was the result of his ignorance of the situation in America, of his long frustration, and of his conception of his obligation to his shareholders. To others, and especially to Bidermann, his largest shareholder, he always defended his son's actions.[107] He made his adverse criticisms and threats only in cipher letters to Irénée.[108] His distance from his son's operations made impossible any sound understanding of the situation.

These troubles could not have come at a worse time for Irénée. He had pledged his credit to assist Victor in starting a woolen mill in partnership with Bauduy. To meet the demand for powder created by the war with England he purchased on mortgage additional land, known as the Hagley Estate, adjoining his original property and constructed more powder mills. He twice had to fear an attack by the British in 1813, when a war squadron sailed into Delaware Bay, and again in 1814, when the British burned Washington. He did not receive prompt payment from the United States Government for all the powder which he manufactured for it. His difficulties with Bauduy increased. There had been hope for reconciliation when, in November, 1813, his daughter Victorine had married Bauduy's son Ferdinand. Young Bauduy died of pneumonia, however, a few weeks after the wedding. Irénée was subjected to unscrupulous competition from others seeking to cut into the immense profits which he was supposed to be making. From his tribulations he gained but one advantage.

A series of financial reverses made Jacques Bidermann more keenly concerned for the status of his shares in the powder company. Disturbed by the rumors spread by Bauduy, Bidermann sent his son Antoine to America in 1814 to carry out a personal investigation. Young Bidermann was only twenty-four but possessed great competence in accounting and a genuine astuteness in business affairs. He had not pored over the company's books very long before he came clearly to appreciate not only the real difficulties which Irénée faced but also the remarkable capability which he displayed in carrying forward the enterprise despite these difficulties. He was able to calm his father's fears and those of others. Madame de Pusy finally returned to France in the fall of 1814, still dissatisfied but less a source of immediate irritation in Europe than she had been in America. Bauduy was bought out of the business in the spring of 1815 on terms very favorable to him but with the payments agreed upon spread over several years. Antoine Bidermann took over Bauduy's place and supplied new energy to the struggling enterprise. Ultimately every share in the business increased many times in value. But Irénée had few moments to savor any feeling of peace or satisfaction. The favorable turn of events in 1815 was destroyed in June, when nine men died in the first fatal explosion at the mills. From that time forward Irénée's life returned to what it had been, a desperate struggle to overcome one crisis after another.

Fortunately, he had Bidermann at his side. In September, 1816, young Antoine married Irénée's daughter Evelina and, thus bound his fortune even more closely to the Du Pont family. He brought new vigor to the selling side of the enterprise, traveling widely in search of new markets for Du Pont powder. His abilities helped to overcome the further efforts of Bauduy to ruin the company. Bauduy went into direct competition, building another powder mill only a few miles from Irénée's mills. He ruthlessly copied the machinery and techniques which he had learned during his former partnership and recruited as many of Irénée's workmen as he could. He did more. Announcing his dissatisfaction with the terms of settlement which had ended his partnership, he began a lawsuit that dragged out over eight years before going against him. During all these years of his struggle to preserve his enterprise, Irénée was plagued by the extra burden thrust upon him by his father, a burden which persisted long after the latter's death. Madame Bureaux de Pusy, though remaining in France, set her American lawyers into action in 1818, the year of a calamitous explosion which destroyed half of the powder mills and killed forty men. She announced her withdrawal from the business and demanded an exorbitant payment, which she agreed to submit to arbitration. The arbitration was never carried out, but Irénée paid her an additional six thousand dollars during the 1820's. Despite these trials, Irénée never displayed any lasting bitterness toward his father. He tried to make the old man's final years of life as comfortable as possible.

The misunderstandings destroyed the hope which Du Pont had cherished of removing himself completely from the world of business. For many years after 1811 he had to spend long hours in efforts to justify his conduct and that of his sons. But he had relieved himself of the primary responsibility for meeting his obligations to his own associates. He wanted also to relieve himself of his debt to Madame Lavoisier, who, in 1804, had entered into a brief and unhappy marriage with Benjamin Thompson, better known as Count Rumford. He had not been able to keep up regular payments on the mortgage which Madame Lavoisier held on Bois-des-Fossés. In 1811 and 1812, when, at Irénée's behest, he sought to buy up some of the powder shares held by his former associates, he decided once more to try to sell the estate in order to obtain ready cash. He was unable then to get Madame Lavoisier to agree to the financial arrangements by which he hoped to retire the mortgage.[109] As in so much else during these years he had to reconcile himself to failure. In 1815, after Du Pont had returned to America, Madame Lavoisier transferred the mortgage on Bois-des-Fossés to Harmand on very favorable terms.[110]

The problem of the unsatisfied mortgage could not, of course, be ignored in the letters which Du Pont wrote to Madame Lavoisier, but it seldom had a prominent place. Du Pont wrote of many other matters and recalled their past intimate relationship. He never permitted his thoughts to dwell too long in his troubles. He was able to surmount his difficulties only because he kept himself so occupied with other thoughts and activities that his worries, though real enough, were reduced to a minor proportion among the influences which shaped his outlook. He spent countless hours at his writing desk. When he was not writing letters or reports, he was turning out essays on a great variety of subjects.

He showed a particular interest in morality and religion. He celebrated the increasing freedom and enlightenment which would bring to mankind a fuller understanding of perfect morality and of man's place in the "celestial hierarchy" reaching from God to the lowest of His creatures.[111] He cried out against unfaithfulness in love and looked to the day when the ever-growing abundance of free agriculture would bring an end to immorality and warfare which, he believed, were principally caused by hunger. He hoped that the conquest of hunger would result in improved relations not only among men, but also between men and the other animals.[112] He stressed the importance of regular religious ceremonies in the home and suggested prayers for use before and after family meals and in the evening before retiring. He expressed his dissatisfaction with the translation of the Lord's Prayer, which he considered the most sublime prayer of all. He offered a new "translation," actually his own extended paraphrase of what he thought the prayer was originally meant to express. His "translation" is about three times as long as the original.[113] He presented again his viewpoint that the true religion was the one which venerated the common elements—reason, humanity, harmony—in the religions of all our forefathers.[114]

In some of his essays, Du Pont was able to forget his uncertain present in happy recollections of his past associations. When he reviewed the four volumes of the posthumous works of Marmontel, he dwelt on the references to Voltaire, Quesnay, Madame de Pompadour, and Turgot. He was careful, however, to point out errors and misunderstandings in which Marmontel had written about Turgot and his ministry.[115] When he prepared a eulogy of Quesnay's grandson, Robert-François-Joseph Quesnay de Saint-Germaine, who died on April 9, 1805, he filled almost half of it with selected maxims of the first teacher of the physiocratic doctrine.[116] Years later he delivered before the Société d'Encouragement pour l'Industrie Nationale a more notable eulogy on a man whose principles and works he long admired—Joel Barlow, American author and diplomat. When he related that President Jefferson had requested Barlow in 1805 to submit ideas for a national university, he could not resist recalling the fact that he had five years earlier answered a similar request.[117]

These excursions into the realm of general ideas and of recollections of the past were not undertaken in order to escape from the realities of everyday life. Du Pont wanted to be useful also in the present. In 1810, when his period of service with the Paris Chamber of Commerce came to an end, he assumed the administration of the system of household relief (*secours à domicile*) in the capital. He felt an especial responsibility to try to establish successfully this method of caring for the indigent ill, since it was fully in accord with proposals which he had made many years earlier in his *Idées sur les secours a donner aux pauvres malades dans une grande ville*.[118] The task was a heavy one and required more time than he had apparently at first thought necessary. He wrote to Madame de Staël on May 18, 1810: "You tell me of the cares of your Empire. These are the cares of mine which have so extraordinarily consumed my every minute, day and night. And mine is populated by about one hundred thousand poor souls, whose blind, septuagenarian, paralytic, one-armed, epileptic, consumptive bodies, some in the first [and] others in the last childhood, have an urgent need of bread, clothing, soup."[119] The public funds available to him fell far short of meeting the need. He had to carry out investigations all over Paris to distinguish the needy from the malingerers. For those who could work he tried to find jobs proportionate to their strength, so that the little money he had could be used for those totally unable to work. In April, 1810, he wrote to Jefferson that he had under his direction 117,000 indigent scattered throughout the city.[120] How many assistants he had he did not indicate, but obviously he could not have carried the burden by himself. Undoubtedly, Madame Du Pont, who gave much of her time to charitable undertakings, provided valuable help. Du Pont was in his seventy-first year in 1810. That he accepted this immense responsibility at his age must arouse respect for his energy and conscientiousness. He was still working at it in 1811.[121] The demands which it made upon him probably contributed to his decision in that year to liquidate the firm of Du Pont de Nemours Père Fils et Cie through the distribution of the shares in Irénée's company.

The human distress which Du Pont witnessed in Paris in 1810 and 1811 was in part at least a reflection of the increasing troubles of Napoleon's empire. The celebrations in 1810 attending the Emperor's marriage to the Austrian princess Marie Louise and those in 1811 upon the birth of the son for whom he had so long yearned in vain during the years of his marriage to Josephine, could not conceal the growing dissatisfaction over the strains of the continuous warfare. With an army of over 350,000 men unexpectedly bogged down in Spain and with the dislocations brought about by the failure of the Continental System to exclude British goods from Europe, France was finally beginning to feel the pinch of Napoleon's ambitious policies. The tide had turned and the flood could not be dammed before it swept back upon the French. The year 1812 witnessed the disintegration of the Grand Army on the bare plains of Russia. Napoleon was not yet finished, but the destiny which years before he had proclaimed as guiding all his actions no longer smiled upon him.[122] With almost incredible drive he raised another army, only to see it also finally collapse near Leipzig in October, 1813. He had eventually to retire behind the frontiers of France, where in a series of brilliant delaying actions against the invading allied forces he demonstrated conclusively that his skill had not deserted him. The odds were too great, but he would make no concessions. Although he might delay the allies, he could no longer control the situation at home. Powerful men, especially his former minister

Talleyrand, were also working against him. The allies entered Paris on March 31, 1814; on April 2, Talleyrand induced a rump Senate to decree Napoleon's deposition. Nine days later the defeated Emperor abdicated unconditionally, having to relinquish his last hope of saving the throne for his infant son. All that was left to him was his title and the rule of the island of Elba, where he arrived on May 4.

Until the very end, Du Pont kept mostly to himself his thoughts on these developments. During the ten years of the Empire, while French armies first overran, and finally retreated from, all parts of the Continent, he remained unusually silent on political affairs. But in April, 1814, he was again suddenly and briefly near the center of the political arena. As the allied armies entered Paris, he had come forward himself to enlist again in the National Guard despite his more than seventy-four years of age. His friend Talleyrand pulled him from the ranks and arranged for his appointment as secretary-general of the Provisional Government which he and his associates were creating.[123] It was not an important post, since it involved only the keeping of records and the certifying of official decrees and addresses of the Government, which, beyond doubt, Talleyrand directed. Of the many official papers which contain Du Pont's name as certifying officer, only a few have historical importance: the Senate decree deposing Napoleon, the copy of Marshal Ney's letter announcing Napoleon's decision to abdicate unconditionally, the broadside printing Napoleon's *acte d'abdication*, which was widely distributed.[124] Du Pont labored as diligently as he had so many years before in his secretarial position with the Assembly of Notables. On April 26, he wrote to his sons: "For sixteen days I was Secretary of the Provisional Government. For two days before that I did my service as sergeant in the National Guard. In those eighteen days I only slept for four nights and not all of them."[125] Exactly a week before he wrote this letter, his tenure of office had ended when the provisional government became the intermediary government under the Comte d'Artois, who was to prepare the way for the accession of his brother Louis XVIII. The Bourbon restoration was firmly underway.

Without power to influence events, Du Pont rapidly reconciled himself to them. There is some evidence that he personally preferred

Extrait du Moniteur universel du 12 avril 1814.

Paris, le 11 Avril 1814.

ACTE
D'ABDICATION
De L'Empereur NAPOLÉON.

Les Puissances alliées ayant proclamé que l'Empereur *Napoléon* étoit le seul obstacle au rétablissement de la paix en Europe, l'Empereur *Napoléon*, fidèle à son serment, déclare qu'il renonce, pour lui et ses héritiers, aux Trônes de France et d'Italie, et qu'il n'est aucun sacrifice personnel, même celui de la vie, qu'il ne soit prêt à faire à l'intérêt de la France.

Fait au palais de Fontainebleau le 11 avril 1814.

Signé NAPOLÉON.

Pour copie conforme :

Signé Dupont de Nemours, secrétaire général du Gouvernement provisoire.

Pour Extrait conforme :

Le Préfet par intérim du département de Saône et Loire,

Signé · CHAPUYS.

A MÂCON, imprimeur de la Préfecture, 1814.

a re-establishment of the republic, since he regarded the Bourbons as "too dangerous." Long out of touch with the situation in France and "surrounded for a dozen years by the weakest, most spiteful, least good part of their former court," they would likely insist upon complete submission to their will and, hence, inherit the arbitrary power of Napoleon.[126] The restored Bourbon, Louis XVIII, soon proved himself to be more amenable than Du Pont expected. He proclaimed the "constitutional charter," which Talleyrand and the Russian Czar Alexander I, then in one of his liberal phases, urged upon him. In some ways this charter reflected ideas which Du Pont had put forward in 1789. It provided for an hereditary monarchy, for a bicameral legislature, with the upper house, or chamber of peers, nominated by the king and the lower house, or chamber of deputies, elected on a limited suffrage, and for guarantees of civil and religious liberty. In the debates during the Constituent Assembly, Du Pont had been an unsuccessful advocate of a bicameral legislature, though he did not favor an hereditary, nominated upper chamber, which he regarded as too much like the English House of Lords. He proposed a constitution "somewhat different" from the Charter of 1814, he told his sons, but yielded to the need for rapid action and did not offer serious objections to "an English constitution."[127] He did not hesitate to accept recognition from the new government. His appointment as secretary of the Provisional Government was legalized in July, although he no longer held the post at that time.[128] His services were acknowledged by his nomination to the Legion of Honor and by his restoration to his former positions on the Council of State and in the Bureau of Commerce.[129] He tried to improve his prospects by sending to Alexander copies of some of his publications, but he got nothing more from this effort than a letter of thanks from the Czar.[130]

Du Pont had gradually to accept the fact that these small honors did not improve his position. He was obviously once again being passed over. His hope for a dignified government post with some influence was in vain. In September he replied sadly to a letter from Victor, who had written of his desire for reappointment to the diplomatic service:

I have only a little esteem and consideration in France, no influence, not the smallest credit; and I am more inclined to go to join you than to call you back here to a position far less important than the one we had before the Revolution. Although I have been returned to the Council of State and to the department of the Committee on Commerce, I have not the authority there that I formerly had; I am considered a man who is to be respected for his age and his honesty but who has dangerous opinions. They think my principles only foolish theories, and men who have been in official positions for two months base their arguments against me on their *experience*, as if fifty-five years of important administration had given me none. . . . They find me interesting; they are most cordial to me; I am convenient when there is sudden work to be done; but they do not care for me, nor my children, nor my happiness, nor my interests.[131]

He had himself hoped to be sent to the United States as minister or, at least, consul-general. As early as April, 1814, he had written that, if he were disappointed in these expectations, he would request his passport and rejoin his sons in America, as they had so long been urging him to do.[132] As his disillusionment mounted, he would likely have carried out this plan, had his wife and Talleyrand not urged him to stay in Paris. His unhappiness was increased when Madame de Pusy returned and took up lodgings in the same house on the Rue de Surenne where he then had an apartment.

Du Pont was not alone in his disillusionment. The new King, Louis XVIII, was sufficiently astute to seek a moderate course for his regime. He could not, however, restrain the reactionary leanings of his brother, the Comte d'Artois, and of the hard-core émigrés who now returned with revenge in their hearts. Louis faced grave disadvantages. Fat, gouty, slow in movement and thought, he was not personally an inspiring figure. The contrast between him and the energetic, decisive Napoleon during the years of imperial glory was inevitably noted by a growing number of his subjects. In order to restore government finances, which had been seriously drained over the period of Napoleon's fall, he had to economize. This policy dictated a decrease in government services and pensions and, especially, a reduction of the army. His Minister of War, General Pierre-Antoine Dupont, who was in no way related to Du Pont de Nemours, forced many of Napoleon's officers to retire and put many more on half pay. This unpopular move was made worse by the yielding of the King and of General Dupont to the claims of the returning émigrés. Many of the latter who had never seen a battlefield were granted army commissions. Some 6,000 men were given officer rank in the re-establishment of the King's Household Guards, a costly and useless body which did little more than add empty pomp and ceremony to the King's court. Army veterans and many civilians could hardly repress their bitterness over the necessity of showing respect for the white flag of the restored Bourbons, a flag which, for almost a generation, had been associated with the enemies of France. Talleyrand, who had performed the major part in the restoration of Louis XVIII, was not on hand to give advice on domestic matters. He had eagerly accepted the portfolio of foreign affairs in the new government and, from September of 1814, was busy attending to French interests at the great congress meeting in Vienna.

At Vienna serious cleavages developed in the policies of the victorious allies. These differences aided Talleyrand in his search for arrangements which he regarded as most favorable for France, though the significance of his actions in Vienna is still a point of some controversy. More important is the fact that rumors of the dissatisfaction in France and of the dissension in Vienna reached Napoleon on Elba. Such tidings made easy his decision to attempt a return. He was eager to leave Elba, a realm too small to exhaust his still considerable energies or to satisfy the authority left to him under his empty title of "Emperor." Besides, the Government of Louis XVIII had refused to honor the commitment placed upon it by the abdication treaty of Fontainebleau to pay him an annual income of 2,000,000 francs. Urged on by his supporters, he laid careful plans for escape. He loaded over a thousand troops on three ships and set sail for France on February 26, 1815. He landed near Frejus on March 1 and, within three weeks, was back in Paris.

Du Pont did not await his arrival in the capital. After Louis XVIII, alarmed by reports that troops dispatched to capture Napoleon had defected to the side of their former Emperor, set out for Ghent on March 13, Du Pont at once decided that he too must leave. His service with the Provisional Government which had deposed the Emperor and his acceptance of honors and office under the Government of the restored Bourbon king were not likely to escape Napoleon's attention. He could hardly expect the Emperor to continue to treat him with the indifference which he had shown in the past. He was now, he thought, in mortal danger. He could no longer postpone his departure for America. The decision to leave was, however, not an easy one. Several weeks earlier his wife had so badly injured her hip in a fall that she was confined to her bedchamber and was unable to accompany him. She urged him to go but, in view of his age, did not want him to travel alone. Since her daughter, Madame de Pusy, was on hand to care for her, Du Pont finally and reluctantly made up his mind to leave her behind, expecting that she would be able to follow him after her injury had sufficiently mended. He agreed to take with him Madame Du Pont's grandson, Maurice Bureaux de Pusy.

He hurriedly arranged an interview with the American Minister to France, William H. Crawford, and somehow persuaded that official to authorize a false passport for one "Monsieur Du Pont (Peter) American citizen of Louisiana, carrying dispatches from the American Legation to his Excellency the President of the United States, accompanied by his secretary, Maurice Bureaux."[133] Two final difficulties had to be overcome. Madame de Pusy refused to consent to the plan that her son accompany her stepfather. A substitute was found at almost the last minute. Alexandre Cardon de Sandrans, a brother-in-law of Madame Du Pont's niece, seized upon an opportunity to escape from his creditors by sailing to America. On March 20, just a few hours before Napoleon reached Paris, Du Pont set out for Le Havre with Cardon de Sandrans. There they could not at once obtain passage. Not until March 30 were Du Pont and his companion, masquerading as "his secretary, Maurice Bureaux," safely launched on the *Fingal*. Napoleon had been too busy to pay any heed to their departure.

Chapter XI

Last Days in America

Du Pont's second voyage to America was infinitely more pleasant than his first. The *Fingal* crossed the Atlantic in a month, putting into New York on May 3. Du Pont spent the days at sea reading and writing. He was principally concerned with Jean-Baptiste's Say's *Traité d'économie politique*, which had first appeared in 1803, when Say was a member of the Tribunate. Say was a disciple of Adam Smith, whose doctrines he put into a more rigid system, while adding special emphases of his own. His *Traité* had won him a considerable reputation and contributed to his retirement from public office, since Napoleon was not pleased with many of its teachings. Du Pont was also displeased with the book, but for a different reason. Though he thought there was much good in Say's work, he did not like its disdainful treatment of Quesnay, whom Say insisted upon designating only as a "physician." He penned a long letter to Say—the "prolix fruit of leisure which a ship provides"—in which he tried to prove that, except for his unjust scorn for Quesnay's achievements and his wrong-headed views on taxation, Say was almost a Physiocrat.[1] The letter is verbose and has the irritating tone of the wise and kindly father who is trying to bring a brilliant and erring son (Say was twenty-eight years younger than Du Pont) back to the path of truth and virtue. Its principal value is in Du Pont's comments on the conformity of the financial decrees of the Constituent Assembly to physiocratic principles and on Napoleon and the recent course of events in France.[2] He mourned the fate of his native land, brought to disaster by the ambitions, the vanity, and the tyranny of "Buonaparte," as he now once again calls the former emperor. Much pent-up hostility towards Napoleon spills forth directly for the first time in the long footnote toward the end of his letter. Despite Buonaparte's crimes the true glory of France, he concludes, will endure.

Du Pont was less optimistic in a letter which he wrote to Talleyrand two days after his arrival in New York. Then he regretted that Talleyrand had not supported his plan to re-establish the republic. Had Louis XVIII been able to control the situation, the monarchy might have succeeded. But he could not overcome the reactionary advisers who surrounded him or the émigrés, "talking, shouting as if they had conquered the Kingdom." The actions of such people, not those of the King, doomed the monarchy and made Napoleon's return easy. Even if the King were restored by the Allies, he would continue to find his way made difficult by the vindictive émigrés. France was threatened by "mob-rule (worse than democracy)." He concluded by placing his hope in Talleyrand's abilities. "If France is partitioned we shall all be in despair. If anyone can prevent that it is you. I have always thought of you as in the highest rank of those men who are statesmen *by the grace of God.* I said so to Calonne twenty-eight years ago."[3]

In this letter he twice mentions a long treatise which he had prepared at the request of several of the "new South American Republics." This *Mémoire aux républiques équinoxiales* is one of the lost manuscripts of Du Pont. His correspondence, the only basis upon which some of the substance of the *mémoire* may be reconstructed, indicates that at least five copies, and probably more, had been prepared by 1817. Only a preface, eight pages in length, has so far turned up.[4] In this *mémoire* Du Pont made detailed recommendations for the government of the Spanish colonies, which, after a long period of mounting discontent, had been in open revolt against the mother country since 1810. The request that he draw up these recommendations and model constitutions seems first to have been made by the Venezuelan patriot Manuel Palacio-Fajardo, whom he met in 1814. After the fall of Napoleon, Palacio had come to Paris to seek the support of the victorious allies for the revolutionary movements in Spanish America. He had almost no success; indeed, his efforts to arrange for the shipment to America of some officers hostile to the Bourbons caused his arrest and the seizure of his papers. According to one undocumented report, Du Pont helped to gain his release in October, 1814.[5] The *mémoire* was completed on March 13, 1815; five days later a copy was delivered to Palacio's agents in Paris to be forwarded to Palacio, then in London. After his arrival in America, Du Pont had several additional copies prepared, one of which he sent to Jefferson. In their correspondence, soon to be considered, the two old friends exchanged their somewhat conflicting views on the scheme of government proposed in the *mémoire*.

After spending a few days in New York, Du Pont set out for Wilmington and was soon safe in the eager embraces of his sons and their families at the powder works along the Brandywine. They had waited many years for the arrival of "Bonpapa" and now surrounded him with every comfort at their disposal, including the best room in Irénée's house. They provided also a commodious writing desk, at which Du Pont was soon busily writing lengthy letters and essays on many subjects. Jefferson sent a letter of welcome on May 15; in his reply on May 26, Du Pont remarked that "we shall not work for empires, but for the world and future centuries." Despite his age he kept himself stolidly to the task. An almost unbelievable quantity of manuscript flowed from his desk in the next two years.

Du Pont wanted very much to visit Jefferson at Monticello and began in May to plan a summer journey there with the Abbé José Francesco Correa da Serra, the brilliant Portuguese scholar and scientist. Correa had been a correspondent of Du Pont's class in the Institute and, when he came to America in 1812, had carried a letter of introduction to Jefferson provided by Du Pont.[6] He had visited Monticello in 1813, where he had been enthusiastically welcomed.[7] The summer trip had, however, to be postponed. Correa and Du Pont could not arrange to leave before late July; by then a combination of circumstances made them decide to give up the trip. Du Pont had barely recovered from a siege of gout and diarrhea, and his sons and daughters-in-law were opposed to his attempting a long journey in the mid-summer heat.[8] Jefferson had planned to leave Monticello early in August for two months and Du Pont did not want to interfere with his plans.[9] Correa set off alone not to visit Jefferson, but to join later with J. W. Gilmer on an expedition to the Cherokee

Indians. Du Pont did not brood over his disappointment. He would go to Monticello at the next available opportunity; besides, he had other worries.

With young Bidermann's assistance, he had been able to examine the financial accounts of the powder works. He gained an understanding not previously possible of the status of the business and of the conscientious labors which Irénée had for so long expended on it. As he recalled the harsh letters he had written to his sons, he suffered deep pangs of regret. He resented as he never had before the unjust attacks which Madame de Pusy had made on Irénée. He expressed his unhappiness in letters to his wife, whose absence he also mourned. Madame Du Pont aggravated her injury in another fall in the late spring of 1815 and could plead physical incapacity as the chief reason for her failure to come to America. She did not want to leave France and hoped that Du Pont would return to her. He might occasionally speak of doing so but made it plain that he wanted to stay in America. Their letters to each other are full of warm affection. Only once did a discordant note arise because of their naturally contradictory attitudes toward Madame de Pusy, and this seems to have come about through another effort of Madame de Pusy to turn to her own advantage in her conflict with Irénée her stepfather's love for her mother. Du Pont saw no hopeful future for his native land, even after Napoleon's defeat at Waterloo and exile to St. Helena, and believed that he would be in real danger as the most reactionary supporters of the Bourbons savored their victory. He was certain that he could not accomplish in France the work which he believed he might yet do. For two long years Du Pont and his wife were to exchange many letters in which they expressed their undying love for each other—Du Pont with a youthful passionateness amazing in a man of his years—and confessed their wretched loneliness over their separation, while finding reasons why they would not end it.[10]

As he had so often in the past Du Pont found relief from his unhappiness in writing. Not a day passed that did not produce numerous letters and other pieces. When he discovered that, in several states, like Delaware and Pennsylvania, there was no regular system for registering vital statistics, he produced a plan to remedy the defect, though no one seems to have paid any attention to his effort.[11] He continued his essay on the Spanish republics, which, by September, 1815, extended through eleven chapters.[12] He began himself to translate into English his book on national education in the United States, which he had written at Jefferson's request fifteen years earlier. In October he went to Philadelphia with Irénée to attend a meeting of the American Philosophical Society.[13] Except for this rare diversion from the regimen he had prescribed for himself, he sought his relaxation among his children and their families along the Brandywine. Sophie and Irénée made him as comfortable as they could in their home. At least once a week he crossed the Brandywine to dine with Josephine and Victor at their home near the wool factory.

His desire to visit Monticello was finally realized in December. Correa was still among the Indians, but Victor agreed to accompany him. They set out in late November and, after resting for two days at Kalorama, the Barlow estate on Rock Creek near Washington, where Madame Barlow, widow of the former American minister to France, graciously entertained them, they arrived at Monticello on December 4. There Du Pont once again faced disappointment and frustration. Not expecting a visit so late in the season, Jefferson was not at home! Correa and Gilmer arrived on December 5, but the longed-for reunion with Jefferson was not to take place. Jefferson's daughter, Mrs. Randolph, was a considerate hostess, and Du Pont stayed for three days, hoping that Jefferson would return. Correa left on the sixth, warning Du Pont not to tarry too long, else he might be indefinitely detained by bad winter weather. Regretfully Du Pont started back to Washington two days later.[14] He spent almost two weeks in the capital, dining once with Secretary of State Monroe. Although he mentioned an invitation to dine at the White House, he may not have seen President Madison during his stay in the city. He quietly celebrated his seventy-sixth birthday there on December 14. He did what he could to support Victor's efforts to gain for his son Samuel Francis an appointment to the United States Navy.

Du Pont had left behind at Monticello a long letter to Jefferson, the first few pages of his English translation of his work on education, the drafts of his constitutions for the republics of New Granada, Cartagena, and Caracas, and a copy of his letter to Say. In his letter he had asked for Jefferson's assistance in gaining for his grandson appointment as midshipman in the Navy. The appointment was made even before Jefferson wrote a letter of recommendation.[15] Samuel Francis du Pont was only twelve years old in 1815, but in future years he was to have a distinguished naval career, retiring as rear admiral after outstanding service in the Mexican and Civil Wars.

A week after his return to Wilmington, Du Pont received a letter from Jefferson expressing his "mortification" over losing the happiness of a visit from his "very dear and ancient friend." Tactfully, Jefferson suggested that Du Pont give up his effort to put into English his treatise on education. He was confident that Correa could find a suitable translator.[16] Gilmer apparently began a translation but did not go very far with it. Du Pont nevertheless accepted his friend's advice and put aside his own poor effort. There was much else to keep him busy for the habitual "twelve hours at least every day," which he had mentioned in an earlier letter to Monroe.[17] In fact, as he himself came to recognize, he was trying to do too much. ". . . I have a great failing," he wrote to Jefferson on March 16, 1816; "pressed by age and circumstances, I am busy with several pieces of work at the same time. I know that this is not a good method—in fact, it is no method at all."[18] He carried on an extensive correspondence with his friends in Europe, an enterprise facilitated by the unusual privilege accorded him by Secretary of State Monroe of sending communications abroad by diplomatic pouch. He continued to prepare papers for the Institute and for the American Philosophical Society.[19] He translated ten additional cantos of Ariosto's *Orlando Furioso*. He did give up his vain attempts to master the English language, admitting to his wife in December, 1816, that he did not know ten more words of English than he knew upon his arrival.[20] Much of his copying he had to do himself, since Cardon de Sandrans, who had served him as secretary, became involved in other enterprises, notably the establishment of a tannery, which ultimately failed.[21]

Du Pont's letters to Jefferson, Madison, and Monroe were full of advice on American policy. Four observations were prominent in these letters: Du Pont's generally gloomy viewpoint on the future of Europe;[22] his belief that another war with Great Britain was inevitable;[23] his eagerness for the establishment of a uniform system of national education, tinctured by regret that so many years had elapsed with nothing accomplished toward the realization of his earlier recommendations;[24] and his hope for the reasonable increase of American industry, primarily as an aid to expanding agriculture.[25] On the last point his natural physiocratic hostility to encouraging the "sterile" activity of manufacture was considerably modified by his study of the American situation. Showing again his willingness to adapt theoretical systems to actual conditions, he argued for a manufacturing establishment in the United States large enough to assure a reasonable independence of foreign manufactures and, especially, to supply a ready market for the products of an expanded agriculture. Although he favored the achievement of a healthful balance between agriculture and industry, he was primarily interested in the latter only insofar as it contributed to the prosperity of the former.

His labors on the proposed constitutions for the Latin American republics offered another opportunity for an exchange of views between him and Jefferson. This part of their correspondence is valuable in gaining some idea of Du Pont's proposals in the absence of any copy of his manuscript on the "Equinoctial Republics." In his arrangements for the government of these future republics, he had remained faithful to his long-held ideas by restricting the electoral right to proprietors and by providing for a hierarchy of assemblies, all but the lowest one (the *commune*) to be chosen by the assemblies immediately below it. These arrangements are essentially those of the *Mémoire sur les municipalités*, which he had composed forty years earlier in 1776. Although Jefferson was willing to concede that such proposals were probably reasonable for the specific areas concerned, he found in general too little democracy provided for in the constitutions. He described the principal difference between his political philosophy and Du Pont's in these terms: "We both consider the people as our children, and love them with parental affection. But you love them as infants whom you are afraid to trust without nurses; and I as adults whom I freely leave to self-government."[26]

Du Pont sprang to the defense of his general political principles. After assuring Jefferson that he had no intention of suggesting his ideas for application to the United States, which, in his view, were susceptible of improvement only in the matter of public finance, he proceeded to reiterate his old arguments in defense of a government controlled by proprietors. He did think that the United States had retained some unfortunate traces of the English heritage, especially that of "absolutely popular elections." To give almost everyone the right to elect was to open the door to popular passions, to demagoguery, and to tyranny. Only those with a real stake in society through the ownership of landed property could be expected to show mature solicitude for the preservation and proper regulation of society. One who possessed nothing beyond his own person and movable property had only the right to liberty of his person, to ownership of his property, and to the faculty of disposing of it as he wished. Such a person was more or less transient, with no firm roots in an organized society, and should enjoy no right to regulate that society unless such right were specifically delegated to him by the proprietors who actually constituted the society.[27] There is here a remarkable conformity to the viewpoints which Du Pont had presented before the Constituent Assembly twenty-seven years earlier. He did make a slight concession when he stated that "there cannot be too much haste in granting full rights of citizenship to the men of red or mixed blood; or at least to such of them as are landowners or will become so." That was the best way, he thought, to encourage men to work, to inspire public spirit, and to guard the interests of capital.[28]

There was no end to the fertility of Du Pont's imagination in planning additional projects, but his basic conception of what had to be done did not noticeably change. The good work which he hoped to accomplish consisted in furthering understanding of those simple, natural truths which should guide men in their government and in all other aspects of their lives. On May 12, 1816, he wrote to Jefferson that he was formulating three philosophical works which "could be printed only in a country completely free." These works would contain his speculations on the limits to the powers of government, on the question why there had never existed a good government, good education, or good religion when the maxims which would assure these things were easily discovered in the head and heart of everyone, and on the extension and application to a large society of those natural laws which would regulate the government of a single family isolated in a desert.[29]

Amidst all these labors and plans, Du Pont's final two years should have been happy. His peace of mind was, however, disturbed by three circumstances—his separation from his wife, his increasing ill health, and his concern for the future of his native land. All three were joined in his thoughts. His desire to return to his wife, since her painful injury made difficult her coming to America, was weakened by his view of the sad state of France and of his inability to contribute to its betterment. His decision to return to France, even though he expected to be in personal jeopardy there, was made impractical by his own physical ills. He had long been accustomed to enduring attacks of gout, though his advanced age now made them more painful. A more serious complaint, a form of nephritis, brought increasing misery during his last year. His discomfort was so intense that he was seldom able to sleep more than a few hours at night. He spent countless dark hours in pain and despair, pacing back and forth in his room or reading and writing by the light of a faulty lamp which his wife had sent him— a lamp so inefficient in its operation that, to Sophie's distress, its smoke blackened the walls and ceiling of his room.

Some of these hours were given over to reading the issues of the *Moniteur*, which his wife sent him from Paris. He could find no cause for elation in what he read of affairs in France. The reaction would triumph, perhaps not completely so long as Louis XVIII lived, but the King was old—actually, he was sixteen years younger than Du Pont. France would become the prey of ambitious rival nations. Had it not been for Alexander I, the brilliant Czar of Russia, France would have suffered much more severely in 1814 and 1815. If Alexander had in Du Pont's eyes played the role of savior, Napoleon, he was more and more convinced, had been the agent of destruction. Buonaparte—no longer did he call the former emperor Napoleon or Bonaparte—had killed France as well as Frenchmen, Du Pont wrote to Monroe; since the French people had not had the wisdom or the ability to dethrone him after his return from Russia and to re-establish the Republic, "we have to resign ourselves to our inevitable misfortunes."[30] As his anger against the Corsican mounted, he easily arranged his recollections to cast himself as a persistent opponent. He became certain, as he wrote to his wife in March, 1816, that "this tyrant has never had an enemy more violent than I; and I have spent twelve years continuously making against him plans, plots, ballads, and epigrams."[31] He wanted to get himself on the right side, not only in his own recollections, but also in the minds of others. On August 3, 1816, he wrote a long letter to the Baron Hyde de Neuville, recently arrived as French Minister to the United States, recalling his past services which, he was certain, the King would remember. He was, he wrote, perhaps the last Frenchman who bore arms in Paris against Buonaparte on March 20, 1815, adding that he left the capital only three hours before Buonaparte's arrival, that he often attended meetings of the Council of State in uniform, that he was not without influence in the National Guard, where he was called "the valiant sergeant." He assured the Minister that he was not in America as a fugitive and that he expected soon to return to France.[32] He wrote other letters to Hyde de Neuville, partly no doubt because he had earlier been acquainted with him in France, but partly also because, as he told his wife in July, 1816, he placed "very much more importance on the life which I shall have after the death of Du Pont de Nemours than on that which I shall have during his lifetime."[33]

The general situation in France after 1815 was so unfavorable to his ideas, he thought, that his reputation would be ruined should he return. In February, 1816, he even sent to his wife a letter to be delivered to the King, in which he resigned his post in the Council of State. Madame Du Pont never delivered the letter, however, since she still hoped that he would come back to Paris.[34] He did not resign from the Institute, although he was unhappy about the reorganization of April 16, which had placed him in the new class of Inscriptions and Belles-lettres.[35]

Du Pont's poor health prevented his attempting any other trips like the visit to Washington and Monticello. During the occasional periods when he was feeling better, he became restless and bored.

On his seventy-seventh birthday, December 14, 1816, he complained in a letter to his wife that he had no one with whom he could really converse. Irénée and Sophie, who understood him best, were too busy. Outside of the family, he had seen no one, he wrote, except "Mr. Monroe and Madame Barlow in Washington and Mr. de Correa here."[36] Because of bad weather and Irénée's absence, celebration of his birthday was postponed until December 16, when a family dinner was to be held at Victor's house across the Brandywine. Dressed in his best finery and eager to go, Du Pont refused to wait for Bidermann, who was to conduct him across the creek, since Irénée had first to visit the Hagley works before he could go to the party. He had Sandrans shove the ferryboat away from the shore, but the ferryman did not hear Sandrans' warning that he was about to do so. When the boatman temporarily lost control of his craft, Du Pont lost his balance and fell into the creek. He was able to keep afloat until Sandrans, holding on to a tree with one hand, grasped the tail of his frock coat with the other and pulled him to safety. Du Pont remained calm amidst the outcries. He permitted Sandrans to lead him to the nearby boardinghouse for the workingmen without families, but then insisted upon walking by himself in his wet clothing through the cold December evening back to Irénée's house. Sophie immediately put him to bed and Irénée rushed in from Hagley, condemning himself for going there in the first place. Amazingly, Du Pont suffered no ill effects. He submitted to his children's ministrations out of regard for them; for himself, as he wrote to his wife, he was glad to have been tested and found able to take care of himself, as on August 10, 1792.[37]

During these months, he devoted most of his time at his desk, when he was not writing letters, to his translation of *Orlando Furioso*, which he hoped to have published in Paris. He had doubts that the effort was worthy of his talents, but was proud to have finished ten cantos in fifteen months—8,516 verses in French, whereas there were only 4,000 in the *Henriade!* He believed, however, that the most enduring of his works would not be *Orlando*, but the *Table of the Principles of Political Economy*, the *Philosophy of the Universe*, and the *Mémoire on the Equinoctial Republics*. In regard to these three works he was not a good prophet. He was, however, occasionally perceptive in some of his remarks in his letters. On February 26, 1817, he warned President-elect Monroe of the dangers to the United States which might be expected from the victorious coalition of powers in Europe. This coalition, which had crushed France through the fault of Buonaparte, still existed and would be hostile to the United States "as long as there are Kings and Peers in Europe. It is the war of Kings and Peers against nations, peoples, and liberty." Du Pont was wrong in believing that England would be the most vindictive member of the coalition but, in his general warning, he seems to be anticipating ideas which six years later contributed to the formulation of the famous Monroe Doctrine. Monroe endorsed this letter as "highly interesting"; still there is no way to determine whether it had any influence on his thinking.[38] Probably it did not; in any event, the important contributions of John Quincy Adams to the authorship of the doctrine which bears Monroe's name has long been generally acknowledged.

Although the unexpected immersion in the cold waters of the Brandywine had no apparent adverse effects on his health, Du Pont's chronic ailments brought him much suffering during the final months of his life. He wrote to his wife in June, 1817, that he had been sleeping very little and that he had actually become thin.[39] Digestive disorders added to his woes. Early in June, when he was still weak from an attack which had made it impossible for him to retain any food in his stomach, he insisted upon going to Philadelphia and Washington. In Philadelphia he wanted to execute a notarized certificate before his friend Peter Du Ponceau to present to the French consul as proof that he was still alive. The reason for this action was to make certain that his wife would continue to draw the small monetary compensations due him from the Institute and from the Government. Sophie insisted that Bidermann accompany him to Philadelphia, where Irénée, who was already there on one of his frequent business trips, could meet him. It was fortunate that he had this assistance, because he became seriously ill in Philadelphia and had to be put to bed in the home of a Madame Benson, an acquaintance of his sons. A doctor was summoned to treat him and, according to Du Pont, rapidly cured his nausea with salt water. A notary public was also brought to his bed so that he could sign the necessary legal papers. Then he felt much better, although he regretfully decided that he would have to give up the trip to Washington. After a few hours of rest, he demanded to be taken home. Helped by Bidermann, he was back on the Brandywine sixteen hours after he had set out for Philadelphia. Again he made an amazing recovery.

A few days later, on July 16, he was worrying in a letter to his wife about the apparent delay in clearing the papers through the French Consulate and decided that he would have to journey again to Philadelphia. He was never to make this journey. Soon after he wrote these words, he retired for the night. He was roused from his first troubled sleep by a commotion outside. The carelessness of a workman in leaving behind smouldering charcoal set the whole charcoal house ablaze. If the fire were to spread to other buildings, one powder mill after another might explode. The watchman's whistle brought everyone running from his bed to combat the deadly flames. Despite his age, his ill health, and the pleading of his family, Du Pont placed himself in the middle of the bucket brigade, whose prompt action brought the blaze under control before it reached the powder stores. Thoroughly soaked and singed, Du Pont returned to bed. The next day he was unable to get up. He became desperately ill; for two weeks he suffered horribly, according to the description of Victor's wife in a letter to her friend Mrs. Manigault.[40] Early in August he lapsed into a coma and never regained consciousness. With his sons and eldest grandson at his bedside, he died in the early morning hours of August 7, 1817.

Madame Du Pont did not learn of her husband's death until sometime in October and continued to write long letters to him from Paris. After hearing the sad news, she could not find the strength or courage to write to Irénée until November 18. Then she mourned her misfortune in surviving "the best man in the world." She took comfort only in the thought that she was old and would "soon join him in a better world where he will receive the reward of his virtues and of fifty-five years of useful work."[41] Although she was wrong in her prediction of her own imminent death—she was to live for twenty-three more years—she was right in her comment about Du Pont's long-sustained efforts to be useful.[42]

Certainly Du Pont's true epitaph must be concerned with this desire to be useful. Sometimes vain, always ambitious, over-sensitive about his reputation and place in history, he did live a life of exuberant activity and of courageous struggle for right and for justice as he understood these terms. One cannot rank him with the prime movers of the affairs of mankind, but one must acknowledge that he set a high standard of ideals and of endeavors not matched by many more famous individuals in the record of man's past. For "upwards of 30 years," wrote Jefferson, "I had witnessed his steady virtue, and disinterested patriotism thro' all the varying scenes, regular and revolutionary, thro' which that unhappy country has been doomed to pass. In these, his object never varied, that of the general good. For this no man ever labored more zealously or honestly; of which he has left abundant monuments."[43]

There can be no doubt of the sincerity and the worthiness of Du Pont's intentions. There may be some question about the fruitfulness of his efforts. Certainly he played an important role in propagating the doctrines of physiocracy between 1765 and 1775, but he made no original contributions to these doctrines. Too much of his thought, especially in the realm of politics, was enclosed within the walls of the "new science." Outside of the affairs of politics, finance, and economics, however, his mind ranged freely over many fields. In the catholicity of his interests—science, literature, religion, philosophy—he was, like Jefferson, an authentic representative of the eighteenth century. Probably, his astounding energy, which endured to the time of his final illness, was too much spent in the resolute accumulation of tedious detail. Undoubtedly he failed to achieve the success which he sought as a philosopher, a writer, or a businessman, but he never ceased to strive and seldom lost his confidence and his hope. Mankind would be poorer if it did not produce such men of determined conviction, of intense desire to be useful, of prodigious industry, and of unconquerable optimism.

An unadorned stone with a simple inscription marks his grave in the du Pont family cemetery near Wilmington.[44] One of his own statements may justly stand as his epitaph and as a summary of his life. It was included in a letter written to Jefferson on July 23, 1808.

If we are disappointed in our hopes, as we must expect, we shall lose a great happiness and a great illusion, but we shall be taught a sound philosophical lesson and as we grow older, we shall leave the world to God for whom centuries hardly count and who knows that Mankind will forever increase its lights and sooner or later will reach a degree of knowledge and morality that will cover the earth with men as happy and as reciprocally kind to each other as their nature permits. Our juvenile impatience makes us believe that these beautiful days will come tomorrow. Poor ants, let us be satisfied with bringing our grain of millet to the ant hill and let us die while looking for another one![45]

Notes

I

1. For the sake of consistency I use throughout the form "Du Pont" when dealing with the subject of this biography. This was the style always used by Du Pont after 1789, when he added to his name the phrase "de Nemours," the name of the *bailliage* which he represented in the Estates General and National Assembly. He made this addition in order to distinguish himself from three other Duponts, none of them related, who were also delegates to the National (or Constituent) Assembly. (See *Table des matières, des noms de lieux et des noms de personnes contenus dans les procès-verbaux des séances de l'Assemblée constituante, depuis le 5 mai 1789 jusqu'au 30 septembre 1791 inclusivement* [Paris, an XIV], II, 476-477.) In his younger years he often wrote his name "Dupont," the form invariably employed by his father, Samuel. Latter-day descendants generally favor a third form—du Pont.

2. The principal source of information on Du Pont's early life is his autobiography. Between September and November, 1792, when he was hiding from the police, expecting at any moment to be seized as a defender of the deposed king, Du Pont began to write an account of his career so that his two sons might be fully informed of their family background in the event that they should lose their father. Unfortunately he never found time to complete it beyond the point at which it breaks off abruptly—just before his first marriage early in 1766. While I am well aware of the caution with which one must treat a document written so long after the events which it describes, I have chosen to tell much of the story as Du Pont presents it. This decision is based not only upon the fact that there is almost no other material available but also upon the belief that the reader, in following Du Pont's account, may gain insights of some value in forming his own viewpoint of the man. H. A. du Pont published an annotated edition of the autobiography: *L'Enfance et la jeunesse de Du Pont de Nemours racontées par lui-même* (Paris, 1906). Although valuable for its footnotes identifying (usually correctly) the relatives and friends of Du Pont de Nemours, this volume cannot be relied upon because of serious omissions and alterations. I have used the original manuscript now at the Eleutherian Mills Historical Library (Greenville, Delaware) in Winterthur MSS, group 2. This manuscript in fifteen separately bound chapters has regrettably been tampered with by a later hand. Two leaves in chapter 10 have been excised and two lines in chapter 7 and sixteen in chapter 10 have been overscored in ink. Part of the excised material can be found in the transcript of the original made by two granddaughters of Du Pont de Nemours, Mrs. T. M. Smith and Mrs. S. F. du Pont, also available at the Eleutherian Mills Historical Library (hereafter EMHL). (See note 35 below.) I have also had the advantage of consulting the translation of Mr. Pierre S. du Pont prepared from a typescript by Mrs. Bessie Gardner du Pont of the granddaughters' transcript. There are numerous variations, mostly of a minor nature, in all these versions. Mr. Earle Coleman, formerly chief bibliographer of EMHL, has prepared a careful study in typescipt of the various forms of "The

360

Mémoires of Du Pont de Nemours" to be found in EMHL. I am grateful to him for assistance in this and numerous other matters. The sentences quoted are Mr. P. S. du Pont's translation of the lines found in the MS autobiography, chapter 1, p. 1. These lines, along with some 500 others, are omitted in H. A. du Pont's *L'Enfance et la jeunesse de Du Pont de Nemours racontées par lui-même* (hereafter *L'Enfance*).

3. Walter M. Gore, *History Genealogical-Biographical of the Barksdale-du Pont and Allied Families* (New York, 1922), p. 144; H. A. du Pont, *The Early Generations of the Du Pont and Allied Families* (New York, 1923), I, 7. Many of the earliest original documents extant today in the Du Pont family are at EMHL, Winterthur MSS, group 1. They deal mostly with landed property in Rouen and nearby parishes.

4. H. A. du Pont, *Early Generations*, vii (preface).

5. See genealogical charts in W. M. Gore, *History Genealogical-Biographical*, pp. 156-157, and in H. A. du Pont, *Early Generations*, I, facing 67.

6. In his edition of the autobiography *(L'Enfance)*, H. A. du Pont deleted all references to the watchmaking trade of the Du Pont family.

7. MS autobiography, chap. 3, p. 1 *(L'Enfance*, p. 47).

8. *Ibid.*, chap. 3, pp. 20-21, 30 *(L'Enfance*, pp. 39-40, 52).

9. Their marriage contract is dated February 23, 1737. EMHL, Winterthur MSS, group 1.

10. George H. Kerr, *Du Pont Romance: A Reminiscent Narrative of E. I. du Pont de Nemours and Company* (Wilmington, Del., *c.* 1938), p. 8.

11. See, for example, the autobiography, chap. 2 (where Du Pont discussed his "maternal family") and chap. 8, pp. 9-10 *(L'Enfance*, pp. 41-42, 135-138).

12. H. A. du Pont, *Early Generations*, I, 367-368. According to H. A. du Pont, the baptismal records were destroyed in the fire of 1871 during the period of the Commune.

13. MS autobiography, chap. 4, pp. 2-4 *(L'Enfance*, pp. 60-62).

14. *Ibid.*, chap. 4, pp. 9-13 *(L'Enfance*, pp. 67-73).

15. *Ibid.*, chap. 3, p. 3 *(L'Enfance*, p. 52). Quoted in a slightly different translation by B. G. du Pont, *Du Pont de Nemours* (Newark, Del., 1933), I, 1 (hereafter B. G. du Pont, *DPdN*). I have used some of Du Pont's own adjectives in describing his father. He called him "bon, généreux, sensible," but also "emporté, colère, opiniâtre, d'un courage ardent et d'une probité sévère. . ." *(ibid.*, chap. 3, p. 1).

16. *Ibid.*, chap. 3, p. 2 *(L'Enfance*, p. 50).

17. *Ibid.*, chap. 4, pp. 7-8 (abbreviated in *L'Enfance*, p. 66).

18. *Ibid.*, chap. 5, p. 6 (P. S. du Pont's translation; *L'Enfance*, p. 84).

19. These are the words quoted by A. Boullée, *Notices sur M. Poivre intendant des Isles de France et de Bourbon, correspondant de l'Académie des Sciences, et sur M. Dupont de Nemours, conseiller d'état, membre de l'Institut . . . suivies du discours de reception de l'auteur à l'Académie de Lyon* (Lyon, 1835), p. 292. Boullée probably extracted them from the earlier eulogy of Du Pont by M. Silvestre in the *Mémoires d'agriculture, d'économie rurale et domestique, publiés par la Société royale et centrale d'agriculture* (Paris, 1818), p. 292. Silvestre's eulogy, read at the meeting of the Royal and Central Society of Agriculture on March 29, 1818, was also published separately: *Notice biographique sur M. Dupont (Pierre Samuel), membre de l'Institut, de la Société royale et centrale d'agriculture, et d'une grand nombre d'autres sociétés savantes et littéraires françaises et étrangères, chevallier* [sic] *de la Legion d'Honneur et de l'ordre de Vasa . . .* Paris, 1818 (p. 3 for this incident). In their brief accounts Silvestre and Boullée merely state that Du Pont's fellow-students presented him with a basket of fruit. The probably more accurate account in the autobiography (chap. 5, pp. 8-9) has been followed here. The incident, again perhaps drawn from Silvestre, also appears in [Bon Joseph] Dacier, "Notice historique sur la vie et les ouvrages de M. Dupont de Nemours," *Histoire de l'Académie royale des inscriptions et belles lettres* (Paris?, 1820?), p. 27. This notice read at a public meeting of the Academy on July 28, 1820, is not listed in the so far most complete bibliography of Du Pont in G[ustave] Schelle, *Du Pont de Nemours et l'école physiocratique* (Paris, 1888; hereafter Schelle, *DPdN*).

Dacier's name is not found in the *Histoire de l'Academie royal* cited above, but has been supplied from the extract of his notice which appears in L. Seb. le Normand et J.G.V. de Moléon, *Annales de l'industrie nationale et étrangère ou Mercure technologique; recueil de Mémoires sur les arts et métiers, les manufactures, le commerce, l'industrie, l'agriculture, etc., renfermant la description des musées des produits de l'industrie française* (Paris, 1820), I, 47-56.

20. MS autobiography, chap. 5, pp. 10-11 (*L'Enfance*, p. 88). The quotation from Horace is from the *Odes*, Book I, the dedication to Maecenas (line 35).

21. Some information on Paul Bosc d'Antic (1726-1784), who became a clandestine Huguenot pastor in January, 1751, has been supplied by Professor Edouard Bosc of Sète (Hérault). (Correspondence in central file of EMHL and *Le Livre de Famille*, mimeographed volume, pp. 9, 120-119—page numbers incorrectly reversed in volume.)

22. *Ibid.*, chap. 6, pp. 4-6. The vigorous attack on Christianity was omitted by Mrs. T. M. Smith and Mrs. S. F. du Pont in their transcript and by H. A. du Pont in *L'Enfance*, pp. 92-93, where only the concluding paragraph about being neither Protestant nor Catholic appears.

23. Was this the notorious Madame d'Urfé to be celebrated in Casanova's *Memoirs?* The Marquise d'Urfé was a rather well-known Parisian character whom Du Pont may have dragged into his autobiographical sketch without warrant. There is no way to vouch for his veracity here, and elsewhere, in his memoirs.

24. *Ibid.*, chap. 6, pp. 15-16 (*L'Enfance*, p. 104).

25. *Ibid.*, chap. 8, p. 3 (not in *L'Enfance*).

26. *Ibid.*, chap. 7, pp. 8-13 (*L'Enfance*, pp. 116-123); EMHL, Winterthur MSS, group 2, for a copy of the farewell letter, which B. G. du Pont translates in full in *DPdN*, I, 23-24.

27. *Ibid.*, chap. 7, p. 18 (*L'Enfance*, p. 127).

28. *Ibid.*, chap. 8, p. 6 (*L'Enfance*, pp. 132-133); an *écu* was a silver coin worth five francs, about one dollar, but with a purchasing power in today's values of over five dollars.

29. *Ibid.*, chap. 8, p. 20 (no mention of watchmaking in *L'Enfance*, p. 146).

30. *Ibid.*, chap. 9, p. 3.

31. *Ibid.*, chap. 9, p. 6 (*L'Enfance*, p. 153).

32. *Ibid.*, chap. 9, pp. 11-12 (*L'Enfance*, pp. 159-160).

33. *Ibid.*, chap. 10, p. 2.

34. These early manuscripts have not been discovered among the family papers; perhaps they never existed.

35. The full story of this duel will never be known. It is at this point in chap. 10 that the MS autobiography has been seriously tampered with. Two sheets (pages 3, 4, 5, 6) have been excised and the first 16 lines of page 7 have been heavily scored out in ink. All we have is that part (not complete) of the excised material which was included in the transcript of Mrs. T. M. Smith and Mrs. S. F. du Pont (see note 2 above). The typescript of this transcript by Mrs. Bessie Gardner du Pont and the translation of Mr. Pierre S. du Pont have been used here.

36. This house still stands, not much changed from Du Pont's day, at 90 Rue de Paris in Nemours. The formerly spacious courtyard in front and garden in the rear have been considerably reduced in size by a new street which now flanks the side of the house. House and garden are briefly described by Dr. Camille Streletski in *Pierre Samuel Du Pont de Nemours (1739-1817); Étude historique, physiognomique et graphologique* (Nemours, 1936), p. 16. Monsieur Léon Petit, curator of the Museum and Library of Nemours, kindly presented me with a copy of this brief study and arranged a visit to the house through the courtesy of the Beguin-Billecocq family, the present owners.

37. H. A. du Pont, *Early Generations*, I, 380, writes "Roccourt," rather than "Raucourt." In the du Pont family materials there is still a third form, "Rencourt," for which, however, there seems to be no authority. "Roccourt" is a possible reading of

the name as it appears upon Marie le Dée's baptismal certificate. I prefer the reading "Raucourt" because there are two Raucourt place names in France, while "Roccourt" and "Rencourt" do not appear. I follow here the suggestion of Mr. Victor de Avenell, formerly Translator on the research staff of EMHL, whose assistance has been significant in various phases of this study.

38. According to Du Pont, MS autobiography, chap. 10, p. 16 (*L'Enfance*, p. 177).

39. *Ibid.*, chap. 10, pp. 10-17 (*L'Enfance*, pp. 174-177).

40. *Ibid.*, chap. 10, p. 18.

41. *Ibid.*, chap. 11, pp. 3-4 (*L'Enfance*, pp. 184-185).

42. These are, at least, the conclusions which Du Pont later stated he had arrived at by 1762; *ibid.* (*L'Enfance*, p. 185). B. G. du Pont (*DPdN*, I, 33-34) gives a slightly different translation.

43. MS autobiography, chap. 11, p. 5 (*L'Enfance*, p. 187).

44. Du Pont included the ode as he remembered it in his MS autobiography (chap. 11, pp. 8-10). H. A. du Pont gives in a footnote the major variations between the poem as reproduced in the autobiography and an earlier version which he found in the family archives (*L'Enfance*, pp. 190-192).

45. MS autobiography, chap. 11, p. 11 (*L'Enfance*, p. 196).

46. *Ibid.*, chap. 11, pp. 13-14 (in part in *L'Enfance*, p. 199).

47. *La Richesse de l'État*, table on p. 7. I have chiefly used the copy of the pamphlet bound with eighteen others on this subject under the title *Riches [sic] de l'État* in EMHL. It is the first pamphlet in this volume. *La Richesse . . .* can also be found as the first pamphlet in volume 86 of political pamphlets in the Jefferson Collection of the Library of Congress. It is perilous to attempt to estimate present-day equivalents of eighteenth century French currency. A rough calculation would make one livre approximate the monetary value of a present-day franc, about 20 cents in United States currency. The purchasing power of a livre then was, of course, much greater than that of a franc today.

48. MS autobiography, chap. 12, p. 2 (*L'Enfance*, pp. 201-202).

49. H. A. du Pont (*L'Enfance*, p. 202) and G. Schelle (*DPdN*, p. 399) are undoubtedly correct in giving Moreau as the bookseller who brought out the pamphlet. In his autobiography (chap. 12, p. 2) Du Pont mentioned Grangé, who, according to Schelle (*ibid.*), printed his second pamphlet in August of 1763. Earlier in the *Éphémérides du citoyen*, 1769, tome 2 (p. xxvi) Du Pont had written in his "notice abrégée" for 1763 under the month of July: "Dans ce mois furent imprimées *à Paris, chez Moreau, rue Gallande*, en deux Éditions, l'une in-quarto et l'autre in-octavo *des Réflexions sur l'Écrit intitulé: Richesse de l'État:* petite brochure d'environ 30 pages." The quarto edition does not contain the dedication or the text of pp. 29-32 of the octavo edition, which were added "gracés à tous les retards de MM les Imprimeurs." There are also about ten minor variations between these two editions (which have been carefully collated by Mr. Earle Coleman). In a footnote on page 4 of his *Réponse demandée par monsieur le marquis de . . . à celle qu'il a faite aux Réflexions sur l'écrit intitulé: Richesse de l'État*, Du Pont states that the octavo edition is "la seule que j'avoue." The Library of Congress copy of this edition (no. 6 of volume 86 of political pamphlets in the Jefferson Collection) bears the notation "Édition de l'auteur" and the following *avis:* "L'auteur avertit que tous les éditions que ont pu paraitre sont incomplettes [sic], fausses et subreptices & que l'on doit regarder comme telles, toutes celles qui ne sont par contresignées des deux lettres ci-après." The two letters were to be *D. P.* (*L'Enfance*, p. 213), but they do not appear in this edition! This copy shows London (Londres) as the place of publication, a common deceit to circumvent the rather loose censorship. The copy of the octavo volume in EMHL lacks a title-page but presumably belongs to the same edition. In his omnibus volume, *Richesse de l'état, à laquelle on a ajouté les pièces qui ont paru pour et contre* (Amsterdam, 1764), M. M. Rey follows the text of the "unofficial" quarto edition. (Two louis, the amount Du Pont was to have received for his manuscript, is equivalent to about 48 francs, or approximately $9.60.)

50. *Réflexions*, pp. 11-16.

51. *Ibid.*, pp. 19-21.

52. *Ibid.*, following p. 28. The small print at the bottom of Du Pont's table must be read carefully, since there he insists upon the subtractions indicated from the figure of 4,000,000 apparent taxables which stands forth clearly in the table. In his *Réponse demandée par Monsieur le marquis de* . . . *à celle qu'il a faite aux Réflexions sur l'écrit intitulé: Richesse de l'État* Du Pont complains about the failure of some readers to make these necessary subtractions from the figure of 4,000,000.

53. MS autobiography, chap. 12, p. 3 (*L'Enfance*, p. 203).

54. *Réponse demandée par Monsieur le Marquis de* . . . , pp. 10 ff. I have used the EMHL copy bound as the fourteenth item in a volume of nineteen pamphlets under the general title *Riches* [*sic*] *de l'État* (cited also in note 47 above). The initials "D.P." appear at the end of Du Pont's *Réponse*. The Marquis apparently arrived at his conclusions by arguing against Du Pont that through import and export duties, merchants and artisans must be included among the taxables. I have been unable to find a copy of the Marquis' letter, which was perhaps never published.

55. MS autobiography, chap. 12, pp. 2-4, 10 (*L'Enfance*, pp. 204-205, 209-212).

56. On this matter consult the doctoral thesis of E. Labiche, *Les Sociétés d'Agriculture au xviii° siècle* (Paris, 1908), especially the conclusion, pp. 185-187.

57. MS autobiography, chap. 12, p. 6 (*L'Enfance*, pp. 207-208). Mirabeau was here paraphrasing John 1:27.

58. The letter may be found in *Œuvres complètes de Voltaire*; nouvelle édition . . . conforme pour le texte à l'édition de Beuchot . . . (Paris, 1877-1885), XLII, 546, or in Theodore Besterman, ed., *Voltaire's Correspondence* (Genève, 1953–), LII, 238-239 (letter no. 10546).

59. For example, G. Schelle, *DPdN*, p. 11; Pierre Jolly, *Du Pont de Nemours Soldat de la Liberté* (Paris, 1956), pp. 15-16; Denise Aimé [Azam], *Du Pont de Nemours Honnête Homme* (Paris, 1933), pp. 57-58.

60. On this point see J. Robert Vignery, "Voltaire's Economic Ideas as Revealed in the 'Romans' and 'Contes'," *French Review*, XXXIII (January, 1960), 263. In addition one can cite Voltaire's constant interest in the *Éphémérides* (see his letter to Du Pont, June 7, 1769, Bestermann ed., LXXII, 63-68 [letter no. 14702]; his remark in his *Défense de Louis XIV*, "Occupé des travaux de la compagne depuis vingt ans, j'ai puissé souvent dans les Éphémérides des leçons dont j'ai profité," in *Œuvres complètes*, XXVIII, 327); his statement about land and labor as the source of everything (letter to Du Pont, July 16, 1779, Besterman ed., LXXVI, 42-44 [letter no. 15507]) and about agriculture as the base of everything (*Diatribe á l'auteur des Éphémérides*, *Œuvres complètes*, XXIX, 359); and his enthusiasm for Turgot's reform program (letters to Du Pont in 1775 and 1776 in *Œuvres complètes*, XLIX, 377-378, 403-404, 486, 501-502, 520-521, 527-529, 538, 554-555, 558-559, 560-561, 563, 572-573, 578-579, 582).

61. Originals of the Voltaire letters are at EMHL, Winterthur MSS, group 2, series A. For references to the published letters of 1775-1776, see the last part of note 60 above. The new edition of Voltaire's correspondence by Theodore Besterman is still in progress. Volume 89 (1963) extends only through December, 1774.

62. I have not seen a copy of the *Réfléxions* which contains these initials (see note 49 above). They do appear clearly at the end of the *Réponse demandée par Monsieur le Marquis de* . . . (note 54 above).

63. This account is taken from Du Pont's version of the incident in his autobiography (chap. 12, pp. 10-12; *L'Enfance*, pp. 213-214). In *Notice sur la vie de Dupont (de Nemours), conseiller d'état, chevalier de Vasa et de la Légion d'Honneur* par M. de M . . . (Paris, 1818), p. 10, the name of the young man summoned to Versailles is given as Du Pont and his native city as Sens (not Soissons). "M. de M . . ." was Jacques-Pierre-Héliodore de Montchanin, Du Pont's first cousin, son of his favorite uncle, Pierre. His *Notice* has in it much of value, but his recollection was probably faulty here. There is no contemporary account of the incident. Du Pont wrote about it

twenty-nine years after it occurred, but Montchanin's *Notice* was penned fifty-five years afterwards.

64. According to M. de M[ontchanin], *Notice sur la vie de Dupont (de Nemours)* . . . , p. 7.

65. MS autobiography, chap. 14, p. 5 (*L'Enfance,* p. 241).

II

1. Eric Roll, *A History of Economic Thought* (revised and enlarged; New York, 1942), p. 132.

2. For an up-to-date list of books and articles on Quesnay and Physiocracy consult the excellent annotated bibliography of Jacqueline Hecht in the co-operative work *François Quesnay et la Physiocratie* (Paris, 1958), I, 317-392, especially pp. 330-392. The great work on Physiocracy is Georges Weulersse, *Le Mouvement physiocratique en France (de 1756 à 1770)* (2 vols.; Paris, 1910).

3. See Du Pont's statement in Carl Knies, ed., *Carl Friedrichs von Baden Brieflicher Verkehr mit Mirabeau und Du Pont* (Heidelberg, 1892), II, 42. Boisguillebert's principal works—*Détail de la France* (1695), *Factum de la France* (1706), *Traité de la nature, culture, commerce et intérêt des grains* (1707), and *Dissertation sur la nature des richesses, de l'argent et des tributs* (1707)—may all be found in Eugène Daire, ed., *Économistes Financiers du XVIIIe siècle: Vauban . . . Boisguillebert . . . Jean Law . . . Melon . . . Dutot* (2d ed.; Paris, 1851), pp. 163-407.

4. See Daire, ed., *ibid.,* pp. 33-146, for Vauban's *Dime royale* (1707), an attack upon the inequitable tax system with a recommendation that it be supplanted by a general tithe borne by everyone.

5. Richard Cantillon, *Essai sur la nature du commerce en général,* edited with an English translation and other material by Henry Higgs (London, 1931), pp. 363-389, has Higgs's summary of his valuable research on Cantillon's career.

6. *Ibid.,* p. 2.

7. Georges Weulersse, *Les Manuscrits économiques de François Quesnay et du Marquis de Mirabeau aux archives nationales, inventaire, extraits et notes* (Paris, 1910), pp. 19-20, gives evidence for concluding that *L'Ami des hommes* was written (and probably printed) in 1756, but not offered to the public until 1757.

8. "La nourriture, les commodités & les douceurs de la vie sont la richesse. La terre la produit, & travail de l'homme lui donne la forme." *L'Ami des hommes, ou Traité de la population* (nouvelle édition; n.p., 1759), I, 22.

9. "La multiplication des hommes s'appelle *Population.* L'augmentation du produit de la terre s'appelle *Agriculture.* Ces deux principes de richesses sont intimement liés l'un à l'autre" (*ibid.,* I, 23).

10. Chapters V ("Inconvéniens qui font languis l'agriculture") and VI ("De la nécessité & des moyens d'encourager l'Agriculture"), *ibid.*

11. A complete bibliography of all Quesnay's publications can be found in *François Quesnay et la Physiocratie,* pp. 301-316.

12. The words "un gout vif, un penchant decidé" from the *Éloge historique de M. Quesnay . . .* par M. le Comte d'A[lbon] (Paris, 1775), p. 40, first appeared in the *Nouvelles Éphémérides économiques ou Bibliothèque raissonnée de l'histoire, de la morale et de la politique,* V [1775], 2e partie, 93-175, quoted in G. Weulersse, *Le Mouvement physiocratique . . .* I, 45. See also Auguste Oncken, ed., *Œuvres économiques et philosophiques de F. Quesnay fondateur de système physiocratique* (Frankfort, 1888), p. 40.

13. Jacqueline Hecht, "La Vie de François Quesnay," in *François Quesnay et la Physiocratie,* I, 245. This essay (pp. 211-293) is the most recent and best brief biography of Quesnay.

14. Lewis A. Maverick, *China a Model for Europe* (San Antonio, Texas, 1946; volume II is a translation of Quesnay's *Le Despotisme de la Chine*) and Adolf Reichwein,

China and Europe: Intellectual and Artistic Contacts in the Eighteenth Century (translated by J. C. Powell; New York, 1925), pp. 101-109. See also the following articles by Maverick: "Chinese Influences upon the Physiocrats," *Economic History (A Supplement of Economic Journal)*, III (1938), 54-67; "The Chinese and the Physiocrats, A Supplement," *ibid.*, IV (1940), 312-319; "Chinese Influences upon Quesnay and Turgot," *Claremont Oriental Studies*, no. 4 (1942). Jacqueline Hecht briefly mentions this aspect in *François Quesnay et la Physiocratie*, I, 268.

15. The article "Fermiers" appears in the *Encyclopédie*, VI, 528-540; "Grains" in VII, 812-831. Both articles are signed with a pseudonym "M. Quesnay le fils" (i.e., Blaise, who occupied the Nivernais estate). These articles have been several times reprinted and may be found more conveniently in E. Daire, ed., *Physiocrates: Quesnay, Dupont de Nemours, Mercier de la Rivière, l'abbé Baudeau, Le Trosne, avec une introduction sur la doctrine des physiocrates, des commentaires et des notices historiques* (Paris, 1846), I, 219-303; A. Oncken, ed., *Œuvres ... de F. Quesnay* (cited in note 12), pp. 159-249; or most recently in *François Quesnay et la Physiocratie*, II, 427-510. The last volume contains also (pp. 396-426) the important anonymous article "Evidence," which Quesnay wrote for volume VI (pp. 146-157) of the *Encyclopédie*. In this article especially section 56 (pp. 422-426), some of Quesnay's basic ideas on man, natural liberty, and natural law are outlined for the first time. Ronald L. Meek has translated into English part of the article on "Grains" in his useful *The Economics of Physiocracy: Essays and Translations* (Cambridge, Mass., 1963), pp. 72-87, a volume containing translations of several of Quesnay's works and five interpretive essays by Mr. Meek.

16. On this point G. Weulersse, *Le Mouvement physiocratique . . .*, I, 51-52, is more convincing than Yves Guyon, *Quesnay et la physiocratie* (Paris [1896]), p. lxxiii, who asserts that the articles "avaient provoqué une grande sensation."

17. In his famous critique of the Physiocrats, Adam Smith goes too far in stating: "This sect, in their work . . . all follow implicitly and without any sensible variation, the doctrine of Mr. Quesnay." *An Inquiry into the Nature and Causes of the Wealth of Nations* (Everyman's Library; New York, 1917), II, Book IV, chap. ix, 172. In "Quesnay and Physiocracy," *Journal of the History of Ideas*, IX (1948), 153-173, especially pp. 166 and 172, Thomas P. Neill insists that there were important differences between Quesnay and his disciples.

18. Louis de Loménie, *Les Mirabeau; nouvelles études sur la société française au XVIIIᵉ siècle* (Paris, 1879-1891), II, 156, 172; J. Hecht in *François Quesnay et la Physiocratie*, I, 256.

19. G. Weulersse, *Les Physiocrates* (Paris, 1931), p. 3.

20. G. Weulersse, *Le Mouvement physiocratique . . .*, I, 58.

21. This edition of the *Tableau Œconomique* appeared as volume VIII of *L'Ami des hommes* (1760). The scheme of the *Tableau* in various applications appears on pp. 23, 51, 101, 119, 131, and 185. For the earlier publications of the *Tableau* by Quesnay see *François Quesnay et la Physiocratie*, II, 667-668, facsimiles between pp. 672 and 673. On the different representations of the *Tableau*, René Suaudeau, *Les Représentations figurés des physiocrates* (Paris, 1947) is brief and informative.

22. Mirabeau's opinion is quoted by Adam Smith in *Wealth of Nations*, II, 173; Du Pont's judgment is in his *De l'origine et des progrès d'une science nouvelle* (London, 1768), p. 11 (p. 9 of the most recent reprinting edited by A. Dubois in *Collection des économistes et des réformateurs sociaux de la France*, Paris, 1910).

23. Cf. analysis of the *Théorie de l'impôt* in Loménie, *Les Mirabeau*, II, 217, 219-220.

24. *Ibid.*, pp. 221-226.

25. G. Weulersse, *Le Mouvement physiocratique . . .* I, 80-81, and see the thesis of E. Labiche, cited in note 56 of chap. I.

26. The seventh chapter of the *Philosophie rurale*, entitled "Les Rapports des dépenses entre elles," was written by Quesnay. MS autobiography, chap. 14, p. 11 (*L'Enfance*, p. 248); *François Quesnay et la Physiocratie*, I, 263, 308. Ronald Meek (p.

278 n.; see note 15 above) holds that the problem of authorship of this chapter is more complicated and that Mirabeau wrote part of it.

27. MS autobiography, chap. 12, p. 13 (*L'Enfance*, p. 215); translated by B. G. du Pont, *DPdN*, I, 39.

28. Abeille's *Lettre d'un négociant sur la nature du commerce des grains* (1763) and *Réflexions sur la police des grains en France et en Angleterre* (1764) are bound with Du Pont's *De l'exportation et de l'importation des grains* (1764) in the edition prepared by Edgard Depitre for the *Collection des économistes et des réformateurs sociaux de la France* (Paris, 1911).

29. MS autobiography, chap. 14, pp. 1-12 (*L'Enfance*, pp. 236-250).

30. *Ibid.*, pp. 14-15 (*L'Enfance*, p. 254). Du Pont does not mention the date of Madame de Pompadour's death. Colonel du Pont supplies it in a footnote in *L'Enfance*.

31. Pp. 28-39 of original edition; pp. 13-18 of the edition in the *Collection des économistes et des réformateurs sociaux de la France* (Paris, 1911).

32. This pamphlet is conveniently included in Depitre's edition of Du Pont's *De l'exportation . . .* on pp. 104-126.

33. For a clear and succinct survey of the principal works which deal with the grain trade, see the introductions which Edgard Depitre wrote for two brochures in the series *Collection des économistes et des réformateurs sociaux de la France:* Cl.-J. Herbert, *Essai sur la police générale des grains sur leurs prix et sur les effets de l'agriculture* (1755) and *Supplément à l'essai sur la police générale des grains* (1757) par J. G. Montaudouin de la Touche (Paris, 1910), pp. v-xliii; and Du Pont de Nemours, *De l'exportation et de l'importation des grains* (1764), L.-P. Abeille, *Premiers opuscules sur le commerce des grains* (1763-1764) (Paris, 1911), pp. v-xlv.

34. "On croit que l'événement funeste arrivé depuis l'impréssion de cet Écrit, ne doit point faire supprimer un hommage que dicta la verité. Malheur à l'homme qui craindrait de jetter quelques fleurs sur la Tombe de ceux auxquels il offrit son encens!" B. G. du Pont, *DPdN*, I, 45, gives a freer, and less exact, translation.

35. MS autobiography, chap. 15, p. 1 (*L'Enfance*, pp. 263-264). Twenty-five louis would be equivalent to around 600 francs ($120) but worth several times that amount today.

36. "Il s'agit de prouver les avantages immense que la Nation trouverait dans la liberté générale, entière, absolue et irrévocable du Commerce extérieur des Grains." Préface, p. vii, in both the original edition and the reprint edited by Depitre.

37. *De l'exportation . . .*, Depitre edition, p. 21.

38. *Ibid.*, p. 56.

39. MS autobiography, chap. 15, p. 1 (*L'Enfance*, pp. 264-265).

40. *Ibid.*, chap. 15, pp. 1-2.

41. Extracts probably taken from this *mémoire* were published in the *Journal de l'agriculture du commerce et des finances*, in October, 1765.

42. *Ibid.*, pp. 17-18 (*L'Enfance*, pp. 286-287). Nearly 300 of the letters which Turgot wrote to Du Pont may be found in EMHL, Winterthur MSS, group 2, series A. Du Pont's letters to Turgot have apparently not survived (*L'Enfance*, p. 287, n. 1). Most of the surviving letters of Turgot to Du Pont have been published by Gustave Schelle, *Lettres de Turgot à Du Pont de Nemours de 1764 à 1781* (Extraites des Œuvres de Turgot et documents le concernant; Paris, 1924).

43. MS autobiography, chap. 15, pp. 4-6 (*L'Enfance*, pp. 271-272). Neither of these letters has been preserved.

44. Du Pont to President Labouret, 15 Septembre 1764; Du Pont to Messieurs de la Société royale d'agriculture de Soissons, au bureau de Laon, 16 Septembre 1764. Archives départementales de l'Aisne, série D 14.

45. "Réflexions ou seconde réponse à une lettre de M. de Montaran"; "Lettre au sujet de la cherté du blé en Guyenne"—*Gazette du commerce*, May, 1764. The latter was separately published by Simon as a seven-page brochure (Schelle, *DPdN*, p. 400).

The *Gazette du commerce* began publication in April, 1763; from May, 1765, it was known as *Gazette du commerce, d'agriculture et de finances*.

46. "Lettre sur la différence qui se trouve entre la grande et la petite culture"; separately printed by Simon (according to Schelle, *DPdN*, p. 400), but I have not seen this brochure.

47. Some 280 letters which Nicole-Charlotte-Marie-Louise Le Dée wrote to her fiancé Du Pont between 1763 and 1765 are in EMHL, Winterthur MSS, group 2, series C. Including her letters to him after their marriage and up to the time of her death in 1784, the body of her correspondence preserved in EMHL totals about 1,070 items.

48. MS autobiography, chap. 15, pp. 13-14 (*L'Enfance*, pp. 281-283, which alters part of the text and omits all mention of the midwife Saulnier).

49. At this point the MS autobiography breaks off, never to be completed. Du Pont does not mention Turgot's request which is related in a letter of Turgot's to L'Averdy, dated December 22, 1766, translated by B. G. du Pont, *DPdN*, I, 59-61. There is an undated draft of a letter from Du Pont to Méliand, requesting payment of the 1,800 francs and mentioning the necessity of making another trip to gather needed information (EMHL, Winterthur MSS, group 2).

50. G. Weulersse, *Le Mouvement physiocratique* . . . I, 95, n. 1, cites the slight evidence for crediting Morellet with recommending him; G. Schelle, *DPdN*, p. 34, suggests Trudaine but without supporting evidence. On the establishment of the *Journal*, see Weulersse, I, 95-96, and Schelle, pp. 33-34.

51. B. G. du Pont, *DPdN*, I, 56, tranlates part of a letter from Marie Le Dée to Du Pont, quoting her father's remarks to her: "Monsieur du Pont wrote to me yesterday. He assures me that he is not a Protestant. I believe what he says; he is an honest man." Since Du Pont's letters to Monsieur Le Dée have not survived, it is impossible to know what he wrote. He could honestly have given assurance that he was not a Protestant; with equal honesty he could have added that he was also not a Catholic, but he must have omitted any such statement.

52. B. G. du Pont, *DPdN*, I, between pp. 56 and 57, reproduces part of the facsimile of the marriage record from the registers of the parish church of Saint Sulpice. A copy of the marriage contract is in EMHL, Winterthur MSS, group 2, series A.

53. In the last number of the *Journal* which appeared under his editorship (November, 1766) Du Pont acknowledged that he was the author of articles signed "M. C." Similar pseudonyms were used for other *économistes:* H. or M., M. de l'isle or M. Nisaque for Quesnay, F. for Mirabeau, G. for Le Mercier de la Rivière, M. for Le Trosne. Cf. G. Schelle, *DPdN*, p. 34.

54. There seems to be no advantage in reproducing the list of Du Pont's contributions to the *Journal* given by Schelle, *DPdN*, pp. 400-401. In my opinion, Schelle was too enthusiastic in his summary of the broad nature of Du Pont's contributions, especially his interpretation of them as bold challenges to governmental policy. It is true that the articles did present physiocratic viewpoints and to that extent may be considered attacks, though not direct, on governmental regulations.

55. Weulersse, *Le Mouvement physiocratique* . . . , I, 97. The conflict between La Chalotais and the Duc d'Aiguillon became the occasion for one of the most famous struggles between the parlements and the royal government. The difficulty arose when La Chalotais led the opposition of the Parlement of Rennes to the attempt of d'Aiguillon, the military governor, to build military roads in the province by levying the royal *corvée*, or labor tax, during the Seven Years' War. The estates (or provincial assembly) received firm support from the parlement. D'Aiguillon and the intendant induced the government to punish La Chalotais by depriving him of the privilege of passing on his office at his death to his son. La Chalotais responded with such vigorous attacks on d'Aiguillon that the latter had him imprisoned. Other parlements joined that of Rennes in denouncing such actions as an unwarranted assault of the government upon their rights. Louis XV was forced to deny their claims through a *lit de justice* in 1766, but the struggle was by no means ended. La Chalotais was a favorite of the Physiocrats

because of his able indictment of the edict of July, 1764, as not affording sufficient liberty to trade in grain.

56. Part of the "avis du libraire" in Tome I of the *Éphémérides* gives this description of the journal: "Les Éphémérides du Citoyen seront un Ouvrage *Périodique, Critique et Moral,* à peu-près dans le goût du *Spectateur Anglois,* petit in -8o. Les Feuilles se distribueront deux fois par Semaine, les Lundi et Vendredi, à commencer le Lundi 4 novembre 1765."

57. The best brief account of Baudeau's conversion is in G. Weulersse, *Le Mouvement physiocratique* . . . I, 104-106. There is in EMHL a copy of a long letter of Du Pont's, dated March 12, 1776, to an unnamed correspondent (probably M. de Pezay; cf. Schelle, *DPdN,* p. 103 n.) recounting his relationships with Baudeau and the *Éphémérides,* wherein he states that he converted Baudeau to physiocratic views after the appearance of the first issues of the journal. In the *Éphémérides du Citoyen,* 1769, tome 5, p. xlvj, Du Pont implies that issues for November and December, 1766, were published, and Weulersse, *Le Mouvement physiocratique,* I, 126 n., states: "Un volume unique avait réuni les feuilles de septembre et d'octobre; et un autre, les feuilles de novembre et de décembre [1766]." None of the known sets of the *Éphémérides,* however, has these issues for these two months. The most careful study of the complex story of the publication of the *Éphémérides* is Earle E. Coleman, "Éphémérides du Citoyen, 1767-1772," *Papers of the Bibliographical Society of America,* LVI (1962), 17-45.

58. Du Pont to Voltaire, September 1, 1769, Bibliothèque Nationale, Manuscrits français, Nouvelles acquisitions 24340; copy in EMHL, Winterthur MSS, group 2.

59. Both G. Weulersse, *Le Mouvement physiocratique* . . . I, 128, and Henry Higgs, *The Physiocrats* (London, 1897), p. 65 n., believe that the word "physiocratie" was probably coined by Quesnay. Luigi Einaudi, 'Apropos de la date de publication de la 'Physiocratie,' " in *François Quesnay et la Physiocratie,* I, 2, points out that the word was used by the Abbé Baudeau in the *Éphémérides du citoyen* of April, 1767 [a typographical error makes it 1757], on page 112, but agrees with Weulersse that Baudeau probably picked it up in one of the discussions which the group held each Friday in Quesnay's entresol in the palace at Versailles.

60. The best evidence for the appearance of *Physiocratie* in November, 1767, is the letter which Turgot wrote to Du Pont, dated November 18, 1767, acknowledging receipt of a copy of the work and criticizing Du Pont's long introduction. This letter is printed in G. Schelle, ed., *Œuvres de Turgot et documents le concernant avec biographie et notes* (Paris, 1913-1923), II, 677. Schelle quotes the letter in *DPdN,* p. 45, and B. G. du Pont translates part of it in *DPdN,* I, 61-63. The book is mentioned in *Éphémérides du citoyen* for December, 1767 (tome xii, pp. 210-212), though it is possible (as Einaudi points out) that this volume of the *Éphémérides* may itself not have appeared until early in 1768. The problem of the exact date for the appearance of *Physiocratie* is complicated by the fact that, with three noted exceptions, every surviving copy of volume (or part) I bears on the title-page the date *1768* (MDCCLXVIII), with Leyden (Leyde) as the place of publication. The second volume (or part) bears the title: *Discussions et Développements sur quelquesunes des notions de l'économie politique: Pour servir de seconde partie au recueil intitulé Physiocratie,* with Leyden as the alleged place of publication and the date *1767* (MDCCLXVII). Several years ago the well-known French book-dealer Michel Bernstein came upon a copy of volume (or part) one which had the date 1767 (M.DCC.LXVII) and which gave Peking (Pékin) as the alleged place of publication. In an enlightening article ("Les Débuts de Dupont de Nemours et la publication de la 'Physiocratie,' " *Revue d'histoire économique et sociale,* XXXIII [1955], 206-223), Jules Conan discusses this copy and the contribution which its discovery made to clearing up the problem created by the different dates of publication in other copies of the two volumes. This copy was apparently purchased from M. Bernstein by Luigi Einaudi, since the latter appears to be concerned with the same copy in his "Apropos de la date de publication de la 'Physiocratie' " (*François*

Quesnay et la Physiocratie, I, 1-9). Einaudi mentions another copy listed in the catalog of the Carl Menger Library in Tokyo. There is in EMHL yet a third copy acquired in 1921 by the late P. S. du Pont from D. L. Passavant, a bookseller of Zelienople, Pennsylvania. The latter is the only one which I have seen. Unfortunately it does not contain the "original" text of page 104 as given by Conan and Einaudi. Rather the leaf (with pages 103-104) is a cancel and has on page 104 the same text as the (later) "Leyde 1768" copies. There are other cancels in the EMHL "Pékin 1767" copy. The printing history of *Physiocratie* is, therefore, probably more complicated than Conan and Einaudi suggest, and the full story must await the careful collating of all known copies by a skilled bibliographer. Until all copies can be brought together, one cannot go beyond the point reached by Conan and Einaudi.

61. G. Schelle, ed., *Œuvres de Turgot*, II, 677; G. Schelle, *DPdN*, p. 45; B. G. du Pont, *DPdN*, I, 61.

62. Weulersse (*Le Mouvement physiocratique* . . . I, 129 n.) remarks correctly that Du Pont was not a scrupulous editor. The adjectives "abstract and logical" are from *ibid.*, p. 128. *Physiocratie* contains the following writings of Quesnay: volume I: "Le Droit naturel" (1-38), "Analyse du Tableau économique" (43-60) with "Résumé" (61-64), "Formule du Tableau économique" (65-66), and "Observations importantes" (67-98), "Maximes générales du gouvernement économique d'un royaume agricole" (99-122), with "Notes sur les maximes" (123-172), which had first appeared as part of Mirabeau's explanation of the *tableau économique* in his *L'Ami des hommes*; volume II: "Problème économique" (181-234), "Dialogues sur le commerce et sur les travaux des artisans" (235-442), and "Second problème économique" (443-488, the only item not previously published).

63. *Wealth of Nations* (Everyman's ed.), II, 172.

64. *De l'origine et des progrès d'une science nouvelle*, pp. 15, 16 (Dubois edition, p. 10).

65. The title-page has the date 1768 and shows London as the alleged place of publication. The most convenient modern edition is by A. Dubois, published in 1910 as a brochure in the *Collection des économistes et des réformateurs sociaux de la France*.

66. *De l'origine* . . ., pp. 17-19 (Dubois edition, p. 11).

67. *Ibid.*, p. 69 (Dubois edition, p. 31).

68. *Ibid.*, p. 70 (Dubois edition, p. 32).

69. This edition showed Yverdon (Switzerland) as the place of publication and, in addition to the works of Quesnay listed in note 62 above, contained the following pieces: Du Pont, *De l'origine et des progrès d'une science nouvelle*; Baudeau, *Lettre d'un citoyen sur les vingtièmes et les impôts*; Du Pont, *De l'administration des chemins*; Baudeau, *De l'utilité des discussions économiques*; Le Trosne, *Lettre à M. B. (sur la concurrence des étrangers)*; Le Trosne, *Discussions sur l'argent et commerce*; Baudeau, *Avis au peuple sur son premier besoin*; Abeille, *Réflexions sur la police des grains en France et en Angleterre*; Abeille, *Faits qui ont influés sur la cherté des grains en France et en Angleterre*; Baudeau, *Lettres sur les émeutes populaires qui causent la cherté des blée*; Abeille, *Effets d'un privilège exclusif en matière de commerce sur les droits de propriété*.

70. *Vom Ursprung und Fortgang einer neuen Wissenschaft*, translated by F. M. Vierordt, Carlsruhe, 1770.

71. *De l'administration des chemins*, à Pékin et se trouve à Paris, 1767 (83 pp.). Du Pont's pamphlet inspired an anonymous publication which, in general, supported his arguments and gave additional details on the reform of the *corvée* in Caen: *Lettre à M . . . ingénieur des ponts et chaussées sur l'ouvrage de M. Dupont qui a pour titre: "De l'administration des chemins," suivi d'une deuxième lettre* (n. p., 1770). The second letter (*Deuxième Lettre à M. N. . . . ingénieur des ponts et chaussées; sur l'administration des chemins*) opposed the arguments of the anonymous M. N. . . . who had, apparently, suggested a *corvée* payable in kind, rather than in labor or money. These

publications are evidence of the interest in the reform of the labor tax without disrupting necessary work on the maintenance of roads.

72. The fourth chapter of the pamphlet describes the changes made by Oreceau de Fontelle, intendant of Caen, and by Turgot in Limoges.

73. John Rae, *Life of Adam Smith* (London, 1895), pp. 197, 215; *Œuvres de M. Turgot, ministre d'état, précédées et accompagnées de mémoires et de notes sur sa vie, son administration et ses ouvrages* (edited by Du Pont; Paris, 1808-1811), V, 136 (note by Du Pont).

74. Du Pont to Franklin, May 10, 1768, in Albert H. Smyth, *The Writings of Benjamin Franklin* (New York, 1905-1907), V, 153-154. For Franklin's relationships with the French Physiocrats, see Edward E. Hale and Edward E. Hale, Jr., *Franklin in France: From Original Documents Most of Which Are Now Published for the First Time* (Boston, 1887-1888), esp. I, 7, 8, 12, 18; II, 382, 389, for references to Du Pont; Alfred O. Aldridge, *Franklin and his French Contemporaries* (New York, 1957), esp. pp. 14, 23, 24, 30, 47, 48, 115, 125, 132, 163, and 220, for relations with Du Pont; Durand Echeverria, *Mirage in the West: A History of the French Image of American Society to 1815* (Princeton, 1957), p. 24; and Carl Van Doren, *Benjamin Franklin* (New York, 1938), pp. 371-373, 417-418.

75. John Bigelow, ed., *The Complete Works of Benjamin Franklin* (New York and London, 1887-1888), IV, 194; also in Smyth, V, 155-156. The great edition of Franklin's papers being published by Yale University (1959-) under the editorship of Leonard W. Labaree has reached only through March 30, 1758, in its first seven volumes. There is a facsimile of Franklin's letter in B. G. du Pont, *DPdN*, I, between pp. 62 and 63.

76. Loménie (see note 18), II, 262-265; G. Schelle, *Turgot* (Paris, 1909), p. 105.

77. The Abbé de l'Ecuy, who had contributed to the *Encyclopédie*, was one of the lesser-known adherents to Quesnay's doctrines.

78. During her husband's absences from home, Madame Du Pont always wrote him several letters a week. While they are mostly concerned with family news and her day-to-day activities, they often have important information on other matters. They are used here as the principal source for Baudeau's unseemly conduct. Especially pertinent are the letters of September 30, October 5, 13, and 26, 1768, EMHL, Winterthur MSS, group 2, series C. B. G. du Pont, *DPdN*, I, 64-75, has translated significant excerpts from Madame Du Pont's letters during this period. (See pp. 68-72 for the four letters referred to above.)

79. Weulersse, *Le Mouvement physiocratique . . .* I, 161-163; Schelle, *DPdN*, pp. 94-95.

80. See note 60 to chap. I (p. 364, above).

81. See note 78, above.

82. Baudeau assisted in the heavy task by editing three volumes in 1770 and one in 1771. A separate supplement was issued to tome XI for 1768. See the excellent article of Earle E. Coleman in the *Papers of the Bibliographical Society of America*, LVI (1962), cited in note 57, above, especially pp. 19-27.

83. The bibliography of these major articles is given by Schelle, *DPdN*, pp. 403-408. He is probably safe in attributing to Du Pont all articles signed "H" (the symbol employed by Du Pont) or "l'auteur des *Éphémérides.*" There seems to be no way to resolve conclusively the problem of authorship of all articles in the *Éphémérides*. See Earle E. Coleman (see note 82, above), pp. 28-31.

84. Many years ago the late Miss Harriet M. Austin, who was for a long time the research assistant of Colonel Henry A. du Pont, found among the Winterthur collections a manuscript list of contributors to the *Éphémérides*. She believed that the list had been prepared by Du Pont himself. Here were listed many short pieces attributed to Du Pont that are not in Schelle's bibliography. Unfortunately for the present-day scholar all that is available in EMHL are Miss Austin's notes based upon this manuscript list, which has not since been located. Eliminating the probable duplications with Schelle's bibliography (caused by some difference in titles), one can count about

forty small pieces and notes presumably contributed by Du Pont. For additional remarks on Miss Austin's listing, see Coleman (see note 82, above), pp. 29-31.

85. Cf. Schelle, *DPdN*, p. 124.

86. EMHL, Winterthur MSS, group 2; Schelle, *Œuvres de Turgot . . .* , III, 373-374; quoted in part by Schelle, *DPdN*, p. 128, and translated in part by B. G. du Pont, *DPdN*, I, 78.

87. Du Pont's malfeasance was later compounded. A separate publication of Turgot's *Réflexions sur la formation et la distribution des richesses* appeared in 1770 without Du Pont's alterations, and a reprint of the work appeared in 1788 after Turgot's death. Very few copies of these editions were printed and they are practically unobtainable today. An English translation of the 1770 edition was published in 1898 in the series *Economic Classics*, edited by W. J. Ashley: *Reflections on the Formation and the Distribution of Riches* by Turgot, 1770 (London, 1898). (This edition gives a concise description—pp. viii-ix—of the alterations which Du Pont made in Turgot's manuscript.) The only copy of the 1788 edition which I have seen is in the University of Kansas Libraries. In his later edition of Turgot's works, published from 1809 to 1811, Du Pont used the altered text which had appeared in the *Éphémérides*, rather than the original as published in 1770 and reprinted in 1788! The most careful study of this matter has been made by G. Schelle; see his article "Pourquoi les 'Réflexions' de Turgot sur la formation et la distribution des richesses ne sont-elles pas exactement connues?" in *Journal des Économistes*, XLIII (1888), 3-16.

88. *Éphémérides*, 1769, tome IX, p. 68. Turgot's letter reprimanding Du Pont for his unsupported assertion about Franklin is printed in Schelle, *Œuvres de Turgot*, III, 13. This incident is mentioned in Aldridge, *Franklin and his French Contemporaries*, p. 24. Six pieces by Franklin appeared in the *Éphémérides* between 1767 and 1769. Aldridge (pp. 24-36) presents a concise discussion of Franklin's contributions. Both Van Doren, *Benjamin Franklin*, p. 372, and Echeverria, *Mirage in the West*, p. 24, supply information on Franklin's views at that time tending to give some support for Du Pont's claim.

89. Turgot to Du Pont, Limoges, March 13, April 12, and May 7, 1771. EMHL, Winterthur MSS, group 2. These letters may be more conveniently consulted in G. Schelle, ed., *Œuvres de Turgot . . .* , III, 476-478, 480-486.

90. The only extant copy of Du Pont's play *Joseph II* seems to be the manuscript copy (not in Du Pont's hand) in the Badische Landesbibliothek in Karlsruhe. It is known that Du Pont sent a copy to Karoline Louise, Margravine of Baden, in 1772, Du Pont to Markgräfin Karoline Louise, Paris, July 12, 1772, in Karl Obser, ed., "Nachträge zu dem Briefwechsel der Markgrafen Karl Friedrich von Baden mit Mirabeau und Du Pont," *Zeitschrift für die Geschichte der Oberrheins*, herausgegeben von der Badischen Historischen Kommission (Neue Folge, Heidelberg, 1909), XXIV, 136-137. I have used the copy of the play in Karlsruhe and, through the courtesy of officials of the Badische Landesbibliothek, have been able to obtain a photographic copy now deposited in EMHL.

91. There is a copy of this letter in EMHL, Winterthur MSS, group 2.

92. In a letter to his wife, dated November 13, 1768, he set down, with characteristic overoptimism, the detailed arrangements to be made for supplying paper and for the printing and binding of the journal (EMHL, Winterthur MSS, group 2, summarized in Coleman [see note 82], pp. 27-28).

93. This series, comprising around 400 printed pages, appeared in the *Éphémérides*, tomes 1 through 6, and 8 and 9 of 1769 and the first tome of 1770. It merits separate publication, such as Jules Conan promised in "Les Débuts de Dupont de Nemours . . . ," *Revue d'histoire économique et sociale*, XXXIII (1955), 209 n.

94. Coleman (see note 82), p. 21.

95. *Éphémérides*, 1771, tome 6, pp. 163-246. This was a review of the third edition of *Les Saissons*. In 1769, tomes 3 (pp. 133-158), 4 (pp. 87-134), and 5 (pp. 169-189), he had presented extensive analyses of parts of the poem without reference to slavery.

96. *Éphémérides*, 1770, tome 3, pp. 104-157: "Eloge de la ville de Moukden et de ses environs . . ."; 1771, tome 2, pp. 69-107: "Extraits du Chou-King . . ."; tome 12, pp. 79-126: "L'Art militaire des Chinois," continued in 1772, tome 1, pp. 112-154, tome 2, pp. 169-187, and tome 3, pp. 102-169, but only in tome 3 is there a similarly clear effort to point up Chinese ideas and practices as models for other nations.

97. *Éphémérides*, 1769, tome 1, pp. 37-69: "De la liberté de commerce des grains" and pp. 70-120; "Objections et réponses sur le commerce des grains et des farines" (the latter also published separately, Schelle, *DPdN*, p. 408); tome 5, pp. 190-199: analysis of *Lettres* [written by Le Trosne] *à un ami sur les avantages des grains et les dangers des prohibitions*; supplement to tome 11 (1769): an analysis of, and reply to, the devastating attack on the physiocratic position made by the Abbé Ferdinando Galiani in his witty *Dialogues sur le commerce des blés* (1770); 1770, tome 1, pp. 200-210: "Liberté du commerce des subsistances en Toscane"; tome 4, pp. 206-230: "Protection sagement accordée par l'autorité à la liberté du commerce" [in Languedoc and Franche Comté]; tome 6, pp. 36-136: "Observations sur les effets de la liberté du commerce des grains et sur ceux des prohibitions" (the only article directly signed by Du Pont, since it was meant as another reply to Galiani). There are numerous additional articles, and parts of articles, supporting free trade in grain, but they cannot be attributed with any assurance to Du Pont.

98. *Éphémérides*, 1769, tome 1, pp. 160-196: commentary on the *Mémoire* [by St. Péravy] *sur les effets de l'impôt indirect relativement au revenu des propriétaires de biens fonds* (this *mémoire* had won the prize offered by the Royal Society of Agriculture of Limoges in 1767), continued in tome 2, pp. 128-136; tome 8, pp. 136-163: commentary on *Du rétablissement de l'impôt dans son ordre naturel* (by Boesnier de l'Orme).

99. *Éphémérides*, 1769, tome 8, pp. 91-135: commentary on the *Lettre à M. N., ingénieur des ponts et chaussées sur l'ouvrage de M. Du Pont, qui a pour titre: L'administration des chemins*; 1771, tome 4, pp. 72-115: commentary on the *Deuxième lettre à M. N., ingénieur des ponts et chaussées, sur l'administration des chemins*, continued in tome 6, pp. 92-117.

100. *Éphémérides*, 1771, tome 10, pp. 43-61: "Des divers moyens que l'on peut employer dans l'état actuel de l'Europe pour procurer la construction et l'entretien des grands canaux de navigation."

101. *Éphémérides*, 1769, tome 8 (pp. 169-180), 10 (pp. 174-209), 11 (pp. 176-192): "Du commerce et de la Compagnie des Indes."

102. Schelle, *DPdN*, p. 133, suggests the possibility that Du Pont may have been requested to employ the *Éphémérides* in the attack upon the privileges of the Compagnie des Indes by Maynon d'Invaut, Controller-General in 1768-1769. Du Pont was well acquainted with D'Invaut, the husband of one of the daughters of his friend Bouvard de Fourqueux. I have been unable to find documentary support for Schelle's conjecture.

103. *Du commerce et de la Compagnie des Indes* (Amsterdam and Paris, 1769), p. 3.

104. Cf. Edouard Mossion, *Dupont de Nemours et la question de la Compagnie des Indes* (Paris, [1918]), pp. 70-112, and André Labrouquère, *Les Idées coloniales des physiocrates* (Paris, 1927), pp. 97-101.

105. Coleman (see note 82), pp. 31-33, provides succinct information on the censors and their work.

106. Turgot to Du Pont, Limoges, February 1, and May 24, 1771, Winterthur MSS, group 2; printed in Schelle, ed. *Œuvres de Turgot*, III, 470, 487.

107. "Bilan général de mes affaires au premier Janvier 1775 [à l'é] poque de mon retour de Pologne" in EMHL, Winterthur MSS, group 2 (special). Cf. Coleman (see note 82), p. 28. Since a livre may be roughly estimated as equivalent to twenty cents, Du Pont was still carrying an indebtedness of some $1,700.

108. Franklin to Du Pont, London, August 12, 1772, in Smyth, ed., *Writings of Benjamin Franklin*, V, 409.

109. For a probably exaggerated statement of the influence of the *Éphémérides* abroad, see Stephen Bauer, "Éphémérides," in Palgrave's *Dictionary of Political Economy,* ed. Henry Higgs (1926), I, 747.

110. Du Pont's announcement of the Correspondence is printed in Carl Knies, ed., *Carl Friedrichs von Baden Brieflicher Verkehr mit Mirabeau und Du Pont,* I, 151-152. The nature of the fortnightly letter is indicated in these words: "Il leur fait passer tous les quinze jours une lettre dans laquelle il a l'honneur de leur rendre compte des livres nouveaux, et particulièrement de ceux qui ont quelque rapport à l'utilité publique ou privée, des inventions remarquables, des actions louables, des travaux des artistes, des changements de législation, des opérations des divers gouvernements de ce qui doit naturellement en résulter en bien ou en mal, de l'opinion qu'en a le public, et de celle qu'il en doit avoir." There are three slightly variant copies of this announcement among the manuscripts of the Badische Generallandesarchiv in Karlsruhe. Microfilm copies of these manuscripts are now available at EMHL.

111. There is no available documentary evidence to support the estimate of B. G. du Pont (*DPdN,* I, 81) that Du Pont received from various princes about $225 a year for twenty-four letters. Knies (I, 143-144) prints a letter to Du Pont, dated November 21, 1772, from the Prince-Evêque of Wilna, who was then in Karlsruhe, containing the sentence: "Le titre en question vous est accordé, et au-dessus pour le correspondance que vous entreprenez avec les souverains, il vous assure 100 ducats pour sa part. . . ." This statement may have been the source of Mrs. du Pont's estimate, but there is no way to prove that it was. (Very few of Mrs. Du Pont's notes for her biography of Du Pont de Nemours can be found at EMHL.) The "Correspondance" was in manuscript only, the main body of it remaining unpublished until Knies prepared his *Brieflicher Verkehr. . . .*

112. Karl Obser, "Nachträge zu dem Briefwechsel der Markgrafen Karl Friedrich von Baden mit Mirabeau und Du Pont," *Zeitschrift für die Geschichte der Oberrheins,* n. f. XXXIV (1909), 127. The Margrave was in Paris from June 12 to September 17, 1771.

113. The "patente de conseiller du margrave de Baden," dated December 31, 1772, and the permission signed by Louis XV for Du Pont to accept the title of Conseiller Aulique from the Margrave of Baden, dated March 22, 1774, are both in the Winterthur MSS in EMHL.

114. With minor omissions, Du Pont's letters have been published in Carl Knies, ed., *Carl Friedrichs von Baden Brieflicher Verkehr mit Mirabeau und Du Pont,* I, 125-283. Microfilm copies of the original manuscripts still preserved in the Badische Generallandesarchiv are available at EMHL.

115. One item not reproduced by Knies is an undated *mémoire* of Du Pont, advising the Margrave to send his son and heir, Carl Ludwig, on a diplomatic mission to the Grand Duke (apparently, Leopold of Tuscany) with the objective of gaining as a bride a princess of the House of Austria (EMHL microfilm from the Badische General-landesarchiv in Karlsruhe).

116. These letters are printed in the second volume of Carl Knies, ed., *Brieflicher Verkehr. . . .*

117. The letter containing the *mémoire* is in Knies, II, 289-300. Knies did not reproduce the diagram which is the essential part of this *mémoire,* because of technical difficulties in setting into type the diagram of the curve which Du Pont drew by hand. We are indebted to Henry W. Spiegel and the Johns Hopkins Press for the reproduction of this curve and for a translation into English of the letter as found in Knies (Pierre Samuel Du Pont de Nemours, *On Economic Curves: A Letter Reproduced in English Translation with the Original Diagram and an Introduction* by Henry W. Spiegel, Baltimore, 1955). Unfortunately, Mr. Spiegel's translation, especially of Du Pont's notations on the diagram, is inaccurate and confusing.

118. Weulersse, *Le Mouvement physiocratique . . . ,* II, 120-129, discusses and criticizes this "arithmetical method" of the Physiocrats.

119. *Lettres de Du Pont de Nemours à la margrave Caroline-Louise de Bade sur les salons de 1773, 1777, 1779* publiées par le Dr. Karl Obser avec le concours de Gaston Brière et Maurice Tourneux (extrait des *Archives de l'art français*, nouvelle série, II, 1908; Paris, 1909). Obser found these letters in the papers of the Margravine Caroline-Louise (volumes XCVI and XCVIII) in Karlsruhe. The letter of 1773 is signed by Du Pont and has corrections in his hand; the one for 1777 (written at Bois-des-Fossés) is entirely in his handwriting; the one for 1779 is a copy.

120. *Ibid.*, pp. 30-31 (Salon of 1773).

121. *Ibid.*, p. 50 (Salon of 1777). Du Pont judged the Salon of 1777 inferior to that of 1773 but admitted that his opinion might have been unduly influenced by his own circumstances (p. 61). He was then living at Bois-des-Fossés after Turgot's disgrace, was in ill health, and, during the visit to Paris to view the exhibits, had been able to go to the Salon only four times. He had to rely for some of his information upon one of the many brochures published on the Salon—probably the anonymous *Lettres pittoresques à l'occasion des tableaux exposés au Salon de 1777* (p. 43 and note).

122. For mention of Chreptowicz's relations with Du Pont in 1769, see G. Schelle, ed., "Lettres inédites de Du Pont de Nemours au Comte Chreptowicz," *Journal des Économistes: revue mensuelle de la science économique et de la statistique*, 6ᵉ série, XIV (1907), 4, and Ambroise Jobert, *Magnats polonais et physiocrates français (1767-1774)* (*Collection historique de l'Institut d'études slaves*, X; Paris, 1941), 38 n.

123. According to M. de M[ontchanin], *Notice sur la vie de Dupont (de Nemours)* . . . , p. 10.

124. *Ibid.*

125. Ambroise Jobert, *La Commission d'education nationale en Pologne (1773-1794); son œuvre d'instruction civique* (*Collection de l'Institut français de Varsovie*, IX; Paris, 1941), p. 185; Knies, I, 168 (Du Pont's letter to Carl Friedrich, Strasburg, March 18, 1774).

126. Du Pont to Carl Friedrich, Paris, February 26, 1774 (Knies I, 167).

127. Du Pont to Carl Friedrich, Strasburg, March 18, 1774, and Rastadt, March 24, 1774 (Knies I, 168-170).

128. Du Pont to Carl Friedrich, Paris, July 4, 1774, Karlsruhe, July 30, 1774, Ratisbonne, August 17, 1774 (Knies I, 170-174).

129. The old house was torn down in 1930 and replaced by a Tudor-styled stucco and timber house erected just to the east of the former Du Pont house. Just west of the house there remains standing a small, square, brick and stucco building which, local tradition maintains, was used as a study by Du Pont. The farm buildings, which probably go back to the seventeenth century, remain generally as they were in Du Pont's time. In the woods on a hillside east of the new house the visitor can still discern the trenches which gave the estate its name. The land is still cultivated but, in the changed conditions of this century, does not provide substantial returns. M. Léon Petit of Nemours made the necessary arrangements to enable me to visit the estate in 1960 through the courtesy of the Henri Mérot family. I am indebted also to Mr. Williams Haynes of Stonecrop Farm, Stonington, Connecticut, for photographs and comments now on file at EMHL.

130. M. de M[ontchanin], *Notice sur la vie de Dupont* . . . , pp. 12-13, prints the letter which Du Pont wrote to his uncle (presumably Pierre) from Bois-des-Fossés on July 18, 1774. It is quoted in part by Jobert, *Magnats polonais et physiocrates français*, pp. 65-66.

131. His passport is dated July 3, and the one for his family, July 8, 1774, but he did not leave until toward the end of the month. Both passports, signed by Louis XVI, are in EMHL, Winterthur MSS.

132. Du Pont to [Quesnay], Battelstedt-en-Saxe, December 18, 1774. EMHL, Winterthur MSS, group 2. The young Adam Czartoryski, whom Du Pont was supposed to tutor, grew up to become well known as the principal Polish adviser of Alexander I of Russia.

133. Jean Fabre, *Stanislas-Auguste Poniatowski et l'Europe des lumières (Collection historique de l'Institut d'études slaves,* XVI; Paris, 1952), p. 147.

134. Jobert, *Magnats polonais et physiocrates français* is the indispensable book on this matter. For the projects considered by the Commission see especially pp. 68, 70, 77, 78. The *mémoire* on the abolition of serfdom has not been found.

135. Jobert, *La Commission d'education nationale en Pologne,* p. 186. Since very little documentary evidence of the work of the Commission survives, beyond the brief *procès-verbal* of its meetings, Du Pont's *mémoires* and correspondence (which Jobert was able to use in Poland) have a special value for students of the subject.

136. Letter dated Warsaw, October 24, 1774 (Knies, I, 174).

137. Turgot to Du Pont, Paris, July 20, 1774 (Schelle, *Œuvres de Turgot* . . . IV, 83-84).

138. The order, dated September 19, 1774, is in EMHL, Winterthur MSS. It is printed in Schelle, *Œuvres de Turgot* . . . IV, 133, and translated by B. G. du Pont, *DPdN,* I, 86.

139. EMHL, Winterthur MSS, group 2; translated by B. G. du Pont, *DPdN,* I, 84-86.

140. The official copy of Du Pont's commission as Inspector General of Commerce is in EMHL, Winterthur MSS, group 2, series F.

141. Du Pont to [Quesnay] "Battelstedt-en-Saxe, entre Haumbourg et Erfert," December 18, 1774. EMHL, Winterthur MSS, group 2; printed in full in Jobert, *Magnats,* pp. 80-83.

III

1. Douglas Dakin, *Turgot and the Ancien Régime in France* (London, 1939), p. 151.

2. *Ibid.,* p. 265; B. G. du Pont, *DPdN,* I, 106. For Turgot's illness see also Schelle, *Œuvres de Turgot* . . . IV, 279-282.

3. For Turgot's succinct and oft-quoted statement of his program in his letter to the King, dated August 24, 1774, see G. Schelle, *Œuvres de Turgot* . . . IV, 109-113. (A study of the rough draft of this letter makes evident the careful effort with which Turgot wrote and revised it; *ibid.,* pp. 113-114.) The letter may also be found in the other two less complete and less satisfactory collections of Turgot's works: [P. S. Du Pont de Nemours], *Œuvres de M*ʳ· *Turgot, ministre d'état, précedées et accompagnées de mémoires et de notes sur sa vie, son administration et ses ouvrages* (Paris, 1808--1811), VII, 2-9; and Eugène Daire and Hippolyte Dussard, *Œuvres de Turgot, nouvelle édition classé par ordre de matières avec les notes de Dupont de Nemours augmenté de lettres inédites, des questions sur le commerce, et d'observations et de notes nouvelles,* etc. (Paris, 1844), II, 165-169. Du Pont also gives the letter in full in his *Mémoires sur la vie et les ouvrages de M. Turgot, ministre d'état;* première partie (Philadelphia, 1782), pp. 138-147.

4. Schelle, *Œuvres de Turgot* . . . IV, 111; Du Pont, *Mémoires sur . . . Turgot,* première partie, p. 143.

5. Du Pont, *Mémoires sur . . . Turgot,* seconde partie, pp. 3-7.

6. Calculations of M. Marion, *Histoire financière de la France depuis 1715* (Paris, 1914-1928), I, 288.

7. Schelle, *Œuvres de Turgot,* IV, provides the most convenient source for a study of the numerous matters with which Turgot had to concern himself. The best scholarly study is the splendid work of Douglas Dakin (cited in note 1 above).

8. See above, pp. 30-31, 37.

9. For the *arrêt du conseil* of September 13, 1774, see Schelle, *Œuvres de Turgot,* IV, 201-210.

10. *Ibid.,* p. 210.

11. Du Pont, *Mémoires . . . sur Turgot,* seconde partie, pp. 10-13.

12. Trudaine du Montigny and Abeille seem to have worked most closely with Turgot in framing the preamble. G. Weulersse, *La Physiocratie sous les ministères de Turgot et de Necker (1774-1781)* (Paris, 1950), p. 17.

13. Schelle, *Œuvres de Turgot*, IV, 415-453.

14. *Ibid.*, 455-466, 480-482; Dakin, *Turgot . . .* , pp. 191-192.

15. Du Pont's review of this incident was written in a letter to Carl Ludwig, heir to the throne of Baden, on January 15, 1783 (Knies, *Brieflicher Verkehr*, II, 356-363). This letter and a subsequent one, dated February 1, 1783, contain a valuable (if, perhaps, not completely reliable) survey by Du Pont of Turgot's Ministry. Both are published by Knies, II, 354-373. There is, unfortunately, no contemporary evidence to support Du Pont's claim that his advice was significant. Although Dakin (*Turgot . . .* , pp. 185-191) sustains the thesis of an organized conspiracy behind the "flour war," the most recent student, Edgar Faure (*La disgrâce de Turgot [12 mai 1776]*; no. 6 of Collection: *Trente journées qui ont fait la France;* Paris, 1961), attempts to destroy this view. Faure regards it as a genuine revolutionary movement among the people (see especially pp. 292-318).

16. Schelle, *Œuvres de Turgot*, IV, 244-257; Dakin, *Turgot*, pp. 195-199.

17. These matters are best studied in some detail in Dakin, *Turgot*, pp. 199-205.

18. Cf. M. Marion, *Dictionnaire des institutions de la France aux XVIIe et XVIIIe siècles* (Paris, 1923), p. 67.

19. Elaborating upon a remark of the Marquis de Mirabeau, Weulersse writes (*La Physiocratie sous . . . Turgot et . . . Necker,* p. 13): "[Dupont] sera de moitié dans la préparation de presque tous ses Édits ou Mémoires, et aux heures difficiles il lui prêtera un concours plus actif encore, qui ne se démentira jamais. . . ." Cf. G. Weulersse, *Les Physiocrates sous le ministère Turgot* (Paris, n.d.), p. 3. I can find no supporting evidence for such a definite statement.

20. The notice of the burial of Samuel Dupont, extracted from the register of the Parish of Saint Roch at Paris, gives no indication that Du Pont was present (EMHL, Winterthur MSS, group 1). Marie Du Pont's letters to her husband prove that he remained at Versailles (excerpts translated by B. G. du Pont, *DPdN*, I, 94, from originals in EMHL, Winterthur MSS, group 2, series C). The date of the funeral on the burial notice is June 8; according to Madame Du Pont's letter, it occurred on June 9.

21. See excerpts translated by B. G. du Pont, *DPdN*, I, 93-94.

22. Copy (not original) of the will of Samuel Dupont (provided by Madame Vaudry, who refused to show the original to Du Pont) in EMHL, Winterthur MSS, group 1.

23. B. G. du Pont translation of letter in *DPdN*, I, 96.

24. EMHL, Winterthur MSS, group 2, series F, contains the warrant of Louis XVI, and the document of investiture. Letters of Madame Du Pont to her husband, translated in part in B. G. du Pont, *DPdN*, I, 97-100.

25. Pierre Bonnassieux and Eugène Lelong, *Conseil de Commerce et Bureau du Commerce 1700-1791; inventaire analytique des procès-verbaux* (Paris, 1900), introd., pp. xlvi-xlvii and p. 429, column 2.

26. Turgot's *mémoire* presenting the Six Edicts may be found in Schelle, *Œuvres de Turgot*, V, 148-162, or E. Daire and H. Dussard, *Œuvres de Turgot*, II, 237-251. For an English translation of these edicts, see Robert P. Shepherd, *Turgot and the Six Edicts (Columbia University Studies in History, Economics and Public Law,* vol. XVIII, no. 2; New York, 1903), Part III, pp. 147-209.

27. Cf. M. Marion, *Dictionnaire des institutions de la France . . .* , p. 68, and D. Dakin, *Turgot*, p. 234.

28. Schelle, *Œuvres de Turgot*, V, 148-154.

29. *Ibid.*, p. 7.

30. G. Weulersse, *Les Physiocrates sous le ministère Turgot*, p. 17; D. Dakin, *Turgot*, p. 255; Schelle, *Œuvres de Turgot*, V, 467-468.

31. *Mémoires . . . sur Turgot*, seconde partie, p. 254. Edgar Faure, *La disgrâce de Turgot (12 mai 1776)*, emphasizes the opposition of the Parlement and the absence of

expressions of popular support as the principal reasons for Turgot's fall (pp. 517, 524-525).

32. The best available presentation of the *Mémoire* and of the circumstances attending its formulation can be found in Schelle, *Œuvres de Turgot*, IV, 568-628. Schelle uses the text found in Knies, *Brieflicher Verkehr*, I, 244-283, but gives also the variants found in Du Pont's edition (1809) of Turgot's *Œuvres*. Schelle (pp. 570-572) and, more briefly, Dakin, *Turgot* (p. 343, note 4 to chap. XVII) relate the story of how Mirabeau, son of the Physiocrat, edited the *Mémoire* for publication in 1787 as the work of Turgot.

33. Schelle, *Œuvres de Turgot*, IV, 576; Knies, *Brieflicher Verkehr*, I, 245-246 (punctuation slightly modified).

34. In his edition of the *Œuvres de M*ʳ· *Turgot* (VII, 482-483) Du Pont remarked that Turgot desired to revise this part of the *Mémoire* in order to give "a clear and complete guarantee" of the liberty of all citizens, whether landowners or not. In a letter to the *Journal de Paris*, dated July 2, 1787 (Schelle, *Œuvres de Turgot*, IV, 571), Du Pont stated that Turgot would give to all citizens some active voice in the government. This need not mean (as Schelle may imply, p. 572) that all citizens, *propriétaires ou non*, would be electors. Du Pont's views on this matter will be subsequently developed (*infra*, p. 168).

35. Schelle, *DPdN*, pp. 261-262, where the later plan of Calonne, based upon this *Mémoire*, is discussed.

36. Letter of July 2, 1787, to *Journal de Paris*, reprinted in Schelle, *Œuvres de Turgot*, IV, 571.

37. Schelle, *Œuvres de Turgot*, p. 676; also quoted in G. Weulersse, *Les Physiocrates sous le ministère Turgot*, p. 11.

38. G. Weulersse, *La Physiocratie sous . . . Turgot . . . Necker (1774-1781)*, p. 41; Schelle, *DPdN*, p. 203. Weulersse and Schelle refer to the position as Inspector of Manufactures. The documents (see note 39) refer exclusively to the position of Inspector General of Commerce, except for one of 1777 confirming Du Pont's salary of 4,000 livres as Inspector General of Manufactures.

39. These documents are in the Archives Nationales (hereafter A.N.), F¹² 740.

40. Du Pont to Vergennes, Paris, May 30, 1776, in Archives du Ministère des Affaires Étrangères (hereafter AAE), Correspondence Politique (hereafter CP), Angleterre, vol. 516, folios 238-239vo.

41. Turgot to Du Pont, La Roche-Guijon, June 1, 1776, in Schelle, *Œuvres de Turgot*, V, 491.

42. Turgot's letters to Du Pont from July 20 through September, 1776, express solicitude for Du Pont's illness. *Ibid.*, V, 499-503.

43. Du Pont to Trudaine, Paris, May 21, 1777, where he writes of his effort to see Trudaine "six or seven weeks ago" and mentions that he has been sick himself most of the time since. From his bed he writes to enlist Trudaine's support in his attempt to have paid to him the 200 écus accorded him annually by Maurepas. A.N., F¹² 740. Du Pont mentions his illness in the letter on the Salon of 1777 to Caroline-Louise of Baden (*Lettres . . . sur les salons de 1773, 1777, 1779*, ed. Karl Obser, p. 43).

44. B. G. du Pont, *DPdN*, I, 110-111. There are preserved in EMHL, Longwood MSS, groups 2 and 3, some of Victor's school copybooks and of Eleuthère Irénée's lessons and notes, though most date from a later period.

45. One must employ caution in using P. Manuel's edition of Mirabeau's *Lettres originales . . . écrites du donjon de Vincennes . . . 1777, 78, 79 et 80* (Paris, 1792). There is, however, in IV, 293, a rather startling passage concerning Du Pont, which merits inclusion here (especially as it does not appear in full in all existing copies of this work). Writing to his mistress, Sophie de Monnier, Mirabeau claims to be quoting from a letter received from Du Pont: "Point du tout, voici ce qu'ajoute pour moi le philosophe Dupont. Pardonne la liberté du langage, et songe que c'était à moi qu'il était destiné: 'Songe à présent, malheureux paillard, que si tu te permets de trousser

une seule de ces femmes, tu te noyeras sans ressource dans ton sperme inconsidéré. *Teterrima belli causa cunnus* [Horace], (ce qui veut dire, mais en langue de mauvais lieu, que l'amour est la source des guerres les plus cruelles). Rien de si doux qu'une femme en tête-à-tête; rien de si tracassier que les femmes en troupeau. Sauve-toi avec elles par le respect, vois-les rarement, étudie et sors. Et si tu ne peux apprendre les vers de Pavillon, sous le nom de Boyer, et l'art de la guerre du marquis de Santa-Crux; (tu sauras que Pavillon conseille pour toute maitresse la *veuve Poignet,* et que le premier principe de guerre de M. de Santa-Crux est qu'un grand général doit savoir s . . . b . . . l . . . v . . . [omissions in original] pour se garer des femmes qui finissent par tout gâter): quand tu viendras voir ta mère, cours chez une fille, libertin, et la vérole exceptée, purge-toi.' " This quotation is taken from the "Longwood" copy at EMHL. The "Winterthur" copy there has a cancel of page 293, expurgating eight lines of Du Pont's letter. Both copies are otherwise defective in part.

46. Oliver J. G. Welch, *Mirabeau: A Study of a Democratic Monarchist* (London, 1951), p. 90.

47. No date appears on the *Table* with the Paris imprint, but it can be dated from references to it in Turgot's letters to Du Pont, dated March 20, June 2, 13, 1778 (Schelle, *Œuvres de Turgot,* V, 548, 556, 558). This notice appears at the lower right side of the *Table:* "Cette Table a été Imaginée Par S.A.S. M. Le Marggrave [sic] régnant de Bade *et redigée en 1775* Par le Citoyen du Pont de Nemours." Weulersse (*La Physiocratie sous . . . Turgot et . . . Necker,* p. 237, and *La Physiocratie à la fin du règne de Louis XV* [1770-1774] [Paris, 1959], p. 9) points out that the table had been worked out in 1773. It was based upon the Margrave's, *Abrégé des principes de l'économie politique,* which first appeared in the *Éphémérides du citoyen,* 1772, tome 1 (Schelle, *DPdN,* p. 409n). In a letter to Benjamin Vaughan (Passy, November 9, 1779), Benjamin Franklin wrote: "I send you M. Dupont's *Table Economique* [sic] which I think an excellent thing as it contains in a clear method all the principles of that new sect called here *les Économistes.*" *Benjamin Franklin's Autobiographical Writings,* selected and edited by Carl Van Doren (New York, 1945), p. 475.

48. Schelle, *Œuvres de Turgot,* V, 576-577. In *DPdN,* p. 203, Schelle suggests that it was probably to please Vergennes that Necker decided to bring Du Pont back to active service. There is no hint of Vergennes' intervention in Turgot's letter. In the preface to the 1812 edition of his *Essai de traduction en vers du Roland Furieux de l'Arioste,* p. 6, Du Pont states bluntly: *"M. de Vergennes m'y rappeler . . . ,"* but his memory might have been faulty.

49. Turgot to Du Pont, March 30, and April 1, 1780. Schelle, *Œuvres de Turgot,* V, 614. The principal source of information on this period of Du Pont's life is the series of letters which Turgot wrote to him (Schelle, *Œuvres de Turgot,* V, 583-641). Unfortunately, Du Pont's letters to Turgot have probably not survived, although they are still being searched for by EMHL.

50. G. Schelle, *Turgot,* p. 3.

51. The exact date of their meeting cannot be determined. In his *Mémoires,* Talleyrand remembers that, somewhat later, Du Pont was one of the group which assembled every morning at his home, Bellechasse (*Mémoires du Prince de Talleyrand,* publiés avec une préface et des notes par le Duc de Broglie [Paris, 1891-1892], I, 36-37; G. Lacour-Gayet, *Talleyrand 1754-1838* [Paris, 1930-1934], I, 58).

52. *Essai de traduction en vers du Roland Furieux de l'Arioste* (Paris: chez Alexandre Jombert, 1781). In a letter, without date, to Stanislas II, King of Poland, to whom he sent a copy of the *Essai,* Du Pont remarked: "Je garde à Paris l'anonime le plus absolu sur ce petit ouvrage. Mais je ne ferai ni ne penserai jamais rien que je veuille cacher à Votre Majesté" (EMHL, Winterthur MSS, group 2).

53. Most of the points made in this brief critique can be illustrated by comparing Du Pont's translation of the first stanza with the original.

Ariosto: Le donne, i cavalier, l'arme, gli amori,
              Le cortesie, l'audaci imprese io canto,

Che furo al tempo che passaro i Mori
D'Africa il mare, e in Francia nocquer tanto,
Seguendo l'ire, e i giovenil furori
D'Agramente lor rè, che si diè vanto
Di vendicar la morte di Troiano
Sopra rè Carlo imperator romano.

Du Pont: Je vais chanter les Guerriers & les Belles,
Et les Amours, & les armes cruelles,
La courtoisie, & la rare valeur
Qu'on vit briller en ces temps de malheur
Où, désertant leur Africain rivage,
Et dans la France apportant le ravage,
Les Sarrasins conduits par Agramant,
Croyaient, au gré de son jeune courage,
Venger le mort de son père Trojan
Sur Charlemagne & sur sa fière armée.

54. *Essai de traduction en vers du Roland Furieux de l'Arioste* (Paris: chez Firmin Didot, 1812), 215 pp.

55. Manuscript copies of cantos 4 through 9 are in EMHL, Winterthur MSS, group 2 special. With the exception of cantos 7 and 8, all have notes attached. There is also a fragment of part of canto 13, but nothing on the intervening cantos (10-12).

56. Du Pont to Malesherbes, April 13, 1781 (Schelle, *Œuvres de Turgot*, V, 653). Schelle mentioned this letter in his remarks on July 30, 1914, at the ceremonies dedicating a monument to Turgot. "Inauguration du Monument de Turgot (30 Juillet 1914): Discours de MM. Yves Guyot, Alfred Neymarche, Gustave Schelle, Mesureur" (extrait de *Journal des Économistes, revue mensuelle de la science économique et de la statistique*, 14 août 1914 [Paris, 1914], p. 14).

57. Schelle, *DPdN*, pp. 208-209, quoting the Marquis de Mirabeau.

58. *Mémoires sur Turgot*, seconde partie, p. 3.

59. *Ibid.*, p. 267.

60. Pierre Jolly, *Necker* (Paris, *c.* 1947), pp. 185-189; Edouard Chapuisat, *Necker (1732-1804)* (Paris, n.d. [1938]), pp. 99-100.

61. Bonnassieux and Lelong, *Conseil de commerce et Bureau de commerce . . .* , p. xlvii (introduction).

62. Du Pont to Vergennes, June 11, 1781, AAE, CP, Angleterre, vol. 534, ff. 95-97vo. There is a brief sketch of Hutton's life in the *Dictionary of National Biography*, X, 353-354. The only attempt at a full-scale biography is the unsatisfactory Daniel Benham, *Memoirs of James Hutton: Comprising the Annals of his Life, and Connection with the United Brethren* (London, 1856). Of the early correspondence only one letter of Hutton's, dated March 3, 1777, is at EMHL. There is also a Hutton letter dated November 15, 1791. All others are only later copies (see note 67, below). Inquiry at the National Register of Archives and at the Moravian Church House in London has turned up no information on the possible survival of a body of Hutton papers, which might contain letters from Du Pont.

63. For some knowledge of these missions I am indebted to an unpublished seminar paper of Mr. Ronald Di Cenzo, graduate student at the University of Kansas: "The Labrador Missions of the Moravian Brethren in the Eighteenth Century."

64. Smyth, *Writings of Benjamin Franklin*, VII, 104.

65. Du Pont to Vergennes, June 11, 1781, as cited in note 62, above. It was widely believed at the time that Hutton was a secret emissary of George III, with whom, he stated, he had had an hour's conversation sometime before he came to Paris. John W. Jordan in his presentation of an interesting collection of letters bearing upon Hutton's visit, contented himself with the comment that Hutton was "supposed to have been the confidential agent of the king . . ." (*Pennsylvania Magazine of History and Biography*, XXXII [1908], 223).

66. See Benham, *Memoirs of James Hutton*, p. 511.

67. In EMHL, Winterthur MSS, group 8, there are copies in the hand of the late Miss Harriet Austin of Vergennes' letters to Du Pont on the Hutton correspondence. There are also copies (by Miss Austin) of three of Hutton's letters to Du Pont and three of Du Pont's letters to Hutton. The originals are not at present available. It is possible that they still exist somewhere in the depositories of the Winterthur estate of Henry Francis du Pont and may some day be uncovered.

68. This exchange of letters can be studied from available contemporary documents only indirectly in AAE, CP, Angleterre, vols. 534, 536, and 537 (only a single reference in last volume at f. 356). (See note 67, above.) Specific references to folio numbers not given here may be found conveniently in Waldo G. Leland, ed., *Guide to Materials for American History in the Libraries and Archives of Paris*; vol. II: *Archives of the Ministry of Foreign Affairs* (by Waldo G. Leland, John J. Meng, Abel Doysié; Carnegie Institution Publication 392; Washington, 1943). Transcripts and photocopies of these volumes in AAE are available in the Library of Congress, although I have here used principally photocopies prepared especially for EMHL by M. Abel Doysié, whose assistance to me in facilitating research in French archives is gratefully acknowledged in the preface to this book.

69. Because of the importance on this point of presumed statements of Hutton in his letters to Du Pont, dated March 26 and June 14, 1782, I subdue my reluctance to cite as authority copies made much later of originals which are not currently available. According to Miss Austin's copy (see note 67, above) Hutton wrote that he had no influence with the new ministers unless Shelburne was one of them and he had not seen Shelburne for a long time. (Shelburne did enter the ministry on March 27 as Secretary of State for the home department and became Prime Minister on July 10, Rockingham having died on July 1.) The former ministry, Hutton wrote, had listened to his ideas arguing for peace but *had never authorized him to do anything*. On June 14, he wrote that he could no longer exchange ideas with the new ministry, that Shelburne and he had long been strangers, that Fox in the Foreign Office didn't even know what he looked like—nor did any of the other ministers. He concluded that there was nothing for him to do in the most august of all trades, that of "garçon ouvrier à la Pacification." I have called these "presumed" statements because I have not seen the originals, although I am personally convinced that they are accurate transcriptions by Miss Austin, who was always a competent and careful scholar.

70. Richard Oswald was the English negotiator of the preliminary peace of November, 1782; David Hartley, of the definitive treaty of September, 1783. Some of Franklin's correspondence with Oswald and Hartley can be found in Smyth, *Writings of Benjamin Franklin*, esp. vols. VIII and IX. I have not exhausted all possibilities but have found no direct or indirect references to Hutton or Du Pont in the Oswald correspondence in AAE, CP, Angleterre, vol. 537 (ff. 151, 307, 308, 379), and vol. 538 (ff. 16, 20, 34). Similarly at the Public Record Office in London I found no references in the Foreign Office correspondence with Oswald in F.O. 97, vol. 157, or in the Hartley papers in F.O. 4 America (Series 1). The most accurate and succinct account of the negotiations of 1782 and 1783 is in Samuel F. Bemis, *A Diplomatic History of the United States* (4th ed.; New York, *c.* 1955), pp. 46-64.

71. Schelle, *DPdN*, pp. 225-226, makes the chief assertions which were followed by B. G. du Pont, *DPdN*, I, 120. Pierre Jolly, *Du Pont de Nemours: Soldat de la Liberté*, p. 47, is only a little more cautious. Henri Doniol, *Histoire de la participation de la France à l'établissement des États-Unis* (Paris, 1886-1892), V, 36-37, also makes unsupported statements about this correspondence, statements which must be especially suspect, since Doniol covered only part of the correspondence and was not completely accurate in his account.

72. William M. Malloy, comp., *Treaties, Conventions, International Acts, Protocols and Agreements Between the United States of America and Other Powers* (61st Congress, 2d. session, Document No. 357; Washington, 1910), p. 478.

73. Du Pont to Vergennes, November 23, 1782, AAE, CP, Angleterre, vol. 539, ff. 21-22vo.; November 25, 1782, *ibid.*, ff. 35-35 *bis*.

74. Useful for this simplified summary has been "Résultat de tous les travaux qui ont été faits depuis trois ans relativement à la ville de Bayonne et au Pays de Labourt, ou Examen de la constitution, des droits et des prétentions de cette ville et de ce pays, des motifs qu'on a pour y établir un port franc et des limites naturelles que l'interêt politique, fiscal et commercial doit fixer à cette franchise," probably prepared by Du Pont (though not in his hand) with the assistance of Boyetet, who was associated with him in studying the Bayonne situation. AAE, Mémoires et Documents (hereafter M. & D.), France, vol. 2011, ff. 209, 210-257vo.

75. The voluminous reports may be studied in AAE, M. & D., France, vols. 1488 and 2011, and AAE, M. & D., Espagne, vol. 209.

76. All of his letters to Vergennes on the Hutton Correspondence, from September 5, 1781, to January 4, 1782, are addressed from Bois-des-Fossés. AAE, CP, Angleterre, vols. 534 and 536.

77. On March 11, 1782, he stated to Vergennes that he had carefully examined and faithfully extracted everything which had been said or written on the matter for seven years. AAE, M. & D., France, vol. 1488, ff. 189-192vo.

78. His attitude is well expressed in a letter to Vergennes, dated June 4, 1784, when he remarks that he can depart from his opinions when the interest of the King requires it. Since we do not live in ideal circumstances, he adds, we must be content with the best *possible* action. AAE, CP, États Unis, vol. 27, f. 396.

79. The best statement of his plan is the "Précis de ce dont il est question relativement à Bayonne, à St. Jean-de-Luz et au pays de Labourt" in AAE, M. & D., France, vol. 2011, ff. 141-142. This document is undated but undoubtedly was penned in the fall of 1782.

80. AAE, M. & D., Espagne, vol. 209, ff. 7-11 (Du Pont to Joly de Fleury, March 1783) and ff. 12-21 (Projet d'articles sur l'affaire de Bayonne).

81. AAE, M. & D., Espagne, vol. 209, ff. 22-23 (Du Pont to Vergennes, March 25, 1783).

82. AAE, M. & D., France, vol. 2011, ff. 272-286vo. The voluminous document is in the hand of a copyist, but Du Pont supplies in his own hand the running summary in the left-hand margin. He suggested an annual indemnity to the General Farm of 24,375 livres.

83. Louis Gottschalk, *Lafayette Between the American and the French Revolution (1783-1789)* (Chicago, *c.* 1950), pp. 25-51 *passim*, covers this matter admirably.

84. AAE, CP, États Unis, vol. 25, ff. 231-241vo., enclosed in a letter from Du Pont to Vergennes, dated August 26, 1783.

85. It seems unwise in an already overburdened account to detail the evidence collected on this point. For the possibly interested reader pertinent documents may be cited here. EMHL, Winterthur MSS, group 2 (special), for the first draft of a letter prepared by Du Pont for Ormesson to send to the Duc de Castries (Minister of Navy) in September, 1783; AAE, CP, Angleterre, vol. 541, folios 191-194vo. (Du Pont to Vergennes, March 16, 1783); AAE, M. & D., France, vol. 1488, ff. 281-282 (Du Pont to Vergennes, January 31, 1783), vol. 2011, f. 265 (same to same under same date); AAE, M. & D., Amérique, vol. 17, ff. 12-32vo. (Du Pont to Vergennes, February 16, 1784, enclosing *mémoire* on American trade with French colonies); and ff. 36-46 (Du Pont to Vergennes, February 21, 1784, enclosing *mémoire* on flour trade in French colonies, arguing against a tariff on American flour). See also *Benjamin Franklin's Autobiographical Writings*, ed. Carl Van Doren, p. 606, where Franklin notes in his Passy journal a visit from Du Pont on June 30, 1784, "to talk . . . about the free port of L'Orient, and some difficulties respecting it. . . ." The difficulties must have concerned American trade, since Franklin referred Du Pont to Barclay, American merchant and commissioner for accounts, and sent along his grandson as interpreter, since Du Pont "said he did not well understand English when spoken, and Mr. Barclay did not speak French. . . ."

86. M. Marion, *Histoire financière de la France depuis 1715*, I, 347-349.

87. These documents, Du Pont to Ormesson, May to August 1783, are in A.N., Série 144 AP 131, no. 11.

88. M. Marion, *Histoire financière*, I, 350.

89. There is a later copy (by Miss Austin) of a letter from Vergennes to Du Pont, dated November 22, 1782, regretting the Minister's inability to assure to his protégé the post of representative of the Prince of Baden because of an adverse decision of the King in EMHL, Winterthur MSS, group 8. On January 31, 1783, however, Du Pont remarks in a letter to Vergennes that M. de Santi, whom Du Pont would succeed "without character" in accordance with the permission which Vergennes had given, was asking for the return of his credentials (AAE, M. & D., France, vol. 1488, ff. 281-282). And on April 12, 1783, Du Pont sent to Vergennes letters of certification of his appointment (Bernhard Erdmannsdörffer, ed., *Politische Correspondenz Karl Friedrichs von Baden, 1783-1806*; herausgegeben von der Badischen Historischen Commission [Heidelberg, 1888-1901], I, 241).

90. A.N., P 2601, folios 13vo.-15vo.: "Lettres d'annoblissement du mois de Decembre 1783 pour Dupont, inspecteur du commerce." B. D. du Pont, *DPdN*, I, 121-124, translates the letter in full.

91. EMHL, Winterthur MSS, group 2, translated by B. G. du Pont, *DPdN*, I, 132-137. There is at EMHL an undated manuscript in Du Pont's hand headed "Discours pour la cérémonie de donner à mon fils sa première epée." Internal evidence indicates that this was written in 1779 and was probably part of the ceremony presenting Victor with his sword—a ceremony justified by Du Pont's position as Chevalier in the Swedish Order of Vasa.

92. Letter in EMHL, Winterthur MSS, group 2, mentioned by B. G. du Pont, *DPdN*, I, 126.

93. The inventory drawn up in December, 1784, after Madame Du Pont's death supplies considerable information on their personal property at this time. It is in EMHL, Winterthur MSS, group 2; B. G. du Pont, *DPdN*, II, 177-213 (Appendix), translates most of it.

94. *Lettres de Mirabeau à Chamfort*, imprimées sur les originaux écrits de la main de Mirabeau, et suivies d'une traduction de la Dissertation allemande sur les causes de l'universalité de la langue française, qui a partagé le prix de l'Académie de Berlin; Traduction attribuée à Mirabeau et imprimée sur le manuscrit corrigé de sa main (Paris, an V [1797?]), p. 86 (Letter XVII, undated).

95. The "Acte d'inhumation de Nicole Charlotte Marie Louise Le Dée épouse de Messire Pierre Samuel Du Pont" is in the Registres de l'État Civil in the Mairie de Chevannes (Loiret) under this date. A photocopy is now at EMHL. B. G. du Pont (*DPdN*, I, 130-131) translates the notice of burial from the Register of the parish church at Chevannes.

96. The present plaque on the right side of the tomb is an exact reproduction of the original and was placed there in 1907. The inscription on the plaque is printed in B. G. du Pont, ed. and trans., *Life of Eleuthère Irénée du Pont from Contemporary Correspondence* (Newark, Delaware, 1923-1927), I, 31. The face of the stone on the left side of the tomb is left vacant, presumably for the plaque which would have been added after Du Pont's death, had he been buried there. Mr. Pierre Samuel du Pont (1880-1954), great-great-grandson of Du Pont de Nemours, provided funds for the restoration of the parish church in 1930, an act gratefully acknowledged by a plaque on a column inside the church. M. Léon Petit of Nemours kindly made the necessary arrangements for my visit to Chevannes.

97. Translation of B. G. du Pont, *DPdN*, I, 140, from a letter printed in full in G. Schelle, "Lettres inédites de Du Pont de Nemours au Comte Chreptowicz," *Journal des Économistes: revue mensuelle de la science économique et de la statistique*, 6ᵉ série, XIV (1907), 15.

98. Henri Pigeonneau and Alfred de Foville, eds., *L'Administration de l'agriculture au controle général des finances (1785-1787): procès-verbaux et rapports* (Paris, 1882), especially pp. 95-96, 119-120, 140-159, 199-202, 224-231, 253-273. There may have been more than sixty-nine meetings of the committee (which usually assembled weekly), but no additional records have been found.

99. Quoted in B. G. du Pont, *DPdN*, I, 141.

100. Du Pont to Vergennes, October 5, 1785 (AAE, M. & D., France, vol. 2006, ff. 271-276vo.).

101. AAE, M. & D., Asie, vol. 11, ff. 15-16: "Parallèle du commerce de la Compagnie des Indes et de celui fait par les negocians particuliers depuis la destruction de cette compagnie."

102. AAE, M. & D., Asie, vol. 5, ff. 121-121vo., and vol. 11, ff. 7-14.

103. The best brief treatment is Frederick L. Nussbaum, "The Formation of the New East India Company of Calonne," *American Historical Review*, XXXVIII (1933), 475-497. The complete history is Henry Weber, *La Compagnie française des Indes (1604-1875)* (Paris, 1904).

104. AAE, M. & D., France, vol. 2006, ff. 262-269vo.

105. *Gazette Nationale, ou le Moniteur universel* (hereafter *Moniteur*, citation being to the original volumes rather than to the later *Réimpression*), II, 382 (no. 93, April 3, 1790). Du Pont's *mémoire* as read by Maury may be found in the later compilation of *Archives parlementaires de 1787 à 1860, recueil complet . . . première série (1787 à 1799)*, ed. Mavidal *et al.* (Paris, 1867-1913), XII, 515-516. It appears also in *Les Actes des Apôtres* (a royalist journal in 11 vols.), IV (no. 93, Affaires de l'Inde), pp. 5-8, together with the *Réponse du conseil des finances*, p. 9. The *mémoire* was separately printed in 1790 as *Mémoire de M. Dupont sur une compagnie messagère des Indes, 1786*, but these separates are very rare. One can be found in the Archives départementales de Seine-et-Marne (Mélun) in Série A₂, Dossier I, 325.

106. Vergennes to Du Pont, November 30, 1786, Winterthur MSS, group 2. Du Pont had announced the happy event in a letter to Baron von Edelsheim on November 10 (Erdmannsdörffer, ed., *Politische Correspondenz Karl Friedrichs von Baden*, I, 264-265).

107. Lafayette to Calonne, no date (but late January, 1786), printed in Albert Mathiez, "Lafayette et le commerce franco-américain à la veille de la Révolution (d'après des documents inédits)," *Annales historiques de la Révolution française*, III (1926), 476.

108. Frederick L. Nussbaum, "American Tobacco and French Politics 1783-1789," *Political Science Quarterly*, XL (1925), 498. This article (pp. 497-516) and Professor Nussbaum's "The Revolutionary Vergennes and Lafayette versus the Farmers General," *Journal of Modern History*, III (1931), 592-604, are essential for a study of this issue. Lafayette's leading role is recounted by Louis Gottschalk, *Lafayette Between the American and the French Revolution*, pp. 202-237 *passim*.

109. AAE, CP, États Unis, vol. 31, ff. 291-311.

110. Gottschalk (see note 83), p. 236.

111. "Documents on the American Tobacco Trade" and Jefferson to Du Pont, October 6, 1787, in Julian P. Boyd, ed., *The Papers of Thomas Jefferson* (Princeton, 1950–), XII, 76-93, 211-212.

112. *Ibid.*, p. 314 (Jefferson to John Jay, November 3, 1787).

113. Du Pont to M. de Beaumarchais Caron, July 21, 1784, in Winterthur MSS, group 2.

114. Du Pont is listed among the *associés-libres* in the *Calendrier et réglemens du Musée de Paris suivis du Tableau de ceux qui composent cette société* (Paris, 1784), p. 40. On Court de Gébelin, see the *Nouvelle biographie général depuis les temps de plus reculés jusqu' à nos jours* (Paris, 1862-1870), XII, 218.

115. The most important documents are in AAE, M. & D., Angleterre, vol. 65, folios 3-8, 9-21, 24-175vo., 180-195vo., 199-223, 225-234vo., 237-290, 327-340vo., 344-356vo. Boyetet (see note 116, below) identifies Du Pont as the author of the *mémoire* on ff.

9-21, the text of which he prints with his comments thereon. The longest and most important of these *mémoires* (the "Troisième," ff. 24-175vo.) has in the left margin a running summary in Du Pont's hand. Similarly the "Quatrième mémoire" (ff. 180-195vo.) has five corrections in Du Pont's hand and the summary in the left margin of the *mémoire* on ff. 344-356vo. is in his handwriting. Du Pont wrote to Edelsheim, July 7, 1787: "I discussed all the bases and all the agreements of the treaty of commerce with [England] and it was adopted according to my plans. . . ." Erdmannsdörffer, ed., *Politische Correspondenz Karl Friedrichs von Baden*, I, 271.

116. Boyetet, *Recueil de divers mémoires, relatifs au traité de commerce avec l'Angleterre, faits avant, pendant et après cette négociation* (Versailles, 1789), I, 14-15, II, 104-173.

117. In the Public Record Office I have surveyed the despatches to and from Eden in the Chatham Papers (30, 8, 333 and 334) and in FO 27, 19 and 20 (France: Mr. W. Eden, 10 March-30 December 1786). Du Pont is not mentioned by P. de Ségur-Dupeyron in the "Fragments historiques—Négotiation du traité de commerce conclu en 1786 entre la France et l'Angleterre" in his *Histoire des négociations commerciales et maritimes de la France aux XVIIe et XVIIIe siècles considerées dans leurs rapports avec la politique générale* (Paris, 1872-1873), III, 297-655, although he remarks (p. 646): "L'influence de la secte économique des physiocrates dominait évidemment les conseils de Sa Majesté Très-Chrétienne; on sacrifiait le fabricant à l'agriculteur, au lieu de tenir la balance égale."

118. Quoted in E. Levasseur, *Histoire du commerce de la France* (Paris, 1911-1912), I, 535 note.

119. ". . . sur 24 millions de produits anglais figurant à l'importation en 1784, on suppose que 10 à 11 étaient entrés en fraude" (*ibid.*, p. 542). Schelle, *DPdN*, p. 243, suggests that French imports from England amounted to around thirty million livres in value and, hence, that two-thirds of these products escaped customs duties. The fact is that there are no reliable statistics, especially of contraband which would not, of course, pass through official channels.

120. AAE, M. & D., Angleterre, vol. 65, ff. 226-234vo. In 1788 Du Pont printed this *mémoire* in his *Lettre à la chambre du commerce de Normandie*, pp. 94-102.

121. Boyetet, *Recueil*, I, 4.

122. These are essentially the conclusions of Camille Bloch, "Le Traité de Commerce de 1786 entre la France & l'Angleterre d'après les papiers de plenipotentiaire anglais" in *Études sur l'histoire économique de la France (1760-1789)* (Paris, 1900), p. 268, and of F. Dumas, *Le Traité de 1786 entre la France et l'Angleterre* (Toulouse, 1904), pp. 43-44.

123. This thesis is well sustained by Léon Cahen, "Une nouvelle interpretation du traité franco-anglais de 1786-1787," *Revue historique*, CLXXXV (1939), 258-270.

124. Lafayette to Washington, Paris, October 26, 1786, *Mémoires, correspondances et manuscripts du Géneral Lafayette*, publiés par sa famille, I (Brussels, 1837), 442; Gottschalk (see note 83), pp. 254-255.

125. *Traité de navigation et de commerce entre la France et la Grande Bretagne, conclu à Versailles le 26 septembre 1786* (Paris: de l'imprimerie royale, 1787).

126. E. Levasseur, *Histoire du commerce de la France*, I, 545.

127. There is a large literature on the Treaty of 1786. In addition to the works of Bloch, Dumas, and Cahen previously cited, I have found helpful suggestions in Charles Gomel, *Les Causes financières de la Révolution française* (Paris, 1892-1893), II, 226-236, and in Germain Martin, *Histoire économique et financière (Histoire de la nation française*, ed., Gabriel Hanotaux, X; Paris, 1927), p. 249. In "The Normandy Chamber of Commerce and the Commercial Treaty of 1786," *Economic History Review*, II (1929-1930), 312-313, Henri Sée concluded that "the Treaty might have stimulated French industry"; and Charles Schmidt, "Le Traité de 1786 et la crise ouvrière en France," *Revue historique*, XCVII (1908), 78-94, insisted that other factors than the treaty must be taken into account in understanding the economic crisis.

128. Cf. L. Cahen in *Revue historique,* CLXXXV (1939), 283.

129. Schelle, *DPdN,* p. 248, names Le Coulteux (i.e., the banker and merchant J. B. Le Coulteux de Canteleu, 1749-1818) as the author of the *Observation,* but I cannot discover the basis of his attribution.

130. *Lettre à la chambre du commerce de Normandie; Sur le mémoire qu'elle a publié relativement au traité de commerce avec l'Angleterre* (Rouen et Paris, 1788). In AAE, M. & D., Angleterre, vol. 74, ff. 140, 141-173, the *Lettre* (without the extensive notes of the printed edition) appears in manuscript in the neat hand of an amanuensis and bears the notation "par du Pont de Nemours." The copying must have been done later, since Du Pont did not add "de Nemours" to his name until after his election to the Estates General.

131. *Ibid.,* pp. 90-91.

132. *Ibid.,* p. 77.

IV

1. A. Goodwin, "Calonne, the Assembly of French Notables of 1787 and the Origins of the 'Révolte Nobiliaire,' " *English Historical Review,* LXI (1946), 209; Jean Egret, *La Pré-Révolution française (1787-1788)* (Paris, 1962), p. 5.

2. *Mémoires du Prince de Talleyrand* (ed. Broglie), I, 105.

3. Goodwin (see note 1). Professor Goodwin's two-part article in *English Historical Review,* LXI (1946), 202-234, 329-377, is the most thorough presentation of the revised view of Calonne. His conclusions are brilliantly summarized in his *The French Revolution* (London, 1953), pp. 27-33. The late Professor Frederick L. Nussbaum and some of his students began a profitable reassessment of the period of Calonne's ministry more than thirty years ago. Prior to Goodwin's significant work, Wilma J. Pugh provided an excellent summary in "Calonne's 'New Deal,' " *Journal of Modern History,* XI (1939), 289-312. A more popular presentation in French is Pierre Jolly, *Calonne 1734-1802* (Paris, *c.* 1949), especially pp. 144-189. The two most recent scholarly works are Jean Egret (see note 1), pp. 5-54, and Robert Lacour-Gayet, *Calonne: Financier, Réformateur, Contre-Révolutionnaire, 1734-1802* (Paris, 1963), especially chaps. viii-xi.

4. Du Pont to Count Chreptowicz, December 25, 1803, in G. Schelle edition of the "Lettres inédites . . . ," *Journal des Économistes* (6ᵉ série, XIV, 1907), 16.

5. Goodwin (see note 1), p. 209 n.; Pugh (see note 3), pp. 291, 293, 295; Egret (see note 1), p. 8. Unfortunately, Egret has nothing of importance to contribute to an appreciation of Du Pont's work, since he relies almost entirely upon Schelle. R. Lacour-Gayet (see note 3), p. 112, remarks that Du Pont "devait être plus écouté que consulté."

6. Draft copy, dated April 13, 1787, in EMHL, Winterthur MSS, group 2.

7. "The Revolt of the Nobility": A. Mathiez, *The French Revolution,* tr. Catherine A. Phillips (New York, 1929), pp. 16-29; "The Aristocratic Revolution": Georges Lefebvre, *The Coming of the French Revolution,* tr. R. R. Palmer (New York, 1947), pp. 7-20. See also G. Lefebvre, *The French Revolution from its Origins to 1793,* tr. Elizabeth M. Evanson (London and New York, 1962), pp. 97-101, and bibliography, p. 313. (The last item is a translation of the first three parts of Lefebvre's great work *La Révolution française,* vol. XIII of *Peuples et Civilisations,* ed. L. Halphen and P. Sagnac; Paris, 1951, reprinted with emendations and corrections, 1957).

8. On this point, upon which there is an expanding literature, see especially Robert R. Palmer, *The Age of the Democratic Revolution: A Political History of Europe and America, 1760-1800*; volume I: *The Challenge* (Princeton, 1959) and two books of Jacques Godechot: *La Grande Nation; l'expansion révolutionnaire de la France dans le monde de 1789 à 1799* (Paris, 1956), and *Les Revolutions (1770-1799)* ("Nouvelle Clio," No. 36; Paris, 1963). Palmer's second volume had not appeared at the time of the final revision of this chapter.

9. Cournot, *Souvenirs,* ed. Bottinelli, pp. 9 ff., quoted in Henri Sée, "The Economic and Social Origins of the French Revolution," *Economic History Review,* III (1931), 8.

10. Quoted in Henry Higgs, "Finance," *The Cambridge Modern History,* ed. **A. W.** Ward *et al.,* VIII (New York, 1934), 70. Cf. Edward J. Lowell, *The Eve of the French Revolution* (Boston, 1892), p. 207.

11. *Travels in France during the years 1787, 1788 & 1789,* ed. Constantia Maxwell (Cambridge, 1929), p. 288.

12. Conveniently summarized in Henri Sée, *Economic and Social Conditions in France during the Eighteenth Century,* tr. Edwin H. Zeydel (New York, 1927), pp. 1-7.

13. H. Sée in *Economic History Review,* III (1931), 5.

14. Ph. Sagnac, *La legislation civile de la Révolution française (1789-1804): essai d'histoire sociale* (Paris, 1898), p. ii (preface).

15. H. Sée in *Economic History Review,* III (1931), 3-4.

16. In a letter to the economist J.-B. Say, published in 1817, and reprinted in E. Daire, ed., *Physiocrates,* I, 410.

17. H. Higgs in *Cambridge Modern History,* VIII, 73.

18. *Ibid.* Mathiez says the cost of the war was estimated at two billion livres (*The French Revolution,* p. 19).

19. E. J. Lowell (see note 10), p. 211. A detailed discussion of Necker's reforms can be found in Charles Gomel, *Les causes financières de la Révolution française,* I, 292-538.

20. M. Marion, *Histoire financière de la France,* I, 346.

21. Martin Göhring, *Geschichte der Grossen Revolution,* I: *Sturz des Ancien Regime und Sieg der Revolution* (Tübingen, 1950), p. 246.

22. A. Goodwin in *English Historical Review,* LXI (1946), 228 n. Assemblies of Notables had met earlier in 1558, 1583, 1596, and 1617.

23. G. Lacour-Gayet, *Talleyrand 1754-1838,* I, 79.

24. *Mémoires du Prince de Talleyrand* (ed. Broglie), I, 105-106.

25. Erdmannsdörffer, ed., *Politische Correspondenz Karl Friedrichs von Baden,* I, 271.

26. Du Pont to Ormesson, June 9, 1787 (EMHL, Winterthur MSS, group 8). Unfortunately, the only copy of the draft of this letter is the one made much later by Miss Harriet Austin.

27. *Procès-verbal de l'Assemblée des Notables, tenue à Versailles, en l'année M.DCCLXXXVII* (Paris, 1788), p. 36.

28. [Bachaumont], *Mémoires secrets pour servir à l'histoire de la république des lettres en France, depuis M. DCCC.LXII jusqu'à nos jours* ("à Londres," 1784-1789), XXXIV, 29-30 (January 11, 1787).

29. G. Lefebvre, *Coming of the French Revolution,* p. 27.

30. A. Goodwin, *The French Revolution,* p. 33. The "Liste des notables convoqués" appears in the *Procès-verbal,* pp. 3-27.

31. *Procès-verbal* (1787), p. 73. Calonne's full speech covers pp. 56-81.

32. O. J. G. Welch, *Mirabeau,* pp. 150-152.

33. *Procès-verbal* (1787), p. 113.

34. Some of these summaries are in EMHL, Winterthur MSS, group 2 (special) and in A.N., C 2, liasses 4 and 5.

35. MS copy in EMHL, Winterthur MSS, group 2 (special).

36. Copy in A.N., C 2, liasse 4, and EMHL, Winterthur MSS, group 2 (special); in the Winterthur copy (marked duplicate No. 92) some pages are in the hand of **Miss** Harriet Austin.

37. This copy, found in the Bibliothèque de l'Arsenal (part of MS 3978), has been edited and published by Pierre Renouvin for the Société de l'histoire de la Révolution française: *L'Assemblée de Notables de 1787: la conference du 2 mars* (Paris, 1920).

38. *Ibid.,* pp. 62 ff. Later, in his *Réponse à Necker* (1788), Calonne gave in detail the differences in the accounts. M. Marion, *Histoire financière de la France,* I, appendice II, prints this "tableau de comparaison du Compte Rendu par M. Necker en 1781, et du Compte effectif de la même année (d'après Calonne)."

39. *Ibid.,* pp. 69-70.

40. *Observations présentées au roi par les bureaux de l'assemblée de notables, sur les mémoires remis a l'assemblée ouverte par le roi, à Versailles, le 23 février 1787* (Versailles, 1787), pp. 1-88. This useful volume contains the observations on all proposals submitted to the Assembly before and after Calonne's dismissal.

41. *Procès-verbal* (1787), p. 138.

42. *Ibid.,* pp. 218-226.

43. *Ibid.,* pp. 141-217.

44. *Observations présentées au roi par les bureaux,* p. 200.

45. *Collection des mémoires présentés a l'assemblée des notables; première et seconde division* (Versailles, 1787).

46. Bachaumont, *Mémoires secrets,* XXXIV, 317 (3 avril).

47. *Collection des mémoires,* p. viii.

48. Bachaumont, XXXIV, 318.

49. *Ibid.,* XXXV, 13-14 (22 avril 1787); *Procès-verbal* (1787), p. 262.

50. Bachaumont, XXXV, 8-9 (20 avril 1787).

51. *Mémoires* (ed. Broglie), I, 107.

52. Du Pont to Edelsheim, July 11, 1787, Erdmannsdörffer, *Politische Correspondenz,* I, 270.

53. *Procès-verbal* (1787), pp. 270-289.

54. *Observations présentées au roi par les bureaux,* pp. 303-352 (first bureau of Monsieur). EMHL, Winterthur MSS, group 2 (special) has a MS book of accounts submitted to the second bureau of the Comte d'Artois, which Du Pont served as Secretary.

55. *Ibid.,* pp. 352-362.

56. *Ibid.,* pp. 397-402 (second bureau of Artois).

57. *Procès-verbal* (1787), pp. 289-290; Bachaumont, XXXV, 81.

58. Du Pont to Edelsheim, July 11, 1787, Erdmannsdörffer, *Politische Correspondenz,* I, 271.

59. Copies of these documents are in EMHL, Winterthur MSS, group 2 (special).

60. *Observations présentées au roi par les bureaux,* p. 430.

61. Erdmannsdörffer, *Politische Correspondenz,* I, 273. These remarks are also quoted by Goodwin in *English Historical Review,* LXI (1946), 369-370, with a keen appreciation of their significance.

62. Of the 696 pages of the *Observations présentées au roi par les bureaux,* 398 are given over to a consideration of the fourth division of *mémoires,* but this consideration was, as is clearly stated, an "examination of the financial situation."

63. *Mémoires . . . du Général Lafayette,* I, 455; Gottschalk, *Lafayette Between the American and the French Revolution,* pp. 314-315. For a less favorable view of Lafayette's conduct, see Jean Egret, "La Fayette dans la première Assemblée des Notables," *Annales historiques de la Révolution française,* XXIV (1952), 1-31.

64. *Mémoires,* I, 455-459; Gottschalk, pp. 315-318.

65. Erdmannsdörffer, *Politische Correspondenz,* I, 268.

66. *Mémoires,* I, 459.

67. C. Bloch, "Les assemblées municipales de 1787; leur caractère économique; leur fonctionnement" in *Études sur l'histoire économique de la France,* pp. 119-156, esp. p. 152.

68. Quoted in Gomel, *Les Causes financières de la Révolution française,* II, 502.

69. *Procès-verbal de l'Assemblée de Notables tenue à Versailles en l'année 1788* (Paris, 1789), p. 1.

70. *Ibid.,* p. 39.

71. Du Pont to his son Victor, October 21, 1788, EMHL, Winterthur MSS, group 2, translated by B. G. du Pont, *DPdN,* I, 149-150.

72. *Ibid.,* p. 150.

73. Du Pont to Edelsheim, July 11, 1787; Erdmannsdörffer, *Politische Correspondenz,* I, 276.

74. Du Pont refers, of course, to Necker's position as Director General of Finances (1776-1781) and errs in calling him a Minister, an honor refused to him at that time.

75. Translation of B. G. du Pont, *DPdN*, I, 150-151; original dated October 21, 1788, in EMHL, Winterthur MSS, group 2.

76. Boyd, ed., *Papers of Jefferson*, XII, 213.

77. Du Pont to Victor, February 21, 1789, EMHL, Winterthur MSS, group 2; Du Pont to Eleuthère Irénée, December 1, 1788, *ibid.*, and translated by B. G. du Pont, *Life of Eleuthère Irénée du Pont from Contemporary Correspondence*, I, 107.

78. R. Dujarric de la Rivière, *E.-I. Du Pont de Nemours élève de Lavoisier* (Paris, c. 1954), p. 157; Du Pont to Victor, February 21, 1789, EMHL, Winterthur MSS, group 2.

79. Letter to Victor, October 21, 1788, in B. G. du Pont, *DPdN*, I, 151.

80. EMHL, Winterthur MSS, group 2 (special).

81. Letter to Victor, October 21, 1788, in B. G. du Pont, *DPdN*, I, 149.

82. For a charming but insignificant vignette of François Robin, who married Poivre in 1766, see Edmond Pilon, "Le Roman de Madame Poivre," *Revue des deux mondes*, 8ᵉ sèrie, XVIII (November 15, 1933), 368-383, which treats of her relationship with the writer Bernardin de Saint-Pierre in 1769-1770.

83. Philadelphie, et se trouve à Paris, chez Moutard, imprimeur-libraire de la Reine, rue des Mathurins, hôtel de Clugny, 1786.

84. *Recueil de pièces concernant l'association de bienfaisance judiciaire fondée en 1787* (Paris, 1788), p. 166.

85. There is in EMHL, Winterthur MSS, group 2 (special) a two-page manuscript, not in Du Pont's hand, headed "Chapitre huitième—De la vie pastorale: troisième état naturel de l'homme; changemens [sic] qu'elle introduit dans le forme de la société; elle n'en apporte aucun dans les droits de ses membres." From a note which she attached to this fragment, it is clear that Miss Harriet Austin once had in her hands the rest of the manuscript. Miss Austin notes that this fragment "is a copy of the last (eighth) chapter of the work . . . with the exception of the last pages—and some slight additions interlined in the original MS." The subject matter of the fragment (pastoral life among Asiatic Tartars) is hardly the topic with which Du Pont planned to end his work. Hence, while it may be part of the last chapter completed, it is not the last chapter which he planned to write.

86. Smyth, *Writings of Benjamin Franklin*, IX, 658-660.

87. Unfortunately, in EMHL, there is only a copy of a translation of Sharp's letter, dated June 8, 1788.

88. EMHL, Winterthur MSS, negative photocopy of letter in Warsaw Archives, dated June 24, 1788.

89. All these manuscripts are in EMHL, Winterthur MSS, group 2 (special). Some are not in Du Pont's hand.

90. Jean Egret, whose article "La seconde Assemblée de Notables (6 novembre-12 decembre 1788)," *Annales historiques de la Révolution française*, XXI (1949), 193-228, is the indispensable study, could count only five commoners among the members (p. 200). More than one-fourth (40 out of 152) of the members had not served in the first Assembly (p. 199). Egret's account in *La Pré-Révolution française* (see note 1), pp. 339 ff., is briefer and less detailed than this article.

91. There were not seven bureaus, as in the first Assembly, because of the "un-availability" of the Duc de Penthièvre, who had presided over the seventh bureau in 1787 (Egret, in *Annales historiques de la Révolution française*, XXI, 199 n.).

92. *Ibid.*, pp. 218-226.

93. *Procès-verbal* (1788), pp. 2-4.

94. *Ibid.*, p. 101.

95. Egret *An. hist. de la Rev. fran.*, XXI, 204, cites in support of this incident the explicit testimony of Lafayette and the indirect testimony of Montmorency-Luxembourg, neither of whom were, however, eyewitnesses, since they were not members of the first bureau.

96. *Procès-verbal* (1788), pp. 108-109, 149-151, 231-232, 269, 330-333, 424-426. Egret, *An hist. de la Rev. fran.*, XXI, 210, gives specific figures at which I cannot arrive from my own study of the *procès-verbal*.

97. Egret, *An. hist. de la Rev. fran.*, XXI, 214, where the pertinent pages of the *procès-verbal* are cited.

98. *Ibid.*, pp. 215-216.

99. The minutes are in A. N., C 6, liasse 7 and C 7, liasses 3 and 4 and in EMHL, Winterthur MSS, group 2 (special).

100. Gottschalk can only speculate on the opinions which Lafayette may have expressed (*Lafayette Between the American and the French Revolution*, pp. 414-415).

101. A. Brette, ed., *Recueil de documents relatifs à la convocation des états généraux de 1789* (Paris, 1894-1915), I, 37.

102. Quoted in Gottschalk (see note 100), p. 420.

103. The most complete list of the membership is in André Bouton, *Les Francs-Maçons Manceaux et la Révolution française (1741-1815)* (Le Mans, 1958), pp. 126-128. See also Egret, *La Pré-Révolution française*, pp. 326-330.

104. G. Lacour-Gayet, *Talleyrand 1754-1838* (I, 83), was one of the most recent able scholars to accept this belief.

105. Bouton (see note 103), p. 129 n., rejects this explanation of the name "Thirty" on this very basis; namely, that among the thirty-five members, he can find only twenty-two known Masons.

106. Lacour-Gayet, *Talleyrand*, I, 83, of course, lists Du Pont as a Mason, as did the Abbé Barruel in his notorious *Mémoires pour servir à l'histoire du jacobinisme* (Hambourg, 1799), IV, 362. In 1787, Victor addressed a letter to his father as follows: "Monsieur du Pont, Commissaire Général du Commerce, rue de la Sourdière, Paris," although Du Pont then resided in the cul-de-sac de la Corderie nearby. The Masonic lodge "Les Amis réunis" was located on the Rue de la Sourdière and there are the possibilities (1) that Du Pont may have received his mail there and (2) that, to do so, he would have to have been a Mason. Later on in his life Victor is known to have been a Mason—see Max Dorian, *Du Pont de Nemours: De la poudre au nylon (Histoire des grandes entreprises*, ed. René Sédillot; Paris, c. 1961), p. 27, where there is sound evidence in an otherwise grossly unreliable book (English translation by E. B. Garside; Boston, 1962, p. 51). Several of Du Pont's letters to Victor contain a curious sign (˙/.) following the signature, a device which Du Pont did not normally employ. In an interesting paper, unfortunately yet unpublished, Mr. Victor de Avenell, to whom I am indebted for most of my information on this subject, has traced this device with several variations in the letters of many prominent men known or suspected to have been Free Masons. Mr. de Avenell is convinced that Du Pont, too, was a Mason.

107. See reference to Barruel in note 106 above.

108. The most reasoned account is in Daniel Mornet, *Les Origines intellectuelles de la Révolution française (1715-1787)* (5th ed.; Paris, 1954), pp. 357-387.

109. Georges Michon, *Essai sur l'histoire du parti feuillant Adrien Duport; Correspondance inédite de Barnave en 1792* (Paris, 1924), p. 28.

110. The *Observations* appeared anonymously in 1787, the author being designated only as "a Farmer of New Jersey." The author then and long afterwards was believed to be Governor William Livingston of New Jersey, but the conclusion that Stevens was the actual author must be accepted on the evidence presented by Archibald D. Turnbull, *John Stevens: An American Record* (New York, c. 1928), p. 91.

111. Boyd, ed., *Papers of Thomas Jefferson*, XII, 325-326.

112. *Examen du gouvernement d'Angleterre comparé aux constitutions des États-Unis; où l'on réfute quelques assertions contenues dans l'ouvrage de M. Adams, intitulé: Apologie des Constitution des États-Unis d'Amérique, & dans celui de M. Delolme, intitulé: De la Constitution d'Angleterre; par un cultivateur de New Jersey; ouvrage traduit de l'Anglois, & accompagné de notes* (London and Paris, 1789), pp. 73-75, 178-182.

113. *Ibid.,* pp. 155-170, 179.

114. Cf. Palmer, *Age of the Democratic Revolution,* I, 281, where the brief analysis does not, in my judgment, sufficiently stress the limitations on legislative power.

115. In B. G. du Pont, *DPdN,* I, 149.

116. Brette, *Recueil de documents relatifs à la convocations des états généraux de 1789,* I, lxx (Introduction).

117. Text of the "Instructions" in *Archives parlementaires,* IV, 215-229, partially quoted in L. Cuny, *Le Rôle de Dupont de Nemours en matière fiscale à l'assemblée constituante* (Paris, 1909), pp. 50-52. A manuscript copy of the "Instructions de la paroisse de Chevannes pour ses députés à l'assemblée du bailliage de Nemours" in the Archives departementales de Seine-et-Marne (Mélun) has corrections in Du Pont's hand. Like many of the parish cahiers, it contains the marks of some of the signatories who were unable to write; four of the thirteen signatories of the Chevannes cahier employed marks.

118. Letter of E. I. Du Pont to Victor, quoted in B. G. du Pont, *DPdN,* I, 152.

119. *Arch. parl.,* IV, 229; Mairie de Chevannes (Loiret), Registre des delibérations, 1 mars 1789—photocopy at EMHL.

120. Arch. dep. de Seine-et-Marne, B 260, 261, 266 (folios 14vo.-15)—photocopies at EMHL.

121. The ruins of the old église des Récollets in Nemours where the assembly met still stand.

122. *Procès-verbal de l'assemblée baillivale de Nemours pour la convocation des états-généraux; avec les cahiers de trois ordres* (Paris, 1789), I, 89. The MS *procès-verbal* is in A.N., C 21, dossier 112 and in the Arch. dep. de Seine-et-Marne, B 266; there is also in the latter depository (B 267) a manuscript copy of Du Pont's speech, with several corrections in his hand.

123. *Procès-verbal,* I, 104-107.

124. This tale, probably considerably embellished, was related by Du Pont to Comte Jacques Beugnot, who placed it in his *Mémoires* (ed. by Albert Beugnot, Paris, 1866), I, 119-120, although he inaccurately ascribed the attack on Du Pont to his desire to abolish the parlements. The story is suspect, since Eleuthère Irénée, who accompanied his father to Nemours, does not mention it in a long letter which he wrote to Victor on March 18 (translated in B. G. du Pont, *DPdN,* I, 153-158).

125. *Procès-verbal,* I, 166.

126. See E. I.'s letter to Victor cited in note 124, above.

127. *Procès-verbal,* I, 171-172.

128. E. I.'s letter (note 124) in B. G. du Pont, *DPdN,* I, 155.

129. *Procès-verbal,* I, 183-186; Brette, *Recueil,* III, 333.

130. *Procès-verbal,* I, 191-194.

131. E. I.'s description in his letter to Victor (note 124 above).

132. Brette, *Recueil,* III, 333, says 150 votes; the *Procès-verbal* is followed here.

133. *Procès-verbal,* I, 196-198. Bordier was seated as deputy on January 23, 1790, after Berthier's death. Armand Brette, *Les Constituants; liste des députés et des suppléants élus à l'Assemblée constituante de 1789* (Paris, 1897), p. 277.

134. Arch. dep de Seine-et-Marne, B 267 (August 6, 1789).

135. "Since the election Papa has written in twenty-five days a Cahier that will be a great credit to him." E. I. to Victor (note 124 above).

136. George Lioret, "Du Pont de Nemours député aux états généraux et à l'assemblée constituante," *Annales de la Société historique et archéologique du Gâtinais,* XXXII (1914-1915), 22n. The living descendant of Pierre Denizet is M. Jean Denizet, formerly Chef des Archives de la Marine, who has obtained for EMHL copies of various archival documents bearing upon Du Pont de Nemours.

137. A.N., C 21, dossier 112².

138. *Procès-verbal de l'assemblée baillivale de Nemours . . . ,* I, 199-458; II, 1-290.

139. *Ibid.,* II, 5-12.

140. *Ibid.*, II, 83-84. Punctuation modified.

141. *Ibid.*, II, 286-289.

V

1. *Noms et demeures de MM. les députés à l'Assemblée nationale* (Paris, 1789), p. 123; *Liste, par ordre alphabétique de bailliages et sénéchaussées, de MM. les députés à l'Assemblée nationale* (Paris, 1789), p. 64. According to the latter list, Berthier, Du Pont's fellow-delegate from Nemours, also lodged at this address.

2. The indispensable book for a study of the first days of the Estates General is Georges Lefebvre and Anne Terroine, eds., *Recueil de documents relatifs aux séances des états généraux mai-juin 1789*; tome I: *Les Préliminaires—la séance du 5 mai* (Paris, 1953).

3. *Ibid.*, pp. 67, 73-74.

4. Translation of B. G. du Pont, *DPdN*, I, 161.

5. *Ibid.*

6. Lefebvre and Terroine (see note 2), p. 285.

7. Robert de Crèvecour, ed., *Journal d'Adrien Duquesnoy (député du tiers état de Bar-le-Duc sur l'Assemblée constituante 3 mai 1789–3 avril 1790)* (Paris, 1894), I, 27.

8. *Arch. parl.*, VIII, 66; *Moniteur*, I (no. 5), 27; *Journal d'Adrien Duquesnoy*, I, 68. The fullest account of the sessions of the National Assembly are usually found in the *Archives parlementaires, première série 1787 à 1799*), but this is a later compilation, begun during the Second Empire in the 1860's. Publication was interrupted by the war in 1914 and has only recently been resumed; hence its coverage actually extends only through January 4, 1794, rather than through 1799. It does, of course, cover all the meetings of the National Assembly, but, unfortunately, the first 71 of the 82 volumes in this *première série* must be used with some caution because of editorial carelessness in combining without specification a variety of sources into the coherent accounts of assembly sessions which it contains. As a general rule, the *Archives parlementaires (Arch. parl.)* will be cited only where it can be checked against other sources. The *Moniteur* (i.e., *Gazette nationale ou le moniteur universel*) began publication on November 24, 1789; subsequently, material was compiled and published in a separate volume to cover the sessions prior to that date. This volume must, therefore, be treated with the same reserve accorded to *Arch. parl.*

9. *Arch. parl.*, VIII, 96; A.N., C* I, 3: MS "Procès-verbal des communes et de l'Assemblée nationale du 12 juin au 27 octobre 1789 inclusivement," folios 10vo.-14.

10. *Arch. parl.*, VIII, 106; *Procès-verbal de l'Assemblée nationale imprimé par son ordre* (Paris, 1789-1791), I, 79-80. In this official *procès-verbal* (hereafter called *PV*) individual speakers are seldom named; hence this document is less useful in tracing the remarks of a specific member of the Assembly.

11. *Journal d'Adrien Duquesnoy*, I, 94.

12. Lefebvre and Terroine (see note 2), p. 36.

13. Unfortunately, EMHL has only a later copy of this long letter dated July 17, 1789 (Winterthur MSS, group 8). It is in the hand of Miss Harriet Austin, who must have seen the original draft. Although replete with Du Pont's self-glorification, it is a valuable document for information about Du Pont's activities and opinions in May and June, 1789. One can only hope that the original will some day be recovered and deposited in EMHL.

14. Copy of letter (July 17, 1789) mentioned in note 13 above.

15. *Moniteur*, introductory volume (a later compilation), pp. 36, 37, 41.

16. A.N., C* I, 3 ff. 43-46. Du Pont's name is on the second of the four pages of signatures. See also *PV*, I (no. 3), 10, and copy of letter in note 13 above.

17. Various versions of their remarks are available. The late master of French revolutionary studies, Georges Lefebvre, apparently favored these succinct renditions: Bailly: "The assembled nation cannot receive orders"; Sieyès: "You are today what you

were yesterday"; Mirabeau: "We will not stir from our seats unless forced by bayonets." (Translations of Mrs. Elizabeth M. Evanson in G. Lefebvre, *The French Revolution from its Origins to 1793*, p. 114.)

18. So Lefebvre entitles his chapter covering the events from the end of 1788 to June 27, 1789—*ibid.*, pp. 102-115.

19. *Journal d'Adrien Duquesnoy*, I, 162.

20. Details on this discussion must, unfortunately, be drawn from publications which appeared after the event and which do not indicate the exact sources of information. See *Arch. parl.*, VIII, 190-194; *Moniteur*, I, 62-63; *Journal des débats et des décrets ou récit de ce qui s'est passé aux séances de l'Assemblée nationale depuis 17 juin 1789* ... (Paris, 1791), I, 98-106. The *Journal des débats* first appeared on August 29, 1789. The volume here cited was, like the first volume of the *Moniteur*, put together after the end of the National Assembly in order to cover the period before September 1, 1789. Future citations to this *Journal* will be designated *JDD* and will be by number of separate issue, since, after volume I, pagination is by issue, rather than by volume.

21. A.N., D XLI, I, dossier 1: pièce 20 is a *projet d'arrêté* in Du Pont's hand; pièce 25 (the second report of the committee) contains extensive revisions in his hand.

22. B. G. du Pont's translation from the prospectus of his print shop, written by Du Pont in 1791 (*Life of E. I. Du Pont* ... I, 142-143).

23. The index of the first thirty-two volumes of the *Archives parlementaires* lists no fewer than 179 separate remarks of Du Pont, some of them very long discourses during the two-year session of the Constituent Assembly (*Arch. parl.*, XXXIII, 334 ff.). The less complete coverage of the *Moniteur* shows ninety-two separate remarks, reports, and speeches (*Révolution française: table alphabétique et chronologique du Moniteur de 1787 jusqu' à l'an 8 de la république* [1799] [Paris, 1802], I, 477 ff.). Even the index of the official *procès-verbaux* of the Assembly, in which individuals are rarely identified, lists Du Pont thirty-one times (*Table des matières, des noms de lieux et des noms de personnes contenus dans les procès-verbaux des séances de l'Assemblée constituante, depuis le 5 mai 1789 jusqu'au 30 septembre 1791 inclusivement* [Paris, an XIV], II, 476-477).

24. H. Sée in *Economic History Review*, III (1931), 11-12.

25. Adrien Duquesnoy described Du Pont on September 26, 1789, as "bon citoyen, homme honnête et éclairé, mais égaré par l'esprit de système . . ." (*Journal*, I, 368). This attitude is echoed in some of the ephemeral publications of the time. In *La Galerie des états généraux* (n.p., 1789), Du Pont is described (perhaps by Mirabeau, who contributed to this pamphlet) under the name "Euxin" in these terms: "Des vues patriotiques, des connoissances réelles, un coeur droit, l'habitude de penser, un désintéressement à l'épreuve, & avec tout cela une réputation incomplette! Est-ce l'esprit de système? Est-ce défaut de connoissance des hommes? Est-ce le malheur des circonstances? Je l'ignore. Mais si je ne me défiois par toujours de l'opinion de la multitude, je pencherois pour l'esprit de système" (p. 121). A later anonymous writer was less kind in *Le véritable Portrait de nos législateurs, ou Galerie des tableaux exposés à la vue du public depuis le 5 mai 1789, jusqu'au premier octobre 1791* (Paris, 1792): "Jamais homme n'a plus assidûment ni plus inutilement travaillé à ce qu'il croyoit le bien public, car son imagination étoit une mine inépuisable de ridicules systèmes" (p. 143). The *Almanach de tous les saints de l'Assemblée nationale qui doivent se réunir dans la vallée de Josaphat après la constitution* (Paris, 1790?) stated: "M. Dupont est le chef actuel de la secte des Économistes; il a eu l'honneur de passer, avec le portefeuille des finances, de Ministre en Ministre. Il est de six Comités, ce qui prouve, au moins, un caractère souple" (p. 33). An anonymous sympathizer wrote in the *Almanach des députés à l'Assemblée nationale* (n. p., 1790): "M. Dupont est connu par ses grandes lumières en économie politique. Il est malheureux que l'assemblée nationale refuse de réaliser le système des économistes. Nous aurions bientôt la plus belle des constitutions, le meilleur des gouvernemens possibles appuyés sur des bases solides: le despotism légal & l'évidence" (p. 130).

26. Duquesnoy commented upon him on June 15, 1789: "Ce Dupont est un homme méprisable, vendu aux ministres, aux Polignac; heureusement il est connu" (*Journal*, I, 94). *Le véritable Portrait de nos législateurs* (see note 25 above) exclaimed: "Dupont ne pouvoit être que ce qu'il avoit été toute sa vie, un valet du ministère" (p. 144).

27. *Arch. parl.*, XVI, 38-39; separately published as *Réclamation faite par M. Du Pont, député du bailliage de Nemours, à l'Assemblée nationale, le premier juin 1790* (Paris, [1790]), p. 6. Paraphrasing the description in *La Galerie des états généraux* (see note 25, above), an anonymous author wrote in *La Glaneur véridique de la galerie nationale, ou les contrepinceaux de cette galerie* (n.p., n.d.): "Dupont. Cet homme a des vues patriotiques & quelques connoissances réelles, une habitude de penser, mais trivialement économique, un desintéressement à toutes épreuves, mais non à celle de l'amour propre: il est par conséquent très-incomplet" (p. 6).

28. A.N., C* I, 3 ff. 80vo.-83vo. In the letter cited in note 13 above, he stated that he had earlier served as secretary of the fifth bureau or committee.

29. A.N., C* I, 3 ff. 94-102.

30. Extract from the *procès-verbal* of the electors of Paris (July 13) in *Réimpression de l'ancien Moniteur . . .* (Paris, 1847-1850), I, 551-552.

31. EMHL, Accession 89: draft signed "Du Pont," dated "Le 15. Juillet à 2 heures et quart du matin" and beginning: "M. Dupont Député de Nemours est arrivé à l'hôtel de Ville et a dit que sur une Députation faite à sa majesté par l'assemblée Nationale, hier soir, le Roy a répondu. . . ." There follows the decision to assist in forming a "Garde Bourgeoise" and to order the troops to withdraw from the Champs de Mars.

32. This account rests, unfortunately, solely upon the copy of the letter cited in note 13 above. Du Pont gives no dates for his visit but states that he spent "two days and two nights" in getting to and from Paris. Dénise Aimé [Azam] is the only one of Du Pont's previous biographers to narrate this story (*Du Pont de Nemours Honnête Homme*, pp. 211-212). She gives more details than I have been able to discover. It is regrettable that, since she was writing for the general reader rather than for the scholar, Madame Azam seldom indicated the sources of her information, except for a brief bibliography at the end of her book.

33. Lefebvre, *The French Revolution*, tr. Evanson, pp. 116-127.

34. The master work is Georges Lefebvre, *La Grande Peur de 1789* (Paris, 1932). Lefebvre gives a remarkably concise summary of his conclusions in *The French Revolution*, tr. Evanson, pp. 127-128.

35. For example, A. Mathiez, *The French Revolution*, tr. Phillips, p. 53.

36. *Arch. parl.*, VIII, 344-345; *Moniteur*, I, 140; *JDD*, I, 362-363. *PV.*, II (no. 40 bis), 12-14, summarizes the discussion, but does not name Du Pont.

37. *Moniteur*, I, 146; *JDD*, I, 378-379.

38. A.N., AD I 38, dossier B; AD I 39; *Moniteur*, II, 397. This list differs somewhat from that in Schelle, *DPdN*, p. 284, and does not include *ad hoc* committees like the two already treated: conference with privileged orders and subsistence. In A.N., AD I, 38, dossier B, p. 22, the Dupont listed on the Committee of Public Instruction must have been one of the other two Duponts in the Assembly, since there seems to be no other record that Du Pont de Nemours served on this committee, though its work would have been close to one of his major interests. An undated letter of Victor Du Pont (in B. G. du Pont, *Life of E. I. Du Pont*, I, 135) indicates that the Committee on the National Treasury was not constituted as planned and that his father did not serve on it.

39. The full title is *De la périodicité des assemblées nationales, de leur organisation, de la forme à suivre pour amener les propositions qui pourront y être faites, à devenir des loix; & de la sanction necessaire pour que ces loix soient obligatoires* (Paris, 1789).

40. *Ibid.*, pp. 4, 7, 8-11, 13-22.

41. *Ibid.*, p. 6.

42. *Arch. parl.*, VIII, 376-377; *Moniteur*, I, 161-162; *JDD*, I, 415; *Journal des états généraux convoqués par Louis XVI le 27 avril 1789; ouvrage accueilli & très interes-*

sant où se trouvent toutes les motions, délibérations, discours, & opérations de l'assemblée, séance par séance (Paris, 1789-1790), II, 474-475. The last publication (hereafter *JEG*) began publication on June 1, 1789. *PV.*, II (no. 46), 1-5, mentions no names.

43. *Arch. parl.*, XI, 667-669; *JDD*, no. 182, pp. 6-7; *JEG*, VIII, 457-459; *PV*, XIII (no. 209), 3 ff., indicates an animated debate, but gives no names.

44. *Arch. parl.*, XVII, 81. Du Pont repeated these views in a letter to his sons, dated August 1, 1790 (B. G. du Pont, *Life of E. I. du Pont*, I, 133-134).

45. G. Lioret, *Annales de la Société historique . . . du Gâtinais*, XXXII (1914-1915), 42.

46. *Arch. parl.*, XVIII, 634-635; *Moniteur*, III, 1036; *PV*, XXIX (no. 404) for the decree adopted. The *projet de décret* (September 7, 1790), signed "Du Pont de Nemours" is in A.N., C 44, dossier 407, pièce 55.

47. *Arch. parl.*, XVII, 578-580 (August 3, 1790), XXV, 700 (May 10, 1791); *Moniteur*, III, 890, 893-894, IV, 544.

48. *Arch. parl.*, VIII, 573 ff.,; *Moniteur*, I, 216 f.; *JDD*, no. 10, p. 89.

49. Translated by B. G. du Pont, *DPdN*, I, 172-173.

50. *Arch. parl.*, IX, 24; *Moniteur*, I, 243; *JDD*, no. 27, p. 3. The constitutional articles finally adopted omitted specific reference to the Spanish Bourbons. Cf. *PV*, IV (no. 77), 8-9, or J. B. Duvergier, ed., *Collection complète des lois, décrets, ordonnances, règlemens, avis du conseil-d'état . . . (de 1788 à 1830 inclusivement, par ordre chronologique) . . .* (Paris, 1834-37), III, 245. The last reference will hereafter be cited as Duvergier. Chap. ii, section i, articles 1 and 2 of the completed constitution of 1791 are the articles in question.

51. *Arch. parl.*, XVII, 15; *Moniteur*, III, 787-788; *JEG*, XIII, 269-270; *PV*, XXIV (no. 344), 11-12, with no mention of Du Pont.

52. *Arch. parl.*, XV, 516; *Moniteur*, II, 550.

53. *Arch. parl.*, XV, 519; *Moniteur*, II, 550.

54. *Opinion de Du Pont, député de Nemours . . . sur l'exercice du droit de la guerre et de la paix* (Paris, 1790). The speech is given in full in *Arch. parl.*, XV, 586-589, but only in summary in the *Moniteur*, II, 567, *JDD*, no. 282, p. 10, and *JEG*, XI, 422-424.

55. *Le Pacte de famille et les conventions subsequentes, entre la France & l'Espagne; avec des observations sur chaque article* (Paris, 1790). Du Pont's pamphlet is valuable for a study of the Compact, since it includes not only the Compact itself, with observations on each article, but the subsequent agreements (again with comments) on interpretation of specific parts of the Compact. (These agreements were drawn up in Conventions dated January 2, 1768, December 27, 1774, and December 24, 1786.)

56. Chap. iii, sec. i, articles 2-3 (Duvergier, III, 248).

57. *Liste des députés plus noirs que les noirs, qui ont quitté la séance au moment de l'appel nominal, sur la question des ministres; avec ceux qui ont opiné pour et contre* ([Paris], 1790), p. 7. This pamphlet is essentially a propaganda piece against the Society of 1789; after the 163 "noms des fuyards" appears the remark "presque tous ces Membres sont du Club de 89" (p. 8). See also the *avertissement* to Du Pont's printed speech cited in note 58.

58. *Principes constitutionnels, relativement au renvoir & à la nomination des ministres; discours prononcé à la Société des Amis de la Liberté & de la Constitution de 1789 dans leur séance du 20 octobre 1790* (Paris, 1790). The complete text is in *Arch. parl.*, XIX, 737-740.

59. *Moniteur*, I, 313; *JEG*, V, 149-150; *PV*, VI (no. 105), 10-12, gives only the decree under discussion.

60. *Arch. parl.*, IX, 597; *Moniteur*, I, 324; *JEG*, V, 241-242; *PV*, VI (no. 110), 6-9, for decree as passed.

61. *Memoires . . . du Général Lafayette*, II, 250 note—from a note found in Lafayette's papers. Du Pont later admitted that he was one of a small group calling for the Republic at this time (Letter to Garat, December 28, 1794; EMHL, Winterthur MSS, group 2).

62. *Liste des députés amis de la liste civile, qui ont formé le projet de donner l'absolution au pouvoir exécutif, contre le voeu de la nation* (n.p., 1791), p. 4, where Dupont de Némour [*sic*] is listed among the 274 names. (Copy in British Museum FR 119/1-51 26.)

63. *Arch. parl.*, XXIX, 267-268; *Moniteur*, V, 915.

64. *Ibid.*

65. *Arch. parl.*, XXIX, 256-257; *Moniteur*, V, 911.

66. *Arch. parl.*, XXX, 168-169; *Moniteur*, V, 1028.

67. *Arch. parl.*, XXIX, 294, 300, 378; XXX, 141; *Moniteur*, V, 932, 1025.

68. *L'Historien* (Du Pont's paper), 1 frimaire, an IV, p. 12, quoted in A. Aulard, *The French Revolution: A Political History, 1789-1804*, tr. Bernard Miall (London, 1910), I, 170 n. There is an earlier reference to this statement in a rare book of the *Correspondance inédite* of the important geologist Déodat Guy Silvain Trancrède Gratet de Dolomieu (1750-1801), who first studied the mineral later known as dolomite. M. Jean Denizet discovered a copy of this book in the library of the Jardin des Plantes in Paris. Letter CI (addressed to M. le Ch^r de Fay at Malta and dated Paris, 30 janvier 1792) contains (p. 32) this form of the statement: "Ils étaient pressés et par la voix publique et par ceux qui devaient leur succéder, *ils ont donc,* comme me le disait, il y a deux jours, Mr Dupont de Nemours, *appliqué une broderie monarchique sur un fond républicain, et ils étaient tellement pressés par les circonstances que souvent l'aiguille a déchiré l'étoffe.*"

69. *Arch. parl.*, IX, 691-695; *Moniteur*, I, 343-344; *JEG*, V, 364-365; *PV*, VI (no. 117), 2 ff., has only the proposals of the committee then discussed (November 5, 1789).

70. *Arch. parl.*, XI, 602-609; *Moniteur*, II, 188—for long committee report regarding a general decree on the division of the kingdom, presented February 13 and 15, 1790 (*PV*, XIII, no. 203, pp. 4-7, has only the decree, while *JDD*, no. 175, pp. 5-7, and *JEG*, VIII, 363-364, state that Du Pont merely substituted for Gossin in delivering the report). According to *Arch. parl.*, Du Pont presented several specific decrees for the establishment and subdivision of separate districts: Bar-le-Duc, January 30, 1790 (XI, 427), Albigeois, February 5, 1790 (XI, 437), Beauvoisis, February 7, 1790 (XI, 438). Other compilations give these minor decrees without mentioning Du Pont: Bar-le-Duc (*PV*, XII, no. 188, pp. 1-4; *JDD*, no. 160, pp. 1-2; *JEG*, VIII, 134-136); Albigeois (*PV*, XII, no. 193, pp. 10-11; *JDD*, no. 166, p. 6; *JEG*, VIII, 232-233); Beauvoisis (*PV*, XIII, no. 195, pp. 4-5; *JDD*, no. 169, pp. 3-4; *JEG*, VIII, 258-259).

71. B. G. du Pont, ed., *Life of E. I. du Pont*, I, 124-125. (In this letter Du Pont announces the sudden death of his colleague Berthier.)

72. G. Schelle, *DPdN*, p. 284. From available evidence, I cannot myself determine how any reasonable statistical estimate of the extent of Du Pont's work in this matter can be made. Schelle's estimate must have been a personal guess.

73. A.N., C* I, 28-44 (MS *procès-verbal* covering April 7 to September 16, 1791).

74. Fernand Gerbaux and Charles Schmidt, eds., *Procès-verbaux des comités d'agriculture et de commerce de la Constituante de la Legislative et de la Convention (Collection de documents inédits sur l'histoire économique de la Révolution française*, Paris, 1906), I, vi (editors' introduction).

75. *Ibid.*, I, vii.

76. At EMHL there are photocopies of the MS "Minute du registre" of the committee meetings in which Du Pont participated, obtained from A.N., AF I, 9-12. My calculations are, however, based principally upon the *procès-verbaux* as printed by Gerbaux and Schmidt.

77. *Arch. parl.*, XXVI, 381; *Moniteur*, IV, 603 (May 24, 1791).

78. *PV*, LVI (no. 660), 10-11.

79. *Arch. parl.*, XX, 748; *Moniteur*, III, 1368; *PV*, XXXVII (no. 482), 19.

80. *Arch. parl.*, XXIV, 409-410; *Moniteur*, IV, 358. *PV*, L (no. 603), 23 ff., giving no names, indicates that this matter was discussed on March 27, rather than March 28.

81. *Arch. parl.*, XV, 431; *JDD*, no. 270, p. 14.

82. *Arch. parl.*, XXVI, 264; *Moniteur*, IV, 591.

83. *Arch. parl.*, XXVI, 50; *Moniteur*, IV, 558.

84. Duvergier, II, 364.

85. *Arch. parl.*, XXVI, 134; *Moniteur*, IV, 574; no details in *PV*, LV (no. 653), 2.

86. *Arch. parl.*, XXVI, 263-264; *Moniteur*, IV, 591; *PV*, LVI (no. 657), 8, with no names or details.

87. Duvergier, II, 397 (full text, pp. 396-399).

88. Ph. Sagnac, *La Révolution (1789-1792)* (*Histoire de France Contemporaine*, ed. E. Lavisse, I; Paris, 1920), p. 125.

89. *Le Point du Jour ou resultat de ce qui s'est passé la veille à l'Assemblée nationale*, III, 105-106 (September 26, 1789). (The *Point du Jour*, well-known journal of Bertrand Barère, began publication on June 19, 1789.) This item is quoted by B. G. du Pont, *DPdN*, I, 167, and, in slightly different translation, in her *Life of E. I. Du Pont*, I, 117-118.

90. B. G. du Pont, *DPdN*, I, 176, 177.

91. *Arch. parl.*, XVII, 352, 444; *Moniteur*, III, 857.

92. *Arch. parl.*, XVIII, 88; *Moniteur*, III, 946; *JEG*, XIV, 394. For Du Pont's remarks upon assuming the presidency, see also *PV*, XXVII (no. 382), 2-5.

93. *Arch. parl.*, XVIII, 120-123; *Moniteur*, III, 950-951; *JEG*, XIV, 420-427. *PV*, XXVII (no. 382), gives no indication of the question at issue nor of the disorder.

94. *PV*, XXVII (no. 391), 2.

95. Augustin Challamel, *Les Clubs contre-révolutionnaires; cercles, comités, sociétés, salons, réunions, cafés, restaurants et librairies* (*Collection de documents relatifs à l'histoire de Paris pendant la Révolution française*; Paris, 1895), p. 391.

96. Gérard Walter, *Histoire des Jacobins* (Paris, 1946), p. 55; Michon, *Essai sur l'histoire du parti feuillant Adrien Duport*, p. 72.

97. *Journal de la société de 1789*, no. IV (26 juin 1790). The banquet was held on June 17, 1790, with 200 members present.

98. Challamel (see note 95), p. 405.

99. *Journal de la Société de 1789*, no. IV (26 juin 1790), pp. 5-32. The *Considérations* later appeared separately as a pamphlet (n.p., n.d., 32 pp.) with a foreword by the author and was translated into English: *Considerations upon the Political Situations of France, Great Britain, and Spain, at the Present Crisis* (London, 1790).

100. A. Mathiez, *The French Revolution*, pp. 78-79.

VI

1. Quoted in Henry E. Bourne, *The Revolutionary Period in Europe (1763-1815)* (New York, 1914), pp. 125-126.

2. Du Pont's prominence in the field of finance is reflected in the important bibliography of René Stourm—*Bibliographie historique des finances de la France au dix-huitième siècle* (Paris, 1895), where there are thirty-eight references to Du Pont, more than for any other person.

3. See the convenient table in J. M. Thompson, *The French Revolution* (New York, 1945), p. 572.

4. Translation of H. Higgs in *Cambridge Modern History*, VIII, 691; for French text, see Duvergier, I, 23-24.

5. No adequate survey of all the taxes of the ancien régime can be attempted within the limited space of this chapter. For the treatment in the text, the following works have been consulted: H. Higgs, "Finance," *Cambridge Modern History*, VIII, 66-78; F. C. Green, *The Ancien Régime: A Manual of French Institutions and Social Classes* (Edinburgh, 1958), pp. 16-21; E. J. Lowell, *The Eve of the French Revolution* (Boston, 1892), pp. 207-229; R. Stourm, *Les Finances de l'ancien régime et de la Révolution: Origines du système financier actuel* (Paris, 1885), I, 1-123; M. Marion, *Histoire financière de la France*, I, 1-62; M. Marion, *Dictionnaire des institutions de la France aux*

XVII⁰ et XVIII⁰ siècles, passim; E. Boursin and A. Challamel, *Dictionnaire de la Révolution française: institutions, hommes et faits* (Paris, 1893), *passim;* and George T. Matthews, *The Royal General Farms in Eighteenth Century France* (New York, 1958), *passim.*

6. H. Higgs in *Cambridge Modern History,* VIII, 67.

7. E. J. Lowell (see note 5), p. 215; cf. G. T. Matthews (see note 5), pp. 24-27.

8. Quoted in H. Higgs, *Cam. Mod. History,* VIII, 67.

9. *The Confessions of Jean Jacques Rousseau* (Modern Library edition; New York, 1945), Book IV, pp. 169-170.

10. This estimate of Higgs without indication of source (in *Cam. Mod. History,* VIII, 67) is probably too high. The accounts which Necker submitted to the Estates General on May 5, 1789, show a total revenue from *all* direct taxes of only 155,655,000 livres (M. Marion, *Histoire financière de la France,* I, Appendix iii, 468). Attempts to reckon the actual state of public receipts and expenditures are uncertain risks. Marion (*ibid.,* I, 447 ff.) discusses some of the difficulties. In his notable speech on finances on September 24, 1789, later to be treated, Du Pont mentioned the impossibility of achieving an accurate picture of the state of public revenues (*Arch. parl.,* IX, 147 ff.; *Moniteur,* I, 253 ff.; *JDD,* no. 38, p. 6; *JEG,* IV, 175 ff.).

11. I follow here M. Marion, *Dictionnaire des institutions de la France,* p. 70, rather than Matthews (see note 5), p. 22 n., where it is alleged that the *capitation* was first promulgated as a temporary tax in 1699.

12. Higgs in *Cam. Mod. History,* VIII, 69 (see note 10, above).

13. *Procès-verbal de l'assemblée baillivale de Nemours . . . ,* I, 234 ff.

14. M. Marion, *Dictionnaire des institutions de la France,* p. 556.

15. Higgs, *Cam. Mod. History,* VIII, 69.

16. R. Stourm, *Les finances de l'ancien régime et de la Révolution,* I, 295-296; M. Marion, *Histoire financière de la France,* I, 17.

17. Marion, *Dictionnaire des institutions,* p. 234.

18. Helpful brief treatments, while not entirely satisfactory, are those of M. Marion, *Dictionnaire des institutions,* pp. 247-250, and R. Stourm, *Les finances,* I, 303-309; in English, G. T. Matthews, *The Royal General Farms,* pp. 88-116 (the most detailed treatment in brief compass), and Theodore Sands and C. P. Higby, "France and the Salt Tax," *Historian,* XI (1949), 145-165.

19. *Arch. parl.,* IV, 22 f., quoted in part in L. Cuny, *Le rôle de Dupont de Nemours en matière fiscale à l'Assemblée constituante,* pp. 120 ff.

20. For additional detail, see L. Cuny, *ibid.,* pp. 100-117; M. Marion, *Histoire financière,* I, 20-21; M. Marion, *Dictionnaire,* pp. 9-12; G. Matthews, *The Royal General Farms,* pp. 145-165.

21. This judgment was expressed much later in a published letter to the economist J.-B. Say. The letter is partially quoted in L. Cuny (see note 19), pp. 60-70, but may most conveniently be read in full in E. Daire, ed., *Physiocrates,* I, 409 ff.

22. The *procès-verbaux* of the Committee of Finances have been published by Camille Bloch in the *Collection de documents inédits sur l'histoire économique de la Révolution française* (Rennes, 1922-1923).

23. Du Pont replaced the Archbishop of Arles on this committee on February 22, 1790 (*Procès-verbaux du comité des finances de l'Assemblée constituante,* ed. Bloch, pp. xxi, 145).

24. *Journal d'Adrien Duquesnoy* (ed. Crevecoeur), II, 140 (December 6, 1789).

25. *Procès-verbaux du comité des finances,* p. 377.

26. EMHL has photocopies of those sections of the MS *procès-verbaux* where Du Pont is mentioned (from A.N., D VI 17, dossiers 186-195, 198-200, 202-203, 208). I have used principally the printed edition of Bloch.

27. For a brief and superficial sketch of the background of the secularization of church property from the days of John Hus, see, for example, William M. Sloane, *The*

French Revolution and Religious Reform: An Account of Ecclesiastical Legislation and Its Influence on Affairs in France from 1789 to 1804 (New York, 1901), p. 94.

28. A. Mathiez, *The French Revolution,* p. 97.

29. *Arch. parl.,* VIII, 354, 369-370; *JEG,* II, 393, 455-456; cf. Georges Lefebvre, *The Coming of the French Revolution,* tr. R. R. Palmer, pp. 166-167.

30. There is no reliable contemporary account which reports in full exactly what Du Pont said in the Assembly. The speech was ordered to be printed by the Assembly (*Le Point du Jour,* III, 102), but in the printed version Du Pont stated that he could not be certain that he had employed the same expressions found in the pamphlet during his discourse before the Assembly (*Discours prononcé à l'Assemblée nationale . . . sur l'état et les resources des finances,* Versailles, 1789, preface, p. iii). It is obvious, indeed, that Du Pont worked over the speech very carefully, because he includes many emendations in footnotes. This is the version reprinted in *Arch. parl.,* IX, 147-168. The substantial summary in *Moniteur,* I, 253-255, was put together long after the speech. Since *JDD,* no. 38, p. 6, provides little more than a mere mention of the speech, *JEG,* IV, 175-181, seems to be the only contemporary account with an extensive summary. *PV,* V (no. 83), pp. 7-8, gives no indication at all of Du Pont's long discourse, although Necker's speech is announced.

31. *Discours . . . sur l'état et les ressources des finances,* p. 13. I have used throughout the printed version of the speech as the best source for Du Pont's considered opinions, even though it probably differs somewhat from his exact remarks before the Assembly.

32. Webster defines the legal term "usufruct" as "the right of using and enjoying the fruits or profits of an estate or other thing belonging to another, without impairing the substance."

33. Cf. M. Marion, *Histoire financière,* II, 42.

34. *Discours,* pp. 133-146.

35. Du Pont's most recent biographer, Pierre Jolly, insists that Du Pont deserves more than mere mention (*Du Pont de Nemours: Soldat de la Liberté,* pp. 99-100).

36. *Discours,* p. 132.

37. Duvergier, I, 55; *Moniteur,* I, 332-335.

38. H. Pigeonneau and A. de Foville, *L'Administration de l'agriculture au contrôle général des finances (1785-1787),* pp. 224-231.

39. *Procès-verbal de l'assemblée baillivale de Nemours,* II, 169-186.

40. *Arch. parl.,* XII, 209; *Moniteur,* II, 318; *JDD,* no. 210, p. 4.

41. *Procès-verbaux* (ed. Bloch), p. 179.

42. See above, p. 160.

43. The best brief present-day defense of the assignats is probably in A. Mathiez, *The French Revolution,* pp. 98-108. The most complete study of the entire matter in English is S. E. Harris, *The Assignats* (Cambridge, Mass., 1930).

44. Text in Duvergier, I, 72-73.

45. *Arch. parl.,* XI, 450; *Moniteur,* II, 155; *JDD,* no. 167, p. 8; *JEG,* VIII, 242-245. *PV,* XII (no. 194), 8-9, as usual does not identify Du Pont.

46. *Arch. parl.,* XI, 520.

47. *Journal d'Adrien Duquesnoy* (ed. Crèvecoeur), II, 373.

48. *Arch. parl.,* XIII, 54-55; *Moniteur,* II, 432-433; *JDD,* no. 244, p. 5; *JEG,* X, 311-313 (April 15, 1790).

49. Art. 3: Duvergier, I, 147 (full text, *ibid.,* 147-148).

50. *Arch. parl.,* XIII, 91; *Moniteur,* II, 441; *JDD,* no. 247, p. 10; *JEG,* X, 350; Duvergier, I, 148.

51. *Arch. parl.,* XVII, 384; *JEG,* XIII, 178-179.

52. *Arch. parl.,* XVIII, 684-685, prints the complete brochure, which may also be found in E. Daire, ed., *Physiocrates,* I, 386-388.

53. *Arch. parl.,* XVIII, 684-685; *Moniteur,* III, 1052.

54. This discourse has been translated by Edmond E. Lincoln: *Du Pont de Nemours on the Dangers of Inflation; an Address by Pierre Samuel Du Pont deputy from Nemours made before the National Assembly of France September 25, 1790* (Boston, 1950). Mr. Lincoln's translation is based on the printed version of the speech published by Baudouin, official printer of the National Assembly. *Arch. parl.*, XIX, 224-237, prints in full the text of the Baudouin pamphlet. It is not possible to ascertain if Du Pont added material not included in his speech as delivered before the Assembly. The account of the speech in *Moniteur*, III, 1115-1116, is far from complete when compared with the text of the printed pamphlet. *PV*, XXXI (no. 422), p. 7, makes no mention of Du Pont, merely stating that several members spoke on the liquidation of the public debt.

55. Lincoln (see note 54), p. 18; *Arch. parl.*, XIX, 225.

56. Lincoln (see note 54), p. 31; *Arch. parl.*, XIX, 229.

57. Lincoln (see note 54), p. 32; *Arch. parl.*, XIX, 229.

58. Lincoln (see note 54), p. 41; *Arch. parl.*, XIX, 232.

59. Mirabeau's speech may be found as a separate report in *PV*, XXXI, following no. 422.

60. Du Pont's long discourse on this occasion had also been printed by Baudouin in a pamphlet of forty pages: *Discours . . . sur les banques en général, sur la caisse d'escompte en particulier, et sur le projet du premier ministre des finances, relativement à cette dernière* (Paris, 1789).

61. Duvergier, I, 391; cf. S. E. Harris (see note 43), p. 16.

62. See no. XLII, p. 124, of the *Révolutions de France et de Brabant*, edited by Camille Desmoulins, conveniently reprinted in L. G. W. Legg, ed., *Select Documents Illustrative of the History of the French Revolution: The Constituent Assembly* (Oxford, 1905), I, 277; also the August 26 and 31, 1790, issues of Marat's *Ami du peuple*, where Du Pont is denounced as "esclave, perfide, filou, déserteur, valet-balai d'antichambre ou de cabinet," etc.

63. A brief account of this incident appears in the October 2, 1790, issue of the conservative *Mercure de France*, p. 44, also reprinted in Legg (see note 62), I, 277.

64. *Procès-verbaux du comité des finances* (Bloch ed.), pp. 153, 158.

65. *Arch. Parl.*, XII, 117-135; *PV*, separate report of 86 pages in XIV after no. 226. (Only a summary appears in *Moniteur*, III, 299, with the date February 13—an obvious typographical error—in *JDD*, no. 202, pp. 5, 6, and *JEG*, IX, 250-253.)

66. *Arch. parl.*, XII, 135; *JDD*, no. 202, p. 5; *JEG*, IX, 250.

67. See Duvergier, I, 127-129; *PV*, XV (no. 237), 6-23; *JDD*, no. 217, 1-9; *JEG*, IX, 411-420.

68. For various amendments debated, see *Arch. parl.*, XII, 178, 192, 262; *Moniteur*, II, 308, 311, 327; *PV*, XV (no. 230), 15-17 (no. 231), 4 (no. 235), 13-17; *JDD*, no. 208, pp. 6-7, no. 209, pp. 2-3, no. 214, pp. 6-8; *JEG*, IX, 313-317, 329-334, 395-397.

69. For final decree, as passed between March 14 and March 30, 1790, see Duvergier, I, 126-127.

70. For examples, see *Arch. parl.*, XV, 271-272, 509-510, XVI, 694; *Moniteur*, II, 465, 547, III, 763; *PV*, XIX (no. 268), 10-14, XXIV (no. 339), 3; *JDD*, no. 253, pp. 8-11; *JEG*, X, 445-450.

71. See *Procès-verbaux du comité des finances* (Bloch ed.), pp. 311-312.

72. *Arch. parl.*, XVIII, 51-67; *PV*, XXVII, separate report of eighty pages, just before no. 380. The report is chiefly concerned with the *gabelles* but includes also material on various other indirect duties; long tables on *gabelle* revenue are appended.

73. *Arch. parl.*, XIX, 426-429; *PV*, XXXII, separately after no. 430 (23 pp.); *Moniteur*, III, 1155 (summary and decree only).

74. Text in Duvergier, I, 402-404 (Decree of October 9-26, 1790). The specific duties suppressed (at least in name) were: the *gabelles*, the *droit de la marque des fers*, the *droit de la marque des cuirs*, the *droit de fabrication sur les amidons et sur les huiles*, and the *droits de circulation sur les huiles et savons*.

75. Cf. M. Marion, *Histoire financière*, II, 88.

76. The interested reader may follow the various reports and debates in *Arch. parl.*, XX, 96-105, 114-126; XXIII, 88-107, 197; XXIV, 445-451; XXIX, 193-197. *PV*, XLVI, has two of the reports following no. 558.

77. In his *Lettre à M. Say* in *Examen du livre de M. Malthus* . . . (Philadelphia, 1817), p. 142. The letter to Say is reprinted in E. Daire, ed., *Physiocrates*, I, 412 (for point at issue).

78. *Arch. parl.*, XV, 265-271, for complete speech and proposed decree; summaries in *Moniteur*, II, 465; *JDD*, no. 253, p. 7; *JEG*, X, 444-445. (As usual, *PV*, XIX, no. 268, 7-9, gives no names in summarizing the discussion.)

79. Du Pont so described his efforts in an undated draft of a letter, translated in B. G. du Pont, *DPdN*, I, 170-171.

80. *Moniteur*, II, 353; *JDD*, no. 222, p. 5; *JEG*, IX, 478, for his attack on the *contribution patriotique* as unjust to taxpayers (March 26, 1790); but *Arch. parl.*, XV, 509, for his insistence that, since this tax had been assessed, no one liable for its payment should escape. See also *Arch. parl.*, XXIV, 150; *Moniteur*, IV, 314 (March 17, 1791) for his argument favoring a maximum limit on the surtaxes which could be added to the direct personal and property taxes so as "not to distress the people with excessive imposts . . . momentarily necessary."

81. *Arch. parl.*, XVI, 179-180; *JDD*, no. 305, pp. 15-16; *JEG*, XII, 287 (June 11, 1790); *Arch. parl.*, XXIII, 432 (February 23, 1791).

82. Complete text of plan in *Arch. parl.*, XXII, 47-51, as annex to meeting of January 6, 1791. The plan was presented to the Assembly on July 23, 1791, but was rejected (*Arch. parl.*, XXVIII, 542; *PV*, LXIV, no. 713, 14).

83. *Arch parl.*, XXXI, 616 (*PV*, LXXIII, no. 781, pp. 45-46, has the decree adopted on this matter).

84. *Arch. parl.*, XXII, 512 (January 27, 1791). Du Pont is not identified in *PV*, XLIV (no. 544), 13-14.

85. *Arch. parl.*, XXIII, 738 (March 8, 1791). The proposal may be found, with no details, in *PV*, XLVIII (no. 584), 9.

86. *Arch. parl.*, XXIV, 12 (March 10, 1791). *PV*, XLVIII (no. 586), 9 ff., has only the article on reorganization under discussion.

87. *Arch. parl.*, XXV, 672 (May 9, 1791), XXX, 298 (September 8, 1791). *PV*, LIV (no. 645), 11, and LXVIII (no. 760), 6, gives only a brief and vague summary of the discussion without identifying individuals.

88. *Arch. parl.*, XVIII, 697. For full text of the report, which Du Pont signed along with six other committee members, see also *PV*, XXX, separately bound just before no. 409.

89. Text in Duvergier, II, 34-39, and of "Instruction de l'Assemblée nationale sur le contribution foncière" in *ibid.*, pp. 39-53.

90. See L. Cahen and R. Guyot, *L'œuvre legislative de la Révolution* (Paris, 1913), chapter iii, for the most convenient summary of financial legislation.

91. *Arch. parl.*, XXIV, 92-93; *Moniteur*, IV, 306.

92. *Arch. parl.*, XXVII, 491-502; *PV*, LX (*viime suite du procès-verbal*), 14, and annex of thirty-eight pages. *Moniteur*, IV, 729, merely mentions the address without giving any of the text.

93. Text of decree in Duvergier, II, 151-155, and of "Instruction" in *ibid.*, pp. 155-164.

94. Article vii of decree of March 2, 1791 (text in Duvergier, II, 230-234). Du Pont later asserted that he had vigorously opposed the *patente—Lettre à M. Say* in *Examen du livre de M. Malthus* . . . , p. 142.

95. Cahen and Guyot (see note 90), p. 243.

96. For examples of such assertions see G. Schelle, *DPdN*, *passim*, L. Cuny (see note 19), *passim*, and R. Stourm (see note 5), I, 141-142.

97. See Du Pont's *Lettre à M. Say* in *Examen du livre de M. Malthus* . . . , p. 141, or in E. Daire, ed., *Physiocrates*, I, 410.

VII

1. EMHL, Winterthur MSS, group 4, contains various papers regarding the establishment of Du Pont's first print shop. Only copies of the original lease survive.

2. The prospectus is translated in full by B. G. du Pont in *Life of E. I. du Pont*, I, 141-144.

3. *Ibid.*, I, 170-181.

4. *Ibid.*, I, 184-189, where B. G. du Pont translates the copy or draft of this letter found in EMHL, Longwood MSS, group 7 ("Longwood Blue Volumes," vol. I). There is no way to determine whether or not it was actually sent to Madame Dalmas. All of the letters translated by Mrs. du Pont in her *Life of E. I. du Pont*—and her *DPdN*—are at EMHL, principally in Longwood MSS, group 7, and Winterthur MSS, group 2. Although her translations are not always reliable (mostly because of occasional omissions without indication), I have not found that they impair the accuracy of the factual content of the letters. Since her published volumes may be more easily accessible to the interested reader than the manuscripts at EMHL, I have made reference to them throughout.

5. *Ibid.*, I, 189-195.

6. EMHL, Winterthur MSS, group 4. The list of employees drawn up at this time was required by the decree of September 2, 1792, providing exemption from National Guard service for those engaged in the printing of assignats.

7. B. G. du Pont, *Life of E. I. du Pont*, II, 23. This building no longer stands, having been demolished to make way for the Rue de la Paix joining the Place de l'Opera to the Place Vendôme.

8. I am indebted to the preliminary study of the "Output of the Du Pont Press" (typescript) by Earle E. Coleman, available at EMHL.

9. A. N., F^{17a} 1305, dossier 2, pièce 298. Georges Bourgin published this letter (then in A. N., F^{10} 369) in "Dupont de Nemours imprimeur," *Revue d'histoire des doctrines économiques et sociales* (1911, no. 4).

10. These contracts are in EMHL, Winterthur MSS, group 4. One of September 13, 1792, with "MM. Pierre Didot et Eleuthère Irénée Dupont fils" for the printing of assignats of 15 and 10 sous is in A. N., C 163, dossier 378, pièce 5.

11. Coleman typescript cited in note 8 above.

12. Maurice Tourneux, *Bibliographie de l'histoire de Paris pendant la Révolution française* (Paris, 1890-1913), II, 624.

13. The most complete, and convenient, bibliography of Du Pont's articles in the first five volumes of the *Correspondance patriotique* is in Schelle, *DPdN*, pp. 417-419.

14. *Correspondance patriotique*, II (no. XII), 334-341; separately published as eight-page pamphlet under the title: *Causes très-légitimes de la diversité des opinions, relativement à l'usage que le roi a fait du veto sur le décret qui concernait des émigrans, et sur celui qui regardait les prêtres non-sermentés; observations propres à décider la question et à réunir les esprits.* There does not seem to be a copy of this pamphlet at EMHL. I have used a copy in the British Museum (FR 1119/1-51 47), bound, without title-page, in one of the many volumes of pamphlets pertinent to the French Revolution (marked *Révolution française* 119, Le Roi, vol. IV).

15. *Correspondance patriotique*, II (no. XIII), 397. This article (pp. 381-397) was separately published in January, 1792, under the title *De la position politique de la France; moyen simple d'en écarter tout peril en lui conservant toute sa dignité*.

16. *Ibid.*, III (no. XV), 74-81, and no. XVII, the latter, a letter of Du Pont to M. Monnot, being separately published as an eight-page pamphlet under the title *Observations sur le décret relatif à la guerre* ("27 janvier de l'an IV").

17. *Correspondance patriotique*, V, 329-356; separately published as *Lettre de M. Du Pont aux citoyens constitutionnaires*. See also Georges Michon, *Essai sur l'histoire du parti feuillant Adrien Duport*, p. 392.

18. The *Lettre de M. Du Pont, à M. Pétion* first appeared in the fifth volume of the *Correspondance patriotique* and was then published as a separate pamphlet of nineteen pages, without the preliminary remarks found in the journal.

19. *Lettre . . . à M. Pétion*, 13 avril de l'an IV (1792), p. 13.

20. F. A. Aulard, ed., *La Societé des Jacobins; recueil de documents pour l'histoire du club des Jacobins de Paris (Collection de documents relatifs à l'histoire de Paris pendant la Révolution française*, Paris, 1889-1897), III, 504.

21. *Réponse de Pétion à Du Pont* in A. N., C 199, dossier 160⁴⁴, pièce 42.

22. The second letter also appeared first in volume V of the *Correspondance patriotique* before being separately published as a twenty-one–page pamphlet. The warning is on pp. 18-20 of the pamphlet, the first part of which is devoted to answering the specific attacks made by Pétion in his reply.

23. A. N., C 154, dossier 292³, pièce 3: "Petition presentée à l'assemblée nationale le 24 juin 1792" (printed). Signatures do not appear on this printed copy; there is only the remark at the end—"suivent deux cent quarante pages de signatures."

24. *Moniteur*, VII, 763.

25. Aulard, ed., *La Société des Jacobins*, IV, 78.

26. Du Pont's account is translated in full in B. G. du Pont, *DPdN*, II, 8-12.

27. Schelle, *DPdN*, p. 330, repeats the story with no citation of source. Du Pont does not mention the incident in his own account of the events of August 10, although he states: "Our whole National Guard was sent to escort [the King] across the Garden" (B. G. du Pont, *DPdN*, II, 11).

28. A. N., Minutier central de Paris et du département de la Seine, Registre no. 1627, XII, 754. There is a photocopy of this document in EMHL, accession 293.

29. B. G. du Pont, *DPdN*, II, 13, is incorrect in stating that Du Pont "escaped to Cormeilles, a village not far from Rouen. . . ." EMHL, Longwood MSS, group 7, has a copy of the certificates of residence which Du Pont had to gather in 1793 in order to prove that he had not emigrated; one of these is his "certificat de résidence en la municipalité de Cormeilles-en-Parisis, pendant la fin de Septembre et le mois d'Octobre." The village of Cormeilles "not far from Rouen" (actually forty miles from Rouen) is 100 miles from Paris.

30. F. A. Aulard, ed., *La Société des Jacobins*, V, 300.

31. Du Pont to Felix Faulcon, 23 Floréal 3 (May 12, 1795), in [Gilbert Chinard, ed.], "Lettres de Du Pont de Nemours à Felix Faulcon 12 mai 1795–25 octobre 1802," *French American Review*, I (1948), 176.

32. B. G. du Pont, *Life of E. I. du Pont*, II, 33-34, 37.

33. *Ibid.*, pp. 38-42, 44-47, 55-57, 59-60.

34. André Martin and Gérard Walter, *Catalogue de l'histoire de la Révolution française* (Paris, 1936-43), V, under number 1277, gives Brosselard as the printer. Any doubt that the Du Pont presses printed *Le Républicain français* is removed by consulting the family letters published by B. G. du Pont (*Life of E. I. du Pont*, II, 39 ff.) and the prospectus of Du Pont's later journal *L'Historien*, which is described as replacing the *Républicain français* in the printing house and bookshop of Du Pont de Nemours. Brosselard probably took over the *Républicain* after Du Pont gave it up for *L'Historien*.

35. B. G. du Pont, *Life of E. I. du Pont*, II, 39.

36. *Ibid.*, p. 57. The convent originally housed girls of Huguenot parents; hence the name "New Catholics."

37. *Ibid.*, p. 62.

38. *Ibid.*, pp. 65, 72.

39. *Ibid.*, p. 69.

40. *Ibid.*, pp. 71-72 (March 13, 1793).

41. *Ibid.*, pp. 113-114 (May 26, 1793).

42. Letter of Sophie to Irénée, December 18, 1793; *ibid.*, p. 211.

43. *Ibid.*, pp. 186-281.

44. *Ibid.*, pp. 112-113.

45. *Ibid.*, p. 178.

46. Sophie to Irénée, January 1, 1794; *ibid.*, p. 223.

47. *Ibid.*, pp. 172-173 (August 30, 1793).

48. Irénée to Sophie, April 24, 1794; *ibid.*, p. 270.

49. Postscript to letter from Sophie to Irénée, July 10, 1794; *ibid.*, p. 280.

50. Most of these details are taken from Josephine's *Souvenirs épars de ma jeunesse*, which she began to write in 1795 and finished in 1802. The *Souvenirs* were rewritten in 1815, and this version was published in 1908 in a private edition of only fifty copies by Josephine's great-granddaughter Mrs. Willard Saulsbury. EMHL has a copy of this edition, together with the original manuscript (among Victor's papers in Winterthur MSS) and a typed translation made by Pierre S. du Pont in 1945. The quotation is from Mr. du Pont's translation (p. 157). Mrs. B. G. du Pont gives some excerpts from the *Souvenirs*, in a slightly different translation, in *Life of E. I. du Pont*, II, 156-158, and 259-262.

51. *Souvenirs* (translated by P. S. du Pont), pp. 169-171; B. G. du Pont, *Life of E. I. du Pont*, II, 261-262.

52. *Philosophie de l'univers* (seconde édition corrigée et augmentée; Paris, an iv), pp. 15-36. My notes are based upon the second edition copy inscribed "à Jefferson, Président du Senat des États unis d'Amérique de la part de l'auteur Du Pont (de Nemours)," now in the Library of Congress. There are numerous textual changes in the body of the work after the first edition, although not in the *Oromasis*. The changes and additions do not alter the basic philosophy expressed. EMHL is the only depository which, to my knowledge, has copies of all three editions of the book and a marked copy designed to serve as the basis of a projected fourth edition, which was never published. The Manichean note of the "system of two principles," good and evil, in Du Pont's *Oromasis* is briefly commented upon by Leslie G. Crocker, *An Age of Crisis: Man and World in Eighteenth Century Thought* (Baltimore, 1959), p. 43, where the title of Du Pont's work is incorrectly given as *Philosophie de la nature*. In several other references to Du Pont's *Philosophie*, however, Professor Crocker gives the correct title.

53. *Philosophie de l'univers*, pp. 41-42.

54. *Ibid.*, pp. 57, 60-61.

55. *Ibid.*, pp. 69-71. Du Pont adopted the words "to love and to know" as the motto to be placed under his portrait.

56. *Ibid.*, pp. 76-88.

57. *Ibid.*, pp. 144-145.

58. *Ibid.*, pp. 205 ff.

59. In 1807, Du Pont published twenty such papers under the title *Quelques mémoires sur différens sujets: la pluspart d'histoire naturelle, ou de physique générale et particulière* (Paris, 1807). A second edition, somewhat expanded, was published in 1813.

60. *Ibid.*, p. 267, with footnote: "Ceci a été écrit en 1793 au Bois-des-Fossés."

61. *Vues sur l'éducation nationale par un cultivateur ou moyen de simplifier l'instruction, de la rendre à la fois morale, philosophique, républicaine, civile et militaire, sans déranger les travaux de l'agriculture et des arts aux quels la jeunesse doit concourir* (Paris, an II). Postscript by Du Pont to letter of Sophie to Irénée, July 13, 1794, in B. G. du Pont, *Life of E. I. du Pont*, II, 284.

62. *Vues sur l'education nationale*, pp. 11-20.

63. *Ibid.*, p. 9.

64. *Ibid.*, p. 45.

65. The copy of the order in A. N., F^7 4571, appears to bear the date 25 messidor, *an IV*, instead of *an II*—a circumstance which must be the result of a clerical error. The text of the order is printed in G. Lioret, *Annales de la Société historique et archeologique du Gâtinais*, XXXII (1914), 63, and translated (from Lioret's sketch) by B. G. du Pont, *Life of E. I. du Pont*, II, 292.

66. Years later Victorine, then Madame Bauduy, wrote in one of her notebooks a brief account of her grandfather's arrest and of her mother's courageous action in going to Paris so that she might be of some assistance to the prisoner. B. G. du Pont, *Life of E. I. du Pont*, II, 293-294, translates this account.

67. *Ibid.*, p. 350. For the French text, see Gilbert Chinard, ed., *Un Epilogue du neuf Thermidor: Lettres de Du Pont de Nemours écrites de la prison de la Force 5 Thermidor—8 Fructidor An II* (Paris, 1929), pp. 64-65. The italics are in the original. Alexandre Beauharnais was, of course, the husband of Josephine, who later married Napoleon Bonaparte. The story of Du Pont's imprisonment is reconstructed chiefly from the family correspondence, which gives a clear and consistent account. Certain archival documents present problems which cannot be resolved by checking against the family letters. A. N., F⁷ 4694, pièce 269, is an order by the Committee of General Security granting Du Pont's request that the Commission of Arms, Powders, and Saltpeter give him a rifle with bayonet so that he can continue "to defend the Republic, the security of persons and property." The order is dated 26 Prairial [June], but no year is indicated. It probably concerns Irénée, who was chosen commissioner for the manufacture of saltpeter by the committees of his section of Paris (Irénée to Sophie, January 23, 1794, B. G. du Pont, *Life of E. I. du Pont*, II, 246). The probable year of the order is therefore 1794. A. N., F⁷ 4694, pièce 270, an order of the Committee of General Security, dated Ventôse an II [March, 1794], places seals on Du Pont's print shop and orders him to appear before the Committee. Here again the reference must be to Irénée, who apparently satisfied the committee, because the notation on the order states that Du Pont was dismissed by the Committee and that the seals on the print shop were removed. The watch committee of the Section Le Pelletier was, however, instructed to keep him under observation. A. N., AF* II, 288, "Registre des arrestations," contains under date of 4 avril an II [1794] an order for the searching of the house of Dupont de Nemours at Choisy sur Seine, where he never resided. This order was probably issued in response to a false rumor.

The most difficult problem is A. N., F⁷ 4694, pièce 271, which is an order of the Committee of General Security, dated 7 Thermidor, with no year indicated, but surely 1794, placing "Dupont dit de Nemours" at liberty and removing the seals from his property. The family letters prove that Du Pont was not released from prison until after August 25, though the date of this order would be July 25, 1794, if the assumption about the year is correct. Perhaps this document led Schelle (*DPdN*, p. 340) and Lioret (*Annales de la Société historique . . . du Gâtanais*, XXXII, 63-64) to state that Irénée was already a prisoner in La Force when his father arrived to join him. This circumstance might explain the document as referring to Irénée. But this obvious, and satisfactory, explanation is not in accord with the family letters, which give no indication that Irénée was at this time arrested—as he clearly was later on, in 1797. Indeed there are letters from Du Pont in La Force to Irénée, obviously outside, dated July 24 and 25 (B. G. du Pont, *Life of E. I. du Pont*, II, 300-303).

68. Translation of B. G. du Pont, *Life of E. I. du Pont*, II, 295-296. The French edition of these *mémoires* is Albert Beugnot, ed., *Mémoires du Comte Beugnot ancien ministre (1783-1815)* (Paris, 1866). For references to Du Pont, see I, 245. ff. There is an English translation: Charlotte M. Yonge, ed., *Life and Adventures of Count Beugnot, Minister of State under Napoleon I* (London, 1871). For Du Pont, see I, 218 ff.

69. Translated in B. G. du Pont, *Life of E. I. du Pont*, II, 297-385. The French text has been published in G. Chinard, ed., *Un épilogue du neuf Thermidor*.

70. B. G. du Pont, II, 297; Chinard, p. 21.

71. B. G. du Pont, II, 300; Chinard, p. 23.

72. B. G. du Pont, II, 300; Chinard, p. 24.

73. B. G. du Pont, II, 301-303; Chinard, pp. 26-28.

74. Beugnot, ed., *Mémoires du Comte Beugnot*, I, 275-276.

75. *Ibid.*, pp. 276-277. B. G. du Pont (II, 308-314) translates this part of Beugnot's *Mémoires*.

76. B. G. du Pont, II, 316-317; Chinard, p. 34.

77. Mairie de Chevannes (Loiret), Registre des délibérations, under date of 25 août 1793.

78. B. G. du Pont, II, 320; Chinard, p. 37.

79. B. G. du Pont, II, 330; Chinard, p. 48.

80. B. G. du Pont, II, 335; Chinard, p. 53.

81. B. G. du Pont, II, 342-343; Chinard, pp. 57-58. Italics are in the original.

82. B. G. du Pont, II, 348; Chinard, pp. 63-64.

83. B. G. du Pont, II, 359; Chinard, p. 74.

84. B. G. du Pont, II, 379; Chinard, pp. 92-93.

85. B. G. du Pont, II, 384; Chinard, pp. 97-98.

86. B. G. du Pont, II, 380, 384; Chinard, pp. 93, 98. At EMHL, there is a copy of a warrant authorizing Du Pont's release, dated August 24, with notation, dated September 4, that it had been executed (Winterthur MSS, group 2).

87. B. G. du Pont, *Life of E. I. du Pont*, III, 11 (letter to Irénée, September 4, 1794).

88. *Ibid.*, p. 41.

89. *Ibid.*, p. 44.

90. *Ibid.*, p. 56.

91. *Ibid.*, p. 96.

92. *Ibid.*, p. 116.

93. *Ibid.*, pp. 122-123.

94. A. N., Minutier central de Paris et du département de la Seine, Registre no. 2002 XII 775 (photocopy in EMHL, acquisition 276).

95. Mairie de Chevannes (Loiret), Registres d'état civil, under date 3 Thermidor an 4 (July 21, 1795).

96. The date of the marriage certificate, a copy of which is in EMHL, Winterthur MSS, group 2.

97. B. G. du Pont, *Life of E. I. du Pont*, III, 68-69.

98. *Ibid.*, p. 75.

99. Draft of letter, dated 16 Brumaire [November 6, 1794] (EMHL, Winterthur MSS, group 2).

100. Du Pont wrote to Irénée on December 12 that he was writing another paper in reply to Boissy's questions about foodstuffs (B. G. du Pont, *Life of E. I. du Pont*, III, 125). His letter to Boissy d'Anglas was offered for sale at a Parisian auction on November 8, 1960. The text of the letter here drawn upon is that printed in the catalog of the sale: "Autographes, historiques, litteraires et scientifiques dont la vente aura lieu à Paris, rue Drouot, Hôtel des Commissaires—Priseurs salle no. 9," lot 33.

101. B. G. du Pont, *Life of E. I. du Pont*, III, 123-124, quoting Madame Victor du Pont, *Notre Transplantation en Amerique*.

102. *Ibid.*, III, 95.

103. *Ibid.*, III, 127.

104. The information in the family letters indicates that Du Pont was in Paris by May 5, 1795 (*ibid.*, III, 181).

105. Du Pont to Faulcon, 23 Floréal 3 (May 12, 1795), ed. Chinard in the *French American Review*, I (1948), 177.

106. *Plaidoyer de Lysias, contre les membres des anciens comités de salut public et de sûreté générale* (Paris, an III).

107. *Du pouvoir législatif et du pouvoir exécutif, convenables à la république française* (Paris, an III), 133 pp.

108. *Ibid.*, pp. 124-127.

109. *Ibid.*, pp. 125-126.

110. *Ibid.*, pp. 127-128.

111. *Ibid.*, p. 8.

112. *Ibid.*, pp. 19, 116-117.

113. *Ibid.*, pp. 26-37.

114. *Ibid.*, pp. 38-41, 118.

115. *Observations sur la constitution proposé par la commission des onze, et sur la position actuelle de la France* (Paris, an III), 60 pp.

116. *Ibid.*, p. 4.

117. *Ibid.*, pp. 57-58.

118. B. G. du Pont, *Life of E. I. du Pont*, III, 242-243. (I have altered Mrs. du Pont's translation of "Conseil des Anciens" from "Council of Ancients" to "Council of Elders.")

119. See above, p. 152.

120. Auguste Kuscinski, *Les Députés au corps législatif conseil des cinq-cents, conseil des anciens de l'an IV à l'an VII; listes, tableaux et lois* (Société de l'histoire de la Révolution française; Paris, 1905), p. 60.

121. *Ibid.*, p. 101; Irénée to Sophie, October 28, 1795 (B. G. du Pont, *Life of E. I. du Pont*, III, 257).

VIII

1. The most substantial defenses of the Directory will be found in the writings of the late Raymond Guyot—see, especially, the section (pp. 285-464) which he prepared for G. Lefebvre, R. Guyot, and P. Sagnac, *La Révolution française* (Halphen and Sagnac, eds., *Peuples et civilisations*, XIII; Paris, 1930) and his *Le Directoire et la paix de l'Europe* (Paris, 1911). Guyot's general interpretation is retained in the revised edition of *La Révolution française* by the late Georges Lefebvre (3rd ed. revised, Paris, 1957). A succinct presentation in English of the revised estimate of the Directory is provided by Crane Brinton, *A Decade of Revolution 1789-1799* (W. L. Langer, ed., *The Rise of Modern Europe*, XII; New York, 1934), pp. 212-231.

2. Irénée to Sophie, October 28, 1795 (B. G. du Pont, *Life of E. I. du Pont*, III, 256-257).

3. Irénée to Sophie, September 25, 1795 (*ibid.*, pp. 248-249).

4. Thus, for example, Georges Lefebvre, *Le Directoire* (Paris, 1946), p. 21, and Albert Mathiez, *Le Directoire du 11 brumaire an IV au 18 fructidor an V* (publié d'apres les manuscrits de l'auteur par Jacques Godechot; Paris, 1934), pp. 246, 251-252. I have found no evidence to support Mathiez' assertions that Du Pont was active in royalist meetings and plots.

5. *L'Historien*, II (no. 50), 157.

6. These committee assignments are too numerous, and too unimportant, to be listed. They may be traced in the parts of the *procès-verbal* of the Council of Elders available at EMHL, either in photocopies of the MS in A. N. (C 485, 489, 490, 492, 493, 494, 496, 497, 501, 514, 516) or in separate copies of the printed *procès-verbal* of various sessions of the Council during the period of Du Pont's service (1795-1797).

7. *Moniteur*, XIII, 1231; A. N., C 490, CIII B 254 (1 Thermidor an IV)—to avoid confusion, dates will not be given in the Republican calendar unless they have historical significance.

8. *Moniteur*, XV, 1216; A. N., C 516, CIV B 140 (1 Thermidor an V).

9. *Moniteur*, XV, issues of 2 Thermidor (July 20), 7 Thermidor (July 25). No further difficulties are apparent in the *Moniteur* accounts from the latter date to the end of Du Pont's term on 1 Fructidor (August 18). The *procès-verbal* gives no indication of any difficulties (A. N., C 516, CIV B 140, 141, 142).

10. Quoted in B. G. du Pont, *DPdN*, II, 36.

11. *Moniteur*, XII, 178; *L'Historien*, I, xxvi-xxvii.

12. P. J. B. Buchez and P. C. Roux, *Histoire parlementaire de la Révolution française ou Journal des assemblées nationales depuis 1789 jusqu'en 1815* (Paris, 1834-1838), XXXVII, 103-104.

13. *L'Historien*, I, xxxii-xxxiii; quoted by A. Mathiez, *Le Directoire*, pp. 37-38; cf. also G. Schelle, *DPdN*, pp. 346-347.

14. Buchez and Roux, *Histoire parlementaire*, XXXVII, 104.

15. *Moniteur*, XII, 227.

16. *Moniteur*, XII, 235-236; *L'Historien*, I, cliv-clviii.

17. *Moniteur*, XII, 243; Mathiez, *Le Directoire*, p. 77; Schelle, *DPdN*, p. 348.

18. Du Pont does not mention Horace, but must have had in mind Horace's verse (in the *Ars poetica*): *Scribendi recte sapere principium est et fons* (*Moniteur*, XII, 240; *L'Historien*, I, ccii).

19. Buchez and Roux, *Histoire parlementaire*, XXXVII, 111-112, where Du Pont is called a "concealed royalist."

20. Since Du Pont's opposition was often on minor points, a full recital of his efforts to restrict the actions of the Directory and the majority in the Councils would be rather burdensome. See, for example, his argument that the Directory had violated the Constitution by citing improper authority for replacing two members of the Council of Elders (Merlin de Douai and Charles Delacroix), who had been named to the Ministry (*Moniteur*, XII, 191; *L'Historien*, I, lxxvi-lxxvii—November 6, 1795); his protest against the alleged urgency and unconstitutional nature of a proposal to name commissioners to supervise the operations of the Treasury (*Moniteur*, XII, 270; *L'Historien*, I, no. 5, pp. 77-78—November 24, 1795); his vigorous objection to the nomination by the Directory of officials to local administrative posts not yet filled by election (*Moniteur*, XII, 366; *L'Historien*, I, no. 30, pp. 475-480—December 16, 1795); his attempt to overturn the results of the elections to choose representatives in French Guiana because he believed the elections to have been illegally controlled by the Directory (*Moniteur*, XIV, 340—December 15, 1796). Occasionally, he was successful. On June 2 and 3, 1796, for example, he induced the Council of Elders to reject a proposal to fill vacancies in the *Corps Législatif* in a manner which he declared unconstitutional (*Moniteur*, XIII, 1036-1038, 1044).

21. Letter dated 16 Ventôse an IV (March 6, 1796), printed in Raymond Guyot, "Du Pont de Nemours et Napoléon," *Foreign Study Notes*, I (no. 3: April-July, 1930), 74; also quoted by Jeanine Dubuisson-Bertin, "Du Pont de Nemours et Napoléon" in *Institut Napoléon: Recueil de travaux et documents* (Paris, 1946), p. 56. The letter was first published in *Révolution française*, XXXV (1898), 376.

22. Letter signed "Miles" in *L'Historien*, V (no. 199), 288-290. In *L'Historien*, IV (no. 150), 244, Du Pont assumed legal responsibility as author or guarantor for all anonymous articles, for those signed with initials, and for those signed with "noms de fantaisie."

23. *L'Historien*, XVI (no. 608), 17. The note was signed "P. N."

24. *Moniteur*, XII, 275 (November 25, 1795); *L'Historien*, I (no. 8), 122-125. Du Pont's attack on the proposal was more extensive than is here indicated, where only one of the seven counts which he brought against it is considered.

25. *Moniteur*, XII, 538, 540 (January 29, 30, 1796); *L'Historien*, II, 483-485, 498-503. Three weeks later, Du Pont replied in *L'Historien* (III, 6-7) to a letter received from a correspondent named Faure that he had found among "les patriots de Montélimart," who had signed the address, the names of eighteen of the twenty-two men accused of having assassinated Faure's brother. These men, he asserted, had a very bad reputation in their community.

26. *Moniteur*, XII, 540.

27. Summary of law in Buchez and Roux, *Histoire parlementaire*, XXVII, 88-89

28. *Moniteur*, XIV, 246-247. Du Pont's speech was printed by order of the Council: *Opinion de Du Pont (de Nemours), sur la résolution relative à la loi du 3 Brumaire; séance du 27 Brumaire, an V* (Paris, an V [1796]).

29. *Moniteur*, XII, 523-524, 527.

30. *Moniteur*, XIII, 1342 (August 16, 1796).

31. Duvergier, IX, 148-149.

32. *Moniteur*, XV, 1388-1389, 1394 (August 28, 1797). Du Pont's speech was separately printed: Corps Législatif, Conseil des Anciens, *Opinion de Du Pont (de*

Nemours), sur le résolution du 19 Messidor, relative aux fugitifs du Haut & du Bas-Rhin; séance du 11 Fructidor (Paris, an V [1797]).

33. A. N., C 485 CIII B 169; *L'Historien*, II, 343.

34. *L'Historien*, II, 330.

35. *Moniteur*, XIV, 496 (January 21, 1797).

36. Schelle, *DPdN*, p. 349, calls Du Pont's modification merely "a new sarcasm," but he does not cover the incident fully.

37. *Moniteur*, XIII, 1172.

38. *Ibid.*, p. 732.

39. *Ibid.*, p. 851.

40. *Moniteur*, XV, 1065; also separately: *Opinion de Du Pont (de Nemours), sur l'imprimerie de la république; séance du 19 Prairial, an V* (Paris, an V [1797]).

41. *Moniteur*, XIV, 434-435; also separately: *Opinion de Du Pont (de Nemours), sur la résolution relative aux canaux d'Orléans et de Loing; séance du 15 Nivôse* (Paris, an V [1797]). The quotation is on page 6 of the pamphlet.

42. *Moniteur*, XIII, 1207-1208 (July 15, 1796).

43. *Moniteur*, XIV, 687, 715-717 (March 8 and 14, 1797); also separately: *Opinion de Du Pont (de Nemours), sur la contrainte par corps; séance du 24 Ventôse, an 5* (Paris, an V [1797]).

44. *Moniteur*, XV, 840-842 (April 13, 1797); also separately: *Opinion . . . sur les projets de loterie & sur l'état des revenus ordinaires de la République; séance du 24 Germinal, an 5* (Paris, an 5 [1797]).

45. *Moniteur*, XIV, 658 (February 28, 1797); separately published: *Opinion . . . sur le projet d'un droit de passe; séance du 9 Ventôse, an V* (Paris, an 5 [1797]).

46. *Moniteur*, XV, 1162 (June 30, 1797); *Opinion . . . sur les postes* (Paris, n. d.).

47. *Moniteur*, XV, 1045-1046; *Rapport fait par Dupont (de Nemours), au nom d'une commission speciale, sur l'organisation & les dépenses de la trésorerie nationale; séance du 17 Prairial, an V* (Paris, an V [1797]); *Opinion . . . sur la résolution du premier Messidor, relative à l'urgence des paimens, & aux négociations à faire par la trésorerie* (Paris, an V [1797]).

48. *Moniteur*, XV, 1405; *Rapport . . . sur la résolution aux dépenses des relations exterieures; séance du 15 Fructidor, an V* (Paris, an V [1797]).

49. S. Harris, *The Assignats*, p. 46, paraphrasing Du Pont's speech of December 10, 1795.

50. H. E. Bourne, *The Revolutionary Period in Europe*, p. 227. For a brief discussion of the financial chaos faced by the Directory, see M. Marion, *Histoire financière de la France*, III, 383-393.

51. Details of the plan can be found most accurately in M. Marion, *Histoire financière de la France*, III, 412-414.

52. *Moniteur*, XII, 341-342 (December 10, 1795); *L'Historien*, I (nos. 22-23), 358-360, 363-368; Schelle, *DPdN*, pp. 350-353.

53. *Moniteur*, XIII, 1244.

54. *Moniteur*, XV, 1042.

55. *Moniteur*, XV, 1147-1148.

56. *L'Historien*, I (no. 35—issue of 5 Nivôse an IV—December 27, 1795). M. Marion, *Histoire financière de la France*, III, 415-416, mentions this article.

57. Text of law in Duvergier, IX, 63-65.

58. *Moniteur*, XIII, 1396.

59. *Ibid.*, p. 726, 839 (March 16 and April 15, 1796).

60. *Moniteur*, XII, 322 (December 4, 1795).

61. *Ibid.*, p. 613 (February 17, 1796).

62. *Ibid.*, p. 636 (February 23, 1796).

63. *Moniteur*, XV, 1111 (June 22, 1797).

64. *Ibid.*, pp. 1403-1404 (September 1, 1797); also separately: *Opinion de Dupont (de Nemours) sur la première resolution du 19 Messidor, relative aux transactions; séance du 15 Fructidor, an V* (Paris, an V [1797]).

65. *Moniteur*, XII, 369; XIII, 875, 1303-1304 (speeches of Du Pont on December 17, 1795, April 23 and August 5, 1796).

66. *Moniteur*, XII, 369.

67. *Moniteur*, XIII, 1303-1304 (August 5, 1796); Duvergier, IX, 134-136 (law of 19 Thermidor an IV—August 6, 1796).

68. *Moniteur*, XIV, 263 (committee report of November 23, 1796, delivered by Jean-Baptiste Créniere).

69. *Moniteur*, XV, 1268.

70. On February 21, 1796, Du Pont submitted observations on Negro slavery and on the usefulness of establishing on the African coast settlements of free Negroes for the cultivation of sugar cane, first published in the *Éphémérides du Citoyen* in 1771; on February 26, he read the letter of dedication to the Lavoisiers, which had appeared in his *Philosophie de l'univers*; on May 1, he submitted his earlier treatise on economic curves (*Des Courbes politiques*); on July 10, he gave his fragment of *Le Serpent*, which had not previously appeared; and on October 5, he put forward his essay on the morality of dogs, foxes, and wolves, which he had written at Bois-des-Fossés almost three years earlier. Institut de France, Académie des sciences morales et politiques, "Registre indicatif des mémoires lus par les membres de la classe des sciences morales et politiques," ff. 26-26vo. (Mémoires lus par Dupont de Nemours) and *Registres des Procès-verbaux et rapports, Ans IV-VI*, pp. 2, 3, 9, 21, 39. (EMHL photocopies.) Du Pont published *Le Serpent; commentaire sur l'ancienne allégorie du serpent et de la vie qui se trouve dans le Boun-Déhesch, et dans plusiers autres mythologies orientales*, together with *Mlle. Dzjerzbicka; anecdote polonaise*, a saccharine and incredible tale of the devotion of a Polish damsel to her loved one (pamphlet of seven pages, with no title-page and no date, but certainly 1796, at EMHL). His essay "Sur la Sociabilité et la Moralité du Loup, du Renard, du Chien sauvage; et sur la manière dont celui-ci est devenue domestique" was read at the public meeting of the Institute on January 4, 1797, where, according to Irénée, it "had a great success" (Irénée to Sophie, March 30, 1797; trans. in B. G. du Pont, *Life of E. I. du Pont*, IV, 53) and was later published as a note in the second edition of the *Philosophie de l'univers* (pp. 252-264) and in *Quelques mémoires sur différens sujets* (Paris, 1807), pp. 263-277.

71. *Quelques mémoires sur différens sujets*, p. 336.

72. *L'Historien*, IV (no. 165), 438 (May 4, 1796).

73. *Ibid.*, pp. 437-439, reprinted in *Quelques mémoires*, p. 236 n. The first of the two stanzas may serve as a measure of Du Pont's imagination:

"Dors, dors, dors, dors, dors, dors, ma douce amie,
Amie, amie,
Si belle et si chérie:
Dors en aimant,
Dors en couvant,
Ma belle amie,
Nos jolis enfans:
Nos jolis, jolis, jolis, jolis, jolis
Si jolis, si jolis, si jolis
Petits enfans."

There follows, Du Pont indicated, "un petit silence," which one should, perhaps, charitably extend over the entire matter.

74. *Quelques mémoires*, pp. 176-178 (footnote). Pierre Jolly reprints most of Du Pont's note, as well as both stanzas of the translation of the nightingale song (*Du Pont de Nemours: Soldat de la Liberté*, pp. 250-252).

75. "Registre indicatif des mémoires lus par les membres de la classe des sciences morales et politiques" (MS, EMHL photocopy), f. 26.

76. *Moniteur*, XV (no. 217), 863.

77. *Quelques mémoires sur différens sujets* (1807), p. 316.

78. *Philosophie de l'univers* (seconde édition corrigée et augmentée; Paris, an IV), pp. 265-293. (The edition did not actually appear until an V—1797—because Du Pont was constantly revising and adding to it.)

79. B. G. du Pont, *Life of E. I. du Pont*, IV, 57 (April 3, 1797).

80. Albert Mathiez, *La Théophilanthropie et le culte décadaire, 1796-1801: Essai sur l'histoire religieuse de la Révolution* (Paris, 1904), p. 109 n. (This is the essential book on the subject. A brief account in English is in the translation of A. Aulard, *The French Revolution*, I, 66-69.)

81. Mathiez, *La Théophilanthropie*, p. 106 n., citing Grégoire, *Histoire des sectes* (1814), II, 102.

82. *Code de religion et de morale naturelles, à l'usage des adorateurs de Dieu et amis des hommes*; rédigé, publié et mis en ordre par J.-B. Chemin, adopté par les différens conseils de direction de la théophilantropie, et constamment suivi depuis l'origine de ce culte (nouvelle edition; Paris, an VII)— in A. N., AD XVII 49. I have not seen an earlier edition; nor have I seen Chemin's *Qu'est-ce que la théophilanthropie*, cited by Mathiez, *La Théophilanthropie*, p. 107, where Chemin names "le sensible Dupont de Nemours" among the first protectors of the cult.

83. Mathiez, *La Théophilanthropie*, p. 122.

84. *Sur le déisme; lettre aux auteurs du Publiciste* (Paris, 6 Brumaire an XIV [October 28, 1805]), p. 5 (italics in original). This six-page pamphlet is bound in volume II of the three-volume collection of *Opuscula par Du Pont de Nemours* at EMHL.

85. Du Pont papers at EMHL are silent on the beginning of their friendship. Their rather extensive correspondence dates from 1800. A present-day descendant of Madame de Staël, the Comte Le Marois, in discussing some of this correspondence in the archives of the family estate, Coppet (near Geneva), does not provide any information on their first association (Comte Le Marois, "Du Pont de Nemours et Madame de Staël," *Cahiers de politique étrangère du Journal des Nations Américaines; supplément bibliographique à France-Amérique Magazine*; nouvelle série, années 1946-1950, cahier LV-LVI, pp. 499-512). Madame de Staël's most recent biographer, J. Christopher Herold, in *Mistress to an Age: A Life of Madame de Staël* (Indianapolis and New York, 1958) does not mention Du Pont.

86. In volume III of the Duchesse d'Abrantès, *Histoire de salons de Paris: tableaux et portraits du grand monde, sous Louis XVI, le Directoire, le Consulat et l'Empire, la Restauration, et le règne de Louis Philippe Ier* (Brussels, 1837-1838), a work which must be used with caution, Du Pont appears among the company in Madame de Staël's salon sometime after July, 1799 (III, 286-308). The date must be in the latter part of 1799, because Talleyrand, who was also present, is described as being "no longer a minister" (he resigned his post in July, 1799) and Du Pont is described as being about "to leave for America." The Duchesse d'Abrantès' statement (III, 288 n.) that Du Pont "aimat M. Necker et en était aimé" seems too strong.

87. Only a copy of this letter, in the hand of Edelsheim, to whom it was probably addressed, is in the Baden archives. It is printed in Knies, *Carl Friedrichs Brieflicher Verkehr . . .*, I, 226-227. This Edelsheim was the brother of Staatsminister Wilhelm von Edelsheim, Du Pont's former correspondent, who died in 1793.

88. Buchez and Roux, ed., *Histoire parlementaire*, XXXVII, 247.

89. *Ibid.*

90. This division into *les directoriaux, les constitutionnels*, and *les royalistes* was the classification adopted by Thibaudeau in his *Mémoires*; cited in Buchez and Roux, XXXVII, 247.

91. Jacques Godechot, *La Contre-Révolution, doctrine et action 1789-1804* (Paris, 1961), p. 304, puts Du Pont "among the first Clichyens." I can find no evidence that he was active in this royalist group and believe that his own statements supporting the Republic, properly governed, must be accepted as sincere.

92. In the view of a careful scholar, there was no warrant for this claim—A. Meynier, *Les Coups d'état du Directoire* (nouvelle edition; Paris, 1932), I, 198.

93. *L'Historien*, XVII (no. 654)—one-page issue.

94. A. N., AF III 463, dossier 2804, pièce 166. Irénée's name was not included in the order of arrest. Further details are in Du Pont to La Revellière-Lépeaux, 20 Fructidor an V (September 6, 1797), A. N., AF III 463, dossier 2806, pièce 278. This letter was translated by B. G. du Pont in *DPdN*, II, 37-39. See also Irénée to Sophie, 20 Fructidor 5, in B. G. du Pont, *Life of E. I. du Pont*, IV, 65-66.

95. The letter from the Directory (signed by Barras and La Revellière-Lépeaux) instructing the Minister of Police to release Du Pont and his son is dated 21 Fructidor (September 7) (A. N., AF III 463, dossier 2804, pièce 277), but Du Pont later said that he spent only one night in jail.

96. For Tallien's denunciation on 25 Germinal an IV (April 14, 1796), see Mathiez, *Le Directoire*, p. 203.

97. This debate can best be followed in Guillaume N. Lallement, ed., *Choix de rapports, opinions et discours prononcés à la tribune nationale, depuis 1789 jusqu'à ce jour* (Paris, 1818-1821), XVI, 287-289.

98. Madame la Baronne De Staël, *Considerations sur les principaux événemens de la Révolution française; ouvrage posthume* (seconde édition; Paris, 1818), II, 188-189. (The translation in the text is that of the English edition, I, 382.)

99. EMHL, Longwood MSS, group 7. This note contains the peculiar sign ·/., which Victor de Avenell, who has studied the matter thoroughly, is convinced is a Masonic symbol.

100. B. G. du Pont (*DPdN*, II, 37-39) translates the letter to La Revellière-Lépeaux. Du Pont to Count Chreptowicz, December 25, 1803, in Schelle, ed., "Lettres inédites de Du Pont de Nemours au Comte Chreptowicz," *Journal des Économistes*, 6e série, XIV (1907), 17.

101. Du Pont to Victor, Paris, "4eme jour complémentaire de l'an cinq"—copy of letter finished by Irénée—EMHL, Winterthur MSS, group 2.

102. *Moniteur*, XV, 1467.

103. *Moniteur*, XVI, 2.

104. A. N., F⁷ 5660 and AD XII 7—*Neuvième liste de radiation, formée en exécution de l'article XXVIII, section III, titre III, de la loi du 25 brumaire IIIe année, des citoyens qui ont obtenu la radiation definitive de leurs noms des listes d'émigres, soit par lois du Corps Legislatif, ou arrêtés du Directoire Exécutif*, p. 38, where Du Pont is inaccurately described as "ex-Représentant du peuple au Conseil des 500." Seine-Inférieure, of which Rouen is chef-lieu, is given under the column of "Départements qui ont constaté l'émigration" and 27 Fructidor an 5, under the column of "Dates des Lois du Corps Législatif ou Arrêtés du Directoire Exécutif, prononçant la radiation."

105. [François-Antoine] Boissy d'Anglas, *Essai sur la vie, les écrits et les opinions de M. de Malesherbes, adressé à mes enfans* (Paris, 1819), II, 294.

IX

1. *Philosophie de l'univers* (3rd ed.; Paris, 1799), p. 326. Gilbert Chinard quotes this passage in his excellent introduction to his edition of *The Correspondence of Jefferson and Du Pont de Nemours* (Baltimore, 1931), p. xxii.

2. Du Pont to unnamed colleague, copy, 1 Vendémiaire de l'an 6 (September 22, 1797), soliciting his vote on "the fifth of this month" (September 26), when Du Pont's class would propose to the other two classes of the Institute that he be chosen one of the *voyageurs* (EMHL, accession 310).

3. Copy of letter dated 10 Frimaire de l'an 6 (November 30, 1797) in EMHL, Winterthur MSS, group 2.

4. B. G. du Pont, *Life of E. I. du Pont*, IV, 68-71, 76-77.

5. Typescript translation of *Notre Transplantation en Amérique* in EMHL, p. 6. B. G. du Pont gives a different translation, less exact but more favorable to Du Pont, in *Life of E. I. du Pont*, IV, 118.

6. EMHL, Winterthur MSS, group 2—the copy of the letter of 8 Nivôse an 6 (December 28, 1797) is marked "triplicata"; that of 27 Ventôse an 6 (March 17, 1798), "duplicata." Where the original drafts are, if they exist, is not known.

7. Chinard, *Correspondence*, p. 7.

8. Translated and printed in full in B. G. du Pont, *Life of E. I. du Pont*, IV, 86-100.

9. Jean Xavier Bureaux de Pusy, who had been imprisoned with Lafayette and Marie Charles César de Fay, comte de Latour-Maubourg, at Olmutz, had married Isle de France Poivre, daughter of the second Madame Du Pont.

10. Victor never assumed this position, of course, because President Adams refused him an exequatur.

11. EMHL, Longwood MSS, group 7—"Note confidentielle sur l'état actuel de la Société."

12. *Ibid.*—"Etat au vrai de notre affaire." The document is undated but must obviously have been written in 1799, after Beaumarchais' death and before the departure for America.

13. A. N., Minutier central de Paris et du département de la Seine, Registre no. 3898 XII 781 (EMHL photocopy, accession 276)—deed of sale by Du Pont to M. J. B. Morel, 14 Pluviôse an 6 (February 2, 1798).

14. Du Pont to Victor (marked "duplicata"), 27 Ventôse an 6 (March 17, 1798), where the sale of the Rouen houses is also mentioned—EMHL, Winterthur MSS, group 2.

15. Irénée to Sophie, May 21, 1799, B. G. du Pont, *Life of E. I. du Pont*, IV, 341.

16. Du Pont to Victor, 27 Ventôse an 6 (March 17, 1798)—"duplicata" in EMHL, Winterthur MSS, group 2.

17. A. N., Minutier central de Paris et du département de la Seine, Registre no. 5270 XII 784 (August 27, 1799)—EMHL photocopy. This power of attorney executed just slightly over a month before Du Pont departed for America casts doubt on B. G. du Pont's statement (*DPdN*, II, 46-47): ". . . Du Pont wanted to sell Bois-des-Fossés also, to pay his debt to Madame Lavoisier and to leave France with no debts on his mind; but Madame Lavoisier refused to permit the sale and he rented the estate to Harmand."

18. Copy of instructions (signed Bidermann Odier and Company) to Odier and Bousquet Brothers of Philadelphia to deliver to Du Pont de Nemours Père Fils et Cᶦᵉ a deed for the Kentucky lands, which they are authorized to sell. Any sum realized from prior sale of part of the lands was to be paid to the company on Bidermann's account. EMHL, Longwood MSS, group 7, document dated 13 Messidor an 6 (July 1, 1798).

19. EMHL, cardboard folder no. 237, titled "Dupont History (Kentucky Lands)." This dossier contains the report of an investigation carried out in July, 1941, by Roland W. Taylor at the request of the late P. S. du Pont. Included are photographs of part of the land and certified copies of deeds conveying the land between 1835 and 1855. Except for 7,000 acres, the land went to Moses L. Moses, creditor of V. Du Pont de Nemours et Cᶦᵉ by instruments of 1805 and 1810. The reserved 7,000 acres were sold in parcels by members of the du Pont family between 1835 and 1855. Mr. Taylor reported: "The land I saw of the original 56,000 acre tract, is very rough and rugged, with narrow valleys and back bone ridges. There is no great quantity of woodland, but trees and bushes are dotted here and there. I understand the woodland was cut off years ago, but I saw no indication of it, such as stumps, etc. There are very few well-

kept farms and not over 2% of the land is now being cultivated. The slopes are so steep that practically all the soil has eroded."

20. Undated four-page printed brochure with the heading *Compagnie d'Amérique*.

21. From an undated MS on the "present status of our project," translated by B. G. du Pont, *Life of E. I. du Pont*, V, 108.

22. Du Pont to Bidermann, December 1, 1800, in *ibid.*, p. 165.

23. The copy of Du Pont's letter (marked no. 7 and dated 18 and 23 Prairial de l'an 7—June 6 and 11, 1799) is not endorsed but was probably written to his wife, who had set out for America (EMHL, Longwood MSS, accession 35).

24. *Mémoires à consulter, et consultations sur les dépots en banque* in EMHL. The four *consultations* are dated 23 Pluviôse an 7 (February 11, 1799), 26 Ventôse (March 15), 1 Germinal (March 21), and 15 Germinal (April 4). The lawsuit is also mentioned in Du Pont's correspondence—for example, in a letter to Cambacérès, Minister of Justice, September 27, 1799 (B. G. du Pont, *Life of E. I. du Pont*, V, 114) and another to Harmand, September 21 (or 22), 1799 (EMHL, Longwood MSS, accession 10).

25. Du Pont to Harmand, 27 Frimaire an 9 (December 18, 1800), EMHL, Longwood MSS, accession 10.

26. Account rendered by Du Pont to the shareholders of his company, April 18, 1808 (EMHL, Longwood MSS, group 7). As usual, Du Pont's figures are not clear. It would appear that the ultimate loss totaled 24,000 francs. The original sum deposited was 36,023 francs, 25 centimes (*Mémoires à consulter et consultations sur les dépots en banque*, p. 22).

27. Institut de France, Académie des Sciences morales et politiques, "Registre indicatif des mémoires lus par les membres de la classe des sciences morales et politiques" (MS, ff. 26-28vo.: "Mémoires lus par Dupont de Nemours"). Some of these papers Du Pont had composed years earlier; thus, he submitted the first two chapters of the still unrecovered manuscript mentioned in chapter IV above ("Observations sur les principes et le bien des Républiques confédérées"). The *mémoire* entitled "Pourquoi la pluspart des chemins sont tortus, et pourquoi il est rare que les hommes et les gouvernemens marchent droit," received on October 9, 1799, was posted to the Institute after Du Pont had left Paris. He continued to mail contributions from America in 1800 and 1801. Several of these papers were later included in the two editions (1807, 1813) of Du Pont's *Quelques mémoires sur différens sujets*.

28. "Mémoire sur le nombre d'écoles primaires qu'il convient d'établir." This *mémoire* was read at a public meeting of the Institute on April 4, 1799, and was mentioned in contemporary journals. See A. Aulard, ed., *Paris pendant la réaction thermidorienne et sous le directoire; recueil de documents pour l'histoire de l'esprit public à Paris* (Collection de documents relatifs à l'histoire de Paris pendant la Révolution française; Paris, 1898-1902), V, 455, where there is the remark: "Quelques traits de ce mémoire ont été applaudis, mais en général il a paru un peu long."

29. In the election for president on 2 Vendémiaire an 7 (September 23, 1798) there was no majority on the first ballot; on the second ballot, Du Pont and Buache received the same number of votes. As the elder in age, Du Pont was thereupon declared elected. Institut de France, Académie des sciences morales et politiques, Institut national des sciences et des arts, *Registre des procès-verbaux et rapports de la classe des sciences morales et politiques (an VII-VIII)*, p. 1.

30. The police documents are reproduced in full by G. Lioret in *Annales de la Société historique et archeologique du Gâtinais*, XXXII (1914), 66-70, and translated by B. G. du Pont, *Life of E. I. du Pont*, IV, 79-84.

31. Bibliothèque nationale, MSS françaises, nouv. acq. 1303—undated, but probably late 1798.

32. Irénée to Sophie, April 27, 1799, B. G. du Pont, *Life of E. I. du Pont*, IV, 260.

33. *Ibid.*, p. 328.

34. Translated in full in *ibid.*, pp. 283-304.

35. *Ibid.*, pp. 297-298, 299-300.

36. *Ibid.*, p. 328.

37. B. G. du Pont, *DPdN*, II, 50; Du Pont to wife, 30 Thermidor an 7 (August 17, 1799), EMHL, Longwood MSS, accession 35.

38. Irénée to Sophie, May 21, 1799 (B. G. du Pont, *Life of E. I. du Pont*, IV, 341); Du Pont to wife [June 6, July 27, August 17, 1799], EMHL, Longwood MSS, accession 35.

39. Family letters in B. G. du Pont, *Life of E. I. du Pont*, IV, 343-380, V, 12-99; in EMHL, Longwood MSS, accession 35.

40. Du Pont to wife (unsigned draft), 30 Thermidor de l'an 7 [August 17, 1799], EMHL, Longwood MSS, accession 35.

41. *Moniteur*, XIX, 1 (issue for September 20, 1799). The exact date of departure from Paris cannot be determined. The earliest letter uncovered from Du Pont at La Rochelle to Harmand is dated 30 Fructidor an 7 (September 16, 1799)—EMHL, Longwood MSS, accession 10.

42. *Le Publiciste*, issue of 3 Vendémiaire VIII (September 25, 1799) in EMHL, Longwood MSS, group 7. The letter is translated in full by B. G. du Pont, *Life of E. I. du Pont*, V, 111-113.

43. Du Pont letter (June 6, 1799), unendorsed, but evidently to his wife, EMHL, Longwood MSS, accession 35. Du Pont called Sieyès "a man of genius."

44. Irénée to Sophie, May 9, 1799, B. G. du Pont, *Life of E. I. du Pont*, IV, 309-310.

45. Du Pont to wife, January 1 and 4, 1800 (typed translation), EMHL, Longwood MSS, group 8.

46. Boissy d'Anglas later wrote in warm terms of the visit and offer of "this constantly generous man"—*Essai sur la vie, les écrits et les opinions de M. de Malesherbes, adressé à mes enfans*, II, 295.

47. An old engraving of the *American Eagle* is reproduced in *The Du Pont Magazine*, XXXVIII (Nov.-Dec., 1944), 10-11.

48. Du Pont to wife, January 4, 1800 (typed translation), EMHL, Longwood MSS, group 8.

49. Silvèstre, *Notice biographique sur M. Dupont* (in *Mémoires . . . de la Société royale et centrale d'agriculture*, 1818), p. 328. Some comment on the journey in Josephine du Pont's *Notre Transplantation en Amerique*—see excerpt translated by B. G. du Pont, *Life of E. I. du Pont*, V, 115-116; also in Du Pont to Harmand [January 16, 1800], EMHL, Longwood MSS, accession 10, and Du Pont to wife (unsigned), January 9, 1800, Longwood MSS, accession 35.

50. January 1, 1800, is the date of landing which has been accepted in the family history and is given by B. G. du Pont, *DPdN*, II, 50. In a letter to Harmand, dated 26 Nivôse de l'an 8 (January 16, 1800), Du Pont gives January 3 as the date of landing (EMHL, Longwood MSS, accession 10).

51. Letter to Harmand cited in note 50 above. The location is today part of the city of Bayonne.

52. Letter from Victor, August 7, 1800 (B. G. du Pont, *Life of E. I. du Pont*, V, 159).

53. Chinard, *Correspondence*, p. 9 The letter is undated, but Dumas Malone (*Correspondence Between Thomas Jefferson and Pierre Samuel du Pont de Nemours, 1798-1817*, Boston and New York, 1930, p. 4) assigns the date January 17, 1800.

54. Du Pont's correspondence in 1800 and 1801 contains various favorable judgments on Napoleon. See, for example, Du Pont to Madame de Staël, 19 Pluviôse an 8 (February 8, 1800) in Comte Le Marois, "Du Pont de Nemours et Madame de Staël," *Cahiers de Politique Étrangère du Journal des Nations Américaines* (supplement bibliographique à *France-Amérique Magazine*), nouvelle série, années 1946-1950, cahier LV-LVI, p. 503; Du Pont to Claret de Fleurien, April 29, 1800, in B. G. du Pont, *Life of E. I. du Pont*, V, 125; Du Pont to Général Constantin Faucher, 10 Fructidor an 8 (September 5, 1800), EMHL, typescript copy from Bordeaux municipal archives supplied by M. Xavier Védère; Du Pont to Desmousseaux (copy), 5 Nivôse an 9 (December 26, 1800), EMHL, Longwood MSS, group 2; Du Pont to Felix Faulcon, 20

Germinal an 9 (April 10, 1801), in Gilbert Chinard, ed., "Lettres de du Pont de Nemours à Felix Faulcon 12 mai 1795–25 octobre 1802," *French American Review*, I (1948), 179.

55. There is a copy of the letter in EMHL, Longwood MSS, group 7; it has been translated in full by B. G. du Pont, *Life of E. I. du Pont*, V, 163-196.

56. Some of these are translated by B. G. du Pont, *Life of E. I. du Pont*, V, 198-212.

57. "Acte d'Association pour l'Establissement d'une manufacture de poudre de Guerre et de chasse dans les États Unis d'Amérique"—2 undated copies, with slight variations, in EMHL, Longwood MSS, group 1; translated (and dated 1 Floréal an 9— April 21, 1801) by B. G. du Pont, *Life of E. I. du Pont*, V, 225-229.

58. Memorandum of E. I. du Pont for Bureaux de Pusy in B. G. du Pont, *Life of E. I. du Pont*, V, 245.

59. Victor to Messrs. Du Pont de Nemours Père Fils & Cⁱᵉ, Paris, August 8, 1801; memorandum in hand of E. I. du Pont—both in *ibid.*, pp. 257-258, 260, 333.

60. Irénée to M. Robin, "superintendent of Powder at Essone," in *ibid.*, pp. 231-232.

61. This interesting but subordinate topic may best be studied in the documents in A. N., F¹⁰ 392: Graines d'Amérique: Rapport de Saulnier et de Du Pont sur les pepinières, an X-1807. The nurseryman signed his letters as Saunier, rather than Saulnier. In 1801-1802, François André Michaux, son of the famous botanist, was sent to America to inspect and, if possible, to re-establish the nurseries. He recommended, however, that they be closed. Du Pont and Saulnier were successful in their efforts to persuade the French Government to retain the nurseries, especially the one in New Jersey (Minister of the Interior to Saulnier, April 27, 1802—in B. G. du Pont, *Life of E. I. du Pont*, VI, 41; the Charleston nursery was eventually disposed of—A. N., F¹⁰ 392, pièce 36). The Du Pont Company advanced funds for the care of the New Jersey nursery and the despatch of seeds to France. It was partially reimbursed by the Government for these services. For several years, at his own expense, Irénée sent to France seeds prepared by Saulnier, who tried vainly to obtain regular and adequate support from France. Apparently, the matter of the nurseries was clearly brought to the attention of the Government through a letter which Du Pont sent to the Institute —report to the Minister of the Interior, 7 Thermidor an 13 (July 26, 1805) by Silvestre in A. N., F¹⁰ 392, pièce 36. J. R. Schramm, "The Memorial to François André Michaux at the Morris Arboretum, University of Pennsylvania," *Proceedings of the American Philosophical Society*, C (April, 1956), 146, is apparently incorrect in stating that the New Jersey nursery was liquidated by early June, 1802.

62. Letters in B. G. du Pont, *Life of E. I. du Pont*, V, 230-241.

63. *Ibid.*, p. 226, article 2 of instrument of incorporation, where, obviously, the names of McCall and Bauduy were added after Irénée's return to America.

64. These details may be followed in the family letters and papers contained in *ibid.*, V, 267-380, and VI, 11-40. They are concisely presented in William S. Dutton, *Du Pont: One Hundred and Forty Years* (New York, 1951), pp. 32-33.

65. The "Articles of agreement," which had been urged by Victor, are printed in B. G. du Pont, *Life of E. I. du Pont*, VI, 108-109.

66. Victor kept a brief daily record of his travels and later wrote an account of them covering the months of January to early May, 1801. These manuscripts in EMHL (Winterthur MSS) have been expertly edited by Charles W. David and published by Cornell University Press: Victor Marie du Pont, *Journey to France and Spain, 1801* (Ithaca, *c.* 1961).

67. B. G. du Pont, *Life of E. I. du Pont*, V, 261-265, 271-277, 282-288.

68. From *Notre Transplantation en Amérique*, translated in *ibid.*, p. 198.

69. Du Pont reported to his shareholders in 1808 that he had sent Bureaux de Pusy to Europe to assist in the negotiation of the Spanish project, which had to be given up with the signing of the peace treaty (B. G. du Pont, *Life of E. I. du Pont*, VIII, 45).

70. Unsigned letter in Du Pont's hand, 20 Pluviôse an X (February 9, 1802), EMHL, Longwood MSS, accession 35.

71. This intention is made clear in his wife's letters to her mother, especially, one dated 1ᵉʳ Xᵇʳᵉ 1801 (December 1, 1801), EMHL, Longwood MSS, accession 35.

72. ". . . These miserable shares which hold no kind of guarantee"—letter of Isle de France Bureaux de Pusy to Madame Du Pont de Nemours, her mother, 3 Messidor an 11 (June 22, 1803); letters of 18 Nivôse (January 8) and 23 Germinal (April 13) also reveal this growing worry and bitterness (EMHL, Longwood MSS, accession 35).

73. Scattered remnants of correspondence with Madame Lavoisier, photocopies of a few letters, and typed translations of other letters, the originals of which are lacking —all available at EMHL—tend to demonstrate beyond doubt that the relationship between her and Du Pont was, at one time, as intimate as such a relationship can be. In the absence of most of the original letters, one would have to rely mostly upon typed translations in trying to substantiate this conclusion. Until the original letters are uncovered, if they ever are, one must refrain from making a case.

74. Du Pont's letters to Harmand from September, 1799, to July, 1802 (by which time he was back in France), are in EMHL, Longwood MSS, accession 10.

75. "Registre indicatif des mémoires lus par les membres de la classe des sciences morales et politiques," folio 26vo. Six of these *mémoires* were later reprinted in Du Pont's *Quelques mémoires sur différens sujets* (Paris, 1807), pp. 1-51.

76. *Early Proceedings of the American Philosophical Society for the Promotion of Useful Knowledge, Compiled by One of the Secretaries from the Manuscript Minutes of its Meetings from 1744 to 1838* (Philadelphia, 1884), pp. 298-301, 313; Du Pont to American Philosophical Society, May 15 and 22, 1800, Du Pont to John Vaughan (secretary of the Society), December 23, 1801, APS archives. Du Pont's paper on vegetables, polypi, and insects was published in volume V of the Society's *Transactions* and his "theory on winds" in volume VI. His *mémoire* "On the Formation of Water in Plants" was judged "ingenious" but "not of sufficient importance to publish" on August 15, 1800.

77. Jefferson to Madison, October 9, 1809, in Chinard, *Correspondence*, p. 152.

78. This treatise was eventually translated and published by B. G. du Pont as *National Education in the United States* (Newark, Del., 1923).

79. *Ibid.*, pp. 16, 18, 34.

80. EMHL, Winterthur MSS, group 2.

81. Du Pont to Madame de Staël, Good Stay, 6 Frimaire IX (November 27, 1800), draft, EMHL, Winterthur MSS, group 2.

82. EMHL, Winterthur MSS, group 2—Eleuthera du Pont Smith autograph collection. This letter, dated Lyon, 6 Pluviôse an 10 (January 26, 1802) is neither addressed nor signed, but seems certainly to have been written by Bureaux de Pusy to his mother-in-law, Madame du Pont.

83. EMHL, Winterthur MSS, group 2.

84. *Ibid.*, letter dated 10 Messidor IX (June 22, 1801), punctuation added. I have profited from a perusal of the unpublished manuscript of Professor Raymond Betts of Grinnell College, Iowa, on "Du Pont de Nemours and Napoleonic France."

85. Copies of both printed documents are in EMHL. B. G. du Pont, *Life of E. I. du Pont*, VI, 41-42, has the English notice. A copy of the circular letter in French is in the Jefferson Papers in the Library of Congress.

86. Translated by B. G. du Pont, *Life of E. I. du Pont*, VI, 44-45.

87. A copy of the deed in English is in EMHL, Longwood MSS, group 1.

88. Letter to Irénée (Paris, 10 Thermidor an X), EMHL, Longwood MSS, group 1, translated in part by B. G. du Pont, *DPdN*, II, 69-70, with date July 30 (actually July 29); see also Du Pont's letter to Victor, August 13, 1802, in *ibid.*, pp. 73-74.

89. The card is in EMHL and is reproduced in *ibid.*, between pp. 80-81.

90. Chinard, *Correspondence*, p. 46; also in Dumas Malone, ed., *Correspondence between Thomas Jefferson and Pierre Samuel du Pont de Nemours 1798-1817*, p. 47.

91. Concise detail on the background and negotiation of the Louisiana issue can be found in the useful volumes of E. Wilson Lyon: *Louisiana in French Diplomacy*

1759-1804 (Norman, Oklahoma, 1934) and *The Man Who Sold Louisiana: The Career of François Barbé-Marbois* (Norman, 1942), pp. 118-123.

92. Gilbert Chinard, *Volney et l'Amérique d'après des documents inédits et sa correspondance avec Jefferson* (The Johns Hopkins Studies in Romance Literature and Languages, I; Baltimore and Paris, 1923), pp. 132 ff.; Chinard, *Correspondence*, Introduction, pp. xxviii-xxix; E. W. Lyon, *Louisiana in French Diplomacy*, p. 162.

93. Chinard, *Correspondence*, p. 45; Malone, *Correspondence*, pp. 49-51, contains an English translation of this letter.

94. E. W. Lyon, *Louisiana in French Diplomacy*, p. 163.

95. Chinard, pp. 46-47; Malone, p. 47; also in B. G. du Pont, *Life of E. I. du Pont*, VI, 26-29.

96. Chinard, p. 54.

97. Chinard, pp. 51-53; Malone, pp. 56-60.

98. Chinard, pp. 55-56; Malone, pp. 62-63.

99. Chinard, pp. 61-62.

100. Chinard, pp. 63-65; Malone, pp. 68-71.

101. Chinard, pp. 65-69; Malone, pp. 72-77.

102. Quoted in Chinard., Introduction, xli. For additional statements on the influence of Du Pont's letter of October 4, 1802, see E. W. Lyon, *Louisiana in French Diplomacy*, p. 177, and G. Chinard, *Thomas Jefferson: the Apostle of Americanism* (2nd ed. revised; Boston, 1943), p. 411.

103. Chinard, *Correspondence*, pp. 69-70.

104. E. W. Lyon, *The Man Who Sold Louisiana*, p. 120.

105. Chinard, p. 71.

106. E. W. Lyon, *Louisiana in French Diplomacy*, p. 211.

107. E. W. Lyon, *The Man Who Sold Louisiana*, p. 121.

108. Du Pont to Jefferson, May 12, 1803, Chinard, pp. 72-75.

109. Chinard, pp. 79-80; Malone, pp. 78-79.

X

1. Especially the letter of 10 Messidor an IX (June 29, 1801) (in EMHL, Winterthur MSS, group 2).

2. Victor to Irénée, March 17, 1803, in B. G. du Pont, *Life of E. I. du Pont*, VI, 183.

3. Schelle, ed., "Lettres inédites . . . ," in *Journal des Économistes*, 6ᵉ serie, XIV (1907), 18.

4. Du Pont to Victor, March 29, 1804 (EMHL, Winterthur MSS, group 2) and to Irénée, January 10, 1806 (EMHL, Longwood MSS, group 1).

5. EMHL, Winterthur MSS, group 2; P. Jolly, *DPdN*, p. 230.

6. EMHL, Longwood MSS, group 1. The letter is incompletely dated as "16 de l'an 13," no month being given.

7. Irénée to Du Pont, October 12, 1804, B. G. du Pont, *Life of E. I. du Pont*, VII, 14. This affair can best be followed in the letters translated in volumes VI and VII of this useful *Life*.

8. This involved matter cannot be dealt with, since it is part of the history of the E. I. du Pont de Nemours Co. and not significantly part of the career of P. S. Du Pont de Nemours, although, of course, Irénée's success was vital to Du Pont, for business as well as personal reasons. There is valuable material on the Bauduy conflict in vols. VII to XI of B. G. du Pont's *Life of E. I. du Pont*.

9. Letter of December 14, 1811, EMHL, Longwood MSS, group 1.

10. EMHL, Longwood MSS, group 1. Du Pont prepared at least four numerical codes, supplying his sons with the keys. Somehow the Napoleonic censorship must have got news of the code—Du Pont never explained the circumstances—and he was required to turn the keys over to the police in 1805 (Letter numbered 56, with illegible date, to Irénée, EMHL, Longwood MSS, group I and Victor to Irénée, April

8, 1805, in B. G. du Pont, *Life of E. I. du Pont*, VII, 130). He continued to employ the codes, however, since, as he aparently explained to the police, they were utilized only for business and personal items.

11. Irénée to Du Pont, May 2, 1807, in B. G. du Pont, *Life of E. I. du Pont*, VII, 296.

12. Irénée to Du Pont, January 22, 1809, in *ibid.*, VIII, 132.

13. Although I have not been able to accept all of his conclusions, I have profited greatly through the opportunity to consult the unpublished paper on the Talleyrand loan prepared in 1959 by Professor Raymond F. Betts of Grinnell College. Professor Betts has traced the history of the negotiation of the loan through a large body of scattered correspondence in EMHL.

14. For some of the difficulties, see Irénée to Durant St. André, Consul General of France, January 22, 1827, in B. G. du Pont, *Life of E. I. du Pont*, XI, 161-162.

15. Victor to Irénée, November 13, 1804, in *ibid.*, VII, 19.

16. *Ibid.*, VI, 311-312.

17. In a letter to Irénée, April 8, 1805, in *ibid.*, VII, 131. A much more favorable view of Pichon will be found in M. Dunan, "Un adversaire du système continental," *Revue des études napoléoniennes*, VII (1915), 262-275.

18. A. N., AF IV 929, dossier II (Thermidor an X), pièce 127.

19. A. N., AF IV 1681A, dossier: États-Unis d'Amérique 1812, pièce 184, ff. 565-566: "Rapport d'Estève, trésorier du gouvernement, 27 frimaire an XI" (December 18, 1802). The "Dubreuil" mentioned in this report must be Francis Breuil, who had a large commercial brokerage and import-export business in Philadelphia.

20. See especially Napoleon's letter to his mother ("Madame Mère"), April 22, 1805, translated in J. M. Thompson, ed., *Napoleon's Letters* (Everyman's Library; New York, 1954), pp. 121-122.

21. B. G. du Pont, *Life of E. I. du Pont*, VI, 318-319.

22. In his letter to Irénée of April 5, 1805, Victor quoted from Bidermann's letter of January 25: "It would have been far more convenient for you to have paper on London; but I thought you so fortunate in getting out of it like this that I did not venture to suggest it. You owe it all to your father's exertions" (*ibid.*, VII, 133).

23. For example, Victor to Irénée, May 1, 1804, and May 27, 1805, in *ibid.*, VI, 311, and VII, 139.

24. Letter of August 10, 1805, *ibid.*, VII, 159.

25. B. G. du Pont, *DPdN*, II, 98. The statement in the text must be tentative because I have not been able firmly to document this arrangement from primary sources. Mrs. du Pont does not cite her evidence. In her *Notre Transplantation en Amérique*, Madame Victor du Pont states that Talleyrand had agreed to lend 50,000 francs (excerpt translated in B. G. du Pont, *Life of E. I. du Pont*, VII, 174).

26. August 25, 1805, B. G. du Pont, *Life of E. I. du Pont*, VII, 165.

27. The third child was Samuel Francis, born at Goodstay in 1803, who later had a distinguished career as an officer in the United States Navy. He bore the same name as the son who had survived only five days in 1799. (See above, pp. 278-279.) Julia Sophie Angélique, second daughter and fifth child of Victor and Josephine, was born at Eleutherian Mills on June 3, 1806, the first du Pont to be born in Delaware.

28. B. G. du Pont, *Life of E. I. du Pont*, VII, 207.

29. *Ibid.*, pp. 189-190.

30. July 29, 1806, EMHL, Longwood MSS, group 1—letter partly in code.

31. *Moniteur* for October 10, 1807 (pp. 1094-1095) under "Decrets Impériaux, Conseil d'État, Extrait des registres des délibérations—Séance du 30 septembre 1807."

32. EMHL, Winterthur MSS, group 2.

33. B. G. du Pont, *Life of E. I. du Pont*, VIII, 52.

34. A. N., AF V 2, dossier: November 1814, pièce 6.

35. *Œuvres de M^r· Turgot, ministre d'état, précédées et accompagnés de mémoires et de notes sur sa vie, son administration et ses ouvrages* (9 vols.; Paris, 1808-1811).

60. In his first pamplet (cited in preceding note), Page (p. 2) admits that Du Pont did not originate the plan to absorb the defaulting bank in the new Chavagnac et Compagnie but points out that Du Pont had become the chief apologist for it. According to Page, the plan was formulated by Choart (who was to be director-general of the new company), Faugé, Laffon-Ladebat, Soufflot de Méré, and other officers or creditors of the original Banque Territoriale.

61. Official document in EMHL, Longwood MSS, accession 224. Levacher-Duplessis, former procurator in the Chambre des Comptes, Felines senior, a retired Parisian banker, and Bergerot, former liquidator-general of the émigré debt, were chosen to the new commission.

62. A succinct account of the *New Jersey* case is the report of the French Minister of the Public Treasury to Napoleon, found in the appendix of the anonymous pamphlet *Examination of the Memorial of the Owners and Underwriters of the American Ship the* New Jersey, *and of the Documents Accompanying It, as Presented to the Senate and House of Representatives of the United States of America at Their Late Session,* by a Friend to Truth and Justice (Philadelphia, 1806). pp. 137-138. This pamphlet, vigorously opposing arguments put forth by Du Pont, is in EMHL and in the Jefferson books in the Rare Book Room of the Library of Congress, where it is bound together with the five pamphlets which Du Pont published on the case.

63. Aside from the *Examination* cited in the preceding note, the best statement of Armstrong's case is his own, found in the extract from his letter to Secretary of State Madison, dated November 26, 1805, as printed in *American State Papers, Class I, Foreign Relations,* vol. II (Documents Legislative and Executive, of the Congress of the United States, from the first session of the First to the third session of the Thirteenth Congress, inclusive; commencing March 3, 1789 and ending March 3, 1815; selected and edited, under the authority of Congress by Walter Lowrie, Secretary of the Senate, and Matthew St. Clair, Clerk of the House of Representatives; Washington, 1832), pp. 774-775.

64. The various powers of attorney are in A. N., Minutier central de Paris et du département de la Seine, Registre no. 5510 XII 802. Through the assistance of M. Jean Denizet, EMHL now has photocopies of these documents (listed as accession 276). The investors in the cargo of the *New Jersey* and the three insurance companies involved granted power of attorney to Nicklin and Griffith, who, in turn, authorized Du Pont to act for them in Paris. The papers were notarized by Peter [Pierre] Duponceau, who may have suggested Du Pont, his fellow-member in the American Philosophical Society.

65. The five *mémoires* were printed and may be found in EMHL and among the Jefferson books in the Library of Congress, since Du Pont sent them to Jefferson. The *New Jersey* affair, which created some stir in 1805, is not now of sufficient importance to warrant an analysis of the arguments presented in the printed *mémoires,* which appeared in the following order: *Observations sommaires et preuves sur le navire le* New-Jersey *et ses propriétaires* (9 pages); *Dernières Observations sur le navire le* New-Jersey (10 pages); *Doutes et préventions relativement à le restitution à faire aux propriétaires americains du navire le* New-Jersey, *réponses a ces doutes, réfutation de ces préventions* (46 pages); *Nouvelles Questions proposées par monsieur le directeur de la quatrième division de la liquidation général, membre du conseil de liquidation, et de la part de ce conseil, aux fondés de pouvoirs et défenseurs des propriétaires du navire le* New-Jersey, *et de leurs co-interressés, réponses à ces questions* (76 pages; this *mémoire* signed also by J.-B. Sirey, "avocat à la Cour de Cassation, et au conseil des prises"); *A leurs excellences les ministres plenipotentiaires français et américains, chargés de prononcer sur les réclamations des citoyens des États-Unis, qui ont droit de prendre part aux avantages stipulés entre les deux nations, par les traités du 8 vendémiaire an IX, et du 10 florréal an XI* (20 pages).

66. Chinard, pp. 99-103.

67. *American State Papers, Class I, Foreign Relations,* II, 774.

68. See *Examination*, etc. (note 62 above), Appendix, p. 138, and *American State Papers, Class I, Foreign Relations*, II, 775 (extract of Armstrong's letter).

69. Letter to Jefferson, September 8, 1805—Malone, p. 87; Chinard, pp. 105-106.

70. Letter to Jefferson, March 10, 1806 (Chinard, p. 108); repeated August 13, 1807 (Malone, pp. 99-100), May 25, 1808 (Malone, p. 104), September 5, 1808 (Malone, pp. 118-120), February 10, 1813 (letter to Madison, Chinard, p. 203).

71. Letter to Jefferson, March 10, 1806 (Chinard, p. 110); repeated May 6, 1807 (Malone, p. 91), August 13, 1807 (Malone, pp. 97-99), May 25, 1808 (Malone, p. 104), July 23, 1808 (Malone, p. 107).

72. Letter to Jefferson, May 6, 1807 (Malone, p. 92); repeated in letter to Madison, October 27, 1814 (Chinard, p. 209).

73. Letter to Jefferson, July 12, 1807 (Chinard, p. 115); repeated May 25, 1808 (Malone, p. 105), July 23, 1808 (Malone, pp. 110-111), January 20, 1810 (letter to Madison, Chinard, p. 156), September 5, 1811 (Malone, p. 135).

74. Letter to Jefferson, July 23, 1808 (Malone, p. 107); repeated September 5, 1808 (Malone, pp. 118-120). It had been determined that the Floridas were not included in the Louisiana territory retroceded to France by Spain in 1800.

75. Letter to Jefferson, July 23, 1808 (Malone, p. 109). This advice came during the commercial stagnation caused by the Embargo Act which cut off manufactures from abroad. Jefferson replied on June 28, 1809, that the stimulus to increase the number of manufacturing establishments was still powerful and would not be stopped (Malone, pp. 124-125).

76. Letter to Jefferson, September 5, 1808 (Malone, pp. 117-118).

77. Letter to Jefferson, January 20, 1810 (Chinard, p. 154); repeated December 12, 1811 (Malone, p. 137) and at length January 25, 1812 (Chinard, pp. 179-193).

78. Letter to Jefferson, September 5, 1811 (Malone, p. 135). Where the letter appears in English translation in Malone, I have cited only that edition. All Du Pont's letters are in French in Chinard's edition. Some are not found in Malone, where there are also occasional but unimportant omissions in the text of the letters printed.

79. Chinard, pp. 182-183, 186, 189.

80. *Ibid.*, p. 194.

81. *Ibid.*, pp. 195-196.

82. See above, chap. III, note 47.

83. Chinard, pp. 197-199.

84. Malone, p. 89.

85. *Ibid.*, pp. 80-81.

86. Institut national des sciences et des arts, "Registre des procès-verbaux de la classe de littérature et beaux arts: Classe d'histoire et de littérature ancienne" (MS, EMHL photocopy), p. 13. Du Pont's name is inserted on left margin, as if it had at first been omitted.

87. Du Pont to Hennin (his former colleague in the Assembly of Notables), 23 Pluviôse 12 (February 13, 1804), where he remarks that he would be happy to have Hennin in the Institute, although, as a result of the new organization, he has no influence, because he was a useful member only in the class of moral philosophy or of political economy (Bibliothèque de l'Institut, MS 1258—EMHL photocopy).

88. Institut de France, Académie des sciences, *Procès-verbaux des séances de l'académie tenues depuis la fondation de l'Institut jusqu'au mois d'août 1835* (Hendaye, 1910-1922), II, 640.

89. Institut national des sciences et des arts, "Registre des procès-verbaux" (see note 86), pp. 280, 289-290. There are numerous mentions of Du Pont in this "Registre" and in the printed *Procès-verbaux de l'académie [des sciences]* (see note 88), where the titles of his *mémoires* may be traced. I have not considered them of sufficient significance to include them in the text. Several of these papers were published in Du Pont's *Quelques mémoires sur differens sujets, la pluspart d'histoire naturelle, ou de physique générale et particulière* (Paris, 1807; seconde édition, 1813).

90. *Mémoires soumis à la 3ᵉ classe de l'Institut sur plusieurs ouvrages historiques, et particulièrement sur celui de M. de Rulhière, intitulé: De l'anarchie de Pologne, concourant pour les prix décennaux* . . . (Paris, 1810).

91. Institut national des sciences et des arts, "Registre des procès-verbaux . . ." (see note 86), p. 367.

92. American Philosophical Society Archives: John Vaughan to Irénée, January 28, 1803, and Vaughan to Victor, November 3, 1803 (photocopies from EMHL, Winterthur MSS); Delambre to Vaughan, 1ᵉʳ Vendémaire an 13 (September 23, 1804); Rob. Andrews to Vaughan, April 18, 1805.

93. *Bulletin de la Société d'Encouragement pour l'Industrie Nationale* ([Paris], 1802-1807), I, 222; II, 53-55, 87.

94. For example: *Rapport fait à la société philantropique, par M. Du Pont de Nemours, au nom de la commission des sociétés de prévoyance, le 6 Pluviôse an XIII* (n.p., n.d.); *Rapport de M. Du Pont de Nemours, à la société philantropique, au nom de la commission des sociétés de prévoyance, sur celle dite des Amis de l'égalité, autrefois Bourse des malades* (n.p., n.d.).

95. Institut national des sciences et des arts, "Registre des procès-verbaux . . ." (see note 86), pp. 181 (April 14, 1809), 268 (April 20, 1810).

96. A.N., F¹⁷ᵃ 1206, dossier 10, pièce 113 (EMHL photocopy); Jolly, *DPdN* (pp. 234-235) quotes part of this letter.

97. A.N., F¹⁷ 3482, dossier 1807 (EMHL photocopy).

98. As Pierre Jolly suggests (*DPdN*, pp. 233-234).

99. A.N., F¹⁷ᵃ 1206, dossier 10, pièce 129 (EMHL photocopy): De Sales to Minister of the Interior, November 17, 1811.

100. There are three copies of this important statement (each in a different hand) in EMHL, Longwood MSS, group 7. B. G. du Pont translates it in *Life of E. I. du Pont*, VII, 40-66. The quotation in the text is her translation (p. 46); the underlining (italics) is Du Pont's.

101. *Ibid.*, pp. 62-63.

102. *Ibid.*, p. 65, 66.

103. Copy of letter, in the hand of Madame Du Pont de Nemours, in EMHL, Winterthur MSS, group 2. The original of this letter is in the archives of the chateau of Coppet, near Geneva, along with thirty other letters of Du Pont to Madame de Staël. The Comte Le Marois, descendant of Madame de Staël, used this correspondence for his article "Du Pont de Nemours et Madame de Staël," published in the *Cahiers de politique étrangère du Journal des nations américaines* (supplément biblographique à *France-Amérique Magazine*), nouvelle série, années 1946-1950, cahier LV-LVI, pp. 499-512. These personal letters, together with sixteen letters which Du Pont wrote to Necker and a number of business letters of Du Pont de Nemours Père Fils et Cⁱᵉ, have not yet been made available to the public. Colonel H. F. du Pont was able to have copied three of the letters to Necker, seven of the letters to Madame de Staël, and three of the letters to Necker-Germany. These typescript copies are available at EMHL, Winterthur MSS, group 8. Manuscript copies of a few of the letters to Madame de Staël and some of her letters to Du Pont are also in EMHL, Winterthur MSS, group 2. In 1960, through the courtesy of the Comtesse Le Marois, M. Abel Doysié was permitted to inspect these papers and to prepare a list of the separate items, without making any transcripts. M. Doysié has given me a copy of his inventory.

104. B. G. du Pont translates the statement in *DPdN*, II, 104-106, and in *Life of E. I. du Pont*, VIII, 303-306. The complete table of distribution was as follows, the first column of figures indicating the number of shares held in Du Pont de Nemours Père Fils et Cⁱᵉ and the second column showing the shares or part-shares in the powder company to be given to each shareholder:

M. Bidermann	13	4 1/3
M. Johannot	5	1 2/3
Mme. de Pusy	5	1 2/3

Du Pont de Nemours	3	1
Mme. de Staël	2	5/6 [*sic*]
M. de Crillon	1 1/2	1/3 [*sic*]
Mme. Du Pont (de N)	1	1/3
M. Lescalier	1	1/3
M. Ochs & children	1	1/3
M. Wischer	1	1/3
M. Forcard Weiss	1	1/3
M. Reinhard	1	1/3
M. Hom	1/2	1/6
	36	12

(I have followed Mrs. B. G. du Pont, *DPdN*, II, 105, in simplifying somewhat Du Pont's original arrangement of the figures. In *Life of E. I. du Pont*, VIII, 305, Mrs. du Pont gives the arrangement as it appears in the manuscript copy in EMHL, Winterthur MSS, group 2.)

105. Irénée to Du Pont, July 4, 1811, in B. G. du Pont, *Life of E. I. du Pont*, VIII, 310-315; and Irénée to Du Pont, December 10, 1811, *ibid.*, IX, 18-21.

106. *Ibid.*, pp. 125-126. The key to the cipher which Du Pont employed in this letter has been lost. Mrs. Bessie du Pont Huidekoper succeeded in deciphering it and reconstructed the key which is printed in *ibid.*, p. 117.

107. See copies of his letters to Bidermann in *ibid.*, pp. 127-142, 200-219, the latter his extensive commentary on a letter severely castigating Irénée's administration, written by Bauduy to Beauchet on June 21, 1814, and sent to Bidermann (*ibid.*, pp. 196-200). See also the undated letter (probably late 1814) in *ibid.*, X, 11-24, and the draft of November 30, 1814, in *ibid.*, pp. 39-52.

108. On August 14, 1814, he was less cruel than he had been the previous October, but still sought to recall Irénée to the path of honor from which he thought he had strayed (*ibid.*, IX, 241-250).

109. Du Pont to Madame Lavoisier, June 27, 1811 (copy), EMHL, Longwood MSS, group 1. Further study of this matter must unfortunately rest, for the present at least, only on typed translations in EMHL of letters dated February 8 and March 12, 1812. The originals of these letters have not yet been uncovered.

110. There is a copy of the notarized instrument by which the Du Ponts turned over their interests in Bois-des-Fossés to Harmand on October 3, 1815, in EMHL, accession 90.

111. *Sur la liberté morale* (n.p., n.d.), read before his class at the Institute on January 20, 1803.

112. *De l'Infidélité* and *Des différens régimes qu'a suivi le genre humaine* (n.p., n.d.). The first piece bears no date but was published along with the second, read at the Institute on September 10, 1803.

113. *Sur les institutions religieuses dans l'intérieur des familles; avec un essai de traduction nouvelle de l'Oraison Dominicale* (n.p., n.d.). Du Pont offered to provide copies of this pamphlet to members of the Institute in October, 1806.

114. *Irénée Bonfils, sur la religion de ses pères et de nos pères* (Paris, 1808). This piece, over the pseudonym "Irénée Bonfils," was first published in the *Journal des Arts et des Sciences*, which had been consolidated with the *Bibliothèque Française*. Du Pont contributed several essays to these journals.

115. *Œuvres posthumes de Marmontel . . . extrait de la Bibliothèque Française* (n.p., n.d.). Marmontel's *Mémoires* in four volumes appeared in 1804, five years after the author's death.

116. *Notice historique sur Mr Quesnay de Saint-Germain; extrait de la Revue philosophique, littéraire et politique* (n.p., n.d.).

117. *Notice sur la vie de M. Barlow, ministre plénipotentiaire des États-Unis d'Amérique auprès de S.M. l'empereur et roi* (Paris, 1813), p. 8. Barlow, who lived

many years in France between 1789 and 1805, had been made an honorary citizen of that country. He was appointed American consul in Algiers in 1795 and returned to the United States in 1805. In 1811 he was sent back to France to negotiate a commercial treaty with Napoleon. He was in Poland in 1812 attempting to contact French officials, when he was caught up in the disastrous French retreat from Russia and died of exposure.

118. See above, chap. IV, p. 131.

119. Quoted by the Comte Le Marois (see note 103), p. 511. In EMHL, Winterthur MSS, group 2, there is a copy of this letter in the hand of Madame Du Pont de Nemours, with slight alterations from the text as printed by the Comte Le Marois.

120. Chinard, p. 157.

121. Du Pont to Jefferson, March 31, 1811—Chinard, pp. 161-162; Malone, pp. 130-131.

122. "Is there a man so blind as not to see that destiny itself guides all my operations?"—Napoleon's Proclamation at Cairo, December 21, 1798, conveniently translated in J. Christopher Herold, ed., *The Mind of Napoleon* (New York, 1961), p. 269.

123. Notice of his appointment, dated April 3, 1814, is printed in the *Moniteur*, no. 94, April 4, 1814, p. 569 (also in *A.P.*, 2ᵉ série, XII, 9). Lacour-Gayet, *Talleyrand*, II, 381, states that Talleyrand chose Du Pont to be secretary-general of the provisional government.

124. See *Moniteur*, no. 93, April 3, 1814, or *A.P.*, 2ᵉ série, XII, 9, for the decree of deposition, dated April 2; the *Journal de Paris, politique, commercial et littéraire*, no. 98, April 8, 1814, p. 2, for Marshal Ney's letter; EMHL, for copy of the broadside containing the text of Napoleon's act of abdication. Du Pont's name appears almost daily in the *Moniteur* for the first half of April, 1814, on government decrees—no. 92 (April 2), p. 565; 95 (April 5), p. 573; 96 (April 6), p. 577, 97 (April 7), p. 580, etc.; also in *A.P.*, 2ᵉ série, XII, 9, 11, 13, 15. There are many other papers connected with Du Pont's brief tenure as secretary-general of the provisional government in A. N., AF V 3, and EMHL, Winterthur MSS, group 2.

125. B. G. du Pont translation in *DPdN*, II, 113.

126. The quotations are from an undated and unfinished manuscript of eighty-three pages in EMHL, Winterthur MSS, group 2 (special) entitled "Rétablissement de la République." According to notations which are probably those of Miss Harriet Austin, a more complete copy of the work was once available in the Winterthur collections. Only a small portion of the unfinished manuscript at EMHL seems to be in Du Pont's hand. That the entire essay is his work cannot be proved from the available incomplete copy. The original decision that Du Pont was unquestionably the author must have been made by Miss Austin on the basis of the larger copy, which is not now at EMHL.

127. Letter of April 26, 1814, in B. G. du Pont, *DPdN*, II, 113.

128. *Moniteur*, July 6, 1814, p. 1: "Ordonnances du Roi."

129. The official papers naming Du Pont to these posts are in EMHL, Winterthur MSS, group 2.

130. The letter is in *ibid.* (the Eleuthera du Pont Smith autograph collection). The Czar wrote: "Ces ouvrages sont le résultat de vos longs et utiles travaux que j'apprécie & je vous remercie de me les avoir offerts."

131. B. G. du Pont translation (*DPdN*, II, 118) of letter in EMHL, Winterthur MSS, group 2.

132. B. G. du Pont translates this letter to his children dated April 26, 1814, in *DPdN*, II, 112-114.

133. Translation in *ibid.*, p. 120. The passport is in EMHL, Winterthur MSS, group 2.

XI

1. The *Lettre à M. Jean Baptiste Say, ex-membre du Tribunat, sur son Traité d'économie politique*—dated "A bord du Fingal, *22 Avril,* 1814, 41 degrés de latitude, 43.30 de longitude"—was later published with Du Pont's *Examen du livre de M. Malthus sur le principe de population; auquel on a joint la traduction de quatre chapitres de ce livre supprimés dans l'édition française* (Philadelphia, 1817). Du Pont's description of his letter as the "fruit prolixe du loisir que donne un vaisseau" are the final words of this edition (p. 159).

2. Du Pont's judgment of the influence of physiocratic principles on the financial decrees of the Constituent Assembly has been mentioned above at the end of chap. VI. His comments on Napoleon and France are in a long footnote, to which he appended an "addition du 30 Septembre 1813" on pp. 150-156 of the edition cited in note 1 above.

3. B. G. du Pont translation (*DPdN*, II, 127) of draft dated May 5, 1815, in EMHL, Winterthur MSS, group 2.

4. The preface, dated June 16, 1815, is in EMHL, Winterthur MSS, group 2 (special). In addition to the Du Pont-Jefferson correspondence, two other letters are useful in gaining an idea of some of the contents of the lost *mémoire*: Du Pont to Pedro Gual, January 15, 1816, and Du Pont to Gonzales da Cruz, June 16, 1817. They are in EMHL, Winterthur MSS, group 2.

5. Victor de Avenell brought to my attention the comments on Palacio in *Tricolor* (May, 1958), p. 20, a magazine published by the Venezuela Ministry for Education. Three letters of Du Pont to Palacio in 1815 (EMHL, Winterthur MSS, group 2) do not mention the incident.

6. Letter dated December 20, 1811, printed in Chinard, pp. 178-179.

7. Jefferson wrote to Du Pont on November 29, 1813, that Correa was "learned beyond any one I had before met with . . ." (Malone, p. 146). For a full account of Correa, see Richard B. Davis, *The Abbé Correa in America, 1812-1820: The Contributions of the Diplomat and Natural Philosopher to the Foundations of Our National Life* (*Transactions of the American Philosophical Society,* vol. 45, part 2), Philadelphia, 1955.

8. Du Pont to wife, July 24 and 25, 1815 (EMHL, Longwood MSS, group 8); Du Pont to Madison, July 25, 1815 (Chinard, p. 224).

9. Jefferson to Du Pont, June 6, 1815, and Du Pont to Jefferson, July 24, 1815 (Malone, pp. 163-164).

10. By a fortunate purchase, arranged in 1945-1946 by Professor Gilbert Chinard, the late P. S. du Pont acquired from M. Pierre Lesage of Paris ninety-four letters which Du Pont wrote to his wife between 1815 and 1817. These are available at EMHL, in Longwood MSS, group 8. In addition to the original letters, the Longwood collections have a typescript in French and an English translation of each letter. Eighty-five letters from Madame Du Pont to her husband during these two years are in EMHL, Winterthur MSS, group 2 (series D).

11. Du Pont to wife, August 14, 1815 (EMHL, Longwood MSS, group 8). B. G. du Pont (*DPdN*, II, 135-138) translates his model "motion," apparently, as Mrs. du Pont remarks, "for the use of any legislator who would introduce the measure." There is no record that any did.

12. Du Pont to wife, letter 14 (dated September 5, 6, 8, 9, 11, 14, 1815) (EMHL, Longwood MSS, group 8). This essay, as previously noted, has been lost.

13. *Ibid.,* letter 18 (October 10, 1815).

14. I have used the dates given by Du Pont in his letters to his wife—letter 24 (dated November 30-December 15), *ibid.* There are slight discrepancies in other accounts, as, for instance, in R. B. Davis, *The Abbé Correa in America,* pp. 102-03, where December 6 is given as the date of the arrival of Correa and Gilmer at Monticello.

15. Du Pont to Jefferson, December 21, 1815 (Malone, p. 170) and Du Pont to Madison, December 28, 1815 (Chinard, p. 233).

16. Malone, pp. 172-174.

17. Du Pont to Monroe, July 15, 1815 (Chinard, p. 224).

18. Malone, p. 176.

19. Two of Du Pont's *mémoires* are noted in the printed proceedings of the Institute: one on "Steam-boats et le steam-frégate" on October 20, 1815, and one on "Crampe" on July 24, 1816—Institut de France, Academie des Sciences, *Procès-verbaux des séances de l'academie tenues depuis la fondation de l'Institut jusqu'au mois d'août 1835*, V, 556; VI, 70. The paper "On Cramp" was read at the American Philosophical Society on February 2, 1816—*Early Proceedings of the American Philosophical Society . . .*, pp. 459-460. A letter suggesting that the Latin words *respublica* and *patria* be substituted in the English language for the words *commonwealth* and *country* was the subject of a committee report on February 2, 1816. The APS committee headed by Peter S. Duponceau was not favorable to Du Pont's suggestion. For detail on this matter, see "Patrie, République et 'Country' d'après Samuel Du Pont de Nemours et Peter Stephen Duponceau," *Institut français de Washington* (1957), pp. 54-62.

20. EMHL, Longwood MSS, group 8. The progress in the translation of Ariosto can be traced in these letters.

21. B. G. du Pont, *Life of E. I. du Pont*, X, 126-127, translates part of the partnership agreement among Cardon de Sandrans, Auguste Dautrement (who had come to America in 1792, becoming a friend of Victor Du Pont at the time of the ill-fated Genesee enterprise; see *ibid.*, VII, 196-197), Charles Dalmas (Irénée's brother-in-law), and Jacques Antoine Bidermann. Irénée advanced over half of the capital in behalf of Dalmas and provided many services through the powder works. The tannery, located on the Hagley property of the powder works, ceased operations in 1825 and was formally dissolved on June 1, 1826. Its debts were assumed by the powder company and eventually charged to Bidermann's account (EMHL, Longwood MSS, group 6).

22. Du Pont to Madison, July 25, 1815 (Chinard, p. 225), to Jefferson, December 10, 1815 (Malone, p. 167), to Jefferson, March 31, 1816 (Malone, pp. 177-179).

23. Du Pont to Jefferson, December 10, 1815 (Malone, p. 167), to Monroe, March 21, 1816 (Chinard, p. 250).

24. Du Pont to Jefferson, May 12, 1816 (Chinard, pp. 265-266), to Jefferson, August 18, 1816 (Malone, pp. 192-193), to Monroe, February 5, 1817 (Chinard, p. 274).

25. Du Pont to Madison, January 18, 1816 (Chinard, pp. 239-250), to Jefferson (Chinard, pp. 254-256).

26. Jefferson to Du Pont, April 24, 1816 (Malone, pp. 181-187; p. 184 for sentences quoted).

27. Du Pont to Jefferson, May 12, 1816 (Chinard, pp. 260-268).

28. Du Pont to Jefferson, August 18, 1816 (Malone, p. 194).

29. Chinard, pp. 267-268.

30. Du Pont to Monroe, November 19, 1816, EMHL, Winterthur MSS, group 2. This letter is not in Chinard.

31. Letter 32 (March 8-19, 1816), EMHL, Longwood MSS, group 8.

32. A.N., 38 AP 10: papiers du baron Hyde de Neuville.

33. *Ibid.; Mémoires et souvenirs du Baron Hyde de Neuville* (Paris, 1888-1892), II, 207-208; EMHL, Longwood MSS, group 8.

34. EMHL, Winterthur MSS, group 2; B. G. du Pont, *DPdN*, II, 152-153.

35. Du Pont to wife, September 6, 1816 (letter 59), EMHL, Longwood MSS, group 8; Institut royal de France, Classe d'histoire et de littérature ancienne (1815-1818), MS, Z 201, pp. 117, 119.

36. EMHL, Longwood MSS, group 8. Du Pont incorrectly spoke of the day as his seventy-sixth birthday.

37. *Ibid.*

38. Chinard, p. 276. Professor Chinard translates part of this letter in his introduction (lxxxi-lxxxii) and points out its possible significance.

39. Letter 92, June 18, 1817, EMHL, Longwood MSS, group 8.

40. B. G. du Pont translates part of this letter of August 5, 1817, in *DPdN*, II, 172.

41. B. G. du Pont, *Life of E. I. du Pont*, X, 264.

42. Madame Du Dont de Nemours died on February 18, 1841. A copy of the death certificate is at EMHL. There are two interesting letters describing visits to Madame Du Pont by two of Du Pont's grandchildren. Irénée's daughter Evelina, who had married Antoine Bidermann, paid a visit with her husband and mother-in-law in November, 1827 (EMHL, Winterthur MSS, group 6) and Victor's son, Samuel Francis, saw her, when she was very feeble, in November, 1840 (EMHL, Winterthur MSS, group 9).

43. Jefferson to E. I. du Pont, September 9, 1817 (Malone, p. 195).

44. The inscription reads:

SACRED TO THE MEMORY OF

PIERRE SAMUEL DU PONT DE NEMOURS

Knight of the order of Vasa, of the

Legion of Honor, and of the order

du Lis; Counsellor of State, member

of the first Constituent Assembly,

President of the Council of Ancients

and member of the Institute of France.

Born in Paris, December, A.D. 1739

Died at the Eleutherian Mills

August 7, A.D. 1817.

45. Translation of Gilbert Chinard in his edition of the correspondence with Jefferson, introduction, p. cxviii; for the French text, *ibid.*, p. 134.

Works Cited

This bibliography brings together materials cited in the notes, though it does not list all the works consulted in the preparation of this book. My original purpose, to provide a bibliography of the works of Du Pont de Nemours more complete than the long list in G. Schelle, *Du Pont de Nemours et l'école physiocratique* (Paris, 1888), pp. 399-432, was abandoned because of Earle E. Coleman's plans for what should be the definitive bibliography.

Manuscript and Archival Sources

With few exceptions I have used photocopies of the archival documents here listed. These photocopies are now available at the Eleutherian Mills Historical Library, Greenville, Delaware.

Archives Nationales (Paris).

C 2, 6, 7, 21, 28, 32, 33, 36, 38, 44, 154, 163, 485, 489, 490, 492, 493, 494, 496, 497, 501, 514, 516; C* I, 3

D VI, 17; D XLI, 1

F^7 4571, 4694, 5660; F^{10} 329; F^{12} 740; F^{17a} 1206, 1302, 3482

P 2601

AD (printed) I, 38, 39; AD XII, 7; AD XVII, 49

AF I, 9-12; AF* II, 288; AF III, 463; AF IV, 929; AF V, 2-3

Minutier central de Paris et du départment de la Seine: Registre no. 1627 XII 754; 2002 XII 775; 3898 XII 781; 5510 XII 802; 5270 XII 784

Archives privées: Série 144 AP 131 No. 11; 38 AP 10

Archives du Ministère des Affaires Étrangères (Paris)

Correspondance politique (Angleterre, vols. 516, 534, 536, 537, 538, 539, 541; États Unis, vols. 27, 31)

Mémoires et Documents (Amérique, vol. 17; Angleterre, vols. 65, 74; Asie, vols. 5, 11; Espagne, vol. 209; France, vols. 1488, 2006, 2011)

Bibliothèque Nationale (Paris): MSS français, nouvelles acquisitions 1303

Institut de France (Paris)

Academie des sciences morales et politiques: "Registre indicatif des mémoires lus par les membres de la classe des sciences morales et politiques" (1796-1803)

Academie des inscriptions et belles lettres: "Registre des procès-verbaux de la classe de littérature et beaux-arts" (1803-1818)

Bibliothèque de l'Institut: MS 1258

Works Cited

Archives de la Chambre de Commerce de Paris
I 2.00; I 2.52; I 2.69; III 1190 (printed); V 3.1; VI 4.1

Bibliothèque de la Société des Amis du Vieux Château de Nemours: Letters by and concerning Du Pont de Nemours

Archives départementales de l'Aisne (Laon): Série D 14

Archives départementales de Seine-et-Marne (Mélun): Série A₂ dossier I; B 260, 261, 266, 267

Mairie de Chevannes (Loiret): Registre des délibérations, 1793; Registre d'état civil, 1784, 1795

Badische Generallandesarchiv (Karlsruhe): Letters of Du Pont de Nemours to Margrave Carl Frederick and others

Badische Landesbibliothek (Karlsruhe): MS copy of Du Pont's drama "Joseph II"

Public Records Office (London): F. O. 97, vol. 157; F. O. 4 America (series 1); Chatham Papers 30, 8, 333-334; F. O. 27, 19 and 20 (France: Mr. W. Eden, 10 March–30 December 1786)

American Philosophical Society Archives (Philadelphia): Letters by and concerning Du Pont de Nemours

Eleutherian Mills Historical Library (Greenville, Delaware)
Winterthur MSS, especially groups 1, 2, and 8
Longwood MSS, especially groups 2, 3, and 8
"Mémoires" of Du Pont de Nemours: manuscript autobiography (see note 2 to chap. I, above)

PRINTED SOURCES

For books in which the date appears only on the copyright page, *c* precedes the year.

Works by Du Pont de Nemours (Arranged Chronologically)

Réflexions sur l'écrit intitulé: Richesse de l'état. [Paris, 1763.]

Réponse demandée par M. le Marquis de . . . à celle qu'il a faite aux Réflexions sur l'écrit intitulé: Richesse de l'état. [Paris, 1763.]

De l'exportation et de l'importation des grains. [Paris], 1764. (Modern edition by Edgard Depitre in the *Collection des économistes et des réformateurs sociaux de la France*, Paris, 1911.)

De l'administration des chemins. Pékin et se trouve à Paris, 1767.

Physiocratie ou Constitution naturelle du gouvernement le plus avantageux au genre humain. 2 vols. (or parts). Pékin et Leyde [Paris], 1767. (See note 60 to chap. II, above.)

De l'origine et des progrès d'une science nouvelle. Londres [Paris], 1768. (Modern edition by A. Dubois in *Collection des économistes et des réformateurs sociaux de la France*, Paris, 1910.)

Du commerce et de la Compagnie des Indes. Amsterdam and Paris, 1769.

Lettres . . . à la margrave Caroline-Louise de Bade sur les salons de 1773, 1777, 1779, publiées par le Dr. Karl Obser avec le concours de Gaston Brière et Maurice Tourneux (extrait des *Archives de l'art français*, nouvelle série, II, 1908). Paris, 1909.

431

Pierre Samuel Du Pont de Nemours

On Economic Curves: A Letter Reproduced in English Translation with the Original Diagram and an Introduction (by Henry W. Spiegel). Baltimore, 1955. (Written *ca.* 1774.)

Table raisonnée de principes de l'économie politique. [Paris, 1778.]

Essai de traduction en vers du Roland Furieux de l'Arioste. Paris, 1781. (Canto 1)

Mémoires sur la vie et les ouvrages de M. Turgot, ministre d'état. Philadelphia, 1782.

Idées sur les sécours à donner aux pauvres malades dans une grande ville. Philadelphia and Paris, 1786.

Mémoire . . . sur une compagnie des Indes, 1786. [Paris, 1790.]

Lettre à la chambre du commerce de Normandie; Sur le mémoire qu'elle a publié relativement au traité de commerce avec l'Angleterre. Rouen and Paris, 1788.

De la periodicité des assemblées nationales, de leur organisation, de la forme à suivre pour amener les propositions qui pourront y être faites, à devenir des loix; & de la sanction necessaire pour que ces loix soient obligatoires. Paris, 1789.

Discours prononcé à l' Assemblée nationale . . . sur l'état et les ressources des finances. Versailles, 1789.

Discours . . . sur les banques en général, sur la caisse d'escompte en particulier, et sur le projet du premier ministre des finances, relativement à cette dernière. Paris, 1789.

Du Pont de Nemours on the Dangers of Inflation; an address by Pierre Samuel Du Pont deputy from Nemours made before the National Assembly of France September 25, 1790. Translated by Edmond E. Lincoln. Boston, 1950.

Considérations sur la position politique de la France, de l'Angleterre et de l'Espagne. n. p., n. d. (English translation: London, 1790.)

Opinion . . . sur l'exercice du droit de la guerre et de la paix. Paris, 1790.

Le Pacte de famille et les conventions subsequentes, entre la France & l'Espagne; avec des observations sur chaque article. Paris, 1790.

Réclamation faite par M. Du Pont, député du bailliage de Nemours, à l'Assemblée nationale, le premier juin 1790. Paris, [1790].

Principes constitutionnels, relativement au renvoi & à la nomination des ministres; discours prononcé à la Société des Amis de la Liberté & de la Constitution de 1789 dans leur séance du 20 octobre 1790. Paris, 1790.

Causes très-légitimes de la diversité des opinions, relativement à l'usage que le roi a fait du veto sur le décret qui concernait des émigrans, et sur celui qui regardait les prêtres non-sermentés; observations propres à décider la question et à réunir les esprits. [Paris, 1791.]

Avant-dernier chapitre de l'histoire des Jacobins. [Paris, 1792.]

De la position politique de la France; moyen simple d'en écarter tout peril en lui conservant toute sa dignité. Paris, 1792.

Lettre . . . à M. Pétion. [Paris, 1792.]

Seconde lettre . . . à M. Pétion. [Paris, 1792.]

Lettre . . . aux citoyens constitutionnaires. [Paris, 1792.]

Observations sur le décret relatif à la guerre. [Paris, 1792.]

L'Enfance et la jeunesse de Du Pont de Nemours racontées par lui-même. Edited by H. A. du Pont. Paris, 1906. (Unfinished autobiography, written late 1792.)

Works Cited

Vues sur l'éducation nationale par un cultivateur ou moyen de simplifier l'in-struction, de la rendre à la fois morale, philosophique, républicaine, civile et militaire, sans déranger les travaux de l'agriculture et des arts aux quels la jeunesse doit concourir. Paris, an II [1794].

Plaidoyer de Lysias, contre les membres des anciens comités de salut public et de sûreté générale. Paris, an III [1795].

Du pouvoir législatif et du pouvoir exécutif, convenables à la république fran-çaise. Paris, an III [1795].

Observations sur la constitution proposé par la commission des onze, et sur la position actuelle de la France. Paris, an III [1795].

Philosophie de l'univers. Paris, 1796. (First draft, 1792-1793.)

Le Serpent; commentaire sur l'ancienne allégorie du serpent et de la vie qui se trouve dans le Boun-Déhesch et dans plusieurs autres mythologies orientales (bound with Mlle *Dzjerzbicka; anecdote polonaise*). [Paris, 1796.]

Opinion . . . sur la résolution relative à la loi du 3 brumaire; séance du 27 brumaire, an V. Paris, an V [1796].

Opinion . . . sur l'imprimerie de la république; séance du 19 prairial, an V. Paris, an V [1797].

Opinion . . . sur la contrainte par corps; séance du 24 ventôse, an 5. Paris, an V [1797].

Opinion . . . sur la première résolution du 19 messidor, relative aux transactions; séance du 15 fructidor, an V. Paris, an V [1797].

Opinion . . . sur la résolution du 19 messidor, relative aux fugitifs du Haut & du Bas-Rhin; séance du 11 fructidor. Paris, an V [1797].

Opinion . . . sur la résolution du premier messidor, relative à l'urgence des paimens, & aux négociations à faire par la trésorerie. Paris, an V [1797].

Opinion . . . sur la résolution relative aux canaux d'Orléans et de Loing; séance du 15 nivôse. Paris, an V [1797].

Opinion . . . sur le projet d'un droit de passe; séance du 9 ventôse, an V. Paris, an 5 [1797].

Opinion . . . sur les projets de loterie & sur l'état des revenus ordinaires de la République; séance du 24 germinal, an 5. Paris, an 5 [1797].

Opinion . . . sur les postes. Paris, n. d. [1797]

Rapport . . . au nom d'une commission speciale, sur l'organisation & les dépenses de la trésorerie nationale; séance du 17 prairial, an V. Paris, an V [1797].

Rapport . . . sur la résolution aux dépenses des relations exterieures; séance du 15 fructidor, an V. Paris, an V [1797].

National Education in the United States. Translated by B. G. du Pont. Newark, Dela., 1923. (Written 1800-1801.)

Sur la liberté morale. n. p., n. d. Read before Institute, January 30, 1803.)

De l'infidélité (bound with *Des différens régimes qu'a suivi le genre humain*). n.p., n.d. (Second essay read before Institute, September 10, 1803.)

Banque Territoriale pamphlets (see note 58 to chap. X). (October-November, 1803).

Œuvres posthumes de Marmontel . . . extrait de la *Bibliothèque Française.* n. p., n. d. (Marmontel's *Mémoires* appeared 1804.)

New Jersey pamphlets (see note 65 to chap. X). (1805).

Rapport . . . à la société philantropique, au nom de la commission de sociétés de prévoyance, sur celle dite des Amis de l'égalité, autrefois Bourse des malades. n. p., n. d. [1805]

Rapport fait à la société philantropique . . . au nom de la commission des sociétés de prévoyance, le 6 pluviôse an XIII. n. p., n. d. [1805]

Notice historique sur Mr Quesnay de Saint-Germain; extrait de la *Revue philosophique, littéraire et politique.* n. p., n. d. [1805].

Sur le déisme; lettre aux auteurs du Publiciste. Paris, an XIV [1805].

Sur la Banque de France, les causes de la crise qu'elle a éprouvée, les tristes effets qui en sont résultés et les moyens d'en prévenir le retour; avec une théorie des banques. Paris, 1806.

Sur les institutions religieuses dans l'intérieur des famillies; avec un essai de traduction nouvelle de l'Oraison Dominicale. n. p., n. d. (Offered to members of Institute, October, 1806.)

Quelques mémoires sur différens sujets: la pluspart d'histoire naturelle, ou de physique générale et particulière. Paris, 1807. Second edition, 1813.

Irénée Bonfiils, sur la religion de ses pères et de nos pères. Paris, 1808.

Œuvres de M. Turgot, ministre d'état, précédées et accompagnés de mémoires et de notes sur sa vie, son administration et ses ouvrages. 9 vols. Paris, 1808-1811.

Mémoires soumis à la 3e classe de l'Institut sur plusieurs ouvrages historiques, et particulièrement sur celui de M. de Rulhière, intitulé: De l'anarchie de Pologne, concourant pour les prix décennaux. . . . Paris, 1810.

Essai de traduction en vers du Roland Furieux de l'Arioste. Paris, 1812. (Cantos I, II, III)

Notice sur la vie de M. Barlow, ministre plénipotentiaire des États-Unis d'Amérique auprès de S. M. l'empereur et roi. Paris, 1813.

Examen du livre de M. Malthus sur le principe de population; auquels on a joint la traduction de quatre chapitres de ce livre supprimés dans l'édition française; bound with *Lettre à M. Jean Baptiste Say, ex-membre du Tribunat, sur son Traité d'économie politique.* Philadelphia, 1817.

Opuscula par Du Pont de Nemours. 3 vols. (Miscellaneous pieces from many years bound together.)

Published letters:

Schelle, G., ed. "Lettres inédits de Du Pont de Nemours au Comte Chreptowicz," *Journal des Économistes: Revue mensuelle de la science économique et de la statistique,* 6e série, XIV (1907), 3-21. (First letter 1778, last 1811.)

Chinard, G., ed. *Un Epilogue du neuf Thermidor: Lettres de Du Pont de Nemours écrites de la prison de la Force 5 Thermidor-8 Fructidor An II.* Paris, 1929.

Chinard, G., ed. "Lettres de du Pont de Nemours à Felix Faulcon 12 mai 1795–25 octobre 1802." *The French American Review,* I (1948), 174-183.

See also items marked by asterisk in next two sections.

Correspondence, Mémoires, and Other Writings by Du Pont's Contemporaries

(Items starred contain important writings of Du Pont de Nemours.)

Works Cited

Abrantès, Laure Saint-Martin (Permon) Junot, duchesse d'. *Histoire de salons de Paris; tableaux et portraits du grande monde, sous Louis XVI, le Directoire, le Consulat et l'Empire, la Restauration, et le règne de Louis Philippe Ier*. 6 vols. Brussels, 1837-1838.

[Bachaumont]. *Mémoires secrets pour servir à l'histoire de la république des lettres en France, depuis M. DCCC. LXII jusqu'à nos jours*. 36 vols. "à Londres," 1784-1789.

Barruel, Abbé. *Mémoires pour servir à l'histoire du Jacobinisme*. 5 vols. Hambourg, 1799.

Beugnot, Jacques. *Mémoires . . . .* Edited by Albert Beugnot. 2 vols. Paris, 1866. (English translation by Charlotte M. Yonge; 2 vols., London, 1871.)

Boissy d'Anglas, [François-Antoine]. *Essai sur la vie, les écrits et les opinions de M. de Malesherbes, adressé à mes enfans*. 2 vols. Paris, 1819.

Boyetet. *Recueil de divers mémoires, relatifs au traité de commerce avec l'Angleterre, faits avant, pendant et après cette négociation*. 2 vols. Versailles, 1789.

Cantillon, Richard. *Essai sur la nature du commerce en général*. Edited by Henry Higgs. London, 1931.

Carl Frederick, Margrave of Baden
Politische Correspondenz Karl Friedrichs von Baden, 1783-1806, herausgegeben von der Badischen Historischen Commission. Edited by Bernhard Erdmannsdörffer. 6 vols. Heidelberg, 1888-1901. (Contains letters of Du Pont de Nemours.)
Carl Friedrichs von Baden Brieflicher Verkehr mit Mirabeau und Du Pont. Edited by Carl Knies. 2 vols. Heidelberg, 1892. (Many Du Pont letters and essays.)

Duquesnoy, Adrien. *Journal d'Adrien Duquesnoy (député du tiers état de Bar-le-Duc sur l'Assemblée constituante 3 mai 1789–3 avril 1790)*. Edited by Robert de Crèvecour. 2 vols. Paris, 1894.

Dolomieu, Déodat-Guy-Silvain-Trancrède Gretet de. *Correspondance inédit*. n. p., n. d.

du Pont, Eleuthère Iréné. *Life of Eleuthère Irènée du Pont from Contemporary Correspondence*. Edited and translated by B. G. du Pont. 12 vols. Newark, Delaware, 1923-1927. (Many letters of Du Pont de Nemours.)

Du Pont, Josephine (Madame Victor). *Souvenirs épars de ma jeunesse*. Privately printed, 1908.

Du Pont, Victor M. *Journey to France and Spain, 1801*. Edited by Charles W. David. Ithaca, c. 1961.

Économistes Financiers du XVIIIe siècle: Vauban . . . Boisguillebert . . . Jean Law . . . Melon . . . Dutot. Edited by Eugène Daire. 2d. ed. Paris, 1851.

Examination of the Memorial of the Owners and Underwriters of the American Ship the New Jersey, *and of the Documents Accompanying It, as Presented to the Senate and House of Representatives of the United States of America at Their Late Session*, by a Friend of Truth and Justice. Philadelphia, 1806.

Franklin, Benjamin
Benjamin Franklin's Autobiographical Writings. Edited by Carl Van Doren. New York, 1945.
The Complete Work of Benjamin Franklin. Edited by John Bigelow. 10 vols. New York and London, 1887-1888.

Franklin in France: from Original Documents Most of Which Are Now Published for the First Time. Edited by Edward E. Hale and Edward E. Hale, Jr. 2 vols. Boston, 1887-1888.

The Writings of Benjamin Franklin. Edited by Albert H. Smyth. 10 vols. New York, 1905-1907.

Guichard, M. *Affaire de la Banque Territoriale*, Précis. Paris, n. d.

Hyde de Neuville, baron. *Mémoires et souvenirs* . . . . 3 vols. Paris, 1888-1892.

Jefferson, Thomas

    *The Correspondence of Jefferson and Du Pont de Nemours, with an Introduction on Jefferson and the Physiocrats. Edited by Gilbert Chinard. Baltimore, 1931.

    *Correspondence between Thomas Jefferson and Pierre Samuel du Pont de Nemours, 1798-1817. Edited by Dumas Malone; translated by Linwood Lehman. Boston and New York, 1930.

    The Papers of Thomas Jefferson. Edited by Julian P. Boyd. 16 vols. to date. Princeton, 1950-.

Lafayette, Marie Joseph Paul Yves Roch Gilbert du Motier, marquis de. *Mémoires, correspondances, et manuscrits du Général Lafayette, publiés par sa famille.* 12 vols. in 6. Brussels, 1837.

Mirabeau, Honoré Gabriel Riquetti, comte de.

    Lettres de Mirabeau à Chamfort, imprimées sur les originaux écrits de la main de Mirabeau . . . . Paris, an V [1797?].

    Lettres originales . . . écrits du donjon de Vincennes . . . 1777, 78, 79, et 80. Edited by P. Manuel. 4 vols. Paris, 1792.

[Mirabeau, Victor de Riquetti, marquis de.] *L'Ami des hommes ou Traité de la population.* 8 vols. n. p., 1759-1760.

Napoleon Bonaparte

    Lettres inédites de Napoléon Ier (an VIII-1815). Edited by Léon Lecestre. 2d. ed. 2 vols. Paris, 1897.

    The Mind of Napoleon. Edited by J. Christopher Herold. New York, 1961.

    Napoleon's Letters. Edited and translated by J. M. Thompson. Everyman's Library. New York, 1954.

    New Letters of Napoleon I Omitted from the Edition Published under Auspices of Napoleon III. Translated by Lady Mary Loyd. London, 1898.

Page, Pierre François. *Banque Territoriale, avis aux créanciers et aux débiteurs de cet établissement.* [Paris, 1803.]

———. *Banque Territoriale, réponse à M. Dupont (de Nemours), avis aux créanciers porteurs de traitres.* [Paris, 1803.]

Pétion de Villeneuve, Jérôme. *Réponse de Pétion à Du Pont.* [Paris, 1792.]

*Physiocrates: Quesnay, Dupont de Nemours, Mercier de la Rivière, l'abbé Baudeau, Le Trosne, avec une introduction sur la doctrine des physiocrates, des commentaires et des notices historiques. Edited by E. Daire. 2 vols. Paris, 1846.

Quesnay, François. *Œuvres économiques et philosophiques de F. Quesnay fondateur de système physiocratique.* Edited by Auguste Oncken. Frankfort, 1888.

Rousseau, J. J. *The Confessions of Jean Jacques Rousseau.* Modern Library edition. New York, 1945.

Roussel de La Tour. *La Richesse de l'état.* [Paris, 1763.]

Works Cited

Smith, Adam. *An Inquiry into the Nature and Causes of the Wealth of Nations.* Everyman's Library. 2 vols. New York, 1917.

Staël, Anne Germaine Necker, baronne de.
Considerations sur les principaux événemens de la Révolution française. 2d. ed. 2 vols. Paris, 1818.
*Le Marois, Comte. "Du Pont de Nemours et Madame de Staël." *Cahiers de politique étrangère du Journal des nations américaines;* supplement bibliographique à *France-Amérique Magazine.* Nouvelle série, années 1946-1950, cahier LV-LVI, pp. 499-512. Letters dated from 1800 to 1810.)

*[Stevens, John]. *Examen du gouvernement d'Angleterre comparé aux constitutions des États-Unis; où l'on réfute quelques assertions contenues dans l'ouvrage de M. Adams, intitulé: Apologie des Constitution des États-Unis d'Amerique & dans celui de M. Delolme, intitulé: De la Constitution d'Angleterre; par un cultivateur de New Jersey; ouvrage traduit de l'anglois, & accompagné de notes.* London and Paris, 1789. (Some of the notes are by Du Pont de Nemours.)

Talleyrand-Périgord, Charles Maurice de. *Mémoires du Prince de Talleyrand. Publiés avec une préface et des notes par le Duc de Broglie.* 5 vols. Paris, 1891-1892.

Turgot, Anne Robert Jacques
Lettres de Turgot à Du Pont de Nemours de 1764 à 1781. Extraites des Œuvres de Turgot et documents le concernant. Paris, 1924.
Œuvres de Turgot et documents le concernant avec biographie et notes. Edited by G. Schelle. 5 vols. Paris, 1913-1923.
Œuvres de Turgot, nouvelle édition classé par ordre de matières avec les notes de Dupont de Nemours augmenté de lettres inédits, des questions sur le commerce, et d'observations et de notes nouvelles . . . . Edited by Eugène Daire and Hippolyte Dussard. 2 vols. Paris, 1844.

Voltaire, François Marie Arouet de
Œuvres complètes de Voltaire; nouvelle édition . . . conforme pour le texte à l'édition de Beuchot. 52 vols. Paris, 1877-1885.
Voltaire's Correspondence. Edited by Theodore Besterman. 89 vols. to date. Genève, 1953- .

Young, Arthur. *Travels in France during the Years 1787, 1788 and 1789.* Edited by Constantia Maxwell. Cambridge, 1929.

Contemporary Journals and Pamphlets

(Items starred contain important writings of Du Pont de Nemours.)

Les Actes des Apôtres. 11 vols. [Paris], 1789-1791. (A few volumes are pertinent to Du Pont de Nemours.)

Almanach de tous les saints de l'Assemblée nationale qui doivent se réunis dans la vallée de Josaphat après la constitution. Paris, n. d.

Almanach des députés à l'Assemblée nationale. n. p., 1790.

Bulletin de la Société d'Encouragement pour l'Industrie Nationale. 2 vols. [Paris], 1802-1807.

Calendrier et règlemens du Musée de Paris suivis du tableau de ceux qui composent cette société. Paris, 1784.

Correspondance patriotique entre les citoyens qui ont été membres de l'Assemblée nationale constituante. 8 vols. Paris, 1791-1792. (Du Pont de Nemours edited the first five numbers.)

Éphémérides du citoyen, ou Bibliothèque des sciences morales et politiques. 66 vols. Paris, 1767-1772. (Numbers edited by Du Pont de Nemours: tome VI, 1768, to tome III, 1772.)

La Galerie des États-généraux. n. p., 1789.

Gazette du commerce (after May, 1765, *Gazette du commerce, d'agriculture et de finances*). (Volumes containing contributions of Du Pont de Nemours in 1764, 1765, 1766.)

Le Glaneur véridique de la galerie nationale, ou les contre-pinceaux de cette galerie. n. p., n. d.

L'Historien. 17 vols. Paris, 1795-1797. (Founded and edited by Du Pont de Nemours. The reports of meetings of the Council of Elders, prepared by Bienaymé, were chiefly consulted.)

Journal de l'agriculture du commerce et des finances. 18 vols. in 7. Paris, 1765-1766. (Volumes edited by Du Pont de Nemours from September, 1765, to November, 1766.)

Journal de la Société de 1789. 15 numbers. Paris, 1790.

Liste des députés amis de la liste civile, qui ont formé le projet de donner l'absolution au pouvoir exécutif, contre le voeu de la nation. n. p., 1791.

Liste des députés plus noirs que les noirs, qui ont quitté la séance au moment de l'appel nominal, sur la question des ministres; avec ceux qui ont opiné pour et contre. n. p., 1790.

Le Point du Jour ou résultat de ce qui s'est passé la veille à l'Assemblée nationale. 26 vols. Paris, 1789-1791. (A few volumes referring to Du Pont de Nemours were used.)

Recueil de pièces concernant l'association de bienfaisance judicaire fondée en 1787. Paris, 1788.

La véritable Portrait de nos législateurs, ou Galerie des tableaux exposés à la vue du public depuis le 5 mai 1789, jusqu'au premier octobre 1791. Paris, 1792.

Collections of Documents, Reports, Debates, etc.

American State Papers, Class I, Foreign Relations. Vol. II (Documents Legislative and Executive, of the Congress of the United States, from the first session of the First to the third session of the Thirteenth Congress inclusive; selected and edited . . . by Walter Lowrie . . . and Matthew St. Clair . . .). Washington, 1832.

Aulard, [F.] A., ed. *Paris pendant la réaction thermidorienne et sous le directoire; recueil de documents pour l'histoire de l'esprit public à Paris.* (Collection de documents relatifs à l'histoire de Paris pendant la Révolution française.) 5 vols. Paris, 1898-1902.

———. *La Société des Jacobins; recueil de documents pour l'histoire du club des Jacobins de Paris.* (Collection de documents relatifs à l'histoire de Paris pendant la Révolution française.) 6 vols. Paris, 1889-1897.

Bloch, Camille, ed. *Procès-verbaux du comité des finances de l'Assemblée constituante.* (Collection de documents inédits sur l'histoire économique de la Révolution française.) Rennes, 1922-1923.

Works Cited

Bonnassieux, Pierre and Eugéne Lelong. *Conseil de Commerce et Bureau du Commerce 1700-1791; inventaire analytique des procès-verbaux.* Paris, 1900.

Brette, A., ed. *Recueil de documents relatifs à la convocation des États-généraux de 1789.* 4 vols. Paris, 1894-1915.

Buchez, P. J. B. and P. C. Roux. *Histoire parlementaire de la Révolution française ou Journal des assemblées nationales depuis 1789 jusqu'en 1815.* 40 vols. Paris, 1834-1838.

Cahen, L. and R. Guyot. *L'Œuvre legislative de la Révolution.* Paris, 1913.

Challamel, Augustin. *Les Clubs contre-révolutionaires; cercles, comités, sociétés, salons, réunions, cafés, restaurants et libraires.* (*Collection de documents relatifs à l'histoire de Paris pendant la Révolution française.*) Paris, 1895.

Chemin, J.-B. *Code de religion et de morale naturelle, à l'usage des adorateurs de Dieu et amis des hommes.* Paris, an VII [1799].

Collection des mémoires presentés à l'Assemblée des notables; première et seconde division. Versailles, 1787.

Duvergier, J. B., ed. *Collection complète des lois, décrets, ordonnances, règlemens, avis du conseil d'état . . . (de 1788 à 1830 inclusivement, par ordre chronologique) . . . .* 20 vols. Paris, 1834-1837.

Early Proceedings of the American Philosophical Society for the Promotion of Useful Knowledge, Compiled by One of the Secretaries from the Manuscript Minutes of its Meetings from 1744 to 1838. Philadelphia, 1884.

Gazette Nationale, ou le Moniteur universal. Paris, 1789-1815. (The *Réimpression de l'ancien Moniteur . . .* [1789-1799]; 32 vols., Paris, 1847-1850, was occasionally used.)

Gerbaux, Fernand and Charles Schmidt, eds. *Procès-verbaux des comités d'agriculture et de commerce de la Constituante de la Législative et de la Convention.* (*Collection de documents inédits sur l'histoire économique de la Révolution française.*) 4 vols. Paris, 1906.

Institut de France. Académie des sciences. *Procès-verbaux des séances de l'académie tenues depuis la fondation de l'Institut jusqu'au mois d'août 1835.* 10 vols. Hendaye, 1910-1922.

———. Académie des sciences morales et politiques. *Registre des procès-verbaux et rapports, ans IV-VI.* [Paris, 1798]; *Registre des procès-verbaux et rapports de la classe des sciences morales et politiques (an VII-VIII).* [Paris], n. d.

Journal des débats et des décrets ou récit de ce qui s'est passé aux séances de l'Assemblée nationale depuis 17 juin 1789 . . . . Paris, 1789-1791.

Journal des États-généraux convoqués par Louis XVI, le 27 avril 1789; ouvrage accueilli & très interessant où se trouvent toutes les motions, délibérations, discours, & opérations de l'assemblée, séance par séance. 35 vols. Paris, 1789-1791.

Lallement, Guillaume, ed. *Choix de rapports, opinions et discours prononcés à la tribune nationale, depuis 1789 jusqu'à ce jour.* 21 vols. Paris, 1818-1822.

Lefebvre, Georges and Anne Terroine, eds. *Recueil de documents relatifs aux séances des États généraux mai-juin 1789.* Tome I: *Les Préliminaires — la séance du 5 mai.* Paris, 1953.

Legg, L. G. W., ed. *Select Documents Illustrative of the History of the French Revolution: The Constituent Assembly.* 2 vols. Oxford, 1905.

Malloy, William M., comp. *Treaties, Conventions, International Acts, Protocols and Agreements between the United States of America and Other Powers.* 61st Congress, 2d session, Document no. 357. 2 vols. Washington, 1910.

Mavidal, L. *et al.*, eds. *Archives parlementaires de 1787 à 1860, recueil complet . . . première série (1787 à 1799), 82 vols.; seconde série (1800 à 1860), 127 vols.* Paris, 1862-1913. (The first series actually ends at January 4, 1794; the second, at July 17, 1839.)

Observations présentées au roi par les bureaux de l'Assemblée de notables, sur les mémoires remis à l'assemblée ouverte par le roi, à Versailles, le 23 février 1787. Versailles, 1787.

Pigeonneau, Henri and Alfred de Foville, eds. *L'Administration de l'agriculture au controle général des finances (1785-1787): procès-verbaux et rapports.* Paris, 1882.

Procès-verbal de l'assemblée baillivale de Nemours pour la convocation des états-généraux; avec les cahiers de trois ordres. 2 vols. Paris, 1789.

Procès-verbal de l'Assemblée des notables, tenue à Versailles, en l'année M.DCCLXXXVII. Paris, 1788.

Procès-verbal de l'Assemblée de notables tenue à Versailles en l'année 1788. Paris, 1789.

Procès-verbal de l'Assemblée nationale imprimé par son ordre. 75 vols. Paris, 1789-1791.

Renouvin, Pierre, ed. *L'Assemblée de notables de 1787: la conference du 2 mars.* Paris, 1920.

Traité de navigation et de commerce entre la France et la Grande Bretagne, conclu à Versailles de 26 septembre 1786. Paris, 1787.

Biographical and Other Studies on Du Pont de Nemours

Aimé [Azam], Denise. *Du Pont de Nemours Honnête Homme.* Paris, 1933.

Betts, Raymond. "Du Pont de Nemours and Napoleonic France." (Unpublished typescript.)

———. "The Talleyrand Loan." (Unpublished typescript.)

Boullée, A. *Notices sur M. Poivre intendant des Isles de France et de Bourbon, correspondant de l'Académie des Sciences, et sur M. Dupont de Nemours, conseiller d'état, membre de l'Institut . . . suivies du discours de reception de l'auteur à l'Académie de Lyon.* Lyon, 1835.

Cuny, L. *Le Rôle de Dupont de Nemours en matière fiscale à l'Assemblée constituante.* Paris, 1909.

Dacier, [Bon Joseph]. "Notice historique sur la vie et les ouvrages de M. Dupont de Nemours," *Histoire de l'Académie royale des inscriptions et belles-lettres* (n. p., n. d.). An extract of this notice appears in L. Seb. le Normand and J.-G.-V. de Moléon, *Annales de l'industrie nationale et étrangère ou Mercure technologique; recueil de mémoires sur les arts et métiers, les manufactures, le commerce, l'industrie, l'agriculture, etc., renfermant la description des musées des produits de l'industrie française* (tome I). Paris, 1820.

du Pont, B. G. *Du Pont de Nemours.* 2 vols. Newark, Dela., 1933.

Jolly, Pierre. *Du Pont de Nemours Soldat de la Liberté.* Paris, 1956.

Lioret, Georges. "Du Pont de Nemours député aux États généraux et à l'Assemblée constituante," *Annales de la Société historique et archéologique du Gâtinais,* XXXII (1914-1915), 1-77.

Works Cited

[Montchanin, Jacques P.-H. de]. *Notice sur la vie de Dupont (de Nemours), conseiller d'état, chevalier de Vasa et de la Légion d'Honneur* (par M. de M . . .). Paris, 1818.

Schelle, G. *Du Pont de Nemours et l'école physiocratique.* Paris, 1888.

Silvestre, M. *Notice biographique sur M. Dupont (Pierre Samuel), membre de l'Institut, de la Société royale et centrale d'agriculture, et d'un grand nombre d'autres sociétés savantes et littéraires françaises et étrangères, chevallier [sic] de la Légion d'Honneur et de l'ordre de Vasa . . . .* Paris, 1818. (Silvestre's eulogy may also be found in *Mémoires d'agriculture, d'économie rurale et domestique, publiés par la Société royale et centrale d'agriculture* [Paris, 1818].)

Streletski, Camille. *Pierre Samuel Du Pont de Nemours (1739-1817); étude historique, physiognomique et graphologique.* Nemours, 1931.

Bibliographies, Dictionaries, Guides, Indexes, etc.

Boursin, E., and A. Challamel. *Dictionnaire de la Révolution française: institutions, hommes et faits.* Paris, 1893.

Brette, Armand. *Les Constituants; liste des députés et des suppléants élus à l'Assemblée constituante de 1789.* Paris, 1897.

Kuscinski, Auguste. *Les Députés au corps législatif, conseil des cinq-cents, conseil des anciens de l'an IV à l'an VII; listes, tableaux et lois.* (Société de l'histoire de la Révolution française.) Paris, 1905.

Leland, Waldo G., ed. *Guide to Materials for American History in the Libraries and Archives of Paris.* (Carnegie Institution Publication no. 392.) 2 vols. Washington, 1932-1943.

Liste, par ordre alphabétique de bailliages et sénéchaussées, de MM. les députés à l'Assemblée nationale. Paris, 1789.

Marion, M. *Dictionnaire des institutions de la France aux XVIIe et XVIIIe siècles.* Paris, 1923.

Martin, André, and Gérard Walter. *Catalogue de l'histoire de la Révolution française.* 5 vols. Paris, 1936-1943.

Noms et demeures de MM. les députés à l'Assemblée nationale. Paris, 1789.

Nouvelle biographie général depuis les temps de plus reculés jusqu'à nos jours. 46 vols. Paris, 1862-1870.

Révolution française: table alphabétique et chronologique du Moniteur de 1787 jusqu'a l'an 8 de la republique [1799]. 7 vols. Paris, 1802.

Stourm, René. *Bibliographie historique des finances de la France au dix-huitième siècle.* Paris, 1895.

Table des matières, des noms de lieux et des noms de personnes contenus dans les procès-verbaux des séances de l'Assemblée constituante, depuis le 5 mai 1789 jusqu'au 30 septembre 1791 inclusivement. 5 vols. Paris, an XIV [1805].

Tourneux, Maurice. *Bibliographie de l'histoire de Paris pendant la Révolution française.* 5 vols. Paris, 1890-1913.

Miscellaneous Secondary Works

Aldridge, Alfred O. *Franklin and his French Contemporaries.* New York, 1957.

Aulard, A. *The French Revolution: A Political History 1789-1804.* Translated by Bernard Miall. 4 vols. London, 1910.

Pierre Samuel Du Pont de Nemours

Bemis, Samuel F. *A Diplomatic History of the United States.* 4th ed. New York, *c.* 1955.

Benham, Daniel. *Memoirs of James Hutton: Comprising the Annals of his Life, and Connection with the United Brethren.* London, 1856.

Bloch, Camille. *Études sur l'histoire économique de la France (1760-1789).* Paris, 1900.

Bosc, Edouard. "Le Livre de famille" (mimeographed). N. p., n.d.

Bourne, Henry E. *The Revolutionary Period in Europe (1763-1815).* New York, 1914.

Bouton, André. *Les Francs-Maçons Manceaux et la Révolution française (1741-1815).* Le Mans, 1958.

Brinton, Crane. *A Decade of Revolution 1789-1799.* (*The Rise of Modern Europe,* ed. W. L. Langer, XII). New York, 1934.

Cahen, Léon. "Une nouvelle interpretation du traité franco-anglais de 1786-1787," *Revue historique,* CLXXXV (1939), 258-270.

The Cambridge Modern History ed. A. W. Ward *et al.* Vol. VIII: *The French Revolution.* New York, 1904.

Chapuisat, Edouard. *Necker.* Paris, [1938].

Chinard, Gilbert. *Thomas Jefferson: The Apostle of Americanism.* 2nd ed. rev. Boston, 1943.

————. *Volney et l'Amérique d'après des documents inédits et sa correspondance avec Jefferson.* (Johns Hopkins Studies in Romance Literature and Languages, I.) Baltimore and Paris, 1923.

Choquet, E. *La Chambre de Commerce de Paris, an XI et an XII de la République (1803-1804).* Extrait du *Bulletin de la Chambre de Commerce de Paris.* Paris, 1900.

Conan, Jules. "Les Débuts de Dupont de Nemours et la publication de la 'Physiocratie,' " *Revue d'histoire économique et sociale,* XXXIII (1955), 206-223.

Crocker, Leslie G. *An Age of Crisis: Man and World in Eighteenth Century Thought.* Baltimore, 1959.

Dakin, Douglas. *Turgot and the Ancien Régime in France.* London, 1939.

Davis, Richard B. *The Abbé Correa in America, 1812-1820: The Contributions of the Diplomat and Natural Philosopher to the Foundations of Our National Life.* (*Transactions of the American Philosophical Society,* vol. 45, part 2.) Philadelphia, 1955.

Doniol, Henri. *Histoire de la participation de la France à l'establissement des États-Unis.* 5 vols. Paris, 1886-1892.

Dorian, Max. *Du Pont de Nemours: de la poudre au nylon.* (*Histoire des grandes entreprises,* ed. René Sédillot.) Paris, *c.* 1961. (English translation by E. B. Garside; Boston, 1962.)

Dubuisson-Bertin, Jeanine. "Du Pont de Nemours et Napoléon," Institut Napoléon: *Recueil de travaux et documents.* Paris, 1946.

Dujarric de la Rivière, R. *E.-I. Du Pont de Nemours élève de Lavoisier.* Paris, *c.* 1954.

Dumas, F. *Le Traité de 1786 entre France et l'Angleterre.* Toulouse, 1904.

Dunan, M. "Un Adversaire du système continental," *Revue des études napoléoniennes,* VII (1915), 262-275.

du Pont, H. A. *The Early Generations of the Du Pont and Allied Families.* 2 vols. New York, 1923.

Works Cited

The Du Pont Magazine, XXXVIII (Nov.-Dec., 1944), 10-11. (Engraving of ship *American Eagle.*)

Dutton, William S. *Du Pont: One Hundred and Forty Years.* New York, 1951.

Echeverria, Durand. *Mirage in the West: A History of the French Image of American Society to 1815.* Princeton, 1957.

Egret, Jean. *La Pré-Révolution française (1787-1788).* Paris, 1962.

———. "La seconde Assemblée de Notables (6 novembre-12 decembre 1788)," *Annales historiques de la Révolution française,* XXI (1949), 193-228.

———. "La Fayette dans la première Assemblée des Notables (Février-Mai 1787)," *Annales historiques de la Révolution française,* XXIV (1952), 1-31.

Fabre, Jean. *Stanislas-Auguste Poniatowski et l'Europe des lumières.* (*Collection historique de l'Institut d'études slaves,* XVI.) Paris, 1952.

Faure, Edgar. *La Disgrâce de Turgot (12 mai 1776).* (*Trente journées qui ont fait la France,* no. 6.) Paris, 1961.

François Quesnay et la Physiocratie. (Institut National d'Études Démographiques.) 2 vols. Paris, 1958.

Godechot, Jacques. *La Contre-Révolution, doctrine et action 1789-1804.* Paris, 1961.

———. *La Grande Nation; l'expansion révolutionnaire de la France dans la monde de 1789 à 1799.* Paris, 1956.

———. *Les Révolutions (1770-1799).* ("Nouvelle Clio," no. 36.) Paris, 1963.

Göhring, Martin. *Geschichte der Grossen Revolution,* I: *Sturz des Ancien Regime und Sieg der Revolution.* Tübingen, 1950.

Gomel, Charles. *Les Causes financières de la Révolution française.* 2 vols. Paris, 1892-1893.

Goodwin, A. "Calonne, the Assembly of French Notables of 1787 and the Origins of the 'Revolte Nobiliaire,'" *English Historical Review,* LXI (1946), 202-234, 329-377.

———. *The French Revolution.* London, 1953.

Gore, Walter M. *History Genealogical-Biographical of the Barksdale-du Pont and Allied Families.* New York, 1922.

Gottschalk, Louis. *Lafayette Between the American and the French Revolution (1783-1789).* Chicago, c. 1950.

Green, F. C. *The Ancien Régime: A Manual of French Institutions and Social Classes.* Edinburgh, 1958.

Guyot, R. *Le Directoire et la paix de l'Europe.* Paris, 1911.

Guyot, Yves. *Quesnay et la physiocratie.* Paris, [1896].

Harris, S. F. *The Assignats.* Cambridge, Mass., 1930.

Herold, J. Christopher. *Mistress to an Age: A Life of Madame de Staël.* Indianapolis and New York, 1958.

Higgs, Henry. *The Physiocrats.* London, 1897.

"Inauguration du Monument de Turgot (30 juillet 1914): Discours de MM. Yves Guyot, Alfred Neymarche, Gustave Schelle, Mesureur," extrait de *Journal des Économistes, revue mensuelle de la science économique et de la statistique,* 14 août 1914. Paris, 1914.

Jobert, Ambroise. *La Commission d'éducation nationale en Pologne (1773-1794); son œuvre d'instruction civique.* (*Collection de l'Institut français de Varsovie,* IX.) Paris, 1941.

————. *La Révolution (1789-1792)*. (*Histoire de France contemporaine*, ed. E. Lavisse, I.) Paris, 1920.

Sands, Theodore and C. P. Higby. "France and the Salt Tax," *Historian*, XI (1949), 145-165.

Schelle, G. "Pourquoi les 'Réflexions' de Turgot sur la formation et la distribution des richesses ne sont-elles pas exactement connues?" *Journal des Économistes*, XLIII (1888), 3-16.

————. *Turgot*. Paris, 1909.

Schmidt, Charles. "Le Traité de 1786 et la crise ouvrière en France," *Revue historique*, XCVII (1908), 78-94.

Schramm, H. R. "The Memorial to François André Michaux at the Morris Arboretum, University of Pennsylvania," *Proceedings of the American Philosophical Society*, C (April, 1956), 145-149.

Sée, Henri. *Economic and Social Conditions in France during the Eighteenth Century*. Translated by Edwin H. Zeydel. New York, 1927.

————. "The Economic and Social Origins of the French Revolution," *Economic History Review*, III (1931), 1-15.

————. "The Normandy Chamber of Commerce and the Commercial Treaty of 1786," *Economic History Review*, II (1929-1930), 308-313.

Ségur-Dupeyron, P. de. *Histoire des négociations commerciales et maritimes de la France aux XVIIᵉ et XVIIIᵉ siècles considerées dans leurs rapports avec la politique générale*. 3 vols. Paris, 1872-1873.

Shepherd, Robert P. *Turgot and the Six Edicts*. (Columbia University Studies in History, Economics and Public Law, XVIII, no. 2.) New York, 1903.

Sloane, William M. *The French Revolution and Religious Reform: An Account of Ecclesiastical Legislation and its Influence on Affairs in France from 1789 to 1804*. New York, 1901.

Stourm, René. *Les Finances de l'ancien régime et de la Révolution: origines du système financier actuel*. 2 vols. Paris, 1885.

Suaudeau, René. *Les Représentations figurés des physiocrates*. Paris, 1947.

Thompson, J. M. *The French Revolution*. New York, 1945.

Turnbull, Archibald D. *John Stevens: An American Record*. New York, c. 1928.

Van Doren, Carl. *Benjamin Franklin*. New York, 1938.

Vignery, J. Robert. "Voltaire's Economic Ideas as Revealed in the 'Romans' and 'Contes,'" *French Review*, XXXIII (1960), 257-263.

Walter, Gérard. *Histoire des Jacobins*. Paris, 1946.

Weber, Henri. *La Compagnie française des Indes (1604-1875)*. Paris, 1904.

Welch, Oliver J. G. *Mirabeau: A Study of a Democratic Monarchist*. London, 1951.

Weulersse, Georges. *Les Manuscrits économiques de François Quesnay et du Marquis de Mirabeau aux Archives Nationales; inventaire, extraits et notes*. Paris, 1910.

————. *Le Mouvement physiocratique en France (de 1756 à 1770)*. 2 vols. Paris, 1910.

————. *Les Physiocrates*. Paris, 1931.

————. *Les Physiocrates sous la ministère Turgot*. Paris, n. d.

446

Works Cited

———. *La Physiocratie sous les ministères de Turgot et de Necker (1774-1781).* Paris, 1950.

———. *La Physiocratie à la fin du règne de Louis XV (1770-1774).* Paris, 1959.

Index

NOTE: Since items in the index begin with a capital, "Du Pont" appears even for the descendants of Du Pont de Nemours—the du Ponts.

"arbitrary" measures (1796), 251-52; defense of private enterprise (1797), 252; on civil code, 252-53; views on financial problems (1795-97), 253-58; on tariffs (1795-96), 258-59; essays on natural history, 260-61, 410n73; arrest and release on 18-19 Fructidor (1797), 266-68; resignation from Council of Elders, 268; plans to go to America, 268-72; difficulties in organization of Company, 272-75; suit for recovery of funds from Corsange, 276; investigated by police (1797), 276-77; sale of print shop, 278; leaves Paris with family, 279; emigration to America, 279-81; voyage on *American Eagle*, 280-81; establishment of business in America, 282-83; interest in French nurseries in America, 285-86, 416n61; visits Jefferson (1802), 286; elected to membership in American Philosophical Society, 289; papers for APS, 289; lack of success in learning English language, 290-91, 350; return to France from America, 292-93; role in negotiation of Louisiana Purchase, 294-300; disappointment in not being named Senator, 301-2; failure to gain appointment to Legion of Honor, 302; unsuccessful efforts to settle accounts with French Treasury, 303, 308-9, 313-14; use of numerical codes in letters to sons, 305, 418n10; arranges loan from Talleyrand, 305-6; business relations with sons, 311-14; attitude on Victor's bankruptcy, 312-13; editor of Turgot's works, 314-16; work in Paris Chamber of Commerce, 316-20, 420n42, 420n43; director of Banque Territoriale, 320-23; part in *New Jersey* affair, 323-24; ideas on American policy, 325-27, 351, 352; opinion of Napoleon's re-organization of National Institute, 327-28, 423n87; *mémoires* for National Institute, 328; member of various societies, 329; appointed sublibrarian of Arsenal, 329; liquidates his company, 330-31, 424n104; threatens to sue sons, 333; essays on morality and religion, 336; administrator of system of household relief, 337-38; secretary of Provisional Government (1814), 339-40; constitutional ideas (1814), 341; return to America (1815), 343-46; criticism of J.-B. Say, 345; life on Brandywine, 347-49; plan for vital statistics, 348-49; visit to Monticello, 349-50; treatise on South American republics, 351-52; illness of, 353, 356-57; ideas on European situation (1815-16), 353-54; fall into Brandywine, 355; fights fire in charcoal house, 357; death, 357; inscription on tomb, 429n44
—autobiography (uncompleted MS), 221,

360n2, 362n35; *Avant-dernier chapitre de l'histoire des Jacobins*, 212; *Considerations sur la position politique de la France, de l'Angleterre et de l'Espagne*, 178; "Correspondance litteraire et politique," 58, 374n110, 374n111; "De Courbes politiques," 58, 374n117; *De l'administration des chemins*, 50, 370n71; *De l'exportation et de l'importation des grains*, 34-35, 36-38; *De l'origine et des progrès d'une science nouvelle*, 48-50; *De la périodicite des assemblées nationales*, 157-59; *Du commerce et de la Compagnie des Indes*, 56, 373n102; *Du pouvoir législatif et du pouvoir exécutif*, 236-37; *Effet des assignats sur le prix du pain*, 194; *Essai de traduction en vers du Roland Furieux de l'Arioste*, 73-74, 379n52, 379n53, 380n55; *Idées sur les sécours à donner aux pauvres malades dans une grande ville*, 131; "Joseph II," 55, 372n90; *Lettre à la chambre du commerce de Normandie*, 96-97; *Lettre . . . à M. Pétion* and *Seconde lettre . . .* (1792), 211; "Mémoire aux républiques équinoxiales," 346-47, 349, 350, 351; *Mémoire sur les municipalités*, 110-11; *Mémoires sur la vie et les ouvrages de M. Turgot*, 74-75; *National Education in the United States*, 290; *Observations sur la constitution proposée par la commission des onze*, 237-38; "Observations sur les principes et le bien des républiques confédérées" (incomplete MS), 132, 389n85; ed., *Œuvres de M^r. Turgot* (9 vols.), 314-16; *Oromasis*, 221-22; *Philosophie de l'univers*, 221-24; *Physiocratie*, 46, 369n60, 370n62, 370n69; *Plaidoyer de Lysias*, 235; *Réflexions sur l'écrit intitulé: Richesse de l'État*, 20-22, 363n49; *Réponse demandée par M. le marquis de . . . à celle qu'il a faite aux Réflexions sur l'écrit intitulé: Richesse de l'État*, 22; "Salons de 1773, 1777, 1779," 59, 375n119, 375n121; *Sur la Banque de France*, 318-19, 420n48; *Table raisonnée des principes de l'économie politique*, 72, 379n47; *Vues sur l'éducation nationale . . .*, 225; *mémoires* prepared for National Institute, 410n70, 414n27, 414n28, 423n89, 428n19
Du Pont de Nemours Père Fils et Compagnie: establishment of, 269-75; lack of business in America, 281-83, 287-88; relations with E. I. du Pont de Nemours and Company, 284, 303, 306, 330-35; transferred to France, 292; seeks to become fiscal agent for U.S. Government, 296, 298, 300; relations with V. du Pont de Nemours et Cie, 303, 307, 311; report to stockholders (1808), 329-31; liquidation of, 331

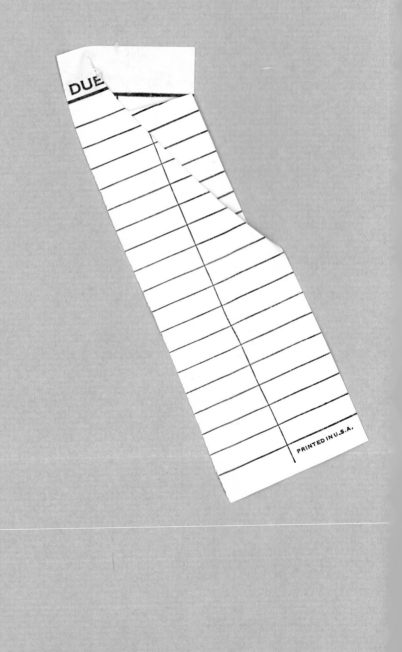

DUE

PRINTED IN U.S.A.